Why Do You Need This New Edition?

6 good reasons why you should buy this new edition of *Thinking through Communication*

Although we communicate every day, we are not always effective. Communication is a complex process, made even more complex by the challenges of new technologies. Communication experts are continually investigating ways to meet these challenges, and this edition of *Thinking through Communication* invites you to share in their insights. Streamlined and edited for greater clarity, this edition includes new material and new features. Pages xvii–xix of the Preface present detailed information on what is new to this edition. An overview is provided below.

1. Just when you've mastered a current technology, a new one comes along. Throughout the text, we have added research on ways new media impact interpersonal, group, and organizational communication. This edition looks at topics such as impression formation on social networking sites, the use of groupware to facilitate organizational communication, ways to succeed in virtual groups.

2. In addition to integrated discussions of mediated communication throughout the text, Chapter 11 specifically addresses media issues, focusing both on the convergence of traditional and new media and on the collabora-

tive media technologies collectively known as Web 2.0, including our expanded ability to create and post media products and the growing popularity of MMOGs and virtual worlds.

3. Research in the areas of interpersonal and group communication grows each year. In Chapter 6 new material on relational maintenance strategies and ways to satisfy face needs has been added. In Chapters 7 and 8, research on transactive memory, group trust, collaborative information sharing, and structural diversity in social and work groups is included, as well as sections on group identity and inter-group conflict.

4. One goal of this text is to make research exciting to students. To this end, studies on Chicago street gangs, human-robot interactions, uses of reality TV, rhetorical strategies in the fight for women's rights, and the creation of a performance piece about Hurricane Katrina have been chosen.

5. In response to requests from reviewers, this edition provides an online glossary of all the key terms in the text. Organized by chapter, students can easily look up definitions and test their understanding of communication concepts.

6. To make studying easier, student review questions have been added for each chapter and are now available online along with chapter outlines on MyCommunicationKit (www.mycommunicationkit.com; access code required).

PEARSON

Sixth Edition

Thinking through Communication

An Introduction to the Study of Human Communication

Sarah Trenholm

Ithaca College

Allyn & Bacon

Boston   Columbus   Indianapolis   New York   San Francisco   Upper Saddle River
Amsterdam   Cape Town   Dubai   London   Madrid   Milan   Munich   Paris   Montreal   Toronto
Delhi   Mexico City   Sao Paulo   Sydney   Hong Kong   Seoul   Singapore   Taipei   Tokyo

Editor in Chief, Communication: Karon Bowers
Editorial Assistant: Stephanie Chaisson
Development Manager: David Kear
Associate Development Editor: Angela Pickard
Media Producer: Megan Higginbotham
Marketing Manager: Blair Tuckman
Managing Editor: Linda Mihatov Behrens
Associate Managing Editor: Bayani Mendoza de Leon
Project Manager: Raegan Keida Heerema
Senior Operations Specialist: Nick Skilitis
Operations Specialist: Mary Ann Gloriande
Creative Director: Leslie Osher
Art Director Cover: Anne Bonanno Nieglos
Designer Cover: Laura Gardner
Cover Image: ©Shutterstock
Editorial Production Services and Electronic Composition: Nesbitt Graphics, Inc.
Photo Researcher: Sarah Evertson

Library of Congress Cataloging-in-Publication Data

Trenholm, Sarah,
 Thinking through communication : an introduction to the study of human
communication/Sarah Trenholm. — 6th ed.
   p. cm.
 Includes bibliographical references and index.
 ISBN 0-205-68809-8
1. Communication. I. Title.

CIP data available

Credits appear on page 408, which constitutes a continuation of the copyright page.

1 2 3 4 5 6 7 8 9 10 EB 13 12 11 10 09

Allyn & Bacon
is an imprint of

www.pearsonhighered.com

ISBN 10:   0-205-68809-8

ISBN 13: 978-0-205-68809-8

Contents

PART II   LISTENING AND LANGUAGE

Contents   xvii

Preface

TO THE INSTRUCTOR

Goals of the Text

This text is designed to introduce your students to basic concepts in speech communication. In writing the text and the instructional materials, I've tried to provide as much flexibility as possible. The text contains core material for the student to read and study. The instructional supplements contain additional materials that allow you to tailor the course to your interests and to students' particular needs.

Whether you take a theory or a skills approach to teaching, this text should give your students a better understanding of communication as a field of study and should help them think about communication in systematic ways. It should provide a conceptual foundation for discussing communication and its effects.

Whereas the text itself provides a general overview, the material in the supplements allows you to fill in details in your own way. Included are standard teaching aids such as chapter outlines and test questions. In addition, I have added suggestions for supplementary lectures, handouts, discussion questions, observation guides, exercises, and assignments. I hope that these materials will allow you to take the course in the direction you want.

Additions to This Edition

Over time, textbooks tend to expand. Authors love to add but have difficulty subtracting. As a result chapters get longer and longer. I've tried to address this problem by streamlining passages that seem redundant or out of date, to make room for new research findings and more current examples and illustrations. Despite these changes, the general structure and organization of the text remain the same. In this edition, you will find new material in the chapters on interpersonal, group, organizational, and mediated communication, as well as new research abstracts in the chapter on research methods.

The chapter on mediated communication (Chapter 11) will always be the chapter in most need of revision because new media are being developed at an ever-increasing rate while traditional media are evolving and converging in response to advances in digital technology. Today's students can, if they want, follow celebrities on Twitter, write on one another's Facebook walls, create avatars in Second Life, engage in transmedia storytelling, and even get involved in sexting. No wonder many experience e-fatigue, the overload that comes with juggling all of these possibilities. Both in Chapter 11 itself and in sections in the context chapters, I have tried to provide a platform for discussing all of ways in which the explosion of collaborative activity loosely known as Web 2.0 affects our lives.

Chapter 6, the chapter on interpersonal communication, has been updated and reorganized for more clarity. New discussions of rejection sensitivity, face-needs, and relational maintenance strategies have been added, as well as a section that examines impression formation and relational maintenance in social networking sites. In Chapter 7, the chapter on small-group communication, the discussion of phases in group development has been simplified, leaving room for new material on ways to build effective teams as well as the importance of, and barriers to, collaborative information sharing. A discussion of social identity and group prototypes allows discussion of inter-group as well as intra-group communication. Finally, attention is given to some of the technologies that allow groups to work online. Chapter 8 has also been expanded to include material on transactive memory and trust as well as the skills necessary to work on virtual teams.

A final change is the substitution of five new research abstracts in Chapter 13. My goal, as always, has been to find studies that illustrate a wide range of topics, are easy to understand, and are interesting to students. This edition describes an ethnography of communication in Chicago street gangs, the creation of a performance piece in the wake of Hurricane Katrina, an experiment that investigates factors in successful human-robot interaction, two surveys on the uses and gratifications of reality TV, and a rhetorical analysis of ways women transformed the act of voting into public performance after the Civil War.

TO THE STUDENT

This book asks you to think about a process that you can do without thinking. It asks you to look at behaviors that most of us overlook. In short, it asks you to rediscover communication.

When we get too close to things, we often take them for granted. People, places, and everyday processes become invisible so that we no longer see their complexity or appreciate their uniqueness. We simply accept them without giving them much thought. Although there are some advantages to taking things as they come, there are also disadvantages. If we were to see the world fresh every day, we would pay a price in time and mental effort. We are often much more efficient when we don't think too much. Yet, we give up something in exchange for efficiency: when we act without thinking, we lose control of our behavior.

This book was written to make you more aware of the invisible process called communication. The first step in mastering communication lies in becoming more conscious of it—in taking time to think it through. It is important that we think communication through because we think through communication. How we see the world and how we act in it are determined by communication practices. When we communicate, we do more than reflect beliefs about the world: we create them.

This book is an introduction to the study of human communication. It is designed to give you the basic concepts you need in order to understand how communication works and to introduce you to some of the most important contexts in which communication occurs. It is also designed to make you more critical of your own communication behavior as both a message sender and a message receiver.

Plan of the Text

The formal study of communication stretches back thousands of years. Like students of today, students in ancient Greece signed up for courses in communication. The first chapter of this book examines the history of communication study. The second chapter provides basic definitions and models of communication. It offers a number of answers to the question "What is communication?" and demonstrates that the way we approach communication determines what we see in it.

Chapters 3, 4, and 5 look at basic encoding and decoding processes. They discuss how we interpret and construct messages. In Chapter 3 we look at listening, the complex process whereby receivers interpret and evaluate messages. In Chapter 4, we turn our attention to the basic material of which most messages are constructed: spoken language. Of course, meaning is not conveyed only through words. Time and space, movement, and appearance also convey meaning. In Chapter 5, we look at the hidden nonverbal messages that sometimes enhance, but often undermine, spoken communication.

Communication comes to us in many forms—from face-to-face conversation to mediated programming. In Chapters 6 through 13, we look at the contexts in which communication occurs. In Chapter 6 we discuss interpersonal communication, the informal, face-to-face interaction that is the most common form of communication. In Chapter 7, we move on to group communication, considering the constraints that speaking in groups places on interaction. Chapter 8 focuses on communication in complex organizations, while Chapters 9 and 10 look at face-to-face public address. Chapter 11 considers the impact of mediated messages on our everyday lives, and Chapter 12 addresses communication between cultures, a topic of increasing importance in today's global village.

Finally, Chapter 13 gives you a glimpse into the way communication scholars make discoveries about communication. Because communication is such an essential part of our lives, the study of communication does not stop when a book ends or a course concludes. Chapter 13 discusses ways we can continue to think through communication throughout our lives.

RESOURCES IN PRINT AND ONLINE

Name of Supplement	Available in Print	Available Online	Instructor or Student Supplement	Description
Instructor's Manual and Test Bank (ISBN: 0-205-79165-4)		√	Instructor Supplement	Prepared by Sarah Trenholm, this comprehensive instructor resource has both chapter-by-chapter teaching material as well as a fully reviewed Test Bank. The Instructor's Manual portion includes the following resources for each chapter: Chapter Outline, Chapter Review Questions with Solutions, Glossary of Key Terms, Questions for In-Class Discussion, Critical Thinking Questions, Student Handouts, and Exercises and Assignments. The Test Bank contains approximately 750 multiple-choice, true/false, and essay questions, all of which are organized by chapter. Available for download at www.pearsonhighered.com/irc (access code required).
MyTest (ISBN: 0-205-79164-6)		√	Instructor Supplement	This flexible, online test generating software includes all of the questions found in the Test Bank section of the printed Instructor's Manual and Test Bank. This computerized software allows instructors to create their own personalized exams, edit any or all of the existing test questions, and add new questions. Other special features of this program include random generation of test questions, creation of alternate versions of the same test, scrambling of question sequence, and test preview before printing. Available at www.pearsonmytest.com (access code required).
PowerPoint™ Presentation Package (ISBN: 0-205-79163-8)		√	Instructor Supplement	This text-specific package, prepared by Ryan Bigler, Kaliegh Mrowka, and Sarah Trenholm, of Ithaca College, provides a basis for your lecture with PowerPoint™ slides for each chapter of the book. Available for download at www.pearsonhighered.com/irc (access code required).
Pearson Allyn & Bacon Introduction to Communication Video Library	√		Instructor Supplement	Pearson Allyn & Bacon's Introduction to Communication Video Library contains a range of videos from which adopters can choose. These videos cover a variety of topics and scenarios for communication foundations, interpersonal communication, small-group communication, and public speaking. Please contact your Pearson representative and a complete list of videos and their contents to choose which would be most useful in your class. Some restrictions apply.

Name of Supplement	Available in Print	Available Online	Instructor or Student Supplement	Description
Allyn & Bacon Digital Media Archive for Communication, Version 3. 0, (ISBN:0-205-43709-5)	√		Instructor Supplement	The Digital Media Archive CD-ROM contains electronic images of charts, graphs, tables, and figures, along with media elements such as video and related Weblinks. These media assets are fully customizable to use with our pre-formatted PowerPoint™ outlines or to import into instructor's own lectures. (Windows and Mac.)
Pearson Allyn & Bacon Introduction to Communication Study Site (Open access)		√	Student Supplement	The Pearson Allyn & Bacon Introduction to Communication Study Site features practice tests, learning objectives, and Weblinks, The site is organized around the major topics typically covered in the Introduction to Communication course. These topics have also been correlated to the table of contents for your book! Available at www.abintrocommunication.com
MyCommunicationKit		√	Instructor & Student Supplement	MyCommunicationKit is an online supplement that offers a glossary of all key terms in the text as electronic flashcards, chapter outlines, and review questions as well as video clips and activities to aid student learning and comprehension. Also included in MyCommunicationKit are MySearchLab and Weblinks, both of which provide assistance with and access to powerful and reliable research material. Available at www.mycommunicationkit.com (access code required).

ACKNOWLEDGMENTS

I am grateful to all my friends and colleagues at Ithaca College for their encouragement and support, in particular to Bruce Henderson and Bob Sullivan, who model what it means to be both scholars and gentlemen. Thanks too to Steve Dalphin who, many years ago, convinced me to do this book, and to Karon Bowers at Allyn & Bacon for guiding subsequent editions, as well as to the excellent production teams I've had the pleasure to work with.

Special thanks go out to all those who have reviewed this and previous editions and offered useful insights and critiques. Although I have not always been able to follow all their suggestions, I have always learned from them. Reviewers include: Isolde K. Anderson, Hope College; Ann J. Atkinson, Keene State College; Bethann Bark, Suffolk Community College; Ferald Bryan, Northern Illinois University; Jerry Buley, Arizona State University; Mary Carpenter, New York University; Dennis Doyle, Central College; Tresha Dutton, Whatcom Community College; Leonard Edmonds, Arizona State University; Larry Galizio, Portland Community College; Katherine Hawkins, Wichita State University; Virginia Kidd, California State University; Thomas J. Knutson, California State University, Sacramento; Mark Lipton, New York University; Rita Miller, Keene State University; Steven Y. Miura, University of Hawaii, Hilo; Teresa Nance, Villanova University; Helen Sterk, Marquette University; John D. Stone, James Madison University; Jo Young Switzer, Indiana University/Purdue University, Fort Wayne; April Trees, University of Colorado, Boulder; Kyle Tusing, University of Arizona; Robin Vagenas, University of Delaware; John T. Warren, Bowling Green State University; Archie Wortham, Palo Alto Community College; and Julie Yingling, Humboldt State University.

The Communication Tradition

It is in the constant interplay between communication and experience that our world is shaped.

After reading this chapter, you should be able to:

- Identify the four periods of rhetorical study.
- Describe the way in which scholars viewed communication in the classical period.
- Describe the five canons of rhetoric.
- Explain the major characteristics of communication study during the medieval period and the Renaissance.
- Outline rhetorical study during the modern period.
- Distinguish between humanistic and scientific approaches to communication study.

Harley Shands once said that "people, in cultures, speaking to each other in the local tongue and following the rules and regulations of the group, are playing a great game, the central game of the human condition."[1] This book is about that game. It's about how the game is played and how playing it affects us and the world we live in. It's about the rewards that come from playing the game well, and it's also about the costs of losing. It's about a game that affects us deeply, both on a cultural and on an individual level.

No society has existed, or ever could exist, without a well-ordered system of communication, and no individual could survive for long without knowing how that system operates. Without the ability to communicate, we could not form relationships with others, nor could we understand the world around us, for it is in the constant interplay between communication and experience that our world is shaped.

In the following pages, we look at how communication affects us as individuals and how it affects us as a culture. We look at the verbal and nonverbal skills that make communication possible and at the many contexts in which it occurs. In short, we'll examine the knowledge and skills necessary to operate successfully in an age that has often been labeled the "age of communication."

A BRIEF HISTORY OF COMMUNICATION STUDY

Before we begin our study of contemporary communication, it is useful to look at the development of the field—the history of communication study. Communication has been studied seriously for many centuries. In fact, many of the communication principles we believe today were taught in ancient Greece over twenty-five hundred years ago. In the remainder of this chapter, we'll see how the formal study of communication began in fifth-century Sicily and developed in ancient Athens; we'll trace it through the medieval period and the Renaissance, discover how it evolved in the modern period, and look at some recent trends (see Table 1.1 for a summary). This brief tour should help you to appreciate the importance of the subject you are about to study and should give you a sense of how it has changed over the years.

> Many of the communication principles we believe today were taught in ancient Greece over twenty-five hundred years ago.

Studying Rhetoric in Ancient Greece

If by some mysterious twist of fate you were to wake up tomorrow and find yourself in ancient Greece, you could still pursue your education, although it's unlikely that you would be able to put together the same class schedule you have today. Many of the courses and majors you now take for granted wouldn't exist. However, if you were interested in studying communication, if you wanted to learn public speaking,

Table 1.1 A Short History of Rhetoric and Communication Theory

Cave paintings attest to the universal human need to record and communicate experience. Written records in all ancient civilizations (Egypt, Babylon, India, China) show that communication has long been an object of study.

Classical Period (500 B.C.–400 C.E.)

With the rise of Greek democracy, public communication became an important tool for problem solving. Rhetoric, the study of "the available means of persuasion," was a respected discipline taught by the great philosophers. The first known communication model, the canons of rhetoric, divided rhetoric into five parts: invention, arrangement, style, memory, and delivery. Classical rhetoric emphasized credibility, ways to ground arguments, and audience analysis. Major figures included Plato, Socrates, Aristotle, Cicero, and Quintilian.

Medieval Period and the Renaissance (400–1600)

In response to the rise of monolithic Christianity, rhetoric became secondary to theology. Major rhetorical acts were letter writing and preaching. Parts of the classical paradigm were kept alive, but the focus was prescriptive, not theoretical. Rhetoricians emphasized methods of embellishing and amplifying rhetorical style. Major figures included Augustine, Cassiodorus, John of Salisbury, and Erasmus.

Modern Period (1600–1900)

Once again, public rhetoric was a major force in determining public policy. The written word became an important medium as books and newspapers became more available. Rhetoric followed four paths: classical rhetoric revived the work of the ancients. Psychological/epistemological rhetoric investigated receivers' psychological responses to persuasive messages. Belletristic rhetoric saw written and spoken communication as art and developed theories of rhetorical criticism. Elocutionists focused on developing elaborate rules for delivery. Major figures were Francis Bacon, René Descartes, John Locke, Fénelon, Lord Kames, George Campbell, Joseph Priestley, and Thomas De Quincey.

Contemporary Period (1900–present)

Modern departments of communication were formed. Communication study took two paths: rhetoricians used humanistic methods to analyze rhetorical effects of public discourse. Communication theorists used scientific methods to analyze communication behavior as a social science. Communication study expanded to include interpersonal and group, as well as public, communication. The rise of electronic media signaled additional changes in communication study.

oral interpretation, argumentation and debate, or communication theory, you would have no problem, for in Athens, about three hundred years before the birth of Christ, communication was as popular a subject as it is today. It would be quite easy for you to find a school, for there were many famous teachers willing to take on new students. You would simply have to keep in mind that in those days, the study of communication was called **rhetoric** and teachers of communication were known as **rhetoricians**.

If you were looking for a place to study rhetoric in Athens around 335 B.C., your best bet would be a school called the Lyceum. The Lyceum was founded by **Aristotle**, whose writings on rhetoric are considered by many to be the single greatest source of rhetorical theory. Born in 384 B.C., Aristotle was a student of the other great Greek philosopher, **Plato**, and attended Plato's Academy. Before starting the Lyceum, Aristotle served as tutor to the young son of Philip of Macedon, the child who grew up to be Alexander the Great.

Those of you who are male would have no difficulty attending the Lyceum, for the school was open to any young man who showed an interest in education. Those of you who are female would, unfortunately, have a problem. Although historical records show that two women managed to attend Plato's school, it was not Athenian custom for women to receive higher education. Indeed, Axiothea, one of the women who attended the Academy, resorted to the strategy of disguising herself as a man.[2]

If you were to attend Aristotle's public lectures (whether or not in disguise), you would have to rise early. Accompanied by your *paidagogos*—the attendant hired by your parents to make sure you didn't cut classes—you would make your way through the busy *agora,* or central marketplace, to the great wall surrounding the city. Outside the wall, you would enter the wooded sanctuary of Apollo the Wolf Slayer, site of the Lyceum. As you passed the huge gymnasium, you might see young men practicing throwing the discus or wrestling. If it were during one of the many periods in which Athens was at war, you could observe troops, clad in bronze breastplates and shields, taking part in military drills on the open parade ground. In Athens, as in other Greek city-states, physical activity was important to education, and teachers of philosophy and rhetoric shared space in the

The need for communication is basic. It allows us to form connections and build community by sharing stories.

public gyms with teachers of physical culture and the military arts. As you neared the school library (one of the first of its kind), you would undoubtedly meet friends, and together you would look for seats in front of the colonnaded portico from which Aristotle customarily spoke.

Aristotle held his public lectures in the mornings, covering philosophy, science, and logic.[3] In the afternoons, he walked along the shaded walkways known as *peripatos*, stopping from time to time to sit in one of the roomy recesses and talk with his students about ethics, politics, and rhetoric. Because much of his private instruction took place as he strolled the peripatos, his school became known as the Peripatetic School.

If you were to study with Aristotle, your focus would be on persuasive rhetoric. Aristotle considered the science of rhetoric to be that of "observing in any given case the available means of persuasion."[4] He lectured about the ways in which successful arguments can be built, and he described methods of arriving at truthful conclusions. He also talked a great deal about proof. Aristotle believed that a speaker could sway an audience in three ways: through personal character, or ethos; through the ability to arouse emotions, or pathos; and through the wording and logic of the message, or logos. In discussing ethos, Aristotle became one of the first communication specialists to point out the importance of source credibility. If you were fortunate enough to study with him, you would leave school knowing the most frequently encountered types of speaking situations, rules for effective reasoning, the part that human emotions play in persuasion, the necessity for audience analysis, ways of improving style and delivery, and the place of rhetoric in maintaining and discovering truth.

The Classical Period: Enchanting the Mind by Arguments

Although he was arguably the greatest of the early Western rhetoricians, Aristotle was not the first. That honor is shared by two Sicilian Greeks, Corax and Tisias, who lived a century before Aristotle. The story of Corax and Tisias illustrates clearly that the study of communication is always prompted by practical problems.[5]

In 466 B.C., Sicily experienced political upheaval; the populace overthrew the existing tyrant and established a democratic constitution. People who had been exiled under the previous regime came back to Sicily and demanded the return of their land and property. This, of course, led to intricate legal problems. Corax recognized that many of the litigants were ill equipped to argue their own cases persuasively. This prompted Tisias to study ways in which speakers could effectively order their ideas. From these early attempts to address practical problems, the rhetorical tradition emerged.

In the next one hundred years, the study of rhetoric expanded rapidly as the great orators and philosophers of ancient Greece added insights and theories about the art of public speaking. Indeed, the rhetoric taught by the Greek philosophers is directly linked to the rhetoric taught in modern communication courses.

Much of the advice a modern teacher of public communication gives a student (advice on building audience rapport, organizing ideas, arguing to hostile audiences, and delivering a speech) was given by Greek and Roman teachers over two thousand years ago.

The **classical period** lasted for about nine hundred years, from the fifth century B.C. to the fourth century A.D. It flowered under Athenian democracy, lasted

> The rhetoric taught by the Greek philosophers is directly linked to the rhetoric taught in modern communication courses.

through the years of the Roman Empire, and closed with the advent of Christianity. Communication study was important in ancient Greece for at least three reasons. First, Greece was a society that revered the spoken word. Although many Athenians could read and write, the stone, wood, or wax tablets they used were unwieldy. There was no light reading, no books, or magazines. Oral expression, in the form of storytelling, poetry reading, dramatic performance, or conversation, was the major source of entertainment, and ornamental speech was greatly admired.

Second, the Greeks put a great deal of emphasis on persuasion and argumentation. Because Athens was a democracy, would-be politicians achieved office through their ability to speak thoughtfully and persuasively. Important political issues were defined and resolved through public debate, and individual politicians gained public notice as a result of their skills in argumentation.

Finally, for many years there was a ban on professional lawyers. Like their Sicilian counterparts, Greek citizens who wished to bring suit in a court of law had to have the forensic skills to argue their cases successfully.

In response to this practical need, a group of itinerant teachers called **Sophists** began to ply their trade. The Sophists were professional speech teachers who advertised their services by posting notices in public places where they could find an audience. Soon the gymnasia became important locations for learning: the Sophists knew they could find a large and receptive audience in the Athenian version of today's health clubs.

The major concern of the Sophists was teaching the "tricks" of persuasive speaking for use in the law courts or assemblies. Often, the Sophists supplemented their income by acting as professional speechwriters and political consultants. Philosophers such as Plato and Aristotle, who believed that the goal of communication was to discover the truth, not merely to win arguments, held the Sophists in great contempt. The Sophists seemed undaunted, however, and bragged about their skill in defeating strong arguments with weak ones.

The Greek and Roman philosophers Plato, Aristotle, Cicero, and Quintilian were more theoretical (and more ethical) than were the Sophists. **Cicero** (106–43 B.C.), a prominent Roman politician, was considered to be Rome's finest orator. He met his death when he joined the forces opposing Mark Antony after the assassination of Julius Caesar. During his lifetime, he delivered many famous speeches and wrote extensively on communication theory. By the time his works were published, the study of rhetoric had stabilized into five major topic areas, the famous **canons of rhetoric**. Cicero did much to elaborate on this early model of communication.

The canons divided communication into five parts: invention, style, arrangement, memory, and delivery (see Table 1.2). The first, **invention**, was the process of deciding on the subject matter of one's speech and of discovering information and arguments that would lead to sound conclusions. Classical rhetoricians shared Aristotle's belief that through communication, one could decide which of several possible "truths" was the most correct. In their writing and teaching, they argued that speakers should have a wide knowledge of current affairs as well as the ability to think clearly. Theories of invention emphasized ways to argue in different contexts.

Aristotle

Style was the second canon. It described the process of selecting the proper words to convey a message. Classical rhetoricians emphasized correct use of language and cataloged major figures of speech. Cicero believed there were three styles of speaking that corresponded to ethos, logos, and pathos, Aristotle's three modes of speech. The **plain style** built ethos by convincing the audience of the speaker's good character, good sense, and trustworthiness; it was

---

Table 1.2 The Five Canons of Rhetoric

Invention

The speaker must begin by discovering what can be said about a given topic and by finding arguments that will allow others to understand it. Classical theory emphasized methods for analyzing audience, subject, and occasion of speech to find material that would move people to belief and action. Through logical thinking and clear topical analysis, the speaker could find grounds for effective arguments. Major speech occasions were three: forensic, deliberative, and epideictic (ceremonial). Modes of proof were three: ethos, pathos, and logos.

Style

The speaker must select and arrange the wording of the message carefully. Style was thought to differ in relationship to speech purpose: it could instruct, please, or persuade. Classical writers believed language should be clear, lively, and appropriate for the audience. Using figurative language was thought to be a way of increasing audience response.

Arrangement

The speaker must arrange ideas for maximum impact. Classical theory divided a speech into several parts that correspond roughly with today's introduction, body, and conclusion. Theorists agreed that the audience must be put into the proper frame of mind for receiving the message, the subject must be set forth clearly, a case must be built, and the speech must end with a summary and conclusion. Writers recognized that order of elements depends on the nature of the audience (whether hostile or friendly) and on the seriousness of the occasion.

Memory

The speaker must find a way to keep the message firmly in mind. Classical writers suggested several mnemonic devices to help orators memorize speeches. Theorists also discussed factors that make speech material memorable, including novelty.

Delivery

The speaker must present the speech in a natural, varied, and appropriate way. Voice should convey interest and emotion, and gestures should match the major ideas in the speech.

logical, clear, and restrained. The middle style emphasized logos by impressing the audience with the soundness of the speaker's position; it consisted of intricate argumentation and careful philosophical distinctions. Finally, the vigorous style was based on pathos; it "pulled out all the stops" and was eloquent and emotional. Cicero, like other classical rhetoricians, mistrusted emotional appeals and warned speakers not to use the vigorous style without elements of the other two styles.[6]

The next canon, arrangement, described ways to order ideas effectively. Speakers were taught that a speech must open with an introduction, follow with a statement of purpose, lead into presentation of arguments, and end with a conclusion. Classical rhetoricians also emphasized the necessity of organizing material according to audience needs and goals.

In an oral society, memory, the ability to hold content, style, and arrangement in one's mind, was exceedingly important. The science of mnemonics was developed during this time to help speakers keep track of complex arguments. One of the most popular mnemonic systems called for the speaker to visualize a villa with the main ideas of the speech situated in each room. During the speech, the speaker could then mentally proceed through the rooms, making each argument in the correct order. The method was developed by a rhetor named Simonides who, after reciting a poem at a banquet, was called away from the banquet hall. This circumstance was fortunate, because no sooner did he leave than the hall collapsed, killing many of the guests. When asked to help identify the dead, Simonides realized that he could remember quite easily where each person had been sitting. The incident brought home to him the power of visual memory and set him to wondering whether visualization might be used to recall other kinds of information.

The final canon was delivery. Delivery was considered necessary for success because if the speaker did not use a pleasing voice and graceful gestures, the effect of the speech would be undermined. Although they considered delivery less important than the other canons, the Greeks and Romans understood the importance of nonverbal communication in speech presentation. Cicero, for example, illustrated the need for nonverbal expression when he warned speakers that they would never be able to make an audience feel indignation, terror, or compassion until these emotions were "visibly stamped or rather branded on the advocate himself."[7]

> For classical rhetoricians, communication was the "queen of disciplines."

For classical rhetoricians, communication was the "queen of disciplines." Because it was through communication that a society determined policies in its own best interest, rhetoric carried heavy ethical weight. In fact, Quintilian (35–95 C.E.), the last of the great classical theorists, defined rhetoric as the study of "the good man speaking well." While the focus of communication study during this time was on legal and political discourse, classical theorists also expressed a concern for all forms of communication. As Plato says in the *Phaedrus*,

> *Is not rhetoric, taken generally, a universal art of enchanting the mind by arguments; which is practised not only in courts and public assemblies, but in private houses also, having to do with all matters, great as well as small, good and bad alike?*[8]

Medieval and Renaissance Communication: Truth Armed against Falsehood

With the fall of the Roman Empire and the rise of Christianity, rhetorical study declined. During the next two important historical periods, the medieval period (which lasted from 400 to 1400) and the Renaissance (1400 to 1600), little insight was added to classical thought. Only at the very beginning of the medieval period, when Augustine wrote, and at the very end of the Renaissance, with the work of Francis Bacon, do we find much original work. During the twelve hundred years following the classical period, most rhetorical works were fragmented versions of earlier thought or handbooks on rhetorical style.

Communication is ubiquitous. In any modern city in any country in the world, messages are everywhere. Communication scholars study the impact of these messages.

The medieval period and the Renaissance were characterized by the rise to power of Christian clergy and the decline of "pagan" theories of rhetoric. With the advent of monolithic Christianity, the goal of communication was no longer to discover possible truth through debate but to instruct the faithful in certain truth, the revealed "will of God." Classic ideas of rhetoric, therefore, fell into disrepute, and "rhetoric ceased to be a vital, developing discipline."[9]

There was, nevertheless, a practical need for training in communication. The two most important communication activities were letter writing and preaching. The first was of great importance because in a world of independently held feudal kingdoms, it was necessary to communicate over large distances. In the so-called Dark Ages, most people were illiterate, and even kings, queens, and priests were forced to hire professional "dictators" who composed and wrote the political decrees, legal mandates, and religious dispensations that connected feudal society.

Preaching was also of great importance, because it was the duty of the Christian clergy to teach the word of God. Augustine (354–430), a major Christian theorist, argued that it would be foolish for truth "to take its stand unarmed against falsehood." If evil speakers were to sway an audience by their eloquence and false arguments, and the good were to "tell the truth in such a way that it is tedious to listen to, hard to understand, and, in fine, not easy to believe in," then wicked and worthless causes would triumph.[10]

The preacher's goal was to interpret the word of God. He (rarely she) had to study the scriptures and pass their meaning on. As a communication theorist, Augustine tried to understand this process. He believed that people communicate through signs. A sign, he said, is something that "causes something else to come into the mind as a consequence of itself."[11] Natural signs (for example, smoke, which causes one to think of fire) are created by God. Conventional signs (for example, the spoken or written word) are arbitrarily created by humans, and their interpretation is more difficult. For Augustine, communication was a process of "drawing forth and conveying into another's mind what the giver of the sign has in his own mind."[12] This view of communication as a process whereby a sender transmits symbols to a receiver who interprets and acts on them is close to the view of many modern theorists.[13]

Augustine

After Augustine, there was little original theorizing about communication. Rhetoric became secondary to theology, its subject matter was dispersed throughout the liberal arts, and what remained was prescriptive rather than theoretical. Most rhetorical works were compilations of form letters or manuals on preaching style. Although the study of rhetoric never died out, it became fragmented; the vigor and originality that had characterized it during the classical period were gone.

The Modern Period: A Rational Science of Rhetoric

The three centuries from 1600 to 1900 are known as the modern period. During this time, new attitudes toward knowledge revitalized the study of rhetoric. James Golden and his colleagues express it this way: "Prior to 1660, the world was viewed as a place of sin, peopled with men who were wicked. God and the devil haunted man. But from 1660 onward religion was less influential."[14] The world became more secular, and a new emphasis on men's and women's ability to determine the truth rationally and independently took hold. The rise of the scientific method meant that ideas and arguments should be empirically grounded (that is, based on observation). The rise of nationalism and democratic forms of government gave new importance to the practice of rhetoric. Once again, people believed that political and moral problems could be solved through the exercise of free speech.

In his analysis of modern rhetoric, Douglas Ehninger identifies four directions of rhetorical study during the modern period.[15] Those who took the classical approach set out to recover the insights of the great classical rhetoricians, adapting them to modern times. Others took a psychological/epistemological approach. They investigated the relationship of communication and thought, trying to understand in a "scientific" way how people could influence one another through speech. The belletristic approach focused on writing and speaking as art forms, developing critical standards for judging drama, poetry, and oratory. Finally, those who took an elocutionary approach designed elaborate systems of instruction to improve speakers' verbal and nonverbal presentation.

Those adopting a psychological/epistemological approach were particularly eager to find a scientific basis for the study of human communication. They wanted to understand how human action could be influenced by speech, and they wanted to describe the thought processes of receivers listening to persuasive messages. This inquiry led them to a consideration of human nature and human thought. Francis Bacon (1561–1626) started things off with an analysis of perceptual bias that seems remarkably modern even today. Writing at the very beginning of the modern period, Bacon identified four "idols" or distortions that get in the way of clear thinking.[16] The "Idols of the Tribe" referred to fallacies in thinking due to human nature. Bacon believed that most of us are, by nature, careless thinkers often ruled by emotion. Thus, our understanding is like a false mirror that can distort reality. The "Idols of the Cave" are the individual prejudices we bring with us because of our own backgrounds and personalities. Each of us lives in a cave or den that "refracts and discolours the light of nature." The "Idols of the Market Place" are social in nature and center on imprecise use of language. "Words," according to Bacon, "plainly force and overrule the understanding, and throw all into confusion, and lead men away into numberless empty controversies and idle fancies." Finally, the "Idols of the Theatre" are fallacies that occur when we accept fashionable ideas uncritically. Bacon felt that received systems of thought represent "worlds of their own creation after an unreal and scenic fashion."[17] According to Bacon, we should be on guard against these prejudices and distortions in our own thought and speech and in those of others. The only true protection is to be as scientific as possible, grounding knowledge in empirical observation and rational thought, and expressing thought in clear, unadorned language.

> Those adopting a psychological/epistemological approach were particularly eager to find a scientific basis for the study of human communication.

Communication takes many forms, from the most sophisticated messages to the simplest of conversations. In every case it affects the quality of our lives.

Other modern thinkers such as René Descartes (1596–1650) and John Locke (1632–1704) also mistrusted normal uses of rhetoric and argued that truth could be obtained only through discourse that was solidly grounded in an understanding of human rationality. The ideas of these early modern thinkers were picked up by George Campbell (1719–1796) and combined with the teachings of the classical rhetoricians. One of Campbell's most modern ideas concerned the relationship between speaker and audience. He believed that receivers were active participants in the persuasion process and that the effective communicator studied the inner workings, or "faculties," of the human mind. Contemporary theorists still emphasize the importance of understanding the experiences and motivations of individual receivers.

The rhetoricians who took a belletristic view were interested less in the psychology of communication than in problems of style and eloquence. Nevertheless, like the classical and psychological theorists, they believed that speakers should be widely read and well educated; should use clear, lively, and concise language; should follow a motivational or psychologically based order of arguments; and should speak with a natural, extemporaneous style, matching gestures and voice to the feeling expressed in their texts.

The elocutionists focused their study of communication on the canon of delivery. Although their initial task was to describe the gestures and vocal characteristics that are naturally associated with different emotional states, their zeal for systematizing soon led to sets of artificial rules for delivery. They developed elaborate charts detailing the appropriate ways to show major emotions such as pride, shame, horror, and admiration (see Figure 1.1). By using the "self-help" books they published, speakers could mechanically map out the nonverbal behaviors that would make their delivery most effective. Unfortunately, this approach led to a florid style that was anything but natural and spontaneous and that gave a bad name to the study of oral communication for many years.

COMMUNICATION TODAY: CONTEMPORARY DEPARTMENTS OF RHETORIC AND COMMUNICATION THEORY

Throughout the history of communication study, new technologies have continually affected our ideas of what communication is. During the modern period, the new technology was printing. As written communication became increasingly important, rhetoricians turned their attention from the study of the spoken word to the study of literary works. Therefore, when American universities and colleges organized themselves into departments, rhetoric was assigned to English departments. In the early years of the twentieth century, however, teachers of public speaking and rhetoric formed their own professional organization and developed their own departments of speech communication. Today, these departments are among the most popular on campuses everywhere, but in the early days, this was not the case. At that time, serious students of communication focused on literary communication, whereas public speaking was associated with the simplistic systems of the elocutionists. Many people considered speech too simple to be studied seriously.[18]

Figure 1.1 An Elocutionary Approach to the Use of Gesture

The Geometric Properties of Easy and Graceful Movement

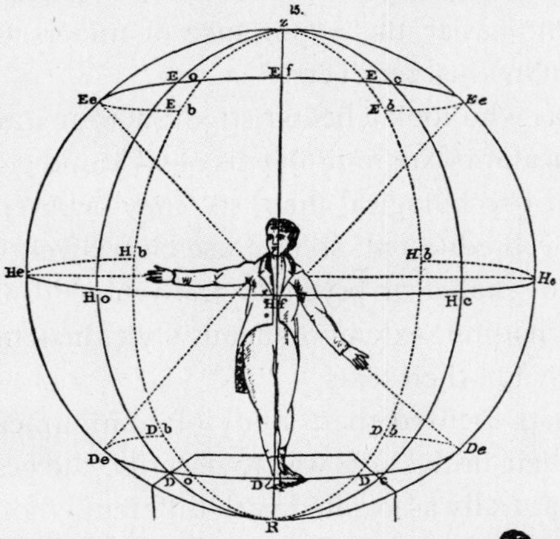

Diagrams Showing the Speaker How to Express Appropriate Emotion

Aversion is expressed by two gestures; first the hand . . . is retracted toward the face . . . then suddenly the eyes are withdrawn, the head is averted, the feet retire, and the arms are projected out extended against the object, the hands vertical.

Veneration crosses both hands on the breast, casts down the eyes slowly, and bows the head.

Horror is seldom capable of retreating, but remains petrified, in one attitude, with the eyes riveted on its object, and the arm held forward to guard the person . . .

From *A Manual of Elocution: Embracing Voice and Gesture, Designed for Schools, Academies and Colleges as Well as for Private Learners* by M. Caldwell, 1845, Philadelphia: Sorin and Ball, pp. 248, 310, 808.

Communication: Humanity or Social Science?

In contemporary departments, two approaches to the study of communication are evident. Many scholars continue in the rhetorical tradition. They use the historical and critical methods of the humanities in their studies of the ways in which symbolic activity shapes public response to political and ethical issues. For these scholars, rhetoric remains a humanistic discipline. Yet although their approach grows out of a long and rich tradition, the problems they address are often very contemporary.

A second school of thought takes a more scientific approach to the study of communication. At the turn of the century, many disciplines were influenced by the scientific method, a belief in controlled laboratory experimentation and careful, objective measurement. Scientists believed that one could understand a phenomenon only by reducing it to its most basic elements or variables, manipulating these variables in a controlled situation, and observing the results.

Scholars in the emerging disciplines of psychology, sociology, and anthropology sought ways of applying the methods of the "hard" scientists to the study of human behavior. Because many students of communication were convinced that human communication should join the social sciences, in the 1920s communication researchers began to look at communication from this new perspective. Rather than relying on introspection, communication scientists decided to observe and measure communication behaviors either in natural, real-world settings or in laboratories. Their first step was to isolate a phenomenon of interest. After looking at relevant theory and finding out what had previously been discovered, they would then pose a research question and determine the kinds of observations and measurements that might allow them to answer their questions or test their hypotheses. For example, a researcher might be interested in the phenomenon that we call source credibility (the extent to which a communicator is considered believable and competent). The researcher might also be interested in how gender affects credibility. He or she might then formulate a research question linking these two variables. For example, the researcher might ask, "Are women considered more credible when they address stereotypically 'female issues,' such as education or health care, than when they speak on stereotypically 'male issues,' such as crime or the economy?" The researcher could then set up a situation in which audience members would listen to a series of speeches by female speakers on different issues and then rate their credibility. As a result of the findings of this study, the researcher could do further work to determine the strategies and approaches that would help or hurt female candidates.[19] The researcher could also determine the extent to which stereotypes affect audience expectations.

In fact, early communication scientists did study phenomena such as credibility in order to understand more about audience psychology and attitude change. They also studied the effects of speech organization, use of evidence, the effects of rational and emotional appeals, and "audience variables such as sex, dogmatism, ego involvement in the subject of the message, and so forth."[20] Today, the areas of interest studied by communication scientists have expanded to include investigations of interpersonal and group interaction as well as investigations of persuasive messages. Chapter 13 discusses in more detail how communication scientists proceed as well as how those who take a more humanistic, rhetorical approach engage in research.

Although their methods may differ, rhetoricians and communication scientists address similar questions.

Whether you believe that communication should be studied by using humanistic or scientific methods, you will find support in contemporary communication departments, where courses both in rhetoric and communication theory are taught. Although their methods may differ, rhetoricians and communication scientists address similar questions. Both want to understand how communicators affect each other as they interact.

What Do Rhetoricians and Communication Scientists Do?

One of the most attractive aspects of studying communication is that it prepares us for so many different professions. People with degrees in rhetoric and communication theory apply their interests in many communication-related professions. They may become speechwriters, political consultants or politicians, legal consultants or lawyers, advertising executives, public relations experts, counselors, organizational training and development specialists, professional negotiators, personnel managers, specialists in information storage and retrieval, radio or television performers, media consultants, and the like. Communication specialists are needed in corporate settings as spokespersons and company representatives. They are also needed in professions that provide information and counseling to the public, such as health-care professions. In fact, opportunities for individuals trained in communication are plentiful throughout the economy. Whether you plan to major in communication or to take some courses simply to explore, what you learn will be useful to you throughout your working life. Knowing how to communicate clearly and effectively will benefit you no matter what career you choose.

Of course, business and professional contexts are not the only settings in which the study of communication is important. Many communication specialists decide to teach or do academic research. Those who do so have large numbers of subjects to investigate and, as we shall see later, a variety of ways to study those subjects. In the past, rhetoricians have studied the rhetoric of films, television, social movements, political speeches, political newscasting, cartoons, popular music, psychotherapy, painting, architecture, and even science.[21] Communication scientists have studied how communication affects the development and maintenance of one's self-image, how message variables affect the way we process and understand information, the factors that lead to attitude change, how interpersonal relationships form and dissolve, how small groups make effective and ineffective decisions, how complex organizations use communication to function effectively, how the media affect audience responses, and the like.[22]

As we've seen, communication has been an important area of study for thousands of years. Now, more than ever, a firm grounding in communication is a personal and professional necessity, for we live in an age in which the ability to process and evaluate communication has become a necessary skill. As you progress through this text, you will gain a greater understanding of how communication works and, in the process, you will begin to develop more control over the way you communicate.

SUMMARY

The study of communication is not a modern invention. We can trace many of today's ideas about communication to earlier periods, in particular ancient Greece and Rome. Although the first Western rhetoricians to be recognized as such were the Sicilian Greeks Corax and Tisias, the study of rhetoric became fully developed only after the Athenian philosophers, particularly Plato and Aristotle, turned their attention to the art of communication. Early rhetorical systems provided practical training for individuals who needed to express their thoughts clearly and eloquently in political and legal contexts.

Aristotle and Plato wrote during the classical period (500 B.C.–A.D. 400). As a result of their work and that of others such as Cicero and Quintilian, by the end of this period a full-fledged communication model had developed. This model, called the canons of rhetoric, divided the process of public communication into five parts: invention, style, arrangement, memory, and delivery. Much of the information we now study in public speaking classes originated in these canons.

During the medieval period (400–1400) and the Renaissance (1400–1600), the focus of rhetoric shifted, owing in part to the political power of the Christian clergy. Particularly important forms of communication were letter writing and preaching. The medieval philosopher Augustine viewed communication as a symbolic process, a view we shall examine in detail in the chapter on spoken language, Chapter 4.

In the modern period (1600–1900), the study of rhetoric followed one of four paths. The classical approach revived ancient Greek and Roman models. The belletristic approach focused on communication as art. The elocutionist approach consisted of elaborate, artificial systems of presentation. And the psychological/epistemological approach investigated the relationship between communication and thought, placing special emphasis on the receiver as an active participant in the creation of meaning.

By the twentieth century, a new method of inquiry, the scientific method, became popular. Some communication scholars began to use experiments and objective measurement to investigate audience response and attitude change. During the same period, a more humanistic, philosophical approach was also used. Contemporary departments of communication acknowledge the importance of both communication science and the rhetorical tradition. Communication study has a rich history. Although methodologies and concerns have changed over the centuries, the fundamental importance of understanding communication remains the same.

KEY TERMS

Listed below are the key terms used in this chapter, along with the number of the page where each is explained.

rhetoric (3)	Peripatetic School (4)	Corax (4)
rhetoricians (3)	ethos (4)	Tisias (4)
Aristotle (3)	pathos (4)	classical period (5)
Plato (3)	logos (4)	Sophists (5)

Cicero   (5)
canons of rhetoric   (6)
invention   (6)
style   (6)
plain style   (6)
middle style   (7)
vigorous style   (7)
arrangement   (7)
memory   (7)
delivery   (7)

Quintilian   (7)
medieval period   (8)
Renaissance   (8)
Augustine   (8)
natural signs   (9)
conventional signs   (9)
modern period   (9)
empiric   (9)
classical approach
   (9)

psychological/epistemological
   approach   (9)
belletristic approach   (9)
elocutionary approach   (10)
Francis Bacon   (10)
René Descartes   (10)
John Locke   (10)
George Campbell   (10)
scientific method   (13)
source credibility   (13)

SUGGESTED READING

Bizzell, Patricia, & Herzberg, Bruce. (2001). *The rhetorical tradition: Readings from classical times to the present* (2nd ed.). Boston: Bedford/St. Martin's.

> Presents readings from the original works of the great rhetoricians; its introductions to each period present excellent summaries of the history of rhetorical thought.

Herrick, James A. (2004). *The history and theory of rhetoric: An introduction* (3rd ed.). Boston: Allyn & Bacon.

> Provides a lively and readable discussion of the history of rhetoric from ancient Greece to current times, using contemporary examples that show the relevance of rhetoric today.

Definitions, Models, and Perspectives

Communication is a complex process that can be viewed in many ways.

As we saw in Chapter 1, communication has had a long history. For thousands of years, scholars have debated the nature of communication, and students have worked to improve their communication skills. Unfortunately, this doesn't mean that it's easy to define communication. As we shall see, communication is a complex process that can be viewed in many ways. In this chapter, we consider issues that arise when scholars try to describe the essence of communication. We examine what it means to create definitions and build models of this complex process, and we explore some of the underlying philosophical perspectives that guide our understanding of communication.

We'll look at three fundamentally different approaches to communication, and as we do so, we'll consider where each locates communication and what each has to say about the characteristics of good communicators. We'll also look at a fourth, evolving perspective.

DEFINING COMMUNICATION

A definition is a useful and logical place to start our exploration of communication. The term definition comes from a Latin word meaning "to determine, bring to an end, or settle." Definitions clarify concepts by indicating their boundaries. They focus attention on what is important about whatever it is we are defining. A good definition of communication tells us which behaviors count as communication and which do not. It also describes the essential characteristics of communication.

Unfortunately, no single definition of communication does this to everyone's satisfaction. In fact, in the early 1970s, Frank Dance identified 126 published definitions.[1] In the last twenty years, communication scholars have been busily adding to that list, so now there

After reading this chapter, you should be able to:

- Explain why definitions are important and why there can be more than one definition of communication.
- Identify how definitions vary in terms of breadth, intentionality, sender/receiver orientation, and importance of symbols.
- Explain the three functions of models as well as their drawbacks.
- Distinguish between the psychological, social constructionist, and pragmatic perspectives.
- Explain for any given model which perspective it belongs to.
- Criticize each perspective by describing its weaknesses.
- Understand the cultural studies perspective.
- Identify the elements of communication in Hymes's SPEAKING model.

are a good many more. Why has the concept of communication produced so many definitions? To understand the reasons for this diversity, we have to look first at what it means to create a definition and then at the specific issues that arise when people try to define communication.

Definitions: Discovery or Construction?

One way to think about the world is to assume that it is made up of phenomena that exist independently of human knowledge. By carefully observing objects and actions, we can discover their essential features and express them in the form of an objective definition. According to this view, a good definition accurately records and describes something that already exists. Understanding the world and expressing that understanding in a definition are objective processes of *discovery;* theoretically, a single correct definition exists for everything we wish to understand.

Even the most mundane of objects can have a number of equally valid definitions.

A second, and quite different, way to think about the world is to assume that most of the things we try to define are human constructions. As we experience the world, each of us tries to make sense of it by creating mental representations of it. Because we each have different needs and experiences, our individual understandings will often vary. According to this view, a definition is a subjective *construction* rather than an objective discovery. If we adopt this approach, then the test of a good definition is not its absolute truth but rather its practical use. Different definitions focus our attention on different aspects of a given phenomenon. A definition is useful if it helps us understand those aspects more fully.

The second approach explains how even the most mundane of objects can have a number of equally valid definitions. Even an everyday object such as a telephone can be defined in many ways. If we were to ask an American teenager, a telemarketer, and a telecommunications engineer to tell us what a telephone is, we might get quite different definitions. The teenager might define the telephone in terms of its social functions, seeing it as a way of maintaining relationships. The telemarketer might view the telephone as a way to reach customers. The engineer might concentrate on the phone's design. Each would visualize and explain the instrument in a different way; and each would be right. All three definitions are useful, because they clarify important aspects of the telephone. Clearly, when it comes to social phenomena such as communication, multiple definitions become even more likely.

Deciding What Communication Is

Table 2.1 lists a number of definitions of communication that differ on several dimensions: breadth, intentionality, role of senders and receivers, and the importance of symbols. Before you read further, consider these definitions and choose the one you like the best. If none appeals to you, try your hand at creating your own definition.

How Broad Is Communication?

One of the first questions to ask is how broad or narrow we want communication to be; this is the issue of breadth. What kinds of behaviors do you call communication? No doubt you include people talking to one another; that's easy. But what do you make of a situation in which one person draws conclusions about another person without the second person's knowledge? Do you call that communication? And how do you class the bond between a pet and its owner, or the signals that animals send to one another? What about someone "communing" with nature; is he or she communicating? Is it possible for people to communicate with computers or for computers to communicate with one another?

If we wish the concept of communication to include all of the activities mentioned above, we need a very broad definition. Definitions 1 and 2 in Table 2.1 are the broadest and most inclusive. Definition 1 ("Communication is a process of acting on information") includes all of the examples given above, whereas definition 2 ("Communication is the discriminatory response of an organism to a stimulus") excludes machine communication but includes behaviors of living organisms.

Table 2.1 Definitions of Communication

Definition 1	Communication is a process of acting on information.
Definition 2	"Communication is the discriminatory response of an organism to a stimulus."[a]
Definition 3	"Communication . . . is an 'effort after meaning,' a creative act initiated by man in which he seeks to discriminate and organize cues so as to orient himself in his environment and satisfy his changing needs."[b]
Definition 4	"Speech communication is a human process through which we make sense out of the world and share that sense with others."[c]
Definition 5	"In the main, communication has as its central interest those behavioral situations in which a source transmits a message to a receiver(s) *with conscious intent to affect the latter's behaviors.*"[d]
Definition 6	Communication is a process whereby people assign meanings to stimuli in order to make sense of the world.
Definition 7	Communication is "the transmission of information, ideas, emotions, skills, etc., by the use of symbols—words, pictures, figures, graphs, etc."[e]
Definition 8	*Spoken symbolic interaction* is the process by which people use words and other symbols to create meaning and to affect one another.
Definition 9	*Nonverbal interaction* is the unspoken, often unintentional behavior that accompanies verbal communication and helps us fully interpret its meaning.

[a]Stevens, S. S. (1950). A definition of communication. *The Journal of the Acoustical Society of America*, 22, 689–690.

[b]Barnlund, Dean. (1968). *Interpersonal communication: Survey and studies*. Boston: Houghton Mifflin, 6.

[c]Masterson, John T., Beebe, Steven A., & Watson, Norman H. (1983). *Speech communication: Theory and practice.* New York: Holt, Rinehart & Winston, 5.

[d]Miller, Gerald A. (1966). On defining communication: Another stab. *Journal of Communication*, 16, 88–98, 92.

[e]Berelson, Bernard, & Steiner, Gary. (1964). *Human behavior*. New York: Harcourt, Brace, & World, 254.

Whereas some people prefer a broad definition, others want one that focuses more directly on human behavior. Arguing that there are essential differences between humans, animals, and machines, these people define communication as a uniquely human process. People who hold this view prefer definition 3 ("Communication . . . is an 'effort after meaning,' a creative act initiated by man in which he seeks to discriminate and organize cues so as to orient himself in his environment and satisfy his changing needs") or definition 4 ("Speech communication is a human process through which we make sense out of the world and share that sense with others"). These definitions set different boundaries for communication.

Is Communication Intentional?

Another question about communication is whether or not it involves intentionality. Let's consider an example of unobtrusive observation. Assume that Brennan comes across Brianne, who is unaware that she is being watched. Brianne does something revealing; perhaps she frowns and looks annoyed. As a result, Brennan draws a conclusion about her mood. Is this communication? According to definition 5 in Table 2.1 ("In the main, communication has as its central interest those behavioral situations in which a source transmits a message to a receiver(s) *with conscious intent to affect the latter's behaviors*"), it is not communication, for Brianne did not mean to send a message.

But not everyone would agree. Some people think that it's impossible to know whether a message is intentional. They argue that what is important about the interaction between Brennan and Brianne is not what Brianne intends but how Brennan interprets her behavior. People who take this view prefer that the definition of communication include unintentional as well as intentional behaviors. Definition 6 ("Communication is a process whereby people assign meanings to stimuli in order to make sense of the world") does just that.

Is Communication Sender- or Receiver-Based?

If we accept the situation involving Brennan and Brianne as an instance of communication, we are faced with yet another question. Which of them is communicating? Some people would argue that it is Brianne who is communicating, because it is her behavior that is the source of information. Others would contend that it is Brennan who is communicating, since it is he who assigns meaning. Those people who locate communication in Brianne's behavior take a sender-based view of communication, whereas those who see Brennan as the communicator take a receiver-based stance. Definition 5 in Table 2.1 ("Communication has as its central interest . . . situations in which a source transmits a message . . . *with conscious intent*") is sender oriented, as is definition 7 ("Communication is the 'transmission of information, ideas, emotions, skills, etc., by the use of symbols—words, pictures, figures, graphs, etc.'"). Definition 4 ("Speech communication is a human process through which we make sense out of the world and share that sense with others") includes both sender and receiver, and the rest of the definitions appear to be receiver oriented.

Is All Communication Symbolic?

A final question concerns the extent to which a definition of communication emphasizes symbolic behavior. As we shall see in more detail in ensuing chapters, humans have two code systems at their disposal. We can express ourselves symbolically through words, numbers, and graphic designs. We can also convey meaning nonverbally through facial expressions, body movements, and physical appearance. Many people believe that it is the ability to use symbols (arbitrary and conventionalized representations) that makes humans unique and that we should focus our study of communication on the way humans use symbols to convey meaning. For these people, nonverbal behaviors are a secondary concern. Definition 7 ("Communication is the 'transmission of [meaning] by the use of symbols'") clearly limits communication to symbolic behavior, whereas the other definitions seem to include both symbolic and nonsymbolic behavior.

Multiple Definitions: Communication as a Family of Concepts

As you move from one definition to another, the boundaries of communication shift, and you focus your attention in a slightly different direction. In choosing one definition over another, consider how that definition expands or contracts the domain of communication. A broad definition is useful when you want to emphasize commonalities between human and nonhuman information processing. A narrow definition is useful when you want to focus on a particular kind of communication, say, human communication or symbolic communication. There is no right or wrong way to make your choice, nor is it necessary to choose a single definition. Indeed, Frank Dance has suggested that instead of talking about communication as a single concept, it may be more useful to talk about several kinds of communication, for example, animal communication, nonverbal communication, spoken symbolic interaction, and so on. Dance asks us to think of communication as a family of interrelated concepts, each of which has its own utility.[2]

If communication is a family of concepts rather than a single concept, then the two family members that receive the most attention in this book are spoken symbolic interaction and nonverbal interaction. Our discipline has focused from its beginning on spoken symbolic interaction, the way people use symbols (primarily words) to create common meaning and to share that meaning with one another. In keeping with this tradition, most of the chapters in this book are devoted to understanding verbal communication. Nevertheless, people are often affected by unintentional behaviors that accompany the spoken word. Therefore, we will also direct attention to nonverbal interaction, the unspoken, often unintentional behavior that accompanies verbal communication and helps us fully interpret its meaning. Although animal and machine communication are valid subjects of study and can add to an understanding of communication in its broadest sense, these topics will receive less attention simply because our goal is to understand human communication.

HOW MODELS HELP US UNDERSTAND COMMUNICATION

In addition to defining communication, scholars build models of it. A model is an abstract representation of a process, a description of its structure or function. Models are useful because they help us understand how a process works. As Cassandra Book and her colleagues point out, models can help us to organize our thinking, generate research questions, and make predictions.[3] And just as there are many definitions of communication, so there are many models. Models are representations; they cannot capture a process in its entirety. Instead, each model describes certain aspects of the total process.

Modeling a social process helps us to think carefully about the form and function of that process. To create a model, we divide the whole process into its basic parts and consider how these parts are connected. Models stimulate creativity; by building models, we may find out interesting things that we might previously have overlooked.

> Models stimulate creativity; by building models, we may find out interesting things that we might previously have overlooked.

In this section, we'll continue our examination of communication by looking at several models. We'll describe each model carefully, consider its assumptions, and discover its strengths and weaknesses. We'll also look at how each model characterizes good communication.

The Forms and Functions of Models

Almost any object or process can be modeled, and models can take many forms. Before we consider ways of modeling communication, consider how you might model another kind of entity: a city. A model of a city could be any of the following: a street map, an organization chart of city government, a computer simulation of traffic flow, a scale model of a city's architecture, a sociological description of changing neighborhoods, even a board game. Each is an abstraction, a simplified version of the city. Each focuses on only a small part of the process. Yet each helps us to answer the questions "What is a city?" and "How does it work?"

Models aid us by describing and explaining a process, by yielding testable predictions about how the process works, or by showing us ways to control the process. Some models fulfill an explanatory function by dividing a process into constituent parts and showing us how the parts are connected. A city's organizational chart does this by explaining how city government works, and the sociological description allows us to see the economic and social factors that caused the city to become what it is today.

Other models fulfill a predictive function. Traffic simulations and population growth projections function in this way. They allow us to answer "if . . . then" questions. If we add another traffic light, then will we eliminate gridlock? If the population keeps growing at the current rate, then what will housing conditions be in the year 2025? Models help us answer questions about the future.

Finally, models fulfill a control function. A street map not only describes the layout of a city but also allows you to find your way from one place to another and helps you figure out where you went wrong if you get lost. Models guide our behavior. They show us how to control a process.

We construct prototypes and models so that we can understand how objects and processes work.

The Drawbacks of Models

Models are useful, but they can also have drawbacks. In building and using models, we must be cautious. First, we must realize that *models are necessarily incomplete* because they are simplified versions of very complex processes. When a model builder chooses to include one detail, he or she invariably chooses to ignore hundreds more. Models can be misleading if they oversimplify a process.

Second, we must keep in mind that *there are many ways to model a single process.* Most of us like certainty. We've grown up believing that every problem has one right answer. Unfortunately, when we study complex processes, we can never be 100 percent certain we understand them. There are many "right answers," all equally valuable but each distinct. Although this may be confusing at first, try thinking of it positively. Looking for single answers limits you intellectually; accepting multiple answers opens you to new possibilities.

Finally, we musn't forget that *models make assumptions about processes.* It's always important to look "below the surface" of any model to detect the hidden assumptions it makes. Communication models, being abstract, make many assumptions. In the next section, we'll look at two of the most important types of assumptions a model makes. We'll examine where each model locates communication; for example, does a given model imply that communication occurs in the minds of human interactants, in social norms and rules, or in patterns of moves and countermoves? We'll also examine what value judgments the model makes; we'll try to discover what good communication is from the

> Models are simplified versions of very complex processes.

standpoint of each model. As we shall see, the answers to these questions are often hidden below a model's surface.

IT ALL DEPENDS ON YOUR POINT OF VIEW: FOUR PERSPECTIVES

Many interesting communication models exist. In this section, we'll look at four, each of which takes a different theoretical perspective. In the next section, we'll look at a fifth model that will provide us with a practical way to observe communication behavior.

A perspective is a coherent set of assumptions about the way a process operates.[4] The first three models we will look at are built on different sets of assumptions. The first model takes what is known as a psychological perspective. It focuses on what happens "inside the heads" of communicators as they transmit and receive messages. The second model takes a social constructionist perspective.[5] It sees communication as a process whereby people, using the tools provided by their culture, create collective representations of reality. It emphasizes the relationship between communication and culture. The third model takes what is called a pragmatic perspective.[6] According to this view, communication consists of a system of interlocking, interdependent "moves," which become patterned over time. This perspective focuses on the games people play when they communicate. As we look at each of these models, you'll begin to understand how these perspectives differ in their emphasis on individual psychology, cultural constructs, or actual behaviors.

Communication as Message Transmission

We'll begin with the most familiar approach to communication. Most models and definitions of communication are based on the psychological perspective. They locate communication in the human mind and see the individual as both the source of and the destination for messages. Figure 2.1 illustrates an example of a psychological model.

Elements of a Psychological Model

The model in Figure 2.1 depicts communication as *a psychological process whereby two (or more) individuals exchange meanings through the transmission and reception of communication stimuli*. According to this model, an individual is a sender/receiver who encodes and decodes meanings. Adam has an idea he wishes to communicate to Betty. Adam encodes this idea by translating it into a message that he believes Betty can understand. The encoded message travels along a channel, its medium of transmission, until it reaches its destination. On receiving the message, Betty decodes it and decides how she will reply. In sending the reply, she gives Adam feedback about his message. Adam uses this information to decide whether or not his communication was successful.

Figure 2.1 A Psychological Model of Communication

In a psychological model, messages are filtered through an individual's store of beliefs, attitudes, values, and emotions.

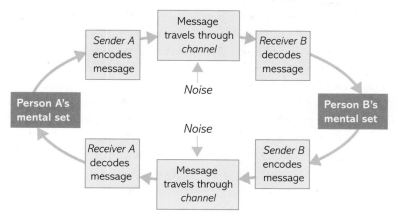

During encoding and decoding, Adam and Betty filter messages through their mental sets. A **mental set** consists of a person's beliefs, values, attitudes, feelings, and so on. Because each message is composed and interpreted in light of an individual's past experience, each encoded or decoded message has its own unique meaning. Of course, partners' mental sets can sometimes lead to misunderstandings. The meanings that Adam and Betty assign to a message may vary in important ways. If this occurs, they may miscommunicate.

> Communication is most successful when individuals are "of the same mind"—when the meanings they assign to messages are similar or identical.

Communication can also go awry if noise enters the channel. **Noise** is any distraction that interferes with or changes a message during transmission. Communication is most successful when individuals are "of the same mind"—when the meanings they assign to messages are similar or identical.

Let's look at how this process works in a familiar setting, the college lecture. Professor Smith wants to inform his students about the history of rhetoric. Alone in his study, he gazes at his plaster-of-paris bust of Aristotle and thinks about how he will encode his understanding and enthusiasm in words. To encode successfully, he must guess about what's going on in the students' minds. Although it's hard for him to imagine that anyone could be bored by the history of rhetoric, he knows that students need to hear a "human element" in his lecture. He therefore decides to include examples and anecdotes to spice up his message.

Smith delivers his lecture in a large, drafty lecture room. The microphone he uses unfortunately emits shrill whines and whistles at inopportune times. That he also forgets to talk into the mike only compounds the noise problem. Other sources of distraction are his appearance and nonverbal behavior. When Smith enters the room, his mismatched polyester suit and hand-painted tie are fairly presentable, but as he gets more and more excited, his clothes take on a life of their own. His shirt untucks itself, his jacket collects chalk dust, and his tie juts out at a very strange angle. In terms of our model, Smith's clothes are too noisy for the classroom.

Despite his lack of attention to material matters and his tendency toward dry speeches, Smith knows his rhetoric, and highly motivated students have no trouble decoding the lecture. Less-prepared students have more difficulty, however. Smith's words go "over their heads." As the lecture progresses, the students' smiles and nods, their frowns of puzzlement, and their whispered comments to one another act as feedback for Smith to consider.

Smith's communication is partially successful and partially unsuccessful. He reaches the students who can follow his classical references but bypasses the willing but unprepared students who can't decode his messages. And he completely loses the seniors in the back row who are taking the course pass/fail and have set their sights on a D minus. Like most of us, some of the time Smith succeeds, and some of the time he fails.

Improving Faulty Communication

According to the psychological model, communication is unsuccessful whenever the meanings intended by the source differ from the meanings interpreted by the receiver. This occurs when the mental sets of source and receiver are so far apart that there is no shared experience, when the source uses a code that is unfamiliar to the receiver, when the channel is overloaded or impeded by noise, when there is little or no opportunity for feedback, or when receivers are distracted by competing internal stimuli.

> According to the psychological model, communication is unsuccessful whenever the meanings intended by the source differ from the meanings interpreted by the receiver.

Each of these problems can be solved. The psychological model points out ways to improve communication. It suggests that senders can learn to see things from their receivers' points of view. Senders can try to encode messages in clear, lively, and appropriate ways. They can use multiple channels to ensure that their message gets across, and they can try to create noise-free environments. They can also build in opportunities for feedback and learn to read receivers' nonverbal messages.

Receivers too can do things to improve communication. They can prepare themselves for a difficult message by studying the subject ahead of time. They can try to understand "where the speaker is coming from" and anticipate arguments. They can improve their listening skills, and they can ask questions and check their understanding. All of these methods of improving communication are implicit in the model in Figure 2.1.

Criticizing the Psychological Perspective

Although the psychological model is by far the most popular view of communication, it poses some problems, which arise from the assumptions the psychological perspective makes about human behavior. What are some of the assumptions?

First, the psychological model locates communication in the psychological processes of individuals, ignoring almost totally the social context in which communication occurs, as well as the shared roles and rules that govern message construction. This model makes individuals appear more independent than they actually are.

Second, in incorporating the ideas of channel and noise, the psychological model is mechanistic. It treats messages as though they are physical objects that can be sent from one place to another. Noise is treated not as a message but as a separate entity that "attacks" messages. The model also assumes that it is possible not to communicate, that communication can break down. All of these are mechanical ideas that may distort the way communication actually works.

Finally, the psychological model implies that successful communication involves a "meeting of the minds." The model suggests that communication succeeds to the extent that the sender transfers what is in his or her mind to the mind of the receiver, thereby implying that good communication is more likely to occur between people who have the same ideas than between those who have different ideas. This raises some important questions: Is it possible to transfer content from one mind to another? Is accuracy the only value we should place on communication? Is it always a good idea to seek out people who are similar rather than different? Some critics believe that the psychological model diminishes the importance of creativity and makes receivers appear to be empty receptacles waiting to be filled with other people's ideas.

Asking Questions from the Psychological Perspective

Models can be used not only to identify potential communication problems and to suggest ways of overcoming them but also to generate research questions. The psychological perspective is usually associated with what is called a **laws approach** to research. Communication scientists who take this approach describe cause-and-effect laws that connect communication variables. A researcher looking for lawful relationships between parts of the communication process might ask the following questions: Are multiple channels more effective than single channels for transmitting complex messages? Does attitude similarity enhance or inhibit communication accuracy? Because the psychological model is linear, it lends itself to these kinds of questions and to related research methods. Chapter 13 takes up this topic in more detail.

Communication as World Building

The social constructionist perspective takes a very different view of communication. In this view, communication becomes a means of world building. Figure 2.2 illustrates an example of a social constructionist model. According to this model, communication is not something that goes on between individuals; instead, communication is something that surrounds people and holds their world together. Through communication,

> Communication is something that surrounds people and holds their world together. Through communication, social groups create collective ideas of themselves, of one another, and of the world they inhabit.

Figure 2.2 A Social Constructionist Model of Communication

In a social constructionist model, people exist within, and perceive
themselves and others through, the communicative practices of their cultures.

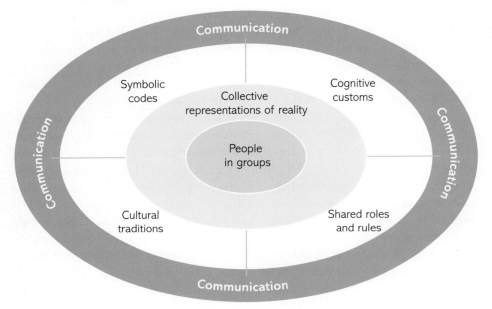

social groups create collective ideas of themselves, of one another, and of the world
they inhabit.

Elements of a Social Constructionist Model

According to the social constructionist model, communication is *a process whereby
people in groups, using the tools provided by their culture, create collective representations of reality.* The model specifies four of these cultural tools: languages, or
symbolic codes; the ways we've been taught to process information, or cognitive
customs; the beliefs, attitudes, and values that make
up our cultural traditions; and the sets of roles and
rules that guide our actions. These tools shape the
ways we experience and talk about our world.

> Most of what we know and believe about the world comes to us through communication rather than through direct experience.

The social constructionist perspective maintains
that we never experience the world directly. Rather, we take those parts of it that
our culture makes significant, process them in culturally recognized ways, connect them to other "facts" that we know, and respond to them in ways our culture
considers significant. According to this perspective, we construct our world
through communication.

This perspective points out that most of what we know and believe about the world comes to us through communication rather than through direct experience. If everyone around us talks about the world in a certain way, we are likely to think of the world in that way and fail to question whether we are seeing things accurately. Thus, when we later encounter people who communicate in different ways, we will have problems during interaction.

Let's take an example. John has been with his company for thirty years and has five more years to go until retirement. When he first started working, there were very few women in managerial positions, but now he finds himself working with many women managers. John thinks of himself as fair-minded and easygoing. He has nothing against the fact that "girls" are now moving up in the company, but he does find it hard to understand why they get so upset over "nothing." When he calls his female secretary "Honey" (which he's done for twenty years), he doesn't understand the prickly reaction of his new colleague, Judy. After all, he's just trying to be nice. It's the way he always talks to women.

Some theorists liken communication to an act of construction, arguing that what we build is larger and more lasting than we realize.

Judy is fresh out of business school and eager to make her way in the professional world. She is appalled by John's behavior. When she hears the way he talks to his secretary, she feels embarrassed and demeaned herself. Furthermore, when John treats Judy like an idiot by explaining everything to her as though she were a child, her blood boils. Judy has come of age in a time when discussions of feminism and sexism are common. She's sensitive to issues John doesn't even notice.

John's attempts to communicate with Judy fail because the two colleagues don't share collective representations of reality. When John was growing up, no one talked about sexism and sexual harassment, so for him these concepts have limited meaning. His views of male/female roles used to work, but now they are outmoded. As a result, he says things that are quite inappropriate in a modern office. In a very real way, John and Judy live in two completely different worlds.

Improving Our Social Constructions

The social constructionist model doesn't give us as many specific guidelines for improving communication as the psychological model did, but it does suggest a few concerns we should think about if we want to be effective communicators. Primarily, it emphasizes that we should take responsibility for the things we talk about and the way we talk about them. Our constructions of reality, according to the model, often distort our communication. Thus, we may accept cultural myths and stereotypes without thinking. Given the fact that symbols have the power to control us, it is useful to develop the critical ability to "see through" cultural constructions and to avoid creating them through our own talk. The ability to decipher our biases is a useful skill.

And whereas the psychological model suggests that individuals create communication, the social constructionist model suggests the opposite, that communication creates individuals. To be successful communicators, it maintains, we must be willing to follow cultural rules and norms. We must take our parts in the social drama our culture has laid out for us. We must also carefully consider whether those roles enhance our identities or inhibit them. If a role is outmoded or unfair to others, we must be willing to abandon it and find a new and more appropriate way of communicating.

Criticizing the Social Constructionist Perspective

For many of you, this model may seem to depart radically from commonsense ideas about communication. To say that we live in a symbolic, rather than a physical, world seems to contradict our most basic notions about the nature of reality. For if we can never gain access to reality but can only experience constructions of it, then how can we tell the difference between truth and illusion? The social constructionist model raises important philosophical questions as it emphasizes a relationship that has been recognized since ancient times: the relationship between rhetoric and truth.

Another troublesome aspect of the social constructionist position is that it defines good communication as socially appropriate communication. Scholars who take this perspective often talk of humans as social performers. To communicate successfully, one acts out a social role over which he or she has little control. For many, this view implies that the good communicator is a social automaton rather than a sincere and spontaneous self. Many people criticize the social constructionist perspective because it places too much emphasis on the social self and not enough on the individual self. They feel that in emphasizing the social and cultural nature of humans, the aspects that make humans unique and individual are forgotten.

Asking Questions from the Social Constructionist Perspective

When social constructionists do research, they pay particular attention to the implicit rules that guide social action. Researchers who are social constructionists often take what is known as a **rules approach** to understanding communication. Rules researchers believe that human behavior is not so much caused as chosen: to accomplish their goals, people choose certain lines of action and follow certain rules laid down by their cultures. We can understand communication behavior by understanding the rules people follow as they act. A rules researcher might ask questions such as these: How do individuals within a given culture use symbols to make sense of the world? Do men and women follow different rules to accomplish their goals? What are the major forms of communication in a given culture, and how are they valued?

Communication as Patterned Interaction

The third model takes yet another view of communication. Instead of focusing on individual selves or on social roles and rules, this perspective centers on systems of behavior. It suggests that the way people act when they are together is of primary importance, and it urges us to look carefully at patterns that emerge as people play the communication game.[7]

Elements of a Pragmatic Model

According to the pragmatic view, communication consists of *a system of interlocking, interdependent behaviors that become patterned over time.* Scholars who take a pragmatic approach argue that communicating is much like playing a game. When people decide to communicate, they become **partners** in a game that requires them to make individual "moves," or **acts.** Over time, these acts become patterned, the simplest pattern being a two-act sequence called an **interact.** One of the reasons certain acts are repeated is that they result in **payoffs** for the participants. Over the course of the game, players become **interdependent** because their payoffs depend on their partners' actions. This analogy between communication and a game is illustrated in Figure 2.3. The analogy between chess and communication holds in a number of ways. First, the game itself, not what goes on around it, is the central concern. Although it is possible to find books on chess that analyze the personality of individual players, most books focus on the structure of the game itself. Who white and black represent is not nearly as important as how they respond to one another. To understand chess, you need to understand the present state of the board and the series of moves that produced it. To understand communication, pragmatists argue, you need to do much the same thing: understand the moves people use as they work out their relationship to one another.

> To understand communication, pragmatists argue, you need to understand the moves people use as they work out their relationship to one another.

Note that in Figure 2.3, the moves are listed sequentially. At every turn, you can see what black did and how white responded. Chess books always list moves in this way, using the exact sequence in which they occurred in the game. It would make no sense to list all the moves of the game randomly. The game consists of ordered, interlocking moves and makes sense only when we follow the sequence. In the same way, an individual act or isolated behavior makes sense only

Figure 2.3 **A Pragmatic Model of Communication**

In a pragmatic model, communication is seen as a game of sequential, interlocking moves between interdependent partners. Each player responds to the partner's moves in light of his or her own strategy and in anticipation of future action. Some moves are specific to this game, and others are common gambits or strategies. All moves make sense only in the context of the game. Outcomes, or payoffs, are a result of patterned "play" between partners.

move	A's moves	B's moves
21	. . . .	B offends A
22	A ignores B	B repeats offense
23	A challenges B	B ignores A
24	A reissues challenge	B offers apology
25	A accepts apology	B thanks A
26	A changes subject	. . . .

in context, that is, when we see it in relationship to previous acts. According to the pragmatic viewpoint, the smallest significant unit of communication is the interact, which consists of two sequential acts. If you merely hear me cry, you know very little about what is happening. To understand what my crying means, you need to know, at the very least, what happened immediately before I cried. I may have become sad or angry, or I may have laughed so hard I began to cry. My crying may be a sincere expression of sorrow, or it may have been a move designed to make you feel sorry for me. The more you know about what happened before I cried, the more you understand the communication game I'm playing.

One of the factors that makes the game analogy appropriate is the interdependence of game players. Each player is affected by what another player does. Players need each other if they are to play. The same is true of communication: a person can't be a sender without someone to be a receiver, and it's impossible for a receiver to receive a message without a sender to send it. The dyad, not the individual, is important. Individuals don't play the communication game; partners (or opponents) do.

In a game, every action is important. Every move I make affects you, and every move you make affects me. Even if I refuse to move, I am still playing: I am resigning from or forfeiting the game. This is even more significant in communication, in which any response counts as a move. According to the pragmatic perspective, *we cannot not communicate*. If a friend promises to write to you and doesn't, his or her silence speaks louder than words. You realize that your friend doesn't want to continue the relationship. It is impossible not to communicate, just as it is impossible not to behave.

Finally, communication resembles a game in that both result in interdependent outcomes, or payoffs. In chess, the payoff is the thrill of victory or the agony of defeat. Communication also has payoffs. Sometimes, they are competitive; for example, someone "wins points" by putting down someone else. But more often than not, the payoffs are cooperative. Each person gets something out of playing. In fact, one way to view relationships is as cooperative improvised games. As people get to know one another, they learn to avoid unproductive moves, and they begin to work out **patterns** of interaction that satisfy both of them. This is what we mean when we say that two people are "working out the rules" of their relationship. They are learning to play the relationship game with style and grace.

Improving Unhealthy Patterns

According to the pragmatic approach, the best way to understand and improve communication is to describe the forms or patterns that the communication takes. If these patterns are destructive, then the players should be encouraged to find more productive ways of playing the communication game. Let's say that George and Martha are having problems communicating and decide to go to a communication counselor for help. The counselor taking a pragmatic approach will try to uncover the communication patterns that are the root of George and Martha's problems.

In the beginning, George may explain the problem by blaming Martha. "Her need for attention is so great," he may say, "that I'm forced to spend all my time catering to her. This makes me so mad that I have to get out of the house. She can't seem to understand that I need my privacy. She's demanding and irrational." Of course, Martha has her own version of events, which may go something like this: "He's so withdrawn, I can't stand it. He never pays any attention to me. I have to beg to get a moment of his time, and when he does give it, he gets angry. George is cold and unreasonable." Without help, George and Martha will each continue to blame the other. Martha may blame George's mother for making him the way he is. George may decide that Martha has a personality flaw.

Some scholars see communication as a complex game, where each move determines the next.

The pragmatic therapist isn't interested in exploring background issues. Instead, the therapist tries to identify the behavior pattern that is causing the problem. In this case, George's and Martha's responses to one another are ineffective and are exacerbating the problem. The therapist will help George and Martha to work out a more effective set of moves that will make them both happy.

Perhaps the most important thing the pragmatic theorist tells us is that to understand communication, we should focus on interaction rather than on personality. When you get into an interpersonal conflict (and it's in the interpersonal and small-group arena that the pragmatic model seems to fit best), how often do you examine the pattern of events that led up to the conflict? Chances are, you don't do so very often; instead, you look for a personality explanation. When you and your roommate have problems communicating, you probably don't ask yourself, "What do I do that causes her to respond the way she does?" Instead, you try to figure out what's wrong with her. This is not the most productive solution to the problem.

Criticizing the Pragmatic Perspective

The principal problem with the pragmatic viewpoint is that it holds that both personality and culture are irrelevant. Pragmatists steadfastly refuse to ask why people act as they do. They dismiss factors such as intentions, desires, and needs. They are interested only in how sets of interacts pattern themselves. They also have little to say about the cultural context surrounding interaction. Look again at Figure 2.3, and notice that only what happens on the board is important. What happens outside the world of the game is never considered. Who the players are, where the game is played, and what other players are doing are all irrelevant questions.

Asking Questions from the Pragmatic Perspective

Communication researchers who subscribe to the pragmatic perspective do not take a laws or a rules approach. The approach most compatible with the pragmatic perspective is the systems approach. Systems researchers are concerned with describing interdependent patterns of behavior rather than individual behavior. A systems researcher looks at the structure, function, and evolution of a communication system, asking how communicators within the system organize their behavior, how patterns of behavior affect the way the system works, and how communication changes over time. A systems researcher might ask the following questions: How do the members of a dyad become interdependent over time? What effect do different patterns of dominance have on long-term relationships? Do small-group discussions go through standard phases?

Cultural Studies: An Evolving Perspective

Perspectives continue to evolve; the perspectives we have looked at are not the only approaches to communication. In recent years, the cultural studies perspective has gained ground and now influences many communication scholars, in particular those who take a rhetorical approach to the study of communication. Unlike the perspectives we have already examined, this approach is overtly political. This is because

scholars in the field of cultural studies see a close relationship between acts of communication (called
discursive acts or texts) and power. According to them,
cultures are constituted through a particular set of dis-
cursive acts. Any given culture is, in fact, a web of interconnected acts of communication, all of which carry meaning, much of which lies below the surface. These texts
play off of one another, as collective beliefs and experiences move from one medium
to another.[8] Because they are linked to social forces such as capitalism, patriarchy,
racism, colonialism, and so on, texts exert power over the people who consume
them.[9] A particularly powerful kind of discursive act can be found in popular culture:
on television, in films, and in other popular art forms. Although these acts of communication may seem innocent of any political content, cultural critics believe that
they serve political interests because they reproduce the structures of domination and
subordination that exist within a culture and because they are often used by receivers
to understand the conditions of their lives.[10] Thus, for example, crime dramas, popular films, or news broadcasts may encourage racism and homophobia, while romance
novels, prom magazines, or beauty pageants may contain messages that encourage
the subordination of women. Sometimes the consumers of these messages are not
aware of their political content and accept them without thought.

> Any given culture is, in fact, a web of intercon-
> nected acts of communication, much of which
> lies below the surface.

The job of the cultural critics is to uncover and make visible the connections
between social forces, particularly forces of oppression, and the messages or texts that
reinforce these forces. A cultural studies critic focusing on race, for example, would
ask questions like the following: How is race symbolically created? How are whole
racial groups relatively empowered or disempow-
ered by exposure to the message comprising the
cultures in which we live? How are people re-
cruited to participate in their own oppression and
devaluation?[11] Cultural studies pays especially
close attention to popular electronic media
because media messages are so pervasive in contemporary society. But cultural criticism is not
only limited to television and film. All aspects of
popular culture are open to examination. In addition to crime dramas, situation comedies, and
popular films, cultural critics have studied "texts"
as diverse as congressional testimony, news stories, rock lyrics, shopping centers, jokes, scientific
papers, public memorials, the AIDS epidemic,
and magazines like *Hustler*.[12]

*TV is a potent source of cultural values, values
that may be largely invisible to media consumers.*

Although power is always at stake, according to the critical studies perspective, public

discourse is not the intentional production of a single individual or even of a homogeneous group of individuals. Instead, it is the product of "multiple voices, in contest over power."[13] Receivers do not always "read" a text in ways that support power structures. It is often possible to do oppositional readings, that is, to resist the political message that may be contained within a given text. Every text offers its readers a subject position, a role or stance to take when responding to the text. Although those who are most oppressed often accept this role by assuming that things are and should be the way they are depicted, they do not need to do so. Part of the political agenda of cultural studies is to help people recognize sources of oppression when they occur in public discourse.

Cultural studies is by no means a unified field. Originating in the 1960s and 1970s, the cultural studies perspective is still being defined, and debates within the ranks about theory and method can often be fierce.[14] Whether you agree or disagree with the specific political stance taken by cultural studies, the perspective raises many interesting questions and draws our attention to the fact that communication has powerful effects, that texts are not always what they seem on the surface, and that it is wise to think carefully about what a given act of public communication is actually saying or doing.

WHAT TO LOOK FOR WHEN YOU LOOK AT COMMUNICATION

Before we move on, we have one more model to consider. This model, developed by Dell Hymes, is a kind of field guide for describing communication.[15] Communication teachers often ask students to develop sensitivity to different speech communities. Students may be asked to describe "locker room talk" or "children's playground talk." Or they may be asked to compare the rules governing female speech with those governing male speech. These assignments put the student in essentially the same situation as anthropologists who try to explain a strange culture; the student must do what is called an ethnography of communication. Hymes presents a systematic way to undertake this kind of observation. Figure 2.4 presents Hymes's model.

Hymes begins by giving a general overview of the contexts in which communication occurs. When people share common ways of thinking about communication and common styles of talk, they have formed a speech community. These communities may be large (as when we describe "women's speech") or small (as when we examine the way athletes on a particular team engage in locker room talk). The first step in doing an ethnography is identifying a speech community. Let's say you are studying the communication patterns of members of the Unification Church, popularly known as

> When people share common ways of thinking about communication and common styles of talk, they have formed a speech community.

Figure 2.4 **What to Look for When Observing Communication**

Contexts for Observing Communication

Speech Community
People who share common attitudes toward speech

Speech Situations
Clearly marked occasion that calls for speech

Speech Events
Identifiable sequence of speech activity

Speech Act
Purpose served by forms of talk

Elements of Communication

S ituations	Setting and scene of interaction
P articipants	Who speaks, who is addressed
E nds	Goals and outcomes of interaction
A ct Sequences	Content, means of expression
K eys	Tone or spirit of interaction
I nstrumentalities	Channels, or media of interaction
N orms	Rules regulating interaction
G enres	Type of communication enacted

Adapted from *Foundations in Sociolinguistics: An Ethnographic Approach* by Dell Hymes, 1974, Philadelphia: University of Pennsylvania Press.

Moonies. You believe that when a member joins the Moonies, he or she becomes socialized into the speech practices of the community, and you want to understand what this process entails. The Moonies, then, are your speech community.

Next, you need to catalog speech situations within the community. A speech situation is a clearly marked occasion that calls for a specific type of speech. By observing church members carefully, you begin to get a sense of what these situations are in this community. Recruitment, weekend retreats, study sessions, and flower sales are four speech situations that call for distinct forms of communication.

Each of these situations consists of a series of speech events, or identifiable sequences of speech. The Moonies build cohesion during weekend retreats by playing simple, competitive games. Recruits are warmly accepted by their teams. As play progresses, group cheering and chanting often lead to an almost ecstatic state. Another weekend workshop activity is called "love bombing." A "love bomber," or church member, follows each recruit everywhere and lavishes attention on him or her. Chanting and love bombing are two different speech events that take place in this retreat setting.

Speech events can often be broken down into speech acts, or individual, purposeful acts of communication. During love bombing, Moonies may engage in one or more of the following speech acts: showing concern, expressing regard, helping a recruit, and so on.

A complete description of all the speech acts and events included in major speech situations of the Unification Church gives us a good idea of the way current members use communication to persuade and influence prospective members. By observing the way communication works in this context, we can also develop a better understanding of persuasive communication in general.

Hymes lists a series of specific items that an ethnographer of communication observes (see Figure 2.4). Conveniently, the first letters of these items spell the word *speaking*. Hymes believes that it is important to describe the specific situation, or the environment in which communication takes place (including the time, place, and physical circumstances), as well as the psychological weight a given situation carries. He also believes it is important to describe the participants who take part in a given form of speech, as well as their goals, or ends. In describing act sequences, the ethnographer carefully records communication content and form, noting not only what is said or done but also how it is expressed.

Key is the tone or spirit (for example, joking, aggressive, or ecstatic) in which a given activity is undertaken. Instrumentalities are the channels of transmission used (for example, verbal or nonverbal, written or spoken). In looking at norms, the observer indicates the values and beliefs attached to a given form of communication, as well as the rules that regulate its use. Finally, a genre is a specialized type of encoded message. Examples of genre include prayers, orations, curses, and so on. Hymes believes the conventions governing each genre should be carefully described to gain a true understanding of communication in a given speech community. Observing communication behavior often seems to be an overwhelming task. By breaking communication down into smaller units, Hymes helps make that task more manageable.

Communication can be understood and modeled in a variety of ways, five of which we've looked at so far (the four models discussed in this chapter and the canons of rhetoric discussed in Chapter 1). Although the methods are quite different, each helps to explain a small part of a very complex process.

SUMMARY

Through the years, rhetoricians and communication scientists have not always agreed about what communication is. This chapter looks at a variety of definitions, models, and perspectives that offer insights into communication.

Definitions help to explain and limit concepts. The process of defining can be thought of as either an objective act of discovery or a creative act of construction. According to the second view, the test of a good definition is not its absolute truth but rather its usefulness, and several definitions of a concept may be valid.

One way definitions of communication vary is in breadth. Narrow definitions limit the domain of communication, whereas broad definitions expand it. Another way in which definitions differ is in the importance they place on intentionality. Further, definitions may be either sender- or receiver-based. Finally, some people believe that all communication is symbolic. We don't have to choose just one definition. Instead, we can think of communication as a family of related concepts. The two members of the family most important in this book are spoken symbolic interaction and nonverbal communication.

Whereas definitions express the essence of a concept, models focus on its structure or function. A good model explains a phenomenon, allows us to predict the future, and gives us control over future events. Even good models are always incomplete; there is no perfect model. Models are based on assumptions. The set of assumptions that we hold about a given concept is called a perspective. This chapter discusses three perspectives (psychological, social constructionist, and pragmatic) and offers a model for each perspective.

The psychological perspective views communication as a process of message transmission. A typical psychological model uses concepts such as sender/receiver, encoding and decoding, message, channel, feedback, and noise. It locates communication in the mental sets of individual communicators. Although the psychological perspective is the most widely used in our field, it has drawbacks: it ignores social context, it is mechanistic, and it places more value on accuracy than on creativity. Researchers who follow this perspective often use a laws approach.

According to the social constructionist perspective, communication is the collective creation of meaning. It is not something that goes on between people but, rather, something that surrounds them and holds their world together. Social constructionist models stress concepts such as symbolic codes, cognitive customs, cultural traditions, roles, and rules. Critics of this view argue that its emphasis on truth as a construction can lead to relativism and that its emphasis on cultural appropriateness leaves out individual action. Researchers who follow this perspective often use a rules approach to research.

The pragmatic perspective views communication as a system of interlocking behaviors that become patterned over time. Pragmatists use concepts such as acts, interacts, outcomes or payoffs, and patterned moves. Critics regard the pragmatic perspective as a form of naive behavioralism and argue that it treats communication as context-free. Pragmatic researchers often use a systems approach to research.

The cultural studies perspective is the most overtly political of the perspectives discussed in this chapter, in that it associates communication and power. According to this perspective, cultures are made up of discursive practices that are embodied in texts. Because many texts uphold a culture's power structures, they need to be examined carefully. By placing receivers in certain subject positions, many texts that look innocent on the surface may oppress receivers. The job of the critic is to offer receivers ways to resist the hegemonic messages contained in popular public discourse.

The chapter closes with a final model that focuses on what to look for as we observe communication behavior. Rather than describing how communication works, this model directs our attention to factors such as situation, participants, ends, act sequences, key, instrumentalities, norms, and genre. It also situates communication within speech communities and gives special emphasis to the identification of speech acts.

KEY TERMS

Listed below are the key terms used in this chapter, along with the number of the page where each is explained.

definition   (17)
breadth   (19)
intentionality   (20)
sender-based communication
    (20)
receiver-based communication
    (20)
symbols   (21)
spoken symbolic interaction
    (21)
nonverbal interaction   (21)
model   (22)
explanatory function   (22)
predictive function   (23)
control function   (23)
perspective   (24)
psychological perspective
    (24)
social constructionist
    perspective   (24)
pragmatic perspective   (24)

sender/receiver   (24)
encoding   (24)
message   (24)
channel   (24)
destination   (24)
decoding   (24)
feedback   (24)
mental set   (25)
noise   (25)
laws approach   (27)
symbolic codes   (28)
cognitive customs   (28)
cultural traditions   (28)
sets of roles and rules
    (28)
rules approach   (30)
partners   (31)
acts   (31)
interact   (31)
payoffs   (31)
interdependence   (31)

patterns   (33)
systems approach   (34)
cultural studies perspective
    (34)
discursive act   (35)
text   (35)
subject position   (36)
ethnography of communication
    (36)
speech community   (36)
speech situation   (37)
speech events   (37)
speech acts   (37)
situation   (38)
participants   (38)
ends   (38)
act sequences   (38)
key   (38)
instrumentalities   (38)
norms   (38)
genre   (38)

SUGGESTED READING

Anderson, Rob, & Ross, Veronica. (2002). *Questions of communication: A practical introduction to theory*. Boston: St. Martin's Press.

An involving, personalized look at theory building in communication and a lively and interesting introduction to theories and models of communication.

During, Simon. (2005). *Cultural studies*. New York: T&F/Routledge.

An introduction to cultural critique, consisting of short essays on core topics in the field, including time, space, identity, sexuality, and gender.

Decoding Messages: Listening and Perception

Listening is the forgotten part of communication, yet being able to listen well is one of the most essential communication-related skills.

Although people may disagree on how to define communication, everyone agrees that we use communication to make sense of the world—in other words, that we think through communication. In the next two chapters, we'll investigate communication from the sender's point of view. In this chapter, however, we'll look at how receivers listen to and process messages. You may be surprised to learn how subjective and fallible perception and listening are. Different people exposed to a single message can come away with very different understandings.

A group of scientists attending a professional conference was waiting for a meeting to begin when a door opened and two men, one wearing a clown's costume and the other wearing a black jacket, red tie, and white trousers, rushed in. The two men yelled at each other and scuffled briefly. Suddenly, a shot rang out, whereupon both men rushed out of the room. The chairperson immediately asked everyone in the room to write a complete description of what had happened. The scientists did not know that the incident had been staged to test the accuracy of their perceptions.

How accurate were their perceptions? Of the forty scientists who responded, none gave a complete description of the incident. Twelve reports missed at least 50 percent of what had happened, and only six reports did not misstate facts or add inaccurate details. The eyewitnesses could not even identify the color of the second man's suit; it was variously described as red, brown, striped, blue, and coffee-colored.

After reading this chapter, you should be able to:

- Explain why listening and perception are active rather than passive processes.
- Describe the difference between hearing and listening.
- Identify the five factors that make up the listening process, and list ways to improve each.
- Distinguish between voluntary and involuntary attention.
- Name and give examples of three kinds of cognitive schema and explain how they enhance and inhibit message interpretation.
- Distinguish between descriptions, inferences, and evaluations.
- Understand the importance of responding in the listening process.
- Know how the use of perception checks and paraphrasing can improve listening accuracy and can signal empathy.
- Recognize that memory is fallible.
- Know how to design messages that capture attention, guide interpretation, ensure acceptance, and enhance storage and retrieval.

In interpersonal interactions failure to listen can lead to frustration and futile attempts to amplify messages.

In relating this story, William D. Brooks comments on the limitations inherent in perception:

> The experiment demonstrated dramatically the fallibility of vision and hearing as avenues of information. Similar demonstrations have been made in numerous college speech and psychology classes since the original incident was carried out. Man does not perceive all he sees, nor does he necessarily perceive accurately what falls on the eye's screen; and yet his intrapersonal communication is limited to and based on the information he has via the process of perception from all the senses.[1]

Although perception and listening are always risky, accurate communication is possible. By understanding how perception and information processing work, you can improve both your receiving and sending skills. In the following pages, we will look at ways to listen and to process information more accurately as well as ways to design messages that are easy for others to understand.

WHAT IS LISTENING?

According to the International Listening Association, listening is "the process of receiving, constructing meaning from, and responding to spoken and/or nonverbal messages."[2] When we listen, we engage in a complex multi-step process that includes (1) attending to the sensory stimuli that make up a message, (2) making those stimuli meaningful by using our own experiences to interpret them, (3) critically evaluating our interpretations, (4) responding to the message, and (5) storing the message for future use. When we listen, we are not passive receivers but active creators of meaning.

Most people think listening and hearing are the same thing. But listening and hearing are quite different. Hearing is a physiological process that occurs when sound waves are translated into electrical impulses and then processed by the central nervous system. Listening, on the other hand, is a social cognitive process. When we listen, we assign meaning, and in assigning meaning, we are influenced by our habits, expectations, and desires. And whereas hearing focuses primarily on sound, listening includes all forms of sensory data. We hear with our ears, but we listen with all our senses. When we listen to a conversation, for example, we process not only what is said but also how it is said. To understand the message fully, we need to be aware of the nonverbal cues that accompany and modify the meanings of words. When we interact through electronic media, we must also listen. We now live in a world where we spend a great deal of time reading and responding to text-based electronic messages. All of the principles that apply to the accurate reception of spoken messages apply to electronic messages as well. The process of interpreting and evaluating text messages is a new but vital form of listening.

> Whereas hearing focuses primarily on sound, listening includes all forms of sensory data. We hear with our ears, but we listen with all our senses.

Why Listening Sometimes Fails

Despite the fact that we spend more time listening than engaging in any other form of communication, most of us have very poor listening skills. How often have you missed the point of a lecture because your attention wandered or you found that your understanding of an assignment was different from your professor's? Have you ever been caught unprepared because you forgot an appointment? Have you failed to pick up on nonverbal cues that signaled a partner's feelings? These kinds of problems are all too common, and they are all tied to poor listening.

Listening takes skill and mental effort. Unfortunately, we are not trained to develop that skill. Years ago, Ralph Nichols and Leonard Stevens conducted a revealing study. They asked teachers at various grade levels to interrupt their lectures and ask students, "What was I talking about before I called time out?" In Grade 1, 90 percent of the students were able to answer the teacher's question. By junior high, only 43.7 percent were listening, and the percentage fell to 28 percent by high school.[3] This and similar studies show that actual listening performance worsens over time. A serious gap exists between what we *can* do and what we actually *do* as listeners.

The gap between ability and actual performance may be partly due to cultural values. As Americans, we value activity and independence. We tend to believe that expressing our own ideas is more valuable than attending to others' messages. And because of the low value our culture places on listening, most of us have learned to be poor listeners. Parents and teachers make sure we develop skills in reading, writing, and speaking. Listening, however, is usually something we learn on our own, and the models that we learn from are not very good. Florence Wolff and her colleagues tell us that our parents often train us to be "nonlisteners." When parents tell a child, "Don't pay any attention to that" or "I don't want to hear that in this family," they model nonlistening. By not paying attention or by interrupting each other in midsentence, parents tell us that it is not important to hear others out.[4] In school, the situation is almost as bad. Teachers, themselves untrained in listening, make

> Because of the low value our culture places on listening, most of us have learned to be poor listeners.

up for students' listening deficiencies by patiently repeating themselves. By failing to demand high levels of listening performance, they too may be reinforcing non-listening.

Why Listening Is Important

If listening is so difficult, why take the time and trouble to improve it? The answer is that learning to listen more effectively has benefits. First, becoming a better listener enhances job performance. A study of listening in the workplace, for example, found that more than 60 percent of business errors are related to poor listening.[5] In another study, 80 percent of the executives questioned rated listening as the most vital skill for accomplishing workplace tasks.[6] As listening expert Judi Brownell tells us, listening has been shown to play a vital role in a variety of organizational settings including health care, the military, sales, and marketing.[7]

Listening is also essential in creating and maintaining relationships. One of the major characteristics that attracts us to others in the first place is their willingness to listen. When people refuse to listen, they send a message that they don't care about us, that we don't exist for them. If we want to develop good relationships, we need to listen carefully not only to what our partners say but also to what they leave unsaid. If we can't listen in an open, accepting way, it is impossible for us to comfort and support our partners. Listening is important in both our professional and personal lives.

THE LISTENING PROCESS

Listening is a complex process. In this section, we will break that process down into parts and try to understand how each part contributes to the whole. We will begin by looking at attention, the first requirement for effective listening. We will then discuss how we interpret, or construct meaning from, the stimuli we attend to. Because listening involves evaluating messages, we will also examine some ways to become more critical receivers. Next we will consider how important it is to respond appropriately to the messages we receive from others. We will end with a discussion of how we retain and retrieve messages. As we look at each part of the listening process, we will also consider ways to improve listening performance. (Table 3.1 summarizes this aspect of our discussion.)

Attention

Because we live in a world that continually bombards us with stimuli, we have to be selective about what we pay attention to. We therefore screen out most of the sensory data that surround us, focusing only on a small subset of the information we could take in. **Attention** is the process of selectively focusing on certain events in the environment. Stop reading for a minute and focus on your surroundings.

You may suddenly become aware of the hum of an air conditioner or the voices of passersby on the street. You may realize that the temperature is a bit too cool or that your chair is a bit too hard. You may also become aware of odors you have blocked out—the smell of food or the faint scent of perfume. While you were reading, all of these stimuli disappeared. When you made a conscious attempt to attend to them, they jumped into focus.

> We screen out most of the sensory data that surround us, focusing only on a small subset of the information we could take in.

Voluntary and Involuntary Attention

Scholars who study information processing often distinguish between two kinds of attention: voluntary and involuntary.[8] **Voluntary attention** occurs when we willfully focus on a stimulus; it is attention guided by personal plans and goals. When we listen to a debate to find out a candidate's position or examine a map to make sure we are going in the right direction, we are engaged in voluntary attention. **Involuntary attention**, by contrast, occurs when the intrinsic properties of a stimulus make that stimulus stand out; this kind of attention lies outside our control. When we jump because a siren starts to blare or when we suddenly stare because someone in an outlandish outfit walks by, we are engaging in involuntary attention.

Improving Attention

Because attention occurs in short bursts and because external stimuli are constantly vying for involuntary attention, it is very easy to get distracted. An effective listener is someone who can focus attention on what is important while

Table 3.1 Ways to Improve Listening Performance

To Improve Attention

- Avoid distractions.
- Be aware of your purpose for listening.
- Notice contextual cues.
- Keep a positive attitude; don't assume that you'll be bored.

To Improve Interpretation

- Recognize the complexity of perception.
- Prepare ahead of time by knowing about the topic.
- Use extra time to summarize and rehearse.
- When appropriate, use perception checks.

To Improve Evaluation

- Test information for adequacy and accuracy.
- Separate inference and evaluation from description.
- Acknowledge your biases and delay final evaluation.

To Improve Responding

- Realize you cannot not communicate.
- See things from the sender's perspective.
- Respond to what is *not* said as well as what is.

To Improve Storage and Retrieval

- Decide what information needs to be stored.
- Rehearse and review material.
- Use mnemonic devices or special memory aids.

Strange or surprising stimuli stand out, capturing involuntary attention.

screening out irrelevant details. One way to improve attention is to *begin by acknowledging how easy it is to be diverted by extraneous details.* A speaker's clothes or mannerisms, unusual environmental details, competing sounds or movements, or our own concerns and feelings can divert voluntary attention. Other sources of distractions are self-consciousness (focusing so much on how you are coming across that you miss what the other person is saying) and competitive turn taking (planning and plotting what you will say next rather than attending to the other person). Luckily, it is possible to refocus attention.

Because voluntary attention is guided by goals and plans, it is especially important to *have a clear purpose in mind on entering a listening situation.* In other words, know what you want to accomplish by listening, and remind yourself of your purpose whenever you find your attention straying. If you are listening to a lecture, your purpose may be to understand and remember the speaker's main points as well as supporting examples. In an interpersonal situation, your goal may be to understand what is bothering a friend. In either case, your goal can direct your attention.

Although a good listener needs to focus primarily on the content of messages while avoiding trivial details, this does not mean that all attention should be directed to what is said. Often, context is an important part of a message, and *how* something is said is a key element in determining *what* has been said. This is particularly important in interpersonal interactions. A friend may say she isn't upset, but if she is wringing her hands and looking away, chances are that something is wrong, something you should be aware of. As an effective listener, then, you should *notice relevant contextual and nonverbal cues.*

> Often, context is an important part of a message, and *how* something is said is a key element in determining *what* has been said.

Finally, you can improve attention if you open yourself to others' messages. *Don't dismiss a message ahead of time because you assume that it will be boring or ignore what someone says because you dislike the person.* If you enter a listening situation expecting the worst, nonlistening becomes inevitable.

Interpretation

Of course, listening is more than attending. It also involves assigning meaning. When we focus on a portion of the sensory world, we immediately label and categorize what we have perceived. We do so by giving incoming stimuli stability, structure, and meaning.[9] You can see how this process works by considering what you do when you watch television. When you turn on the TV, what you actually sense are a series of flickering lights and a jumble of undifferentiated sounds. You quickly **structure** these sounds and shadows into images and words; for example, you perceive a group of six teenagers hanging out in what appears to be a restaurant. As the show progresses, you also impose **stability** on what you see. When the camera moves in for a close-up on one character, you are not disoriented. You understand that you are viewing a single character from a new perspective. When the camera pans across the room, you know that the character still exists even though he or she is no longer in view. Finally, you give the scene **meaning**. You begin to identify the characters, recognizing them as stereotypical high school students: the wisecracking schemer who can get away with anything, the pretty head cheerleader, the nerd, the shopaholic and gossip queen, the serious feminist, and the athlete. If you have seen the show before, you recognize it as *Saved by the Bell,* and with this knowledge, you can predict that Zack, the handsome troublemaker, will spend most of the episode trying to get a date with the beautiful (but not too bright) Kelly, while Screech, the nerd, will show once again that he is incurably accident-prone. All of this happens so quickly that you may not realize that complicated social knowledge is involved. Yet without this knowledge to guide you, you could not organize your sensations in any meaningful way.

Using Cognitive Schemata

Psychologists agree that we use shared social understandings, past experiences, and our knowledge about the world to help us interpret what we see or hear. To do so, we draw on mental guidelines, or what psychologists call **schemata** (singular: schema), to help us identify and organize incoming information. Schemata are internal representations of objects and sequences of actions. When we encounter a perceptual object, we store its image in short-term memory while we search for a schema to make sense of it. Perhaps you have a *Saved by the Bell* schema. You know the characters and typical plots, and it is easy for you to follow the story and identify who is who. If you have never seen the show, on the other hand, you must work out your own understandings, although a general situation-comedy schema can help you to make sense of the format. If you were from a culture without this kind of TV show, however, you would lack the interpretive schemata needed to understand the conventions we take for granted. Schemata make processing rapid and effortless, although, as we shall see, they can sometimes distort perception.

> We use shared social understandings, past experiences, and our knowledge about the world to help us interpret what we see or hear.

We have schemata for physical objects, types of people (including ourselves), personal traits, relationships, and sequences of actions. For our purposes, the three most important types of schemata are person prototypes, personal constructs, and scripts.[10] (See Table 3.2 for an overview of these schemata.)

Person Prototypes.   We often use schemata to form impressions of other people and to interpret their messages. Person prototypes are idealized representations of a certain kind of person. For example, you may have a prototypical image of a professor, a used car salesman, a scientist, or a quiz show host. These images allow you to identify whether a person belongs to one of these categories. The information contained in prototypes consists of traits, patterns of behavior, and role relations that fit our idea of a certain type of person. If a person appears to have a sufficient number of these traits, and if he or she exhibits no incompatible traits, then that person is easily recognized and understood.[11]

In helping us to identify and categorize people, person prototypes make our lives easier. But they also can color the way we interpret and evaluate messages by affecting expectations. If, for example, we class Kristin as "a typical airhead," then we are unlikely to take what she says seriously, regardless of the quality of her message. On the other hand, if we decide that Sam is "an expert in the field," then we're likely to accept whatever he says, even when a moment's reflection would tell us that he's not making any sense. In both cases, we allow a prototype to affect our ability to listen.

Personal Constructs.   In our daily interactions, we often use another kind of schema, called a personal construct.[12] Personal constructs are characteristics that we notice on a daily basis about others. Whereas prototypes are global categorizations, constructs are specific descriptors.

Some personal constructs are suggested to us by events. We use them because they have recently been "primed." For example, if we have just come back from a religious service, constructs such as "forgiving" and "kind" may be uppermost in our minds, and we may interpret others' behavior in terms of generosity

Table 3.2 Cognitive Schemata

Person Prototypes

Person prototypes are idealized representations of a certain kind of person. They are used to identify and classify people. If you can form a mental image of any of the following, you are using a person prototype: cowboy, beauty queen, stand-up comic, feminist, politician, type-A personality. Although prototypes give us a quick take on someone, they ignore individual details and can lead to stereotyped responses.

Personal Constructs

Personal constructs are the characteristics that we habitually notice in others. They are the specific descriptors we use to answer the question "What is he or she like?"

Part of the mental apparatus of the observer, they appear to be characteristics of the observed. Like other schemata, they can make perception easier and more efficient, but they can also be inaccurate and unfair.

Scripts

Scripts are representations of sequences of action. They tell us what to do next in a given situation. When communication is scripted, we can rattle off a routine without thinking about it. Well-learned scripts free us from making conscious decisions about our actions and give us the confidence that comes from knowing what to say or do next. However, they can lull us into mindlessness and repetitive routines.

and concern for others. If, on the other hand, we have been reading about the latest political scandal, constructs such as "manipulative" may occur to us.

In addition to constructs that we use temporarily because they are suggested to us by events, we also have habitual ways of judging others. Constructs that are important to us and that we frequently use, regardless of circumstances, are called chronically accessible constructs, and these constructs are likely to color and bias our interpretation of others and their messages. Psychologist John Bargh tells us that there are wide personal differences in construct accessibility and that this accessibility does not often overlap between individuals. Thus, two people may "pick up very different information about a third person, and interpret the same information in very different ways."[13] For example, Sheldon (who is suspicious of others) may use constructs such as *manipulative, insincere,* and *ingratiating* to interpret Judi's offer of help, while Marla may see the same behavior as *friendly* and *sincere.* Each of us sees what is important to us and may miss what others see. Clearly over-reliance on chronic constructs can lead to problems in interpreting messages.

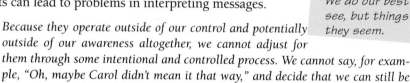

We do our best to interpret what we see, but things are not always what they seem.

Because they operate outside of our control and potentially outside of our awareness altogether, we cannot adjust for them through some intentional and controlled process. We cannot say, for example, "Oh, maybe Carol didn't mean it that way," and decide that we can still be friends with her, because as with the color of the sky, we do not question the validity of automatically produced perceptions.[14]

To examine your own personal constructs, consider a number of people you know, and write down adjectives to describe them. Looking at your completed list, you'll see the kinds of judgments you habitually make about others. Are the constructs you listed based on physical or psychological characteristics? Are they fair or unfair? What do they tell you about how you evaluate people and their behaviors and motivations?

When individuals use only simple, undifferentiated constructs, we say that they lack cognitive complexity. Cognitive complexity occurs when an individual has a large, rich, and varied set of personal constructs.[15] The cognitively complex person is willing to combine seemingly contradictory characteristics in creative ways, realizing that people are not all good or all bad. The person who lacks cognitive complexity tends to use one or two simple constructs, ignoring contradictory information. Cognitive complexity is a mark of maturity and is necessary for good communication. Incidentally, cognitive complexity

> The cognitively complex person is willing to combine seemingly contradictory characteristics in creative ways.

is itself a personal construct, one that communication scholars use to explain perceptual behavior.

Scripts.   So far, we have focused on how we use schemata to process information about other people. We also have schemata that allow us to interpret sequences of behavior. These are called **scripts**.[16] A script tells us what comes next in a sequence of actions. When we experience a situation repeatedly, we abstract its essential features and identify the order in which things happen. We have scripts for all kinds of simple actions: eating in a restaurant, working out at a gym, walking to class. Scripts allow us to behave effortlessly, without having to think much about what to do next. When we find ourselves in highly scripted situations, we feel confident. When we encounter unusual or novel situations for which we have no script, we feel uncomfortable and unsure of ourselves and have trouble figuring out what is going on.

We have scripts for a variety of communicative events: simple greetings, public speeches, interviews, and so on. When speakers follow these scripts, we have no trouble understanding what is going on. Part of being an effective listener is being familiar with common scripts. For example, if we know that in a public speech, the introduction will present the main idea, the body of the speech will provide supporting evidence, and the conclusion will include a summary, then it will be relatively easy to follow the speech and interpret its message correctly.

Despite the fact that scripts can help us to interpret messages, there are times when they can impede rather than enhance interpretation. If we rely too heavily on a script, we may see or hear what we expect rather than what actually occurs.

> If we rely too heavily on a script, we may see or hear what we expect rather than what actually occurs.

All schemata have embedded within them **schematic default options**, details that are supplied when actual information is missing. Assume that you witness a car crash. Later, when a lawyer asks you whether or not glass from broken headlights was on the ground, you may answer, "Sure," even if the headlights were not actually broken. Your schema for a car accident contains this detail, one that exists in your mind rather than in the actual situation.[17]

The use of schematic default options often occurs in simple greetings. For example, when we greet a friend with a "How are you?," we assume that the answer will be, "Fine." If the other person says, "I'm terrible," we may not even notice and may respond with a cheery, "That's good. See you later." The story that opened this chapter shows another example of how schemata can distort perception. The scientists described what they thought they had seen rather than what they actually saw, filling in details in ways that made sense to them but did not correspond to reality. And evidence shows that after a period of time, the problem only gets worse; as time progresses, people have more and more trouble distinguishing inferred from observed information.[18]

Becoming More Mindful

As our discussion of schemata has shown, we often process information automatically, without much conscious thought. We frequently act like "lazy organisms" or "cognitive misers," saving our conscious attention for important situations and spending much of our time in what is called **mindless** or **automatic processing**.[19] We process mindlessly when we rely on old routines and mental habits to give us information about the world. Of course, mindless processing has its advantages: it can free us to attend to "the new, the unusual, the potentially dangerous, the most informative, and the most important events going on around us at any time."[20] On the other hand, mindlessness has serious disadvantages when we rely on incomplete or inappropriate schemata.

The opposite of mindless processing is **mindful processing**. According to psychologist Ellen Langer, when we are mindful, we are in a state of "alert and lively awareness."[21] When we act mindfully, we actively think about the world, creating new understandings rather than relying on old. Effective listeners know when to rely on familiar scripts, but they also know how and when to switch from mindless to mindful processing.

> Effective listeners know when to rely on familiar scripts, but they also know how and when to switch from mindless to mindful processing.

Improving Interpretation

As this section has shown, the process of interpretation depends heavily on subjective factors. Listening to a message is not simply a case of recording what we hear; rather, it is a complex process involving shared social knowledge, personal expectations, and individual schemata. The first step in improving interpretation, therefore, is to *recognize how complex perception is and how easy it is to get things wrong*.

When listening for complex information, you may need to *prepare ahead of time. The more you know about a topic, the easier it will be to process information about it*. If you can identify a speaker's purpose and the way he or she has structured a presentation and you know something about the subject, it will be a great deal easier for you to interpret the presentation correctly. Consider the following example:

> *The procedure is quite simple. First you arrange items into different groups. Of course one pile might be sufficient depending on how much there is to do. If you have to go somewhere else due to lack of facilities, that is the next step; otherwise you are pretty well set. It is important not to overdo things. That is, it is better to do too few things at once than too many. . . . After the procedure is completed one arranges the material into different groups again. They then can be put into their appropriate places. Eventually they will be used once more and the whole cycle will then have to be repeated. However, that is part of life.*[22]

At first, the passage seems so incomprehensible that you may be tempted to give up and stop processing. But it instantly becomes interpretable once you discover that it is about washing clothes and once you relate what you know about clothes washing to what the speaker has said. As a listener, you should constantly ask yourself, "What's going on here?" And you should *relate what the speaker says to what you already know*. Luckily, there is a gap between speaking and processing speed that allows you time to do just that.

One of the interesting facts about listening is that we can listen much faster than we can speak. The normal rate of speaking is approximately 150 words per minute, but studies have shown that we can process messages at rates of 300 words per minute or even higher. This means that as we listen, we have plenty of time to think. When processing complex information, we should *use the time differential between speaking and processing to focus on message content and structure*. In public speaking situations, you can fill time by identifying main ideas, recalling supporting details, and looking for transitions that will identify the structure of the speech. In interpersonal contexts, you can focus on identifying a partner's feelings and checking his or her nonverbal communication. In either case, the time differential can be used to paraphrase content and relate it to prior knowledge.

> We can listen much faster than we can speak. This means that as we listen, we have plenty of time to think.

In formal, public situations, communication may be primarily one way. In such a situation, there is little opportunity for you to check your interpretation of the speaker's message during the speech itself. But in less formal settings, it is often possible to *ask for clarification by using what is called a perception check*. A perception check is a response that allows you to state your interpretation and ask your partner whether or not that interpretation is correct. When your professor gives you an assignment, you can check your perception by saying, "So, you want us to hand in our papers by ten o'clock on this Friday, is that right?" This allows the professor to agree or to explain, "No, not this Friday. It's due next Friday." You can also comment on contextual cues when you do a perception check. Say, for example, a friend says to you, "I don't want to go. You go without me." A perception check might consist of the following: "I know you say you don't want to go, but you seem a bit disappointed. Would you rather we both went at another time?" In this case, not only does perception checking clarify the message, but it allows you to avoid potential hurt feelings and misunderstandings.

Evaluation

Living as we do, in an age of information, we are bombarded with messages. It would be absurd to accept everything we hear or to believe everything we see. Some of the messages we receive are accurate and useful, and some are not. Part of being a good listener is evaluating message quality—knowing what to reject, what to believe, and what to question. That means listening critically. Being critical, however, does not mean being negative or rejecting everything we hear out of hand; instead, it means thinking carefully about the messages we receive. It means being aware of a speaker's purpose, evaluating the quality of the information that is being presented, and recognizing logical inconsistencies.

Identifying Communicative Purpose

The first step in evaluating a message lies in determining its purpose. In some cases, the purpose is clear. When candidate Smith says, "Vote for me," we know that we are listening to a persuasive message. But in other cases, the speaker's intent may not be so obvious. An apparently objective lecture may actually have a hidden persuasive intent. And when the interaction is interpersonal, its purpose may be even more difficult to determine. For example, a stranger at a bus stop who remarks, "It's a beautiful day" probably is not working for the Weather Channel. The comment may be a way of passing the time, of striking up an acquaintance, of flirting, or even of softening you up so that the person can borrow the bus fare. And when someone says to you, "I'm only telling you this for your own good," it's probably wise to be suspicious; the speaker may have a hidden agenda that is unclear to you and not even very clear to the speaker. Knowing what a speaker is trying to do puts us in a much better position to evaluate the message.

Censoring or restricting stimuli often makes them more interesting and appealing.

Judging Information

Critical listeners are also adept at judging the quality of the information contained in a message. Although we know that we should be suspicious of new information, especially if it appears to be too good to be true, we also have a tendency to believe what we want to believe. If a message supports current beliefs, attitudes, and values, we tend to find it compelling. If it enhances our sense of self-worth, we may accept it without question. Yet it is in exactly these situations that we should be wary. By demanding good evidence and by considering the trustworthiness and expertness of message sources, we increase our ability to think critically about messages.

As we saw in Chapter 1 and will explore more fully in Chapter 9, source credibility is an important factor in judging the quality of information. Communicators who are both expert and trustworthy are much more believable than sources that are not. Whether you

> If a message supports current beliefs, attitudes, and values, we tend to find it compelling. If it enhances our sense of self-worth, we may accept it without question. Yet it is in exactly these situations that we should be wary.

are communicating in a dyad or a group or are part of an audience, you should remember the old adage "Consider the source."

Identifying Loaded Language

Finally, effective evaluation means identifying logical inconsistencies and emotionally charged language. Critical listeners understand that appeals to emotion are often tied to questionable conclusions. In Chapter 9, we will consider logical fallacies in more detail, as we look at ways public speakers bypass reason in an attempt to sway audiences. At this point, it is probably enough to note that critical listeners carefully judge the language choices of speakers. Many years ago, Richard Weaver suggested that we react especially strongly to what he called god and devil terms.[23] **God terms** are terms that are so positive that they go unchallenged; **devil terms** express negative values and repel the listener. For most Americans, *homeland security, patriotism,* and *democracy* are unquestionably good, while *weapons of mass destruction, terrorism,* and *insurgency* are unquestionably evil. Words like these may inspire us to action, but they can also short-circuit rational debate because of their powerful connotations. Of course, using loaded language for persuasive ends is not new. As social psychologists Anthony Pratkanis and Elliot Aronson explain, our forefathers used loaded language to stir up patriotic feelings. Early American patriots, they tell us, "were able to increase revolutionary fervor by terming a minor skirmish with the British the *Boston massacre*."[24] To get current versions of the use of loaded language, all you need do is turn on your TV and tune in to one of the many political commentary shows, look at blogs with a political agenda, or listen to talk radio.

Evaluating Information on the Web

We noted earlier that nowadays, we spend a great deal of time processing electronic messages. When you want to look up a "fact," where do you go? Chances are, you turn to the World Wide Web for the information you need. Why not? After all, the Web is a rich source of information. Unfortunately, it is a rich source of misinformation as well. Because anyone can post anything on the Web and because sources are often anonymous, evaluating information gleaned from Web pages is particularly challenging.

Librarian John Henderson offers some simple guidelines for using the Web as an information source. First, he tells us, make sure that the Web is the appropriate place to find the information you are seeking. Not everything, he reminds us, is on the Web. "An hour on the Web may not answer a question that you could find within two minutes of picking up a reference book."[25] If you decide to go to the Web, be suspicious: when in doubt, doubt. Look for ambiguity, loaded language, poor reasoning, and bias. Check several sources to verify that the fact you've just found isn't pure fiction. And always consider the source. You might assume that anyone posting information about a serious topic has credentials, but this isn't always the case. Susan Barnes reports one case in which a 15-year-old California high school student presented himself online as a legal "expert," despite the fact that almost all of his legal knowledge was gleaned from watching Court TV. In fact, he was such a popular contributor to the Website in question that even after he confessed, members still sought out his advice.[26]

As we suggested earlier, identifying the purpose of a message is an important aspect of listening. Henderson reminds us that we should try to determine why a given Website was created. "Since money talks, try to notice who is paying for the site, either through advertising or sponsorship. Both can affect content and objectivity."[27] Ask yourself whether the main purpose is to inform or to persuade. Looking at details can also help you to determine the accuracy of a Website's facts. Misspelling, poor grammar, lack of organization, distracting graphics, and links that do not work suggest carelessness and a lack of professionalism that may carry over into content.

Finally, Henderson reminds us that not all pages found on the Web are Web pages. Some Web content is created by individuals with an idiosyncratic view or by advertisers with persuasive intent, but books, periodicals, and government research reports are now accessible on the Web as well. These online sources are no more or less reliable than the same information found in print and must be evaluated like any other source. See Table 3.3 for a summary of things to keep in mind as you evaluate information from the Internet.

Improving Evaluation

As we've already seen, to be good listeners, we need to be critical consumers of information and to *question the adequacy and accuracy of the messages we receive.*

Table 3.3   A Guide to Evaluating What You See on the Web

- **Make Sure You Are in the Right Place.**
  Ask yourself: *Is this site the right place to get the information I need?*

- **When in Doubt, Doubt.**
  Ask yourself: *Do I have good reason to believe the information on the site is accurate? Can I confirm this information from another source?*

- **Consider the Source.**
  Ask yourself: *Who is responsible for the site? Do the authors have any authority or expertise?*

- **Know What Is Happening.**
  Ask yourself: *What is the main purpose of the site? Is it to inform, to persuade, to entertain, or to sell something?*

- **Look at Details.**
  Ask yourself: *Did the authors spend time making the site clear and professional, or is it full of careless errors? Are graphics helpful or distracting?*

- **Distinguish Web Pages from Pages Found on the Web.**
  Ask yourself: *Was the page designed for the Web, or was it originally something else? If it was something else, what was it?*

Adapted from *ICYouSee: T Is for Thinking,* by John R. Henderson, Ithaca College Library, www.ithaca.edu. Used by permission of the author.

One of the stumbling blocks to doing this is misunderstanding the difference between a description, an inference, and an evaluation.[28]

A **description** of fact is an actual observation of a state of affairs, made with a minimum of distortion. "John is making direct eye contact with me" is a description. An **inference**, by contrast, is a personal interpretation of the meaning behind the behavior being described. "John is aggressive" is a possible inference, as is "John is interested in what I have to say" or even "John finds me attractive." An **evaluation** goes even further, adding a positive or negative judgment. "John has a rotten attitude" and "I like the way John listens" and even "How dare John react to me in that way?" are all evaluations. It is easy lose sight of the fact that a given behavior can be interpreted in multiple ways. Consider the following: "Elissa stamped her foot, screamed, and threw the book across the room"; "Elissa is angry"; "I hate it when Elissa acts like a child." These three statements are doing very different things. The second is an inference, but it is only one possible explanation for Elissa's behavior. What other possibilities might there be? And how might your evaluation of her change as a result? As effective listeners we need to *separate descriptions of fact from inferences and evaluations.*

Refusing to accept inferences without considering the facts they're based on is one way to improve listening. But we can't do this if we respond emotionally. It is human nature to jump to conclusions—to accept blindly what we want to hear and to reject without thinking what we don't want to hear. And the more ego involved we are with an issue—that is, the more we have a personal stake in the outcome—the more likely we are to lose our objectivity by not listening or by distorting the message. If you're like most people, some things that people say drive you crazy. Can you identify some of these statements? How do you respond when one of these hot button issues is raised? Most likely, you either shut down or begin to argue back before you have actually heard the speaker out. You will be a better listener if you *become aware of your biases and delay final evaluation until you have had time to think about the message.* If your interpretations of messages are biased, your responses will be biased as well.

> It is human nature to jump to conclusions—to accept blindly what we want to hear and to reject without thinking what we don't want to hear.

Responding

Picture this. You pour your heart out to a friend. As you talk, your friend stares at you blankly. When you're finished, your friend looks at you with a neutral expression, gets up, shrugs, and walks out of the room. How would you feel? Chances are that you would be hurt and confused. When we communicate, we expect a reaction. In social situations, the role of the listener involves more than simply understanding and storing information. Listeners have an obligation to respond either verbally or nonverbally. Responding in a way that lets a speaker know you are listening is called **active listening**.

Active listening takes many forms. It can consist of overt verbal responses, or it can simply be a nod, a smile, or a frown. In any form, active listening shows the speaker that you are paying attention. It also allows senders to gauge the success of their messages and receivers to check the accuracy of their perceptions. Although it can be awkward—even painful—to give or get negative feedback, even negative feedback is better than silence and a frozen expression.

Styles of Listening

Not only is it important to give feedback during listening, it is crucial to do so in the right way. Just as there are styles of speaking, there are also styles of listening, ways in which listeners indicate understanding and interest. Sometimes these styles are individual; some people are more nonverbally expressive than others. And sometimes these styles are cultural. European Americans, for example, usually expect listeners to listen silently, fixing their eyes on the speaker until he or she signals that talk is concluded. In this cultural group, such behavior shows respect. In the African American rhetorical tradition, however, a different pattern occurs. "Speaker and listener urge one another on with call and response, with messages and expressions of delight, amplification, encouragement, and echoes of words just said."[29] Eye behavior also differs; in the African American group, the speaker gazes and listeners look away. Likewise, individuals in other cultural groups listen in their own distinctive ways. Given how much we all rely on cues to tell us that our conversational partners are listening, it is important to keep in mind that listening style varies both individually and culturally and to become familiar with different listening styles.

> Not only is it important to give feedback during listening, it is crucial to do so in the right way. Just as there are styles of speaking, there are also styles of listening.

Empathic Listening

Active listening is perhaps most important in close dyadic relationships when individuals want to show their concern for one another. In these relationships, active listening is a way to offer support and counsel. One of the most important ways to show empathy is to use paraphrasing. When we paraphrase, we repeat the sender's message in our own words.

Assume for a moment that a friend says to you, "I'm so far behind in my classes, I'll never catch up. I might as well drop out." How would you respond? Some people might offer immediate advice, telling their friend to work more efficiently. Others might try to reassure their friend that the problem is not serious and that everything will turn out all right. These responses are based on the same assumption: that the listener understands the speaker's problem. But problems are not always easy to understand, and people don't always clearly articulate what is bothering them. If your friend's problem goes deeper than the issue of time management, the only way to find out is to encourage more discussion, and the best way to do this is to paraphrase.

Paraphrasing enables you to check your understanding of what someone else is saying. In the example above, you might paraphrase by saying, "So you're very discouraged about your classes and ready to give up." This allows your friend to think more about the problem; it invites elaboration. Because it is a tentative statement, it encourages your friend to tell you what's really wrong. As a result, not only will you understand your friend better, but your friend will have a better understanding of the problem as well. Only when you both understand the problem can you go about solving it.

Of course, using paraphrasing should be more than just a technique. If you are simply applying a formula in a mechanical way, your response will sound as though you are playing psychologist. But if your motivation is honest, then paraphrasing will come naturally, and you will find that in your role as listener, you have given useful help.

Clearly, listening is an active process that takes attention and energy. Like other goal-directed behaviors, it can be improved with practice. Because listening is the forgotten part of communication, we seldom spend much time or effort on it. Yet being able to listen well is one of the most essential communication-related skills.

Improving Responding

The best way to improve responding is to realize that you cannot not communicate. In other words, you are always responding in some way to the people around you, whether you are saying anything or not. No matter what you do, you are sending a message. Let's say you slip into your 9:00 A.M. communication class after catching only a few hours of sleep the night before. You sit in the back and hope that by the time class is over, you will be fully alert. You are much too tired to answer questions or do much more than stare. Luckily, all you have to do is listen; there is no need for you to communicate. But you *are* communicating, even though you may be unaware of the message you are sending. Whether or not you are processing what is going on in class, your lack of responsiveness is sending the message that you aren't listening and that you aren't interested. Without knowing it, you create a negative impression. Or let's say that someone sends you a text message just to say hi, but you don't bother to reply. Don't assume that in ignoring the message, you are not communicating. Your lack of response is a message in itself, one that can have unintended but very negative results.

The point here is not that you should answer every question in class or respond to every text message or email within minutes; it is simply that you should be aware of how your responses are likely to be read and *see things from the perspective of the sender.* This means focusing on your partner instead of yourself and imaginatively feeling what he or she is feeling.

Responding may also mean reading between the lines. For example, Carlos, age nine years, suddenly says that he hates school and doesn't want to go back. To respond effectively, you need to figure out what is actually going on. Responding by saying, "Nonsense, you love school," won't help if a bad experience has made him think the other kids don't like him or if he is having trouble with math. What he needs is sympathy and reassurance and a way out of his dilemma. As a good listener, you need to *respond to what is not said as well as what is said.*

Storage and Retrieval

No matter how effectively you attend, interpret, evaluate, and respond, if you cannot remember a message, then listening fails. Telling your professor after a test that you knew the information last night won't be enough to get you a passing grade. Explaining to your significant other that you knew her birthday was today but just forgot isn't much of an excuse. Effective listeners must do two essential things: store messages in memory and then retrieve them at the appropriate time.

Factors Affecting Memory

A number of factors can interfere with storage and retrieval. First of all, most of us are highly suggestible. The sad fact is that memory is fallible. Information that is painful or unpleasant can be pushed aside, while things that never happened can be remembered as though they were true. There have been several dramatic instances of false memory. Anthony Pratkanis and Elliot Aronson report a fascinating case in which a previously law-abiding deputy sheriff confessed to abusing his daughters and leading a satanic cult.[30] Why did he confess to and supply false details about a crime that experts now agree never happened? The answer lies in the social pressures he endured as the case unfolded. During interrogation, he was told that it was common to repress memories of crimes of this type. In addition, everyone in his environment—members of his church, his family, and other members of the sheriff's department—behaved as though the allegations were true, and confession was held out as the only way to atone for his transgression. But perhaps the most important factor leading to his false confession was that he had to choose between believing that his daughters were lying and believing that he had committed a horrible crime. Psychologically, he responded to this untenable situation by creating a false memory.

Of course false memories are usually not this extreme; many average, well-balanced people have very vivid childhood memories of things that could never have happened. In fact, psychologist Elizabeth Loftus has demonstrated that it is quite easy for parents or family members to implant childhood memories simply by talking about events as though they were true.[31] The fact is, many of us remember doing things it turns out we never did. And many of us choose to forget information that challenges our assumptions or desires.

> Many average, well-balanced people have very vivid childhood memories of things that could never have happened.

In addition to psychological defense mechanisms and social pressures, the situation in which listening occurs can also affect memory. Stress is one of the biggest impediments to memory. When we are rushed, when we are in unfamiliar surroundings, when a situation is interpersonally unpleasant, or when we have simply worked ourselves up into a state of anxiety, we are unlikely to remember events accurately.[32]

Another factor that can affect storage and retrieval is information interference. This occurs when information from multiple sources merges and details from one situation become attached to another. If, as a child, you spent many summers at the lake, your memories may run together. A picnic that occurred when you were six years old may include a storm that actually happened two years later. And you may remember how your dog jumped into the water, even though that didn't happen until you were twelve. The tendency of one memory set to interfere with another can also influence how well you do on tests. An effect called retroactive inhibition occurs when new learning interferes with early stored material. To avoid this problem, before a test, you should study only the subject you will be tested on, get a good night's sleep, review, and take the test. Any extraneous information that you acquire between studying and taking the test can cause interference.

Improving Storage and Retrieval

As we have seen, memory is fallible. Yet it is possible to improve storage and retrieval, especially when you are listening intently and your purpose is to retain knowledge. Sometimes, especially in a college setting, you may feel overwhelmed by the sheer amount of information you are expected to remember. Just keep in mind that you seldom have to remember everything you hear exactly as you heard it. In most cases, it is better to store main ideas rather than specific phrasing. In fact, if during listening you concentrate too specifically on wording or descriptive

> If during listening you concentrate too specifically on wording or descriptive details and not enough on ideas, you'll miss the meaning of the message.

details and not enough on ideas, you'll miss the meaning of the message. The first principle in improving retention, then, is to *decide what needs to be stored*.

Once you decide that something should be remembered, you must actively work to retain it. One way is to *mentally rehearse and review ideas that need to be stored*. Another is to take notes to ensure that you have a permanent record of a spoken message. Of course, special problems can arise during note taking. The first is that as we struggle to write something down, we may tune out the rest of the message. If you have to take notes, jot down main ideas along with brief examples. Be sure you understand the idea before you start writing. In addition, notes are of little use if they are not reviewed. The information ultimately has to go into memory, and writing it in a book does not guarantee that you will remember it later. Experts on note taking suggest that you go over your notes as soon as possible after taking them, filling in details.

In special cases, you may wish to use mnemonic devices or special memory aids. When simple repetition fails to fix things in memory, other devices can be used. If you are visually oriented, you may find it easier to memorize something (say, a list) by visualizing its parts or items placed in a familiar setting—a technique that we discussed in Chapter 1. Another way to remember items is to link them visually to one another. For example, if you have to shop for a light bulb, suntan lotion, a quart of orange juice, and pencils, you could visualize a cartoon of a light bulb wearing sunglasses, lounging in the sun writing a postcard with the pencil and drinking a cool glass of orange juice. This unusual image is likely to stay with you as you pick up each item at the store. Acronyms, or made-up words, each letter of which stands for an idea you want to remember, are also useful, as are rhymes, such as "*I* before *e,* except after *c.*" Whatever aid you choose, you must spend time and effort to ensure that what you have attended to and interpreted will come back to you when you need it.

DESIGNING MESSAGES THAT ARE EASY TO LISTEN TO

Not all speakers capture attention, and not all messages are easy to understand and remember. There are things the sender of a message can do to ensure that audience members do not tune out or get confused. In this section, we look at ways in which speakers can capture attention, increase comprehension, enhance message acceptance, and increase retention. Table 3.4 summarizes this discussion.

Capturing Attention

Earlier, we noted that there are two kinds of attention: voluntary and involuntary. A skilled communicator must consider both when designing messages. Voluntary attention can be increased by relating message content to receiver's needs. An unemployed person, for example, will be receptive to a speech on how to get a good job. To someone with a job, the same speech is less interesting, and the speaker will have to show the receiver that the information will be useful in the future or can lead to job advancement now. In either case, *voluntary attention can be increased by giving receivers a reason to listen.*

Involuntary attention works differently. *To increase involuntary attention, one must create vivid and compelling message elements that cannot be ignored.* Marvin Zuckerman explains that involuntary attention is part of our biological makeup:

> *One of our hominid ancestors in a relatively relaxed state on a plain in Africa might have little engagement of attention by the environment, but the sound of something moving in the brush, the sight of something moving in the distance, or a new smell wafting about must have had the instant capacity to engage attention and arouse the brain. Novel stimuli do have this intrinsic capacity to stop ongoing activity and to engage the attention mechanism.*[33]

What kinds of stimuli have the potential to arouse involuntary attention? Stimuli that are intense, novel, complex, surprising, and incongruous.[34] Vivid colors, loud sounds, and sharp contrasts instantly capture attention. In addition, evidence suggests that we prefer visual over other sensory modalities—that a picture really is worth a thousand words. In terms of verbal material, therefore, vivid, concrete, easily visualized information draws attention more easily than does drier, more abstract information.[35] People also pay special attention to information that is surprising or that violates well-established schemata.[36]

> What kinds of stimuli arouse involuntary attention? Stimuli that are intense, novel, complex, surprising, and incongruous.

Of course, vivid stimuli are not always desirable. If listeners are anxious, intense stimuli may make them feel uncomfortable. And competing stimuli in the speaking environment can distract attention. When deciding where to deliver a message, it is important for communicators to choose environments that are interesting enough to keep receivers alert but not so interesting that receivers miss the intended message.

Guiding Interpretation

Message elements can be vivid and compelling, but if the message is unintelligible, it will not be effective. Therefore, senders must design messages that are easy to understand. Message comprehension can be increased in a number of ways. The first is to *relate new information to old.* Our discussion of schemata showed that when we encounter new information, we search for schemata that will make sense of it. A skillful message sender helps the receiver to do this by using analogy, comparison, and contrast—methods that help receivers to interpret a new experience in terms of prior meaning structures.

Table 3.4 Design Elements That Make Listening Easier

Elements That Capture Attention

- Increase voluntary attention by giving receivers a reason to listen.
- Increase involuntary attention by including vivid and compelling message elements.

Elements That Guide Interpretation

- Relate new information to old.
- Adapt content to audience's learning level.
- Use a clear-cut organizational pattern.
- Ask for feedback.

Elements That Ensure Acceptance

- Show the audience that new information is supported by prior beliefs.
- Offer an incentive for acceptance.
- Encourage favorable cognitive responses by involving receivers.

Elements That Enhance Storage and Retrieval

- Use repetition within the message.
- Personalize the message.
- Tie information to appropriate triggers.

Listeners have different levels of experience to draw on and process information at different levels. A fundamental principle of good communication is that *effective senders adapt to the learning level of their listeners, using familiar, concrete, and clear language and appropriate and unambiguous images.* This does not mean that speakers should talk down to listeners, but it does mean they must make a reasonable assessment of receivers' intellectual ability, degree of expertness, and past experience with the topic.

When complex information is presented, it is often necessary to link ideas and to construct interconnected arguments. *Use of a clear-cut organizational pattern that guides a receiver through a message enhances comprehension.* Whether people are reading an article, listening to a story, or hearing a joke, they expect message details to be delivered in a logical order. Organization is as important in a comedy routine as it is in a persuasive speech. All good communication must exhibit coherence.

Message comprehension can also be increased when the sender provides opportunities for feedback. One friend asks another, "Do you understand what I mean? Have you ever felt like that?" A person on duty in an information booth gives directions and then encourages the receiver to repeat them. A teacher quizzes students to find out whether or not they understand. In each case, the communicator is prepared to offer more information if the original message is unclear.

Ensuring Acceptance

Because receivers may understand what is said but may still block out or dismiss a message, effective senders do their best to ensure that message content is evaluated positively. *One way to increase acceptance is to show receivers that new information agrees with other elements in their belief system.* Most of us find it difficult to accept information that contradicts cherished beliefs or values. If you were to hear something shockingly negative about a close and respected friend, you probably wouldn't believe it—at least not initially. If you were to take a course with a professor who contradicts everything you have been taught, you would not know what to think. Accepting radically new information often means abandoning or reorganizing old beliefs, a difficult process. Senders can make the process easier by indicating how new information is supported by old beliefs or, when cognitive realignment is necessary, by helping receivers to reorganize belief structures.

Acceptable messages offer receivers an incentive. It is important that receivers see value in a message proposal. Receivers should understand why the information conveyed is useful and why following the speaker's recommendations might be rewarding. After all, message processing takes time and effort, and receivers won't want to expend that time and effort on irrelevant or erroneous messages.

Persuasion theorists called cognitive response theorists point out that people accept messages not on the basis of what a speaker says but on the basis of their own responses to the speaker's message.[37] During listening, receivers hold a kind of internal conversation with themselves. They agree or disagree, supplying supporting examples or counterarguments. These cognitive responses are what ultimately convince them to accept or reject a message. The cognitive response principle suggests that *senders who wish to increase acceptance should encourage favorable cognitive responses*. This can be achieved by getting receivers actively involved in message processing. Teachers, for example, may use experiments or exercises because what people discover for themselves is often more powerfully convincing that what they are told. Therapists may use role-playing for the same reason. And public speakers may ask audience members rhetorical questions to make them think about a topic.

Enhancing Storage and Retrieval

As we have seen, memory is not always perfect. How can senders help receivers to remember message content? First, *senders can encourage message retention by using repetition within the message*. During a message, they can also ask questions that encourage receivers to repeat what they have heard. They can provide follow-up activities that reinforce information rehearsal. They can also personalize their messages, making sure that information is relevant to receivers' experiences. *Information related to self-perception appears to be stored and retrieved more readily than is less relevant information.*

Message retrieval is often "triggered" or set off by some external stimulus. For example, we pass a restaurant and suddenly remember that we were supposed to meet a friend for lunch. Or we see an acquaintance going to the gym and suddenly recall that we vowed to exercise more often. In both cases, something in the environment jogged our memory. *Senders can increase information retrieval if they tie their message to an appropriate trigger.* Assume, for example, that a father wants his child to refuse rides from strangers. To ensure that the child retrieves the message at the appropriate time, the parent may set up a role-play. He may take the child outside, have a partner pretend to lure the youngster into a car, and make sure the child says no and runs away. In this way, the child knows when and under what circumstances to retrieve the desired response.

> Because listening is the forgotten part of communication, we seldom spend much time or effort on it. Yet being able to listen well is one of the most essential communication-related skills.

Clearly, listening is a complex process that takes attention and energy. It can be enhanced when senders design clear and interesting messages. And like other goal-directed behaviors, it can be improved with practice. Because listening is the forgotten part of communication, we seldom spend much time or effort on it. Yet being able to listen well is one of the most essential communication-related skills.

SUMMARY

Listening is a complex, multi-step process during which we attend to, interpret, evaluate, respond to, and store messages. Listening is not the same as hearing. When we hear, we translate sound waves into electrical signals to be processed by the brain. When we listen, we engage in a social cognitive process that focuses not just on sound but on other sensory data as well. Unfortunately, Americans are quite poor listeners, a situation that can negatively affect career and personal success.

Listening begins with attention, a process of selectively focusing on some stimuli while filtering out others. Attention can be voluntary or involuntary. In addition to being aware of distractions, we improve attention by listening with a clear purpose, by focusing on relevant contextual cues, and by maintaining a positive attitude.

As we listen, we give incoming stimuli structure, stability, and meaning. In doing so, we rely on cognitive schemata—mental models of the world that help us to process information. Person prototypes label and categorize people, personal constructs describe individual differences, and scripts describe action sequences. People who have rich construct systems and accurate schemata are more cognitively complex and therefore better able to interpret messages than are individuals who are limited to small sets of chronically accessible constructs. People who act mindfully are also better listeners than those who act mindlessly. In addition to recognizing the fallibility of perception, listeners can improve interpretation by being well informed, relating new information to old, using the speech–listening time differential effectively, and, when appropriate, employing perception checks.

Not all messages are believable. Effective listening involves evaluating information. By identifying a sender's purposes and credibility, demanding good evidence, and being sensitive to loaded language, listeners improve evaluation. Special problems exist in evaluating mediated messages. Some ways to be more critical of Web-based information include being suspicious of information that cannot be confirmed, understanding purpose and origins of a site, and being cautious about sites that are poorly or carelessly designed.

Responding is an often overlooked part of listening. Listeners are obligated to listen actively, that is, to react in ways that let speakers know they are listening. Active listening is an important part of empathic listening—listening designed to offer support or comfort to others. One effective way to show empathy is to use paraphrasing, a practice that allows listeners to check understanding, that invites elaboration, and that signals concern. Listeners improve responding by monitoring their nonverbal behaviors, seeing things from the perspective of the sender, and being aware of what is not said as well as of what is said.

The final factor that affects listening is message storage and retrieval. Memories are constructed and fallible and are affected by information interference, stress, anxiety, and social pressure. Storage can be improved when listeners consciously decide what needs to be stored, mentally rehearse and review important ideas, and use mnemonic devices or special memory aids.

Although a large part of the responsibility for effective listening lies with receivers, senders also have a part to play. Senders can help receivers by designing messages that are easy to listen to. By giving receivers a reason to listen, employing vivid and compelling message elements, and setting up proper environments, senders make attending easier. The probability that receivers will understand and interpret messages correctly is increased when speakers relate new information to old, adapt to the learning level of their listeners, use clear-cut organizational patterns, and provide opportunities for feedback. Sometimes receivers are resistant to messages. One way to increase acceptance is to show receivers that new information agrees with existing elements in their belief systems. Another is to offer incentives. Senders also increase the likelihood that receivers will agree with them by encouraging favorable cognitive responses. Finally, techniques like repetition and personalization make messages more memorable, as does associating a message with an appropriate trigger.

Listening is the forgotten part of communication, yet being able to listen well is an essential skill that can improve with practice.

KEY TERMS

Listed below are the key terms used in this chapter, along with the number of the page where each is explained.

listening (42)	personal constructs (48)	god terms (54)
hearing (42)	chronically accessible	devil terms (54)
attention (44)	constructs (49)	description (56)
voluntary attention (45)	cognitive complexity (49)	inference (56)
involuntary attention	scripts (50)	evaluation (56)
(45)	schematic default options	active listening (56)
structure (47)	(50)	paraphrasing (57)
stability (47)	mindless/automatic	false memory (59)
meaning (47)	processing (51)	retroactive inhibition (60)
schemata (47)	mindful processing (51)	cognitive response
person prototypes (48)	perception check (52)	theorists (63)

SUGGESTED READINGS

Brownell, Judi. (2006). *Listening: Attitudes, principles, and skills* (3rd ed.). Boston: Allyn & Bacon.

> A thorough discussion of listening as a complex, interrelated process, including a discussion of emotional intelligence and listening. In addition to providing a solid foundation, this book has many good activities and exercises.

Blake, Randolph, & Sekuler, Robert. (2006). Perception. New York: McGraw-Hill.

> Provides a detailed examination of perception as a physical, social, and cognitive process and includes chapters on visual perception as well as speech perception and hearing. For the student who is interested in the science of perception.

Encoding Messages: Spoken Language

Language gives us the power to affect and persuade others. But language also exerts power over us.

After reading this chapter, you should be able to:

- Identify four important characteristics of language.
- Explain what a symbol is.
- Explain the Sapir-Whorf hypothesis and give examples of ways language affects thought.
- Identify and describe the four subsystems of language.
- Explain the four levels of context described in CMM theory.
- Describe how public and private discourses differ from one another.
- Name the functions of conversational closings.
- Identify differences between men's and women's communication.
- Explain how ambiguity, abstraction, and metaphor use affects our interactions.

"**I**t was a bright cold day in April, and the clocks were striking thirteen." These words usher us into the bleak world of *1984,* George Orwell's chilling anti-utopia. Written in 1949, the novel describes a future world where freedom of thought has vanished—a world where Big Brother is always watching.

In *1984,* the government controls the masses through a special kind of language: "Newspeak." In Newspeak, any idea that diverges from party principles is literally unthinkable. Words such as *honor, justice, morality, internationalism, democracy, science,* and *religion* no longer exist, and words such as *free* have been stripped of connotations deemed troublesome by the government. The architects of Newspeak have reduced the number of words in the language because "the smaller the area of choice, the smaller the temptation to take thought."[1]

Orwell's novel illustrates a truth we often overlook: we think through language. This is as true of the everyday English we speak as it is of Newspeak. Language gives us the power to affect and persuade others. But language also exerts power over us. In this chapter, we look at what we do with language and what language does to us.

We'll begin by defining language and discussing its structure. We'll then move on to consider how we use language during interaction. We'll look at some pragmatic rules that govern language use, and we'll see how language is tied to group identity. Finally, we'll discuss how everyday language choices can sometimes result in unintended effects.

WHAT IS LANGUAGE?

Newspeak is frightening because it is dehumanizing. It is language "designed not to extend but to *diminish* the range of human thought, to make only 'correct' thought possible and all other modes of thought impossible."[2] Like other thinkers before him, Orwell understood the connection between language, thought, and humanity, a connection that can be found in the stories, myths, and religions of many cultures. Linguist Victoria Fromkin tells us that language is often experienced as the source of human life and power:

> *To some people of Africa, a newborn child is a kuntu, a "thing," not yet a muntu, a "person." Only by the act of learning does the child become a human being. According to this tradition, we all become "human" because we all come to know at least one language.*[3]

There are many kinds of languages. The most common are those built around the spoken word. Spoken languages are called "natural languages," emphasizing the close link between language and its expression in speech. Not all languages, however, depend on speech. Some "artificial" languages, such as computer languages, employ electrical signals, and sign languages use gestures. In this chapter, we'll focus on understanding spoken languages. In the next, we'll widen our discussion by looking at nonlinguistic codes.

In its most general sense, language can be defined as a rule-governed symbol system that allows its users to generate meaning and, in the process, to define reality. As we shall see, spoken language has four important characteristics: it is made up of symbols, it is a kind of knowledge, it is rule governed and productive, and it affects the way we experience the world.

Language Is Symbolic

To communicate, people must find a way to express the ideas that originate in their minds. A sign is the vehicle for this expression. It consists of two parts: the private idea located solely in the mind of a communicator (known as the signified); and the form in which the idea is expressed (or the signifier). In natural languages, the signifier is a sequence of spoken sounds. In artificial languages, the signifier may consist of electrical pulses, gestures, plastic shapes, marks on a page, or any of the other ingenious ways humans use to express meanings. In each case, the sign connects content and form. The French linguist Ferdinand de Saussure compared the sign to a sheet of paper, the front of which is the signifier and the back of which is the signified. Creating a word is like cutting a shape out of the paper, a shape that is both conceptual and representational.[4]

The sign relationship can be natural, or it can be produced by humans. An example of a natural sign is the smoke that indicates fire. In this case, the relationship between signifier (smoke) and signified (fire) does not depend on human intervention. In other cases, humans create signs. For example, English speakers use the sound sequence "dog" to represent a domesticated canine. The word *dog* is a special kind of sign called a symbol. A **symbol** differs from other signs in that it is arbitrary and conventional. The symbol *dog* is an **arbitrary symbol** because there is no natural connection between the idea of dog and the signifier *dog*. There is nothing particularly doglike about the word *dog*. In fact, in northern China, the signifier *gou* is used to represent the same idea. The symbol *dog* is a **conventional symbol** because its meaning depends on social agree-

Every culture develops its own set of symbols. Clear to members of the culture, they are impenetrable to outsiders.

ment. Speakers of English have agreed to use the word *dog* in certain ways that speakers of other languages have not. In our language, the sound sequence "dog" has meaning; in Chinese it does not.

Of course, words are not the only vehicles to carry meaning. Cultures can assign meaning to shapes (a hexagonal sign at the end of a street means stop) and to colors. For most Americans, red means love, sex, anger, or heat; white stands for innocence and purity; and black is associated with mourning. That this color symbolism does not hold true in other cultures shows how arbitrary and conventional color symbols are. Guo-Ming Chen and William Starosta explain, "for instance, to the Chinese, Japanese, and Koreans, red represents a color of longevity, splendor, and wealth; the color black is very much welcome in the Caribbean and Africa; green is a holy color to Moslems but means adultery to the Chinese; and yellow is a noble color for the Chinese and Indians."[5]

The fact that symbols call up similar thoughts in the minds of communicators even though no natural relationship between sign and idea exists has fascinated scholars for thousands of years. Aristotle recognized that symbols were ways of making inner thoughts discernible through sound, and (as you may recall from Chapter 1) Augustine thought and wrote about the nature of symbols. The Port-Royal grammarians of the seventeenth century also recognized this connection, describing language as

> *the marvellous invention of composing out of 25 or 30 sounds that infinite variety of words, which tho' they have no natural resemblance to the operations of the mind, are yet the means of unfolding all its secrets, and of disclosing unto those, who cannot see into our hearts, the variety of our thoughts, and our sentiments upon all manner of subjects.*[6]

Language Is a Kind of Knowledge

Language is mental rather than physical. Language is a body of knowledge stored within our brains. As such, it can never be examined directly but must be inferred from speech. Speech is the external, physical side of language, and language is the internal, mental side of speech. When we are born, we have not yet acquired the knowledge we call language. As we grow, we listen to the speech of those around us and figure out the rules that make up language. Every infant has the potential to learn the sounds, words, and sentence structures of any language. Had you been born into a language community other than the one in which you were raised, you would have mastered its language quite easily.

Language Is Rule Governed and Productive

One of the most amazing things about linguistic knowledge is that it lets us understand sentences we have never heard before. It is unlikely that you have ever before read this sentence: "The large, gray pachyderm wearing the pink tutu ate cherry vanilla ice cream and dreamed of Africa." Yet you know what the sentence means. Your ability to understand and create unusual sentences like this one is called linguistic productivity, and it shows that language learning is more than a matter of trial and error. When we learn language, we don't learn a set of specific word combinations; instead, we learn rules that allow us to generate meanings. Of course, most of us can't consciously explain the rules we follow as we speak and listen, but we can use them to make ourselves understood. These rules are complex and interrelated. They tell us how to make the sounds of our language, how to combine those sounds into words, how to order those words into sentences, and how to use sentences in interaction.

> One of the most amazing things about linguistic knowledge is that it lets us understand sentences we have never heard before.

Language Affects the Way We See the World

Human language is closely related to thought. Although some thought is purely visual, most is filtered through language. You can see this connection if you watch very young children think: they invariably talk or whisper at the same time. As we grow, overt verbalization gives way to silent, inner speech, but we still do a lot of our thinking through language.

Not only do we think in language, but we also store many memories in words. This phenomenon was demonstrated in a classic experiment performed in the 1930s. Leonard Carmichael and his colleagues asked people to view a set of twelve ambiguous figures (see Figure 4.1). Those taking part in the study were told to reproduce the figures as accurately as possible. As each figure was flashed before the subjects, it was labeled. A figure consisting of two circles connected by a short line, for example, was alternately labeled "eyeglasses" or "dumbbell." Results showed that subjects distorted the ambiguous figure to better fit the verbal label. Those who were shown the "eyeglasses" drew a picture in which the line

Figure 4.1 Figures Carmichael Used to Illustrate the Effect of Language on Memory

Figures in the middle column are the stimuli Carmichael presented to subjects. Figures in both outer columns show how verbal labels distorted subjects' recall.

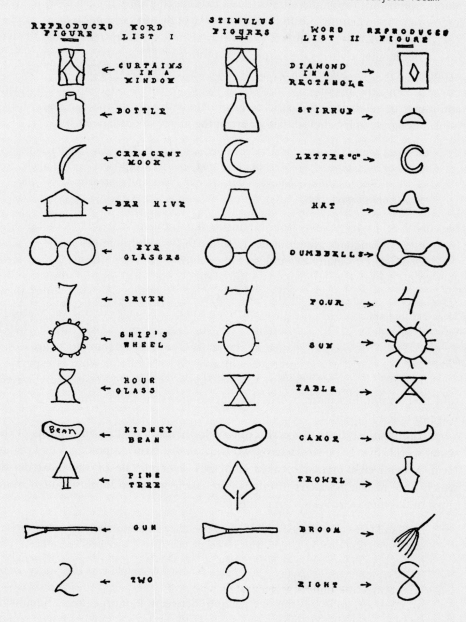

From "An Experimental Study of the Effect of Language on the Reproduction of Visually Perceived Forms" by L. Carmichael, H. P. Hogan, and A. A. Walter, February 1932, *Journal of Experimental Psychology, 15,* pp. 73–86.

connecting the circles was rounded to look like the bridge of a pair of glasses. Those shown the "dumbbell" thickened the center piece, making it look like a training weight. Evidently, people stored the verbal labels and then produced matching images, rather than storing the images themselves. As linguist Dan Slobin points out, verbal memory is thus a two-edged sword: it enables us to store and retrieve information, but in the process, it can distort perception.[7]

If we think and remember linguistically, then it stands to reason that the nature of our language affects the nature of our thought. The Sapir-Whorf hypothesis expresses this idea. Named after the linguist Benjamin Lee Whorf and his teacher Edward Sapir, the hypothesis consists of two corollaries: linguistic determinism and linguistic relativity. Linguistic determinism is the theory that language determines thought. Sapir believed that we are at the mercy of our language:

> the "real world" is to a large extent unconsciously built up on the language habits of the group. . . . We see and hear and otherwise experience very largely as we do because the language habits of our community predispose certain choices of interpretation.[8]

Linguistic relativity follows from linguistic determinism. It theorizes that people from different language communities perceive the world differently.

Linguists cite many examples of the Sapir-Whorf hypothesis. If you have ever studied a foreign language, you know that some concepts and ideas that are easily expressed in one language are difficult to translate into another. Languages divide the world in different ways. In fact, some people argue that a glance at the most frequently occurring words in a language will give you an idea of what is especially important to speakers of that language. Thus, we are told that Arabic has many words for horses and that the Eskimos have many ways to talk about snow.

> Some concepts and ideas that are easily expressed in one language are difficult to translate into another. Languages divide the world in different ways.

Grammatical distinctions also draw our attention to different aspects of the social world. French speakers have two ways to say "you": a polite and a familiar form. Whenever a French speaker addresses someone, he or she must decide which form to use. Speakers of English are not required to think about relationships in the same way. As Slobin points out,

> If we suddenly all switched to French, we would find our attention focused on many aspects of social relations which were previously not of central concern. . . . In speaking French, or some other language, we would almost certainly have to pay more daily attention to such matters.[9]

Another example of the connection between language and thought is discussed by psychologist Carol Cohn, who studied the ways that "defense intellectuals" discuss nuclear strategy. In her year-long study at a nuclear think tank,

Cohn found that policy makers used a specialized language to talk about life and death. As Cohn learned to use this language, she found her own attitudes and feelings changing.

Cohn found that the language of defense strategists is highly euphemistic. Euphemisms are inoffensive words that are used instead of highly charged terms. Although euphemisms allow us to avoid talking about painful or offensive situations, they can also act as blinders. Cohn tells us that defense strategists often used terms "so bland that they never forced the speaker or enabled the listener to touch the realities of nuclear holocaust that lay behind the words."[10] For example, a nuclear expert "sanitizes" bombs that are one thousand times more powerful than the one that destroyed Hiroshima by calling them "clean bombs." When civilian deaths are called "collateral damage," they become easier to dismiss. And when delivery of ordnance equipment results in "friendly casualties," the fact that American troops are being killed by American bombs goes almost unnoticed.[11]

Technostrategic language is a specialized jargon known only to members of the in-group. Cohn reports that gaining access to this jargon gave her a feeling of power. Knowing the jargon also made talking about defense strategy fun, in part because the language used many short, snappy words. Referring to a missile guidance system as a "shoot and scoot" made it easy to forget the darker and more serious side of nuclear scenarios.

The better Cohn got at speaking the language, the more difficult it became to express her own ideas and values. As she accepted a new way of talking, she also came to accept a new way of thinking:

> As I learned to speak, my perspective changed. . . . Speaking the language, I could no longer really hear it. And once inside its protective walls, I began to find it difficult to get out. . . . I had not only learned to speak a language: I had started to think in it. Its questions became my questions, its concepts shaped my responses to new ideas. Its definitions of the parameters of reality became mine.[12]

Language, then, has powerful effects on the ways that we think about and experience the world. Although we are not completely prisoners of language, it is easy to overlook the extent to which our language habits affect our views of the world.

Language Takes Many Forms

Languages can take a variety of forms. People who share a common language do not necessarily speak in the same manner. If you've ever conversed with an Australian or a New Zealander, for example, you know that the English language can vary in pronunciation and vocabulary. If you've attended a professional convention, you've seen jargon in action. One of the things that makes language so interesting is the way it changes to meet the needs and express the values of its users. Table 4.1 shows some of the forms languages can take.

THE SUBSYSTEMS OF LANGUAGE

No matter what form it takes, language is a carefully structured system of meaning. In this section, we'll look briefly at how language is put together, and we'll examine what it means to master the sounds, the words, the sentences, and the social context of language. Table 4.2 summarizes our discussion.

The Sounds of Language

When you first experience a foreign language, all you hear is a string of unintelligible sounds. As you learn the language, however, you learn how to pronounce these sounds and how to combine them with one another. When you have

Table 4.1 Forms of Language

Dialects

When a subgroup speaks a language using a different vocabulary, grammar, or pronunciation from others who speak that language, they are using a dialect. Problems occur when one dialect is defined as standard and given greater status than other dialects. Black English in the United States (sometimes called Ebonics) is an example. "Because language will naturally show variations, showing respect and open-mindedness is more important than arguing which dialect should be . . . standard. Today's preferred dialect may be tomorrow's relic."

Pidgins

There are no native speakers of pidgins. A pidgin is a simple language deliberately invented so that people new to an area (often colonizers) can communicate with those who live in that area. During wartime, soldiers may use pidgins to speak to locals. The grammar and vocabulary of pidgins are often very simple. "Long time no see" is an expression originating in the pidgin used by Chinese immigrants when they first arrived in America.

Creoles

A language that occurs when a pidgin becomes permanent is called a creole. Haitian Creole, based on French and African languages, can be traced to a slave-trade pidgin. Gullah, spoken on the coast of South Carolina, is another example. Creoles are often devalued because

of the frequently marginalized social status of their speakers.

Lingua Francas

When people from different language communities choose one language to use for trade and commerce, the chosen language is called a lingua franca. Swahili is used in this manner in Africa, and English has now become the lingua franca of international business.

Jargon

The special or technical words used by members of professions are called jargon. Legal, medical, and computer jargon are examples.

Argot

Argot refers to words whose meanings have been changed so that outsiders cannot understand them. They are often used by nondominant groups for protection and concealment. Prostitutes and prisoners, for example, use such words to refer to their activities.

Taboo

Words that are unacceptable in polite society are taboo. In the United States, frank discussions of bodily functions are usually considered taboo. In Chinese, the word that means "four" may be avoided because it sounds the same as the word for "death."

Adapted from Guo-Ming Chen and William J. Starosta, *Foundations of Intercultural Communication*. Lanham, MD: University Press of America, 2005. Reprinted by permission of Rowman & Littlefield Publishing Group.

accomplished this, you have mastered the first subsystem of language: the sound system. We humans have a rich and varied repertoire of sounds that we combine in countless ways to make up the lexicon of our language. Because we can articulate distinct sounds, we can build a sophisticated system for expressing meaning. The ability to articulate sounds is a vitally important part of being able to communicate.

The study of the significant sound patterns of language is called **phonology**. Of all the possible sounds we humans can make, only a small portion enter our language. In any language, some sounds are important and others are not. In English, for example, only one kind of "b" sound is significant. Different English speakers pronounce that "b" differently, but these variations can be overlooked. In Hindi, however, there are two kinds of "b" sounds: one is aspirated (accompanied by a short puff of air), and the other is unaspirated. Hindi speakers hear an aspirated and an unaspirated "b" as very different sounds, whereas we hear no difference at all. English, of course, contains some sounds not found in other languages. French speakers, for example, often pronounce the English

Table 4.2 The Subsystems of Language

Phonology: Study of the Sound System of a Language

- Phonology is the study of ways in which speech sounds form systems and patterns in human language.
- Its smallest unit is the phoneme.
- Phonological knowledge allows us to pronounce familiar words correctly, to know how unfamiliar words should sound, to know which sound variations are important in a language and which are not, to recognize foreign accents, and to make up new words that sound right.

Semantics: Study of the Meaning System of a Language

- Semantics is the study of linguistic signs (symbols), including word formation and the internal structure of words.
- Its smallest unit is the morpheme.
- Morphological knowledge allows us to divide a stream of sound into meaningful words, to store and recall both the forms and meanings of words, to understand a word's morphemic components, to recognize how the addition or subtraction of a morpheme can change meaning, and to inflect unfamiliar words (e.g., to make plurals, to change tenses, etc.).

Syntactics: Study of the Structure of Phrases and Sentences

- Syntactics is the study of the rules that govern the combination of words into permissible strings.
- Its smallest unit is the sentence or utterance.
- Syntactic knowledge allows us to distinguish grammatical from ungrammatical combinations of words, to combine words in the correct order and to understand how changes in order change meaning, to produce sentences we have never heard before, and to recognize ambiguous sentences and decode their ambiguity.

Pragmatics: Study of the Social Context of Language

- Pragmatics is the study of ways in which people use language forms to achieve goals in social contexts.
- Its basic unit is discourse.
- Pragmatic knowledge allows us to interpret another's communicative intent, to understand how context affects linguistic choices, to make language choices that communicate our intentions effectively, and to take into account information about the social world and our partner's knowledge of it.

words *this* and *that* as "zis" and "zat." Their language does not have a sound comparable to our "th."

The significant sound distinctions in a given language are called its **phonemes**. In English, "b" and "th" are phonemes; they are used to construct words, and no English speaker will confuse "bat" and "that." All English speakers have learned how to pronounce the English phonemes and know their basic characteristics. They also know how to use pitch, intonation, and word stress in acceptable ways. All of these skills are part of their knowledge of the sound system of language.

Written language lets us display our values and broadcast our messages at a distance.

The Words of Language

In every spoken language, sounds are combined into meaningful sequences called words. The study of the structure of the units of meaning in a language is called **semantics**. We all carry a kind of mental dictionary that equates word meanings with sound structures. When you memorize the words that make up your language, when you can hear a sound sequence and assign it meaning, you are acting on your knowledge of this subsystem of language.

So far, we have been talking about words as though they were the basic unit of meaning. Actually, the smallest unit of meaning in language is the **morpheme**. Some morphemes, called **free morphemes**, are equivalent to words. The words *boy* and *girl* are free morphemes. Other morphemes, called **bound morphemes**, must always be attached to other morphemes. The morpheme *ish,* meaning "having the quality of," is never found alone but must be combined with a noun, as in *boyish.* The plural morpheme *s* when added to *girl* creates *girls,* a new word with a new meaning. *Antidisestablishmentarianism* is one word made up of six bound morphemes attached to the free morpheme *establish* (anti-dis-*establish*-ment-ari-an-ism). A list of all the words of a language is known as a **lexicon**.

To know language is to know the rules of word formation. Young children often make errors because their morphological rules are not quite right. They learn that *s* indicates a plural form and *ed* indicates a past form, so they form words such as *dogs* and *barked.* But they may also construct words such as *sheeps* and *runned.* These errors show that children have inferred basic morphological rules but have not yet learned exceptions and irregularities.

The Sentences of Language

If a foreign student memorized an English dictionary, he or she would not know English, for he or she would not know how to construct sentences. To speak English, one must know the grammatical rules that govern English sentence construction. The study of the sentence structure of a language is known as syntactics.

Syntactic knowledge enables us to sequence words appropriately and to determine meaning based on word order. An English speaker who wants to indicate that Elliot surprised Mary on Tuesday would not say, "It was that on Tuesday Elliot Mary surprised." This way of ordering words defies the rules of English sentence structure. Neither would the speaker say, "It was on Tuesday that Mary surprised Elliot," for that would confuse Elliot's and Mary's actions. Clearly, word order and sentence structure are important elements of communication.

What do we know about syntactic knowledge? Grammarians believe that to use language, we must have a basic sense of how the different parts of a sentence (subject, verb, object, and the like) are related. To prove that we do have this knowledge, grammarians often point to ambiguous sentences; for example, "He decided on the train." This string of words can have two meanings. One meaning is "He made a decision while riding on the train." Here, "on the train" is a phrase that modifies the verb *decided.* On the other hand, the sentence could mean "He decided to take the train [rather than some other form of transportation]." Here, *train* is the object of the verb *decided on.* This sentence has two meanings not because the words are ambiguous but because the sentence has two different grammatical structures. If we couldn't understand this, we couldn't recognize the ambiguity.

Grammarians believe that syntactic knowledge contains information about the basic structures of sentences; the grammatical functions of words (for example, whether a word is a noun or a verb and where it fits in a sentence); rules for generating new sentences; and rules for transforming base sentences into different forms. Attempts to describe the syntactic knowledge necessary for even the simplest conversation are extraordinarily complex, and grammarians are still working on mapping syntactic structures. Luckily, we don't have to know complicated grammatical theories to use language. We can use syntactic knowledge automatically and unconsciously to generate new sentences and to recognize the sentences we hear.

The Social Context of Language

Knowing how to form grammatical sentences is a necessary, but not a sufficient, condition for good communication. To be really effective, speakers have to say the right thing at the right time in the right way. The fourth subsystem of language, the study of how we use language in social contexts, is known as pragmatics.

Speech Acts

People seldom make sentences just to show off grammatical competence. We talk to accomplish goals. Pragmatic knowledge allows us to understand the intentions of others and to make our own intentions clear. The goal a speaker intends to accomplish through speech is called a speech act. Successful communication involves understanding the relationship between words and sentences and the speech acts they represent. To do this, we have to go beyond grammatical knowledge and draw on social knowledge.

Earlier, we saw that a single utterance can have two syntactic structures. A single utterance can also have more than one pragmatic structure. Let's look at an example that has at least two interpretations and identify the speech act in each case. Consider the words "Do you have a watch?" The most likely interpretation of this sentence, if it is uttered by a stranger in the street, is that the speaker wants to know the time. Your knowledge of social behavior tells you that in our culture, people often phrase a request for the time in this roundabout way. If you believe that the speech act being performed is a request for the time, then the appropriate response is "Yes, it's 12:05."

Of course, the speaker may have other speech acts in mind. If he or she is carrying a clipboard and seems to be interviewing every passerby, the question might be part of a marketing survey. Then the proper response is yes or no or, perhaps, "I'm not interested in being in a survey." If the speaker is your teacher and you have just walked into class ten minutes late, the speech act is probably a criticism rather than a request for information, and the expected response is an excuse or an apology. Finally, if the speaker is a six-year-old who has been asking you a series of silly questions, the question may be part of a game, and you may decide to respond by asking silly questions of your own. To understand what is really meant by a speech act, you have to make inferences about the speaker's intentions.

Communication and Context

To make correct pragmatic choices, speakers must be sensitive to context, for context offers us, as listeners, the social information we need to understand speech acts. Context tells us who our communicative partners are and gives us clues about their assumptions and their expectations of us.

> To make correct pragmatic choices, speakers must be sensitive to context, for context offers us, as listeners, the social information we need to understand speech acts.

Table 4.3 shows some of the contextual information that we use to make pragmatic interpretations. This material is drawn from a larger theory of communication called the Coordinated Management of Meaning theory, or CMM.[13] CMM theory provides a framework for understanding how individuals use context to assign pragmatic meaning. CMM theorists believe that to communicate successfully, we must take into account four levels of context: episode, relationship, life script, and cultural pattern.

An episode simply means the situation we find ourselves in during a given interaction. Relationship refers to the role obligations that we feel toward one another. Life script is our professional or personal identity, and cultural pattern consists of the cultural norms we share with others. Communicators who understand these factors interpret the messages they receive correctly and communicate clearly. Communicators who can't read these contextual cues are at a disadvantage.

Language must always match context. Thus, if a speaker's professional identity is that of an aggressive defense attorney (life script) engaged in cross-examining (episode) a hostile witness (relationship) in a U.S. court of law (cultural pattern), he or she must communicate accordingly. When the speaker leaves the courtroom to have dinner with his or her spouse, however, the speaker's language style must change. A spouse can't be treated like a witness if a marriage is to survive. What is admirable in the courtroom may be unforgivable in the dining room.

Pragmatic knowledge is essential for good communication. In linguist Robin Lakoff's words,

> Pragmatics connect words to their speakers and the context in which they are speaking: what they hope to achieve by talking, the relation between the form they choose and the effect they want it to have (and the effect it does have), the assumptions speakers make about what their hearers already know or need to know.[14]

Pragmatic knowledge also includes knowledge about the type of discourse employed in any situation.

PRAGMATIC STYLES AND STRUCTURES

As we move from one situation to another, we use what linguists refer to as different discourse styles. Just as the basic unit of syntax is the sentence, so the basic unit

Table 4.3 Levels of Context: The CMM Hierarchy

Speech Act

An act done by the speaker to the hearer. Speech acts identify the speaker's intention.

Examples: to persuade, to flatter, to inform, to comfort, to gather information

Episode

A sequence of communicative behaviors that exist as a unit and has a beginning, a middle, and an end. Episodes identify the purpose of an interaction.

Examples: a friendly chat, playing a game, solving a problem

Relationship

All of the episodes that can reasonably be expected to occur between self and other, given reciprocal roles. Relationship identifies who communicators are to one another.

Examples: friends, lovers, strangers, business associates

Life Script

A person's ideas about the kind of communication that matches his or her personal identity. Life script is the individual's sense of self.

Examples: aggressive executive, creative artist, loving parent, gifted orator, sensitive friend

Cultural Pattern

General agreements shared by members of a particular cultural group about how to act in and respond to the world. Cultural patterns legitimize all lower contextual levels.

Examples: identity based on class, national, religious, or ethnic membership of pragmatics is discourse. **Discourse** is a unit of language larger than a single sentence; it consists of connected sentences that form an identifiable structure to fulfill a communicative function. In a typical day, you may read a newspaper article, study a college textbook, listen to a professor's lecture, take part in a group discussion, write a personal essay, give a public speech, or hold a casual conversation. All these activities are forms of discourse, and each has its own structure and rules. As we shall see in Part III of this text, different communication contexts call for different kinds of discourse. One aspect of being a good communicator is understanding and following the rules that govern common forms of discourse.

Forms of Discourse: Classifying Kinds of Talk

In this section, we'll compare two forms of discourse, one relatively private and the other slightly more public. These two forms of discourse, conversation and classroom interaction, are so familiar that we engage in them effortlessly. Yet when we go from one to the other—when we move from friendly talk with friends to interaction with classmates and teachers—our pragmatic rules change quite dramatically.

Understanding Conversation

The most common mode of spoken communication is the conversation. Through conversations, we create and maintain relationships, explore and develop personal identities, and accomplish daily tasks. Because this form of discourse is essential for social survival, conversation has been one of the most studied of all the discourse modes.

> Through conversations, we create and maintain relationships, explore and develop personal identities, and accomplish daily tasks.

Conversation analyst Margaret McLaughlin defines a **conversation** as "a relatively informal social interaction in which the roles of speaker and hearer are exchanged in a nonautomatic fashion under the collaborative management of all parties."[15] As the most private and most personal mode of communication, conversation differs from other forms of discourse.[16] It is the most reciprocal and egalitarian of all discourse forms because participation is equally distributed. Generally speaking, conversation allows partners a degree of freedom not present in any other kind of communication. In most cases, informal language forms are chosen and personal information is shared. Conversations are also spontaneous, or locally managed; that is, participants make up a conversation as they go along, taking their cues from one another. Thus, conversations are characterized by hesitations, restatements, repairs, and fillers, devices that signal the absence of strategy.

Some forms of discourse are publicly accessible; they are open to a large audience and are "on the record." Conversations, on the other hand, are private; in many cases, it is a violation of trust to repeat what is said. Outsiders may have difficulty making sense of conversations because participants use implicit, private codes and personal "shorthands" that reinforce the participants' unique bonds. This is important because the overall orientation of conversation is often relational.

Although people may accomplish tasks through conversation, they often use conversation to get to know one another. More formal kinds of talk seldom focus on purely relational matters.

Describing Classroom Interaction

Classroom discourse is quite different in both style and substance from conversation. Whether or not we admit it, the defining characteristic of classroom discourse is a nonegalitarian distribution of power. In almost all cases, a teacher has more power than a student does. The teacher chooses the text, makes the assignments, and gives the grades. As a result, interaction is nonreciprocal. In a typical lecture-discussion class, teachers talk more than students do, and teachers set the topics for discussion. Although both students and teachers ask questions, the functions of these questions differ. Presumably, students ask questions to acquire information, whereas teachers already know the answers to the questions they ask.

Conversation is the most private and personal form of communication. Through conversation we create and maintain relationships.

Degree of language formality varies, but generally, the syntax and vocabulary used in the classroom are formal, and topics are relatively impersonal. Certainly, classroom discourse contains more jargon than do private forms of talk. Teachers' talk is also scripted. If being too prepared in a conversation makes a speaker seem manipulative, being unprepared in the classroom destroys a teacher's credibility. Most teachers preplan their lectures, and some use the same jokes and examples from one year to the next. One of the most difficult tasks in good teaching is finding a way to make standard material fresh.

Classroom material is publicly accessible and generally explicit, and clarity is required. Finally, although teachers and students do build personal relationships, the business of the classroom is instruction, and most classes stay task oriented.

Dimensions of Discourse

The dimensions we have used to describe conversations and classroom discourse are summarized in Table 4.4. These dimensions define some of the important differences between private and public forms of talk and demonstrate how language use changes in different situations. Every time you adjust the way you talk to a different social context, you show your tacit understanding of these dimensions. We will return to these differences in more detail in Chapters 6 through 9, in which we'll discuss the nature and goals of interpersonal, group, public, and mass communication.

Interactive Discourse: Coherence and Structure

In addition to knowing general forms of discourse, communicators must coordinate communication. This knowledge is of particular concern in interactive discourse, in which communicators must be particularly sensitive to coherence and structure.

Coordinating Conversational Moves

In his discussion of the cooperative principle and conversational maxims, H. P. Grice has described the most basic and simple of the conventions that guide talk.[17] The cooperative principle asserts that for talk to work, communicators must be willing to cooperate with one another by speaking in socially approved ways. To cooperate, they must follow four conversational maxims, or rules. First, they must make sure their contributions contain enough, but not too much, information. This is the quantity maxim. Second, speakers must be truthful. If they say something patently absurd, they violate the quality maxim. Speakers must also be sure their contributions are direct and pertinent; otherwise, they fail to follow the relevancy maxim. Finally, speakers should follow the manner maxim; they should be direct and clear. When communicators don't follow these rules, conversation becomes impossible. No one can carry on a conversation with someone who has no regard for truth or relevance, whose style is unclear, and who has no concept of an appropriate amount of talk.

> For talk to work, communicators must be willing to cooperate with one another by speaking in socially approved ways.

This does not mean that maxims are never violated, however. Sometimes we violate a maxim intentionally to send an indirect message. If, for example, Harry

Table 4.4 Dimensions of Public and Private Discourse

Private Discourse	Discourse Dimension	Public Discourse
reciprocal	interaction pattern	nonreciprocal
egalitarian	power distribution	nonegalitarian
personal/informal	language choice	impersonal/formal
spontaneous	amount of forethought	scripted
privately owned	information accessibility	publicly accessible
implicit	meanings	explicit
relational	orientation	task oriented

asks Sally a personal question and she responds, "Nice weather," her violation of the relevancy maxim probably means that she finds Harry's question too personal. If he's sensitive to pragmatic rules, he understands her indirect meaning and has the good grace to change the subject. In this example, interpreting Sally's meaning is complex, for her meaning is not just in her words but also in the fact that she purposefully violates a conversational maxim. What lesson can we draw from Grice's analysis? It suggests that *to make sense, communicators must act cooperatively; when they fail to do so by violating conversational conventions, meaning is affected.*

An important factor is that conversation is sequential. For conversation to work, each move must follow the previous move and must fit into the overall conversation. This means that *communicators must keep track of what is going on as they talk and must build off others' contributions without losing sight of their conversational goals.* This is by no means easy, and conversation analysts have spent a great deal of time and effort debating and describing the rules that make such coordination possible. Communicators must do something more as well. *Communicators must know when it is time to make a conversational move.* In conversation, knowing whose turn it is can be tricky. In formal classroom discourse, the convention of raising your hand helps to regulate turn taking. In informal conversations, communicators must rely on subtle linguistic and nonverbal cues that indicate whether one speaker wants to continue or is relinquishing a turn. Although conversational turns commonly overlap a bit, true interruptions are social blunders that are often read as attempts to dominate.

Given the complexity of conversation, it isn't surprising that people occasionally lose track of what is going on and misunderstand one another. A final skill that communicators need is conversational repair. *Conversational partners must be able to head off problems before they occur or, if these attempts fail, to repair misunderstandings.* By using disclaimers and licenses, communicators can ask their partners for special understanding. "I'm not sure if I have this right,

> Given the complexity of conversation, it isn't surprising that people occasionally lose track of what is going on and misunderstand one another.

but I heard . . ." or "Now, hear me out before you object . . ." keep the conversation from breaking down. If these efforts fail, communicators must be able to explain misunderstandings and repair the conversation.

Conversational Closings

Each form of communication, from the nightly newscast to the everyday conversation, has its own internal structure. A speech, for example, can be divided into a beginning, a middle, and an end, each of which does something different. In this section, we'll illustrate the importance of structure by taking a brief look at conversational endings. We'll see that even in this relatively spontaneous form of interaction, people have definite expectations for what should occur—expectations the competent communicator must meet.

Endings play an important role in conversation. They signal that interaction is about to wind down, establish a sense of closure, reassure participants that the interaction has been successful, and establish conditions for future interaction. Often, they also contain specific directions for future behavior on the part of both speaker and listener.

Because walking away abruptly the instant talk ceases is unconscionably rude, the end of a conversation is signaled in advance. A statement about upcoming commitments ("I suppose I should get back to work soon") or a comment on the interaction ("I'm so glad we could get together") lets others know the conversation is drawing to an end and establishes closure. A good conversational ending also contains a statement of concern and goodwill ("It was great to see you") as well as a brief summary of the conversation ("Now, don't worry; things will work out"). Finally, it's a good idea to mention future contact ("I'll call you"). As Robin Lakoff points out, "Farewells stress the speaker's unwillingness to depart, offering it as a necessity imposed by cruel circumstances rather than the speaker's desire. We say, 'Gotta go!' not, 'Wanna go!'"[18]

Endings are equally important in other forms of discourse. In courtroom communication, for example, the summation is a lawyer's last chance to impress the jury; it is here that he or she will summarize arguments and make the strongest appeals. Conclusions are also vital in public speeches, because a weak ending can undermine the entire effect of a speech.

Yet endings are only one part of discourse structure. To be truly competent communicators, we must understand the entire structure of a given kind of discourse. (Beginnings, for example, are another important part of messages.) Although some forms of discourse are structured and formulaic and others are open and spontaneous, all must be well organized to be effective.

Guidelines for Understanding Discourse

To communicate successfully, we must master many types of discourse. We must know the purpose, rules, and stylistic properties of each type, and we must be aware of hidden assumptions and unintended effects. To become more aware of the way a specific form of discourse works, we should ask ourselves the four sets of questions listed below.[19]

1. **What is the purpose of this discourse?**

   What do I and my partners hope to achieve? Do we agree about the purpose of this interaction? What would mark the success of this discourse, and what would mark its failure?

2. **What rules regulate this discourse?**

   What speech acts are expected of each participant? What speech acts should participants avoid?

3. **What are the normal style and structure of this discourse?**

What specialized language choices are called for? How does one begin and end interaction? How might meanings here differ from those elsewhere?

4. **What are the effects of engaging in this form of discourse?**

What values and assumptions are presupposed in this discourse? Do I agree with these beliefs? Can this discourse be used to manipulate or dominate? How?

LANGUAGE AND SOCIAL IDENTITY

Although modes of discourse dictate certain language choices, they do not completely control communication. Not every teacher or public speaker or lawyer communicates in the same way. In this section, we will look at how group memberships affect language use, beginning with one of our most important group identities: gender.

Gender and Language

Men may not be from Mars, nor women from Venus (as a popular book proclaims), but it sometimes feels as though we might as well be from different planets. Let's look at a few examples.

> Men may not be from Mars, nor women from Venus (as the popular book proclaims), but it sometimes feels as though we might as well be from different planets.

On the way to visit friends in another part of the city, Juan and Rick and their friend Denise get lost. Denise suggests that they stop and ask the way, but both Juan and Rick refuse. They are uncomfortable asking for help and believe that there's no guarantee that a stranger will give accurate information anyway. They would prefer to drive around until they find the way. This doesn't make sense to Denise, who isn't at all embarrassed about asking for information and believes that anyone who doesn't know where he or she is should admit it.

Maria can't wait until Tom gets home from work so that they can talk about the day. As Tom enters the house, Maria begins a barrage of questions. What did he do? How was his presentation? Where did he and his colleagues go for lunch, and what did everyone order? She is interested in every detail, and his evasive answers hurt her. Tom, on the other hand, feels overwhelmed by Maria's "third degree" about things he barely noticed.

Not only do we teach children to act in gender-appropriate ways, we teach them to speak like "ladies" and "gentlemen." These lessons go largely unchallenged, yet they affect us in important ways.

Michael's friends ask whether it's okay to come over to watch the game on Friday. Michael says, "Sure." When he tells his girlfriend, Alyssa, she's upset—not because the friends are coming but because Michael didn't consult her first. Had the situation been reversed, she would have asked. In fact, "I have to check with Mike" would have been a way for her to let others know that she's part of a couple. For Michael, however, asking Alyssa implies he needs to get permission. As a result of these differences, Michael thinks Alyssa is unreasonable, and she sees him as insensitive.

Deborah Tannen believes that misunderstandings like these occur because men and women grow up in different cultures. Women's culture, she believes, stresses intimacy and connection, whereas men's culture values autonomy and individual achievement. These orientations affect men's and women's topics of conversation, their conversational styles, and their interpretations of one another's meanings.

As a linguist, Deborah Tannen believes that these misunderstandings occur because men and women grow up with different expectations about how to use language.[20] Women are encouraged to focus on intimacy and connection, whereas men are taught to display autonomy and individual achievement. These orientations affect the ways men and women think they are supposed to communicate and determine their topics of conversation, their conversational styles, and their interpretations of one another's meaning.

The Development of Gender Differences

We are the victims of gender expectations from the moment we're born. The first question most people ask after a child is born is "Is it a boy or a girl?" And once this question has been answered, perceptions and expectations change markedly. Psychologists John and Sandra Condry asked people to interpret why a newborn was crying. Those who were told that the baby was a boy were likely to interpret his first act of communication as anger. Those who were informed that the baby was a girl assumed she was afraid.[21]

As boys and girls grow up, they learn the expectations associated with their gender. Play is a case in point. Games traditionally associated with boys stress freedom and competition, whereas girls' games focus on matters of inclusion and exclusion. Boys are encouraged to interact in large, hierarchically structured groups, playing rule-bound games with winners and losers. Boasting, mocking insults, and teasing often accompany boys' play. Girls, on the other hand, often play in smaller groups within which everyone gets a turn. Girls try to avoid the appearance of conflict by proposing rather than ordering. Instead of saying, "You stand over there," girls are more likely to say, "Let's get in a circle, okay?" or "What if you stand at that corner?" This is not to say that girls do not find ways to exclude one another, but they do it in ways that allow them to display "appropriate" gender identities.[22] Later in life, men continue to bond through shared physical activity and women through talk.[23]

As boys and girls grow older, they develop characteristic conversational styles. One example is the way each gender responds to trouble talk. A number of studies show that boys often respond to other boys' reports of a problem by dismissing or downplaying it or by giving straightforward advice on how to solve it. Girls, on the other hand, are likely to respond with trouble talk of their own.

This characteristic holds true in storytelling as well. Males often tell stories about contests in which they acted as either protagonist or antagonist and in which they ultimately succeeded. Females often tell stories about times when they or others violated social rules and consequently looked bad. Females exorcise their social failures by talking about them. Males, on the other hand, prefer to ignore failures and to focus on achievement. Tannen comments, "If men see life in terms of a contest, a struggle against nature and other men, for women life is a struggle against the danger of being cut off from their community."[24]

In adulthood, these patterns persist, and a verbal division of labor takes place. Women specialize in relationally oriented talk, whereas men specialize in task-oriented talk. Tannen uses the terms **rapport talk** and **report talk** to get at these differences. Rapport talk focuses on relational meaning; it is most appropriate for interpersonal topics and feels most natural in intimate contexts. Report talk focuses on content; as a style, it is appropriate in public situations when decision making or opinion exchange is expected.

Throughout their lives, men and women learn, to varying degrees, how to use language to display stereotypical gender identities. Men know that being competitive is a way of being masculine. Women recognize that stressing connection is part of being feminine. This can explain why many men would rather drive around for hours than ask directions (and reveal their lack of control). It can explain why many women want to know every detail of a man's day the minute he walks through the door (to build intimacy through shared talk). And it can also explain why a simple statement such as "I have to check with X" can be interpreted in entirely different ways.

Of course, men and women do not act stereotypically all of the time, nor do all men and women feel comfortable fitting into expected gender identities. Just as we grow up knowing how to display gender identities through language, we also make choices about whether or not to act in expected ways. Feminist scholars frequently make a distinction between "women's language" (the way women are supposed to talk) and the "language of women" (the way women actually communicate). The same can be said for men's language. One of the tasks faced by researchers who want to understand gender and language is finding out how stereotypical expectations interact with actual behaviors.

> Just as we grow up knowing how to display gender identities through language, we also make choices about whether or not to act in expected ways.

Research on Gender and Communication

Over twenty-five years ago, Cheris Kramer, Barrie Thorne, and Nancy Henley took on the task of investigating the relationship between gender and language. They posed the following questions: "Do women and men use language in different ways? In what ways does language—in structure, content, and daily usage—reflect and help constitute sexual inequality? How can sexist language be changed?"[25]

In the ensuing years, a great many answers have been given to these questions. Scholars have described and documented sexist language, and experimental researchers have found evidence that the use of this language has a negative impact on both men and women. For example, there is evidence that women's recall for facts is better when those facts are presented using inclusive, nonsexist language than when they are presented in noninclusive terms.[26] And it has also been demonstrated that when women are referred to as "girls" they are judged as being less responsible than when referred to as "women."[27] As a result of these and other findings, it is now common practice to avoid the use of language that denigrates, disrespects, or makes women invisible.

The answer to the question of whether there are differences between the ways men and women use language is more problematic. On one hand, our own experiences as well as many hundreds of studies attest to the fact that men's and women's language differs. So, in one sense, the answer to the question "Do men and women communicate differently?" is a resounding "Yes." On the other, as Ann Weatherall points out, there is no agreement on the exact nature of these differences nor is there any consensus about their theoretical explanation.[28] Table 4.5 describes some of the many findings in this area.

Problems in Interpreting Gender Differences

But how significant are these differences, and what do they mean? In recent years, feminist scholars have urged caution in interpreting research on gender differences. As Deborah Cameron points out, many of our most familiar generalizations exhibit what Shan Wareing has called the **hall of mirrors effect**: "in the course of being cited, discussed, and popularized over time, originally modest claims have been progressively represented as more and more absolute, while hypotheses have been given the status of facts."[29]

Psychologist Elizabeth Aries agrees, pointing out that although there are many statistically significant differences between male and female communication styles, they are generally quite small. She reminds us that "men do not form a homogeneous group, nor do women. There is considerable variability in the interaction styles of members of the same sex because of differences in personality, age, race, class, ethnicity, or sexual orientation."[30] In many studies of communication differences, gender accounts for only a small proportion of subjects' behaviors. It is therefore useful to keep in mind that we are much more similar than we are different.

Aries also cautions us to remember that context makes a difference when it comes to gendered communication. For example, it would not be accurate or fair to conclude that overall men are more likely than women to take on leadership roles. In point of fact, research shows that men are most likely to emerge as leaders in short encounters with strangers or when the task draws on skills that are typically associated with men. In longer encounters, when women have been given equal status and power, there are fewer gender differences in leadership behavior.[31]

More problems arise when we try to evaluate communication differences. For example, for many years, women's talk was denigrated as trivial, gossipy, and uncertain, while men's speech was seen as competent and authoritative. Using a male model, women's speech was considered deficient. When women used **tag**

Table 4.5 Conclusions Drawn from Research on Gender Differences in Communication

Quantity of Talk: *Who Talks the Most?*

- In task-oriented cross-gender groups, men talk more than do women.
- In friendly same-gender dyads, women prefer to spend time talking; men prefer to share activities such as sports or hobbies.

Topics of Talk: *What Do Men and Women Talk About?*

- Women talk more about private matters (family, relational problems, other women, men, clothing) than do men.
- Men talk more about public matters (sports, money, and news) than do women.
- Women and men both talk about work and sexual relationships.

Vocabulary: *Do Women and Men Use Different Words?*

- Women are reported to use more detailed color terms (*mauve, teal*) than do men.
- Women more often use weaker expletives ("Oh dear," "Oh my"), whereas men more often use stronger expletives, including obscenities.
- Women use certain evaluative adjectives (*adorable, cute, fabulous*) that men do not use.

Grammatical Constructions: *Do Men's and Women's Syntax Differ?*

- Women use more qualifiers (*somewhat, kind of, I guess*) than do men.

- Women use more disclaimers ("I'm no expert, but . . . ," "Don't get mad, but . . .") than do men.
- Women use more tag questions ("Right?" "You know?") than do men.
- Women are more likely to use polite forms than are men.

Turn Taking: *Who Controls Interaction Flow?*

- In cross-gender dyads, men interrupt women more than women interrupt men.
- Women ask more questions, and men make more statements during interaction.
- Men often respond to women using delayed minimal responses ("Oh" or "right," said after a brief pause) that discourage interaction; women's minimal responses ("Hmmm, I see") occur within turns and seem to encourage talk.

Topic Control: *Who Chooses the Topics of Talk?*

- Men successfully initiate topics more often than do women.

Humor: *Do Women or Men Tell More Jokes?*

- Boys and men offer more jokes and witticisms than do girls or women.
- Girls and women laugh more than do boys or men.

Self-Disclosure: *Are Men or Women More Open?*

- Women tend both to disclose more and to receive more disclosures from others than do men.

Note: Current research supports these conclusions; however, not every study concurs, and some contradictory findings exist.

Adapted from research reviewed by Laurie P. Arliss in *Gender Communication,* 1991, Englewood Cliffs, NJ: Prentice-Hall.

questions (fragments such as "right?" or "okay?" at the end of sentences), qualifiers (words such as "maybe" or "perhaps"), or disclaimers (phrases such as "now don't get me wrong, but" or "don't get mad until you hear me out"), they were criticized for being passive and powerless. They were advised to become more assertive and direct to become credible; in other words, to be more like men. More recently, women's speech has been reevaluated. Now, use of tag questions and the like is interpreted as attempts to build mutual support and solidarity. And men's speech, now viewed against a female model, is often seen as deficient in intimacy, connectedness, and expressiveness. But turnabout is not necessarily fair play. As Aries states, "We now misrepresent and devalue men just as women were misrepresented using masculine models, and we continue to define men and women in position to one another and to polarize differences."[32]

One way to avoid making the mistake of viewing male/female differences as essential is to consider the performative aspects of language. Although it may look as though we differ in essential ways, many of these differences can be explained as social performances rather than as innate characteristics. Candace West and Don Zimmerman tell us, "A person's gender is not simply an aspect of what one is, but, more fundamentally, it is something that one *does*, and does recurrently, in interaction with others."[33] Many current language scholars argue that we do not use language the way we do because of our gender, we create gender identity through language. Deborah Tannen explains, "Ways of talking and behaving that are associated with gender are a matter not of identity but of display. In other words, the behavior is not a reflection of the individual's nature (identity) but rather of some performance that the individual is accomplishing (display)."[34] An interesting example of this idea can be found in the fact that some of the most eager readers of books on gender differences and communication are transgendered individuals "looking for guidance on how to mount an 'authentic' performance of their chosen gender identity."[35] But it is not only transsexuals or drag queens who perform gender. Most of us know how to "talk like ladies" or "act like men" in order to fit in and display an appropriate gender identity. Aries reminds us that:

> Many current language scholars argue that we do not use language the way we do because of our gender, we create gender identity through language.

> Men and women behave in different ways because of their different placement within the social hierarchy, the different statuses and roles they fulfill, the different skills and abilities they acquire in these roles, their desire to display behavior to confirm their gender identities, and the consequences they face for violating expectations for gender-related behavior.[36]

Adapting to Gender Differences

None of the scholars we have quoted denies the fact that men and women do communicate in different ways; they simply believe that these differences are more complex than was originally thought. It would be as wrong to deny true differences as it would be to accept false ones. In fact, understanding that men's and women's approaches to communicative situations often vary can be useful. Knowing, for example, that the behaviors that annoy or perplex us about another person may be based not on personality defects but on the need to perform gender roles can make us more accepting of one another.

Today's language scholars call on us to be both more cautious and more tolerant, and to be willing to experiment with traditional communicative behaviors. If habitual styles of communicating are not serving us well, we should find new forms of communication that suit us better. We should also learn to accept people who do not fit traditional gender roles, valuing them for their ability to imagine new ways of being as they find ways to escape the stereotyped expectations that control most of us.

Language and Cultural Difference

If men and women within a single language community confuse one another, you can imagine how difficult it can be when people from different countries try to communicate. Even when they have learned the vocabulary and grammar of each other's language, they may still experience problems, for languages differ in many other ways. Students of cross-cultural communication have described some of these differences; in particular, they have focused on the extent to which context is part of a message, the directness with which thoughts can be expressed, the amount of emotional expressiveness that is appropriate, and the extent to which formality is expected.[37]

Context Dependence

Some cultures value verbal precision; in such cultures, speakers must explicitly say everything they mean. The language is structured so that nothing is left to conjecture. Cultures that find meaning in the words rather than in the shared context in which communication occurs are called low-context cultures. In such cultures, the speaker assumes that the listener doesn't know very much about the situation and must be told everything explicitly. England, the United States, and other English-speaking nations are considered low-context cultures, as are many of the countries in Western Europe.

High-context cultures, on the other hand, don't consider it necessary to spell out messages as explicitly. Speakers don't bother to say what they believe listeners already know. They also believe that where and how something is said is as important as what is said. The Chinese language, for example, is highly contextual: many of the grammatical details we regard as important, such as verb tense or the distinction between the pronouns *he* and *she,* are not usually indicated. In Chinese, the same string of words can mean "he is going" or "she went." How do Chinese speakers know which is the intended meaning? From context. If the speaker has been discussing a past event and the subject of the conversation has been a woman, then everyone will know that the speaker means "she went." On the other hand, if the topic of conversation has been the current actions of a man, then everyone will understand the sentence to mean "he is going." In Chinese, it is often not necessary to say explicitly what can be inferred from context.

In other high-context cultures, such as Japan, business meetings may open with talk about nonbusiness issues such as family, food and drink, the weather, and so on. During discussion, words are sometimes less important than tone of voice, eye contact, and other nonverbal cues. A "yes" may mean a number of things including "yes," "I don't know," "perhaps," or even "I hope I have said this unenthusiastically enough for you to understand that I mean no."[38] As you can imagine, these differences can cause problems. To the high-context speaker, low-context language can seem abrupt and insulting. And low-context speakers can become extremely frustrated and confused in high-context cultures.

Verbal Directness

Closely related to context is the dimension of directness. Generally, people from low-context cultures exhibit verbal directness: they get to the point quickly and say what they mean. People in high-context cultures often prefer verbal indirectness: they prefer to discuss matters in a more subtle and roundabout way. Thus, they may say things in ways that members of low-context cultures would consider "hinting" or "beating around the bush."

The following example, cited by Lustig and Koester, is a perfect example of indirectness.[39] A Malaysian teacher is talking to a European American teacher. The Malaysian, who doesn't have a car, wants the American to drive him off campus for lunch but is too polite to ask directly. Instead, the Malaysian says, "Can I ask you a question?" "Yes, of course," the American answers. "Do you know what time it is?" "Yes, it's two o'clock," answers the American. The Malaysian then asks, "Might you have a little soup left in the pot?" Puzzled, the American asks for clarification, forcing the Malaysian to be more explicit. "I will be on campus teaching until nine o'clock tonight, a very long day for any person, let alone a hungry one!" Finally, the American catches on: "Would you like me to drive you to a restaurant off campus so you can have lunch?" The Malaysian teacher answers, "What a very good idea you have!" Although the authors do not reverse the dialogue, we can imagine that if it were the American who was hungry, the request would be much more direct: "I'm starving. Can you give me a lift off campus? I need to get lunch."

Members of indirect cultures use a variety of methods to get meanings across, including refraction (letting someone overhear what you want him or her to know), covert revelation (letting personal views out in a disguised way), or mediation (waiting for someone else to relay the message).[40]

Expressiveness

Expressive cultures are open when it comes to displaying emotions. Hugging, touching, laughing, and crying may not be out of place, even in the workplace. Eloquence is often valued. In other cultures, the opposite is true. In many cultures, emotional displays are seen as inappropriate and unprofessional. Iranians, for example, are very emotionally expressive. When angry, an Iranian's behaviors may consist of "turning red, invoking religious oaths, proclaiming his injustices for all to hear, and allowing himself to be held back."[41] Many southeast Asians, in contrast, value evenness and restraint and try to neutralize emotions. European Americans, in general, are somewhere in the middle.

Formality

A final dimension of intercultural language use is formality. Some cultures use language in a formal way. Protocol is very important, deference should be shown to superiors, and all messages should flow through proper channels. This kind of language use is found in cultures in which there is a distinct power hierarchy. Conversely, the goal of cultures favoring informal language is to reduce this hierarchy, get rid of red tape, and treat individuals as equals. The United States and Australia are well known for such informality.

We will look at cultural differences again throughout this text, and in Chapter 12 in particular. For the time being, it's important to realize that there are many different ways to use language and that our attitudes toward language are culturally determined. People say what they mean in very different ways. If you find yourself communicating with someone from another culture or co-culture, it's probably a good idea to keep this in mind and recognize the potential for misunderstanding.

LANGUAGE CHOICES AND PRAGMATIC EFFECTS

One of the themes of this chapter is that language gives us power. Our linguistic choices count: they make a difference in our lives and in those of others. If we use language wisely, we can control communication; if we do not, communication can have unintended effects. In this section, we look at some of the effects of using four kinds of language. We'll discuss ambiguity, immediacy, abstraction, and figurative language.

Ambiguity: When Not Making Sense Makes Sense

As we have seen, U.S. culture values directness and clarity. You've probably been told that language should be concrete, simple, direct, and straightforward. You've been warned that ambiguity diminishes communication. Often, this is true. In many situations, clarity is the measure of the success of a message. Legal documents or technical instructions, for example, must be precise. But clarity is not always advantageous, even in a low-context culture like ours, and ambiguity can sometimes help, rather than hinder, communication.

> Clarity is not always advantageous, even in a low-context culture like ours, and ambiguity can sometimes help, rather than hinder, communication.

Eric Eisenberg, an expert in organizational communication, discusses positive effects of using **ambiguous language**, language that can be interpreted in more than one way.[42] First, ambiguous language can give an organization the flexibility to adapt to future contingencies. When a university issues the statement "The University shall be responsive to its surroundings," the university is being deliberately ambiguous. It is assuring members of the surrounding community of its intention to act in good faith while leaving itself room to develop policy. On an interpersonal level, ambiguity allows members of organizations to perceive themselves as similar rather than different. Because similarity is a basic factor in attraction, ambiguity can increase group solidarity. We often employ strategic ambiguity unconsciously. For example, the first stages of group formation involve a great deal of ambiguity. Here, ambiguity allows members to avoid disagreements until the group is cohesive enough to deal with stress.

Eisenberg points out that people with high credibility often benefit most from ambiguity. If one's credibility is already high, clarity is more likely to decrease than to increase it. Strategic ambiguity also allows one to deny a stand if it should become unpopular. "That's not what I meant at all" gives a person a way to back down gracefully.

Janet Beavin Bavelas and her colleagues suggest that **equivocal communication**, another term used to describe ambiguous communication, is most often used when a communicator feels trapped between two unpleasant alternatives. When speaking the truth and lying are both problematic, people often equivocate. Ask yourself which response you would choose in each of the following situations:[43]

A fellow student has just given a class presentation. It was very badly done. After class he asks you, "How did I do?" Which response is best?

    a. You did very well. I really liked it.
    b. You were terrible; bad job.
    c. Not well, but don't feel bad about it.
    d. You were braver than I would be!

You have received a gift from someone you really like a lot, but the gift is awful. How would you respond?

    a. The gift is perfect; I really love it.
    b. I don't like the gift and am going to exchange it.
    c. I like you, but I don't like the gift.
    d. I appreciate your thoughtfulness.

You are torn between loyalties to two people you know and like equally well. Ann worked for you at one time. Bob is thinking of hiring Ann. Unfortunately, Ann is nice but incompetent. You must write a letter of reference. What would you say?

    a. Ann was an excellent employee; I recommend her.
    b. Don't hire Ann; she was not a good employee.
    c. Ann is a nice person but not a good employee.
    d. It's been years since I employed Ann, so I can't answer specifically.

In each case, *d* is the equivocal response. If you are like most people, you were probably tempted to use ambiguity in at least one of these cases, for it is a way of responding to an uncomfortable situation without lying or hurting someone's feelings. Communication specialists differ in their evaluation of this form of communication. Some decry it as deceptive and misleading and tell us we should always be honest. Others, like Bavelas, defend it:

> *Equivocation is not the deliberately deceitful "dirty old man" of communication. It is subtle, often commendable, and entirely understandable, if only the observer will expand his or her analysis to include the communicative situation. . . . In our experience, real living messages do not fit prescriptive and judgmental models; they are more subtle, more skillful, and more interesting.*[44]

Immediacy: Up Close and Personal

Language can be inclusive or exclusive. It can place the listener at a distance or forge a close and personal bond.[45] **Immediate language** is personalized language, and it can be very effective in persuasive situations. Consider the following excerpt from a televised speech:

> *This historic room and the presidency belong to you. It is your right and responsibility every four years to give temporary custody of this office and of the institution of the presidency. You so honored me, and I am grateful—grateful and proud of what together we have accomplished.*

The speaker was President Ronald Reagan, and the occasion was the 1984 announcement of his decision to run for a second term.[46] This speech illustrates an effective use of immediacy. Reagan involves us directly and personally. We feel we are a part of his presidency, although what exactly "we" did together is not specified. Critics might say that this use of immediacy is misleading, yet it is certainly effective.

Empirical studies show that the use of verbal immediacy in public situations has positive effects, increasing ratings of a speaker's competence, character, similarity to audience members, and degree of relaxation, especially when the speaker agrees with audience members.[47] Immediacy is also effective in interpersonal contexts. If, however, it is blatantly used to create a bond where none exists, it can backfire. A low-status speaker might offend someone of higher status by being too familiar. Sometimes, norms for considerateness preclude being too immediate. As communicators, we must find a balance between familiarity and polite deference.[48]

Abstraction: Creating General Categories

I remember my grandmother's house in complete detail. If I close my eyes, I can picture the garden in back and the broad veranda where I played as a child. When

I speak of this place, I use the word *house*. Yet no single thing called "house" exists, only particular houses, such as the ones you and I grew up in. A house has no particular color, shape, or size. It is simply a structure used for human habitation. "House" is an abstraction, a synthesis of what many houses have in common. All words are abstractions, although some are more general than others. To call my grandmother's house a "dwelling unit" or an "abode" is to abstract it even further, and to abstract something is to make it less real.

Of course, abstraction is necessary. Abstract concepts allow us to talk about the future, to make predictions, and to think logically and mathematically. In Robin Lakoff's terms, abstraction is "the basis of science, crucial to human understanding and the growth of our intellect and to our power as a species over the physical universe. It has made us what we are."[49]

Abstract language can also be false and dangerous. It is the basis of stereotyping. When my grandmother's house becomes merely a "house," it loses its individuality; it is reduced to a series of general qualities. Similarly, when my neighbor becomes a "New Yorker" or a "teacher" or an "American," she loses her uniqueness. Your idea of what she is like is shaped by these abstractions. Finally, when some people become "we" and others "they," the way is paved for misunderstanding and abuse.

Figurative Language: Metaphors We Live By

We usually think of metaphors as devices that poets use, not as a feature of everyday talk. Metaphors, however, are a figurative form of language that is found in every kind of discourse, and their presence affects us in interesting and important ways. A metaphor is a linguistic usage that allows us to understand and experience one thing in terms of another. Metaphors guide our thoughts and actions.

George Lakoff and Mark Johnson illustrate the pervasiveness of metaphors by looking at the common ways we talk about argument.[50] What underlying comparison is common to the following statements?

He *attacked every weak point* in my argument.
His criticisms were *right on target*.
I *demolished* his argument.
He *shot down* all my arguments.

The metaphor is that argument is a war—a common way of viewing argument in our culture. Lakoff and Johnson ask us to imagine instead another kind of culture,

> [where] argument is viewed as a dance, the participants are seen as performers, and the goal is to perform in a balanced and aesthetically pleasing way. In such a culture, people would view arguments differently, carry them out differently, and talk about them differently.[51]

Metaphors allow us to grasp abstract or difficult concepts in terms of more understandable ideas. In doing so, however, they highlight some aspects of the concept and downplay others. Let's look at some common metaphors used to describe love. Love can be thought of as a physical force ("There's electricity between us," "When we're together, sparks fly"); as mystic power ("She's bewitching," "The magic is gone"); as madness ("I'm crazy about him"); or as war ("She conquered my heart," "He's besieged by women"). Each of these metaphors calls our attention to a different kind of experience and legitimizes a different kind of behavior. If love is a physical force or mystic power, it is beyond our control; there's nothing we can do but let it wash over us. If love is madness, then irrational behavior is defensible. What if, however, we were to think of love in a new way, as a collaborative work of art? Following from this metaphor, love would be something to be worked on, something that takes shape over time, and something that is beautiful and precious. Our reactions to and experience of love would be significantly different.

Lakoff and Johnson believe that the metaphors we live by have a political dimension. Metaphors are often imposed on us by people in power: politicians, religious leaders, economists, and advertisers control us by creating metaphorical values. Once we come to believe in a given metaphor, say, "Bigger is better" or "More is good," then it becomes difficult to see the world in any other way. Accumulation is valorized, and behaviors such as conservation are devalued. When, in *1984,* the architects of Newspeak force the masses to believe that war is peace, freedom is slavery, and ignorance is strength, they create ideological metaphors. Although metaphors can illuminate the way we see the world, they can also blind us. Metaphors, like other language choices, can shape our actions and experiences. They can give us power, or they can control us. For a discussion of how metaphors work in complex organizations, see Chapter 8.

Improving Language Choices

Language is a powerful tool. It allows us to abstract and store experiences and to share them with others. It allows us to make contact with and to influence, regulate, persuade, and dominate one another. It makes us the humans we are. Yet, despite the great power it gives us, language also exerts power over us. Our thoughts and perceptions are filtered through language and can be distorted by it. In the words of Aldous Huxley, "Possessing language, we are . . . capable of intellectual achievements beyond the scope of any animal, but at the same time capable of systematic silliness and stupidity such as no dumb beast could ever dream of."[52] It is important, then, that we use language with care and sensitivity, realizing that it can lead us astray as often as it can lead us to the truth.

> Language is a powerful tool. It allows us to influence, regulate, persuade, and dominate one another. It makes us the humans we are.

Throughout this chapter, we've explored the social nature of language. We've seen that words are social agreements, agreements to express ideas in similar ways. We get into trouble if we start believing that words are complete and accurate reflections of reality. We should *always remember that talking about something doesn't necessarily mean it is real*. Language has a peculiar tendency to **reify** concepts, to make us believe that they are tangible and real rather than fallible human constructions. Two old sayings remind us not to confuse reality with talk: "The map is not the territory" and "The word is not the thing."

Another important principle to keep in mind is that meanings are in people, not in words. Although we share a language with others, we each shade its words and phrases with our own experiences. Meanings are by no means objective, and, as our discussion of speech acts points out, we often mean more than we say and say less than we mean. *Uncovering meaning involves making inferences about the communicative intentions of others*. Only a madman would take as literal everything others say. A sane and competent communicator recognizes that language involves a great deal of social inference. One should always be careful to *take context into account both when interpreting others' messages and when creating one's own*.

When we encode messages through spoken language, we have to make choices. *There is no single right way to use language; language choices must depend on our purposes, our audience, and the conventions of the discourse form we use*. We use a specific kind of language to sell a used car, host a TV talk show, tell a joke, deliver a public speech, or talk to a stranger at a party. Each form of communication has its own linguistic conventions. Although most of the time language that is direct, clear, concrete, and straightforward is preferred, there are also appropriate times for ambiguity, abstraction, and figurative language. Making language choices is no simple matter. It requires sensitivity to others, a clear sense of one's own communicative intent, a great deal of social knowledge, and an overall understanding of the communication process.

SUMMARY

Although we use many encoding systems, the one most natural to us is spoken language. Spoken language has four important characteristics: it is symbolic, it is a kind of knowledge, it is rule governed and productive, and it affects the way we experience the world. The first step in understanding language is to grasp the concepts of symbol and sign. A sign is any mode of expression that connects an idea (the signified) to a form (the signifier). When the signifier is an arbitrary and conventional creation of the human imagination, it is a special kind of sign known as a symbol.

Language learning is not a matter of rote repetition. When we learn language, we learn implicit rules that allow us to generate and understand novel utterances. These rules are complex and interrelated, allowing us to make the sounds in our language and to combine these sounds into words and sentences. Ultimately, language practices affect the way we see the world, as the Sapir-Whorf hypothesis shows.

Language can be divided into several subsystems. The first is the sound system. Each language recognizes certain sounds as significant and ignores others. The significant sound distinctions in a given language are called phonemes. Phonemes are combined into units of meaning called morphemes. Morphemes are roughly equivalent to words, although a single word may consist of several morphemes. In practice, human utterances are made up of strings of words. The rules that govern the way words can be combined make up the syntax of language. Although knowing how to form words and make sentences is important for communication, an understanding of pragmatic rules, or rules governing language use, is also important.

When we talk, we do so for specific reasons. The goal we want to accomplish when we talk is called a speech act. According to CMM theory, speech acts are affected by four levels of context: episode, relationship, life script, and cultural pattern. The kind of communication appropriate to a given social context is called discourse. Each form of discourse has its own style and structure. Perhaps the most common form of discourse is everyday conversation. To be successful at conversation, individuals must work together cooperatively. Their talk must follow the conversational maxims of quantity, quality, relevancy, and manner. Communicators must keep track of the conversation as it unfolds, making sure their contributions fit into what has been said previously. They must also coordinate turn taking and be able to repair problems when they occur.

All forms of discourse, whether formal or spontaneous, have a certain shape or structure. One example of structure is the conversational closing. Closings must be carried out in specific ways. They must be signaled in advance and must include an explanation of why the conversation is ending. Often, they include statements of concern as well as summaries of what has happened. A communica-tor who does not understand discourse conventions such as the conversational closing will be at a social disadvantage.

People from different social groups use language differently, and this difference is often a source of social identity. Men and women, for example, grow up learning to use language to display gender identities. Studies suggest that men learn to prefer task-oriented, or report, talk, whereas women are encouraged to use relational, or rapport, talk. Although current researchers do not deny that there are differences in the ways men and women communicate, they believe that many of the generalizations we have come to accept should be treated with caution. They recognize that men and women do not form homogeneous groups, that context affects whether or not gender communication will be displayed, and that the meanings often associated with gender differences are problematic. They also urge us to think of gender as a performance rather than as an essential characteristic of humans.

Gender, of course, is not the only group membership that affects language use. Students of cross-cultural communication have described some of the ways in which languages are affected by national or ethnic background. In particular, they have focused on the extent to which context is part of a message, the directness with which thoughts can be expressed, the amount of emotional expressiveness that is appropriate, and the extent to which formality is expected in various cultures.

Although social memberships affect language usage, we do make language choices, and the way in which we make these choices affects communicative success. The chapter closes with a discussion of the advantages and disadvantages of four choices: the choice between ambiguity and clarity, immediacy and distance, abstraction and concreteness, and figurative and nonfigurative language.

KEY TERMS

Listed below are the key terms used in this chapter, along with the number of the page where each is explained.

language   (68)
sign   (68)
signified   (68)
signifier   (68)
symbol   (69)
arbitrary symbol   (69)
conventional symbol   (69)
linguistic productivity   (70)
Sapir-Whorf hypothesis   (72)
linguistic determinism   (72)
linguistic relativity   (72)
euphemisms   (73)
dialect   (74)
Ebonics   (74)
pidgin   (74)
creole   (74)
lingua franca   (74)
jargon   (74)
argot   (74)
taboo   (74)
phonology   (75)
phonemes   (76)

semantics   (76)
morpheme   (76)
free morphemes   (76)
bound morphemes   (76)
lexicon   (76)
syntactics   (77)
pragmatics   (77)
speech act   (77)
CMM theory   (78)
episode   (78)
relationship   (78)
life script   (78)
cultural pattern   (78)
discourse   (80)
conversation   (80)
cooperative principle   (82)
conversational maxims   (82)
quantity maxim   (82)
quality maxim   (82)
relevancy maxim   (82)
manner maxim   (82)

trouble talk   (86)
rapport talk   (87)
report talk   (87)
hall of mirrors effect   (88)
tag questions   (89)
qualifiers   (90)
disclaimers   (90)
performative aspects of
   language   (90)
low-context cultures   (91)
high-context cultures   (91)
verbal directness   (92)
verbal indirectness   (92)
expressive cultures   (92)
formality   (93)
ambiguous language   (94)
equivocal communication
   (94)
immediate language   (95)
abstraction   (96)
metaphor   (96)
reify   (98)

SUGGESTED READING

Ravitch, Diane. (2004). *The language police: How pressure groups restrict what children learn.* New York: Vintage.

> Describes some of the ridiculous lengths people go to to guard against politically incorrect language, raising important questions about the political implications of language.

Tannen, Deborah. (2006). *You're wearing that?: Understanding mothers and daughters in conversation.* New York: Random House.

> An examination of the meta-messages that lurk underneath the words mothers and daughters use to work out their relationships.

Encoding Messages: Nonverbal Communication

Even when we are silent, invisible messages crowd around us: colors excite us, sounds calm us, the smell or look or feel of another human attracts or repels us.

After reading this chapter, you should be able to:

- Name the four characteristics that distinguish nonverbal from verbal communication.
- Identify the six basic nonverbal codes.
- Explain the kinds of meaning that are best conveyed nonverbally.
- List some of the ways nonverbal and verbal messages interact.
- Distinguish emblems, illustrators, regulators, affect displays, and adaptors.
- Describe how facial expression, eye behavior, and vocal behavior are used to communicate.
- Describe some of the ways in which time and space communicate.
- Describe how physical appearance and object language affect interaction.
- List some ways in which communicators can improve their nonverbal skills.

We live not only in a world of words but also in a world of silent messages. Every day, we accompany our talk with the languages of gesture and posture, space and time. Even when we are silent, invisible messages crowd around us: colors excite us, sounds calm us, the smell or look or feel of another human attracts or repels us. To communicate fully, we must learn to speak these unspoken languages.

This chapter is about nonverbal communication, the study of communication systems that do not involve words. As we will see, many human behaviors convey messages—messages that can be understood as clearly as words. Picture, for example, the following scene, familiar from countless movies and TV shows. Two men, standing several yards apart, face one another in a dusty, deserted street at high noon. One man, clean-shaven, dressed in a light-colored Western-style hat with a tin star on his vest, stands straight and tall, his face betraying no emotion, his eyes steady and intent. The other, all in black, a sneer on his face and a glint of hatred in his eye, stands opposite, his body tensed, his hands near the holsters he wears at his side. Though not a word has been spoken, we know that we are on the main street of a small town in the Old West, about to witness a gunfight. We also know something about the character and motivation of the two men. By reading their posture and gesture, their facial expressions and the symbols in their dress, we know which is the "good guy" and which is the "bad guy." All this has been coded nonverbally in a familiar language of sight and sound.

In this chapter, we examine the unspoken language that allows us to find meaning not only in this scene but also in the more typical scenes that we encounter every day. We begin by defining nonverbal communication, looking at its nature and purpose. We then examine each of the codes that make up the nonverbal system: body movement and gesture; facial display and eye contact; vocal characteristics; time, space, and touch; and physical appearance and the use of artifacts. Once we have considered each code in turn, we will list some skills that can increase nonverbal effectiveness.

WHAT IS NONVERBAL COMMUNICATION?

One of the problems of defining nonverbal communication is deciding what counts as a nonverbal message and what does not. Because all human behavior has the potential to create meaning, is all behavior communication? This question is more than academic; it has real-life implications. Consider an example. As Lorene sits waiting for her boyfriend, Jack, she swings her foot back and forth and repeatedly taps her keys on the edge of a chair. Is Lorene's behavior nonverbal communication? If we also know that Lorene is completely alone and is totally unaware of her behavior, most of us would answer no. Lorene is behaving, but she is not communicating. But what if the situation is slightly different? What if Lorene is angry with Jack and wants him to observe her anger? What if her impatient behaviors are meant to let Jack know that he should be more punctual in the future? Is Lorene's behavior nonverbal communication in this case? Most of us would answer yes. Lorene is communicating, because she is intentionally creating a message for Jack's consumption.

So far, it has been easy to see the difference between behavior and communication in our examples. Unfortunately, however, it's not always this simple. Assume now that Lorene is simply bored. She is not trying to send a message to Jack; she is totally unaware of her behavior. An observer, however, watches her and thinks, "That young woman looks tense and troubled. I wonder what's wrong." The observer received a message that Lorene did not intend to send, one that she would very likely deny sending if asked. This kind of unintended message is harder to classify. Some would argue that Lorene's behavior is not communication, because Lorene is not aware of her observer. Others would argue that Lorene is nevertheless sending a message, and therefore she is communicating.

Because unintended messages occur frequently and have powerful effects (and because it is often difficult to determine whether or not a message is intended), we will take the second view, including as nonverbal communication any instance in which a stimulus other than words creates meaning in either a sender's or a receiver's mind. According to this view, the first scenario cannot be called nonverbal communication because no meaning was created. Both the second and third scenarios, however, can be called nonverbal communication.

How Can We Know What Nonverbals Mean?

If some nonverbal communication is unintentional, how can we be certain that our interpretations are accurate? Unfortunately, we can't ever be completely sure, but we can take steps to increase our chances of making correct interpretations. Consider the following scene: Kelly shudders, crosses her arms, and moves away from Cliff. Should Cliff take this to mean that he has offended Kelly? Perhaps. But what if Kelly is just cold? Cliff can't be sure unless he gets additional information. He can increase his probability of being correct in three ways. First, he can *check the context*. If a breeze is blowing through an open window and Kelly is covered with goose bumps, Cliff shouldn't lose sleep over her behavior; she is probably physically cold rather than irritated with him. A second way for Cliff to increase his accuracy is to *compare current behavior to baseline behavior*. If Kelly usually stands quite far from people, if her body posture is generally closed, and if she habitually crosses her arms, Cliff may conclude that she is simply the kind of person who needs a lot of personal space. If Kelly is normally quite open, however, she is more likely responding to something Cliff has done. Cliff can use one final method to check his understanding. He can *ask for verbal feedback*. He can ask Kelly what her behavior means. Like Cliff, we should be aware that every nonverbal act has several different interpretations, and we should be careful not to settle on one too soon.

Characteristics of Nonverbal Communication

Nonverbal communication has a number of characteristics that distinguish it from other communication systems. We'll look at four.

Nonverbal Communication May Be Unintentional

This characteristic has important implications for our behavior as both senders and receivers. As receivers, we should not assume that every nonverbal act is an intentional message. We should always check for alternative interpretations, and we should realize that reading nonverbals is a risky business. As senders, we should be aware that unintended nonverbal messages can easily undermine and contradict what we really want to convey. We should try our best to make our verbal and non-verbal messages congruent and clear.

Nonverbal Communication Consists of Multiple Codes

The nonverbal system is made up of a number of separate codes. To be successful communicators, we must become aware of how each of these codes works. We must also learn to coordinate codes. When nonverbal codes work together to send the same message, their impact is intensified. When they work at cross-purposes, confusion

When nonverbal codes work together to send the same message, their impact is intensified. When they work at cross-purposes, confusion results.

results. In an interview, for example, a confident smile can be undermined by nervous foot tapping, and a firm handshake can be offset by a too-rigid stance. The competent communicator is able to use the full range of nonverbal codes in ways that enhance messages. Later in this chapter, we will look in detail at how these codes work. For now, Table 5.1 presents an overview.

Nonverbal Communication Is Immediate, Continuous, and Natural

Because nonverbals are physical extensions of our bodies, they are immediate. We can weigh our words, carefully compose our verbal messages, and wait for the right time and place before we speak. But we can't delay most nonverbal messages. They occur whenever we are face to face with one another. In this regard, we cannot not communicate.

If we try to isolate and separate nonverbal gestures, they lose meaning. Whether a raised arm is a greeting or a sign of impending attack can only be decided by its context.

Nonverbal messages are also more continuous than verbal messages. Nonverbal displays flow into one another without the discrete beginnings and endings that characterize words. If we try to isolate and separate nonverbal gestures, they lose meaning. Whether a raised arm is a greeting or a sign of impending attack can only be decided by its context.

Finally, nonverbal messages are more natural and less arbitrary than their verbal counterparts. In most, form and meaning are connected. When we gesture to someone to come nearer, the gesture traces the path we want the person to take. When we show our concern by hugging someone, the hug is part of the natural act of comforting.

Table 5.1 Some Basic Nonverbal Codes

Body Movement and Gesture (Kinesics)	Vocal Characteristics (Paralanguage)	Space (Proxemics)
• Emblems	• Vocal qualities	• Territoriality
• Illustrators	• Vocalizations	• Spatial arrangement
• Regulators	• Vocal segregates	• Personal space
• Affect displays		• Touch (haptics)
• Adaptors	**Time (Chronemics)**	
Facial Expression and Eye Behavior	• Psychological time orientation	**Physical Appearance and Object Language**
• Cultural display rules	• Biological time orientation	• Body type
• Professional display rules	• Cultural time orientation	• Dress
• Personal display rules		• Object language

Nonverbal Communication Is Both Universal and Cultural

Although not completely free of cultural convention, many nonverbals are understandable the world over. Paul Ekman and Wallace Friesen have shown, for example, that happiness, anger, disgust, fear, surprise, and sadness are conveyed in much the same way in many different cultures. Some hand gestures, such as pointing, also transcend culture. At a very basic level, therefore, we can communicate nonverbally with people whose verbal language we do not know.[1]

Not all nonverbal behaviors, however, have universal meaning. Even emotional displays are modified by cultural rules. Although a smile conveys happiness in most cultures, in some cultures it conveys other emotions, such as embarrassment or submission. In addition, the rules for how often and when to smile vary in different cultures. And when it comes to other kinds of nonverbal meanings, such as the use of time and space, quite dramatic cultural differences occur. The implication is clear: do not assume that everyone shares your own nonverbal rules.

What Meanings Are Best Conveyed Nonverbally?

Verbal and nonverbal codes do not operate in quite the same way. What may be expressed easily in one may often be quite difficult to express in the other. We therefore tend to rely on each of these codes in slightly different situations. As we shall see, nonverbal codes are especially useful for giving us information about personal and relational topics we would be embarrassed to talk about. They allow us to express certain emotional themes that are hard to describe verbally. Nonverbal codes also allow us to refine and expand upon verbal meanings. When something can't be put into words, we turn to nonverbal channels.

> Nonverbal codes are especially useful for giving us information about personal and relational topics we would be embarrassed to talk about.

Making Initial Judgments

Nonverbal cues are often used to size up other people. It is important, sometimes even vital, to know the characteristics, attitudes, and intentions of others. In the early stages of an acquaintance, we seldom volunteer much verbal information about ourselves, nor do we feel comfortable asking others personal questions. This does not mean that we ignore personal information; it simply means that we turn to nonverbal channels. In addition to information about gender, race, and cultural identity, we can pick up cues about personality, attitude, and individual style. Nonverbal behaviors tell us whether others are friendly or hostile, shy or confident, gullible or worldly wise. They help us to determine the credibility and approachability of those around us.

Relational Information

Once we have sized up others and have decided to interact with them, nonverbal cues convey relational information, helping us keep track of how an interaction is going and what others think of us. According to Albert Mehrabian, three kinds of relational messages are exchanged nonverbally during every interaction: liking, status, and responsiveness.[2]

Liking is indicated through facial expression, eye contact, proximity, and the like. If a conversational partner smiles frequently and makes eye contact, we can be relatively sure that he or she likes us. If the partner avoids touch, however, and stands at some distance, there's a good chance that he or she does not like us very well. **Status** is often conveyed through posture and gesture, through touch and proximity, and by the objects we display. Of two individuals, the one who controls the most space, initiates the most touch, and seems the most relaxed is probably the one of higher status. A person's display of expensive or rare objects is also a good indication of high status.

Responsiveness, the degree to which we are psychologically involved in an interaction, is shown by such cues as rate and volume of speech, amount of gesture, and variability of facial display. Someone who responds to us in a monotone, staring straight ahead with a dull, expressionless look, is indicating low involvement and low responsiveness. All of these messages tell us how we are faring in an interaction and give us cues about how to communicate. Although we can ask people whether they like us, whether their status is higher than ours, and how involved they are in an interaction, this approach is rather awkward. Luckily, asking is usually unnecessary. Nonverbal communication gives us a clear picture of where we stand.

Emotional Expression

Another area in which nonverbal is more effective than verbal communication is emotional expression. When a child is frightened or unhappy, a comforting hug is worth more than a verbal explanation of why it doesn't help to cry. When we care about someone, we want to reach out and touch him or her. Talk is not an entirely adequate substitute for human contact, despite what telephone company slogans would have us believe. When people have something emotionally important to say, they need the full range of nonverbal channels. Of course, when they want to break off a relationship but also want to avoid an emotional scene, they may take the coward's way out and use a purely verbal channel, sending a "Dear John" or "Dear Joan" letter rather than announcing the breakup face to face.

Nonverbal Codes and Verbal Messages

Finally, nonverbal cues expand on and clarify verbal messages. Nonverbal experts such as Paul Ekman and Mark Knapp have cataloged some of the ways nonverbal messages are used in conjunction with verbal messages.[3] Table 5.2 summarizes the six ways in which nonverbal messages modify verbal messages.

Sometimes we use nonverbal cues to repeat what we say verbally. If I'm giving you directions, I may say, "To get to my office, go down the stairs," and, to make sure you understand where I want you to go, I may point toward the stairs. This kind of redundancy helps to ensure that verbal messages are accurately received. Nonverbal cues are also used to contradict verbal messages. Jason may turn to his wife, Isabel, and say, "I don't know why I ever married you. For two cents I'd get a divorce." His smile and friendly tone, however, contradict the harshness of his words and let her know he is just joking. Sarcastic comments are another example of contradiction. The words may be friendly, but the tone of voice gives the real message.

Joking and sarcasm are culturally recognized patterns; most people understand what their meaning really is. But other forms of contradiction are not easily deciphered—for example, when a close friend says to you, "I'm fine," but grimaces with pain, or when someone says, "I love you," in a cold, distant way. Communications like these send two opposing messages at the same time. They are potentially harmful to relationships and should be avoided.

Sometimes nonverbal messages can substitute for verbal ones. At the end of a difficult and boring meeting, two people can just sigh and roll their eyes. They don't need to put their frustration into words. We also use substitution when verbal channels are unavailable. While scuba diving or during the filming of a TV show, we can't yell out a message, so we resort to sign language.

Nonverbal messages can also complement, that is, modify or elaborate on, a verbal message. When Don says to his roommate, "I had a terrible day today," the slope of his shoulders and the weariness in his voice indicate just how bad the day

Table 5.2 Some Ways Nonverbal and Verbal Messages Interact

Repeating	The nonverbal message repeats the verbal message; resulting redundancy can increase accuracy. *Example:* "I'll give you three minutes," said while holding up three fingers.
Contradicting	The nonverbal message undermines the verbal message, often causing confusion and uncertainty. *Example:* "I'm glad to see you," said with a sneer.
Substituting	A nonverbal message is used instead of a verbal message. *Example:* In answer to "How was your day?" the communicator just sighs and shakes his or her head.
Complementing	The nonverbal message modifies the verbal message, letting the receiver know how to take it. *Example:* "I love your gift," said with a huge smile.
Accenting	Nonverbal cues emphasize part of the verbal message. *Example:* "And the most important thing is . . . ," said with vocal emphasis on the most important words.
Regulating	The nonverbal message manages and controls verbal behavior. *Example:* Looking at one's watch to let the speaker know it is time to go.

Liking is indicated nonverbally, through posture, touch, and facial display.

really was. These behaviors add to Don's message, telling us the extent of his feeling. Without the proper accompanying nonverbals, people do not believe others' verbal messages. If a winning contestant on a game show reacts by saying, "I'm glad I won," but fails to scream and clap and jump up and down, the audience doesn't believe that the message is sincere or that the contestant deserved to win.

Sometimes, nonverbal behaviors accent the important parts of a verbal message. A teacher may emphasize the main points in a lecture by nonverbally stressing certain words. A parent may make eye contact with a child to make sure the child hears an important bit of advice. The eye contact says, "Now listen carefully. I expect you to remember this and to follow through."

Finally, nonverbal cues regulate, or control, social interaction. When we converse, we must carefully coordinate our contributions, finding a way to take the field when it is our turn to speak and a way to relinquish it when we are finished. Because we must do this instantly, without awkward pauses or interruptions that disrupt the flow of speech, we turn to nonverbal channels. Through changes in speech tempo, eye contact, head nodding, and the like, we manage conversations. To claim our turn to talk, we raise our index finger or lean slightly forward, taking a breath as though we are about to speak and nodding our heads to hurry up the other speaker. If the other speaker responds with decreased eye contact and begins to talk faster and louder, we know that our bid to talk has been turned down.[4] Knowing the meaning of and abiding by these nonverbals are aspects of the important interpersonal skill called interaction management. People who are skilled in interaction management are considered highly competent communicators.[5]

THE NONVERBAL CODES

So far, our discussion of nonverbal communication has been general. Now we'll look at the specific channels that make up the nonverbal system. We'll start with body movement and gesture, move on to facial expression and eye behavior, and then consider the way vocal quality is related to verbal expression. We'll also discuss the messages conveyed by time, space, and touch, and we'll end by looking at the effects of personal appearance and object language.

The Kinesic Code I: Body Movement and Gesture

Our bodies are an important source of nonverbal meaning. Whether we lean in toward someone or move away, whether our stance is wide and strong or narrow and weak, whether we talk with our hands or remain completely still—we tell others a lot about us. Even the way we walk can give off signals. When prison inmates arrested for assault were asked to look at tapes of people walking along a city street, they had little trouble agreeing on which were "muggable" and which were not. People classed as "easy rip-offs" moved awkwardly, taking either very long or very short strides, and their arm movements followed their leg movements rather than alternating with them. They appeared to walk around in a daze. Their walk signaled to potential muggers that they would put up little resistance.[6]

The study of body movement (including movement of the face and eyes) is called kinesics. People who study kinesics often classify body movement into five categories: emblems, illustrators, regulators, affect displays, and adaptors.[7]

Emblems

Emblems are kinesic behaviors whose direct verbal translations are known to all of the members of a social group. Emblems are like silent words. If you are at a noisy party and want to send a message to a friend across the room, you can use nonverbal emblems. You can "say" to your friend, "Shame on you" (by rubbing your right index finger across your left), "All right! Excellent!" (by turning your clenched fist inward at about head height, then drawing it rapidly down and back), "What time is it?" (by pointing at your wrist), or "I'm leaving now" (by pointing to yourself and then to the door). In fact, you can have a fairly lengthy (if not intellectually stimulating) conversation using emblems. In the United States, we have emblems that allow us to tell others what to do ("Wait a minute"; "I can't hear you"; "Come over here"; "Sit down next to me"; "Calm down"), that convey our physical state ("I'm hot"; "I'm cold"; "I'm sleepy"; "I don't know"; "I'm confused"), that act as replies ("Yes"; "No"; "Maybe"; "I promise"), that evaluate others ("He's crazy"; "That stinks"; "He [or she] has a great figure"), and that serve as insults, including obscenities.[8]

> Whether we lean in toward someone or move away, whether our stance is wide and strong or narrow and weak, whether we talk with our hands or remain completely still—we tell others a lot about us.

One of the defining characteristics of emblems is that they are culturally defined. We must be very careful when using them with members of different cultural groups. The sign that we in the United States recognize as the A-OK sign (thumb and index finger touching in a circle, the rest of the fingers outstretched) can in other countries stand for money, can indicate that something is worthless, or can obscenely signify female genitalia. Judee Burgoon comments on the way emblems vary in different cultures:

> For example, the head throw for "no" displayed by Greeks, Southern Italians, Bulgarians, and Turks could be mistaken for "yes" in cultures where nodding signifies affirmation. The Bulgarian turn of the head for "yes" is likely to appear to be shaking the head, a sign of negation in many cultures. Beckoning gestures are also a source of misunderstandings. The palm-down fluttering fingers beckoning

gesture observed in Asian and Latin American cultures may be interpreted as "go away" by North Americans. In sum, although emblematic differences allow us to identify cultural group membership, they can also create cross-cultural misunderstandings and unfavorable attributions.[9]

Illustrators

Sometimes, the best way to describe an object is to use gestures that indicate its size or shape or movement. If someone doesn't know what a scalloped edge looks like or isn't familiar with the term *zigzag*, you can use hand movements to illustrate what you mean. Gestures like these accompany speech and add to the meaning of utterances; they are called **illustrators**. Illustrators need not describe physical objects; they can also be used to indicate the structure of utterances. A public speaker may gesture each time a new point is raised. The gesture illustrates the central structure of the argument. People differ in the number of gestures they use. Some people are so used to talking with their hands that if their hands were tied behind their backs, they would find it almost impossible to speak.

Regulators

Regulators are nonverbal behaviors that act as "traffic signals" during interaction. They consist of the head nods and eye and hand movements that allow us to maintain, request, or deny others a turn to talk. As their name implies, they fulfill a nonverbal regulating function. Regulators usually occur so rapidly and automatically that we are not consciously aware we are using them. At a subconscious level, however, we are certainly aware of them, for without them conversations grind to a halt.

Regulators are seldom noticed—unless they are used inappropriately. Then negative attributions are likely. This can be a problem in communicating with people from other cultures, for the rules governing regulators can differ. In comparison to the Japanese, Americans tend to dominate conversations. Whoever has something to say has the floor and tends to keep it for as long as he or she has something to say. The Japanese, on the other hand, distribute the talk more equally, making sure that everyone has equal talking time.

Affect Displays

Body movements that convey emotional states are called **affect displays**. When we want to know what someone is feeling, our first instinct is to look at that person's face. The rest of the body, however, is equally expressive. In fact, experts on deception tell us that to determine whether someone is lying, we should not necessarily look at the face but at the body. When people lie, they generally experience heightened emotional arousal. If this arousal is not suppressed, it will act as a **leakage cue**, letting the observer sense guilt, anxiety, and excitement. Facial cues are least likely to leak this information, because liars pay close attention to and control their facial expressions. Body movements are less controlled and are therefore a better source of information. The voice is also a good source of leakage cues.[10]

In addition to leakage, liars may also give themselves away through their use of **strategic cues**.[11] Strategic cues are behaviors that liars use to disassociate themselves from their messages and to reduce their responsibility for what they've said. Liars sometimes seem uncertain or vague, less immediate, and more reticent than non-liars as they try to "back away" nonverbally from their lies. These cues, shown by body movement and spatial behavior, may be detected if one knows where to look. Unfortunately, the average receiver is not very good at detecting deception, perhaps because liars control those very types of behaviors that most of us associate with lying: facial and eye behaviors. If you want to detect deception, attend instead to a sender's body and vocal channels, and compare any suspicious behavior to the sender's baseline behavior.

> Experts on deception tell us that to determine whether someone is lying, we should not necessarily look at the face but at the body.

Of course, not all emotional displays are attempted deceptions. Most affect displays are honest depictions of internal states and are easily detected. In attempting to read emotions, remember to look at the behaviors of the other person's whole body, including those behaviors that fall into our next category, adaptors.

Adaptors

Have you ever noticed how often people engage in odd, repetitive, nervous mannerisms? The next time you're in public, say, in a classroom, watch your fellow students tap their pens, kick their feet, twirl their hair, play with their jewelry, groom themselves, and so on. As often as these behaviors happen in public, they are even more frequent in private. Called **adaptors**, they are behaviors that people use to adapt to stresses and to satisfy personal needs. Some (such as scratching) are behaviors that satisfy immediate needs, whereas others (such as pen tapping) may be residual displays of behaviors that were once functional. Fist clenching or foot kicking, for example, may be residual hitting or running motions. Rocking back and forth may be a way of re-creating early childhood experiences. And playing with jewelry may be the next best thing to carrying around a security blanket. Regardless of where they originate, most adaptors are used to manage stress.

People are often completely unaware that they are using adaptors, and for this reason, adaptors are a good source of information about emotions. When people touch their own bodies (for example, by rubbing their necks or playing with their hair), they are using **self-adaptors**. When they touch objects (for example, by playing with cigarettes or shredding styrofoam cups), they are using **object adaptors**. By observing these behaviors, you may uncover hidden information about people's emotional states.

The Kinesic Code II: Facial Expression and Eye Behavior

The face is the arena most people turn to for information about others. We believe that "the eyes are mirrors of the soul" and that people's character can be "written all over their faces." We like people with open, friendly faces, and we avoid "two-faced" people with shifty eyes or thin, mean lips. And when we want to look particularly honest or friendly, we smile and widen our eyes. All these behaviors indicate our faith in the face and eyes as sources of nonverbal communication.

Facial Displays

Where do facial displays come from? Experts believe that they are partly innate and partly learned. That is, the form that emotional expressions take is "prewired" into the human brain, but the way these expressions are exhibited is governed by culture-specific rules. Evidence for the basic innateness of facial expression comes from several sources. Studies show, for example, that blind and sighted children have very similar facial expressions, and cross-cultural studies show that basic expressions are shared across many different cultures.[12] These studies suggest that the reason we smile when happy and cry when sad is that smiling and crying are part of our biological inheritance.

When we consciously make a face, we're well aware of what we're doing. At other times, we may not realize how much of what we feel is displayed for everyone to see.

When and where and how much we smile or cry, however, depend on learning and imitation. Within each culture, certain expressions are encouraged and reinforced, whereas others are discouraged.[13] People in every culture learn to modify their facial displays, intensifying certain emotions and deintensifying others. For example, most Americans feel that it is impolite to show disappointment over a gift or to gloat at our own good fortune. We may therefore pretend to like a birthday present more than we actually do, or we may downplay pleasure at our own success if a friend has failed. We also learn to neutralize other emotions, swallowing our disappointment by pretending not to care. Finally, we may mask one emotion with another. When the first runner-up hears she is not being crowned Miss America, not only does she not show her disappointment and jealousy, she looks positively joyful as she rushes up to hug the winner. Becoming a good communicator includes learning how to modify facial displays. The rules that govern these modifications occur at three levels: the cultural, the professional, and the personal.

By following what are called cultural display rules, people in some cultures learn to be "stone-faced" and stoic, whereas those in other cultures learn to be highly expressive. In American culture, for example, men follow a cultural display rule that tells them not to show fear in public. Women, on the other hand, are free to show fear but must keep anger in check. Women are also expected to express pleasant emotions and smile more frequently than men. In Japan, smiling is equally important, although the display rules governing smiling differ. There the smile is not only a way to express happiness, but also a way to reduce embarrassment and promote harmony. Guo-Ming Chen and William Starosta tell us that Japanese hosts are expected to smile at guests, even at funerals. An athlete who loses a competition or a student who receives a failing grade must also cover his or her concern with a smile.[14]

In addition to modifying facial displays to meet cultural expectations, people learn to follow display rules at work. Service personnel, such as flight attendants, are taught to inhibit any irritation they feel and to smile no matter what. Nurses learn to be cheerful, calm, and caring, whereas lawyers learn when to put on a "poker face" and when to show justified outrage. Rules for facial expression based on career considerations are called **professional display rules**.

Finally, people also follow **personal display rules**. These rules are learned through individual experience and are often, but not always, shared with family members. Researchers have made a number of attempts to identify personal styles in emotional expression. Ross Buck argues that people are either externalizers or internalizers.[15] **Externalizers** are good at portraying emotion, whereas **internalizers** are less adept at showing emotions.

Eye Behavior

For centuries, the eyes have been associated with mystic power. The Greek philosopher Empedocles explained vision as a flow of fiery corpuscles that pass from the eye to an object of vision and back again. This image of the glance as a fiery stream persisted; it can also be found in Renaissance love poetry, in which eyes were thought to "shoot arrows, daggers or swords [and] project fiery beams which burn the soul and kindle love's flame."[16] In addition to possessing the ability to engender love, the eyes have also been associated with suffering and death, perhaps because of our instinctive fear of the predatory gaze. Whatever the reason, primitive people in all ages have guarded themselves from the evil eye, a hostile glance reputed to kill instantly. Gerald Grumet reports that a certain mental disorder reverses the evil-eye superstition: the afflicted person avoids others in fear that his or her glance will injure them.[17]

Although modern Americans do not believe in primitive superstitions, we do recognize that eye behavior serves a number of important functions. Grumet tells us that dominant animals place themselves where they can watch their subordinates and where they themselves can be watched. Similarly, human leaders tend to situate themselves where they will command the center of visual attention, such as at the head of a table or the front of a conference room. Thus, *eye behavior serves to maintain social position.*

> For centuries, the eyes have been associated with mystic power. The Greek philosopher Empedocles explained vision as a flow of fiery corpuscles that pass from the eye to an object of vision and back again.

Eye behavior is also a good indication of both positive and negative emotions. We stare at sights we find agreeable and avert our eyes when a sight disgusts or horrifies us. Studies also show that when our interest and attention are high, our pupil size enlarges. Furthermore, research shows that people with enlarged pupils are judged more physically attractive than those with constricted pupils, a fact known as early as Cleopatra's time, when women used eyedrops made of belladonna to darken and enlarge their eyes.[18]

The eyes also signal our willingness to relate to one another. Mutual gaze is the first step in most relationships, for it signals both parties' awareness of one another.[19] During conversation, eyes act as nonverbal regulators, displaying typical patterns for listening and speaking. Listeners gaze more than do speakers, perhaps to pick up turn-taking cues. Speakers look away while formulating their thoughts, perhaps to cut down on visual stimuli that might interfere with concentration. As any student who does not want to be called on in class knows, avoiding eye contact closes communication channels, whereas inadvertently looking up virtually guarantees being called on.

> As any student who does not want to be called on in class knows, avoiding eye contact closes communication channels, whereas inadvertently looking up virtually guarantees being called on.

Finally, like other nonverbal cues, *eye behavior is associated with specific character traits.* People who make eye contact are judged as friendlier and more natural and sincere than those who avoid direct gaze. People who shift their gaze, on the other hand, are judged as cold, defensive, evasive, submissive, or inattentive.[20]

Paralinguistics: Vocal Behavior

A lot of the meaning in everyday talk lies not in our words but in how we say those words. If we were to read transcripts of conversations, we would have to mentally supply what is left out: the speakers' intonations, tones of voice, volume, pitch, timing, and the like. Characteristics that define how something is said, rather than what is said, are part of paralinguistics, the study of the sounds that accompany words. The importance of paralanguage was clearly demonstrated in 1974, when former president Richard Nixon, under investigation by the House Judiciary Committee, refused to supply audiotapes of his conversations and instead sent transcripts. Committee members, who needed to determine the truth value and meaning of the tapes, argued that the transcripts were incomplete, because vocal qualities and characterizers were missing.[21] The committee recognized how important vocal modifications are.

> Although the judgments we make based on vocal qualities are not necessarily accurate, we think they are. People generally agree about the connotations of different kinds of voices.

Paralanguage includes vocal qualities (characteristics of the voice, such as pitch, tone, and intonation patterns), vocalizations (special sounds that convey meaning, such as groans, cries, moans, giggles, and yawns), and vocal segregates (pauses and fillers, such as "um" and "uh"). All of these kinds of sounds affect the meaning of our spoken communications. They can be eloquent testimonies to emotional states, but they can also be cues used to make stereotypic judgments of personality characteristics.

It is a matter of interest that although the judgments we make based on vocal qualities are not necessarily accurate, we think they are. People generally agree about the connotations of different kinds of voices. A light, breathy voice connotes seductiveness and a lack of intelligence. A nasal voice may lead others to perceive the speaker as dull, lazy, and whiny. And the big, full, orotund voice associated with preachers and politicians can signify authority and pomposity.[22]

Judgments of social status are also associated with the way we speak. Most cultures define certain accents and ways of speaking as "prestige speech." People whose grammar, word choice, or accent deviates from these standards are likely to be judged less credible and less intelligent than people who meet paralinguistic norms. On the other hand, speaking a regional or subcultural dialect may lead to higher ratings of benevolence and attractiveness. That is, the person who speaks in perfect, pear-shaped tones may appear distant and snobby, whereas someone whose language patterns are more regional may seem like a "regular guy." Certainly, to people within a social group, accent similarity can enhance group solidarity.[23]

An often overlooked aspect of paralanguage is silence. Just as sound creates meaning, so too does the absence of sound. One use of silence is to create interpersonal distance. By not talking to someone, we can send the message "I refuse to admit your presence." The Amish use a form of silence called "shunning" to punish those who have violated important social norms.

A sudden silence can also indicate that a specific remark or behavior is inappropriate. If after telling an off-color joke at a dinner party you are greeted with stunned silence, you have likely committed a major social faux pas.

Of course, silence is not always negative. If filled by other nonverbal cues (a tender gaze, a touch), silence can signal intimacy and comfort. Silence can also be a mark of respect or reverence. We often fall silent on entering places of worship, both to show our respect and to concentrate on inner, spiritual concerns. We also become silent when someone of high status appears, indicating that his or her words are more important than our own.[24]

But although there are times when we value silence, in general, Americans like to talk. This is not true in other cultures. According to Keith Basso, who has studied Western Apache culture, silence in this culture is generally valued over talk. For example, strangers who jump into a conversation too quickly are treated with suspicion. Their desire to speak seems to indicate a kind of greed or selfishness that imposes on listeners. The Apache suspicion of those who speak too much extends to a dislike of detailed descriptions. As Basso explains:

A person who speaks too much—someone who describes too busily, who supplies too many details, who repeats and qualifies too many times—presumes without warrant on the right of hearers to build freely and creatively on the speaker's own depiction. . . . In other words, persons who speak too much insult the imaginative capabilities of other people, "blocking their thinking" . . . and "holding down their minds."[25]

Chronemics and Proxemics: Time, Territory, and Space

So far, we have looked at ways we use our bodies to communicate. In this section, we will look at how the dimensions of space and time can serve as nonverbal messages. We will begin by looking at chronemics, the study of time as it affects human behavior. We will then move on to a discussion of proxemics, the study of how we use space and what space means to us.

Time Orientations

Are you the kind of person who enjoys dwelling in the past? Do you retell old stories, pore over scrapbooks, and spend your time remembering past events? Or do you like making plans and imagining what the future will hold? Do you place high or low value on being punctual? Do your friends always end up waiting for you, or are you the one who is always early? The answers to these questions can tell you

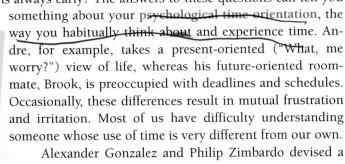

something about your psychological time orientation, the way you habitually think about and experience time. Andre, for example, takes a present-oriented ("What, me worry?") view of life, whereas his future-oriented roommate, Brook, is preoccupied with deadlines and schedules. Occasionally, these differences result in mutual frustration and irritation. Most of us have difficulty understanding someone whose use of time is very different from our own.

Alexander Gonzalez and Philip Zimbardo devised a scale called the Stanford Time Perspective Inventory to measure individual differences in time orientation. Using a variation of this scale, they surveyed more than eleven thousand readers of *Psychology Today* and found seven different time perspectives: two related to the present, four focused on the future, and one concerned with the effects of time pressures.[26] Interestingly, past orientations were so infrequent that they were eliminated from analysis. The overwhelming emphasis on the future makes sense, given the values our culture attaches to progress. As we shall see, members of other cultures have a much different sense of time.

Two of the perspectives that Gonzalez and Zimbardo describe focus on the present. The present, hedonism orientation involves living for the moment. People who fall into this category are impulsive sensation seekers who like to spend their time playing and going to

The importance we attach to time and how we manage it are important nonverbal signals.

parties. In contrast, respondents who score high on present, fatalism orientation focus on the present not because they are pleasure seekers but because they feel they have no control over fate. These people believe that it doesn't make sense to plan, because events will occur unalterably no matter what one does.

Four time orientations focus on the future. The first is labeled the future, work-motivation orientation. People who hold this orientation believe in hard work, recognizing the importance of meeting obligations and completing projects no matter how difficult or uninteresting. People who take this view believe that it is their duty to work hard. Future, goal-seeking respondents are more positive about the future. They enjoy thinking about what will happen to them and spend their time imagining the success they will achieve when their goals are met. People falling into the future, pragmatic-action category view the future in practical, down-to-earth ways. For them, the future is something to be prepared for in the present. They value behaviors that make the future secure, such as saving money and buying insurance. Future, daily planning respondents are obsessed with controlling the details of day-to-day events. They are the list makers and daily planners who map out their lives in specific detail. The final orientation is slightly different from the others. Labeled the time-sensitivity orientation, it describes people who feel anxious and pressured by time obligations and who are somewhat compulsive about both their own and others' punctuality.

Gonzalez and Zimbardo believe that time orientation may be related to the kinds of employment we seek. Thus, semiskilled or unskilled occupations may be attractive to and appropriate for people with present orientations, whereas managerial and professional occupations call for future-oriented individuals. The authors also suggest that we can all benefit from developing more flexibility in our relationship to time. Although punctuality is important for success, we should not let it become an obsession. The world will not come to an end if we are occasionally late. On the other hand, although taking a present orientation may be a fine way to approach one's social life, it can be a disaster in the world of work. A professional who is consistently a half hour late to meetings will soon be asked to look for other employment. Think about your own time perspective. When does your orientation work for you, and when does it get you into trouble? Are your relationships with others hurt or helped by the way you think of time?

In addition to being influenced by our psychological orientation to time, we are also controlled by our biological time orientation. Humans, like other animals, seem to have built-in biological clocks that govern our daily rhythms. Metabolic processes, as well as neurochemical activities in the brain, are tied to biological rhythms. When these processes are upset by changes in clock time (for example, by flying into a different time zone or by changing work shifts), we may feel irritated, tired, and even physically sick until we find a way to reset our internal clocks. Some people are extremely sensitive to seasonal changes in the amount of available light. In the short, dark days of winter, they can fall into a depression called seasonal affective disorder, which can sometimes be treated by using artificial light. We are beginning to find out that our mental alertness, as well as our emotional stability, is affected by biological time.

A third way time affects us is through our cultural time orientation. People from different cultures think differently about the value and uses of time. Judee Burgoon tells us that the Sioux have no words for "late" or "waiting," that the Pueblo people start ceremonies whenever "the time is right," and that the traditional Navajo are extremely present oriented.[27] Gonzalez and Zimbardo point out that clashes between different cultural time orientations account for cross-cultural misunderstandings between North Americans and people from Latin American and Mediterranean countries:

> From their strong present and past perspectives, they see us as obsessed with working, efficiency, rationality, delaying gratification and planning for what will be. To us, they are inefficient, lazy, imprudent, backward and immature in their obsession with making the most of the moment.[28]

The silent language of time is an extremely important part of nonverbal communication.

Territory and the Use of Space

Managing territory and distance is another important aspect of nonverbal behavior. Like birds and mammals, humans need to maintain uniform distances from one another and to occupy and defend territories. Proxemics commonly consists of three areas: territory, spatial arrangement, and personal space.

The need to create boundaries, to control areas of space and make them ours, is called territoriality. Territoriality is a basic human need. We need to have a place to call our own, a place where we are safe from attack and, even more important, where we are free to do what we want without being observed and judged. People often feel most truly themselves when they are in familiar territory.

People occupy several kinds of territories. Stanford Lyman and Marvin Scott describe four: public, home, interaction, and body territories.[29] Public territories are territories that we share with others. City parks and shopping malls, for example, are open to everyone in the community, although what people are allowed to do there is often restricted. To avoid the potential disorder that can occur when strangers interact, public territories are usually patrolled by police, and anyone who is thought to be threatening community standards may be asked to leave. When we occupy public territories, we are expected to follow the rules. At most beaches, for example, we are free to play Frisbee but not to sunbathe nude.

Home territories are areas owned and controlled by individuals. In these spaces, we have much greater freedom to do whatever we want. A child's clubhouse with its sign warning "Keep Out, This Means You!" is a home territory, as is his or her parents' bedroom. The need to control space is so great that people may even try to make home territories out of public territories. We may, for example, consider a favorite table in a local restaurant "our" table and be irritated or outraged when it is occupied by someone else. In cities, gangs may lay claim to certain streets, marking nearby buildings with graffiti to indicate "their" turf. You may even consider your seat in your communication classroom as an extension of your home territory.

Whereas public and home territories may be bounded by physical barriers, such as walls, gates, or fences, interaction territories are socially marked. Groupings of people at a party or lovers in private conversation occupy interactional territories. Like other territories, these arenas may be made off limits to outsiders. By the way they position their bodies, make or avoid eye contact, or focus their attention, those who are inside the interaction separate themselves from those who are outside and indicate how permeable their invisible boundaries may be.

Body territories are the most private of all our territories. Our rights to touch and view one another's bodies are strongly restricted. From the

> Body territories are the most private of all our territories. Our rights to touch and view one another's bodies are strongly restricted.

time we are children, we are shown which parts of our own (and others') bodies can and cannot be touched. We are told how much clothing to wear, and we are expected to decorate our bodies in acceptable ways. In some cultures, practices such as tattooing or nose piercing are encouraged; in others, they are thought to be disgusting.

Lyman and Scott believe that our territories may be encroached in three ways: through contamination, violation, or invasion. In contamination, a territory is polluted or made unacceptable. After contamination, the territory must be cleansed before it can be used again. In caste societies, the presence of a low-caste person is thought to pollute sacred spaces. Vandalism can encroach on home territories, and dirty jokes can contaminate an interaction. Soiling one's clothes or spattering someone else with mud are examples of body contamination.

A second form of encroachment is violation, any unwarranted entry into or use of a space. Homeless people sleeping in a park, an outsider stumbling into a private conversation, a dog digging in a neighbor's flower bed, or a stranger brushing against someone in a crowded subway are examples of violations.

Invasion is perhaps the most serious form of encroachment. It occurs whenever people who are not entitled to use a space enter and take control of that space. When a motorcycle gang takes over a public park, when a visiting relative won't leave after two weeks, or when an insensitive boor dominates a conversation, public, home, and interaction territories are invaded. Rape and assault, of course, are invasions of body territories; most cultures consider these acts to be so serious that they are punishable by imprisonment or even death.

Territories are important to us. We build barriers against the approach of others, and we are often willing to defend these barriers to the death. Some barriers are easy to identify. Barbed-wire fences and border guards let us know when we are crossing national boundaries. Picket fences or hedges tell us where one yard ends and another begins. But other barriers are not as easy to identify. We do not always know when we are not wanted or when our behavior has violated a social norm. The ability to recognize the nonverbal signs that indicate we are encroaching on another's territory is an important communication skill.

Spatial Arrangement

The ways we arrange home and public territories affect our lives. Architects and interior designers know how important spatial arrangement can be. The way walls and furniture are arranged within structures affects the amount, flow, and kind of interaction in them. Seating choice in classrooms, for example, often predicts which students are likely to talk and which are not. In a seminar-style classroom, students who sit directly next to the teacher are less likely to be called on than are those who sit farther down the seminar table. In a regular classroom, most participation comes from the so-called action zone, a roughly triangular area beginning with the seats immediately in front of the teacher and diminishing as it approaches the back of the room.[30]

> The way walls and furniture are arranged within structures affects the amount, flow, and kind of interaction in them.

Furniture arrangement in offices also delivers a number of messages. To observe this phenomenon yourself, visit several of your professors' offices, and note factors such as the overall amount of space and the presence or absence of barriers between instructor and student, as well as the relative amount of space "owned" by each. Ask yourself how these arrangements affect your comfort level and how they define the role of student. Figure 5.1 shows several examples of seating arrangements and furniture placement and summarizes their effects on communication in the United States.

U.S. workers in general prefer private offices or cubicles, but not every culture divides up work space similarly. Bruce Feilor, who lived and worked in Japan, describes a very different arrangement. In Feilor's office, a large open space, desks were arranged in groups of nine. Within each group, four desks were lined up next to and directly facing another four desks opposite, while a desk for the section chief was placed at one end, perpendicular to the two rows. With all of the desks touching, the work surface was like a giant table top. As Feilor explains, "every conversation and every minor memo became the business of the whole group."[31]

Such an office arrangement promotes group interaction, but it does not, as it might first appear to an American, promote equality. In Japan, group membership and hierarchy are valued at the same time, and status markers are often subtly revealed. Feilor goes on to explain:

> *Younger people sat at the bottom of each line, seniors higher along, and the section chief alone at the end. As a worker advanced along this route, he was allowed to keep more paper on his desk, more cushions on his chair, and perhaps even a pair of*

Figure 5.1 Effects of Furniture Placement on Communication

Seating Arrangements at Rectangular Tables

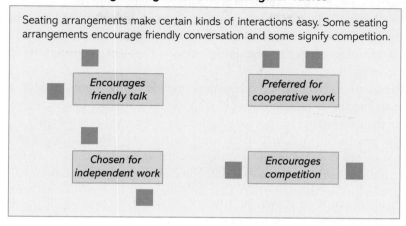

Seating arrangements make certain kinds of interactions easy. Some seating arrangements encourage friendly conversation and some signify competition.

Encourages friendly talk

Preferred for cooperative work

Chosen for independent work

Encourages competition

Office Arrangements

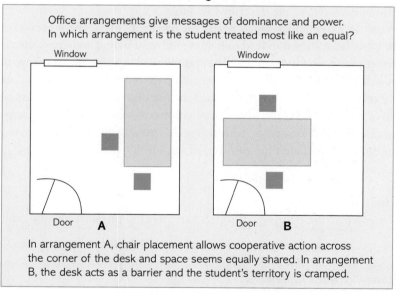

Office arrangements give messages of dominance and power. In which arrangement is the student treated most like an equal?

Window

Window

Door **A**

Door **B**

In arrangement A, chair placement allows cooperative action across the corner of the desk and space seems equally shared. In arrangement B, the desk acts as a barrier and the student's territory is cramped.

slippers underneath. In this office, one desk stood out. It was placed in the center of the room, separate and unequal from the rest. . . . Above the desk a lone sign dangled from a fluorescent light. It read simply, shocho: *Director.*[32]

Personal Space

Each one of us varies in how close we prefer to be to other people. This preference, called personal space, acts as a kind of portable territory that we carry with us wherever we go. If others come too close, we move away until we feel comfortable.

> People who like one another usually stand closer together than do strangers; in fact, closeness is often used as a measure of attraction.

Similarly, if people stand too far away, we move in to establish more intimacy. People with the same personal space norms have little trouble interacting. Those who vary greatly, however, find it difficult to coordinate their needs. They can be observed engaging in a complex dance; as one moves closer, the other counters by backing away.

Factors that affect personal closeness include liking, status, gender, and the way we define the interaction. People who like one another usually stand closer together than do strangers; in fact, closeness is often used as a measure of attraction. The amount of personal space one controls can also indicate status, with people of higher rank being given more personal space than those with low rank. In our culture, gender too makes a difference in the way we use personal space: males generally take up more space than do females. Of course, our personal space also depends on the nature of our interaction. We expect to be at a greater distance from a teacher delivering a lecture than from a friend talking to us. Edward T. Hall investigated American cultural norms for personal space and found four kinds of interaction zones. These are described in Table 5.3.

When one's personal space needs are violated, one experiences crowding. Crowding has been shown to lead to heightened arousal and anxiety, decreased cognitive functioning, and increased verbal and physical aggression. To relieve discomfort, crowded individuals often avoid eye contact or verbal interaction, use body blocking to decrease their sense of contact, or use objects to build barriers between themselves and others. People whose occupations cause them to violate the personal space of others (such as servers, hairdressers, or massagers) are often given the status of nonpersons and are thus absolved of responsibility for the violation.

Touch

The extreme of personal closeness is touch. To touch and be touched is a basic need. People who are deprived of touch may develop physical, mental, and social

Table 5.3 Interaction Zones for Most Americans

Intimate Distance	Extends from contact to about eighteen inches. It is reserved for intimate interaction and very private conversations.
Personal Distance	Extends from eighteen inches to about four feet. It is used for casual, friendly interactions.
Social Distance	Extends from four to twelve feet. It is used for impersonal business relationships.
Public Distance	Extends from twelve feet to the limits of visibility or hearing. It is used for public performances, lectures, and the like.

For a more extensive discussion, see Edward T. Hall (1966). *The Hidden Dimensions*. New York: Doubleday.

disorders. In fact, studies have linked touch deprivation to depression, alienation, and violence.[33] Touch is
an important form of nonverbal communication, and
its study is sometimes called haptics.

> People deprived of touch may develop
> physical, mental, and social disorders. In fact,
> studies have linked touch deprivation to
> depression, alienation, and violence.

All cultures regulate how and how often their
members touch. Judee Burgoon and Thomas Saine feel that, compared to other societies, our culture is "restrictive, punitive, and ritualized" in regard to touch.[34] Affectionate contact between people outside the family is discouraged, and strict
norms regulate touch within the family. Mothers, for example, are encouraged to
touch male children, but fathers are not. Fathers also face strict taboos about
touching post-adolescent female children. In general, touch declines from early in-
fancy on, with senior citizens suffering the most deprivation and isolation.[35] Strong
antitouch norms also affect heterosexual male–male touch. As Loretta Malandro
and Larry Barker tell us, "Physical contact by a man with another man remains so
potentially dangerous and unspeakable for many American males that other than a
constrained handshake, no one but the dentist and doctor are permitted to touch
the skin surface."[36]

Touch conveys a number of messages. First, the type of touch (a pat on the
back versus a lingering caress) indicates how we feel about others and defines a
given relationship as playful, loving, friendly, sexual, or even aggressive. In most
cultures, negative feelings such as derision are shown by touch avoidance. Touch
also communicates status, the person who initiates touch being of higher status.
It is a social error, for example, for a management trainee to casually pat his or
her manager on the shoulder. Touch initiation is generally considered a dominant
behavior; in fact, we often use touch to control or direct the action of others. For
this reason, touch initiation is governed by the rules that control other forms of
dominance.

Touch also satisfies our own emotional needs. When we feel stressed or
lonely, we may curl up our bodies and hug our knees, wring our hands, or stroke
our hair. The use of these kinds of self-adaptors shows a need for body contact.
When we feel the need for touch, we may also gain comfort from touching animals. Some nursing homes have introduced house pets or encourage visiting pets.
Being able to stroke a cat or dog and feel its warmth helps residents to overcome
isolation and loneliness.

Physical Appearance and Object Language

Professional designers—whether they design clothing, graphics, or interiors—are
trained in the selection and arrangement of elements to create an overall effect. In
a certain way, we are all designers. When we go out to face the world each morning, we take with us a material self that is created by the way we look and dress
and by the objects we display. Whether or not we realize it, our design efforts

matter. Personal appearance affects the way others act toward us, as well as how we feel about ourselves. As Mark Knapp has pointed out,

> *Physical attractiveness may be influential in determining whether you are sought out; it may have a bearing on whether you are able to persuade or manipulate others; it is often an important factor in the selection of dates and marriage partners; . . . it may be a major factor contributing to how others judge your personality, your sexuality, your popularity, your success, and often your happiness.*[37]

Body Type

People have strong reactions to body shape and appearance. All cultures favor certain **body types**, subjecting to ridicule people who don't fit the ideal. Cultures also form stereotypes about the characteristics that are thought to go along with various body types. Whether there is any truth to these stereotypes is less important than that we believe and act on them.

Researchers who study body types classify people according to how closely they approximate three extremes. The **endomorph** is short, round, and fat; the **mesomorph** is of average height and is muscular and athletic; the **ectomorph** is tall, thin, and frail. A person's **somatype** is a composite score, using a seven-point scale, of each of these extremes. The somatype of an extremely fat person, for example, is a 7/1/1; that of a trained athlete, a 1/7/1; and that of a very tall, skinny person, a 1/1/7. Mark Knapp reports that the late comedian Jackie Gleason scored roughly a 6/4/1, that former heavyweight boxing champion Muhammad Ali rated a 2/7/1 at the peak of his career, and that Abraham Lincoln is considered to have been a 1/5/6.

Certain personality characteristics are generally associated with each of the three body types that make up the somatype. Descriptors such as placid, contented, affable, generous, and affectionate are used to characterize endomorphs. Mesomorphs are seen as energetic, enthusiastic, competitive, reckless, and optimistic. Ectomorphs seem more self-conscious, precise, shy, awkward, serious, and sensitive.[38]

One's height and body type can put one at an advantage or a disadvantage when it comes to love and career. In America, height is an advantage, especially for men. A number of studies show that—all else being equal—tall men are hired more frequently than are short men.[39] Tall men are also more successful in romance. Few women seek out a man who is "short, dark, and handsome."

Generally, North American cultural norms value men who are muscular and women who are slender, even though most Americans are overweight. Obesity is especially disliked, and fat people are often ridiculed and avoided. To escape being perceived as endomorphic, Americans will go to great lengths in exercise and diet. Victims of anorexia nervosa are quite literally willing to starve themselves to death to achieve what they consider a desirable body type.

Dress

According to Desmond Morris, clothing, or **dress**, serves three major functions. First, it provides **comfort-protection**, shielding us from extremes of heat and cold.

Second, it preserves our **modesty** by covering areas of the body that are considered taboo. Most important, it serves as a **cultural display**, telling others about our place in a variety of culturally defined hierarchies. In earlier times, laws dictated the clothing appropriate for each profession and social class. People who dressed above their station in life could be arrested. Rank could be read in the shape of a coat or the color of a ribbon. In modern, more democratic times, we are freer to dress as we wish. Yet we are still constrained by unwritten laws, and we may still read information about socioeconomic class in others' clothing choices.

Like other nonverbal signs, clothes are often read as a sign of character and are especially important in creating first impressions. The courtroom is one place where the messages of clothes are carefully scrutinized. Heiress Patty Hearst did not appear at her trial for bank robbery wearing the beret, dark glasses, and fatigues she had assumed as a member of the "urban guerrilla" band, the Symbionese Liberation Army. Instead she wore a modest skirt and blouse several sizes too large for her. Her clothing was chosen to ensure that she looked frail and worn—the victim rather than the victimizer.[40]

> Whether or not clothes should be taken seriously, they are. Most businesses and schools have written or unwritten dress codes, and violations of dress norms are still a potent outlet for social rebellion.

Clothing choice is important not only for defendants but for witnesses and lawyers as well. If you were going to appear in court, say, as a character witness on behalf of a friend, how would you dress? Take a moment to imagine what you would wear. Then compare your choices to the following descriptions of clothing that, according to Lawrence Smith and Loretta Malandro, increase perceptions of credibility and likeability in a courtroom setting.[41]

To increase their credibility, men are advised to wear classic, conservative two-piece suits made of wools and wool blends. Trendy styles, unusual fabrics, and large patterns are to be avoided. Acceptable suit colors are gray and navy, but the only acceptable color for the shirt is white. Jewelry should be limited to one conservative ring, a watch, and a tie bar or tiepin. Conservative tortoiseshell eyeglasses can enhance the image. Hair should be short and conservatively styled.

Advice for women is similar. A traditional two-piece suit consisting of matching jacket and skirt in a solid color should be worn with a cotton or silk (not polyester) blouse with a simple collar. The skirt length should range from just below the knee to two inches below the knee. Shoes should have closed toes and heels approximately two and one-half inches high. Acceptable suit colors include gray, white, off-white, beige, and navy, with a white or

Appearance and adornment are often considered to be indicators of taste and status as any fashion-victim knows.

light blue blouse. Jewelry should be limited to five points, for example, nondangling earrings, a simple ring, a single strand of pearls, a watch, and a pin on the jacket. As with men, eyeglasses increase women's credibility. Makeup should be moderate.

Men and women who wish to emphasize their approachability and likeability may modify their dress by wearing jackets that contrast with the rest of the suit. Men are advised to wear tans, beiges, or browns; women may wear colors in the brown, gray, and blue families, as well as pinks and roses. Eyeglasses should be removed occasionally to increase the perception of approachability.

Although it seems patently obvious that dressing conservatively will not make one any more intelligent or more expert, violating dress norms can have serious effects. Whether or not clothes should be taken seriously, they are. Most businesses and schools have written or unwritten dress codes, and violations of dress norms are still a potent outlet for social rebellion.

Object Language

The objects or artifacts we own and display can also be an important mode of communication. Object language can be defined as "all intentional and nonintentional displays of material things, such as implements, machines, art objects, architectural structures, [as well as] the human body, and whatever clothes or covers it."[42] As we have already discussed body and dress, we will concentrate on material possessions, giving special attention to environmental design.

In the 1890s, philosopher William James talked about three aspects of the self: the social self, the spiritual self, and the material self. James believed that a person's possessions are a fair measure of his or her sense of self. As Franklin Becker notes, James defined a man's material self as:

> the sum total of all that he can call his, not only his body and his psychic processes, but his clothes and his house, his wife and children, his ancestors and his friends, his reputation and works, his lambs and horses, his yacht and bank account. All things give him the same emotions. If they wax and prosper, he feels "triumphant"; if they dwindle and die away, he feels cast down—not necessarily in the same degree for each thing but in much the same way for all.[43]

> Our possessions act as public symbols of our values, status, and financial success, informing others of our identity and reinforcing our own sense of self.

Even today our possessions act as public symbols of our values, status, and financial success, informing others of our identity and reinforcing our own sense of self.[44]

Nowhere is our status so clearly displayed as in the buildings we construct. From the outside, the look of a building tells people what to wear, how to act, who is allowed in, and what services they can expect. Once inside, interior design elements give off additional messages. Burgoon and Saine list a number of factors that affect communication in built environments. In addition to furniture arrangement (which we have already discussed), Burgoon and Saine cite size,

Figure 5.2 Linear Perspective and Meaning

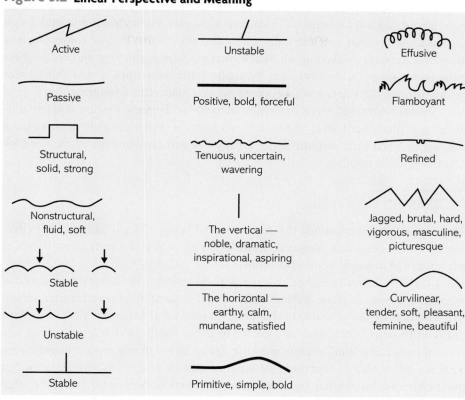

Active

Passive

Structural, solid, strong

Nonstructural, fluid, soft

Stable

Unstable

Stable

Unstable

Positive, bold, forceful

Tenuous, uncertain, wavering

The vertical — noble, dramatic, inspirational, aspiring

The horizontal — earthy, calm, mundane, satisfied

Primitive, simple, bold

Effusive

Flamboyant

Refined

Jagged, brutal, hard, vigorous, masculine, picturesque

Curvilinear, tender, soft, pleasant, feminine, beautiful

From *Landscape Architecture* by J. O. Simonds, copyright 1961, New York: F. W. Dodge Corporation. Used by permission of McGraw-Hill Book Company.

shape, and texture of materials, linear perspective, lighting, color, temperature, noise, and sensory stimulation as important communicative factors.[45]

In terms of size, massive spaces create a sense of awe, whereas smaller spaces are cozier and more comfortable. Of course, if spaces are too small, we can feel cornered. The size of furnishings within spaces also sends messages. Large furniture (for example, a massive desk with a high-back swivel chair) often indicates power. The boss's and the secretary's desks are usually not the same size. The materials used to decorate a room can affect mood and comfort level. Rough surfaces give an effect different from smooth ones; softness invites us to relax, whereas hardness makes us more tense. A hard-edged modern office with highly polished metal furniture creates an atmosphere very different from a more traditional, wood-paneled room with leather-upholstered furniture.

Linear perspective refers to the ways in which lines created by walls or furnishings relate to one another. Figure 5.2 illustrates the meanings that can be created by different linear perspectives.

Lighting can vary our perception of the size of a room, as well as make us want to linger or to escape. A restaurant that wants to encourage leisurely dining usually uses muted lighting, whereas a restaurant designed for high volume and quick turnover uses harsher, brighter light. Color also affects moods; cool colors (such as blues and greens) are relaxing, whereas warm colors (reds, oranges, and yellows) are more stimulating. Colors also carry symbolic value. Most men would think twice before painting their dens pink, because pink is considered a feminine color.

Temperature and noise can either increase or decrease tension and irritability, as can the overall level of sensory stimulation. Environments must strike a balance between satisfying the needs for novelty and excitement and the need for consistency and stability.

INCREASING NONVERBAL SKILLS

This chapter has emphasized the importance of being aware of and making effective use of the unspoken languages available to us. In this last section, we'll look at a few ways to improve nonverbal skills.

The first lesson we should learn is to *be cautious in interpreting nonverbal messages*. Most of us share the folk belief that it is possible to read another person like a book if we are sensitive to that person's nonverbal behavior. Most of us have our own theories about what to look for to judge another's character, and we use these theories as a kind of early warning device to avoid unpleasant interactions. That we never stop to test these stereotypes seldom bothers us. Yet many of our most cherished nonverbal stereotypes are false. It's important to remember that nonverbal behaviors can have many different meanings. When Anne crosses her arms over her chest, she may be inadvertently indicating a need to protect herself from contact, or she may simply find that posture comfortable. When Larry's eyes shift during a conversation, he may be lying, he may be nervous, or he may have been distracted by some extraneous stimulus.

It is not a good idea to read deep meaning into every gesture, yet it is important to *give proper attention to nonverbal cues*. Just as some people seem too sensitive to nonverbal cues, others seem completely insensitive. People will sometimes tell us nonverbally what they will not tell us with words, and we should not ignore those silent messages. Jim, for example, never seemed to notice other people's leave-taking cues. As a consequence, his employees didn't know how to get out of a conversation with him. The usual nonverbal cues— glancing toward the door, looking at one's watch, making small movements of escape—were always ignored, while more overt methods (such as saying, "Jim, stop talking. I'm leaving now") seemed too rude. The problem was so bad that people who were scheduled to have a meeting with Jim would often ask a friend to phone Jim a half hour into the meeting. When Jim would stop

> People will sometimes tell us nonverbally what they will not tell us with words, and we should not ignore those silent messages.

to pick up the phone, the employee would sneak out the door. Although this fact-based example may be extreme, it nevertheless illustrates that some people aren't very sensitive to nonverbals. If you're the kind of person who needs to have things spelled out, if you're often the last person to figure out what everyone else seems to know, then you may not be paying enough attention to nonverbal communication.

In addition to becoming more aware of others' messages, you should also *become aware of the messages you may be inadvertently sending.* As we've seen, people jump to conclusions about nonverbal behavior. And if they form judgments about other people in this way, you can bet that they also form judgments about you. Remember that what you do is as important as—and sometimes more important than—what you say. We're used to considering our words but much less used to monitoring our nonverbals. Think about the ways in which you habitually use all of the nonverbal codes. Some of these ways will be obvious to you, but others will not. Most people check out their clothes in a mirror, but fewer are aware of vocal habits, and still fewer stop to think about their use of space and time. If you're not sure what messages you're sending, ask someone you trust to give you feedback.

It's also wise to *remember that nonverbals you consider to be perfectly innocent can be invasive and even threatening to others.* When we stare at people, enter their personal space, use objects that belong to them, or make them wait for us, we may be offending them in ways we scarcely realize. That these things don't bother us doesn't mean that they don't bother others. And the potential for inadvertently committing offense is compounded whenever cultural differences exist. Take the time to find out the nonverbal meanings of others, and try to respect those meanings.

The silent messages that make up the nonverbal codes are subtle and are easily misinterpreted. Yet they are powerful modes of communication, and complete communicators are as aware of their own nonverbal messages as they are of their spoken words. If we overlook nonverbal communication, we overlook a world of meaning.

SUMMARY

Although language is an important source of human messages, words are not our only means of communication. Messages can be encoded nonverbally. In this chapter, we have looked at the nature and purpose of nonverbal communication and at the codes that make up the nonverbal system. Nonverbal communication occurs whenever a stimulus other than words creates meaning. This broad definition includes virtually all meaningful human behavior, whether intentional or not. Because behavior can convey a variety of meanings, we should be careful in interpreting nonverbal communication to remain aware of context, to compare current to baseline behavior, and to ask for verbal feedback to clear up misunderstandings.

Nonverbal communication is unique. It is often unintentional; it consists of multiple codes; it is immediate, continuous, and natural; and it may carry universal meaning. Nonverbal communication is particularly useful when direct verbal communication is socially inappropriate or difficult (e.g., when making initial judgments; when conveying relational messages of liking, status, and responsiveness; or when expressing emotion). Nonverbal communication can also expand upon, clarify, or even contradict verbal messages.

Body movement and gesture make up the first of the nonverbal codes. We use a variety of kinesic cues, including emblems, illustrators, regulators, affect displays, and adaptors. All are potential sources of nonverbal meaning. Facial displays are another important nonverbal code. People in every culture learn to modify and to manage facial expressions by following cultural, professional, or personal display rules, and each of us develops our own display style. The eyes are a particularly important part of the face. They can signal positive and negative emotions and attraction, and they are often used as cues to character. The voice is a third nonverbal code. Paralanguage includes not only the quality of the voice but also the sounds we make and the pauses and fillers we add to our talk. Even silence can communicate.

The dimensions of time and space are rich sources of meaning. Chronemics includes the study of psychological time orientation (how we think about and experience the past, present, and future), biological time orientation (how biological clocks govern our lives), and cultural time orientation (social rules for managing time). Proxemics is the study of space. One important aspect of proxemics is territoriality. We humans need to own and control a variety of territories (public, home, interaction, and body). When these spaces are threatened, we feel compelled to defend them. This is especially true of personal space; every society has implicit rules regulating personal closeness and touch, to convey both emotional and power messages.

A final nonverbal code consists of physical appearance and object language. The way we look and dress and the objects we display affect not only the way others see us but also the way we see ourselves. For many, self-concept is tied to appearance and possessions.

With all of its complexity, the nonverbal system is a powerful source of information as well as a powerful source of misunderstanding. It is important to become more aware of our own and others' silent messages.

KEY TERMS

Listed below are the key terms used in this chapter, along with the number of the page where each is explained.

nonverbal communication (101)	accenting (108)	leakage cue (110)
liking (106)	regulating (108)	strategic cues (111)
status (106)	interaction management (108)	adaptors (111)
responsiveness (106)	kinesics (109)	self-adaptors (111)
repeating (107)	emblems (109)	object adaptors (111)
contradicting (107)	illustrators (110)	facial displays (112)
substituting (107)	regulators (110)	intensifying (112)
complementing (107)	affect displays (110)	deintensifying (112)
		neutralizing (112)

SUGGESTED READING

Ekman, Paul. (2004). *Emotions revealed: Recognizing faces and feelings to improve communication and emotional life.* New York: Holt/Owl Books.
    An examination of the ways in which people express and control emotional displays; written by one of the foremost researchers in nonverbal communication.

Knapp, Mark L., & Hall, Judith A. (2005). *Nonverbal communication in human interaction* (6th ed.). Belmont, CA: Wadsworth Publishing.

    A comprehensive and popular review of research and theory on nonverbal communication.

Manusov, Valerie, & Patterson, Miles L. (2006). *The Sage handbook of nonverbal communication.* Thousand Oaks, CA: Sage.
    Offers a comprehensive overview of the field in a series of chapters written by nonverbal scholars.

Interpersonal Communication

Our survival as social beings depends in large part on our interpersonal communication skills.

It is easy to underemphasize the importance of everyday communication. Whereas public speakers often deal with issues of national importance and members of decision-making groups often design important new products, members of interpersonal dyads tend to spend their time in what seem to be less significant pursuits: gossiping, joking, or simply passing the time. Viewed in this light, interpersonal communication hardly seems to be a topic worthy of serious study.

The goal of this chapter is to show you that interpersonal communication is far from insignificant. It is, in fact, the most frequently used and, arguably, the most important form of communication humans undertake. It's possible to make it through life without ever giving a public speech or joining any decision-making group. None of us, however, can avoid interpersonal communication. In fact, our survival as social beings depends in large part on our interpersonal communication skills.

In this chapter, we look at how the everyday exchanges that make up interpersonal communication shape our lives. After defining interpersonal communication, we look at some of the problems that can affect interpersonal interactions; examine the stages in building interpersonal relationships; and review some basic skills that can enhance communication in everyday life.

WHAT IS INTERPERSONAL COMMUNICATION?

In a sense, all communication is interpersonal, because all communication occurs between people. The term interpersonal communication, however, is generally reserved for two-person, face-to-face interaction and is often used interchangeably with the term dyadic communication. Whenever we tell a joke to a friend, ask a professor a question, succumb to a sales pitch, share news with a family member, or express our love to a romantic partner, we are engaging in interpersonal communication. Compared to other forms of communication, dyadic communication has several unique characteristics. It is direct, personal, immediate, spontaneous, and informal.

> Compared to other forms of communication, dyadic communication has several unique characteristics. It is direct, personal, immediate, spontaneous, and informal.

Characteristics of Dyadic Communication

The first characteristic that distinguishes the dyadic context from other communication contexts is its *directness*. We can hide in the back of a classroom or make ourselves unobtrusive in a committee meeting, but when we communicate face to face with one other person, we cannot hide. Because we are in such direct contact, dyadic communication is also very *personal*. Public speakers cannot adapt to every audience member's specific needs. Dyadic communicators, on the other hand, can get to know one another more intimately. They can adapt their contributions to their partner's intellect and interests.

Dyadic interaction is more *immediate* than other forms of communication because the quality of feedback is high. As a member of a dyad, we can instantly sense when our partner is losing interest, can note when we are speaking too rapidly or too slowly, and can correct ourselves on the spot if our partner looks confused or puzzled. In other communication contexts, feedback is less immediate.

Compared to other kinds of communication, dyadic communication is the most *spontaneous*. Members of dyads rarely, if ever, outline and rehearse what they will say to each other; public speakers almost always do. Finally, whereas communication in other contexts is often characterized by formal role relations that signal a communicative division of labor, in dyads the roles of speaker and listener are usually *informal*.

Are All Dyads Interpersonal?

For many scholars, the defining characteristic of interpersonal communication is that it occurs between two people. This view suggests that all dyads are equally interpersonal. But are they? Is the communication between a clerk and a customer in a busy store interpersonal in the same way as the communication between a parent and a child or between two best friends? Does the quality of communication stay the same as partners get to know one another? A number of scholars say "No." They believe that dyadic communication and interpersonal communication are not the same thing. According to those who take a developmental approach to interpersonal communication, something special must occur to turn ordinary, impersonal, dyadic interaction into interpersonal communication. When the rules governing the relationship, the amount of data communicators have about one another, and the communicators' level of knowledge change, dyadic communication becomes interpersonal.

Gerald Miller and Mark Steinberg argue that communication is governed by rules that tell us how to communicate with one another.[1] Cultural-level rules are general and apply to all of the members of a particular culture. We use cultural-level rules with people we do not know well. When we greet strangers, for example, we follow rules that tell us to use polite, fairly formal forms of address. We usually nod, shake hands, and say something such as, "Hello, how are you?" Our choice of topics is limited. With strangers, we talk about the weather, sports, or current events, not about personal concerns and fears.

When we interact with people who belong to specific groups within our culture, we use sociological-level rules, rules that are tied to group membership. When college students greet each other, informal modes of address, such as "What's up?" are preferred. Topics concern classes, upcoming social activities, and campus events. Each of the many groups we belong to employs a slightly different set of communication rules.

Relationships can be troublesome, but they give us support when life gets risky.

Finally, when we interact with people we know quite well, we abandon the sociological rules and move to the use of psychological-level rules. We make up the rules ourselves. Part of the joy of being in a close relationship is the knowledge that we are free to break everyday rules. Friends, for example, may greet each other with hugs, screams of delight, or mock blows. They may even insult one another. They use behaviors that would never do with strangers, because in the course of their relationship, they have made these behaviors their own. With our close friends, we can talk about very personal and emotional matters, topics we would hesitate to mention to people we don't know well.

Part of the joy of being in a close relationship is the knowledge that we are free to break everyday rules.

As we get to know one another, our sources of information also deepen. When we interact at the cultural level, we have very little data to go on. As we become more familiar, however, we can understand our partners better because we know about their attitudes and values. We begin to recognize when they are happy or upset or hiding their feelings. We pick up on cues that would not be obvious to outsiders. As a result, our level of knowledge deepens. Now, not only can we describe our partners' behaviors, but we can predict and explain them as well.

Miller and Steinberg argue that interpersonal communication is "a special kind of dyadic communication, characterized by the development of personally negotiated rules, increased information exchange, and progressively deeper levels of knowledge."[2] Interpersonal communication occurs over time, as partners put effort and energy into building a personal relationship. For Miller and Steinberg, dyads start off as impersonal; only a few undergo the changes that make them interpersonal.

Why Do We Build Dyads?

In the movie *Annie Hall,* the narrator, Alvie Singer, tells a joke about a man whose uncle had convinced himself he was a chicken. When asked why the family didn't send his uncle to a psychiatrist, the man replies, "We would have, but we needed the eggs." Singer goes on to explain that that's how he feels about relationships. No matter how "totally irrational and crazy and absurd" they are, we keep going through them "because most of us need the eggs."[3] Singer understands that relationships can be difficult, but he also understands that they serve us well. Among the many other things they do, dyads give us security in an often insecure world, tell us who we are, and allow us to maintain our self-esteem.

> We choose our friends in part because they tell us it is okay to be the person we want to be.

One reason we form dyads is that *without interpersonal relationships, we would fail to thrive.* Recent studies have found a surprising connection between interpersonal relationships and physical and mental health. Dyads, it turns out, "have major effects on immune, cardiovascular, and neurotransmitter systems."[4] Children raised in isolation or in threatening environments, for example, are likely to develop stress-related illnesses and suffer depression in later life.

We also form dyads because *interpersonal relationships help us develop stable self-concepts.* Our sense of self is a product of the approval and disapproval of those with whom we come in contact. To use Charles Horton Cooley's metaphor, the appraisals of others act as a kind of mirror, reflecting back to us our looking-glass self.[5] The other people in our lives show us ways to live and teach us who to be. They validate our perceptions of ourselves and our social worlds. We choose our friends in part because they tell

Dyads provide us with comfort and support. With friends we don't have to worry about putting on a front; we can relax and be ourselves.

us it is okay to be the person we want to be. In this sense, "friendship is the purest illustration of picking one's propaganda."[6]

Finally, *interpersonal relationships offer us comfort and support*. In an often insecure world, knowing that we have someone to turn to when things get bad provides a feeling of security. To cope with everyday life, we need to make connections with others.

MANAGING INTERPERSONAL COMMUNICATION

Although close relationships bring enormous benefits, they also involve costs. In joining a relationship, individuals take on duties and responsibilities that can leave them feeling stressed. In this section, we look at some of the inevitable tensions of relational life. We begin by reviewing three dialectical forces that must be balanced if relationships are to be successful. We then discuss the need to acknowledge and protect identity needs. Finally, we look at some of the dysfunctional patterns that can beset dyads. As we shall see, all of these problems arise through, and are resolved by, interpersonal communication.

Balancing Interpersonal Tensions

A number of authors, including Leslie Baxter and William Rawlins, have written about the tensions that beset individuals as they try to balance the demands of a relationship and their own personal needs.[7] Individuals must face three sets of tensions as they decide how much of themselves to invest in relationships. These are called the expressive–protective, the autonomy–togetherness, and the novelty–predictability dialectics.

The **expressive–protective dialectic** involves finding a balance between the need to share personal information and the need to maintain privacy. When we become close to someone, we have a natural desire to share our thoughts and feelings with that person. Close relationships are built on shared information, and we usually expect a high level of self-disclosure (the voluntary revealing of information that would normally be unobtainable) in interpersonal relationships.

On the other hand, we can feel very uncomfortable when others ask for information that is too personal. Just as we have a need to be open, we have a need to keep some of our thoughts and feelings to ourselves. The problem of how much information to reveal and how much to keep private must be negotiated by every couple. Managing self-disclosure is a basic interpersonal skill, one we will return to at the end of the chapter when we discuss ways of increasing relational competence.

> Just as we have a need to be open, we have a need to keep some of our thoughts and feelings to ourselves.

A second dialectic is the **autonomy–togetherness dialectic**. Here, friends and couples decide how interdependent they want to be. This problem is often experienced by first-semester college roommates. Some people come to school expecting to spend all their time with their roommates. Others feel overwhelmed by too much closeness. Of course, roommates are not the only people to feel this tension. Dating and married couples must also decide on the proper level of autonomy and togetherness. Wilmot points out that

> some of the "craziness" and unpredictability in close, intimate relations comes from the oscillations between autonomy and interdependence. As we get farther away, we miss the other, and when we feel at "one" with the other, we sense a loss of the self.[8]

The only way to resolve this tension is to realize that others' needs may differ from our own and to talk about our feelings openly as soon as they become a problem. In the final section of this chapter, we will look at ways of expressing one's feelings without offending one's partner.

Finally, partners must resolve the novelty–predictability dialectic. On the one hand, as individuals interact, they fall into patterns of behavior. After a time, these behaviors become predictable, and the couple spends much of their time repeating old routines. Obviously, a certain amount of predictability is necessary for coordinated activity. A long-term relationship couldn't sustain itself at the level of uncertainty found in a developing relationship.

On the other hand, when behavior gets too patterned, partners can feel bored, and everyday interaction can become flat and stale. After all, relationships do not occur in a vacuum; they occur in a constantly changing world. Relationships that aren't open to change may become obsolete. Therefore, every couple must spend some time adapting to changing conditions and finding new ways to interact. The novelty–predictability dialectic is a matter of finding ways to balance the familiar and the new.

It's important to remember that over time, relationships change. Small children are dependent on their parents, but during adolescence, older children strive to become more autonomous. Both child and parent must adapt to the changing shape of their relationship and must make adjustments according to the "cultural" rules they follow. Likewise, competent communicators must be willing and able to negotiate new relational understandings as time goes by.

Respecting Identity and Protecting Face

Communication is inherently risky. There is always the chance that others may not like us or may not see us as we want to be seen. Several communication scholars have directed their attention to describing what happens when we experience rejection. In this section we will examine the relationship between communication and identity first by looking at the concept of face, and then by describing ways we may inadvertently cause others to feel disconfirmed.

Approval and Autonomy: Balancing Face Needs

One way to think about the effects of communication on identity is to consider the significance of face. Face is the "conception of self that each person displays in particular interactions with others."[9] It is the person we try to be when we are with other people. Because having one's sense of self questioned or rejected is painful and disheartening, communicators must make efforts to honor and support each other's face needs. Penelope Brown and Stephen Levinson argue that we have two face-related needs.[10] We need to be respected and accepted by others and we need to feel we are free to control our own lives. The first of these face needs is called positive face; it is threatened whenever people criticize or disagree with us. The second face need is called negative face; it is threatened whenever others impose on our autonomy. Assume, for example, that you disagree with a friend and want to convince her she is wrong. This act can threaten her positive face (after all, you are disapproving of her current views) as well as her negative face (you are attempting to control and change her behavior). In order to communicate effectively, you need to recognize that your behavior is potentially face threatening and find a polite way to balance your need to persuade and your duty to support your friend's face. Instead of saying, "Your views are absurd; you can't really do that," you might instead say, "You know I respect you, but in this case I can't agree. I know you'll make up your own mind, but I hope you'll consider my position." The latter choice diminishes threats to face and keeps the relationship on an even keel. Politeness, then, is more than a social nicety. It is a way of acknowledging others' identities and saving face.

Giving advice, asking favors, enforcing obligations, and refusing requests are common communication activities that have the potential to threaten participants' social selves. So too are attempts to initiate, intensify, or terminate relationships. All necessitate careful attention to the face needs of both self and others.[11]

Disconfirmation

One way to respect face is to avoid disconfirmations, rejecting messages that leave recipients with a diminished sense of self-respect. Evelyn Sieberg argues that whenever we communicate we present ourselves to others. Their responses can either confirm our sense of self or can make us feel diminished and rejected. She identifies seven ways in which we can (sometimes unknowingly) disconfirm one another.[12] These are shown in Table 6.1. The first occurs when one partner ignores the other. A parent who is too busy reading the paper to listen to a child's story is giving an impervious response. The message is, "You are not worth noticing." A second way people disconfirm one another is by giving an interrupting response. An interruption is a move that sends the message "You are not worth listening to." Occasionally, we encounter people who burst into conversations and immediately change the subject to something that has absolutely no bearing on what was said before. This is an example of an irrelevant response. A variation on this pattern is the tangential response, wherein an individual briefly acknowledges the topic but then goes on to discuss his or her own interests. Both responses send the message "My concerns are more important than yours are."

Impersonal responses are also disconfirming. The person who uses stilted, formal, distant language is signaling "I feel uncomfortable being close to you." Another response that indicates a desire to escape from interaction is the incoherent response. When someone seems embarrassed and tongue-tied, he or she says, in effect, "I feel uncomfortable with you." A final way to disconfirm a partner is by sending incongruous responses, messages wherein the verbal and nonverbal cues don't match. These double messages imply "I don't want to deal with you directly and openly."

Table 6.1 Disconfirming Responses

Response	Example
Impervious B fails to acknowledge, even minimally, A's message.	A: "Hi!" (B continues talking on the phone, ignoring A.)
Interrupting B cuts A's message short.	A: "So I said—" B: "Got to go. Bye!"
Irrelevant B's response is unrelated to what A said.	A: "He really hurt me." B: "Do you like my coat?"
Tangential B briefly acknowledges A, then changes topic.	A: "He really hurt me." B: "Too bad. I got dumped once. It was last year. . . ."
Impersonal B conducts a monologue or uses stilted, formal, or jargon-laden language.	A: "I don't understand." B: "The dependent variable is conceptually isomorphic. . . ."
Incoherent B's response is rambling and hard to follow.	A: "Do you love me?" B: "Well, gosh, I mean, sure, that is, I. . . ."
Incongruous B's verbal and nonverbal messages are contradictory.	A: "Do you love me?" B: "Of course" (said in a bored, offhand way).

Adapted from *Speech Communication: Concepts and Behavior* by Frank E. X. Dance and Carl E. Larson, 1972, New York: Holt, Rinehart and Winston, pp. 141–143.

Most people are disconfirming from time to time. Out of carelessness or irritation, we may use one of the responses just described. An occasional lapse is not necessarily problematic. However, if disconfirmations become habitual, they can destroy others' self-esteem and can severely damage relationships.

Avoiding Dysfunctional Patterns

In the process of working out the general shape of their relationship, individuals create specific patterns of interaction. Unfortunately, these patterns often go unnoticed. When relationships run into trouble, partners rarely analyze their behavior patterns. Instead, they each place the blame on the other's character or personality. This is unfortunate because although patterns can be changed, people usually can't.

Dysfunctional patterns—especially our own—are often difficult to describe. We are so used to them that they become invisible to us. Yet with a little effort and a willingness to be objective, we can begin to identify and correct problematic behaviors. In the next section, we look at some common dysfunctional communication patterns. In particular, we look at what happens when partners fall into rigid role relationships, disconfirm one another, become the victims of paradoxes, and get swept away by spirals.

Rigid Role Relations

Over time, one of the major relational themes that partners address is *dominance*. Partners must distribute power within the relationship. Each must decide whether he or she feels more comfortable playing a dominant part, or one-up role, or a more submissive part, or one-down role. Although some couples share power equally, relationships often fall into one of two patterns: complementary or symmetrical.

In a complementary pattern, one partner takes the one-up position and the other takes the one-down. Parents and their children generally have a complementary relationship. The parent controls the child, making most of the decisions and exerting most of the influence. For the most part, the child complies, although occasional temper tantrums show the child's dissatisfaction with the one-down role.

This division of relational labor has an advantage: decisions can be made rapidly and easily. Problems occur, however, when complementarity becomes too rigid. When the submissive partner begins to resent always giving in or when the dominant partner begins to tire of being in charge, dissatisfaction can result.

The second common pattern is the symmetrical pattern. In *competitive symmetry,* both members fight for the one-up position. Although there are times (for example, when two athletes train together) when competition can encourage both members to do their best, in typical relationships this pattern can be stressful and frustrating and can take its toll on the patience of the partners. In *submissive symmetry,* both parties struggle to relinquish control. If you and a friend have ever spent all night deciding where to eat ("I don't care, you decide." "No, anything's okay with me; you decide"), you have experienced the problems associated with submissive symmetry. This is an especially interesting pattern, because it is paradoxical. Although both partners ostensibly avoid control, each does his or her best to control the other by forcing the other to make the decision.

Complementary or symmetrical patterns can occasionally be satisfying, but they can also take over a relationship and limit partners' options. Partners can feel trapped by a pattern they hardly realize they have created. Learning how to share the one-up and one-down positions gives a couple the flexibility they need to adapt to changing circumstances.

Paradoxes

Couples sometimes fall into the habit of sending one another contradictory messages. These kinds of double messages are called paradoxes. For example, we may make statements such as "I know you'll do well, but don't worry if you fail" or "I don't mind if you go camping this weekend; it doesn't matter if I'm lonely and miserable." These kinds of responses are confusing and annoying, and they place the receiver in an awkward position.

Another, and a potentially more serious, form of paradox is the double bind. A double bind is a particularly strong and enduring paradoxical communication wherein the receiver is simultaneously given two opposing messages but is prohibited from resolving them. When a parent says to a child, "Come give me a hug," but recoils in disgust when the child approaches, the parent is delivering a double message. The child has no way to do the right thing. Over a long period of time, double binds can damage a partner's sense of rationality and self-esteem.

Spirals

The final dysfunctional pattern we will look at is the spiral. In a spiral, one partner's behavior intensifies that of the other. William Wilmot gives an amusing example of how spirals can escalate:

> My son Jason at age three saw a sleek, shiny cat. With the reckless abandon of a child his age, he rushed at the cat to pet it. The wise cat, seeing potential death, moved out of Jason's reach. Not to be outdone, Jason tried harder. The cat moved farther away. Jason started running after the cat. The cat, no dummy, ran too. In a short ten seconds from the initial lunge at the cat, Jason and the cat were running at full tilt.[13]

The same thing can happen to couples. In some spirals, called progressive spirals, the partners' behaviors lead to increasing levels of involvement and satisfaction. Claudine shows trust in Michele, who decides to earn that trust by working hard. Michele's hard work earns her more trust, and so on; over time, Claudine and Michele's relationship becomes stronger. Unfortunately, not all spirals are positive. When misunderstanding leads to more misunderstanding, eventually damaging a relationship, partners have established what is called a regressive spiral. Leslie begins to suspect Toby of being unfaithful. Toby becomes defensive and denies being in the wrong, but the denials only increase Leslie's suspicions. Finally, figuring, "If I'm going to be blamed, I might as well get something out of it," Toby actually is unfaithful. The relationship has spiraled out of control, and, in the process, Leslie and Toby have created an **interpersonal self-fulfilling prophecy**. Leslie's original prophecy (that Toby could not be trusted) has become true.

What can be done to stop spirals? In many cases, the partners need only sit down with one another and analyze the situation to determine what triggered the spiral and how it got out of control. In other cases, if the spiral has gone too far, the partners may need to turn to an objective third party who can help them describe their behaviors objectively and without defensiveness. The key to dealing with spirals is the same as that for dealing with any relational problem: partners must focus on patterns rather than on personalities.

> The key to dealing with spirals is the same as that for dealing with any relational problem: partners must focus on patterns rather than on personalities.

RELATIONAL DEVELOPMENT: STAGES IN INTIMATE DYADS

Relationships are in a constant state of flux. Over time, couples redefine themselves, moving toward and away from deeper involvement. In an attempt to understand more about the ways in which relationships change, several theorists have looked for global patterns of relational development. Although these theorists recognize that each couple's relational journey is slightly different, they have nonetheless attempted to chart the paths that couples take into and out of intimacy.[14] In this section, we examine two aspects of this journey. We begin with one of the most widely known of the relational stage models, Mark Knapp's relational development model. We then consider some of the factors that lead couples to become attracted to one another in the first place, reviewing Steve Duck's filtering theory of attraction.

Paths to and from Intimacy

Mark Knapp provides us with a ten-step model of the way relationships grow and dissolve. These steps are summarized in Figure 6.1.

The Journey toward Intimacy

The first of the **relational development stages** occurs during a couple's initial encounter as communicators and is known as the **initiating stage**. In this stage, partners work to create a favorable initial impression; observe cues about personality, attitudes, and willingness to engage in further interactions; and look for ways to open communication channels. Communication tends to be cautious, and topics are relatively shallow as individuals use tried-and-true opening lines and conventional formulas to initiate conversation.

Figure 6.1 Knapp's Relational Development Model

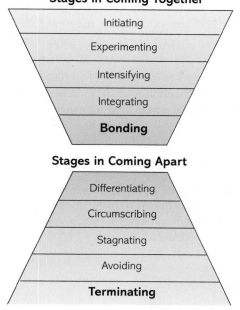

Stages in Coming Together

- Initiating
- Experimenting
- Intensifying
- Integrating
- **Bonding**

Stages in Coming Apart

- Differentiating
- Circumscribing
- Stagnating
- Avoiding
- **Terminating**

Stages are described in *Interpersonal Communication and Human Relationships,* 2nd ed. by Mark L. Knapp and Anita L. Vangelisti, 1992, Boston: Allyn and Bacon, pp. 35–45.

If all goes well and initial evaluations are positive, a couple moves on to the **experimenting stage**. Here, partners search for common ground on which to begin to build their relationship. Communication at this stage consists primarily of small talk. Although the talk may be small, it is not unimportant, for it uncovers topics for further conversation, gives individuals information that reduces their uncertainty about one another, and allows them to reveal their personalities. Communication at stage two is generally relaxed, uncritical, noncommittal, and somewhat ambiguous.

> Experimenting-stage communication uncovers topics for further conversation, gives individuals information that reduces their uncertainty about one another, and allows them to reveal their personalities.

Most relationships stop somewhere in stage two, but others move on to the **intensifying stage**. Here, individuals make initial moves toward greater involvement. Self-disclosure increases, and the use of nicknames and terms of endearment becomes more common. Inclusive pronouns such as *we* and *us* begin to be used, as do tentative expressions of commitment and private symbols for shared experiences. Finally, as partners become more familiar with each other's verbal and nonverbal styles, they start to use verbal shortcuts and may even complete each other's thoughts. In this stage, satisfaction and excitement are high.

In the **integrating stage**, the individuals become a couple both in their own and in others' eyes. Attitudes and interests are shared, and social circles merge. As body rhythms synchronize, partners may even begin to talk and move in similar ways. Shared experiences and artifacts become personalized, and a couple can be overheard talking about "our" restaurant or "our" song. Finally, partners may exchange **intimacy trophies**. By wearing the other's athletic jacket or by displaying the other's picture, partners signal to the rest of the world their official status as a couple. This perception of unity is often reinforced by friends or acquaintances who now think of the partners as halves of a whole, and who may show their approval or disapproval of the relationship.

For the couple, the loss of individual identity that comes with integrating may be welcome or upsetting. Knapp emphasizes the fact that

> *as we participate in the integration process, we are intensifying and minimizing various aspects of our total person. As a result, we may not be fully conscious of the idea but when we commit ourselves to integrating with another, we also agree to become another individual.*[15]

Maintaining relationships requires balance and coordination.

With commitment often comes insecurity. An individual may wonder whether his or her partner is truly involved in the relationship and may (either consciously or subconsciously) use **secret tests** to measure the other's commitment. Leslie Baxter and William Wilmot discuss four of these secret tests: indirect suggestions, separation tests, endurance tests, and triangle tests.[16]

Indirect suggestions include flirting and joking about the seriousness of the relationship. They let partners observe each other's response. If, for example, a comment on living together is greeted with laughter, this shows that the relationship is not intensifying. If the comment is taken seriously, however, this response indicates that commitment is high. **Separation tests** let individuals see how their partners feel about being apart. It's not a good sign if one's partner doesn't even notice a week-long absence. Daily phone calls, on the other hand, indicate strong commitment. **Endurance tests** involve making demands on the time or energy of one's partner; they show individuals just how far a partner is willing to go to maintain the relationship. Finally, individuals use **triangle tests** to see whether or not their partners are prone to jealousy. Although secret tests are frequently used, they are not necessarily good for a relationship, and they can easily backfire.

Once all tests are passed and both parties are sure of their feelings, they move on to bonding. Bonding consists of a public ritual to legitimize the relationship. Romantic couples may bond through marriage or commitment ceremonies. Friends may bond by exchanging friendship rings. Even groups can bond, as when social clubs initiate new members. In any case, bonding rituals officially legitimize the relationship and, in subtle and not-so-subtle ways, change participants' attitudes toward and feelings about one another.

> Throughout the entire journey toward intimacy, partners expand the boundaries of their relationship.

Throughout the entire journey toward intimacy, partners expand the boundaries of their relationship. According to Irwin Altman and Dalmas Taylor, relationships grow in breadth and depth as time progresses.[17] Figure 6.2 illustrates this idea. To expand relational breadth, individuals progressively share more aspects of themselves and communicate about more topics. To increase relational depth, they let their partners get closer to their core identities. For Altman and Taylor, the process of relational development is a matter of social penetration.

If the relationship lasts, partners continue to share intimate ideas and emotions. If the relationship cannot stand up to internal or external stresses, however, it gradually weakens; patterns of communication narrow and become more shallow, and the relationship starts to break apart. Figure 6.1 illustrates the relational dissolution stages.

Figure 6.2 Social Penetration: Relational Depth and Breadth

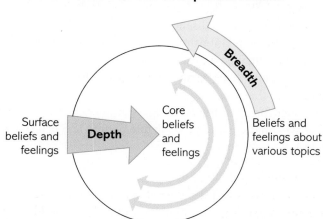

The original social penetration model was developed in *Social Penetration: The Development of Interpersonal Relationships*, by Irwin Altman and Dalmas A. Taylor, 1973, New York: Holt, Rinehart and Winston.

The Retreat from Intimacy

In the retreat from intimacy, a couple emphasizes differences rather than similarities. In the first or **differentiating stage**, a couple begins to notice and comment on previously overlooked disparities. Instead of using the pronouns *we* and *us*, they begin to talk about "you" and "me." Arguments may be prefaced by comments such as "I don't understand how you could possibly like her" or "I can't believe you agree with him." Overt argument and conflict are hallmarks of this stage. One reason for differentiation is that bonding may have taken place too rapidly, before the partners were able to negotiate a satisfactory relational culture.

Short periods of differentiation occur in all relationships. By reaffirming relational goals and focusing on similarities, partners may reverse their movement away from intimacy. Sometimes, however, differentiation leads to the second stage of relational breakdown, the **circumscribing stage**. In this stage, members carefully restrict their communication. Certain topics are placed off limits because they are too painful. "Let's just skip it" or "I'd rather not discuss that" indicate that communication has become a minefield of potentially explosive topics. As a result, very little information is exchanged, and expressions of commitment decrease.

In a failing relationship, the next stage is the **stagnating stage**. This stage is characterized by silence and inactivity. Communication is infrequent, and when it occurs, it is stylized, rigid, and awkward. Talk may be overly formal and polite, with negative emotions being conveyed nonverbally. One might think that this uncomfortable stage cannot last long. Unfortunately, a couple may stagnate for months or even years.

In the **avoiding stage**, partners separate either physically or emotionally. In a dating situation, one partner may suddenly stop answering the phone or disappear for weeks at a time. In a marriage, one spouse may spend more time at the office or visit relatives for the summer. If physical separation is impossible, couples may isolate themselves psychologically, behaving as though the other does not exist.

The final stage in relational disengagement is the **terminating stage**. If both parties are aware that their relationship is dissolving, termination may come as a relief. In other cases, it may be a heart-wrenching surprise. Either way, termination is the time when individuals come to terms with the fact that the relationship is over. Knapp believes that communication during this stage fulfills the three basic functions of other forms of leave-taking. It announces the upcoming separation, summarizes what has occurred during interaction, and determines the future of the relationship.

Variations in Relational Development

Keep in mind that Knapp's model is a general overview, not a specific prediction. It describes what often happens in relationships, not what inevitably happens. If you and a partner find yourselves in the differentiating stage, for example, you should not pack your bags and decide there is no hope for the relationship. Couples can turn relationships around by going back to and replaying earlier stages. If they care enough, they can repair troubled relationships by exploring alternative forms of relating; taking on more functional roles; eliminating unhealthy interaction patterns; or searching for new ways to make the relationship rewarding.

In real life, couples do not always go through the stages together. One partner may think the relationship is at the casual, experimenting stage, whereas the other may believe the partners are ready to bond. Or one partner may be so busy that he or she doesn't notice that the other partner is circumscribing. Furthermore, not all couples take the same length of time to complete the steps, even when partners are in sync. Some couples take a long time before risking commitment. Others rush through the early stages. This latter course is dangerous; if one of the early stages is skipped or rushed, later stages may be unstable, like a building constructed with a faulty foundation. For relationships to last, couples must work out agreements and develop healthy interaction patterns, processes that take time.

Interpersonal Attraction: Filtering Theory

We have seen how relationships change over time. But what causes people to enter relationships in the first place? Steve Duck feels that attraction is really a process of elimination. According to his **filtering theory**, we use a series of filters to judge how close to others we want to become.[18] At each filter, some potential partners are eliminated and some move on. Figure 6.3 shows how this process works.

What are the filters we use to regulate attraction? Duck identifies four filters: sociological or incidental, preinteraction, interaction, and cognitive cues. **Sociological or incidental cues** are the demographic or environmental factors that determine probability of contact. They include factors such as where we work and live, how frequently we travel, and so on. Obviously, we cannot form relationships with people we have never met, and maintaining contact with someone thousands of miles away is extremely difficult. **Physical proximity** seems to be a key factor here. Numerous studies show that marriages and close friendships are most likely to occur between people who live close to one another. *By carefully choosing where to live, work, and play, people can increase the nature and frequency of their interpersonal bonds.*

Preinteraction cues are also important filters. People use nonverbal impressions to determine whether they wish to interact with others. We use body type, physical beauty, dress, and related artifacts to give us some idea of what others are like. Whether or not they should, surface details often determine whether future interaction will occur. At least some of the time, the old expression "You never get a second chance to make a first impression" is true. Therefore, *it is important to become more aware of the ways silent nonverbal messages affect impression formation.*

Interaction cues occur once we have made initial contact. Some interactions are smooth and comfortable, whereas others are awkward and difficult. When topics flow easily, turn taking is smooth and effortless, eye contact and facial expression indicate friendliness and approval, and attraction is high.

Figure 6.3 **Duck's Attraction Filter**

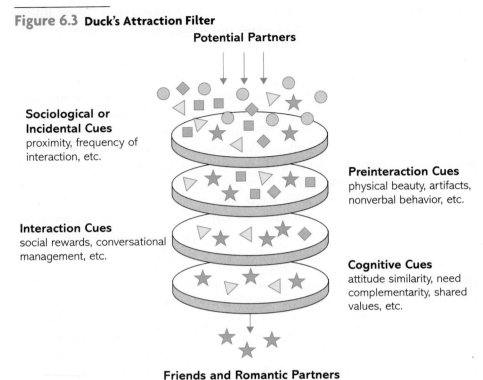

Potential Partners

Sociological or Incidental Cues
proximity, frequency of interaction, etc.

Preinteraction Cues
physical beauty, artifacts, nonverbal behavior, etc.

Interaction Cues
social rewards, conversational management, etc.

Cognitive Cues
attitude similarity, need complementarity, shared values, etc.

Friends and Romantic Partners

Adapted from "Interpersonal Communication in Developing Acquaintance" by Steven Duck, 1973, in *Exploration in Interpersonal Communication,* Gerald R. Miller, ed. Beverly Hills, CA: Sage, pp. 127–148.

The ability to manage conversations and to make interaction rewarding is an important factor in increasing attractiveness.

Cognitive cues constitute the last, and most important, filter. Studies show that the strongest factors in creating solid, long-lasting relationships are psychological. In the long run, the extent to which values are shared and attitudes and beliefs are similar is a more important determinant of friendship than is physical appearance. How do we get to know another person at this level? By communicating openly about our beliefs, attitudes, and values. This is why *it is important to disclose one's own beliefs and values and to elicit disclosure from others.* It is also important to be open to the possibilities in others. If we let initial filters keep us from getting to know people, we may be missing out on potentially rewarding relationships.

INCREASING RELATIONAL SKILLS

As we've seen, relationships wax and wane. How long a relationship lasts, and how successful it is, depends in large part on the partners' skills as communicators. Over the last twenty years, communication scholars have directed a great deal of attention to identifying the ways people keep their relationships in good working order. In this section, we address this research and look at some of the skills necessary for successful relational maintenance.

Relational Maintenance

Relational maintenance strategies are the behaviors people use to keep their relationships at a desired level. When asked how they routinely go about maintaining relationships, people report a range of strategies. Although most people report using positive behaviors such as expressing affection, comforting one another, avoiding hurtful topics, and so on, others report using antisocial methods like inciting jealousy or guilt.[19] Obviously not all of these strategies are widespread or successful. The five most often identified by scholars are: positivity (being positive and cheerful), openness (being willing to disclose personal information), assurance (offering reassurance), networks (spending time with one another's family and friends), and task sharing (sharing the workload.)[20] Conflict management (handling conflict effectively) and advice (offering advice and support) are also frequently cited.[21] Table 6.2 lists these strategies and gives some examples of the kinds of communication they entail.

Table 6.2 Relational Maintenance Behaviors

Positivity

Relational partners are cheerful and optimistic, build each other's self-esteem, are patient and forgiving, and refrain from criticizing one another.

Openness

Relational partners have periodic talks about the relationship, are able to disclose their own feelings and needs, and encourage their partners to be open.

Assurance

Relational partners indicate their commitment to one another, demonstrate that they are faithful, and talk in ways that show they believe the relationship has a future.

Networks

Relational partners like to spend time with each other's families and with mutual friends, and include them in their activities.

Task Sharing

Relational partners take joint responsibility for the relationship and help equally with tasks that need to be done.

Conflict Management

Relational partners know how to work out disagreements, listen to their partners' needs, and apologize when conflict occurs.

Advice Sharing/Offering

Relational partners share opinions, offer support, and use feedback effectively.

These seven behaviors are not only common but also successful. The more these behaviors occur in relationships, the more people report positive outcomes such as increased liking, commitment, satisfaction, and trust. These strategies have been found to be important in marital and romantic,[22] friendship,[23] parent-child,[24] and even friends-with-benefits relationships.[25] Secure people use them more often than do anxious or avoidant people,[26] and chronically lonely people use very few of them.[27] There is a great deal of evidence, then, that these are important communication behaviors to master if you want your interpersonal relationships to thrive.

Although these behaviors might, at first glance, seem easy, they take interpersonal skills. In the remainder of this section, we look at some of the specific skills that allow us to use these strategies effectively. In particular, we focus on self-disclosure, conflict management, and ways to offer helpful feedback and advice.

Toward More Effective Self-Disclosure

One of the most important interpersonal skills is the ability to self-disclose effectively. Self-disclosure occurs when we reveal information to others that they are unlikely to discover on their own: when we voluntarily open up to them. The ability to disclose in appropriate ways has many benefits. Being open about traumatic events, for example, typically diminishes anxiety and stress and can increase physical and mental health.[28] In fact, there is evidence that talking or writing about disturbing events can actually increase immune system functioning and prevent physical ailments. In addition, the support that comes from disclosing to a close and trusted friend can be comforting, and a frank discussion can help one put a problem into perspective. Disclosure can also strengthen relationships by signaling trust and commitment. Studies have shown that the partners of people who conceal information and refuse to be open often feel excluded and find such relationships unsatisfactory.[29] Disclosure, then, seems to draw people together and strengthen their bonds.

Yet not all statements about the self are true self-disclosures. "I have to be honest and share this with you. No one around here can stand you," is not a disclosure, it's an attack. This kind of "open" communication is not something that will strengthen a relationship and is not what communication experts mean when they discuss self-disclosure.

Rules for Disclosing

True disclosures can be healthy for a relationship, but only if certain guidelines are followed. The first is that *self-disclosure is not appropriate in all relationships*. In deciding whether or not to reveal personal information, try to match the level of your disclosure to the level of your relationship. We usually don't tell our personal experiences to strangers (except, perhaps, for bartenders, therapists, and people sitting next to us on long-distance airline flights). We do tell our personal experiences to close friends and romantic partners. One of the reasons for not disclosing to everyone is that disclosure is a risk. People are not always sympathetic and understanding. Disclosures can come back to haunt us, for not everyone can be trusted to keep a confidence.

Another reason for not disclosing indiscriminately is that disclosures put a burden on others by creating intimacy. The chance acquaintance who confides that he or she is in terrible trouble is asking for more than polite attention. He or she is asking for involvement. A close friend may be happy to provide the necessary counsel and comfort; a stranger usually is not. Therefore, it is important to *consider the effect your disclosures will have on others.*

Even when you know that your partner will be open to disclosure, you should nonetheless be cautious about when and where to hold the discussion. It is important to *choose the right time and place for your disclosures.* Running up to your best friend in the hall and revealing a major problem ("Guess what? I think I'm pregnant. Got to run.") right before a major test is insensitive and foolish. Disclosures should not be bolts from the blue. They should take place in an environment and at a time that allows recipients to react appropriately.

> Disclosures should also be related to what is happening in the "here and now." They should be connected to what is currently going on in the relationship.

Disclosures should also be related to what is happening in the "here and now." They should be connected to what is currently going on in the relationship. Any disconnected topic—particularly an unrelated disclosure—disrupts a conversation. If Elena and her roommate are discussing what to do next weekend and Elena suddenly says, "Dad lost his job when I was ten. We were so poor that I didn't get a birthday present for years," the disclosure is inappropriate. Elena doesn't seem to have a reason to bring up such a sensitive issue. The same disclosure might make perfect sense in another context. For example, if the roommate has just given Elena a small gift and Elena bursts into tears, the disclosure allows the roommate to understand Elena's behavior.

In general, *disclosure should be gradual.* It is a good idea to start out with fairly safe disclosures and then move on to more personal topics. As we have seen, relationships take time to develop and to deepen. We don't dive headfirst into them; we test the waters first. The same is true for disclosures.

Finally, *disclosures should be reciprocal.* In general, we expect a disclosure by one party to be met with a disclosure by the other. If one person in a relationship does all the disclosing, the imbalance may signal opposing attitudes toward openness. Participants should encourage their partners to disclose without making them feel uncomfortable. They should also learn to modify their own disclosures until an appropriate atmosphere has been established.

Responding to Disclosures

If disclosing is tricky, so too is responding to others' disclosures. It takes sensitivity to respond in useful ways. Imagine this: you run into your best friend from high school, who turns to you and says, "I'm really depressed. I have a good job and I make an adequate salary, but I'm not happy. . . . I didn't do too well in school before, but maybe I will quit work and go back to school. I don't know what I should do." What do you say? Your response probably falls into one of five categories identified by David Johnson. You may give advice, analyze your friend's problem, offer reassurance and support, ask questions, or help your friend clarify his thinking by paraphrasing his statement.[30] Each of these ways of responding bears a closer look.

Most people respond to disclosures by offering advice. They think about the problem, make a judgment about what ought to be done, and offer a simple (and sometimes simplistic) solution. If your response is to tell your friend what to do, you are using an **advising and evaluating response**. People don't always want you to offer them a plan of action. Note that in this example, your friend didn't say, "Tell me what to do," but instead said, "I don't know what I should do." The advice you give may be more appropriate for you than it is for your friend. In most cases, you won't have enough information about a problem to offer advice right away. You may eventually help your friend come up with his own plan, but it's probably best to use one of the other responses first.

If your response is to analyze the causes of his dilemma, then you are using an **analyzing and interpreting response**. Telling your friend that depression is often internalized anger and suggesting that he may feel angry with himself because he dropped out of school is an example. Such a response may be insightful (if you know your friend very well), but it may be way off base (e.g., if your interpretation is based on something you heard on a daytime talk show). In either case, it is likely to cause defensiveness. As Johnson points out, "people will usually respond better when you help them think about themselves and their feelings than if you try to figure out what causes them to do the things they do."[31]

Many of you may respond to your friend's disclosure by telling him not to worry, assuring him that it will all work out. By offering sympathy, you have chosen a **reassuring and supporting response**. If your friend is so distraught that he needs to be calmed down, this kind of response may be okay. It runs the danger, however, of cutting short the discussion and of making your friend feel he has no right to be unhappy.

If your immediate reaction is to gather more information, then you choose a **questioning and probing response**. This response can be useful, especially if your friend can benefit from considering the problem more fully. Obviously, different questions define the problem in different ways. And questions can also be evaluative. "How in the world did you get yourself in such a mess?" may sound like a question, but it is really an evaluation.

Often it is a good idea to turn questions into reflective statements for the other person to respond to. Phrased as a question, "Why aren't you happy?" seems judgmental (as well as very difficult to answer). But phrased as a statement, "You're feeling very unhappy now," the response loses its judgmental tone, and the listener can more easily clarify his feelings. If your response to your friend's dilemma is something on the order of "In other words, you're depressed and puzzled because your job isn't fulfilling. Yet you're not sure going back to school will work out either," then you choose a **paraphrasing and understanding response**.

Many communication scholars believe that paraphrasing is the best of the alternatives, at least as a first step. It allows you to check your understanding of what is troubling your friend, it allows your friend to hear and think about what he has just said, and it shows that you are listening to him.[32] Its major disadvantage is that it may seem awkward until you get used to it.

Make sure that when you paraphrase, you do not parrot back exactly what was said. Instead, offer your own understanding of what your friend was trying to say. And be careful not to get carried away in your paraphrasing. "So, what I hear you saying is that you're so depressed you don't want to live, because you're a failure at everything" puts the problem into your own words; unfortunately, it also completely misinterprets what was said. When paraphrasing, try to get at the gist of the problem without diminishing or enlarging it. This may take some practice, but the practice will pay off.

> When paraphrasing, try to get at the gist of the problem without diminishing or enlarging it. This may take some practice, but the practice will pay off.

Managing Interpersonal Conflict

Relationships don't always run smoothly. It's natural for people in relationships to experience bouts of conflict from time to time. If conflict is managed successfully, it need not lead to termination; indeed, it can strengthen a relationship.

Conflict occurs whenever two people have incompatible goals. If one roommate, for example, wants to watch TV and the other wants to sleep, they'll feel that they are in conflict. Whether they resolve this conflict or whether it escalates will depend on their attitudes toward conflict and their conflict styles.[33]

We each have preferred ways of dealing with conflict. Some people opt for **withdrawing**. The minute they sense conflict, they walk away or change the subject. If the issue is unimportant and there is no need to build a strong relationship with the other party or if engaging in conflict would lead to dangerous escalation, the decision to withdraw may be appropriate, but most of the time, withdrawing just postpones a problem and makes it worse.

Unaddressed conflict can undermine relationships and lead to relational dissolution.

Some people use a tactic called forcing to get their way. When they sense conflict, they put aside the other's needs and go all out to win. If an issue is personally very important and you are not deeply invested in a relationship you may want to use this technique; for example, when buying a used car from someone you don't know, it is okay to push hard for the price and terms you want. However, forcing is an inappropriate tactic with a loved one because too much domination can destroy equality in a relationship.

Some people try accommodating in conflict situations. When they sense conflicts, they give in immediately. It's all right to accommodate on unimportant issues to please someone you care for, but when important issues are at stake, it's not a good idea to give in. In long-term relationships, accommodation can often lead to unstated resentment.

What about compromising? Compromise usually means that each party gives up part of what he or she wants. Although this can be effective, remember that even in the best of compromise situations, both parties are somewhat unsatisfied. There is actually a better alternative than compromise: problem solving. Problem solving means negotiating until you come up with a new, creative solution that satisfies both parties. This is better than reaching a middle ground that satisfies no one.

If problem solving is the best alternative, why don't we use it more often? One reason is that we tend to specialize in one of the five strategies. People who withdraw or accommodate are often fearful of conflict and aren't used to arguing for what they believe in, whereas aggressive people often see problem solving or compromise as weakness. As David W. Johnson points out:

> It's important to remember that the use of certain strategies may increase the probability that other strategies will appear. When individuals cannot withdraw any more, when they feel backed into a corner and have to deal with the conflict, they are likely to strike out and try to force the other person into letting them have their way. When a person attempts to smooth, and the other person responds with forcing and anger, withdrawal may follow. That, in turn, may be followed by forcing if the other person continues to be angry and competitive.[34]

It takes time and skill to think of creative solutions, which is another reason why we don't use problem solving as often as we should. Most people seize a single position and argue for it exclusively, rather than addressing the conflict in terms of mutual interests. A position is a concrete solution to a problem; an interest is the overall goal we want to achieve. Take the example of Mandy, who wants some time alone because she is tired. She decides that the only way she can get the break she needs is to go on vacation by herself. However, when Mandy suddenly announces this decision to her partner, Diane, who has made plans to spend the vacation with her, Diane feels angry and confused. Worsening the situation is the fact that Mandy states her position (a separate vacation) and doesn't let Diane know the thinking behind it. If Mandy would discuss her thinking with Diane rather than insisting on her decision without explanation, it's possible they could resolve the problem.

Problem solving means sitting down together, directly expressing interests, defining problems clearly, and finding positions that best serve everyone's interests. This process often involves the ability to see things from the other person's point of view and a commitment to seeking options that benefit everyone.[35] It also involves a willingness to be open and direct.

Directness is learned. In general, directness is a cultural value in today's United States. Most of us believe that we should confront rather than avoid problems. After all, our needs cannot be met if no one knows what they are. The process of avoiding and postponing conflict is known as **gunnysacking**; when we gunnysack, we store up all our grievances and carry them around until the burden gets too heavy and we explode in anger. To prevent this, the best time to confront conflict is when the issue is immediate, small, and manageable.

Direct confrontation may work well for people in our culture, but it is certainly not the norm everywhere. In some cultures, direct expression of feelings is looked on with disapproval. In such cultures, smoothing and indirect statements are favored. In China, for example, indirect communication is preferred. Often, conflicts are solved by unofficial intermediaries, friends, or acquaintances of the parties to a conflict, who take it on themselves to intervene. In this way, group harmony is not disturbed. According to Guo-Ming Chen and William Starosta, "the intermediary approach to interpersonal conflict tends to be as functional in East Asia as is the assertive approach in North America."[36]

According to Richard Reeves-Ellington, "For Americans, self-disclosure is a strategy to make various types of relationships work; for Chinese, it is a gift shared only with the most intimate relatives and friends."[37] It's clear, then, that there's no one correct way to deal with conflict. When we handle conflict, we should take into account the cultural backgrounds and individual styles of the participants.

Making Feedback Effective

During conflict, as well as during other forms of interaction, it's important to give and receive feedback. **Feedback** is information that helps individuals to control and adjust their behavior. It tells people how they are doing and what they may need to change to be more effective. Competent communicators are open to feedback about their own behavior and know how to give useful feedback to others. In many cases, feedback presents no problem. "That was great!" is easy to say and is usually well received. Giving feedback about more sensitive issues, however, is not quite so simple. We will end this chapter by looking at five ways to make sure your feedback is effective.[38]

> Competent communicators are open to feedback about their own behavior and know how to give useful feedback to others.

The first rule is to *own your own message*. When we have to give others unwelcome feedback, we often avoid blame by refusing to acknowledge that the message is ours. We may use phrases such as "everyone's angry" or "we're all beginning to worry," when what we really mean is "I'm angry" or "I'm worried." Attributing the feedback to others is basically dishonest and confusing. Your partner is left with the idea that some unspecified others are upset, but he or she has no idea what you think. If you want to give feedback, own up to it.

Also, *avoid apologizing for your feelings.* To avoid hurting someone else, you may place all the blame on yourself. If you aren't at fault, don't act as though you were. A statement such as "I guess it's my fault that you borrowed my shirt and ruined it. Maybe I just didn't make it clear that I wanted it back in one piece" is not good feedback. This statement gives the impression that you don't really care about the shirt and that you don't expect any repayment, when in fact you do (and have every right to). The receiver of a message such as this can't be blamed if he or she doesn't understand the depth of your concern.

It is important to *make your messages specific and behavioral.* The object of good feedback is to give useful information. Saying something such as "Oh, I don't know, it's just your attitude" is not useful. "I was hurt when you didn't call me last week. It made me feel as though I don't count" is better because it relates to behavior. Your partner now knows what he or she did and what your feelings were. This kind of direct statement paves the way for a discussion of what each of you expects from the other and allows you to set norms for future behavior. People often hurt others simply because they are unaware that their behavior is a problem. In many cases, they would have been happy to change if only they had known. Specific behavioral information gives them this knowledge.

Verbal and nonverbal behaviors should support one another. People often have trouble expressing their emotions nonverbally. This is particularly true of anger. In an attempt to remain calm, an individual may smile and say (in a perfectly pleasant voice), "You know, I'm very angry right now." This double message is confusing and potentially double binding. In effective feedback, the verbal and nonverbal channels are congruent.

Finally, it is important to keep your partner from feeling defensive. This means that you should *avoid evaluating and interpreting your partner unless he or she specifically asks you to do so.* As we have seen, there are times when your partner may want to know your interpretation. In most cases, however, unsolicited judgments cause defensiveness. How helpful would it be if someone were to turn to you and say, "I think you should hear this for your own good. You are the craziest, most narcissistic, most sociopathic personality I've ever met"? Attacks like this are never helpful and can only hurt relationships.

UNDERSTANDING MEDIATED RELATIONSHIPS

Traditionally, interpersonal communication has involved dyads communicating face to face (FtF). What happens when technologies emerge that allow people separated in time and space to form relationships? How does computer-mediated communication (CMC) affect interpersonal communication? In this section we'll look at some of the ways new media technologies impact relationships. After describing the characteristics of mediated channels, we'll look at the nature of relationships that occur solely online and then consider how face-to-face relationships are supported through the use of online communication.

Characteristics of Electronic Channels

One of the most important characteristics of electronic communication is that it allows us to transcend space and time. When we communicate online, "difficulties, delays, and costs do not increase in relation to geographic distance between communicators."[39] Email messages travel at the speed of light, whereas it can take days or even weeks to send messages back and forth by traditional post. Seconds after being written, an email may be received, and the receiver can be transmitting a reply.

Not only does electronic communication transcend time, but it transforms space as well. We are no longer limited by geography. We can form relationships with people thousands of miles away. This is especially important for people who live in isolated areas where no one shares their special interests. Now, they can easily find like-minded people to talk to. As Martin Lea and Russell Spears point out, "one of the effects of the connectivity afforded by computer networks is that it vastly increases the 'field of availables' for forming relationships far beyond the limits set by physical proximity—or even the extended horizons offered by other communication media."[40]

Another significant characteristic of text-based electronic channels is visual anonymity. As we have already noted, when we communicate over email no one need know who we are. Physicality no longer matters; we reveal details about personal identity and appearance as we see fit. As a result, it is possible to use electronic communication to try on new "selves."

In addition to changing how we establish identity, visual anonymity online also frees us from the emotional constraints. When others are not physically co-present, we often experience disinhibition; that is, we feel free to express our emotions in nonnormative ways. A positive aspect of disinhibition is that people may be more willing to self-disclose or feel freer to ask for help and advice from others. As one online communicator puts it, "It can be very useful to have someone completely outside of one's normal life to whom you can tell what is bothering you, because the people who are in your life are often the cause of what's bothering you."[41] The negative side of disinhibition occurs when people feel that anonymity makes them unaccountable for their actions.

Online Relationships

Every year, more people become involved in computer-mediated relationships. Online dating services offer the possibility of new kinds of romantic attachments. Chat rooms and discussion groups provide places to meet new acquaintances. And social networking services make it possible to collect hundreds of Internet "friends." Other media such as cell phones, text message systems, email, and instant messaging (IM) are an integral part of everyday interactions. Nowadays, few, if any, relationships are conducted solely offline.

Given the relative lack of nonverbal cues in CMC, communication scholars used to believe that it was impossible for individuals to form deep and lasting relationships online. Recent research studies, however, have shown the opposite: online interpersonal relationships develop quickly and are often more intimate than FtF relationships.[42] Joseph Walther's hyperpersonal theory explains why this is the case: (1) online senders often carefully emphasize those aspects of self that make them attractive to others, thus increasing their appeal; (2) they edit their messages before sending them, creating high-quality conversations; (3) in the absence of cues to the contrary, there is a tendency for receivers to overemphasize similarities and form idealized views of their partners; and (4) the lack of emphasis on physical presence removes inhibitions to free and genuine communication.[43] Although in the initial stages of online relationships individuals are less open, they quickly adapt to the characteristics of the medium and exhibit increased self-disclosure.[44] The upshot is that relationships formed in cyberspace can be meaningful and the factors that lead to satisfaction in computer-mediated communication are similar to those emphasized in offline relationships, including trust, honesty, and commitment.[45]

Impression Management on Social Networking Sites

Forming accurate impressions of others is an essential part of interpersonal communication. This is equally true whether those we judge are virtual or real, although the cues we use to form impressions differ when we move from FtF to CMC environments. Impressions online are based, among other things, on language use, paralinguistic cues, stereotypes and exemplars, and personal markers.[46] Because of the absence of nonverbal cues, verbal behaviors such as word choice, sentence structure, spelling errors, and the like become important sources of information. Paralinguistic cues such as emoticons or using capital letters to SHOUT can modify the meaning of a message. Social labels that categorize people, such as "professor" or "physician," help us decide what others may be like as well. Finally, personal markers are a rich source of information. Personal markers are individual ways we present ourselves in cyberspace. They can range from screen names or choice of avatar to the photos and personal disclosures contained in our posted profiles.

Social networking sites like Facebook, MySpace, Friendster, and the like are popular places to observe and form impressions of others as well as to keep tabs on romantic partners and keep in touch with friends.[47] Posted profiles are one way members of social networking sites try to manage impressions. By choosing flattering photos and by describing themselves in socially acceptable ways, members seek to control the way others view them. However, most users take the content of profiles with a grain of salt, realizing that people often think of their online profiles "as resumes, or strategic tools intended for marketing their 'best' selves, rather than providing completely candid self-representations."[48] To make up for this fact, observers may use information other than what is presented in a profile to validate impressions. In an interesting set of studies on Facebook, Walther and his colleagues found that visitors form impressions of a user from the content of wall postings and the attractiveness of photos of the user's friends;[49] they also found that users are judged by the number of "Facebook friends" they claim to have, with the popularity and desirability of users who claim too many friends becoming suspect.[50] It would appear that in cyberspace as well as in the "real world," we are judged by the people we know and we can know too many people for our own good.

Relational Maintenance in Cyberspace

Nowadays we have a large number of choices when it comes to communicating with family, friends, and romantic partners. In addition to FtF conversations, we use telephone, email, instant messaging, and social networking sites to keep existing relationships from eroding. CMC is especially useful for college students because it is a readily available, cheap, and convenient channel of communication. Although CMC frequently is used to check in with geographically close friends, it is particularly important in maintaining long-distance relationships. Indeed, today's students can easily stay in contact with absent friends and extended family, "resulting in their having greater numbers of social ties than their parents."[51]

For many reasons such as going away to college, military deployment, immigration, and work-related travel, people find themselves separated from friends, family, and romantic partners. For these people, mediated channels provide a means for self-disclosure and other relational maintenance behaviors. Hua Wang and Peter Anderson report that telephone, email, and IM are the primary communication channels used in long-distance friendships, followed by FtF interactions, letters, and other types of CMC. They argue that "the more intimate the relationships become, the more communication channels people adopt, and the more frequently they use these tools to keep the relationship going."[52]

Although there is evidence that the more channels people use to keep in contact with one another, the better able they are to keep their relationships in tune, using IM or email is not a magic solution to relational maintenance. If, for example, one's long-distance relationships are based on "distorted pleasant memories, then the reality of a friend changing over time may lead to faster deterioration of an otherwise dormant relationship."[53] And if one's mediated messages are not reciprocal and fair, one partner may feel "under-benefitted" and dissatisfied. The key in using mediated communication is to negotiate which channels to use and to agree about how often and when to communicate. We have more options than ever before, but we must use them wisely.

BECOMING A MORE RESPONSIBLE COMMUNICATOR

The childhood taunt "Sticks and stones can break my bones, but words can never hurt me" suggests that talk is unimportant—that words don't count. But of course, they do. Careless talk can wound others, sometimes irreparably. It's important, therefore, to reflect on our responsibilities as communicators.

There are no hard and fast rules that can tell you what is right or wrong in any given situation, yet there are some questions you can ask yourself to determine whether a given act of communication is ethical or not. Melinda Kramer offers two simple tests for ethical decision making.[54] The first, which she labels the **public scrutiny test**, consists of three questions:

1. Am I personally proud of this action?
2. Am I comfortable with this decision?
3. Would I feel uncomfortable or embarrassed if this decision were known to my colleagues, friends, spouse, or children?

The second, which she calls the **four-way test**, comprises the following four questions:

1. Is it the *truth*?
2. Is it *fair* to all concerned?
3. Will it build *goodwill* and *better friendships*?
4. Will it be *beneficial* to all concerned?

These tests are not exhaustive, but remembering to ask these questions may serve to focus your attention on the consequences of communicative behavior.

Here and at the end of the next four chapters, you'll find brief sections on some of the ethical issues involved in different communication contexts. As you read the following guidelines for becoming more interpersonally responsible, think about other criteria you would add to the list. The guidelines are as follows:

- Interpersonal communication has consequences. Everyday talk may seem inconsequential, but as we've seen throughout this chapter, our notions of who we are and what we are worth evolve through interactions with others. Careless comments over a period of time can have serious repercussions. Because people make themselves vulnerable whenever they communicate, communication that belittles, attacks, or otherwise takes advantage of this vulnerability is irresponsible.

- Communicating responsibly does not mean that we have to agree with or even like everyone with whom we interact. It does mean that we should show others respect and be willing to listen with an open mind to their points of view. Too often, we dismiss other people's ideas because we assume that we have nothing to learn from them. In doing so, we limit ourselves. In an ideal world, communicators would not only listen to one another, but would actively seek out each other's opinions.

- Respectful communication also involves honesty. If we truly disagree with a proposal or if we believe that what someone is doing is self-destructive or wrong, we have an obligation to offer honest and helpful feedback, even if that feedback may not be welcomed. Of course, in expressing our opinion, we should take into account our own motives as well as the needs of our partners. Selfish or manipulative comments can sometimes masquerade as honest feedback. It's important to be rhetorically sensitive while communicating honestly.

- Whenever people form long-lasting relationships, they reveal themselves to others. Sometimes, in order to be accepted, we may be tempted to present ourselves dishonestly. Although there's nothing wrong with accentuating the positive, lying about who we are in order to create a false impression is a violation of a basic interpersonal contract. Any serious, long-lasting relationship must be built on trust.

- As we build relationships, we create relational cultures. And in these cultures, we take on roles vis-à-vis one another. For example, one person may dominate while the other submits. Some division of interpersonal labor is fine, as long as the roles are mutually negotiated and mutually satisfying. But sometimes, people force others into roles that are rigid and limiting. In general, we should use communication to create roles that allow participants maximum freedom and equality.

SUMMARY

In this chapter, we begin our consideration of communication contexts with a discussion of interpersonal communication. The most frequently encountered of all communication contexts, interpersonal communication refers to two-person, face-to-face interaction. Communication of this type is direct, personal, immediate, spontaneous, and informal. If we take a developmental view, interpersonal communication is also governed by psychological-level rules. In long-term dyads, we understand our partner at a very personal level and develop unique ways of interacting.

Managing communication is never easy. In every context, we must balance conflicting demands that pull us in different directions. In interpersonal relationships, we must balance the goals of expressiveness and protectiveness, autonomy and togetherness, and novelty and predictability.

We must also respect one another's positive and negative face needs and avoid disconfirmations. Finally, we should avoid dysfunctional patterns such as rigid role relations, paradoxical messages, and spirals. Each of these patterns limits the freedom of participants and sends ambiguous and destructive messages. One key to avoiding these potential problems is to focus as much as possible on patterns rather than on personalities.

Relationships are always changing. As individuals get to know and trust one another, they go through a series of stages: initiating, experimenting, intensifying, and integrating. As they pass through these stages, a couple often use secret tests to gather information about each other's level of commitment. Once tests have been passed, the couple may decide to engage in bonding, a public legitimation of their relationship. Unfortunately, relationships don't always work out. When relationships dissolve, they pass through the stages of differentiating, circumscribing, stagnating, and avoiding until they reach termination. During each of these stages, including the last, partners do important relational work that calls for different sets of relational skills. The extent to which a couple pass through the stages of forming a relationship is often determined by their level of attraction. Interpersonal theorists have likened attraction to a sequential filtering process whereby potential relational partners are judged and eliminated.

Relationships are built and maintained through communication. By using relational maintenance strategies such as positivity, openness, assurance, networks, task sharing, conflict management, and advice, we can keep relationships healthy. An essential relational skill is self-disclosure, the ability to offer our partners access to personal information. In responding to others' disclosures we should recognize when it is appropriate to advise, interpret, support, question, or paraphrase.

Relationships don't always go smoothly, so effective communicators must learn to manage conflict. Most people handle conflict in one of

five ways: by withdrawing, forcing, accommodating, compromising, or problem solving. The last is usually most effective, although each approach has its place. In managing conflict, it's important to focus on interests rather than positions. Americans in general handle conflict openly to avoid gunnysacking. Members of other cultures use more indirect methods. In everyday interaction, as well as during conflict, communicators need to give feedback in clear, nonevaluative ways.

Nowadays, more and more of us communicate via computer. To do so effectively, we need to be aware of the special characteristics of online communication. Ease and speed of transmission coupled with visual anonymity often lead to forms of disinhibition such as flaming. Identity establishment and trust are also difficult, as people use the Internet to try on different selves.

It is becoming much more common for people to develop relationships online. According to hyperpersonal theory, online interpersonal relationships develop quickly and can often be more intimate than face-to-face relationships. One reason is that we can control what we reveal to others online. Studies of impressions management in social networking sites have shown that people judge others on language use, paralinguistic cues, stereotypes and exemplars, and personal style markers. We are even judged by the photos and comments people leave on our Facebook walls and by the number of Facebook friends we amass. Mediated channels are used not only to initiate relationships, but also to maintain current bonds. Studies show that most people use multiple channels to keep in contact with one another. However, CMC is not a cure-all. If it is not used wisely it can lead to feelings of inequity and dissatisfaction.

It is easy to lose sight of the fact that our communication decisions have an impact on those around us. Yet they do, and this means we should act responsibly when we communicate. One way is to use either the public scrutiny test or the four-way test of ethical decision making to determine whether an act of communication is ethical.

KEY TERMS

Listed below are the key terms used in this chapter, along with the number of the page where each is explained.

interpersonal communication (132)
dyadic communication (133)
developmental approach (133)
cultural-level rules (134)
sociological-level rules (134)
psychological-level rules (134)
looking-glass self (135)
expressive–protective dialectic (136)
autonomy–togetherness dialectic (136)
novelty–predictability dialectic (137)
face (138)
positive/negative face (138)
disconfirmation (138)
impervious response (138)
interrupting response (138)
irrelevant response (138)
tangential response (139)
impersonal response (139)
incoherent response (139)
incongruous response (139)
one-up role (140)
one-down role (140)
complementary pattern (140)
symmetrical pattern (140)
paradoxes (141)
double bind (141)
spiral (141)

interpersonal self-fulfilling prophecy (142)
relational development stages (142)
initiating stage (142)
experimenting stage (143)
intensifying stage (143)
integrating stage (144)
intimacy trophies (144)
secret tests (144)
indirect suggestions (144)
separation tests (144)
endurance tests (144)
triangle tests (144)
bonding (145)
relational breadth (145)
relational depth (145)
relational dissolution stages (145)
differentiating stage (146)
circumscribing stage (146)
stagnating stage (146)
avoiding stage (146)
terminating stage (146)
filtering theory (147)
sociological or incidental cues (147)
physical proximity (147)
preinteraction cues (147)
interaction cues (147)
cognitive cues (148)
relational maintenance strategies (149)
positivity (149)

openness (149)
assurance (149)
networks (149)
task sharing (149)
conflict management (149)
advice sharing/offering (149)
self-disclosure (150)
advising and evaluating response (152)
analyzing and interpreting response (152)
reassuring and supporting response (152)
questioning and probing response (152)
paraphrasing and understanding response (153)
conflict (153)
withdrawing (153)
forcing (154)
accommodating (154)
compromising (154)
problem solving (154)
position (154)
interest (154)
gunnysacking (155)
feedback (155)
visual anonymity (157)
disinhibition (157)
hyperpersonal theory (158)
public scrutiny test (160)
four-way test (160)

SUGGESTED READINGS

DeVito, Joseph A. (2007). *Interpersonal messages: Communication and relationship skills.* Boston: Allyn & Bacon.

An interactive text that emphasizes interpersonal skills.

Guerrero, Laura, Andersen, Peter A., & Afifi, Walid. (2007). *Close encounters: Communication in relationships.* Thousand Oaks, CA: Sage Publications.

Discusses how close relationships begin, escalate, maintain themselves, and end.

Spitzberg, Brian H., & Cupach, William R. (Eds.). (2007). *The dark side of interpersonal communication.* Mahwah, NJ: Lawrence Erlbaum.

Discusses destructive elements such as secrets, complaints and criticisms, bullying, infidelity, and the like.

Trenholm, Sarah, & Jensen, Arthur. (2008). *Interpersonal communication.* (6th ed.) New York: Oxford University Press.

A comprehensive introduction to the study of interpersonal communication.

Group Communication

Groups tell us what to think and feel and how to act. We are who we are because of the groups we have been a part of.

After reading this chapter, you should be able to:

- Identify the characteristics of "groupness."
- Distinguish tasks best done by groups from those best done by individuals.
- Explain group socialization processes.
- Identify task, maintenance, and negative group roles.
- Recognize the danger signs of groupthink.
- Understand how group identity affects in-group and out-group relations.
- Explain the normal phases of group development.
- List four approaches to leadership. Describe behaviors that keep individuals from leadership positions.
- Describe methods and findings of hidden profile research.
- Recognize behaviors that lead to defensive and supportive climates.
- Understand how the standard agenda, brainstorming, and nominal group technique can be used to enhance problem-solving.
- Describe special formats for public discussion.
- Discuss ways new technologies affect group communication.
- Describe ethical responsibilities involved in group discussion.

Groups affect us throughout our lives. We are born into family groups, play and learn in friendship and school groups, and spend much of our adult life in work groups. Most Americans think of the individual as the basic social unit, but others believe that the group is even more basic, that individuals are merely products of group interaction.[1] In fact, R. E. Pittinger and his colleagues argue that it is

> not really useful to think of individuals as the units out of which groups and societies are constructed; it is more fruitful to think of an individual as the limiting case of a group when, for the moment, there is no one else around.[2]

In many ways, Pittinger is correct, for we are shaped by the groups we've belonged to, and, even after we leave them, they continue to live on in us. Much as we may hate to admit it, groups tell us what to think and feel and how to act. For good or ill, we are who we are because of the groups we have been a part of.

WHAT IS A GROUP?

Not every aggregate is a group. Groups, like dyads, develop over time. A **group** is a special kind of entity. It is a collection of individuals who, as a result of interacting with one another over time, become interdependent, developing shared patterns of behavior and a collective identity.

Characteristics of Groups

One way to see how "groupness" develops is by considering the development of a team. The athletes who show up for tryouts at the beginning of a season are not yet a group. At this point they are merely a collection of individuals. As they begin to train together, however, they gradually take on the characteristics of a true group.

A collection of people develops into a group through interaction. It is through interaction that an aggregate of individual athletes becomes a functioning team. If the team is relatively small, communication is direct and participation is equal. If it is larger, specialized roles such as trainer, captain, and assistant coach develop and messages are conveyed through specialized networks. Whichever is the case, without communication the team could not exist.

As a result of communication, *the behaviors of group members become interdependent; in a true group, any action by one affects all.* Interdependence is an important characteristic of groups, for it means that separate individuals have become a functioning whole. In athletics, it is not the individual but the team that wins or loses. If team members act independently, pursuing individual goals rather than team goals, the team never gels and may eventually disintegrate.

In the process of becoming interdependent, *members develop and share stable and predictable norms, values, and role structures.* Each group develops a unique culture that sets it apart from other groups, a culture that tells group members how to behave, what to value, and who to be. Once these shared behavioral standards develop, *members experience a sense of identity and psychological closeness.* They take pride in their shared membership, and being part of the team becomes a primary identity for them. The stronger and more cohesive their sense of membership, the stronger is their collective identity and the more they become a true team. When all these characteristics develop—interaction, interdependence, shared behavioral standards, and a sense of membership—"groupness" has been achieved. Without these characteristics, individuals remain separate and isolated. Table 7.1 summarizes the characteristics of groups.

When a collection of individuals becomes interdependent, begins to share a sense of identity, and learns how to work together for a common purpose, they have become a group.

Group Size: How Big Is a Small Group?

In discussing the characteristics of groups, we have so far avoided one topic: group size. Exactly how big is a small group? The answer to this question is not

as straightforward as it seems. Although most people agree that the lower limit of a small group is three, they disagree on a small group's upper limits. We say that a group begins at three because something special happens to communication when a third person enters a relationship, something that does not occur in a dyad.

Newscaster Jane Pauley once remarked, "Somehow three children are many more than two."[3] Pauley is right. For a number of reasons, triads, or groups of three, are much more complex than dyads, and three-person communication is different from two-person. One reason is that the number of communication channels increases dramatically with three people. In a dyad, partners don't need to choose whom to talk to; there is only one channel, A to B. In a triad, there are suddenly six channels: A to B, A to C, B to C, A to B and C, B to A and C, and C to A and B. And as the number of people in a group increases, the number of channels rises dramatically. In a seven-person group, for example, the number of potential relationships is 966. Members in large groups must work harder to include one another and to ensure equal participation. Often, groups solve this problem by developing formal roles, such as leader, follower, or harmonizer, and by using specialized networks.

Groups also tend to break down into smaller units. If you have ever lived with two other people, you may have experienced the tendency of a triad to break down into a primary dyad plus one outsider.[4] Three-person groups have to work hard to maintain cohesion. If more people join a group, the tendency to divide into subunits increases markedly.

As groups increase in size, they become more unwieldy. At some point, they become too large for the members to interact directly with one another. At the

Table 7.1 Characteristics of Groups

Interaction	Groups are constructed through communication. As members interact with one another regularly, interaction networks develop, and repeated use of these communication channels links group members.
Interdependence	Member behaviors become interconnected. In a true group, each member affects every other member. People who are interdependent share common goals and a common fate.
Shared Behavioral Standards	Groups develop unique ways of doing things. Each member takes on a role within the group, and the group as a whole abides by shared norms. Members implicitly know and follow the kinds of behaviors that are appropriate within the group. In this way, the group develops a group structure.
Collective Identity	In true groups, members perceive themselves as part of a whole. They feel a sense of closeness to other members. In addition to having an "I" identity, they develop a "we" identity based on group membership.

> At the point when members no longer recognize and relate to one another as equal individuals, the small group ceases to exist, becoming a large group or an organization.

point when members no longer recognize and relate to one another as equal individuals, the small group ceases to exist, becoming a large group or an organization. Under extraordinary circumstances, a small group may include as many as twenty people, but most of the time the upper limit is much smaller, around ten or twelve. In reviewing a study of jury deliberations, Ernest Bormann tells us that in twelve-person groups, five to seven people often hold the discussion while the others listen silently.[5] Bormann also found that groups of more than ten or eleven tend to break into smaller cliques.

What is the ideal size for a group? Dan Rothwell tells us, "the appropriate size for a group is the smallest size capable of performing the task effectively."[6] Other experts are more specific. They feel that the optimum size for a problem-solving group is from five to seven people. A group of this size has enough members to ensure a large pool of ideas and information yet not so many members as to inhibit equal participation.

Why Communicate in Groups?

If groups are unwieldy and unstable and if one needs special skills to communicate in groups, why bother? Why not work by oneself? Because there are advantages to working in groups. Whereas some tasks are best done by individuals, other tasks benefit from the input of several people. In general, the more complex the task and the more difficult its implementation, the more it needs the multiple inputs that occur in group interaction.

The first advantage of working in a small group is that *groups provide more input than do individuals*. Often, complex problems need knowledge that goes beyond that of a single individual. Having five or six heads rather than one means that more ideas can be generated and explored. Researchers who have studied small groups often speak of an effect known as **group synergy**. Put simply, group synergy is the idea that groups are often more effective than the best individuals within them. Something extraordinary happens to people when they work with others: their output surpasses what it would have been if they had worked alone. People working in groups can pool information, share perspectives, and use one another's ideas as springboards. They can also motivate and energize one another to keep searching for a solution.

A second advantage of working with others is that *cohesive groups provide support and commitment*. Sometimes, tasks are too large for a single individual, either because they require a great deal of planning or because special effort is needed to implement them. Sometimes, problems are too serious to face alone. By sharing the workload and by offering encouragement and support, groups can take on difficult and complex tasks that individuals would hesitate to undertake by themselves.

A final advantage of groups is that *groups can meet members' interpersonal needs*. We often work with others because we like being with people and because we feel that they can help us meet individual needs. One way to think of need satisfaction in groups is to consider the three basic interpersonal needs described by psychologist William Schutz: the needs for inclusion, control, and affection.[7]

The inclusion need is the need to establish identity by associating with others. As we saw in the previous chapter, other people give us a sense of self. Groups are especially important for enhancing identity. They tell us who we are, and, even more, they tell us that it is okay to be who we are. People with especially high needs for self-definition can find a stable sense of self in working with others.

In addition, groups satisfy control needs. The control need is the need to prove one's worth and competence by making effective decisions. By providing opportunities for leadership, groups can validate members' feelings of self-worth. Groups can also provide guidance and control for people who feel overwhelmed by responsibility.

Finally, groups can satisfy affection needs. The affection need is the need to develop close, caring relationships with others. By establishing friendships and by getting to know one another intimately, group members can satisfy their need to receive affection, as well as their need to show affection to others.

When Are Groups More Effective Than Individuals?

Although there is evidence that mature, cooperative groups often make better decisions than do individuals working alone, groups are not always superior to individuals. Group synergy occurs only under certain conditions: when the task is appropriate and when the group structure is such that each member is encouraged to do his or her best.

What kinds of tasks are most appropriate for groups? In general, the most appropriate tasks are those that are complex, need a wide range of insights and information for their completion, and depend on group commitment to be put into practice. When tasks are relatively simple and straightforward, time is limited, and implementing decisions is easy, then

Groups allow us to pool our talents and create an end product that is more than the sum of its parts.

a single talented individual can be as effective as a group. Table 7.2 lists some of the factors that determine whether group or individual decision making is more effective.

The manner in which group members work together also makes a big difference in whether a group will be more productive than an individual. When members support one another, are accountable for the work they do, and feel committed to group goals, group synergy occurs. However, sometimes groups do not work effectively. Group synergy is unlikely in at least two situations: when social loafing occurs and when members take a free ride by letting others do their work.

Social loafing occurs when members get "lost in the crowd" and don't fulfill their work potential. This effect often arises during additive tasks, in which the productivity of the group is determined by adding up the efforts of each member—for example, when the entire group has to produce as many products as possible in a given time. In theory, the output from additive tasks should be directly proportional to the number of group members. This is not always the case, however. Although a ten-member group will produce a lot more than an individual will, it often will not produce ten times as much because of social loafing. Some researchers believe that social loafing can be reduced if groups build cohesion among members, set clear performance goals, and identify individual contributions.[8]

Another effect, called free-riding, also decreases group productivity. This effect occurs in disjunctive tasks, tasks in which if one person does a job, no one else has to. For example, if one person does all the research for a project, the work is done, and no one else has to contribute. In this kind of situation, it's easy for members to sit back and let others do the work for them; we call this "taking a free

Table 7.2 Individual versus Group Decision Making

Tasks Are Best Left to Individuals When	Tasks are Best Done by Groups When
1. the decision is simple and its rationale is apparent to all members;	1. the decision is complex and needs an innovative, creative solution;
2. a single individual clearly has the expertise to make the decision, and that individual is trusted by the group;	2. the resources of the entire group are needed;
3. time pressures are great and it is difficult to get group members together;	3. there is adequate time for group members to meet;
4. implementing a decision does not necessitate the committed action of all group members;	4. full commitment of all group members is needed to get the job done;
5. little risk is involved;	5. a good solution is risky;
6. there is substantial agreement within the group.	6. the possibility for disagreement or misunderstanding exists unless members talk about the problem.

ride." The effects of free-riding are especially destructive because they tend to escalate; when working members perceive that others are getting a free ride, they in turn reduce their efforts. It is important, therefore, to make sure that group members feel their contributions are valued and that everyone is encouraged to participate equally. Table 7.3 indicates some of the factors that can decrease social loafing and free-riding to make groups more productive.

MANAGING GROUP COMMUNICATION

To get the most from groups, members need to understand how to manage group interaction. They must be aware of potential problems that can beset inexperienced groups. In this section, we turn our attention to some of these problems and look for ways to overcome them. We'll begin by discussing two group dialectics: the need for group members to balance individual and group needs and the need to resolve the tension between task and maintenance goals. We'll then examine how poor communication can result in poor decision making, how groups can avoid the serious problem called groupthink, and how identifying with one group can damage relationships with another.

Balancing Group and Individual Needs

In discussing interpersonal communication, we saw that couples are often beset by contradictory needs—the needs for individuality and interdependence, openness and privacy, and novelty and familiarity. Couples must work out these relational dialectics if they are to create a stable and satisfying relational culture. As we shall see, groups experience similar pressures. And unless a group balances its opposing needs, group communication can fail. The first dialectic is between the needs of the group as a whole and the needs of the individual members.

Table 7.3 Factors Related to Group Productivity

Factors That Increase Group Productivity	Factors That Decrease Group Productivity
Members have a variety of different skills and knowledge.	The group is too large to use all members' resources adequately.
Everyone is committed to group goals.	Members feel their individual efforts don't make a difference.
There is individual accountability.	There is a perception that others are taking a free ride.
All members have an opportunity to contribute.	Members lack commitment to the group.
Members have critical skills.	There is too great a desire for unanimity.
There is an atmosphere of positive interdependence.	Members have hidden agendas or conflicting goals.

Group Socialization Processes

Richard Moreland and John Levine, two social psychologists who study group behavior, see **group socialization** as a kind of contest between the individual and the group.[9] Throughout the life of their relationship, individuals try to influence the group to meet their needs, whereas the group as a whole seeks to influence individuals to do what is best for it.

Members have their own reasons for being part of a group. They join groups, at least in part, to receive individual rewards. Throughout their membership, they repeatedly measure the extent to which they are receiving these rewards. Moreland and Levine call this **process evaluation**. As a result of evaluation, the level of member satisfaction, or **commitment**, either stays the same, rises, or falls. In the first case, members determine that no change is necessary, and they simply maintain their relationship with the group. In the latter two cases, members decide that some kind of change, or **role transition**, is necessary, and they become either more or less engaged in the life of the group.

The evaluation process begins when a *prospective member* scouts out and evaluates prospective groups, committing himself or herself to the one that he or she evaluates most positively. If the group agrees to accept the person, he or she experiences the role transition from prospective member to *new member*. Often, this transition is marked by an official ceremony and is followed by some kind of orientation. Over time, new members experience additional transitions. If commitment rises, they become *full members*. If commitment falls, they become either *marginal members* or *ex-members*. (Figure 7.1 shows the major role transitions that members go through as they enter, find acceptance in, diverge from, and, finally, exit group life.)

> If a group has high status, if it can get things done, and if its social atmosphere is positive, members will feel group commitment.

What factors cause a rise in commitment and therefore a deeper involvement in the life of the group? If a group has high status, if it can get things done, and if its social atmosphere is positive, members will feel group commitment. In addition, members become committed to groups that allow them to act in desired ways. One member may turn to a group to demonstrate leadership ability. Another member may seek friendship or security. Only if the group gives members what they want will members continue the relationship.

At the same time that members try to influence the group, the group tries to influence members. Just as prospective members shop around for the best group available, so groups try to recruit the best members, admitting only those who meet entry criteria. Think for a minute of yourself as the prospective member and the school you are now attending as the group. In deciding to admit you and to reject others, the school was attempting to maintain its standards and identity. When you decided to attend, you became a new member. In the administration's eyes, first-year students are on a kind of probation and aren't given full status until they prove themselves.

Figure 7.1 Group Socialization Processes

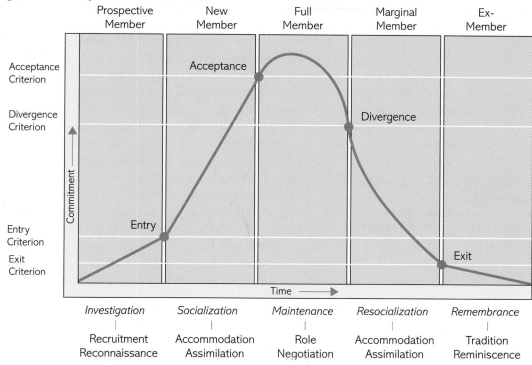

Reprinted from *Advances in Experimental Social Psychology*, 15, edited by Leonard Berkowitz, "Socialization in Small Groups: Temporal Changes in Individual-Group Relations" by Richard Moreland and John Levine, pp. 137–193, Copyright 1982, with permission from Elsevier.

If you are at or beyond the sophomore level, you have achieved the status of a full member of your school. Of course, at any time, if your grades fall or if your conduct violates school standards, you may become a marginal member, and the school will make special efforts to resocialize you. If these efforts fail and you completely refuse to meet the school's requirements, the administration may ask you to leave.

From summer orientation to graduation, ceremonies mark your progress. Along the way, the school tries to make you into its idea of the model student, and you either go along or resist. This process happens not only in large organizations such as colleges but also in everyday small groups. Fraternities or sororities, work or friendship groups, and even families attempt to socialize members. In each case, member and group must reach agreement on what they are to receive from one another. Both must have realistic expectations, and both must be willing to meet some of the others' needs while maintaining their own standards.

Adapting to Group Pressures

How can members adapt most easily to group socialization and find a balance between individual and group needs? One way is to *recognize that full membership comes only with time*. At different stages in one's relationship with a group, different behaviors are expected. Rookies can't make the same demands on a team that veteran players can. A first lieutenant doesn't have the same status as a general. And the brand-new, just-out-of-school management trainee doesn't sit down at the head of the table and tell the third-line manager what to do.

Before a new member can be accepted, he or she must earn the right. Using an economic metaphor, Edwin Hollander created the concept of idiosyncrasy credit to explain how groups regulate the behavior of inexperienced members.[10] An **idiosyncrasy credit** is a kind of symbolic currency earned through conformity. By meeting group expectations, members build up a "credit balance" that can later be traded in for innovative behavior. Group members who try to take over leadership too soon or who deviate from group consensus before they have earned enough credit are usually rejected by more established members. Hollander's research reinforces the idea that new members should proceed slowly, gradually increasing their participation once they have earned the group's trust.

> Group members who try to take over leadership too soon or who deviate from group consensus before they have earned enough credit are usually rejected by more established members.

Another way to make a successful transition into a group is to *recognize the written and unwritten norms that govern each level of membership*. These norms may be explicit rules, written down and available to all, or they may be implicit norms that can only be picked up through imitation. Whether or not members decide to follow all of the group's norms, they should be aware of what the norms are. This awareness takes careful and sensitive observation on the part of the member and clear messages on the part of the group.

Adapting to group life is usually easier with support from others. This support can come from more experienced members or from other new members. A full member who knows the ropes and who is willing to initiate a new member into the group culture is called a **mentor**. Mentors can help to smooth role transitions for new members by instructing them how to fit in. Support is also essential for members who decide to resist group norms. By banding together with other newcomers, new members can sometimes successfully challenge old ways of doing things. Whereas a lone member usually cannot exert enough pressure to change a group, several new members sometimes can.

Successful role transition is a matter of negotiation and balance. Perhaps the most important thing to keep in mind is that *members have a right to expect the group to meet some of their needs, just as the group has a right to expect members to contribute to its goals*. Only by recognizing the legitimacy of both parties' goals can groups and individuals successfully work together.

Taking on Task and Maintenance Roles

Another dialectic is important in group life: the tension between task and maintenance goals. Most groups exist for a reason. Often, they form to solve a problem or
to reach a decision. This dimension of group behavior is called its task dimension,
and the output of this dimension is called productivity. We expect groups to produce results.

At the same time, groups must also fulfill social functions. Groups must de-
vote some of their efforts to creating a positive group climate. This dimension of a
group's behavior is called its maintenance or social dimension, and its output is
called group cohesiveness. Although productivity and
cohesiveness are sometimes in conflict, they are closely
related. Successful groups must achieve both. A group
that works so hard on its task that it neglects members'
feelings eventually dissolves. Cohesiveness is the glue
that holds a group together. Similarly, a group that

> A group that works so hard on its task that it
> neglects members' feelings eventually
> dissolves. Cohesiveness is the glue that holds a
> group together.

avoids work to focus entirely on maintenance ends up losing members, for no one
wants to be part of an unproductive group. One of the keys to managing group
communication is to behave in ways that advance both productivity and cohesion.

All of us find some behaviors easier than others. Often, we specialize in either
task or maintenance behaviors. The key to being an effective group member, however, lies in being able to take on both kinds of behaviors, depending on the needs
of the group. Behaviors that help the group to accomplish its task are called task
roles. They include acting as information giver, information seeker, evaluator-
critic, and so on. Behaviors that en-
hance the social climate of the group
are called maintenance roles. Roles
such as encourager, standard setter, or
harmonizer are examples. Finally,
personal goals that do not help the
group reach either of its basic goals
are called negative roles. Negative
roles are generally dysfunctional and
indicate that a member is having trouble balancing group and individual
needs. Table 7.4 lists some of the roles
necessary for group productivity and
cohesiveness, and Table 7.5 outlines
negative, dysfunctional roles.

How can one person increase
group effectiveness? First, it is important to *become as flexible as possible in both task and maintenance roles.*

*Groups allow people with unique and similar interests to
create bonds.*

The best group member is the one who can recognize and provide whatever the group needs at a particular time. Such a member must watch the group process carefully, realizing that what the group needs is not necessarily what the member likes to do best. Highly task-oriented members often lose patience with the group when it gets off track; they fail to understand that occasional jokes, friendly

Table 7.4 Task and Maintenance Roles

Task Roles

Role	Description
Initiator–Contributor	Suggests new ideas to group or offers new way of regarding group problem
Information Seeker	Asks for clarification of suggestions and for information and facts pertinent to problem
Opinion Seeker	Asks for clarification of values associated with group problem or with decision suggestions
Information Giver	Offers facts or generalizations or relates experiences relevant to group problem
Opinion Giver	States beliefs or opinions pertinent to group problem or to decision suggestions
Elaborator	Thinks of examples, offers rationales, or works out details of previous suggestions
Coordinator	Pulls together ideas and suggestions and coordinates work of various subgroups
Orienter	Summarizes what has occurred or asks questions about the path the group will take
Evaluator–Critic	Develops standards for group functioning and compares group performance to standards
Energizer	Prods group to action and stimulates greater levels of group activity
Procedural Technician	Expedites group movement by taking on routine tasks
Recorder	Writes down suggestions, records decisions, and takes minutes

Maintenance Roles

Role	Description
Encourager	Accepts and praises others' contributions
Harmonizer	Relieves tension and mediates disagreements
Compromiser	Seeks to find solution for conflict that involves own ideas
Gatekeeper–Expediter	Keeps communication channels open and facilitates others' participation
Standard Setter	Expresses maintenance standards or applies standards to group process
Group Observer	Observes group process and offers feedback about maintenance procedures
Follower	Accepts ideas of group and serves as audience

Adapted from "Functional Roles of Group Members," by Kenneth Benne and Paul Sheats, 1948, *Journal of Social Issues*, 4, pp. 41–49. Copyright SPSSI.

chitchat, and well-timed breaks are not a waste of time but are ways to build group cohesion. Instead of giving a steady barrage of opinions, the task-oriented group member should learn to stop and make sure other members are comfortable.

Similarly, the maintenance-oriented member should learn how to enhance task development. A harmonizer, for example, should realize that the line between relieving tension and being a clown is thin. Although maintenance is a good thing, there are times when the group must get down to work. One way to increase your own flexibility is to look at Tables 7.4 and 7.5 and determine the roles you play most frequently. Then practice playing different roles until you feel comfortable with a large repertoire.

In addition, it is important to *avoid disruptive individual roles*. We all bring our own hidden agendas to the groups we belong to. A hidden agenda is a personal goal that lies below the surface and that can get in the way of group performance. Sometimes, hidden agendas are compatible with group goals (for example, when a group member channels a need for recognition into effective task leadership), and sometimes, they are incompatible (as when a team member grandstands or hogs the ball instead of passing it off). Members should examine their own agendas and guard against dysfunctional behavior. At the same time, the group should be aware of members' needs and try to satisfy them. If this is impossible, the group should discuss members' dysfunctional behaviors with those members, pointing out the effects of the behaviors on the group as a whole.

Table 7.5 Negative Roles

Role	Description
Dominator	Refuses to allow others to express their opinions and dominates discussion
Blocker	Prolongs or stops decision making by foot-dragging and nit-picking
Self-Confessor	Distracts group by disclosing personal problems and by using group for personal therapy
Help Seeker	Constantly expresses own inadequacy and asks group for sympathy and compliments
Recognition Seeker	Spends time boasting about own accomplishments in order to be center of attention
Special-Interest Pleader	Manipulates group in interests of some other group; has hidden agenda
Playboy or Playgirl	Fails to take group seriously; spends time playing around and mocks serious behavior
Joker or Clown	Uses humor and horseplay to divert group from task

Combating Groupthink

We have seen that it is important for task groups to feel cohesive and confident. Sometimes, however, a group gets too confident and begins to make poor decisions. We call this state groupthink, and it can have very serious repercussions. A number of communication scholars have argued that the 1986 explosion of the space shuttle *Challenger* was a classic example of groupthink. They contend that poor decision making on the part of Thiokol engineers and NASA officials led these experts to underestimate risks, overestimate the likelihood of success, and ignore warnings and their own misgivings.[11] In this case, a failure of group communication may have led to death and disaster.

What exactly is groupthink? Irving Janis, who coined the term, defines it as "a mode of thinking that people engage in when they are deeply involved in a cohesive in-group, when the members' strivings for unanimity override their motivation to realistically appraise alternative courses of action."[12] In groupthink, group members believe that they can do no wrong. This problem can occur when cohesion is too high, when group members are too similar (so that no new ideas challenge group consensus), or when the group is isolated from outside influences.

Groupthink has several symptoms. The first is an *illusion of invulnerability*. A group that is immersed in groupthink believes so strongly that it is the best that it loses all sense of reality. The second symptom is *belief in the group's own morality*. Members feel that their actions and beliefs are more valuable than those of people outside the group. This symptom is closely related to a third symptom, the tendency to hold *shared stereotypes*. Members take on an "us versus them" mentality, believing that anyone who opposes the group is stupid or wrong. Problems or failures are explained away by *collective rationalizations,* which allow members to stick to an ill-advised course of action even in the face of contrary information. Individual members who begin to doubt the group feel strong pressures toward *self-censorship*. They hesitate to speak up because they know they will encounter disapproval. In fact, an *illusion of unanimity* arises, whereby a doubting member believes that everyone else agrees with the group's chosen action. Should a dissenting member speak up, he or she is severely sanctioned as other members place *pressure on dissenters*. Finally, the leader and key members of the group are protected from outside information by self-appointed *mind-guards* who "protect" them from negative information.

As a result of the groupthink atmosphere, problem solving is disrupted. Members ignore alternatives, fail to test their ideas against reality, and refuse to make contingency plans. When people believe that they are superior and invincible, they feel no need to examine their ideas carefully. Janis analyzed several historical fiascoes and showed that symptoms of groupthink occurred in all of them, including America's failure to secure Pearl Harbor, its decision to invade the Bay of Pigs, the escalation of the Vietnam War, and the Watergate cover-up. And we can add the *Challenger* disaster to this list.

Groupthink does not occur only in famous historical cases; it also character-izes everyday groups. Any speech communication teacher who has taught a course in small-group communication can give exam-ples of classroom groups that spent all their time telling themselves how great their project would be and almost no time working on the project. Talented people have a natural tendency to get lazy and over-confident unless they make special efforts to avoid groupthink.

> Talented people have a natural tendency to get lazy and overconfident unless they make special efforts to avoid groupthink.

How can groups guard against this kind of overconfidence? Groups can as-sign a member to take on the role of critic or devil's advocate. They can take criti-cisms and warnings seriously. When they hear themselves denigrating the competition or bragging about their own talents, they can become aware that they may be slipping into groupthink. And they can also make a rule that once a deci-sion has been made, they will hold a second-chance meeting to review it and find its flaws. By carefully monitoring their behavior as they pass through the common stages of group development, groups can avoid serious errors in problem solving.

Improving Communication with Out-Groups

So far we have focused on communication within groups. But what about interac-tion between groups? How does being a part of one group affect how we think about and act toward members of another group? In this section we discuss how group membership offers us social identity, and how this identity may cause us to depersonalize and compete with people who belong to other groups.

But identity may be more complex than you think. Rather than having one identity, we have many. Each of us has a personal identity consisting of the charac-teristics that distinguish us from those around us. At the same time we have a social identity or, more accu-rately, a series of social identities that define us in terms of our similarities to others. When you describe yourself as cheerful or kind or brave, you are talking about your personal identity. When you describe yourself as a Republican or

> Identity is arguably our most prized possession; it shapes the way we see ourselves, it affects our self-esteem, and it guides our actions.

Democrat, a man or woman, a Christian or Muslim or Jew, you are referencing a social identity, an identity based on group membership. Scholars who take a *social identity approach* to studying groups go so far as to define them as collec-tions of three or more people who "have the same definition of who they are, what attributes they have, and how they relate to and differ from specific out-groups."[13] Social identity theorists believe that groups create socially shared worldviews. They also believe that we favor in-group members (people in our own groups) and try to distinguish ourselves from out-group members (people in other groups.) So strong is this need to see ourselves as similar to some and different from others that even when our ties to others are tenuous and artificial, we still allow those ties to affect us.

A series of studies demonstrated this effect by using what is known as the *minimum group paradigm*. In a typical minimum group study, subjects are labeled as belonging to one of two groups and then asked to give money to each of the groups. Despite the fact that they get no money themselves, and despite the fact that they have no interaction with those who share their group label, subjects divide the money so that members of "their group" get more than members of the other group. Identification with a minimum group can be extremely tenuous. In one study, college students were asked to play a competitive game with someone they thought either had the same birthday as they did or had another birthday. Results showed that students tended to cooperate with those individuals with the same birthday but to compete against those with a different birthday.[14] If simply being categorized as similar to someone else leads to in-group bias, imagine how much influence real-life groups have over their members.

Social identity theorists believe that we hold group prototypes for every group we belong to. Group prototypes are mental images of the characteristics of group members, the values and norms they hold, and the differences between group members and outsiders. Within a given group, we will like members who match the group prototype and dislike members who fail to conform to the group prototype.[15] Furthermore, if we are strongly committed to a group, we ourselves internalize the group's norms and values, doing our best to fit the prototype by being like other group members. Research shows that members who act in accordance with the norms and values embedded in a group prototype gain the ability to influence others.[16]

We also use group prototypes to categorize and depersonalize members of out-groups, ignoring their unique characteristics. How can we explain this tendency to categorize others on the basis of their group identities? One reason is that depersonalizing allows us to reduce uncertainty. Assigning someone to a category suggests that he or she is like other people in that category; it allows us to say to ourselves, "I know who that person is because I know the group he belongs to." When people are uncertain or when the times in which they live are complex and confusing, they often join groups that have clearly defined or ideologically extreme prototypes.[17]

In addition to reducing uncertainty, holding strong positive in-group prototypes can increase self-esteem. By creating prototypes that favor in-group members, people can convince themselves, "My group is the best. Thank goodness I'm not one of *them*." Over time, this kind of thinking results in polarized perceptions such that out-group members are seen as more different than they actually are. Social identity theory, then, offers an explanation for prejudice and ethnocentrism and emphasizes the importance groups have in our lives. By being aware of our tendency to categorize and depersonalize others based on group membership, we may be able to, at least partially, make fairer and more reasoned evaluations of others.

> By being aware of our tendency to categorize and depersonalize others based on group membership, we may be able to, at least partially, make fairer and more reasoned evaluations of others.

GROUP DEVELOPMENT: PHASES IN PROBLEM-SOLVING GROUPS

Groups are not static. Over time groups develop and change. Norms develop, roles are embraced, and leaders emerge. As we saw in our discussion of interpersonal communication, couples go through recognizable stages as they create their relational cultures. So too do groups. In this section we begin by looking at phases in group development and then take up the topic of leader emergence in groups.

Phase Models: Mapping the Life of a Group

A number of scholars have tried to describe the phases that groups go through as they find ways to work effectively and productively. Despite slight differences in their models of group development, most scholars agree that groups go through approximately five phases.

In the initial phase, called by Bruce Tuckman the *forming* phase, members focus on getting to know one another and in deciding how to fit in to the group.[18] This stage is often characterized by tentative and awkward communication as members experience primary tension.[19] The best way to deal with primary tension is simply to *act in an open, friendly, and positive manner and to give members time to feel comfortable with one another*. It is not a good idea to force decisions during this period. In most cases, this tension will dissipate naturally; however, if it persists groups will be blocked from further development.

The second phase is generally described as a conflict phase, or, in Tuckman's term, a *storming* phase. Here a new form of tension, called secondary tension, arises as group members work out leadership and role distinctions. Susan Wheelan explains that "issues of power, authority, and competition are debated at this stage."[20] She believes that the conflict experienced in this stage, if properly resolved, can serve to define common values and can lead to increased cohesion. Members should *learn to expect periods of conflict and find ways to benefit from the energy and ideas that are generated during these periods*.

Once secondary tension has been resolved, the third phase, a *norming* phase, occurs as members openly work out group goals, norms, and roles, preparing themselves for the fourth, or *performing phase*. Groups are now ready to settle down to work. The goal here is to make good decisions, get the job done, and remain a cohesive unit. Members now feel comfortable in exchanging ideas.

In groups that have a formal end point, a fifth, *adjourning,* phase occurs. Depending on the success of the group in achieving its task, expression of positive feelings and congratulations may emerge, although occasionally anxiety about termination may occur.

Whereas most scholars see group development as passing through a series of orderly phases like these, others have argued that progress may not always be so clear-cut. Marshall Scott Poole, for example, offers a multiple-sequence model, in which he argues that groups often work on different problems simultaneously and may backtrack or even need to repeat earlier work.[21] Wheelan believes that the fact that groups do not always progress in an orderly fashion does not invalidate global phase models. She compares groups to individuals. While most people mature over time in fairly orderly ways, not all do. Some experience developmental delays or failures while others regress temporarily. "Some groups," she tells us, "like some people, will not mature. However, the majority of groups will develop cultures, structures, and processes that facilitate goal achievement."[22]

Leadership: How Groups Choose Leaders

What does it take to be a good leader? There is no easy answer to this question. Theorists who take a trait approach believe that the key to leadership lies in the personal characteristics of leaders. In his review of leadership research, Peter Northhouse found evidence that individuals who show intelligence, self-confidence, determination, integrity, and sociability are likely to emerge as leaders, although it is not yet clear if these same factors lead to successful group influence.[23] Other researchers argue that people who are charismatic, visionary, intellectually stimulating, and considerate of followers are likely to emerge as transformation leaders and may be in a position to influence others.[24] Still others take a different tack, identifying factors, or traits, that keep a person from becoming a leader, such as lack of participation, rigidity, authoritarian behavior, or negative communication.[25] Unfortunately, no one has been able to come up with a list of traits that, in all cases, distinguish leaders from nonleaders.

If traits can't always identify a leader, perhaps communication style can. Theorists who take a styles approach contend that what is important is not the personality of the leader but rather how he or she acts. A series of studies have argued, for example, that leaders who choose a democratic or participatory style are more effective than those who are either authoritarian or use a "hands-off" style.[26] Although a democratic style has been associated with positive outcomes, it too is not universally effective.

Perhaps, rather than looking for the one best style of leadership, it makes more sense to argue that different styles work in different situations. This is exactly what those who take a situational approach believe. But what aspects of the situation affect leadership? Kenneth Hershey and Paul Blanchard have argued that the maturity level of a group should dictate the leader's style, with a more directive style being suitable in the early stages of group development and a more delegating style being effective later in the life of the group.[27] Robert J. House and Gary Dessler, on the other hand, believe that the most important factors in determining leadership style are members' attitudes, in particular whether members believe they have the ability and opportunity to do their tasks effectively and whether they view completing the tasks as potentially rewarding.[28] Fred Fiedler offers another suggestion. He feels that variables such as the leader's relationship with group members, his or her power, and whether a task is structured or unstructured dictate the kind of leader who will succeed.[29] Finally, leader-member exchange theory contends that leaders should match their styles not to the situation, but to the characteristics of each member, substituting sensitivity to member needs for consistency.[30]

One of the factors that complicates research into leadership is the ambiguity of the term "leader." Some people think of a leader as a single individual, someone who is appointed to manage a group. Others, however, believe that a leader is any-one who performs behavior that moves a group toward its goals. Under this latter view, called the functional approach, leadership can be shared, and what is impor-tant in understanding leadership is knowing the functions that have to be fulfilled in the group. Dennis Gouran offers an interesting way of thinking about leader-ship. He argues that leadership is the "art of counteractive influence."[31] By this he means that leadership is the art of getting a group back on track when it encoun-ters obstacles such as arguments over authority, conformity pressures, disruptive behavior, lack of motivation, and the like.

Clearly, leadership is a complex process that cannot be summed up neatly. It is possible that there is a grain of truth in all of these theories. It is likely that lead-ership calls for personal traits that make the leader attractive to members. But it is also likely that leadership necessitates the flexibility to take on differing styles de-pending on the situation as well as the sensitivity to know how to keep the group moving in a positive direction. Gouran points out that leadership is more an art than a science:

> There does appear to be a kind of intuitive feel that some individuals have and others do not for the enactment of certain types of communicative behavior; it is very difficult to detect but it nonetheless can produce differences in leadership success . . . Capitalizing on those subtleties that give one greater advantage def-initely appears to be something of an art.[32]

How Not to Be Chosen Leader

Although the qualities that make people succeed as leaders appear complex, those associated with poor leadership are much easier to list. Fisher gives eight rules for how not to emerge as leader.[33] Although his intent is humorous, his list holds more than a little truth. If you don't want the responsibility of group leadership, try these suggestions. If, on the other hand, you want to help your group accom-plish its tasks, these are behaviors to avoid.

RULE 1 **Be absent as often as possible.** And if you want to increase your chances of avoiding leadership still more, refuse to provide any excuse for your absence.

RULE 2 **Contribute as little as possible.** Here it helps to appear incompe-tent and uninterested as well as to be silent.

RULE 3 Volunteer to be secretary or record keeper. You run the risk of demonstrating your value to the group in this way, but because the secretary role is generally a secondary role, you can probably avoid major leadership responsibilities.

RULE 4 Be subservient and acquiescent, showing a total inability to come up with useful ideas of your own.

RULE 5 Be rude and verbally aggressive early in the discussion, and sulk and become apathetic later on when people are sharing ideas.

RULE 6 Become the group's joker. In this way, you get to be the center of attention, yet at the same time, you warn others not to take you seriously.

RULE 7 Come across as a know-it-all. The use of big words and a desire to talk about every topic under the sun should do the trick.

RULE 8 Show contempt for leadership, and attack and label others when they try to contribute.

STRENGTHENING GROUP DISCUSSION SKILLS

Communicating in groups is not always easy. In this section, we'll look at a few ways to become a more effective group member. We'll begin by discussing the importance of sharing information, we'll then look at ways to create positive group climates, and examine some ways to organize problem-solving discussions. Finally, we'll review some of the standard formats for group discussion used in public settings.

The Importance of Information Sharing: Uncovering Hidden Profiles

Groups thrive on information, yet too often group members fail to communicate what they know. The area of research that focuses on how and why members fail to share information has come to be called hidden profile research.[34] In a typical hidden profile study, group members are given information (the hidden profile) before discussing a problem. Some of the information is given to all members and some unique information is given only to individual members. Only when all the information is used can the group make a high-quality decision. What happens? Often the unique information is never discussed, and as a result optimal solutions are not reached.

One of the reasons that unique information is not offered is because information that everyone possesses is encouraged and repeated during deliberations and may overpower individual information. When members hear that others have the same information they do, they may take this as a validation that the shared information is important, and, as a consequence, unique information falls by the wayside. In addition, members may consciously decide to withhold unique information because they don't want to run the risk of losing credibility by contradicting the group.[35] They may also be motivated by a desire to avoid looking like a troublemaker, by a need to get their decision supported by the group, or by a desire to fit in to the group and make it more cohesive. Discussing something everyone agrees on can help members develop trust and interpersonal closeness and can establish common ground.[36]

Whatever the reasons, withheld information can lead to poor decision making. There are several ways to increase information sharing. Choosing group members who possess a range of information and encouraging them to discuss all possible alternatives before trying to solve the problem can lead to higher-quality solutions.[37] In addition, developing norms for critical evaluation can increase information exchange. Finally, studies have also shown that simply encouraging members to recall as much information as possible before deliberating will lead to better results.[38]

Creating a Positive Climate

Some years ago, Jack Gibb described the kinds of behaviors that can lead to competitive, defensive climates and those that can lead to cooperative, supportive climates.[39] Gibb believed that in a **defensive climate**, in which group members feel threatened, the group is unproductive. To the extent to which group members sense evaluation, control, strategy, neutrality, superiority, and certainty on the part of others, they close down and refuse to cooperate. By replacing these behaviors with description, problem orientation, spontaneity, empathy, equality, and provisionalism, a group can create a **supportive climate**.

Evaluation occurs when individuals are judgmental toward one another, when their comments imply that they are appraising and criticizing one another's behavior. **Description**, on the other hand, arouses little defensiveness, because it focuses on presenting feelings or opinions without assigning blame. It is better for a group member to express concern about a deadline by describing his or her feelings ("I'm concerned about getting the work done as soon as possible, because I have commitments at the end of the month") than by evaluating ("This group has got to stop wasting time and being lazy"). **Control** is another behavior that increases defensiveness. When members try to impose their will on others ("The only way to get this done is to . . .") rather than trying to collaborate ("Does anyone have ideas about how to get the job done?"), they are likely to meet resistance. The opposite of control is taking a **problem orientation**.

> By recognizing the need to be more supportive and open and by listening empathically, members can improve the social climate of their groups.

Strategy occurs when group members' behavior is prompted by hidden agendas. Feeling manipulated naturally leads to defensiveness. The corresponding supportive behavior is **spontaneity**, whereby the member communicates in an open and honest manner. **Neutrality**, although it sounds positive, can often signal indifference and a lack of commitment. On the other hand, **empathy** tells others that you understand their thoughts and feelings. As we saw in Chapter 6, the use of the paraphrasing response can indicate concern and empathy.

Superiority should be avoided as much as possible, for superior responses lead to jealousy and resentment. Instead, members should be careful to indicate **equality** by asking for others' opinions and weighing everyone's contributions equally. Finally, having too great a sense of **certainty** can lead to an unpleasant group climate. **Provisionalism**, by contrast, signals a willingness to listen openly to others' ideas. Group members should monitor themselves to make sure they are not inadvertently making others defensive. It is easy to come across as superior or certain even when you may not mean to. Without realizing it, we can easily hurt one another's feelings and make groups frustrating and unpleasant. By recognizing the need to be more supportive and open and by listening empathically, members can improve the social climate of their groups.

Enhancing Problem Solving

When left to their own devices, groups often jump from one idea to another. In fact, studies have shown that the average attention span of a group—the time it stays on a single topic—is approximately fifty-eight seconds.[40] One of the reasons group problem solving is so difficult is that groups have trouble staying on track.

To facilitate more orderly thinking, group members sometimes turn to the use of logical plans, or agendas, to guide their discussion. Agendas are often very useful when time is limited and task pressures are strong, because they focus on the task dimension. Their major disadvantage is that they may neglect maintenance issues. Following a task agenda too closely or using agendas at every meeting may increase productivity at the cost of cohesiveness. Nevertheless, there are times when agendas can be extremely useful.

The Standard Agenda

In 1910, philosopher John Dewey described a rational process for solving problems that he called reflective thinking. Dewey believed that reflective thinking begins with a felt difficulty. We then examine that difficulty, think of possible solutions, evaluate them, choose the best one, and then implement it. The **standard agenda** is a six-step guide to solving problems that derives directly from Dewey's theories about reflective thinking.[41] Table 7.6 summarizes the six steps.

The first step in the standard agenda is **problem identification**. Too often, groups jump into a discussion without a complete understanding of what the problem that they need to solve really is. A **problem** can be defined as a discrepancy between a present state of affairs and a desired state of affairs.[42] Defining the problem can often be the most difficult step in problem solving.

> Too often, groups jump into a discussion without a complete understanding of what the problem that they need to solve really is.

Let's look at an example. Most of us feel that our campuses have a parking problem. But what does that really mean? Does it mean that there are currently not enough spaces? Or does it mean that there are plenty of spaces but that they are too far from classroom buildings? Or could it be that spaces are available at some times of the day but not at others? In the first case, the solution may involve setting aside new spaces or cutting down on campus traffic. In the second, it may necessitate moving spaces or classes or providing shuttle service. In the third, it may mean rescheduling some activities. Only when the definition of the problem is concrete and clear can the group move on to the next step.

Dan Rothwell gives two interesting examples of how the way a problem is framed affects the way it is ultimately solved.[43] In the first example, a service station manager learned that his soda machine was out of order when customers who lost their money complained. To solve the problem, he put an "Out of Order" sign on the machine. Customers ignored the sign, continued to lose money, and continued to complain. He finally solved the problem by changing the sign to read $2. No one bought the soda, and no one complained. In a second example, a convenience store had a problem with teenagers loitering outside. Instead of looking for ways to confront the students, the store owners simply piped Muzak into the parking lot. The kids found the bland music so objectionable that they soon found another hangout.

Rothwell explains that in both cases, the solution became achievable as soon as it was framed in the right way. In the first example, the service station manager stopped asking himself, "How can I let the customers know the machine is out of order?" and instead asked, "How can I stop customers from putting money in the machine?" In the second example, the proprietors were successful only after they stopped thinking in terms of force and started to ask, "What will motivate the teenagers to leave on their own?"

Table 7.6 Steps in the Standard Agenda

STEP 1 *Problem Identification*
Group members clarify the problem, often by specifying the difference between a present state of affairs and a desired state of affairs. Problems should be concrete, clear, and solvable.

STEP 2 *Problem Analysis*
Group members collect information about the problem, identifying factors that are causing the problem and factors that may help in solving the problem.

STEP 3 *Criteria Selection*
Group members decide on the characteristics of a valid solution prior to discussing specific solutions.

STEP 4 *Solution Generation*
Group members generate as many solution alternatives as possible.

STEP 5 *Solution Evaluation and Selection*
Group members use previously selected criteria to evaluate each solution. The solution that best meets evaluation criteria is chosen.

STEP 6 *Solution Implementation*
Group members follow through by putting the solution into effect.

The second step in the standard agenda is problem analysis. David Johnson and Frank Johnson, drawing on the work of Kurt Lewin, suggest that one of the best ways to diagnose a problem is to view the current state of affairs as a balance between two opposing forces: restraining and helping forces.[44] Restraining forces are forces that are negative in direction. If they prevail, the current state will get worse. Helping forces, on the other hand, are forces that are positive in direction. If they are strengthened, the current state will move closer to the ideal. This kind of analysis is called force-field analysis. By listing restraining and helping forces, group members understand the problem better. They know what they have going for them and what they must overcome. When it comes to solving the problem, they can look at solutions that either increase helping forces or remove restraining forces.

Assume that a school curriculum committee has decided that a new experimental course is needed to update current offerings. Through force-field analysis, the committee finds that one of the major restraining factors is parents' resistance to the course and that this resistance is based on a misunderstanding of what the new course is all about. The committee also finds that the helping forces include the fact that current faculty members can teach the new course and that the faculty as a whole supports the idea. The group now knows that it can enlist the teachers' aid and that they should remove parents' fears.

The third step in the standard agenda is criteria selection. Before they begin to offer suggestions, group members should establish the criteria they will use in judging solutions. One group may decide, for example, that its solution must be rapid and reasonably cheap and that it must change the status quo as little as possible. Another group addressing another problem may decide that it wants a long-term solution and that money is no object. The time to decide on criteria is before members' egos get too involved in specific decision proposals.

The fourth step is solution generation. Here, group members attempt to generate as many alternative solutions as possible. To do this, they may use methods such as brainstorming, a method we will look at shortly when we examine ways to enhance group creativity. The important point is identifying a number of alternatives rather than being satisfied with the first one.

In step five of the standard agenda, solution evaluation and selection, alternative solutions are evaluated, and the best one is selected. Now it is a simple matter of looking at each solution and measuring it against each criterion. The solution that meets the most criteria (without causing additional problems) is the best solution. Finally, in step six, the group follows through with solution implementation.

Brainstorming: Increasing Creativity
Although a standard agenda can keep a group focused and can encourage members to think critically, it doesn't tell us much about how to generate new and creative

ideas. One of the major blocks to idea generation is the tendency to reject potentially good ideas by evaluating them prematurely. **Brainstorming** is a technique for overcoming this problem. In brainstorming,

One of the major blocks to idea generation is the tendency to reject potentially good ideas by evaluating them prematurely.

members are encouraged to generate as many ideas as they can, as quickly as possible. They are instructed to say whatever pops into their heads, no matter how ridiculous it may sound. The idea is to collect a large pool of ideas and then go back and criticize them. Only after all ideas have been suggested is evaluation allowed.

David Johnson and Frank Johnson discuss several ways to encourage idea generation, methods that can be used by themselves or in conjunction with brainstorming.[45] One is called the **part-changing method**. Here, members think of new products or ideas by identifying old parts that might be altered. A group of furniture designers, for example, might decide to think of ways to change each part of a chair. They would then generate as many different colors, shapes, sizes, textures, styles, and so on as possible without worrying whether or not the ideas were feasible.

In the **checkerboard method**, the group draws up a matrix. One set of behaviors or characteristics is written in columns across the top of the matrix, and another set is written in rows along the left-hand side. Members then examine the spaces where rows and columns intersect to see whether they can generate any creative combinations. For example, a group with the task of inventing a new sport might list equipment or materials across the top of a matrix and actions or playing surfaces along the side. Although many of the resulting combinations might seem ridiculous, some just might work.

Finally, in the **find-something-similar method**, group members are encouraged to think of analogies. A group that wants to solve a parking problem might think of how bees, squirrels, shoe stores, dry cleaners, and so on store things. All of these methods encourage members to break away from standard ways of thinking and to become more open minded and daring.

Nominal Group Technique

The standard agenda, brainstorming, and the Johnsons's methods for generating ideas are only some of the many techniques that have been devised to increase group problem-solving efficiency. An interesting variation combines parts of these procedures but cuts actual interaction to a minimum. This is **nominal group technique**.[46] In this technique, individuals generate solution ideas on their own and then meet to clarify these ideas. After all ideas have been listed and explained, members individually rank their favorite ideas. The rankings are then averaged, and the idea with the highest average is chosen. By asking members to work individually, the method avoids the problem of more aggressive members overpowering quieter members. By refusing to allow members to evaluate one another's ideas, the method eliminates potential conflict. This method is also less lengthy than full-blown discussion.

More recently, Brilhart and Galanes have modified this technique to involve more discussion.[47] In their model, the group leader defines the problem. Each member, working alone, then generates as many solutions as possible without discussion. Once members are finished, each idea is posted so that everyone can see it. Each member then individually indicates his or her top five choices, and the aggregate rankings are computed and displayed. At this point, members begin to discuss the merits of the top ideas. The discussion continues until consensus is reached or until a vote is called.

Many additional methods exist to guide group problem solving, each with its own advantages and disadvantages. A skilled group leader has a number of agendas at his or her disposal to use with different kinds of groups and different kinds of problems. Being able to control a group and enhance its ability to work effectively are important skills for anyone who is interested in working with people. The more you learn about group dynamics, the more fascinating this subject will become.

Using Special Formats for Public Discussion

The techniques we have looked at so far were designed for groups to use in private deliberations. Occasionally, group discussion takes place in public, in front of an audience. In such a case, group discussion is used to increase audience understanding of a particular issue. **Public discussion formats** designed with this goal in mind include the symposium, the forum, the panel discussion, the buzz group, and the role-playing group.[48]

The Symposium

A **symposium** is a form of public discussion in which a number of experts give brief, prepared speeches on a topic. Although each participant speaks independently, participants often hold planning sessions in advance to decide how to divide up a problem and to determine speaking order. A typical symposium might concern a public issue such as child abuse. A sociologist might be invited to outline the extent and causes of the problem, a psychologist to discuss the symptoms and effects of abuse, a school administrator to speak on the role of teachers in discovering and reporting suspected cases, and so on. The role of the chairperson of a symposium is to introduce the problem, to present each speaker, and to sum up the discussion. The symposium is a fairly formal format that involves little interaction between participants and audience. To encourage more interaction, planners often combine the symposium with another format, the forum.

The Forum

A **forum** is a much more freewheeling form of discussion than is a symposium. In a forum, audience members are the discussants. They share their comments and opinions with one another and are led by a moderator whose job is to announce the topic, to provide necessary background information, to set the ground rules for participation, and generally to control the discussion. When a forum follows a symposium, it allows audience members to express their feelings and to add their comments to those of the experts. Much of the success of the discussion lies with the moderator, who must keep the audience on track and make sure everyone is heard. When talk show hosts such as Oprah Winfrey or Dr. Phil go out into the audience to solicit comments, they are using a forum format.

The Panel Discussion

In the **panel discussion**, experts interact with one another in a small group while an audience listens. Panels may be formed around a number of topics. After the Los Angeles riots of 1992, for example, many communities organized panel discussions on the topic of police–community relations. These panels included police representatives as well as leaders from minority communities, educators, and local politicians. The goals were to allow interested parties to share their feelings and to discover ways to increase cooperation between law enforcement agencies and the public.

In a well-organized panel discussion, the moderator formulates the major topics to be discussed and informs the participants of these topics ahead of time. The moderator introduces participants, organizes the discussion, and summarizes panelists' contributions. The moderator may decide to follow a modified problem-solving agenda or may allow the discussion to follow its own path, but in either case, he or she controls the shape of the discussion. It is up to the moderator and participants to ensure that the discussion follows a logical plan, that participation is fair, and that enough time is allocated for each topic.

The key to moderating or participating in a panel is to be well informed, to listen carefully to others, and to make sure that the discussion is coherent. The panel format is particularly interesting because it combines small group and public communication. Panelists must share ideas and reach conclusions within the group while also communicating to an audience. This is no easy task.

The Buzz Group

Some discussion formats are expressly designed to be used as supplements to formal presentations. Their goal is to increase audience response to a speech or public discussion. One such format is the **buzz group**. Once the initial presentation is finished, audience members are divided into small discussion groups and are asked to respond to the speaker's topic. For example, a conference on the topic of wellness might begin with a speech on the importance of a healthy diet. To reinforce the speaker's points, audience members might be asked to divide into groups of seven or eight people, to make a list of factors that reinforce unhealthy eating habits, and then to think of ways to resist these negative influences. After members of each group have had time to discuss their ideas, a spokesperson reports the group's conclusions to the assembly as a whole.

The buzz session increases audience involvement by placing audience members in a small, friendly group. Members who might be intimidated by speaking up in a large forum often feel comfortable in the small-group context. In addition, discussion makes the speaker's points more personal and more memorable.

The Role-Playing Group

An even stronger way to involve audience members is through role-playing. In role-playing, people are placed in small groups, are given a scenario, and are asked to act out their responses. By experiencing a situation rather than passively discussing it, members can get in touch with their emotions and can practice new behaviors. After a role-play is over, the actors discuss what occurred and what they learned from the experience.

> By experiencing a situation rather than passively discussing it, members can get in touch with their emotions and can practice new behaviors.

Role-playing is often used to help people understand one another's point of view. In a workshop designed to increase child–parent interaction, for example, children and parents might be asked to switch roles, each playing the part of the other. This role reversal may help them understand one another's concerns and motivations. Role-playing is also often used to help people practice new or difficult behaviors. A campaign against drunk driving might ask high school students to practice taking the keys away from a friend who has had too much to drink. By rehearsing this response in a supportive group context, the students learn what to do if they are ever actually confronted with the problem.

Role-playing is not for everyone. If group members are too inhibited to play their roles or do not take them seriously, this technique will not work. If the scenarios revolve around highly sensitive issues, role-plays can become highly emotional and can get out of hand. In such cases, the presence of a moderator with training and experience is a must.

COMMUNICATING IN VIRTUAL GROUPS

In the past, most group communication occurred face to face. Increasingly, however, group communication is becoming mediated. Communication technologies now exist that can link group members at remote sites to one another, connect group members to information databases, allow members to communicate with individuals outside the group, and help to structure group tasks.[49]

Computer-mediated groups have unique features that distinguish them from face-to-face groups. As Robyn Parker has argued, virtual groups are not simply groups at a distance.[50] Not only are group members physically separated as they communicate, they may never even have met one another in person. In addition, their messages are often asynchronous, with members sending and responding to messages at various times of the day. Because virtual groups do not share a common location, the identification that comes from seeing each other daily or being familiar with on-site events does not occur.

These characteristics offer unique challenges to group members. Members may be slow to develop trust, and the reduction of social cues that is a result of computer mediation can lead to misunderstandings. In addition, incidental communication that might occur when members of FtF groups meet by chance at lunch or carry on a casual conversation in the parking lot is obviously restricted. Informal channels, which often support formal channels in on-site groups, are severely limited. Parker argues that virtual dynamics are more unpredictable than traditional group dynamics, and that virtual members have a more difficult time fulfilling the group maintenance functions that are necessary to build cohesion and trust. Finally, virtual groups depend on the ability of members to use technology effectively. When members lack access to or are unfamiliar with computer-supported technology, group communication can become impossible.

Are computer-mediated groups as successful and productive as face-to-face groups? In some cases, they are; in others, they are not. Certainly, strong commitments can and do emerge in Internet forums and problem-solving groups; nevertheless, effective group cooperation is not always the result. On tasks that involve idea generation, for example, computer-mediated groups appear to be more effective than face-to-face groups. On problem-solving and negotiation tasks, however, face-to-face groups have the advantage.[51] Members of mediated groups have also been found to be more negative and less polite than are individuals in face-to-face groups, although this depends on the group. Some groups allow uninhibited interaction, while others have strong politeness norms.[52]

A number of studies have also found a participation equalization effect in mediated groups. That is, at least in initial interactions, people communicating electronically participate more equally, presumably because the status cues that would normally make reticent members inhibited are not present. Over time, however, this effect dissipates as members establish status hierarchies.[53] Group members gain status online in many ways, including loquacity, skilled use of software, expertise and control of information, and clever performance.[54]

Working effectively in virtual groups is not always easy. Some people find it more challenging than others.[55] What does it take to be an effective virtual group member? One factor is the ability to work independently. Another is the ability to tolerate uncertainty and ambiguity. In addition, a willingness to trust others makes members valuable to a virtual group because trust fosters cohesiveness and satisfaction with group process. As Marshall Scott Poole points out, there is a cyclical relationship between trust and group effectiveness. When members trust one another, they are more likely to fulfill their obligations, which builds more trust and more commitment to the group.[56] Finally, the ability to accept and understand people who may be culturally different has been found to increase group effectiveness.

Whatever the challenges of computer-mediated group interaction, most organizations today find benefits in linking people who are geographically separated. Andrea Hollingshead and Noshir Contractor point out that organizations see real competitive advantages in having employees located in different time zones:

> In some cases the members of these teams are "e-lancers" (electronic free-lancers) who coalesce on a short-term project and then disperse. In other cases, the technologies have the potential to enable the organization to hire and retain the best people, regardless of location. . . . These changes have led scholars to call for a reconceptualization of groups as much more fluid, dynamic, multiplex and activity based.[57]

> Indeed, many group scholars now think of groups not just as collections of people but as knowledge networks made up of people and the media they use.

Indeed, many group scholars now think of groups not just as collections of people but as **knowledge networks** made up of people and the media they use.[58] We will have more to say about the importance of using technology to manage information flow and about the challenges of working in virtual groups in the next chapter when we look at virtual teams in organizational settings. For now, it is enough to realize that learning to use technology skillfully is not a choice but a necessity, one that affects every aspect of communication, including group interaction.

BECOMING A MORE RESPONSIBLE COMMUNICATOR

Groups can bring out the best or the worst in us. At their best, they can produce the kind of synergy in which members outdo themselves. At their worst, they can be hotbeds of disagreement and personal ambition. It's easy for members to lose sight of group goals as they pursue individual agendas. This means that group members need to work hard to be responsible communicators for the sake of the group and shared goals. Following are issues to keep in mind as you interact with others in small groups:

- The behavior of each group member has consequences. As we saw in our discussion of groupthink, when policy-making groups go awry, there can be serious repercussions. Although the kinds of policy decisions we make in everyday life may not be earth-shaking, they still have an impact on the people who must live with them.

- In addition to showing concern for those outside the group who will be affected by group decisions, members should also show concern and respect for one another during group deliberations. This means giving each member's ideas a complete hearing. In some cases, it also means encouraging quiet members to speak up and listening patiently to those with whom you may disagree.

- Responsible group communication is unselfish. Of course, no one enters a group without a personal agenda; nevertheless, it's important to be as honest as possible about personal goals. It is irresponsible to manipulate others to gain selfish ends or to exercise personal power. Participants should not be coerced or manipulated into making decisions that have hidden outcomes and should make up their own minds on the basis of the best possible information available.

- To ensure high-quality decisions, it is important to enter deliberations with information that is as accurate as possible. You must also be willing to admit when you need further data; pretending to know more than you really do in order to save face or dismissing data that do not fit your personal biases is irresponsible. Because group members are under many pressures to solve problems rapidly, it's also important to avoid carelessness and premature consensus. Questions that arise during deliberations should be explored fully and thoughtfully.

- Group members have an obligation to express their views. Although it is often difficult to speak up, especially when groups are in the throes of groupthink, it is irresponsible to agree with a decision you do not support. Honest disagreement can only benefit group deliberations.

SUMMARY

We spend much of our social and work lives communicating in groups. This chapter looks at the special characteristics of group communication and offers advice for increasing group effectiveness.

A group is a collection of individuals who interact over time, becoming interdependent, developing unique patterns of behavior, and achieving a collective identity. Although it is difficult to say exactly how large a group can be before it ceases to be a group, it is safe to say that a small group must consist of at least three people. The ideal group size for effective communication is realized when the group is large enough to generate creative ideas yet small enough for equal participation.

People communicate in groups because the presence of others increases information, provides support, and helps members achieve individual goals. Successful groups create group synergy and are often more effective than their best members. Sometimes, however, groups take on tasks that are inappropriate, and social loafing or free-riding can occur. Like members of dyads, group members experience dialectical tensions. They must satisfy group and individual needs and must learn to balance task and maintenance roles. In groups, both the individual member and the group as a whole try to influence one another. If each meets the other's needs, commitment is high, and members pass through stages that deepen their involvement. If either party fails to meet its obligations, the group becomes unstable, and members drop out. To function effectively, members must also fulfill task and maintenance roles, working to get the job done and to ensure that the group atmosphere is pleasant, while avoiding negative individual roles and hidden agendas. When a group becomes too confident and fails to think realistically about its task, groupthink can occur. By assigning a member to act as critic, by taking criticisms seriously, and by holding second-chance meetings, groups can avoid groupthink.

Group membership is an important source of social identity. Members try to fit their groups' prototypes, and they often depersonalize those who don't fit. Categorizing others on the basis of group membership allows members to reduce uncertainty and bolster self-esteem.

Like dyads, groups go through phases. Often, the first is an orientation or forming phase and the second a conflict or storming phase. The third phase is usually characterized by norming, as members work out rules and roles. In the fourth, or performing, phase, groups settle down to work. Finally in the final or adjourning phase, members prepare to separate. Some groups pass through these phases in an orderly way, while others may simultaneously work on task, maintenance, and topic issues, returning to earlier stages if development is not smooth.

Groups must resolve issues of leadership as they develop. Scholars have used a variety of approaches to study leadership. The trait approach focuses on personal characteristics, the styles approach on the methods leaders use to influence members. The situational approach looks at the way external factors affect style choices, and the functional approach examines shared behaviors that help move the group forward. There are definite behaviors would-be leaders should avoid, including being absent, uncooperative, domineering, rude, or irresponsible.

Members can increase effectiveness by sharing hidden profiles, avoiding defensiveness, and using techniques such as the standard agenda, brainstorming, nominal group technique, and the like. Finally, they should be aware of the kinds of formats used in public discussions.

Groups today are often computer-mediated. Virtual groups are not just groups at a distance; they have unique characteristics that call for special skills. In addition to technological competence, members must be able to work independently, willing to trust others, and sensitive to cultural differences. On tasks involving idea generation, computer-mediated groups outdo face-to-face groups, but they fall behind when it comes to negotiation or problem solving. Online groups can also be uninhibited. In the early stages of group development, online members participate more frequently than do their offline counterparts, although over time, status hierarchies develop online too. Because more and more organizations find it advantageous to create computer-mediated groups, learning to take part in mediated group interaction is a necessary communication skill.

When individuals interact in groups, they bear an added ethical burden because their actions affect not only themselves but also the group as a whole. Honesty, concern for others, willingness to listen, and the ability to admit ignorance are necessary qualities of the ethical group member.

KEY TERMS

Listed below are the key terms used in this chapter, along with the number of the page where each is explained.

group   (165)
interaction   (166)
interdependence   (166)
shared behavioral
    standards   (166)
collective identity   (166)
triads   (167)
group synergy   (168)
interpersonal needs
    (169)
inclusion need   (169)
control need   (169)
affection need   (169)
social loafing   (170)
additive tasks   (170)
free-riding   (170)
disjunctive tasks   (170)
group socialization   (172)
process evaluation   (172)
commitment   (172)
role transition   (172)
idiosyncrasy credit   (174)
mentor   (174)
task dimension   (175)
productivity   (175)
maintenance or social
    dimension   (175)
group cohesiveness   (175)
task roles   (175)
maintenance roles
    (175)

negative roles   (175)
hidden agenda   (177)
groupthink   (178)
social identity   (179)
group prototypes   (180)
trait approach   (182)
styles approach   (182)
situational approach   (182)
functional approach   (183)
hidden profile research
    (184)
defensive climate   (185)
supportive climate   (185)
evaluation   (185)
description   (185)
control   (185)
problem
    orientation   (185)
strategy   (185)
spontaneity   (185)
neutrality   (185)
empathy   (185)
superiority   (186)
equality   (186)
certainty   (186)
provisionalism   (186)
agendas   (186)
reflective thinking   (186)
standard agenda   (186)
problem identification
    (186)

problem   (186)
problem analysis   (188)
restraining forces   (188)
helping forces   (188)
force-field analysis   (188)
criteria selection   (188)
solution generation   (188)
solution evaluation and
    selection   (188)
solution
    implementation   (188)
brainstorming   (189)
part-changing
    method   (189)
checkerboard
    method   (189)
find-something-similar
    method   (189)
nominal group
    technique   (189)
public discussion
    formats   (190)
symposium   (190)
forum   (191)
panel discussion   (191)
buzz group   (191)
role-playing   (192)
participation equalization
    effect   (193)
knowledge networks
    (194)

SUGGESTED READINGS

Beebe, Steven A., Masterson, John T., & Sherblom, John C. (2007). *Communicating in small groups: Principles and practices.* Boston: Allyn & Bacon.

Provides a combination of theory, application, and skills, with expanded coverage of team building and critical thinking.

Hirokawa, Randy, & others. (2003). *Small group communication theory and practice: An anthology.* (8th ed.). Los Angeles: Roxbury.

A collection of readable essays from major scholars in the field; especially strong on small-group theory.

Wheelan, Susan A. (2005). *The handbook of group research and practice.* Thousand Oaks, CA: Sage.

A comprehensive review of major theories and approaches with articles by group scholars from a variety of disciplines.

Organizational Communication

Each of us is affected by and, in turn, affects organizations.

Organizations are everywhere. In the United States today, there is no way to escape their influence. Public school systems, organized religions, groups such as the Boy and Girl Scouts, hospitals, banks, charities and relief agencies, fast-food restaurant chains, and certainly the U.S. government, are all examples of organizations that have an impact, large or small, on our lives. Each of us is affected by and, in turn, affects organizations. As such, we are all "stakeholders" in the complex, goal-directed, social systems we call organizations.

This chapter is about communication in complex organizations. In looking at this communication context, we'll combine traditional and contemporary views of what organizational communication is. We'll begin by considering how information flows through organizations, examining informal pathways such as the organizational grapevine as well as more formal communication routes. We'll also consider the importance of building healthy workplace relationships. We'll then take a more interpretive view and discuss ways in which organizational cultures are created and maintained through communication. Finally, we'll focus on two specific skill areas, interviewing and use of organizational technology. Throughout, we'll concern ourselves with some of the ethical issues that confront organizations today.

WHAT IS AN ORGANIZATION?

An **organization** is a system consisting of a large number of people working together in a structured way to accomplish multiple goals. The college or university you attend, for example, is a complex organization that involves many people working together to achieve a common educational goal. Each person plays a different role depending on his or her position within the organization. Faculty, administrators, staff, and students have their own organizational identities and their own ways of behaving, and the success of the university depends in large part on each group's willingness and ability to fit into the university's structures. If, for example, faculty started to behave like students or students like administrators, the whole enterprise would likely fall apart (although the results might be quite interesting). So as you read this chapter, remember that you're already part of a complex organization. Consider how communication flows through your campus. Think about how power is distributed and used. And try to use what you learn about organizational communication to diagnose problems and understand the climate of the complex organization of which you are currently an integral member.

Characteristics of Organizations

Organizations have several characteristics that make them unique. Among these are interdependence, hierarchical structure, linkage to the environment, and a dependence on communication.

Perhaps the characteristic that best defines an organization is interdependence. Interdependence means that all the members within an organization are connected to one another. They share a common fate: what affects one part of the organization affects every other part. Interdependence is the reason people join organizations in the first place. People in organizations know that by working together, they can accomplish goals they could not achieve on their own.

In addition, organizations are hierarchical. A hierarchy is a system that is divided into orders and ranks. In a hierarchy, status and power are not distributed equally: some people are subordinate to others. The classic form of the hierarchical organization is the bureaucracy. In a bureaucracy, there is a clear chain of command. Jobs are usually specialized, and employees are rewarded on the basis of performance. When we use the term *bureaucracy* now, we generally equate it with red tape and inefficiency. However, when sociologist Max Weber first used the term, the bureaucracy was thought to be the ideal organization for Western industrial democracies because of its efficiency and impersonality.[1] Since Weber, the concept of strict hierarchical control has been criticized. Nevertheless, division of labor and recognition of status differences are still characteristic of most complex organizations.

It is important to keep in mind that, like other living systems, organizations are linked to their environments. Just like living creatures, organizations cannot survive without a healthy environment. And just like living creatures, organizations change (and sometimes destroy) their environments. An obvious example occurs when a manufacturing company depletes local resources. But there are other, less apparent, instances as well. When a large corporation moves its corporate headquarters its former community suffers. When a college or university expands, it creates pressures (for example, energy, transportation, and housing needs) as well as opportunities (both economic and cultural) for those who share its environment. Organizations must be aware of the damage they can sometimes cause. They must also be capable of adapting to changes in the environment that surrounds them.

It's common practice to talk about organizations as though they had an identity independent of the activities that define them. When the newspaper reports that "the Fed is lowering interest rates," the Fed seems to be a "thing." When we announce, "I'll be working at MTV next year," MTV sounds like a place. But Tom D. Daniels and his colleagues point out that we should not think of organizations as "things," or as "places," but rather as elaborate and complicated forms of human behavior. In other words, "an organization is not merely a container for behavior. Rather, an organization literally is human behavior."[2] And one of the most important kinds of organizational behavior is communication. People in organizations argue, cooperate, make decisions, solve problems, and forge relationships.

One of the things that make organizational communication so important is that the very nature of the organization depends on the way members communicate. Marshall Scott Poole and Robert McPhee have pointed out the importance of communication in creating and maintaining organizational identity, or climate.[3] Taking what is called a structurational approach, they believe that there is a reciprocal relationship between organizational structures and organizational communication. How does this work? Well, as individuals settle into organizations, they begin to communicate in ways that they feel are appropriate to the organization. For example, they may learn that complaints and excuses are considered unprofessional. By following perceived rules—for example, by hanging tough when things get bad and taking criticism on the chin—they create an organizational climate that stresses personal accountability and individual responsibility. This climate, in turn, may generate new rules of behavior—such as the rule that employees should take tough stands and argue forcefully for their beliefs. Poole and his colleagues base their theories on the work of sociologist Anthony Giddens. Giddens believes that social structures (including organizational structures such as climate) are continually produced and reproduced by

Unless the organization works hard to build connections, workers can get lost in corporate bureaucracies.

human interaction. Giddens once said that the structures in human societies are "buildings that are at every moment being reconstructed by the very bricks that compose them."[4] Organizations, too, are structures—structures built on a foundation of human communication.

Why Communicate in Organizations?

Good communication skills are absolutely essential to organizational life. It's through communication that people in organizations coordinate their efforts and achieve their goals. When communication succeeds, the organization is likely to be effective and efficient and workers satisfied and committed. When it fails, both the organization and its individual members suffer. Charles Redding, a scholar who studied organizations for many years, lists just a few of the problems that can occur when communication is faulty:

> When communication succeeds, the organization is likely to be effective and efficient and workers satisfied and committed. When it fails, both the organization and its individual members suffer.

> insensitive supervision, confusing instructions, fruitless meetings, deceptive announcements, vicious defense of "turf," biased (or entirely omitted) performance evaluations, misleading reports, empty promises, backstabbing tête-à-têtes with the boss, privacy-invading questions, sexist or racist harassment, scapegoating memorandum, clumsy explanations, paucity of information, conflicting orders, ambiguity (both intentional and unintentional), worship of inane regulations, refusal to listen to bad news, and rejection of innovative ideas—not to mention stubborn reliance upon autocratic, downward-directed messages in general.[5]

Only by learning to communicate effectively in organizations can we recognize and avoid problems such as these.

Being skilled in organizational communication can also enhance our careers. Organizations look for and reward employees "who understand how communication functions in an organization, who have developed a wide repertory of written and oral communication skills, and who have learned when and how to use those skills." Such employees have "more successful careers and contribute more fully to their organizations" than do people without these skills.[6]

Modes of Discourse in Organizations

Communication in the organizational context differs in some fundamental ways from everyday interpersonal or group communication. First, because organizations are hierarchical, members are expected to act not just as individuals but as incumbents of organizational positions. This latter identity puts some restrictions on communication. As Charles Conrad points out, even a strong personal relationship with a supervisor doesn't mean that we can communicate with that supervisor as we would with a friend. While at work, we have to maintain at least some degree of relational distance and detachment.[7] Because organizational communication is driven not only by our own personal goals but also by the need to work together to achieve common goals, it is more formal and deferential than communication in other contexts.

Second, there are unique types of communications, or communication genres, that occur only in organizations. Business letters, memoranda, meetings, interviews, and so on are widely recognized genres in American business.[8] Each genre is governed by rules of discourse that define not only what should and should not be conveyed but also how it should be conveyed. Letters of recommendation, for example, must speak to the qualifications of the candidate while avoiding irrelevant information. A recommendation letter (and this is a true example) that starts out, "Although she is no beauty, you can count on her to get the job done," violates the rules of proper business etiquette, betrays a sexist bias, and gives irrelevant information. Part of fitting into an organization is knowing what you can and cannot say in certain situations and choosing the correct genre to convey your message.

> Part of fitting into an organization is knowing what you can and cannot say in certain situations and choosing the correct genre to convey your message.

Communication genres and the rules that define them are, of course, culture-specific. The American coffee break, for example, could be considered an informal communication genre. But what goes on there is not the same as what occurs when Japanese stop for tea. Bruce Feilor, who worked as a teacher in Japan, provides a perfect example when he describes the meaning of a uniquely Japanese organizational genre, the *aisatsu* tea-break. When Feilor first reported to his office, work ground to a halt as he and his principal were served cups of green tea and a plate of intricately wrapped sponge cakes. As he explains:

> *Aisatsu greeting ceremonies like this occurred in school and in my office no fewer than eight times in the course of a normal day. . . . That meant eight times a day everyone must rise and bow to the guest. Eight trays of tea that must be made, served, drunk, retrieved, and cleaned. Eight plates of sponge cakes stuffed with bean paste, fancy rice crackers, cookies, or plastic containers of jelly that must be eaten. It didn't seem to matter what was said in these meetings. Their purpose was to establish the unofficial paths along which tacit deals and arrangements are made. As I was . . . drinking tea and bowing to strangers, I was creating lines along which I could later walk, if need be.*[9]

Although the lines of communication may be different in the United States, they still serve the same ends: creating an atmosphere in which the work of the organization can be accomplished. To work effectively in organizations, one must know when to stick to well-worn paths and when to blaze new trails.

MANAGING ORGANIZATIONAL COMMUNICATION

Early scholars in the field of organizational communication were quick to realize that information is a precious organizational resource. They recognized that high-quality information is the fuel that powers organizational decision making and that the ability to create, analyze, store, and retrieve information is a source of power within any organization.

Understanding Formal and Informal Channels

It is common to distinguish between two kinds of channels: formal and informal. Formal channels of communication occur when information flows through a structured chain of command officially recognized by the organization. For example, if a worker hands in a report to his or her manager, who then sends it on to an immediate supervisor, information flows through formal channels. When information takes a more personal and less structured path, informal channels of communication come into play. When a sales representative meets the head of personnel's secretary in the lunchroom and discusses rumors about cutbacks, the worker is taking advantage of informal channels. Both forms of communication are essential to the life of the organization.

Formal Organizational Structure

Formal channels are often made explicit in an organizational chart, a visual representation of the organization's chain of command. Organizational charts, such as the Campus Safety Organizational Chart shown in Figure 8.1, specify formal relationships between organizational positions. They indicate where, in a hierarchy of responsibility and power, each job is located. They show who supervises whom, and they also illustrate preferred communication pathways.

As you can see in Figure 8.1, information can flow in several directions. Downward flow occurs when someone near the top of the organization sends a message to someone near the bottom (for example, when the associate director of campus safety sends a memo to the escort service supervisor). We find upward flow when a message travels from the bottom of the chart toward the top (for example, when a message from a records clerk ends up on the desk of the operations director). Finally, horizontal flow takes place when communication occurs between people at the same level (for example, when an investigator discusses an automobile break-in with a parking attendant and a patrol officer or when the heads of the community service, training, and administration departments meet to discuss budget needs).

Communication overload is a common problem in complex organizations.

Figure 8.1 Organizational Chart: Campus Safety Department at XYZ University

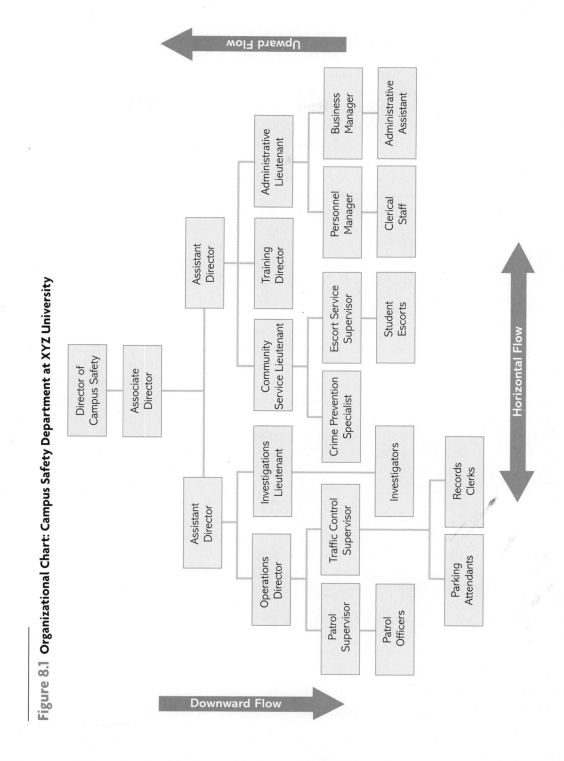

Downward Communication.   Instructions, appraisals, and announcements are examples of communications that typically flow downward. When a supervisor discusses the results of a yearly evaluation with a subordinate or explains travel policies to new employees, the supervisor is using downward communication. Unfortunately, employees in most organizations report dissatisfaction with downward communication. Daniels and his colleagues list some of the problems responsible for this dissatisfaction. Included are "inadequacy of information, inappropriate means of diffusing information, filtering of information, and a general pervasive climate of dominance and submission."[10]

Dissatisfaction with the amount and type of information received is a serious problem in most organizations. Employees report, on the one hand, that they often don't receive enough information to do their jobs. On the other hand, they report receiving too much information. Often, they feel buried under an avalanche of forms, letters, memos, bulletins, reports, and emails. Given these seemingly contradictory responses, it is reasonable to conclude that organizational members receive a lot of information but that, unfortunately, it is not the information they want or need. This may occur because managers don't consider the needs of employees when they send out messages or because they don't choose the correct medium. Several scholars have found that organizational members receive too much mediated communication and not enough face-to-face communication from their superiors.[11]

> Dissatisfaction with the amount and type of information received is a serious problem in most organizations. Employees feel buried under an avalanche of forms, letters, memos, bulletins, reports, and emails.

Downward communication often contains information that is misleading or downright wrong. If you've ever played the game called "telephone," in which players pass on a message by whispering it to the person next in line, you know that messages change as they pass from person to person. This change is known as message filtering, and it is a serious problem in formal communication. As messages flow downward, the gist of the message may get lost in the process. The more links through which information must pass (the "taller" the organization), the more likely messages are to undergo distortion. Table 8.1 lists some of the kinds of distortion that occur during serial transmission (transmission of a message in a one-way direction from one person to the next).

Table 8.1 Effects of Serial Transmission

Leveling	Details are left out as the amount of information in the message is reduced. The message grows shorter.
Sharpening	Certain high points are given special significance and elaboration.
Assimilation	Memory of the message is affected by the sender's frame of reference. Unfamiliar material is changed so that it makes sense to the sender.

Adapted from David W. Johnson and Frank P. Johnson, *Joining together: Group theory and group skills* (5th ed.). Boston: Allyn and Bacon, 1994, p. 159.

A number of things can be done to improve accuracy during serial transmission. Managers can build redundancy into their messages and employees can ask for clarification when messages are ambiguous. Unfortunately, these simple solutions are rarely used because superiors are often too rushed to think carefully about their communications and subordinates are often reluctant to ask questions of their supervisors. Furthermore, both superiors and subordinates may not know that there is a problem. Managers in particular tend to overestimate the clarity and frequency of their communications.[12]

Information may also be deliberately withheld. If managers anticipate that a piece of news will anger employees, decrease the organization's competitive edge, or be criticized by external stakeholders, they may decide to keep the information to themselves or even to lie about it. Unfortunately, this practice creates a climate of mistrust, damaging the credibility of future downward communication.

> Some message distortion is inevitable in any system that uses serial transmission, even when those involved do their best to communicate accurately.

Upward Communication.   Although most organizational messages flow downward, some flow from the bottom up. Typical of these are progress reports, warnings of job-related problems, and suggestions or feedback about organizational policies. When employees submit project reports, alert their superiors to changes in client needs, or express their objections to reorganization efforts, they are using upward communication.

Research shows that organizations often neglect upward communication, especially when it is negative or when it calls for organizational change. As a result, suggestion programs may be implemented in name only, with very little attention paid by either superiors or subordinates. Furthermore, upward communication is often distorted. Subordinates fear being seen as the bearers of bad tidings and tend to withhold information that will reflect badly on them. Research shows, for example, that subordinates who are insecure, who don't trust their superiors, or who are very ambitious tend to distort upward flow and withhold negative information.[13]

In addition, gatekeepers may affect upward flow. A **gatekeeper** is someone (such as an administrative assistant or receptionist) who is in a position to pass on or discard information. While gatekeepers can provide a valuable service by filtering out trivial messages, they can also suppress information that is badly needed. As we saw in Chapter 7, one of the characteristics of groupthink is the presence of self-appointed mind-guards who paint an unrealistic picture of events in order to protect the leader from negative information.

What can an organization do to improve upward flow? First, managers can seek out bad news and encourage subordinates to tell the truth, no matter how negative it may be.[14] In addition, unnecessary gatekeepers can be eliminated, or special channels can be provided to bypass cumbersome serial transmission. Some organizations have a special position called **ombudsman**. This person's job is to listen to workers at lower levels of the organization and pass their concerns directly to the top. Finally, the most important thing managers can do to increase upward flow is to establish a climate of trust and openness.

Taking Advantage of Informal Structures

In everyday life, people are connected to one another in complex and intriguing ways. It's not uncommon to meet a stranger and, after talking awhile, discover that you have friends in common, that you are in fact connected to one another through a network of acquaintances. It may be a small world after all. To find out exactly how interconnected the world is, psychologist Stanley Milgram set up an experiment in which he asked individuals from Nebraska and Kansas to try to contact strangers in Massachusetts.[15] His subjects were each given a message and asked to send it to a personal acquaintance. The acquaintances were then asked to forward the message to someone they knew personally. This continued until the message reached its goal. Surprisingly, it took on average only five or six links. Milgram discovered that we are all part of a giant network, connected to others (including Kevin Bacon) by "six degrees of separation."

Acquaintance networks like those studied by Milgram also occur in organizations. People are linked to one another through personal relationships that often do not mirror the formal channels found in organizational charts. The problem with formal channels is that they are artificially constructed. Because they fail to take into account employees' social bonds and friendship choices, employees often bypass them by creating informal links to people they trust or like.

> We are all part of a giant network, connected to others by "six degrees of separation."

Informal channels serve to counterbalance the inefficiency and distortion found in formal channels. When employees want to find out what's really going on, they may turn to informal channels. As Charles Conrad points out, "if organizational communication really was restricted to formal channels, most people, in most organizations, most of the time could honestly say that they do not know what is going on."[16]

The Grapevine.   Informal channels are often referred to as the grapevine. When someone says, "I heard it through the grapevine," he or she means that the news came through an informal channel. Where did this usage arise? Evidently, during the Civil War, telegraph lines were threaded through trees in a complicated pattern resembling a grapevine. Later on, the term was adopted to describe any system of messages that does not follow a straight-line, predictable pattern.

Susan Hellwig and Keith Davis have both studied grapevine communication and have come to a number of conclusions. First, the grapevine arises because individuals have personal interests and needs that are not satisfied by formal channels. According to Keith Davis, "a lively grapevine reflects the deep psychological need of people to talk about their jobs and their company as a central life interest. Without it, the company would literally be sick."[17]

Second, although it's common to equate the grapevine with rumor, rumors make up only a small proportion of the information on the grapevine. The grapevine contains useful and valid information as well. Third, information on the grapevine may be incomplete, but it is quite accurate. In fact, it has been estimated to be anywhere from 75 percent to 95 percent accurate. Sometimes, it may even be more reliable than formally conveyed information. Conrad argues that it is also richer in content than formal communication, and because it usually operates on a face-to-face basis, it also allows for immediate feedback and clarification. Although managers may caution employees not to use the grapevine, their concern may be due to their own lack of control rather than to the grapevine's accuracy.

Fitting into an organization means understanding and accepting organizational culture. Usually, the rules are not expressed as clearly as they are in this photo.

Network Analysis. Informal communication can be very influential. Organizations should therefore understand and take advantage of informal networks. One tool for understanding networks is called network analysis, a method of mapping informal communication patterns. Network analysts can identify who is connected to whom in the organization. They can also specify the role each individual plays in an informal network. For example, some individuals, called opinion leaders, are at the center of things; they are the first people others go to for information. Other individuals, called isolates, have very few connections with coworkers; they are "out of the loop" when it comes to information. In times of institutional change, it makes sense for management to seek out and discuss the situation with opinion leaders rather than with isolates. If opinion leaders can be persuaded that a proposed change is good, they can influence others in their networks. It also makes sense to try to reintegrate isolates into the organization, especially if the isolates are keeping valuable ideas to themselves. Table 8.2 lists some other key network roles. As you look at the table, ask yourself how you, as a manager, could use network analysis to enhance organizational communication.

Loose and Tight Coupling

Another distinction that describes organizational communication is the construct of coupling. Organizations may be either tightly or loosely coupled. Subunits within an organization that are closely connected and highly interdependent are characterized by tight coupling. In such an organization, anything that influences one part of the organization influences all parts. Information flow is rapid. Tightly coupled organizations are easy to control and standardize. But because subsystems are so closely connected, a problem that affects one part of the organization can affect all parts: in essence, subsystems are like dominoes—when the first goes down, the rest follow.[18] In fact, sociologist Charles Perrow suggests that one of the factors that led to the Three Mile Island nuclear accident was the fact that the system was so complex and so tightly coupled.[19]

> Sociologist Charles Perrow suggests that one of the factors that led to the Three Mile Island nuclear accident was the fact that the system was so complex and so tightly coupled.

When the relationship between subunits in an organization is relatively weak, the organization is characterized by loose coupling. Each unit acts in a relatively independent fashion, and an event that influences one unit may have only indirect effects on others. Here, information flow is more gradual. One of the apparent disadvantages of loose coupling, lack of standardization, may sometimes be an advantage. Because loosely coupled units are relatively independent, a given unit can respond rapidly and creatively to change. Of course, loose coupling does not always lead to positive results; units can also "preserve archaic, outmoded traditions."[20] Colleges and universities are prime examples of loosely coupled organizations. Individual departments are usually fairly autonomous and will defend to the death any attempt by an outsider to interfere with the academic decisions they make.

Table 8.2 Network Roles

Boundary Spanner or Cosmopolite	An organizational member who has contact with individuals outside the organization's boundaries. Often, boundary spanners tend to occur at the top or bottom of organizations. They represent the organization and can bring valuable information into the organization.
Bridge	A member of a clique who has connections with another clique.
Clique	A group of people who communicate more with each other than they do with others in the organization. Members of cliques may have similar jobs or share a common status.
Isolate	Someone who is outside the informal network. An isolate has no links to any clique.
Liaison	Someone who connects two cliques without being a member of either one. A liaison may help spread information between people who might normally not speak to one another.
Opinion Leader	Someone within a clique who can influence the attitudes and actions of members.
Star	The member of a network connected to the most members.

Building Effective Teams: Structural Diversity, Transactive Memory, and Trust

In the last section, we looked at downward and upward communication. In this section we focus on *horizontal communication*, the kind of communication that is used between people at the same level in the organization. Whenever we work with coworkers on team projects, we are engaged in horizontal communication. And more and more, organizations expect individuals to take part in teams. Unfortunately, not all teams are effective.

In the last chapter we saw that when group members pool resources they can be more productive than single individuals. We also saw, however, that group members do not always share unique information with one another, preferring instead to solve problems in familiar ways using commonly held information. Because information is the life-blood of organizations, and because single individuals can no longer know everything they need to in order to make optimal decisions, it is necessary for organizations to encourage information sharing. This section looks at several ways organizations can encourage knowledge-sharing including composing teams with diverse experts, keeping track of who knows what in the organization, and encouraging trust.

When people on a team come from the same organizational unit, share the same work methods, or have the same kind of training, there is often a danger that they will stay with the tried and true and be reluctant to accept creative ideas or try new approaches. To counter this danger, organizational experts now recommend the creation of work teams that exhibit structural diversity, that is, teams with members from different units within the organization and with different training and knowledge. For example, rather than composing a team entirely of employees from the research and development division at a single location, organizations who are creating new products may include employees from their marketing, sales, and human factors divisions as well. In this way the team can call on many areas of expertise. It has been shown that structurally diverse teams have a greater range of knowledge and see problems from more vantage points.[21]

But how does the organization determine who has expertise? And how does it make sure that information flows to the people who can best use it? The answer lies in keeping track of who knows what. When the organization has a systematic way to remember and identify who possesses expert knowledge, that is, when it possesses an effective transactive memory system, it is no longer necessary for everyone to know everything. Transactive memory systems "expand the total amount of knowledge available to members of work groups in organizations," because they allow the organization to make effective use of their employees' knowledge.[22]

Optimal transactive memory depends on an organization's ability to recognize expertise, to distribute new information to those who can make the best use of it, and to identify where to go when information is needed. How important is transactive memory? In some cases, it can be a matter of life and death. It has been argued, for example, that the *Columbia* space shuttle disaster of 2003 was at least partly due to the fact that the right information did not get to the right people.[23]

Despite the advantages that accrue when teams of experts work together, there can be communication challenges. It is sometimes difficult for individuals with different backgrounds to see things from one another's perspectives. Vocabulary can also be a problem when members use the technical jargon of their respective fields. The vocabulary of a senior chemist may be unintelligible to the people from advertising and vice versa. In addition, when organizational resources are limited, departments often compete for their share of the pie and may not communicate openly. For all of these reasons, the development of trust in teams is extremely important. **Trust** is an expectation that others will act in consistent and dependable ways. It is necessary for effective communication because it encourages employees to take risks and express themselves openly. Scholars have found that trust is associated with enhanced group and organizational performance, innovative behavior, effective crisis management, and overall satisfaction.[24] Trust has also been found to be an important predictor of success in virtual teams, a topic we will return to toward the end of this chapter.

INCREASING ORGANIZATIONAL SKILLS

To succeed in an organization you need to use all of the interpersonal and group skills we've talked about in previous chapters. In addition, you need to develop specific organizational skills. In this section, we look at the interviewing skills that gain you entry, the interpretive skills that allow you to fit into the organization's culture, and the relational skills that allow you to communicate professionally.

Interviewing Skills

An **interview** is a form of two-way communication having a predetermined and serious purpose in which participants ask and answer questions.[25] Interviews are used for many purposes: to orient and train employees, to survey their attitudes, to evaluate job performance, and to resolve complaints.[26] And of course interviews are used to select new employees. Since this latter form of interview is of immediate concern to most college students, we will look at it in some detail.[27]

Preparing for the Interview

Interviews are serious business. Talking off the cuff may be fine in everyday conversation, but it is not acceptable in a job interview. Preparation is a must. Interviewees should begin with a clear idea of their own strengths and weaknesses. They should also research the organization and prepare a cover letter and resume.

Before the interview, prospective employees need to review skills gained through coursework, personal experience, or previous employment. Facility in using computers, research ability, and graphic design skills are examples of **work-content skills**, skills that are directly related to a particular job. Skills that apply to a variety of situations and settings are called **transferable skills**. The abilities to define and solve problems, teach others, and manage time are examples. Finally, **self-management skills** include personal strengths such as flexibility, enthusiasm, and persistence. In addition to listing skills in these three areas, prospective employees should be prepared to discuss specific situations involving these skills. It is not enough for a candidate to tell an interviewer, "I can deal effectively with the public." The interviewer wants examples.

Before the interview, job candidates need to know as much as possible about the job they are seeking. By consulting standard reference books such as *Dun and Bradstreet's Career Guide* or *Hoover's Handbook of American Companies*, business magazines such as *Business Week* or *Fast Company*, company brochures and annual reports, and, of course, the Internet, candidates can walk in ready to answer two of the most frequently asked interview questions: "What do you know about our organization?" and "Why do you want to work here?"

Interviews are like exclusive parties: you can't crash the gate; you have to be invited. That means sending out resumes and cover letters that catch the eye of potential employers and make them want to meet with you. The **cover letter** highlights one's ability to do the job and motivates the employer to examine the resume. In the cover letter, prospective employees identify the position they are interested in, explain how they heard about it and why they are applying, emphasize how their qualifications meet job requirements, and make specific requests for an interview.

> Interviews are like exclusive parties: you can't crash the gate; you have to be invited. That means sending out resumes and cover letters that catch the eye of potential employers and make them want to meet with you.

The **resume** is a profile of the candidate's background and qualifications. It communicates who the job seeker is. Because resumes are generally limited to a single page, every word counts. The resume should include contact information, a statement of career objectives, a summary of education and work experience, a list of special skills or interests, and the names, addresses, and phone numbers of references. It goes without saying that both letter and resume must be completely error free. A single misspelled word or grammatical error can be enough to eliminate the writer from further consideration. Employers have come to expect a certain format for resumes. An excellent source of information about current resume formats is the career services office at your school. Career counselors can offer more specific advice and show you models to follow. In the meantime, Table 8.3 gives you an example of what a resume should *not* look like. See if you can spot all the mistakes.

Answering and Asking Questions

Success in the actual interview is measured by how well candidates answer (and ask) questions. Although there is no way to anticipate all the questions the interviewer will ask, preparation and practice can help. Table 8.4 lists some frequently asked interview questions. By thinking about how to answer these questions and by practicing responses, you can increase the likelihood that you will present yourself effectively. As Table 8.4 also shows, not all the questions come from the interviewer.

Table 8.3 What's Wrong with This Resume?

PAT SUNDANCE

Local address:	Generic College, Generic, New York, 14850 **Permanent address:** 55 Main Street, Hometown, New Jersey.
Career Objective:	To use my people skills.
Education:	Generic College, Generic, New York Bachelor of Arts, May 2000 **Major:** speach communication **Minor:** Business **GPA:** 1.02 **Extracurricular Activities:** American Marketing Society, Skateboarding, Following Phish.
Experience:	Safety Patrol: John Paul Jones Elementary School. September 1990–June 1991. Asisted other students at crossings; gave out hall passes. Night clerk at Hollywood and Vine Video Store Anywhere, New York September 1999–June 1999. Rewound videotapes; learned names of all academy award nominated films since 1947; demonstrated people skills by talking with customers. Retail Salesperson at The Fissure Jeans Store Hometown, New Jersey June 2000–August 2000 Interacted courteously with customers; generated high volume of sales; solely responsible for handling customer complaints and returns; chosen salesperson of the month, July.
Special Skills:	Know how to use the computer, Lead singer in garage band.
References:	Robert Berlin High School Music Teacher George Patton High School Hometown, New York Illeana Cannes T.A., French 101 Anywhere College Anywhere, New York

Key to errors: No zip on permanent address. Phone number and e-mail should be included. Career objective vague. Several misspelled words, including name of major. GPA should not be listed if below 3.00. Some extracurricular activities are better left unsaid. Experience should be noted in reverse chronological order, beginning with most recent employment. List only relevant experience. Describe work-related aspects of prior experience. Be specific about special skills and make sure they're job related. Why are there no references from Hollywood and Vine or the Fissure? Overall layout is poor. Incidentally, description of employment at Fissure is fine.

Interviewees are expected to ask questions. But watch what you ask. If your only concern is with salary, office size, and benefits rather than with the nature and challenges of the job itself, you will come across as self-absorbed. In most cases, it is best to avoid questions about salary in the first interview and to focus instead on learning about the organization and the position. Throughout the entire process, it's essential to demonstrate self-confidence, openness, and respect.

Like many things in life, the interview is not over until it's over. It is common nowadays for job candidates to follow up with a brief, professional letter thanking the interviewer for his or her time and restating your interest in the company. This gives a candidate one more chance to stand out from the crowd and make a positive impression.

Table 8.4 Typical Interview Questions

Questions about Career Objectives and Goals
Some Typical Questions in This Category:

- What are your long-range career goals? How have you prepared yourself to reach these goals? What other personal goals do you hope to accomplish in the next ten years?
- Describe what you consider to be the ideal job.
- What characteristics do you believe are necessary for success in this field? Do you have those characteristics?

Interviewer wants to know: how your future plans relate to the organization, whether you have a realistic view of your career area, how goal directed and serious you are.

Use these questions to: demonstrate your knowledge of the field in which you hope to be employed, assure the organization that you have realistic goals, show a serious commitment to your career.

Questions about the Organization Itself
Some Typical Questions in This Category:

- Why are you interested in our organization?
- What do you know about us? What do you like best about our organization?
- What can you offer us?

Interviewer wants to know: whether you've done your homework, if you're a good match for the organization, if you intend to stay with the organization.

Use these questions to: show that you've taken the time to research the organization, demonstrate a positive interest in the organization, show that you understand the job that you're applying for.

Questions about Your Education
Some Typical Questions in This Category:

- How did you choose your college? Your major? If you had it to do over again, what would you change about your education?
- To what extent does your scholastic record reflect your abilities?
- What was your most rewarding college experience?

Interviewer wants to know: how thoughtful and goal directed you are, what your level of training and preparation is, whether you have the personal characteristics needed for the job.

Use these questions to: show your level of preparation; indicate characteristics, talents, and skills that are *job* related; indicate that you are serious and eager to learn.

Questions about Your Work Experience
Some Typical Questions in This Category:

- Tell me about the jobs you've held. What did you do exactly? Did you enjoy working there? Why did you leave?
- Did you encounter any problems at those jobs? How did you respond?

(continued)

Handling Inappropriate Questions

Although there are laws governing what can and cannot be asked in interviews, not all interviewers are sensitive about what they ask. Questions about marital status, plans for having a family, religious affiliation, politics, ethnic identification, and so forth are illegal. Yet it is possible that an interviewee may be asked such a question. What's the correct response? That's really up to each individual. There are a number of choices. The interviewee can

1. simply answer the question (although one should not feel pressured to do so).
2. politely refuse to answer and make the interviewer aware that the question was not appropriate.

Table 8.4 Typical Interview Questions (*continued*)

- What is your greatest strength as an employee? Your greatest weakness?

Interviewer wants to know: what you will be like as an employee, what skills you possess, how your previous experience has prepared you for this position.

Use these questions to: demonstrate that you have what it takes to be an effective employee; show that you are responsible, willing to work, good with people, and so on.

Questions about You as a Person
Some Typical Questions in This Category:

- Tell me about yourself.
- What are your hobbies? How do you spend your free time? What kinds of books, magazines, or newspapers do you read?
- What personal accomplishment has given you the most satisfaction? Why?
- What is the most embarrassing thing that ever happened to you?
- What have you done that shows initiative?

Interviewer wants to know: how you relate to the profile of a successful employee, whether you have the necessary traits to fulfill job requirements, how articulate and focused you are.

Use these questions to: show concrete examples of job-related characteristics such as drive, ability to get along

with others, and leadership; indicate that you have a positive self-concept and are both confident and realistic about your abilities and experience.

Questions *You* Should Ask
Some Typical Questions the Interviewee Should Bring Up:

- How would you describe the organization's management style?
- Describe typical assignments for someone in this position during the first year. What are some typical problems that the person in this position may encounter?
- Tell me about your training programs.
- What industry trends do you feel will affect this company in the next five years?
- Earlier you mentioned . . . . Could you elaborate?

Interviewer will be looking for questions that: show a sincere interest in the field and organization, indicate that you want to continue learning, demonstrate that you want realistic information on which to base your decision.

Use these questions to: show a sincere interest in the organization and its future, demonstrate a desire to advance, indicate that you want to grow professionally, show you were listening during the interview, let the interviewer know that you are interested in more than just salary.

3. discuss the underlying concern that may have prompted the question. For example, in asking a question about the candidate's family life, the interviewer's concern could be about the amount of overtime required by the job. An interviewee could respond by saying, "I understand that the job requires substantial investment of time. Let me assure you that there is nothing in my personal life that would keep me from performing any of the duties associated with this job."

Of course, if the questions are extremely offensive, the incident should be reported. In any case, it's important to remain calm and behave politely.

Understanding Organizational Cultures

The traditional approach to understanding organizations has been expanded, in recent years, by efforts to understand how organizational members make sense of organizations and share their understandings with others. In this section, we'll begin by looking at what new employees do to understand new organizational cultures. We'll then expand the notion of culture by looking at how cultural understandings are conveyed through metaphors, stories, and rites.

Fitting in: Entering New Organizational Cultures

Whenever a collection of people share common understandings, values, and perceptions, we can think of them as belonging to a common culture. Because people in organizations need to find a way to understand and manage what goes on around them, they create organizational cultures. In the words of Gary Kreps, organizational culture consists of collectively held "logics and legends about organizational life and the organization's identity."[28]

If you have ever lived or traveled abroad for an extended period of time, you may have experienced culture shock, a sense of disorientation that occurs when the rules you're used to playing by no longer work. That same sense may occur as individuals enter new organizational cultures. They need to know what's going on, and they need to find some way to adapt to their new surroundings.

Meryl Reis Louis argues that newcomers should be helped to make sense of organizations.[29] When newcomers enter an organization, they often have trouble understanding what is going on because

Maneuvering through employment interviews is a challenge for both interviewer and interviewee.

their old scripts and schemata no longer work. As a result, they experience surprise, an emotional reaction to differences between life in the organization and life outside it. For Louis, surprise is the emotional state that occurs when one's expectations about the job or about oneself are disconfirmed. And surprise triggers the need for sense making.

> Newcomers should be helped to make sense of organizations. When newcomers enter an organization, they often have trouble understanding what is going on because their old scripts and schemata no longer work.

When insiders in an organization encounter a surprising event, they can use their knowledge of the culture to help explain it or they can turn to friends and colleagues. But newcomers lack cultural knowledge and have no one to turn to. Their only way of understanding organizational events is to use models based on past experience. Unfortunately, these forms of sense making may not be useful. A newly employed recent college graduate who uses college experience to define what it means to "put in a hard day's work," for example, may be in for a rude awakening.

Louis believes that organizations must help newcomers learn the ropes. By linking newcomers with mentors and instituting early appraisal meetings in which superiors give newcomers feedback, organizations can eliminate many transition problems. "Secrecy norms, the sink-or-swim, learn-on-your-own philosophy, and sanctions against sharing information among office members," she argues, "are dysfunctional for newcomers and for their employing organizations as well."[30] Louis believes that newcomers should also be taught to understand the nature of entry experiences. They should learn to anticipate surprise and actively seek information from insiders. The newcomer who expects to experience organizational culture shock and who makes active efforts to learn the culture will be at a real advantage during his or her first year on the job.

Organizational Culture: Metaphors, Stories, and Rites

Newcomers can learn a lot about organizational culture by observing what goes on around them. But what, exactly, should they observe? In their classic article on communication cultures, Michael Pacanowsky and Nick O'Donnell-Trujillo suggested that organizational culture can be seen in communication practices, including metaphors, stories, and rituals.[31] By carefully observing these forms of communication, they argue, we can better understand an organization's underlying values, beliefs, and attitudes.

Metaphors and Stories

As we saw in Chapter 4, metaphors are linguistic expressions that allow us to experience one thing in terms of another. Metaphors both reflect and shape the way we see the world. This is as true in organizations as it is in our private lives. The metaphors that are used in corporate settings interest communication scholars because they embody basic aspects of organizational culture. For example, one organization may encourage the use of a family metaphor ("Here at Acme, you're part of a family who cares"), while another may see itself as an armed force ("We've got to go out there and blast the competition"). Cynthia Stohl explains how the family metaphor can affect employees:

> If we "see" our office group as a traditional family, then we expect people to take care of and protect one another. . . . [D]ominant behavior would be interpreted as fatherly or motherly[;] . . . weaker members would be treated as children, with fewer rights but much support. Our personal lives would be appropriate topics for discussion and rituals surrounding birthdays, the birth of a child, and other personal landmarks would be enacted.[32]

In an organization that uses a military metaphor, by contrast, life would be quite different. Charles Conrad describes a large West Coast toy manufacturer that takes a more military approach to organizational life. In this company, employees habitually talk about "fighting the battle" (working hard) and "taking no casualties" (being obsessed with quality). But, Conrad tells us, the most powerful expressions of the metaphor come directly from military slogans:

> "Be all that you can be" is used to justify voluntary overtime, and "lean, mean fighting machine" is used to explain reduction in the number of middle managers. Almost every normal work experience is explained in language reflecting the "army under siege" metaphor; almost every behavior desired of workers can be justified by referring to the metaphor.[33]

Clearly, the organizational cultures of these two companies are quite different.

Stories also help us make sense of organizational culture by reflecting company values. Conrad gives an example of how a story from the 3M Corporation embodies the key value "innovation should be encouraged."[34] According to the story, a junior employee discovered Scotch Tape by accident. His superiors didn't believe that there was a viable market for the product. So he slipped into the boardroom and taped members' materials to the conference table. The board members decided to give the new product a chance, and the rest, as they say, is history. Any new 3M employee hearing the story will quickly draw the conclusion that it is important to fight for one's ideas.

Another example of an organizational story concerns the actions of a young receptionist at IBM whose job it was to stop anyone from entering restricted areas without a badge. When Thomas Watson, Jr., then chairman of the board, walked up without a badge, she stopped him. According to a former IBM employee, this story was still circulating several years ago, and its interpretation was clear: at IBM, the boss gets no special treatment; everyone follows the rules. This interpretation is even clearer when it is compared to another story employees liked to tell. According to this companion story, the same situation occurred in a different organization, but instead of being understanding, the boss is reported to have said, "Don't you recognize my name? You should. It's on the checks you *used to* get. You're fired." Clearly, at least in these stories, IBM characterizes itself as a humane organization that "plays fair."

Rites and Ceremonials

A more elaborate form of cultural life can be found in organizational rites and ceremonials. Harrison Trice and Janice Beyer define **rites** as publicly performed, "relatively elaborate, dramatic, planned sets of activities that consolidate various forms of cultural expressions into one event." A **ceremonial**, by contrast, is a "system of several rites connected with a single occasion or event."[35] Graduation, for example, is a ceremonial consisting of a number of different rites, including receptions, parties, award presentations, and the conferring of degrees. According to Trice and Beyer, rites have both manifest and latent consequences. The manifest (or public) consequence of graduation is recognition of the passage from student to graduate. The latent (or hidden) consequences, however, are more interesting. Graduations also celebrate the status of the college or university, reiterate the value of a college education, and remind participants that they are taking part in a practice that has a rich historical tradition. At the very least, they encourage both parents and students to believe that their sacrifices were worth it. Table 8.5 lists some of the kinds of rites that occur in organizations.

Table 8.5 Organizational Rites

Rites of Passage

Purpose: Rites of passage celebrate new role identities

Example: Army basic training, freshman orientation

Consequences: Facilitate transformation into new role while ensuring new member is as much as possible like previous members

Rites of Degradation

Purpose: Rites of degradation strip away power or remove incumbent from role

Example: Impeachment, student judicial hearing

Consequences: Strengthen organizational boundaries by defining who belongs and who doesn't; reaffirm value of role by punishing out-of-role behavior

Rites of Enhancement

Purpose: Rites of enhancement reward organizational achievement

Example: Academy Awards, student honor society induction

Consequences: Enhance status and value of organization, motivate individuals to strive, give organization credit for individual achievement

Rites of Renewal

Purpose: Rites of renewal improve functioning of organization

Example: Diversity awareness training, student government retreat

Consequences: Make members believe something is being done to solve problems; focus on some problems and avoid others; reinforce existing power structures

Rites of Conflict Reduction

Purpose: Reduce conflict and aggression

Example: Collective bargaining, grievance procedures

Consequences: Deflect attention away from problems; compartmentalize conflict

Rites of Integration

Purpose: Create common identity and commitment to organization

Example: Mardi Gras, end-of-semester party

Consequences: Permit catharsis; loosen norms temporarily in order to reaffirm their moral rightness; channel aggression

Adapted from Harrison Trice and Janice Beyer, "Studying Organizational Cultures Through Rites and Ceremonials," *Academy of Management Review, 9* (1984), pp. 653–669.

Trice and Beyer believe that rites play an important role in the creation and maintenance of strong organizational cultures and that strong cultures, in turn, help to produce effective organizations.[36] They advise managers to assess the hidden consequences of rites in their organizations in order to find out whether the rites are achieving desired effects. They also suggest

> Rites play an important role in the creation and maintenance of strong organizational cultures.

that managers learn effective ceremonial skills. "Some flair for the dramatic and the ability to be expressive in speech, writing, and gestures," they tell us, "could be an asset in meeting the ceremonial requirements of managerial roles."[37] They go on to quote Karl Weick, "Managerial work can be viewed as managing myth, symbols, and labels. . . . [B]ecause managers traffic so often in images, the appropriate role for the manager may be the evangelist rather than the accountant."[38]

Promoting Professionalism in Workplace Relationships

Getting along in an organization means more than simply passing on information efficiently or getting one's reports in on time. It also involves creating healthy relationships with one's coworkers. Too often, however, organizational relationships are marked by petty jealousies, resentments, stereotyping, and the like. In this section, we'll look briefly at why building good relationships is so important and so difficult in the organizational setting.

Workplace Relationships

Most of us treat strangers very differently than we treat those we know and trust. But where exactly do coworkers fit on the continuum between stranger and intimate? The answer is that they fit somewhere in between. Because we spend so much time with them, it is natural to feel a personal connection and want to be friends. Yet we are in the organization to get a task accomplished; we certainly aren't paid to have fun and hang out. In the workplace, relationships must be professional, and part of fitting into an organization is figuring out just exactly what professional relationships are all about.

> Getting along in an organization means more than simply passing on information efficiently or getting one's reports in on time. It also involves creating healthy relationships with one's coworkers.

Professional relationships differ from personal relationships in at least two dimensions: choice and power. Choice is important. Although we choose our friends, we do not choose our coworkers; they are chosen for us by the organization. As professional consultant Bob Wall points out, "Companies do not bring people together to be friends. We are not there to develop some form of an extended family. Our primary purpose is to accomplish work, and the company is depending on us to be able to work together to make that happen."[39] Because employees are chosen for competence rather than personal compatibility, we may find ourselves working with people we would not otherwise choose as friends. Yet to work effectively together, we often have to put aside personal feelings of like or dislike.

Power is an added complication. Organizations are hierarchical; therefore, differences in power and status are natural and expected. This means that while organizational members should recognize that everyone in the organization, regardless of status, has a contribution to make, they should also understand and acknowledge role and status differences. It doesn't work to pretend that everyone is equal. The CEO and the guy or gal in the next cubicle don't do the same work, and the organization does not expect that they be treated exactly the same way.

Acknowledging status differences and putting aside personal feelings may not come naturally. Deferring to authority may make us feel uncomfortable. Because we are usually encouraged to be open and candid, being polite may appear phony. Therefore, when we enter the world of work, we may have to learn new sets of behaviors in order to act professionally. Table 8.6 lists some general guidelines for communicating on the job. As you read them, think about whether you

Table 8.6 Some Rules for Professional Behavior

- *Understand and acknowledge that different people have different roles to play in the organization.*
Acknowledge roles, but don't grovel or condescend. In addressing others, use formal titles until you're told to do otherwise. Let your superior initiate and set the tone and content of a conversation. In other words, don't corner the CEO in the hall and launch into a long conversation about your vacation.

- *Remember that you're there to work.*
Take care of personal business before or after work. It is inappropriate to make personal phone calls at the office if you are in an entry-level position. Similarly, you are not being paid to play computer games, download music, flirt, spend hours rehashing your personal problems, and the like. If others do so, disengage yourself politely.

- *Manage time and responsibilities effectively.*
Arrive on time and stay until closing. Take deadlines seriously. You may have managed to get extensions while you were in college, but the rules change after graduation. When you say you're going to do something, follow through.

- *When it comes to relationships, balance inclusion and distance.*
Greeting coworkers with a few friendly words, offering to help out in small ways, and inviting others to be part of group activities help build a positive climate. Refraining from asking nosy questions or looking through their desks shows that you respect coworkers' privacy. Find a way to be pleasant without being overly familiar.

- *Remember that you share public space with others and must therefore take their comfort and concerns into account.*
Your office is not your home, no matter how many hours you spend there. Don't assault others with heavy cologne, smelly sandwiches, or loud music. An office should look like an office, not a picnic area.

- *Know when to put aside personal feelings.*
Open expression of like and dislike (either to others' faces or behind their backs) can destroy a cooperative climate. Personal feelings are often irrelevant in a work environment, so learn to bite your tongue.

- *Figure out how to handle disagreement and criticism.*
Disagreement and criticism are normal parts of office life. Without criticism, how could we learn? When negative feedback is directed at you, don't take it personally. And when you're the one disagreeing, make sure that you focus on the issues, not the person.

agree or disagree with them and about how easy or difficult they might be to follow. Also ask yourself what other rules you would add. And keep in mind that different organizations will call for different kinds of communication, so general rules must always be modified in specific situations.

Of course, acting professionally doesn't mean keeping everyone at arm's length and never developing friendships. Professional relationships can and do turn into personal ones. But workplace relationships should be grounded in professional behavior. As Wall suggests, "It will be easier to build personal relationships when we know that we can work powerfully together and disagree without taking things personally. . . . It is simply easier to like people when we are able to work out the mechanics of working together."[40]

The Office Romance

People not only make friends at work but also occasionally fall in love. Handling workplace romance is particularly complicated. In the past, most organizations forbade office romances. If they were discovered, one partner (for heterosexual couples, it was usually the woman) would be asked to leave. Nowadays, attitudes are more relaxed. Several studies have surveyed both participants and observers and found the majority of respondents accepts office relationships and feels that they make little difference in terms of work performance.[41] Indeed, so common have they become that several modern etiquette books include advice for handling them. Grace Fox, for example, advises romantic partners to be discreet and tells them not to spend too much time together or send each other cute emails or faxes. She also advises them about what to do if the romance ends: "Don't tell your side of what happened around the office. Don't take it out on the person in meetings or in private. Treat each other as kindly as you can."[42]

Office romances are not without risks. They can disrupt work, cause perceptions that one of the partners is being given unfair advantages, isolate the lovers from the rest of the office, and affect the credibility of the organization in the eyes of clients. Because they play out in public, participants may lose control. Office romances are, in a sense, no longer dyadic relationships; they can affect the attitudes and behaviors of all coworkers. Indeed, Gary Alan Fine criticizes office romances and even goes so far as to suggest, "If the company is a family, an organizational romance is incest."[43]

> Office romances are not without risks. They can disrupt work, cause perceptions that one of the partners is being given unfair advantages, isolate the lovers from the rest of the office, and affect the credibility of the organization in the eyes of clients.

Sexual Harassment

Although dating coworkers is becoming more accepted, there is a thin line between pursuing a personal relationship and assaulting coworkers with offensive displays of affection and intimacy. Pursuing a coworker who is not interested in a romantic relationship can be a form of sexual harassment and can destroy a working relationship. According to the Equal Employment Opportunity Commission (EEOC), **sexual harassment** consists of

> *unwelcome sexual advances, request for sexual favors, and other verbal or physical conduct of a sexual nature . . . when submission to or rejection of this conduct explicitly or implicitly affects an individual's employment, unreasonably interferes with an individual's work performance or creates an intimidating, hostile or offensive work environment.*[44]

It should be noted that the harasser may be a woman or a man and the victim does not have to be of the opposite sex. In fact, anyone affected by the offensive conduct—for example, a bystander who is forced to witness harassment—can be considered a victim. Sexual harassment is not a laughing matter. It violates Title VII of the Civil Rights Act of 1964 and can lead to serious legal repercussions.

According to Charles Conrad, harassment is more likely to occur in certain kinds of organizations than in others. When the organization defines the "normal" employee as male, when support systems for women and people of color are weak or nonexistent, when the organization is loosely coupled, and when power relationships between superiors and subordinates are unequal, there will be more incidents of harassment. Unfortunately, as Conrad points out, "each of these factors is present in most colleges and universities."[45]

Although some sexual harassment is intentional and egregious, some may be the result of stupidity or insensitivity rather than malice. While anyone would agree that unwanted touch, requests for sexual favors in return for job advancement, or sexual taunting clearly fall within the bounds of sexual harassment, is it sexual harassment if the victim overhears an off-color joke being told in the hall? Experts disagree. As Daniels puts it, "It is very clear that you cannot do something such as put a pornographic photo with a sexual proposition couched in vulgar language on a coworker's office desk to taunt that person. Whether you can play songs with explicit lyrics on your portable CD for your own amusement during lunch break remains to be seen."[46] What constitutes a hostile work environment is currently being clarified in the courts. Regardless of the results, sexually suggestive behavior in any form has no place in the workplace. Restraint and respect should characterize all workplace relationships.

USING ORGANIZATIONAL TECHNOLOGY

Some of you may love technology; others of you may hate it. But whatever your attitude, you will be exposed during your working life to an array of new devices designed to make your work easier and more efficient. Whether these advances in technology live up to their promise or whether they complicate your life will depend on your ability to use them wisely. To be successful in today's workplace, it's essential to keep informed about new technologies. More important, it's necessary to recognize the ways in which technology changes the structure and operations of organizations.

Telecommuting

For many people, the virtual office is replacing the real office. Growing numbers of employees are telecommuting, working from their homes via electronic media. Champions of telecommuting have pointed out potential advantages. Organizations will be able to save the money they normally spend on providing office and work sites, and workers will not have to relocate to get that perfect job. It has even been suggested that telecommuting can decrease traffic and pollution. In Los Angeles, for example, 60 percent of the city's notorious air pollution comes from automobile emissions.[47] Imagine how much more livable Los Angeles and other major cities could be if physical commuting were replaced by virtual commuting.

> As it becomes more feasible to work at home, the traditional separation between workplace and home may gradually disappear. When we can work anywhere, there is no way to escape the demands of the office, no time when parents are available exclusively to their children or husbands and wives to their spouses.

On the other hand, as it becomes more feasible to work at home, the traditional separation between workplace and home may gradually disappear. When we can work anywhere, there is no way to escape the demands of the office, no time when parents are available exclusively to their children or husbands and wives to their spouses. In *The Wired Community,* Stephen Doheny-Farina describes a typical telecommuter. Peg Fagen lives in Massachusetts and telecommutes to a New York office. She has equipped her home office with a "dedicated phone and fax line, computer and modem, e-mail and file-transfer connectivity, copier, and so on." She also hires a baby-sitter to supervise her preschool children. She is single-minded about her work time. "When she goes into her office, she is at work. When the sitter leaves or when the children awaken, she is at home. If the day's work is not completed when the sitter leaves, she returns to her office after the children have been put to bed."[48] She telecommutes successfully because she can manage her time wisely and because her boss knows and trusts her. Nevertheless, her decision has not been without costs: "Co-workers with similar education, on-the-job experience, and time with the company have moved up the company's management ladder faster than Peg."[49]

Despite its convenience, telecommuting has drawbacks. Undisciplined workers may find it difficult to work without direct supervision, while workaholics may find themselves writing memos well past midnight. According to a report commissioned by *Mobile Office* magazine, home workers work more hours and experience more stress to meet deadlines than do office workers.[50] In addition, face-to-face informal networking and relationship building are not possible. Surveys show that telecommuters often fear a loss of "visibility and career momentum" when they don't have the opportunity to form direct, offline relationships with those who evaluate their job performance.[51] A final cost is to the development of a strong organizational culture. Corporate culture is created through the minutiae of everyday communications. As employees interact, they forge alliances and develop cohesion. Some of this interaction can be accomplished via corporate chat lines; however, text-based bulletin boards and video teleconferences don't allow the informality and frequency of face-to-face communication.

Virtual Teams

Although you may not end up working from home, it is quite possible that you will one day be part of a work group that communicates online. Because of advances in information and communication technologies (ICTs) and because of economic globalization, many organizations now ask their employees to join **virtual teams**, work groups whose members are separated geographically and whose communication is mediated by technologies such as email, telephone, groupware, videoconferencing and the like.[52]

Virtual teamwork calls for heightened communication skills. Due to the fact that communication is often asynchronous, members can experience frustrating time lags during communication. Although slow response time is often due to time zone differences or difficulty in accessing ICTs, it can lead members to believe their communication partners are lazy or nonproductive. Feelings of isolation can also occur in groups where members have never met face to face. Differences in cultural background can lead to misunderstandings. Finally, trust and group loyalty may be difficult to achieve. As Marshall Scott Poole and Huiyan Zhang point out:

> *Trust is the substrate of effective virtual teams. It substitutes for direct physical contact and the expectation that others will deliver, and it encourages members to meet their own commitments in order to maintain the trust that others have in them.*[53]

Although Sirka Jarvenpaa and Dorothy Leidner have argued that swift, depersonalized, goal-directed trust can develop in virtual teams, this trust is quite fragile and temporal.[54]

To combat some of the problems encountered by virtual groups, organizations should use software that lets members know who is available online and what everyone has been doing. They should also create strong norms to coordinate and schedule work. To combat isolation, most communication experts suggest that virtual teams meet face-to-face at the beginning of every project and that leaders stay in telephone contact with every member. Organizations should also provide cross-cultural training for international teams. In addition, all members should also be trained to use a variety of ITCs, and access to up-to-date technology should be assured. Finally, organizations must choose the right people when composing teams.

What kinds of people should organizations look for? Research suggests people who are able to work independently, tolerate ambiguity, and motivate themselves are particularly effective in virtual teams.[55] In addition, individuals who are quick to trust others and are accepting of cultural differences seem to do well in this kind of setting. And, of course, facility in using ICTs is an important requirement. If you plan to work for a modern organization the ability to use and choose technologies wisely is a necessity you should prepare for now.

Finding the Right Medium for the Right Job

Computer-mediated communication (CMC) may be the latest thing, but that doesn't necessarily mean that it is the best thing. One of the drawbacks is that such communications use lean media rather than rich media. **Rich media** use a variety of channels to carry information whereas lean media use fewer channels. Face-to-face conversation, for example, is the richest medium because it contains the most verbal and nonverbal cues. Generally speaking, rich media are better than lean media when immediate feedback is important, when communicators need to know each other's emotional responses, or when the message contains very personal, highly charged news.[56] CMC may also discourage mutual problem solving, which is probably better done in a face-to-face context. On the other hand, CMC does provide a great deal of information very rapidly. Not only does it enhance distribution of simple announcements, it may actually improve information efficiency by bypassing formal channels. What is important is that communicators think carefully about what they want to accomplish with their messages and that they choose an appropriate medium.

Melinda Kramer offers a list of some of the factors that should affect choice of medium in a business context. Included are speed (How quickly does the message need to be there?), timing (Do you need an answer immediately or can you leave information to be dealt with later?), distance (How far does the message need to travel?), size of audience (How many people do you need to reach?), intimacy (How personal is the message?), talent (What media are both you and your receiver most comfortable with?), and cost (What is your budget?). Thus, if a message has to get out right away, if it doesn't need an immediate reply, if it is to go to many people at the same time, and if it is not personal, then email may be the way to go. On the other hand, if the material is sensitive, then a medium such as the telephone (where the receiver can hear your voice) or, better yet, a face-to-face meeting (with the full complement of verbal and nonverbal cues) is the right choice. Kramer reminds us, "Many business people choose the communication medium with which they are most familiar . . . without thinking about which medium will actually be the most effective. Instead of following old habits, you should evaluate the available media and select the one that best fits your communication goals."[57]

Alan Zaremba gives an example of what can happen when people react without thinking about the appropriateness of the medium. He reports that, in 1999, a counseling center in Boston received a phoned-in bomb threat. Taking the threat seriously, administrators knew that they had to notify the staff. How did they do it? By using a mass email asking everyone to vacate the building. The problem? Most of the employees were in a conference at the time, and even had they been in their offices, it's not likely that they all would have checked their email quickly enough. Luckily, the threat was a hoax. Had it not been, choosing the wrong medium could have led to disaster.[58]

In choosing the best way to send a message, it can be helpful to keep in mind the distinction made by Lee Sproull and Sara Kiesler between first-level and second-level effects of technology.[59] A first-level effect refers to what the technology is designed to do. For example, the first-level effect of email is that it allows us to communicate cheaply and immediately. A second-level effect is an unforeseen side effect of technology. Zaremba explains that second-level effects of email may be to make face-to-face encounters rarer, create a digital divide between those with access to computers and those without, and encourage flaming.[60] When choosing media, it is important to keep both kinds of effects in mind.

Etiquette in the Wired Workplace

Just as there are rules of etiquette to help people develop workable relationships in the modern organization, so there are rules for the civil use of technology. If you've ever had to listen to someone else's cell phone conversation during a meal at your favorite restaurant or if you've been the recipient of an abrupt, dismissive email, you know how rude people can be in their use of electronic media. Table 8.7 lists some rules to follow as you employ electronic media.

> If you've ever had to listen to someone else's cell phone conversation during a meal at your favorite restaurant or if you've been the recipient of an abrupt, dismissive email, you know how rude people can be in their use of electronic media.

BECOMING A MORE RESPONSIBLE COMMUNICATOR

In today's business environment, issues of responsibility are extraordinarily complex and critical. As the power of multinational organizations increases, so do troubling ethical issues. In an article on social responsibility in international business, Stanley Deetz lists just a few of the questionable business practices that occur in an organizational world where high-speed decision making hinders thoughtful ethical debate and internationalization and outsourcing make surveillance and control difficult. Values such as human rights, environmental protection, fair competition, and equal opportunity for all workers are abused in activities such as

> *using prisoners as workers, moving operations to environmentally less restrictive communities, offering and taking bribes and payoffs, creating environmentally unsound or wasteful products, closing of economically viable plants in takeover and merger games, growing income disparity, declining social safety nets, malingering, harassment, maintaining unnecessary and unhealthy controls on employees, and advocating consumerism.*[61]

In a world where practices like these can and do occur, organizations must work to create responsible and humane environments for those both inside and outside their boundaries. Listed below are a few guidelines that can help members of organizations act more responsibly.

- In most organizations, it's easy to pass the buck when it comes to ethical issues. As Charles Conrad points out, in bureaucratic structures, responsibility often falls between the cracks. Employees at lower levels who implement unethical procedures often excuse their behavior by pointing out that they were just following company policies and procedures. Employees at higher levels, who make the policies, do not feel any responsibility because they themselves don't actually have to make illegal or unethical decisions. As a result, in irresponsible organizations, unethical practices are always someone else's fault. Responsible organizations, on the other hand, encourage all employees to take an ethical stance.[62]

Table 8.7 Etiquette for an Information Age

As new technologies enter the world of work, a new code of electronic manners has emerged. Letitia Baldrige offers some advice on using a variety of communications media.

Cellular Phones

"No one should intrude on anyone's privacy by talking on a cellular telephone in a restaurant, during a concert, in the middle of a hot love scene at the movies, or during a church service."

Answering Machines

"Try not to make jokes, play weird music, or be flip in your recorded messages. The CEO or the Japanese ambassador may be calling."

"Don't use an answering machine that allows . . . only very short messages. It's aggravating and expensive to have to make repeated calls."

When you leave a message, give adequate information and "don't leave mysterious, teasing, or ambiguous messages that you might find amusing but which could be confusing to the person you have called."

Conference Calls

When participating in a conference call, "remember to identify yourself each time you speak, for the benefit of people not in the room," and "don't lower your voice to make sarcastic comments or to tell a joke [you don't want everyone to hear]. It's just plain rude and bad business procedure."

Faxes

Don't fax long, unannounced, or unwelcomed materials. When you do fax, "call the would-be recipient's office first and ask if it's all right to transmit material during a certain period."

And always remember that "a fax may be seen by many people in an office, so don't send anything personal or sensitive via fax."

Timing Your Communications

Finally, always remember to time your calls and faxes so as not to disturb your recipient at home, and be cautious about beeping anyone on a car phone: doing business while driving can be dangerous.

Screen Names and Ring Tones

The screen name you chose when you set up your first Internet account may have seemed funny then, but is it appropriate now? And when it comes to ring tones use discretion, especially in professional settings.

Quotes taken from *Letitia Baldrige's New Complete Guide to Executive Manners*, by Letitia Baldrige, 1993. New York: Maxwell MacMillan International, pp. 139–142, 145–148.

- Organizational cultures can be humane or inhumane. When they are humane, workers feel comfortable and supported and are able to work creatively. When they are inhumane, workers feel criticized and defensive and may be pressured to act in unethical ways to protect themselves. When organizations encourage mutual trust and support, employees are more satisfied with their jobs and display more commitment and loyalty to the organization. By refusing to play politics, engage in gossip, follow hidden agendas, or attack coworkers, employees can enhance the organizational climate and build a more humane culture. D. K. Banner and T. E. Gagne express it this way:

  > [W]e create and maintain organizational forms consistent with our level of collective maturity and our shared identity. If we see ourselves as separate, fearful, shameridden people whose best hope for happiness is to manipulate our external circumstances so that they please us, we get the bureaucratic form. If we are willing to accept personal responsibility for expressing transcendent values, for living in true, spiritual identity, we will create flexible, nonhierarchical politics-free organizations. We create our own reality.[63]

- Responsible organizations encourage open communication. Since the 1960s, organizational communication experts have argued that effective organizations must establish an open communication climate in which subordinates have access to information on matters that affect their work lives and feel free to express their ideas and participate in decision making. Both scholars and practitioners have argued that when communication networks are open and participation is encouraged, organizations are likely to be productive and effective. To ensure open communication, organizations must provide forums for the voicing of opinions. But because many current forums are actually used to suppress conflict and to increase compliance rather than to foster a genuine exchange of ideas, companies must find new ways to encourage employees to express their own opinions, interests, and feelings.

- For too long, organizations have excluded large portions of the population. By opening up to employees who were formerly denied entry, organizations not only do the right thing, they also increase their ability to compete in a global economy. When organizations limit membership to people who think and act alike, they diminish creativity and problem-solving ability. When they expand their membership, they expand their perspectives. According to Deetz, "The presence of diverse goals, rather than creating costly conflict and impasse, creates the conditions whereby limited decisional frames are broken and the company learns."[64] But diversity must be more than an organizational policy. Members at every level in the organization must learn to value diversity and to overcome their discomfort with others who are different.

- It's a common belief that the only people affected by an organization are its employees and stockholders. In fact, the impact of organizational decisions is far ranging. Organizations affect the communities in which they are located, the customers who use their products or services, and even the physical environments that surround them. The groups that can affect or are affected by organizations—that have a "stake" in the organization—are called **stakeholders**. In a sense, they are as much a part of the organization as employees, and, as members of the organization, their values and needs must be taken into account. Responsible organizations recognize the legitimacy of their relationships with a wider community of stakeholders, acting as their stewards.

SUMMARY

An organization is a system made up of people working toward a common goal. Organizations have four characteristics: interdependence, hierarchical structure, linkage to their environments, and, most important from our point of view, dependence on communication. When communication fails, organizations experience problems in productivity and member satisfaction. Poor communication practices can also make the organization an unpleasant place to work by creating a negative organizational climate. By focusing on communication, managers and their employees can avoid problems and can increase their chances of organizational advancement.

To communicate competently in an organization, members must communicate with more formality than in other contexts. They must also master organizational genres, the unique forms of communication common to organizations. Of course, each organization will have its own rules for communication. What works in one organizational culture will not necessarily work in another.

Information is the lifeblood of organizations. As it circulates through the organization, it can follow a formal chain of command (the formal network) or a more unstructured pathway based on personal contacts and friendships (the informal network). Formal communication can move in an upward direction (from subordinate to superior), a downward direction (from superior to subordinate), or a horizontal direction (between employees with equal status). In U.S. organizations, most information flows downward. Unfortunately, employees are often dissatisfied with the amount and quality of downward flow. Sometimes, they receive too little information; sometimes, they receive too much; and sometimes, they receive deceptive or false information. Part of the problem is due to the fact that as messages pass between individuals, details are left out, elaborated, or changed to fit the communicator's own frame of reference. By building in redundancy and asking for clarification, communicators can overcome some of these difficulties in serial transmission.

Upward flow is less common in organizations, but it, too, can be distorted by employees who don't want to be the bearers of bad tidings or by gatekeepers who want to protect their superiors.

Informal structures, such as the grapevine, are also prevalent in organizations. Although we tend to think of the grapevine as a hotbed of gossip and false rumor, studies have shown it to be quite accurate, although often incomplete. One way to determine the informal structures in an organization is to do network analysis.

Horizontal communication can also be beset by problems. When people at the same level work together in teams, they may be reluctant to try new approaches, they may be unable to locate important information, or they may lack trust, especially in organizations in which departments are in competition. For this reason it is important for team leaders and managers to create teams that exhibit structural diversity, to maintain effective transactive memory systems, and to encourage trust.

Employees must know how to interview effectively, understand and fit into organizational culture, and act professionally. In order to gain admittance to an organization, individuals must prepare carefully for employment interviews by assessing their skills, preparing compelling resumes and cover letters, and researching the organization. During the interview itself they should use their answers to demonstrate competence and confidence as well as intelligence and respect. Once hired, individuals must find a way to fit into the organization's culture. By observing norms of conduct, metaphors, stories, and rites, the perceptive employee can uncover hidden values and assumptions and can begin to understand what is expected of him or her. Finally, organizational members must build professional relationships. By recognizing role differences and by remembering that personal desires and feelings must sometimes be subordinated to those of others, employees can create productive work relationships.

When sex and romance enter the workplace, interaction becomes complicated. Nowa-days, more and more people are engaging in office romances. These interactions can be risky and must be handled with a great deal of discretion and skill. Sometimes, the presence of sexual attraction in the workplace can lead to serious problems, including sexual harassment. Any communication that creates an intimidating, hostile, or offensive work environment on the basis of verbal or physical conduct of a sexual nature counts as sexual harassment and is illegal under the Civil Rights Act of 1964.

In today's work culture, keeping up with technology is a must. At some time in their work lives, most members of organizations will be asked to join virtual teams composed of members who are separated geographically and whose communication is mediated. Virtual teamwork calls for heightened communication skills because working in cyberspace presents challenges such as frustrating time lags, unfair attributions about other members, feelings of isolation, and lack of trust. To combat these problems, organizations should work hard to connect members, provide cross-cultural training when necessary, and train members to use a variety of Internet communication technologies. Individuals who are independent and self-motivated, can tolerate ambiguity, are open to trusting others, and can choose the right medium for the right job do well on virtual teams.

Organizations should also encourage members to use the right medium for each job. Factors such as speed, timing, distance, audience size, intimacy, talent, and cost should be taken into consideration when choosing how to convey a message. It's also important to be aware of second-level effects associated with every medium.

Every communication context raises ethical dilemmas. The organizational context is no different. By taking responsibility for one's actions, by trying to create a culture that respects the dignity of others, and by encouraging open discussion and respecting diversity, organizational communicators can create humane workplaces. In addition, organizational members should not develop an "us" versus "them" mentality; they should recognize that they are part of a wider community and take into account the needs and feelings of multiple stakeholders.

KEY TERMS

Listed below are the key terms used in this chapter, along with the number of the page where each is explained.

organization (199)	grapevine (208)	organizational culture (217)
interdependence (200)	network analysis (209)	culture shock (217)
hierarchy (200)	opinion leaders (209)	surprise (218)
bureaucracy (200)	isolates (209)	metaphors (218)
climate (201)	tight coupling (210)	stories (219)
structurational approach (201)	loose coupling (210)	rites (220)
genres (203)	boundary spanner (210)	ceremonials (220)
formal channels of	cosmopolite (210)	rites of passage (220)
communication (204)	bridge (210)	rites of degradation (220)
informal channels of	clique (210)	rites of enhancement (220)
communication (204)	liaison (210)	rites of renewal (220)
organizational chart (204)	star (210)	rites of conflict
downward flow (204)	structural diversity (211)	reduction (220)
upward flow (204)	transactive memory	rites of integration (220)
horizontal flow (204)	system (211)	sexual harassment (224)
message filtering (206)	trust (212)	telecommuting (225)
serial transmission (206)	interview (212)	virtual team (226)
leveling (206)	work-content skills (213)	rich media (227)
sharpening (206)	transferable skills (213)	first-level effect (228)
assimilation (206)	self-management skills (213)	second-level effect (228)
gatekeeper (207)	cover letter (213)	stakeholders (231)
ombudsman (207)	resume (213)	

SUGGESTED READING

Conrad, Charles, & Poole, Marshall Scott. (2004). *Strategic organizational communication in a global economy.* Belmont, CA: Wadsworth.

   An intelligent survey of organizational communication with an excellent section on organizational culture.

Papa, Michael J., Daniels, Tom D., & Spiker, Barry K. (2007). *Organizational communication: Perspectives and trends.* Thousand Oaks, CA: Sage.

   An overview of traditional, interpretive, and critical approaches to organizational communication combining case material and up-to-date research.

Wheelan, Susan A. (2005). *The handbook of group research and practice.* Thousand Oaks, CA: Sage.

   A comprehensive collection of essays by noted organizational communication experts.

Public Communication

Public communication does not belong only to the famous; —every day, all over the country, average people stand up and speak to audiences and, in doing so, make a difference.

Consider the following situations in which public communication had a major impact on personal fortune and national consciousness.

- In one of the first of a long line of cases to be dubbed "the Crime of the Century," a celebrated lawyer took on the defense of two college students who had confessed to murder. In a summation that reportedly lasted for twelve hours, the lawyer presented one of the most eloquent attacks on capital punishment ever delivered.[1]

- During the Great Depression, when millions of Americans were struggling to survive, a president took office and rallied the nation, promising that there was "nothing to fear but fear itself."[2]

- A politician who had been accused of corruption resurrected his career with a single speech and was eventually elected president. Twelve years later, during his second term as president, he once again addressed the nation, this time as he resigned in disgrace.[3]

- Speaking the night before he was assassinated, the most famous civil rights leader in the United States celebrated the accomplishments of the movement and urged followers to continue their struggle. "I may not make it with you," he said, "but I want you to know tonight that we, as a people, will get to the Promised Land."[4]

- The wife of a TV star, a young mother with AIDS whose seven-year-old daughter had already died, addressed a national political convention and described the kind of America she believed in.[5]

Clarence Darrow, Franklin Delano Roosevelt, Richard Nixon, Martin Luther King Jr., Elizabeth Glaser—none of these speakers is with us today, yet their words live on as compelling examples of how single individuals, communicating in the public sphere, can use the spoken word to influence audiences and sway public opinion. These speakers were all well known at the time they spoke. But public communication does not belong only to the famous; every day, all over the country, average people stand up and speak to audiences and, in doing so, make a difference.

In previous chapters, we looked at communication that involved relatively small numbers of people in face-to-face interaction. In this and the next chapter, we examine a different kind of communication: communication in which a single speaker addresses an audience to inform, persuade, or entertain. This chapter will provide a brief and very general introduction to the study of rhetoric, the art of designing public messages that can change the way in which audiences think and feel about public issues. Here, our concern will be in understanding the factors that make communicating in the public sphere unique and in discovering ways to evaluate public speeches. The next chapter is designed for those of you who want to gain practical speaking skills. It will examine some specific techniques that you, as a speaker, can use to construct and deliver effective public presentations.

WHAT IS PUBLIC COMMUNICATION?

Public communication is a one-to-many form of communication wherein a single speaker addresses a large audience. Although audience members may ask questions afterward, their major role during the speech is to listen to and evaluate what the speaker has to say. Clear organization, careful preplanning, and formal language style are the hallmarks of public speeches, which are the most traditional form of public discourse.

Characteristics of Public Communication

Public speaking differs from the forms of communication we have already studied. In the public context, the spontaneity and informality of interpersonal communication and the give-and-take of group discussion are replaced by relatively formal, preplanned messages and more rigidly defined communication roles. Public speakers and their audiences do not run into each other by chance, nor do they sit around and discuss whatever comes into their minds. Public speaking is usually prompted by an important event or issue. As a consequence, public messages are constructed with more care than are interpersonal messages.

> Public speaking is usually prompted by an important event or issue.

One factor motivating that care is audience size. Public speakers may address tens, hundreds, or even thousands of people. Their messages must therefore make sense to large, sometimes quite heterogeneous audiences. As we shall see, audience adaptation is one of the central challenges of communication in the public context. In addition, time is an important variable that affects public communication. Speakers do not have the luxury of slowly developing a relationship with receivers or of going back to reexplain poorly expressed ideas. Most public speeches are one-time-only occasions. The speaker must therefore make an immediate impact and must be completely clear from the outset. Public speeches are also relatively long. In conversations, turns are exchanged rapidly and rarely last longer than a minute or so. In public speeches, a single speaker may retain the floor for an hour or even longer. Audience members must therefore listen attentively for extended periods of time. Because this is hard work, the speakers must make the receivers' work as easy as possible. They must use simple structures that are easy to follow, employ transitions and repeated summaries, and do everything they can to capture attention.

The public speaker is also physically distanced from the audience. Conversational partners sit within a few feet of one another, but public speakers may be twenty or more feet from the audience. They must therefore speak loudly and clearly and use gestures and visual aids that can be seen at a distance.

A final characteristic of public communication is that it takes place in a different sphere from interpersonal or group communication. In interpersonal communication, talk focuses inward on personal matters. In public communication, the focus is wider. Issues and topics are focused outward, toward a community of individuals with shared interests. In other words, public communication occurs within the public sphere.

Communicating in the Public Sphere

When we communicate solely with our own interests in mind, we are acting in the private sphere. However, when we communicate as members of a larger community and our topic is of concern to many, then we are operating in the public sphere. Rhetorician Martha Cooper explains that

> *the public sphere . . . is not a real place . . . in which you could sit down and have a conversation. Instead, it is an orientation that people take to parts of their lives. When something happens that seems to affect groups of people rather than single individuals, the public sphere is emerging. . . . [W]e can recognize that we have entered the public sphere when we find ourselves motivated by the needs of others as well as ourselves, by the needs of the community, rather than our own personal needs.*[6]

When we communicate solely with our own interests in mind, we are acting in the private sphere. However, when we communicate as members of a larger community we are operating in the public sphere.

What we say in the public sphere can affect the well-being of hundreds or even thousands of others. When sports celebrity Magic Johnson tested positive for HIV, he went public with the news. Had he kept his illness a secret, he could have retained some measure of personal privacy—at least for a while. By announcing the news immediately, however, he became a major figure in the battle against AIDS.

His decision to make a public issue of his private circumstances had a dramatic impact on the attitudes of thousands of people.

Making a decision such as Johnson made would take a great deal of courage, for public communication involves risks and responsibilities. In fact, in contemporary society, many people shy away from public involvement. In discussing the reluctance of modern Americans to enter the public realm, Cooper argues that the mobility of modern society and the technical, specialized nature of the modern workplace weaken our ties with our communities. In addition, the diversity of contemporary society keeps many people from forming close bonds with those around them. As a result, our society emphasizes individualism more than community; we are constantly urged to make it on our own, to be our own person, and to look out for number one.[7]

One reason for communicating in the public sphere is to create social change.

Despite these difficulties, many people do take part in public debate. Environmental issues, in particular, have awakened people to the necessity of public involvement. And the success of grassroots groups such as MADD (Mothers Against Drunk Driving) has demonstrated that public communication is a powerful tool not only for dealing with public issues but for creating them as well. A generation ago, people bragged about how well they could drive while drunk, and driving with open containers was legal. Now our attitude is very different: drunk drivers are considered criminals. This change in attitude occurred in part because one woman, Candy Lightner, entered the public sphere. After a drunk driver caused the death of her daughter, Lightner formed MADD and began to take her message to the public. Today, she is a nationally recognized figure who delivers hundreds of speeches a year. She illustrates that one determined person can make a difference.[8]

WHY IS PUBLIC COMMUNICATION IMPORTANT?

Most people's attitudes to public communication are mixed. On the one hand, we recognize how essential public discussion is to a democracy. Most of us believe that part of the responsibility of citizens in a free society is to take stands on public issues, and we know that public communication allows us to take that stand.

> Distrust of the art of rhetoric is not a modern phenomenon. Indeed, as early as the beginning of the fourth century B.C., Plato wrote about the fact that skilled public communicators could use rhetoric to dupe their audiences.

Yet at the same time, we distrust much of what we hear in the public realm, dismissing the speeches of politicians or the arguments of lawyers as "empty rhetoric" or, worse, as manipulation or deception. This distrust of the art of rhetoric is not a modern phenomenon. Indeed, as early as the beginning of the fourth century B.C., Plato wrote about the fact that skilled public communicators could use rhetoric to dupe their audiences.[9] Plato recognized the power that knowledge of rhetoric can convey, a power that can be used to hide the truth as well as to reveal it.

Social Functions of Rhetoric

Rhetorician James Herrick admits that rhetoric can be used deceptively, but he also believes that it fulfills at least six positive social functions. By understanding and applying rhetorical principles, he argues, we discover facts about our worlds, test ideas, learn how to persuade others, shape knowledge, build community, and distribute power.[10] These six factors serve as an answer to the question: Why is public communication important?

Discovering Facts

An important aspect of rhetoric is the discovery of facts. Public speakers are expected to be well informed. This means that they must research their topics. Often, this process reveals new information. Engaging in the rhetorical enterprise means that both speaker and audience find out things about the world they had not previously known.

Testing Ideas

Rhetoric also provides us with "an important and peaceful means for testing ideas publicly."[11] In the process of putting together a public address, communicators test ideas, rejecting those that are illogical or unsupported and accepting others. Audience members too are part of the testing process. By listening with intelligence and by responding critically, audiences can demand that rhetoric be well reasoned and well supported.

Persuading Others

The art of rhetoric is one of the most important resources available to groups or individuals engaged in persuasive argumentation—"second only to the merits of their ideas." Knowledge of rhetoric helps lawyers prepare cases, candidates get elected, lobbyists make their cases, constituents persuade their representative, and committees debate the merits of proposals.[12]

Shaping Knowledge

Once facts have been discovered and presented and the ideas that derive from them have been tested, individuals within cultures come to accept these facts and ideas as true. Thus, public communication serves to create a body of knowledge. In this sense, truth is not something independent of communication; instead, it is a product of communication.

Building Community

If rhetoric is the tool that allows us to establish truth, it is also the tool that allows the establishment of community. After all, community consists of groups of people "who find common cause with one another, who see the world in a similar way, who identify their concerns and aspirations with similar concerns and aspirations of other people."[13] And it is through public discourse that people come to share visions of the world.

Much of the time, the communities we build are local, but increasingly, communities can be electronically mediated. It is not uncommon to look for others who share our interests online. Anyone who has ever logged onto *Facebook* (and there are hundreds of thousands of college students who use this service) knows how easy it is to create and join groups with common interests.

> If rhetoric is the tool that allows us to establish truth, it is also the tool that allows the establishment of community.

Distributing Power

Finally, knowledge of rhetoric and the ability to speak publicly give us power. Herrick believes that rhetoric is connected to power in three ways. It gives us *personal power* by providing the skills needed for personal success and career advancement. It gives us *psychological power* by giving us the knowledge to shape the way other people think. And it grants us *political power* in that it gives us a voice. This latter point is important, for, as Herrick argues, "how influence gets distributed in a culture is often a matter of who gets to speak, where they are allowed to speak, and on what subjects."[14]

Personal and Professional Consequences

In addition to its social functions, skill in public communication has personal consequences. The ability to communicate in public is a necessary skill in most professional and managerial positions. As we saw in Chapter 8, modern businesses are held together by information. The ability to convey that information clearly and effectively is essential for professional advancement. As James van Oosting points out,

> *speechmaking is integral to the business enterprise. Information must be conveyed; personnel must be motivated and directed; reports must be given; policies must be articulated and defended; meetings must be chaired; products and services must be sold. . . . Whether one gets up in front of a public gathering to introduce the company president or addresses a small sales staff the first thing each morning, one is engaged in public communication. . . . [P]ublic communication is [a] workaday expectation and not some extraordinary assignment reserved for special occasions.*[15]

EVALUATING PUBLIC COMMUNICATION

Whether or not you end up doing a great deal of public speaking, your life will be affected by those who do. Politicians will try to persuade you, religious leaders will try to inspire you, and lawyers may try to sway you. It is therefore important to think about ways to evaluate the strength and impact of the public speeches you are exposed to. In this section, we look at three factors that critics should use in evaluating public messages: the nature of the context in which public communication occurs, the relationship between speaker and audience, and appeals within the message itself.

> Whether or not you end up doing a great deal of public speaking, your life will be affected by those who do.

Context and Rhetorical Situation

Like all acts of communication, public speeches are situated within contexts. When communication and context don't "fit," speakers stop being effective. To evaluate the impact of a public speech, it's necessary to begin with context. Factors such as the physical setting of the speech, the medium through which it is delivered, and the specific nature of the occasion are part of context. But so also are its wider historical and cultural setting and its argumentative history.

Physical Setting, Medium, and Occasion

As rhetorical critics James Andrews, Michael Leff, and Robert Terrill point out, "physical surroundings can have a real impact on the way a message is constructed and how it is delivered" because audience expectations are tied to settings.[16] For example, the style and delivery of a speech given in an open-air stadium to an audience of ten thousand are quite different from the style and delivery of a speech given in a college classroom, even when the purposes of the two speeches are similar. Vocal tone and language choices that are suitable for the first context will embarrass the audience in the second because the stadium demands a larger and more emotional style than does the classroom.

The medium of transmission is another aspect of context that affects public messages. A speech designed for TV will differ from one delivered in person because the conditions for reception are so different. Not only are television viewers distanced from the speaker, they are situated in a "noisier" environment, where they may be interrupted by the phone, by the dog asking to go out, or by a sudden urge to make a sandwich and grab a beer. Audiences in face-to-face contexts have less freedom to move around or multitask. On the other hand, they are freer to direct their attention to different aspects of the speech situation. The home viewer's perspective is entirely in the hands of the director who decides when to zoom in and when to get a shot of audience reaction. This is just one example of how media affect communication. In Chapter 11, we will deal with this topic in more detail, looking at how traditional and emerging media affect the way in which we process and send messages.

Another aspect of context is the nature of the occasion that has prompted the speech. An address that does not match its occasion cannot achieve its purpose. A speech delivered at a celebrity roast, for example, is stylistically very different from a State of the Union address. The form and substance of a funeral oration are not the same as those of a political keynote address or an opening argument in a murder trial. All the factors that make up the speech—its purpose, organization, language style, use of supporting materials, and the like—depend on the nature of the occasion. Receivers have a sense of what fits into a particular context and will be unsettled if the speech does not meet expectations.

> All the factors that make up the speech—its purpose, organization, language style, use of supporting materials, and the like—depend on the nature of the occasion.

History as Context

There are broader aspects of context to consider as well. Every speech is given at a particular time in history and the events that surround the speech affect its reception. The attacks of September 11, 2001, for example, affected the way Americans thought about the world and their place in it. A speech criticizing America's posture in the Middle East would have been received very differently on September 12 than on September 10. Of course, events do not have to be of national significance to be part of a historical context. Campus or community events could well affect reactions to a speech. A recent hazing accident may well make an audience less receptive to a speech praising the fraternity and sorority system. Or a local case of police brutality may make it harder to argue for a stronger police presence on campus.

It is not just historical events that are of concern. Issues have a history as well. Unless an issue is completely new, it has been argued before, and these prior arguments may be known to an audience. Speakers who don't bother to find out what an audience has already heard are likely to spend valuable time "reinventing the wheel" by arguing points that have already been made or bringing up proposals that are likely to be rejected. Andrews and his colleagues refer to knowledge about how an issues has been treated in the past as **argumentational history**, and it is an essential aspect of context.[17]

Rhetorical Situation

The importance of context is probably best summed up by rhetorician Lloyd Bitzer.[18] In an article entitled "The Rhetorical Situation," Bitzer argues that of all the factors affecting public communication, situation is the most important because it both prompts a speaker to act and shapes the nature of his or her message.

For Bitzer, **rhetorical situations** consist of three parts: exigence, audience, and constraints. Bitzer believes that all acts of rhetoric are motivated by some

exigence, or problem. Speakers decide to speak because they feel that something is wrong and hope, by speaking about it, to make it right. They therefore address an **audience** of people who can change the problem, either by altering their beliefs and attitudes or by taking direct action. Of course, the ways in which speakers respond to their audiences are affected by **constraints**, factors that control and shape the nature of the communication. The kinds of contextual features we've already discussed, such as medium of transmission or argumentative history, are constraints, as are things like the current beliefs and values of the audience and speaker characteristics such as credibility and argumentative skill.

Good speakers, no matter what their age, build a relationship with their audience.

Bitzer goes on to argue that every rhetorical situation demands a **fitting response**, a response that meets the demands of exigence, takes into account the audience, and is sensitive to constraints. For example, if a major natural disaster occurs, as it did in 2005 when Hurricane Katrina struck the Gulf Coast, and the government officials responsible for disaster relief fail to speak in a timely way, spend their time making excuses, or show a lack of understanding of the victims' plight, then we can rightly say that their rhetorical response failed. The rhetorical situation demanded a response, but the response that occurred did not fit the situation.

Bitzer's analysis is simple, yet it provides a powerful guide both for the speaker and for the rhetorical critic. Speakers must fully understand the rhetorical situation if they are to be effective; and audience members, if they are to respond thoughtfully and critically, must evaluate whether or not a given speech meets the demands of the situation. Bitzer's essay also offers a strong justification for the study of rhetoric. "In the best of all possible worlds," he tells us, "there would be communication perhaps, but no rhetoric—since exigencies would not arise. In our real world, however, rhetorical exigencies abound; the world really invites change—change conceived and effected by human agents who quite properly address a mediating audience."[19]

The Audience–Speaker Relationship

It is a truism in the field of rhetoric that speakers must understand and adapt their messages to audiences. Of course, the need to understand and set up a relationship with one's receivers is true of every kind of communication. We've seen its importance in interpersonal interactions as well as in group settings. In the public context, in which communicators often have no personal acquaintance with audience members, understanding where the audience is coming from is challenging. In this section, we look at some of the things that speakers must know about audiences and at how speakers create perceived relationships with their receivers.

> It is a truism in the field of rhetoric that speakers must understand and adapt their messages to audiences.

Audience Attitudes and Change

When audience members come to hear a speech, they bring prior beliefs, attitudes, values, and life experiences with them. In constructing messages, speakers must take into account what audience members may already be thinking. If speakers fail to do so, their messages will be misunderstood or rejected.

> When audience members come to hear a speech, they bring prior beliefs, attitudes, values, and life experiences with them.

Psychologist Milton Rokeach believes that the human mind uses three kinds of cognitive structures: beliefs, attitudes, and values.[20] Because these structures organize perception and motivate action, it is essential that public speakers understand them. Table 9.1 summarizes these structures.

Beliefs. **Beliefs** are the opinions that individuals hold about the world and about their place in it. "The world is round," "I am a worthwhile person," "Police can [or cannot] be trusted," "The capital of New York is Albany," and "Chocolate ice cream is delicious" are all examples. Obviously, beliefs differ in nature and importance. According to Rokeach, some beliefs are **peripheral beliefs**—that is, they are

---

Table 9.1 Structures in the Minds of Audience Members

Beliefs

Opinions about what is or is not the case. Beliefs differ in nature and importance.

- **Core Beliefs**
Fundamental beliefs held for a long period of time. Some are shared with others ("The sun rises in the east"), and others are highly personal ("I believe that the world is an unfriendly place").

- **Peripheral Beliefs**
Relatively inconsequential and less resistant beliefs about who is or is not an authority ("My dad will know what to do"), facts derived from authorities ("It's not good to bottle up your feelings"), or matters of personal taste ("Green is an ugly color").

Attitudes

Opinions that link an individual to a topic. Attitudes predispose a person to respond to a topic in a particular way. Attitudes have three dimensions.

- **Cognitive Dimension**
What an individual knows about a topic ("There are X number of hungry children in America").

- **Affective Dimension**
What an individual feels in regard to a topic ("I feel sad whenever I think about hungry children").

- **Behavioral Dimension**
What an individual intends to do in regard to a topic ("I will donate money to feed hungry children").

Values

General and enduring opinions about what should or should not be the case.

relatively inconsequential and easy to change. Matters of taste (such as one's belief about the relative merits of chocolate ice cream) and simple, unemotional facts (such as where the capital of New York is) are more peripheral than are beliefs about whether police can be trusted. Beliefs about whether the world is round or flat and about one's self-worth are more central, or core, beliefs. Core beliefs are basic long-term beliefs that cannot be changed without disrupting our entire belief structure. Core beliefs are more difficult to change than are peripheral beliefs. People defend core beliefs against attack. Yet when core beliefs are changed, other related beliefs change as well. Rokeach argues that beliefs are tied to one another in complicated ways. For this reason, a speaker must understand not only what an audience believes but also how that belief is connected to other beliefs and how central it is to audience members.

Attitudes.   In addition to beliefs, people also hold attitudes. Attitudes are evaluative mental structures that predispose us to act in certain ways. "Studying is important and worthwhile" (or "Studying is a waste of time"), "Welfare programs help people" (or "Welfare only encourages idleness"), and "Candidate X's policies are nonsense" (or "X's policies are absolutely brilliant") are all attitudes. Attitudes are partially products of beliefs, but they are also products of emotions and desires.

Attitudes can manifest themselves in three ways. They can affect how we think, feel, and behave. Attitudes toward homelessness are an example. The cognitive dimension of our attitude toward homelessness consists of everything we know or choose to believe about it: its causes, its effects, and its solutions. An attitude's affective dimension consists of emotional reactions to the attitude object. Some people respond to the homeless with fear and distaste, others with pity and understanding, and still others with a mixture of emotions. How we feel about an issue is important because it can motivate us to take action. This leads us to the third way in which we exhibit attitudes: the behavioral dimension. An attitude's behavioral dimension consists of what we think should be done about the attitude object—for example, whether we intend to ignore homelessness or to take action.[21]

Most public speeches are designed either to reinforce or to change existing attitudes. Speeches may be designed to give people information about an attitude object and thus to affect the cognitive dimension, to stir our feelings and thus to change the affective dimension, or to get audience members to make a direct response and thus to act on the behavioral dimension. Often, a speaker's goal may be to affect all three dimensions at once.

Values.   Values are the strongest and most personal of the three cognitive structures. Values are convictions about what ought to occur or about what is or is not desirable and right. "World peace ought to be our highest goal," "Honesty is the best policy," and "Cleanliness is next to godliness" are examples. Values are stronger and more personal than attitudes, but they are less numerous. An individual may have thousands of beliefs and hundreds of attitudes but only ten or twenty values. Values are deeply held and are closely tied to audience members' identities. Making reference to a cherished value can be a powerful way to touch an audience. In the 1992 presidential election, for example, "family values" became an important catchphrase as each presidential and vice presidential candidate tried to show that his commitment to the family was greater than his opponent's.

Many authors have attempted to classify values. Rokeach, for example, lists eighteen values he believes people strive to achieve.[22] Table 9.2 defines these values. Which values do you think are important in your community? How committed are you to each value, and how would you respond to an appeal focused on that value?

Source Characteristics and Audience Response

From its inception, Western rhetoric has emphasized the importance of source characteristics in persuading an audience. As you may recall from Chapter 1, the Greek philosopher Aristotle believed that speakers have three tools with which to persuade an audience: logos refers to logical reasoning, pathos to emotional appeals, and ethos to the impression the audience forms of the speaker's character. Aristotle advises speakers to demonstrate intelligence, character, and goodwill in order to establish ethos. Although modern investigators take a slightly different approach to classifying the characteristics that indicate a speaker's character, they agree with Aristotle's basic premise that the success or failure of a speech depends on how the speaker is perceived by the audience.

It is quite natural for receivers to consider the source. Most of us would find a lecture on the dangers of avian flu more believable if its source was a noted research scientist than if it was delivered by someone with no medical credentials. In deciding on a vacation spot, most of us would respect the word of a friend we liked and trusted who had been there more than we would an advertising brochure. And most employees would comply with a directive from a boss more readily than they would

Table 9.2 Rokeach's Terminal Values

A comfortable life (a prosperous life)	Inner harmony (freedom from inner conflict)
An exciting life (a stimulating, active life)	
A sense of accomplishment (making a lasting contribution)	Mature love (sexual and spiritual intimacy)
	National security (protection from attack)
A world at peace (free of war and conflict)	Pleasure (an enjoyable, leisurely life)
A world of beauty (beauty of nature and the arts)	Salvation (saved, eternal life)
Equality (brotherhood, equal opportunity for all)	Self-respect (self-esteem)
Family security (taking care of loved ones)	Social recognition (respect, admiration)
Freedom (independence, free choice)	True friendship (close companionship)
Happiness (contentedness)	Wisdom (a mature understanding of life)

an order from a summer intern. People who appear to us to be credible, attractive, and powerful have an advantage when it comes to communication and persuasion.

Herbert Kelman and William McGuire are two contemporary writers who have analyzed how source characteristics are related to audience response.[23] According to Kelman, audiences are influenced by sources in three ways: through internalization, identification, or compliance. Internalization occurs when audience members incorporate message content into their belief systems. When audience members think, "Yes, I agree; that argument makes sense to me and fits in with what I believe," they are experiencing internalization. What source quality leads audience members to internalize messages? According to McGuire, internalization occurs when the source possesses credibility; that is, when he or she is perceived to be believable and trustworthy.

Without audience or exigence, the public speech has no purpose.

In addition to internalizing a message, audience members may accept a message because they identify strongly with the source. Identification is based on the presence of a perceived relationship (either real or imaginary) between source and receiver. When audience members think, "By agreeing with the source, I will be more like him or her; we will have something in common," they are experiencing identification. Identification occurs when the source possesses attractiveness; that is, when he or she offers audience members an emotionally rewarding relationship.

Finally, audience members often respond favorably to sources who can meet audience needs or offer material incentives. This influence process is called compliance. Audience members experiencing compliance say to themselves, "It is in my own best interest to agree with the source." Compliance occurs whenever the source is perceived as possessing power, when he or she controls material resources desired by audience members. Table 9.3 summarizes these three influence processes and gives examples of ways in which speakers can increase ethos in each area.

Credibility.   Of the three kinds of source characteristics, credibility has captured the most attention in communication research. Although different authors identify different dimensions of credibility, most agree on two: expertness and trustworthiness. Speakers who show that they are knowledgeable about a topic establish expertness. Speakers who indicate a concern for audience interests demonstrate trustworthiness. Both characteristics increase credibility and consequently enable the speaker to influence and educate audience members.

Even before a speech begins, audience members have some feelings about the speaker's credibility; that is, they have preconceived notions of how expert and how trustworthy the speaker is. These notions may be the result of direct experience, advance publicity, or information given as the speaker is introduced. Once the speech begins, this initial credibility can rise or fall. A speaker without particularly impressive titles and credentials can increase credibility by delivering a carefully prepared and well-argued speech. Conversely, the credibility of a highly

Table 9.3 Source Characteristics That Enhance Influence

The following table shows the kinds of characteristics that audiences value in public speakers. Note that the effectiveness of a given characteristic varies according to type of influence.

Influence Type	Source Characteristic	Ways of Exhibiting Characteristic
Internalization Influence based on convincing an audience to accept an argument as part of their belief system	**Credibility** Perception that the speaker can be believed	Speakers increase credibility by emphasizing expertness and trustworthiness.
Identification Influence based on creating a personal and positive relationship with audience members	**Attractiveness** Perception that the speaker is likeable and is someone with whom audience members would be comfortable	Speakers increase attractiveness by emphasizing familiarity, similarity, physical attractiveness, and liking.
Compliance Influence based on persuading audience members they have something to gain by agreeing or something to lose by disagreeing	**Power** Perception that the speaker controls a resource desired by the audience or has the ability to affect audience members' lives directly	Speakers increase power by emphasizing their legitimacy, control of rewards, and ability to act coercively as well as their access to scarce information and their willingness to associate with audience members.

Influence types are based on a taxonomy in "Processes of Opinion Change," by Herbert C. Kelman, 1961, *Public Opinion Quarterly, 25,* pp. 57–78. Classification of source characteristics follows that in "Attitudes and Attitude Change," by William McGuire, 1985, in *Handbook of Social Psychology,* Gardner Lindzey and Elliot Aronson, Eds. New York: Random House.

respected speaker can be undermined if the speech seems to have been thrown together at the last minute or if the speaker seems insincere.

Attractiveness.   All else being equal, the more attractive a speaker is, the more effective he or she will be. McGuire divides attractiveness into four dimensions: familiarity, similarity, physical attractiveness, and liking. Although new ideas are sometimes appealing, most of the time people are attracted by familiarity. Audiences often respond best to sources and ideas that seem "normal." Studies have also shown that the more often audiences hear an idea, the more attractive the idea becomes. Many years ago, Robert Zajonc demonstrated what he called the mere-exposure hypothesis, the idea that "simple repeated exposure to a stimulus" results in attraction.[24] These findings suggest that speakers will be perceived as more attractive if their ideas resonate with ideas already accepted by audience members. The findings also suggest that it takes time for audience members to become comfortable with new ideas. The speaker who pushes new ideas too rapidly may be rejected.

> All else being equal, the more attractive a speaker is, the more effective he or she will be.

Closely related to familiarity is similarity. Typically, people are attracted to others who share their characteristics. Apparently, audience members identify more strongly with speakers who are like them than with speakers who are very different. This same effect occurs in modeling, wherein receivers are shown someone else being rewarded or punished for a given action. The more similar the model is to the receiver, the more likely the receiver is to act like the model.[25]

A source's physical appearance also affects an audience. A speaker whose physical appearance is average or above average has an advantage over one who is less physically attractive. Of course, physical attractiveness can sometimes backfire. Occasionally a speaker is too good-looking. Audiences who value credibility may be turned off by glamor. Nevertheless, if the audience is not overly concerned with expertise and if emotional identification is at stake, then a positive physical appearance is desirable.

Finally, a person who offers liking, who provides the social rewards of warmth, humor, and respect, will be perceived as attractive. Taken to an extreme and used as a tactic, presenting oneself as likeable is known as ingratiation.[26] Although ingratiation strategies such as flattery can be overdone and obviously insincere, audiences enjoy speakers who are genuinely warm, outgoing, and friendly.

Power.   The final way in which sources can influence others is through power. John French and Bertram Raven believe that power is exercised whenever an individual controls a valued resource.[27] According to their analysis, sources can achieve power in five ways: by occupying an important position in society, by offering material rewards in exchange for compliance, by threatening to punish disobedience, by gaining access to scarce information, and by exhibiting personal characteristics that others admire.

The last two of these power bases—the possession of information (which French and Raven call **expert power**) and the ability to offer social rewards through personal characteristics (which French and Raven label **referent power**)—are similar to expertness and liking, which have already been discussed. The first three power bases, however, are new to our discussion. The first of these, **legitimate power**, is evident when a source represents an important social institution. In such a case, the individual is powerful not because of personal characteristics but because of his or her position in the institution. The primary reason we obey police officers, judges, teachers, and the like is that we consider them legitimate authorities.

The second power base, **reward power**, is involved when an individual has a material possession that another person values. An employer who can give employees bonuses, raises, and promotions has reward power. The final power base, **coercive power**, exists when an individual can harm another or can take away valued possessions. A boss who can fire or demote a worker has coercive power. Employees usually comply with the requests and suggestions of their bosses because they realize both the harm and the good their bosses can do them.

Audiences differ in their attitudes toward power. Some people, called **high authoritarians**, are preoccupied with power and tend to identify with authority figures.[28] An audience made up of this kind of person is extremely impressed with symbols of power and will respect high-power sources. Other people are less likely to defer to the powerful. To assess their impact on an audience, sources should have a realistic view of their own power bases.

Relationships among Source Characteristics.   As we have seen, many characteristics affect responses to public communications. Generally, receivers look for characteristics that are relevant and appropriate to a given rhetorical situation. When the topic is serious and the goal is to inform or persuade, audiences want speakers to be expert and trustworthy. When the topic is less serious and the speaker's goal is to entertain, attractiveness may be more important. The relationships among source characteristics are complex. Indeed, factors that increase audience acceptance in one way may decrease it in another. Humor, for example, can increase attractiveness but may do little to enhance credibility or power. Perceived intelligence may increase credibility but may not make a speaker particularly well liked.

From the speaker's point of view, it is important to control audience perceptions. This does not mean, however, that speakers should try to be something they are not. Speakers are always better off sticking to their strengths. If they're not particularly funny, they should avoid telling jokes; if they're not well informed, they should not try to pass themselves off as experts; and if they don't have reward power, they would be foolish to make false promises.

From the audience's point of view, it is important to think carefully about how speakers affect us. If we let ourselves be swept away by warmth or charm when we should be considering whether or not the speaker actually knows anything about the topic, then we lower the standards for public discourse. Because audiences ultimately get the kind of speakers they deserve, it is important to consider the source.

> If we let ourselves be swept away by warmth or charm when we should be considering whether or not the speaker actually knows anything about the topic, then we lower the standards for public discourse.

Arguments and Appeals

Although perceived ethos can be an indication of the quality of public communication, it is a perception, and like other perceptions, it can be faulty. People who sound credible may have hidden agendas. Folks who seem attractive can be deceptive. And those with power do not necessarily have our best interests at heart. Therefore, it is important to pay close attention to the message itself and to the reasoning it employs.

The Structure of Argument: The Toulmin Model

Sometimes, we accept a speaker's message without question; at other times, we need to be convinced. In the latter case, the speaker must provide an **argument**, an explanation of his or her reasoning. But not all arguments are equally valid. One method of testing arguments is to employ the Toulmin model.

Parts of an Argument. What constitutes a good argument? According to Stephen Toulmin, everyday arguments, the kind we use to convince one another, are made up of six parts: claim, qualifier, data, warrant, backing, and rebuttal or reservation.[29] Although a speaker may not refer explicitly to all six parts during a speech, preferring to keep some parts hidden, audience members who wish to test the validity of an argument should try to uncover the argument in its entirety. The Toulmin model, illustrated in Figure 9.1, is a great help in this regard.

The **claim** is what the speaker wishes the audience to accept. An argument succeeds if the audience accepts the claim, and it fails if the audience rejects the claim. Claims may be facts ("Smoking cigarettes is hazardous to one's health"), values ("Health is a positive value and should be safeguarded"), or policies ("Cigarette advertising should be banned").

Claims vary in strength. Some claims are absolute; others are less certain. The **qualifier** indicates the strength of the claim. Modifiers such as "always," "sometimes," "probably," "nine out of ten times," and the like are qualifiers that indicate the strength of a claim. Although some facts in this world are absolute, most knowledge is conditional. Unqualified claims often indicate that a speaker is overstating the case.

Figure 9.1 **The Toulmin Model**

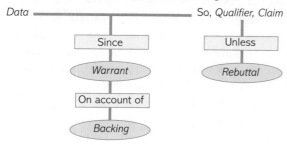

A General Diagram of an Argument

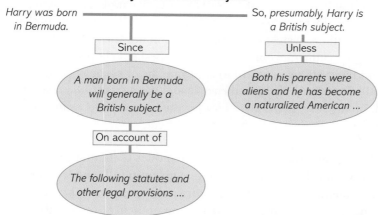

**Example of an Argument Seeking to Justify the Claim
"Harry Is a British Subject"**

From *The Uses of Argument* by Stephen Edelston Toulmin, 1985. Cambridge, UK: Cambridge University Press; p. 105. Reprinted with permission of Cambridge University Press.

Intelligent audiences do not accept unsupported claims, even if the claims are qualified. Instead, audience members want evidence, or **data**, to support claims. In making public claims, speakers use statistics, illustrative examples, research results, expert testimony, eyewitness accounts, and the like as data.

Citing data does not guarantee that an argument will be accepted. Audience members must see a relationship between data and claim; that is, they must understand the reasoning that lets the speaker move from evidence to conclusion. The connecting link between data and claim is called the **warrant**. Ultimately, the argument lives or dies on the strength of the warrant. Warrants may or may not be spelled out explicitly during the speech, but they are always a hidden part of the argument.

Let's suppose that a speaker's claim is that the proportion of women faculty at a given school should be increased.[30] The data show that only 7 percent of the faculty are women and that, as a consequence, very few students have the opportunity to study with a woman teacher. What is the warrant that ties data to claim? In this case, the warrant is based on a value; the speaker is arguing that the presence of women faculty is worthwhile and desirable. Audiences who share the speaker's values will accept the warrant with little difficulty. Others will need additional evidence, called backing. Outlining the educational and social advantages provided by women faculty will provide this backing. When a warrant is well understood and acceptable, it needs no backing; when it is less acceptable, it may require detailed explanation.

The final part of the Toulmin argument is the rebuttal, or reservation. This consists of a statement of the conditions under which the claim does not hold true. What might constitute the reservation in the argument about employing female teachers? If women were less competent scholars or teachers than men or if their contributions were not particularly unique, then the warrant would not hold, and the argument would crumble. If a speaker believes that the audience has significant reservations in regard to a warrant, he or she may bring up the reservations and refute them. If the audience favors the warrant, the reservation may be omitted. In any case, it is a good idea for the creator of an argument to search for reservations to test the strength of the argument.

Using the Toulmin Model.   Speakers often offer their audiences only part of an argument. When should an argument be given in full, and when is the use of a partial argument justified? Most rhetoricians agree that when the warrant and its backing are known and accepted by an audience, the speaker need not go through a detailed explanation of the entire argument. If, for example, I live in a state where the speed limit is 65 mph, I will accept the state trooper's claim "You were speeding" on the basis of the data "I clocked you going 73 mph." The trooper does not need to spell out the warrant ("Anyone who exceeds 65 mph is guilty of speeding") or provide backing for it ("According to provisions of New York state traffic laws"). A visitor from a state where the maximum speed limit is more than 65 mph, however, might need to hear the entire argument.

Since the time of Aristotle, rhetoricians have argued that when a speaker is confident that audience members will correctly fill in missing parts of an argument, it is not only more efficient but also more effective to allow them to do so. That is, when people supply their own reasoning, they are more likely to be convinced than when the speaker presents the argument to them.

Of course, not every audience member fills in an argument as the speaker wishes. Reasoning that seems completely self-evident to a speaker may be flatly rejected by some audience members. In deciding how fully to frame an argument, the speaker must carefully consider the kinds of conclusions the audience will draw and the kinds of warrants it will accept.

When we make arguments, we are often vague about them. We know the conclusion we wish the audience to reach, and we usually have some data to support it, but at times we have trouble articulating the warrant, backing, qualifier, and rebuttal. By using the Toulmin system to lay out our arguments, we can examine and clarify our thinking. And in evaluating a speaker's argument audience members should carefully examine the speaker's reasoning.

Types of Arguments

Adapting Aristotle's distinction between ethos, pathos, and logos, Wayne Brockreide and Douglas Ehninger argue that speakers have three kinds of warrants or ways of appealing to an audience.[31] Arguments can be based on authoritative, motivational, or substantive appeals.

As audience members we can easily be swept away by emotional appeals; it is our responsibility to carefully evaluate a speaker's arguments.

Authoritative and Motivational Arguments. An authoritative argument depends entirely on the authority of a source. Some sources are automatically trusted. In matters of health, the surgeon general is a good example. Let's assume the surgeon general has stated that a particular drug is dangerous and believes that it should not be sold. A speaker can use this statement as data to support the claim that the drug ought to be removed from the market immediately. We can outline the argument, including its implied authoritative warrant.

> **Data:** *According to the surgeon general, drug X is dangerous to public health.*
> **Claim:** *Drug X should be removed from the market immediately.*
> **Warrant:** *The surgeon general is an expert and trustworthy source whose recommendations should be followed.*
> **Reservation:** *Unless the surgeon general is politically motivated or her data are incorrect*

When parents tell their children to do something "because I said so," they too are using an authoritative warrant.

A motivational argument is based on the emotional needs of the audience. When a speaker uses a highly emotional appeal or urges audience members to accept a claim because doing so will satisfy a personal desire or need, he or she is using a motivational warrant. In the following example, the speaker relies on a visceral reaction of audience members. The argument is based on the speaker's belief that he and the audience share common feelings of pity and horror.

> **Data:** *Baby seals are being slaughtered.*
> **Claim:** *Laws should be enacted to protect the seals.*
> **Warrant:** *Brutality toward animals is emotionally repellent.*
> **Reservation:** *Unless animals do not have rights to humane treatment*

Whereas some motivational arguments are directed toward audience members' passions, others are directed toward members' needs. These kinds of motivational appeals assure audience members that a basic need will be fulfilled if the claim is accepted. To construct a need-focused argument, a speaker must understand the basic emotions and needs that drive an audience. Although needs are classified in several ways, the most familiar is **Maslow's needs hierarchy**. According to Abraham Maslow, humans have five basic needs.[32] The most urgent and basic of these needs are called **physiological needs**, the needs for food, water, air, warmth, and so on. Once these needs are satisfied, we concern ourselves with **safety needs**, our needs to be safe from external harm. Next come our needs for **love and belongingness**, and **self-esteem**. Finally, we experience the need for **self-actualization**, the need to reach our full potential. Later, Maslow came to believe that people may also be motivated by **curiosity needs**, the needs to explore and understand the environment, and by **aesthetic needs**, the needs for beauty, harmony, and balance.

Arguments can focus on any of these needs. Let's consider as an example a hypothetical advertisement for a new perfume.

> **Data:** (Visuals showing attractive male models being irresistibly drawn to a woman wearing Jungle Passion perfume.)
> **Claim:** *Buy Jungle Passion today.*
> **Warrant:** *If you buy Jungle Passion, you too will be irresistible to men, and your needs for belongingness and love will be satisfied.*
> **Reservation:** *Unless men find women attractive for reasons other than their scent*

Although this is not a particularly rational argument, it may be emotionally compelling if audience members' needs are strong enough and if members identify psychologically with the models in the advertisement.

Substantive Arguments. A **substantive argument** connects data and claim through logic and reasoning. When a speaker shows audience members that the claim is the only rational conclusion, given the data, he or she is using a substantive warrant. As we shall see, certain standard patterns of argument are considered acceptable in our culture. These patterns include arguments from cause, sign, generalization, and analogy. Each takes a slightly different form and must stand up to different tests to be considered valid. Each also can be misused and can lead to faulty conclusions.[33]

Arguments from cause are common in the public context. Whenever a speaker tries to establish why something happened, he or she is using a causal argument. The following example shows how a causal argument might work.

> **Claim:** *If my opponent is reelected, the economy will grow worse.*
> **Data:** *Since my opponent took office, inflation has risen and unemployment has grown dramatically.*
> **Warrant:** *These economic disasters were caused by my opponent's unwise fiscal policies.*
> **Reservation:** *Unless these economic disasters were caused by factors beyond my opponent's control*

Establishing causal connections is not always easy. A valid argument from cause must establish four things: (1) that the presumed cause (Y) preceded the presumed effect (X) in time; (2) that Y can, in fact, lead to X; (3) that there is no other, more plausible cause that might explain X; and (4) that both X and Y were not due to a third, unexplained factor. Only when all four propositions are established can we be confident that a cause really does exist.

In attempting to prove cause, people often commit a **fallacy** (an error in reasoning) called the **post hoc fallacy** or doubtful cause fallacy. They assume that Y caused X simply because it preceded X. Superstitions are examples of post hoc fallacies. The driver who has an accident right after a black cat crosses the road and who assumes that the cat caused the accident is committing a post hoc fallacy.

Although the flaw in the black cat argument is fairly easy to see (unless you are unusually superstitious), some post hoc fallacies can be harder to spot. Assume, for example, that right after a new coach is hired, a team has a losing season. It is tempting to blame the loss on the coach, because bad coaching can sometimes cause a team to lose. But before we recommend firing the coach, we need to rule out other possible causes. We need to be sure that nothing about this year's team (say, the players' lack of experience) makes them uncoachable. We also must assure ourselves that no third factor (say, budget cuts) has kept both team and coach from doing an effective job. Assigning cause is a common activity, but it is more difficult to do correctly than it appears.

Arguments from sign are a second kind of substantive argument. An argument from sign seeks to predict one condition (X) by pointing to another condition (Y) associated with it. Arguments from sign should not be confused with causal arguments. Smoke, for example, is a sign of fire, but it is not the cause of fire. Most people would accept the claim "This building is on fire" on the strength of the data "The hall is full of smoke." Not all arguments from sign, however, are this straightforward. Let's look at a slightly more controversial example.

Claim: *This year's freshman class will not do as well as previous classes.*
Data: *The class SAT scores are substantially lower than previous class scores.*
Warrant: *SAT scores are a good indicator of academic success.*
Reservation: *Unless SAT scores are biased or other factors intervene that contradict their validity*

For an argument from sign to be valid, four things must be established: (1) that Y is a reliable sign of X, (2) that nothing has occurred to change the relationship between X and Y, (3) that a sufficient number of signs point to X, and (4) that there are no signs that contradict X. Let's look at the argument about test scores. People who oppose using standardized scores to predict success in school often argue that although test scores may indicate some students' achievement potential, other equally reliable and less biased predictors are overlooked. When people rely on only one sign and ignore others or when they imperfectly associate the sign in question with what they think it predicts, they are using fallacious reasoning.

Arguments from generalization seek to establish a general conclusion on the basis of data taken from a small sample of cases.

Claim: *Jones will win the election.*
Data: *Of 1,000 people surveyed, 57 percent said that they would vote for Jones.*
Warrant: *The rest of the public will act as did the sample.*
Reservation: *Unless the sample was unusual in some way*

Although professional pollsters following scientific procedures can generalize with amazing accuracy, the kinds of generalizations we make every day are often flawed. Four conditions must be met for a generalization to be valid: (1) the cases examined must be representative; (2) a sufficient number of cases must be examined; (3) the data must be up to date; and (4) any negative cases must be negligible.

In everyday life, we often generalize on the basis of one or two instances. Unfounded stereotypes and prejudices are examples of a kind of fallacy called **hasty generalization**. Hasty generalizations are based on too few cases or on unusual cases. If I were to draw conclusions about what students on your campus are like by surveying one student (say, the student who usually sits next to you in class), my generalization would probably be flawed. When I generalize on the basis of one case, I run the risk of choosing an atypical individual. The more cases I look at and the more careful I am to avoid selection biases, the more likely I am to reach valid conclusions.

Arguments from analogy seek to establish that two situations, X and Y, are alike.

Claim: *As president, I will be able to balance the budget.*

Data: *As governor, I balanced the budget.*

Warrant: *Being governor is similar enough to being president that success at the former level means success at the latter level.*

Reservation: *Unless I have not anticipated additional difficulties*

The validity of an argument from analogy depends on two conditions: (1) that the cases being compared are alike in all important respects and (2) that any differences between the cases are insignificant. Arguments such as "It worked for me, so it will work for you" are good examples. This argument obviously fails if the two people involved are very different from one another.

Some analogies are purely figurative. They are rhetorical devices a speaker uses to explain an idea to an audience, but they should not be taken literally. Such a false analogy was used by King James I. He argued that the monarch is the head of state and that just as the body dies when the head is cut off, so the nation dies without its king.[34] Although the analogy may be emotionally compelling, it is not substantive. Nations and bodies are not, in most important respects, governed by the same principles.

STRENGTHENING CRITICAL RECEPTION SKILLS

Much as we like to believe that people are rational and logical, it simply isn't true. Much of the time, we jump to conclusions, engage in wishful thinking, and believe what is easiest for us to believe. Psychologists who study the ways people reason find that most of us hold cognitive biases that distort our conclusions about the world. Evidence suggests, for example, that people exaggerate responsibility for their successes and minimize responsibility for their failures; give themselves more credit than they deserve for collective activities; exaggerate the extent to which others agree with them; and believe that they have a great deal more control over their destinies than they actually do.[35]

As audience members, we also often act as lazy processors.[36] We make up our minds about a speaker not by listening carefully to what he or she has to say but rather by looking at surface details. A less-than-confident listener, for example, may assume that a speech was good simply because everyone else liked it. An audience member with math anxiety may decide that any speaker who uses statistics must be intelligent. This kind of cognitive carelessness puts us at risk of being fooled by ignorant or unscrupulous speakers who feed us half-truths and fallacies. The only way we can guard ourselves against lazy processing is to learn to recognize some of the techniques used to fool audiences. Table 9.4 lists some ways speakers either deliberately or inadvertently create false arguments.[37]

BECOMING A MORE RESPONSIBLE COMMUNICATOR

It is common to think that the ethical responsibility for public communication lies only with the speaker. Certainly, anyone who takes on the role of public speaker bears the burden of being well informed and trustworthy. But audiences too have a responsibility for the outcomes of public communication. In the next chapter, we consider how speakers can become more responsible communicators. We would like to end this chapter by briefly turning our attention to the role of the listener.

> Anyone who takes on the role of public speaker bears the burden of being well informed and trustworthy. But audiences too have a responsibility for the outcomes of public communication.

Table 9.4   Fallacies in Argument: Usages That Mislead Audiences

Ad Hominem

The speaker attacks someone's character in areas not necessarily relevant to the issue. By accusing a political opponent of infidelity, atheism, or a flamboyant lifestyle, the speaker diverts attention from the issue under discussion.

Slippery Slope

The speaker predicts that taking a given line of action will inevitably lead to undesirable effects. For example, it was once seriously argued that "If women are educated, they will be unable to bear children and the family will be destroyed." Slippery slope predictions often play on our fears.

False Dilemma

The speaker sets up an either–or situation, ignoring other possibilities. "America. Love it or leave it" and "You're either with me or against me" are two examples.

Straw Man

The speaker characterizes an opponent's view in simplistic terms and then easily demolishes it. Nixon's famous "Checkers speech" suggested that his only crime was in keeping a little cocker spaniel as a gift for his children. He had actually been accused of misappropriating campaign funds.

Non Sequitur

From the Latin, meaning "it does not follow." The speaker, using connectives such as *therefore, so,* or *hence,* makes two unrelated ideas seem logically connected. "It's been used for years; therefore, it must be good" is a non sequitur.

Glittering Generality

The speaker associates self or issue with a vague virtue word. "I believe in the American dream; my opponent will create the American nightmare" sounds good, but what does it mean?

Transfer

The speaker links own ideas with popular people or issues and links opponent's ideas with unpopular people or issues. Presidential candidates may portray themselves as following in the path of Washington or Lincoln, for example.

Plain Folks

The speaker attributes an idea to a member of the audience's own group rather than to self. Politicians often read letters from "average citizens" asking for help or thanking the politicians for enacting a given law.

Bandwagon

The speaker makes it appear that anyone who does not agree will be left out or will fall behind. "Fifty thousand people have already donated" legitimizes the act of donating and makes the nondonor feel abnormal.

Ad Populum

The speaker appeals to popular prejudices. "Unless we act now, the Japanese will soon own everything of value in this country" relies more on fear and ethnic prejudice than on a realistic threat.

As listeners, we act irresponsibly whenever we passively accept whatever we hear or when we allow personal needs and prejudices to blind us to facts. As audience members, we need to inform ourselves on important issues, follow arguments carefully, judge the adequacy of evidence, and critically evaluate the consequences of proposals. When unethical speakers persuade audiences to draw questionable conclusions audience members are themselves partly to blame. Taking on the role of listener does not absolve a communicator from ethical responsibilities.

SUMMARY

This chapter examines the character of public communication and offers advice about factors audiences should consider in evaluating public messages. Public communication is a face-to-face, one-to-many form of communication wherein a single speaker addresses a large audience. It is more formal and less spontaneous than communication in other contexts and is affected by factors such as audience size, time, and space. Public communication also differs from interpersonal or group communication in that it takes place in the public sphere.

Rhetoric is the art of designing messages that can change the way audiences think and feel about public issues. Understanding rhetorical principles has both social and personal advantages. Socially, it allows us to discover facts, test ideas, advocate positions, shape knowledge, build community, and distribute power. Because the ability to communicate in public is a necessary skill in most careers, knowledge of rhetoric also leads to personal and professional success.

Three factors that audiences should consider in evaluating public messages are context, audience–speaker relationship, and message appeals. First, public messages must fit the context in which they are situated. Context includes factors such as physical setting, medium, and occasion as well as historical setting and argumentational history. That is, events that surround a speaking occasion have an effect on audience response, as does the way an issue has been argued in the past. One of the simplest yet most powerful discussions of the importance of context can be found in Bitzer's discussion of rhetorical situation. Bitzer believes that situation both motivates and shapes public discourse. Rhetorical situation consists of three parts, exigence (the problem addressed by a speaker), audience (receivers who have a stake in the outcome), and constraints (factors that affect the way messages are shaped). Rhetoric succeeds if it matches the demands of the rhetorical situation.

When speakers communicate in rhetorical situations, they seek to influence audiences. They can do this by targeting the beliefs, attitudes, or values of audiences. Audience members are also influenced by the personal characteristics they believe speakers possess. Three characteristics that affect audiences are a speaker's credibility, attractiveness, and power. Credibility refers to the extent to which a speaker is believable; it is affected by perceptions of expertness and trustworthiness. Attractiveness refers to the extent to which audience members want to maintain a relationship with the speaker and is affected by familiarity, similarity, physical appearance, and liking. Finally, power refers to the extent to which a source controls a valued resource. In addition to referent and expert power, legitimate power, reward power, and coercive power allow speakers to persuade audiences.

In evaluating public communication, audiences should not rely solely on their perception of source characteristics. It is also important to look at the appeals and arguments contained in a message. The Toulmin model provides one way of analyzing arguments and identifying gaps in logic. Audiences should also consider the nature of appeals. In authoritative appeals, arguments are based on expert opinions. In motivational appeals, arguments focus on audience needs such as the physiological, safety, love, esteem, self-actualization, curiosity, and aesthetic needs outlined by Maslow. In substantive appeals, logical argumentation based on cause, sign, generalization, and analogy is used.

KEY TERMS

Listed below are the key terms used in this chapter, along with the number of the page where each is explained.

SUGGESTED READINGS

Borchers, Timothy. (2006). *Rhetorical theory: An introduction*. New York: Thomson/Wadsworth.

An excellent introduction to the history of rhetoric, Borchers takes on topics such as style and delivery, argumentation, theories of meaning, and rhetorical criticism as well as interesting discussions of gendered and non-Western rhetorical theories.

Herrick, James A. (2005). *The history and theory of rhetoric: An introduction* (3rd ed.). Boston: Allyn and Bacon.

If you are interested in learning more about rhetorical approaches to the study of public communication, Herrick provides an excellent, readable summary of rhetorical theory from Sophists of ancient Greece to the works of contemporary writers.

10

Preparing and Presenting Public Speeches

After reading this chapter, you should be able to:

- Understand how public speeches differ from other forms of discourse.

- Explain why it is important for speakers to understand audiences, and list some of the demographics that describe audience characteristics.

- List sources speakers can go to for information about audience motivations and attitudes.

- Explain the functions of the introduction and conclusion of a speech and describe techniques used in both.

- Identify the stock organizational patterns used to structure material in the body of a speech.

- Be able to write a formal speech outline.

- Know the difference between impromptu, extemporaneous, and manuscript delivery.

- Understand ways to manage speech anxiety.

- Identify effective and ineffective use of visual aids.

- Discuss the ethical responsibilities of the public speaker.

Public speaking offers the opportunity to speak up when it is important to do so, to develop ideas in one's own way, and to make a difference in the public sphere.

Consider the following situations in which you or someone you know might well be called upon to give a public speech.

- At your parents' twenty-fifth wedding anniversary celebration, you are asked to propose a toast and give a speech of congratulation.

- Your boss decides that you should explain the company benefit package to an assembly of new employees.

- Your child's teacher invites you to talk about your job during the school's career week.

- You are so outraged by a local politician's proposed law that you stand up and oppose it at a town council meeting.

Occasions like these are common. They are the kinds of everyday speaking situations that most of us encounter sometime in our lives, and it matters if we do them well. Some people respond to the challenge of public communication with fear and hesitation; others respond with grace and confidence. Luckily, a little knowledge and a lot of practice can transform the former into the latter. In this chapter, we look at ways to improve public speaking. In particular, we focus on audience analysis and adaptation, speech organization, delivery, and ways to use technology to enhance presentations. Reading this chapter cannot turn you into a Clarence Darrow or a Martin Luther King Jr. overnight, but it can give you some of the basic knowledge you need to prepare and organize presentations. And coupled with practice, it can give you the confidence to stand up and speak when you are called on to do so.

WHAT IS A PUBLIC SPEECH?

A public speech is a form of communication that is quite unlike most everyday interactions. It is an organized, purposeful, continuous presentation delivered in the presence of a relatively large group of receivers. In everyday interactions, receiver and sender roles switch back and forth; when giving a public speech, however, the speaker is the primary sender. In normal conversations, speaker and listener are usually personally acquainted. In the public speaking situation, by contrast, the speaker addresses a largely anonymous audience. In most informal settings, the communicators are situated within a few feet of one another. In public venues, they are commonly separated in space.

> In planning a public speech, speakers must find a way to establish a relationship with audience members, structure the speech so that it is both persuasive and easy to understand, and, to keep the audiences' attention over an extended period of time, develop a compelling vocal and gestural style.

PLANNING THE PUBLIC SPEECH

The conditions described above present the public speaker with a complex set of challenges. In planning a public speech, speakers must find a way to establish a relationship with audience members, structure the speech so that it is both persuasive and easy to understand, and, to keep the audiences' attention over an extended period of time, develop a compelling vocal and gestural style. In addition, speakers have to find ways to manage speech anxiety. This sounds like a tall order, but it is one that most of us can achieve with practice.

Creating a Relationship with the Audience

As we saw in Chapter 9, speakers need to create relationships with their receivers. To do so, they need to adapt their messages. We don't speak the same way to everyone, because every individual is different. For a kindergarten teacher to treat schoolchildren as though they were graduate students would be ridiculous. It would be equally ridiculous to confuse the life experiences of adolescents with those of senior citizens or to assume that people reared in remote rural communities have

Being able to stand and deliver in everyday speaking situations is a basic competence that can serve all of us well.

exactly the same experiences as do those from crowded urban centers. When we take into account the beliefs and life experiences of audience members and use that information in constructing a message, we are engaging in **audience adaptation**. Audience adaptation doesn't mean lying to please an audience; it means making a message relevant and understandable to the audience.

Audience Adaptation

A good communicator uses information about the audience in constructing at least three aspects of a speech: its central idea and structure, its supporting materials, and its style. A speaker must first decide on the purpose and central idea of the speech. If the speech is intended to inform, the speaker must present new and interesting information that is not too difficult or detailed. If the speech is intended to persuade, the speaker must avoid alienating audience members by advocating a proposal that is too extreme. In choosing the central idea of the speech, the speaker must know what the audience currently believes, what positions it might be willing to accept, and what positions it definitely rejects.

A successful communicator adapts to the audience. These children are clearly delighted with the performance being put on for them.

Assume for a moment that you are planning to argue that there is too much sex and violence on television. If members of your audience agree with you, you might advocate strong measures to combat the problem, including a boycott of products advertised on offensive programs. If your audience is less concerned about current programming, a better approach might be to show why current programming is objectionable. When an audience doesn't share your concern at all, you should identify the problem rather than offer a solution. In adjusting your proposal in this way, you are taking a realistic, incremental approach to persuasion.

The structure of the speech should also be adapted to the beliefs of audience members. With a hostile audience, for example, effective speakers begin by establishing common ground and then gradually move into their argument, presenting both sides of an issue rather than arguing for just one. With a favorable audience, however, a direct, one-sided appeal may be most effective.

Speakers should also choose supporting materials with audience characteristics in mind. Assume that you support bringing a professional athletic team to your community and that meeting this goal involves raising money to build a new stadium. When speaking to a group of business leaders, you might stress the economic advantages of your proposal; when speaking to the local PTA, however, you might mention that increased spending may provide additional dollars for education and that the team will provide a new source of family entertainment. Good speakers choose appeals that are relevant to the audience.

> People come to a speech with expectations. They want your speech to resemble their idea of the way a speech should sound.

Finally, the style of a speech should be adapted to the audience. Above all else, speeches must be understandable. It is not a good idea to try to clarify a concept by comparing it to a computer if the people in your audience are computer illiterate. If you are speaking to a group of engineers, however, this type of clarification might be a very good idea—provided that you know what you are talking about. It is also important to remember that people come to a speech with expectations. They want your speech to resemble their idea of the way a speech should sound. If you violate their expectations by using an unusual style, the speech will probably fail.

Audience Analysis

To make the adjustments just described, you must gather information about your audience. This can be done in a number of ways. **Demographic analysis** tells you about the groups to which audience members belong. Knowing the age, sex, educational level, religious affiliation, occupation, economic status, and cultural identification of audience members can help a speaker draw inferences about current beliefs and interests.

Age is an important audience variable. A story or example that appeals to a teenage audience may mean very little to listeners in their forties, whereas personalities and issues familiar to older listeners may be over younger listeners' heads. References to the 1960s, for example, can effectively build interest or illustrate a point if the audience is full of baby boomers, but these references can mystify an audience of teens.

Gender is another demographic factor that affects audience responses. Men and women are likely to have different views and concerns in some cases and identical responses in others. The trick is understanding which case is which. In earlier times, when women's place was thought to be in the private sphere and men's in the public sphere, audience adaptation was easy. Those days are, fortunately, long past, and men and women are now more equal. Nevertheless, even today's liberated men and women were raised in gender-specific environments and were encouraged to pursue sex-typed interests. This makes adaptation based on gender a difficult process. Stereotypic assumptions will only offend large segments of the audience, yet ignoring differences can be insensitive. As Stephen Lucas explains, "you must avoid false sex distinctions that do not exist and acknowledge true sex distinctions where they do exist."[1] To see just how difficult this is, try making your own lists of topics that are suitable for men and women without offending or stereotyping either group.

Lucas's rule should also be applied to other demographic categories, such as ethnicity, cultural identity, and geographic location. Speakers who address groups to which they themselves do not belong should be especially careful to check their assumptions by asking for feedback from people who belong to those groups. Speakers should also remember that collecting demographic data is not an end in itself. Data are useful only to the extent that they allow a speaker to answer specific questions: What motivates the people I am preparing to speak to? Why will they attend, and how do they feel about my topic? What approach will best help me inform or convince them?

A skilled speaker uses a number of sources to gather information about audiences.[2] One source is the local media. Bert Bradley suggests that speakers listen to local news broadcasts and subscribe to a local newspaper prior to a speaking engagement. News items show the kind of information that interests members of the community, editorials indicate opinions and concerns, and classified ads can provide useful information about economic conditions. Another source is personal interviews with individuals who are similar to audience members. Finally, if invited by an organization to speak, the speaker should spend some time with people in the organization and should read its official publications.

Structuring the Speech

Because public speeches are purposeful and because speakers communicate for extended periods of time, organization and structure are extremely important. Unless the speech is carefully constructed, audience members can lose interest or misinterpret the speaker's message. For this reason, public speeches are generally structured into three parts: introduction, body, and conclusion.

Introductions and Conclusions

Research shows that the beginnings and endings of arguments are remembered more than middle sections. Because introductions create initial impressions and conclusions sum up a speaker's points, they are extremely important to the structure of the presentation.

Functions of the Introduction.   The first function of the introduction is to create a desire in the audience to listen to the speech. As the speaker begins, audience members judge whether the speech will be lively or boring. If the speaker does not create interest at the outset, listeners are likely to tune out. Audience members also judge the speaker's qualifications. Therefore, the second function of the introduction is to increase audience confidence in the speaker. The speaker must introduce himself or herself to the audience and establish positive ethos. Finally, the third function of the introduction is to let the audience know what the speech is about. If audience members cannot figure out what the point is, they will stop listening. At some point in the introduction, the speaker must announce the thesis, or central purpose, of the speech. He or she may also use the introduction to foreshadow major points and themes (if the speech topic is complex) or to provide special information and definitions (if the topic is unfamiliar).

How does a speaker actually accomplish these goals? There are some standard ways in which speakers begin speeches: referring to the topic or occasion, offering a personal allusion or greeting, asking a rhetorical question, making a startling statement, using a quotation, telling a humorous anecdote, and offering an illustration. Table 10.1 lists and illustrates these techniques and explains how they are related to the functions of the introduction.

Functions of the Conclusion. Just as the introduction is the speaker's first opportunity to make an impression on the audience, so the ending of the speech, or the conclusion, is the speaker's last chance to convince the audience. Both the introduction and the conclusion are extremely important, because audiences listen most closely and most critically at the beginning and at the end of a communication. Many novice speakers fail to take advantage of this phenomenon. They trail off or simply stop without warning the audience that the speech is ending.

> Just as the introduction is the speaker's first opportunity to make an impression on the audience, so the ending of the speech, or the conclusion, is the speaker's last chance to convince the audience.

The conclusion must be as carefully crafted as the introduction and must generally do three things: signal that the speech is ending, reiterate the significance of the topic, and summarize the main ideas of the speech. If these functions are fulfilled, the audience leaves with a feeling of closure and an understanding of what the speaker expects them to know or to do.

As with the introduction, a speech may conclude in many stock ways. These ways, summarized in Table 10.2, include issuing a challenge or appeal, summarizing main ideas, using a relevant quotation, returning to an earlier illustration, offering an inducement for action or belief, and expressing one's own intention in relation to the speech topic.

Organizing the Body of the Speech

The part of the speech that lies between the introduction and the conclusion is called the body of the speech. Here, major ideas are developed and supported. It is important to organize these ideas so that audience members can follow the flow of the speech. Receivers who are exposed to written arguments can always reread a puzzling message. Receivers of spoken messages, however, must follow an argument as it is presented. To help them do this, speakers employ several devices. They preview the speech structure ("I'm going to give you three reasons why you should take action today"), use transitions to move the audience from one idea to

Table 10.1 Ways to Open a Public Speech

Type of Opening	Example
Reference to Topic A direct statement of subject; works well with motivated audience; less effective with skeptical or apathetic receivers	"I am here tonight to speak to you about a concern we all share, the problem of . . . ."
Reference to Occasion A reference to the reason for the speech; allows speaker to acknowledge special occasions	"On the 100th anniversary of the founding of this great institution, it is fitting that we gather here to celebrate."
Personal Reference or Greeting An indication of one's relation to topic or audience; builds common ground; can backfire if greeting is too familiar or intrusive	"It's a pleasure to be here today. Ten years ago, I too was a new student. Like you, I wondered what the next four years would bring."
Rhetorical Question A question the speaker wants the audience to consider; involves audience; can offend if it makes assumptions about audience or asks members to make an uncomfortable choice	"What would you do if you had no place to live and no one to turn to for help? How long would you survive on the streets?"
Startling Statement A shocking statement of fact or opinion; increases attention and interest; can offend if silly or melodramatic	"Every six seconds another child becomes a victim of . . . ."
Quotation A relevant quotation from a respected source; links speaker to source; can be trite or inapplicable	"As Shakespeare said, 'All the world's a stage. . . .'"
Humorous Anecdote A joke or story related to topic; shows speaker's warmth; can offend if poorly chosen	"This puts me in mind of a story. It seems there were three shipwrecked sailors . . . ."
Illustration An extended example; makes topic vivid and concrete; can divert attention if point of illustration is not clear	"Let me tell you about what happened to one family whose lives were changed by our program . . . ."

From D. Ehninger and A. Monroe, *Principles and Types of Communication*, 7/e. Published by Allyn and Bacon, Boston, MA. Copyright © 1974 by Pearson Education. Reprinted by permission of the publisher.

the next ("Now let's look at the second reason"), and employ internal summaries ("So far, we've seen that there are financial and social reasons to act"). Even more important than these stylistic devices is the use of an overall organizational scheme that arranges materials in ways that make sense to an audience. Several stock organizational patterns have been identified. These patterns include chronological, spatial, topical, causal, and problem–solution orders, as well as a special pattern known as the motivated sequence.

A chronological order arranges ideas according to a logical time sequence. If you were giving a speech on the history of the United States (putting aside for the moment the fact that this is too broad a topic for a single speech), you might decide to talk about North America before Columbus, the colonies prior to the Revolution, the Revolutionary period, the early Republic, and so on up to the present.

Table 10.2 Ways to Close a Public Speech

Type of Closing	Example
Challenge or Appeal A direct request for action; lets audience know what to do next; not as appropriate if change desired is attitudinal rather than behavioral	"I encourage you to join with us now. . . ."
Summary A restatement of main ideas; increases audience comprehension	"There are, then, four ways we can protect ourselves. . . ."
Quotation A relevant quotation from a respected source; increases speaker credibility and inspires audience	"Let me close with the words Thomas Jefferson used when he stood in this hall exactly 200 years ago today. . . ."
Illustration An extended example; makes speech content concrete; can tie conclusion to earlier material	"So the next time you're ready to give up on yourself, remember what happened to the Jackson family. . . ."
Added Inducement A final reason for believing or acting; increases audience acceptance; can confuse if inducement is not clearly tied to proposal	"And if we work together now, not only will we be a happier and healthier community, but we will also . . . ."
Personal Intention A statement of what the speaker is prepared to do; speaker leads by example and illustrates own trustworthiness	"I know I will be at the rally on Sunday, and I hope I will see you there too."

From D. Ehninger and A. Monroe, *Principles and Types of Communication*, 7/e. Published by Allyn and Bacon, Boston, MA. Copyright © 1974 by Pearson Education. Reprinted by permission of the publisher.

It makes more sense to follow a past-to-present chronology. If you were given the job of orienting new students to your campus, one way would be to take them through a typical day, from morning to evening. In both cases, use of a time sequence would help you to order your thoughts in a way that audience members could easily follow.

A spatial order arranges ideas according to physical location. The speech on U.S. history, for example, could be arranged geographically from east to west. In the orientation speech, you could employ a spatial order by taking your audience on an imaginary tour of the campus. As you would mentally pass each building or location, you could talk about a different aspect of campus life. For example, you might start at the theater and discuss the cultural life of the campus, move on to the gym and talk about athletics, proceed to the classrooms and discuss academic life, and so on. Of course, the success of this approach would depend on whether audience members were familiar with a map of the campus. For those unfamiliar with the campus, the use of slides or other visual aids could add interest and clarity.

A topical order divides the speech into familiar subtopics. Yet another way of organizing the orientation speech might be to divide the college experience into separate components: academic, social, cultural, and so forth. Or if you were explaining the kinds of majors available, you might discuss them in clusters: natural sciences, social sciences, humanities, and fine arts. Topical order works only when the subtopics seem to be sensible divisions of a field and when they are reasonably exhaustive. If a subtopic is unfamiliar to the audience, it should not be used. For example, if a student is not familiar with the term *social science,* this way of organizing the speech will be confusing.

The next two stock patterns are useful when a problem is the topic of the speech. When the speaker's goal is to discuss the causes and effects of the problem, a causal order may be used. Here, the speech is divided into two main parts. In the first, the factors that have led to the problem are discussed; in the second, the results of these factors are explained. Imagine a speech on the depletion of the ozone layer. The speech might first explain major causes of the problem and then talk about what will result if the problem continues. For speeches that offer a solution, problem–solution order is often used. As the name suggests, the two main divisions of this type of speech are the problem and the solution. Imagine a speech urging voluntary recycling. The speaker first establishes that a problem exists— that in many communities, landfills are completely full and alternative forms of waste disposal are unavailable. Having convinced the audience that a serious problem exists, the speaker then offers a solution (or a partial solution): voluntary recycling.

A final stock organizational pattern is called the motivated sequence. This five-part organizational plan focuses on making the topic and the claim relevant to audience needs. According to Alan Monroe, who developed this approach, the sequence follows a natural progression; that is, it mirrors the psychological reactions of receivers as they consider issues related to their needs.[3]

The five steps in the motivated sequence are attention, need, satisfaction, visualization, and action. In the **attention step**, which occurs in the introduction, the speaker's goal is to focus audience members on the message and to give them a reason for listening. Let's assume a speaker wants to convince audience members to begin to make financial investments for their old age. An audience of college-age people may not find this a very compelling topic. A startling statistic may serve here to gain attention. The speaker might say something such as, "In 2038, the year most of you will reach retirement, a dollar will be worth only X percent of its value today, a week's groceries will cost Y dollars, and rent on the most modest apartment will be Z dollars per month." If the numbers used are extreme, the audience will probably take note of them. Of course, the speaker's statistics should be taken from a reliable source so that they are believable as well as shocking.

The next step is the **need step**. Here, the speaker shows audience members that a present state of affairs is undesirable. In the investment speech example, the speaker uses the need step to establish that Social Security benefits alone will not be enough to allow audience members to live comfortably. The speaker's goal is to get the audience to think, "These things could happen to me if I don't take action."

Following the need step is the **satisfaction step**. Here, the speaker offers a plan to meet the need. In the example we have been discussing, the speaker has used the need step to induce fear of the future. Now he or she must show the audience that there is a simple and effective way to reduce the fear. Without this step, audience members may simply refuse to think about the issue. With a successful satisfaction step, however, they will see how their fear can be alleviated. At this point, then, our speaker shows how a reasonably modest amount of money can, over time, create a substantial retirement fund. The investment plan should be simple and easy to understand, and the use of complicated computations should be kept to a minimum, especially if the audience is not comfortable with numbers.

If the satisfaction step has worked, audience members are now thinking, "The plan seems simple and effective." To cement this idea and to motivate the audience to take action on the speaker's recommendations, the speaker next uses the **visualization step**. Here, the speaker describes concretely what will happen if the solution is adopted. In the investment speech, the speaker paints a picture of a retirement free from worry, a time when audience members can travel, pursue special interests and hobbies, and generally live comfortably.

Finally, in the **action step**, the speaker asks the audience to implement the proposal outlined in the satisfaction step. "So pick up one of our brochures, and open an IRA today" might constitute the action step and conclude the investment speech.

Outlining Main Points and Subpoints

Whichever organizational pattern you choose, be sure to develop your ideas fully and clearly in ways an audience will find sensible. One way to check your organization is to outline your speech. An outline is a kind of blueprint that shows the basic ideas in your speech. When you outline, you write out each of your main points and, below each main point, indicate the subpoints you wish to make. An outline allows you to see at a glance whether you are mixing up your ideas. Main points are usually indicated by Roman numerals and are written next to the left-hand margin; subpoints are indented. Table 10.3 illustrates an outline form and provides a summary of our discussion of speech structure.

MANAGING DELIVERY

In an everyday conversation, it's hardly necessary to worry about delivery. You talk in your natural tone, and if your partner wants you to speak more softly or more loudly or more clearly, he or she will ask you. In public, however, factors such as rate, volume, and articulation are important. Novice speakers often speak way too quickly, have trouble speaking loudly enough to be heard by everyone, and may not speak clearly.

> In an everyday conversation it's hardly necessary to worry about delivery. In public, however, factors such as rate, volume, and articulation are important.

Table 10.3   An Example of Outline Form

How to Organize a Public Speech

I. A well-organized speech opens with an introduction.

   A. The introduction gets attention.

   B. The introduction establishes goodwill.

   C. The introduction orients listeners to the subject.

II. Every speech should have a thesis, or central purpose statement.

   A. The thesis explains the central idea of the speech.

   B. Ideas unrelated to the thesis should be eliminated.

   C. The audience must be able to identify the thesis.

III. Main ideas are included in the body of the speech.

   A. Organizing main ideas in outline form allows the speaker to check the organization.

      1. In outlines, subpoints are subordinated to main points.

      2. If an idea is subdivided, it should include at least two subpoints.

   B. Stock organizational patterns help the speaker arrange points in a sensible order.

      1. Chronological order arranges ideas according to time.

      2. Spatial order arranges ideas according to location.

      3. Topical order arranges ideas according to subject.

      4. Causal order arranges ideas into causes and effects.

      5. Problem–solution order arranges ideas into problems and solutions.

      6. Motivated sequence arranges ideas psychologically.

IV. Speeches end with a conclusion.

   A. A conclusion should provide a sense of closure.

   B. A conclusion should sum up the argument or present a proposal for action.

   C. The conclusion is the last thing an audience hears.

Type of delivery is also important. Public speakers must match topic, occasion, and their own personal style in deciding whether to speak off the cuff, plan their speech ahead of time but deliver it conversationally, or read it from a manuscript.

Types of Deliveries

Traditionally, teachers of public speaking talk about three styles of speaking: impromptu, extemporaneous, and manuscript. **Impromptu speaking** occurs when the speaker is suddenly confronted with a rhetorical situation and is able, on the spur of the moment, to organize a message. Impromptu speaking does not mean disorganized speaking. In fact, in impromptu situations, clear organization is a must. The more practiced a speaker is at public presentations and the more familiar he or she is with the topic, the more successful an impromptu speech will be.

Extemporaneous speaking is carefully preplanned but nonmemorized delivery. The extemporaneous speaker has researched and outlined the message but has not memorized its exact wording. Extemporaneous speeches are usually more immediate than memorized speeches; they allow the speaker to connect with the audience and choose the words that will have the greatest impact at the time. This is the method of delivery that is most favored in beginning public speaking classes.

Manuscript speaking, by contrast, involves very careful composition. In this form of delivery, the speaker reads from a printed page or TelePrompTer. Although beginning speakers often imagine that it would be easier to speak from a manuscript than to speak extemporaneously, it is actually very difficult to read with expression and quite easy to lose one's place. It takes a great deal of skill to avoid appearing wooden when reading. On the other hand, when precise wording is important, it is advisable to use a manuscript. No one form is better than the others. The nature of the rhetorical situation should dictate the type of delivery, and good public speakers become adept at all kinds of speaking.

Speech Anxiety

Most people who speak before large audiences experience some amount of **speech anxiety**. They may experience problems in speaking too fast or too slow, stammering, speech blocks, dry mouth, rapid heartbeat—the list goes on. This is entirely normal, and in most cases, the fear disappears over time. While you're waiting for it to subside, there are two measures you can take to reduce your apprehension. One is **cognitive restructuring**, in which you substitute adaptive thinking for negative thoughts. For example, instead of thinking, "I'll look like an idiot up there," you could think, "I know a lot more about this topic than anyone else in the class does, and besides they're just as scared as I am." The other is to use some form of **physical relaxation**, such as breathing deeply or consciously relaxing tense muscles. Both measures are based on the principle that it is impossible to experience

Speakers' use of gestures can be a powerful way of communicating.

two different mental or physical states at the same time. When you're thinking positively, it's hard to feel fear; when your body is relaxed, it's impossible to feel tense.

For most people, practice and a few simple actions will reduce tension. Raymond Ross lists six useful ways to become more confident. First, you should recognize and, if necessary, talk to someone about your fright; your instructor is a good source. By talking about it, you normalize your fear. Second, find a way to burn up excess tension by engaging in a simple, repetitive physical activity before you begin. Third, redirect your attention, for example, by concentrating on a given audience member or on objects on the back walls of the auditorium (but be sure you don't lose eye contact with your audience for long). Fourth, use a clear organizational pattern or a simple outline to keep from losing your place or forgetting a point. If you do blank out, try summarizing what you've said so far, as this will generally reawaken your memory. Fifth, unless you're giving your first Inaugural Address or accepting a Nobel Prize, your speech will not be recorded for posterity, so be realistic about its importance. Finally, concentrate on your message more than on yourself.[4]

If you are unusually apprehensive and find that your fear is debilitating or that it transfers to other communication situations, then you may want to take part in a program of **systematic desensitization**. In this process, you will learn to substitute deep relaxation for fear responses. You will be asked to list the situations that make you apprehensive, in order of severity; you will then be instructed on how to relax; finally, you will be asked to imagine each fear-producing situation while remaining relaxed. Over time, your fear reactions can be extinguished or at least reduced to the point at which they are manageable. Most college or university counseling centers offer some form of desensitization. Don't be afraid to use their services if you experience severe speech anxiety. Your reactions are something you learned along the way, and they can be unlearned with a little work.

INCREASING PUBLIC SPEAKING SKILLS

Many people avoid giving public speeches because they think that to speak in public, one must be a "born speaker." The truth is, of course, that no one is born able to speak in public. Even the greatest public speakers had to start somewhere. For many great speakers, that starting point was the realization that public speaking offers opportunities: an opportunity to speak up when it is important to do so, an opportunity to develop ideas in one's own way, and an opportunity to make a difference in the public sphere.

Some Guidelines for Speakers

Keep in mind that although each speech you give will be different, some general principles will help you to prepare to speak in public. Before speaking, you must *do serious research and preparation*. Researching your subject will increase your understanding of your subject area, build up your self-confidence, and, when incorporated into your speech, increase your ethos. It will also provide convincing data to back up your claims.

Once you have done sufficient research, you can start to develop your main points and arguments. First, make sure that your ideas make sense to you; then make sure they will make sense to your audience. This means that you must *make a special effort to be organized and clear*. Keep in mind that the audience has not researched and thought about the topic as you have and that conclusions that seem self-evident to you may not seem so to them.

Listening is a difficult, draining process, and audiences often become bored or distracted. *Incorporate vivid and interesting elements into your speech*. By using personal examples, concrete and immediate language, interesting anecdotes, and the like, you can keep your audience interested. Try also to make what you say relevant to audience members' life experiences.

Finally, you should *develop your own individual style*. What will make you worth listening to is the unique perspective you bring to a problem. If you can find a way to express original ideas in a personal style, you will have gone a long way toward becoming a good speaker.

Using Technology to Enhance Public Speeches

Although it is possible to give a compelling public speech without sophisticated audiovisual aids, most speakers realize that a well-placed chart, picture, or film clip can enhance a presentation. Nowadays, computer-generated multimedia presentations are a part of many traditional public speaking situations. They have been used effectively during final summations in trials and during nominating speeches at political conventions. Community groups employ them during year-end reports; teachers use them during lectures; and they are a large part of day-to-day business presentations. Certainly, slick visuals can never replace carefully organized and well-thought-out content; nevertheless, if visuals are well designed, they can add to the impact of a speech. Nowadays, none of us can afford to ignore a tool that is becoming an expected part of public communication.

> Nowadays, computer-generated multimedia presentations are a part of many traditional public speaking situations. Slick visuals can never replace carefully organized and well-thought-out content; nevertheless, if visuals are well designed, they can add to the impact of a speech.

Why Visual Aids Are Important

When used effectively, visual aids can increase audience attention, comprehension, and retention. First of all, visual images are often more compelling and emotionally powerful than words. As we saw in Chapter 3, receivers automatically attend to vivid images, especially if they are colorful or novel. Visual aids can also increase comprehension by making difficult concepts clear. A graph or diagram can help us to understand concepts that would be hard to put into words. In addition, visual images are often highly memorable, so they can stick with us long after we have forgotten the actual words a speaker used. Finally, use of well-designed visual aids can make a speaker appear credible to an audience. Of course, if visual aids are not carefully thought out, they can backfire. PowerPoint slides can bore an audience, graphs can be confusing, and video clips can act as distractors. And visuals that seem carelessly made or awkwardly presented can actually decrease credibility judgments.

Visual aids can capture attention, but to be effective they should match the occasion and purpose.

How to Make Visual Aids More Effective

What are some things that make visual aids ineffective? Basically, visual aids don't work if:

- They draw attention away from the idea they are meant to illustrate
- They are difficult to see or understand
- They present too much information at once
- They are awkward or difficult to handle during the presentation
- Their relationship to the idea they are meant to illustrate is not clear

Visual aids should not distract. Because visual aids are so compelling, it is important that they not take attention away from the speaker. If you are going to display an object, for example, you should keep it hidden until it is needed. If you are using PowerPoint slides, show a blank slide until you reach the point in your speech at which you want to introduce the idea illustrated on your slide. In general, you should avoid using visual aids that need to be passed around the room. Stephen Lucas tells us that putting visual aids in the hands of the audience spells trouble. "At least three people will be paying more attention to the aid than to you—the person who has just had it, the person who has it now, and the person waiting to get it next."[5]

> Because visual aids are so compelling, it is important that they not take attention away from the speaker.

Visual aids must be easy to see. If a visual aid is too small or if it is messy and hard to decipher, it will work against you. On slides, you must consider font size, color, balance, and a variety of other design elements. Charts should be easy to understand and clearly labeled.

Visual aids should be simple. Generally, visual aids are used for illustrative or summarizing purposes. Don't try to get your entire presentation onto a poster or handout. A single slide with a picture, a chart, a quote, an animated cartoon, and five lines of text may show how clever you are at using PowerPoint, but it won't be effective. Remember, people come to hear a speech, not to read it.

Visual aids should be easy to handle. This rule is especially important with computerized or multimedia presentations. Electronic aids that need complex equipment to operate can invite disaster if the speaker isn't comfortable with the equipment or if something breaks. This means that you need to practice until you are completely confident. Asking the audience, "Hey, does anyone know how to turn on the projector?" doesn't create a positive impression. It is also necessary to have a backup plan. If your videotape breaks or the DVD player is not in the room, you should be prepared to give the speech the old-fashioned way.

Visual aids should be subordinate to the ideas they are meant to illustrate. The basic idea to remember is that visual aids are just that—aids. Their relationship to the points in a speech should be clear. Randomly chosen photos, no matter how beautiful, won't advance an argument or illustrate a thought. It is also important not to overuse slides; they should be used only when they will have maximum impact.

If these warnings are kept in mind, audiovisual aids can make a presentation polished and professional. Many software packages are available that can help you to design your presentation. Perhaps the most widely known is PowerPoint, which is, in fact, a very powerful tool. It can allow you to create and display text, photographs, clip art, charts, graphs, video clips, and audio clips with relative ease. It is definitely worth the time to become familiar with how this software works. But be careful. The more features you use, the more careful you need to be to make sure your style and tone are consistent and that every choice you make works to enhance your purpose.

BECOMING A MORE RESPONSIBLE COMMUNICATOR

From the very beginning of the study of rhetoric, ethics and communication have been linked. For the Greeks, ethical behavior was an important characteristic of the ideal communicator. Isocrates, for example, believed that dishonest communicators could do great harm; he therefore taught that "the argument which is made by a man's life is of more weight than that which is furnished by words."[6] Today, when technology has increased the ability of all communicators to reach mass audiences, the importance of ethical communication is at least as important as it was in classical times. Here are some simple guidelines to keep in mind as you engage in public communication, either in the community or in the classroom:

- A distinguishing characteristic of public communication is the power that is given over to the speaker. In the public context, the primary communication role is given to the speaker, and audience members expect facts that are true and proposals that are well considered. Whenever you speak publicly, even if only in the classroom, you are responsible for what you say. Delivering false information or half-formed ideas is a misuse of this power and a violation of trust.

- It is also a violation of trust for speakers to advocate positions that they themselves do not hold. As we've noted throughout this chapter, skillful public communicators adapt to their audiences. But adapting to an audience does not mean adopting their point of view. It means presenting your own ideas in a form that the audience can comprehend and appreciate. It is irresponsible to compromise personal ideals to tell an audience what it wants to hear in an attempt to gain acceptance or popularity.

- Skillful speakers can use their power either to inform or inflame. They can appeal to the best in people or to bigotry and hatred. They can use rational argument or resort to innuendo and simplistic slogans. In so doing, they demean their audiences. Assuming audiences are too stupid to understand or too weak-willed to make their own moral and ethical choices does great disservice, and possible harm, for people who are lied to learn not to respect the truth and people who are treated as though they are irrational can become so. Responsible speakers treat their audiences with respect by rejecting these abuses of power.

- Speakers also show respect to audience members by encouraging independent decision making. They do so by presenting clearly and completely the best information available on a given topic at a given time. It is irresponsible to use methods that interfere with an audience's ability to make an informed choice, such as intentionally falsifying data, lying about one's own interest and intents, or misrepresenting the consequences of a proposed action. Paul Campbell expresses this idea when he instructs communicators on how to act more ethically:

  > You avoid all hidden pressures and prejudices; you point out the consequences of given viewpoints whether they are favorable or unfavorable to your cause[,] . . . and you always, always make it totally apparent that the audience must consciously and freely make its own choices.[7]

- Finally, as was pointed out in Chapter 9, audience members, too, have responsibilities. Listeners act irresponsibly when they passively accept whatever they hear or allow personal needs and prejudices to blind them to facts. Responsible listeners inform themselves on important issues, follow arguments carefully, judge the adequacy of evidence, and critically evaluate the consequences of proposals. When unethical speakers persuade audiences to draw questionable conclusions, audience members are themselves partly to blame. Taking on the role of listener does not absolve a communicator from ethical responsibilities.

SUMMARY

Most people, at some time in their lives, will be given the opportunity to speak in public. Those who have studied public speaking will be able to take best advantage of this opportunity. A public speech is quite different from the kind of communication we do every day: public speeches are organized, purposeful, continuous presentations in which a single sender talks to a large, anonymous audience for an extended period of time. This form of communication presents special challenges to speakers, who must create relationships with the audience, structure their speeches, and deliver them with confidence and force.

In planning their speeches, successful public speakers must adapt to the audience, keeping the audience in mind as they decide on the central idea they wish to convey, the structure of their speech, the supporting materials they will use, and the presentation style they will employ. This means that they must gather demographic information about the audience. Knowing things such as age, sex, educational level, religious affiliation, economic status, and cultural or ethnic identification can help speakers to understand audience motivations and attitudes. Demographic data can be obtained in a number of ways, including reading local newspapers, watching local news programming on TV, and interviewing individuals like those who will be in the audience.

Public speeches must be carefully organized. A typical speech is made up of an introduction, a body, and a conclusion. The introduction creates interest, establishes credibility, and orients the audience to the speaker's thesis. The conclusion signals the end of the speech, underscores the significance of the topic, and summarizes main ideas. The content in the body must be arranged in a logical order, often following a stock organizational pattern. By creating a formal outline, the speaker can check organization and subordination of ideas.

Delivery is an important aspect of public speaking. In planning the speech, speakers must decide whether to use impromptu, extemporaneous, or manuscript delivery. Speakers must also find a way to manage anxiety. Luckily, there are some simple actions that can ward off apprehension. In addition to cognitive restructuring and physical relaxation, speakers can talk about their fears, burn off tension before speaking, redirect their attention, and use clear organization. Being realistic about their roles as speakers and focusing more on their message than on themselves can also help. In severe cases of stage fright, systematic desensitization can be used.

One cannot learn public speaking overnight; it takes practice and instruction. Nevertheless, some general principles can help a speaker to prepare. To ensure audience attention, comprehension, and retention, speakers should be organized and clear and should use vivid and interesting material. Finally, although they must adapt their speech to the audience members' needs and interests, speakers should never lose the unique perspective that makes a message their own.

Although there was a time when speakers used nothing but the spoken word to sway audiences, today's audiences expect speeches to be accompanied by sophisticated multimedia support. Well-designed visuals can compel attention, increase comprehension, make a speech memorable, and increase speaker credibility. Whether a speaker's audiovisual aids consist of posters and charts or computer-generated slides, they should be carefully planned. Efforts should be made to make sure they are not distracting, are easy to see, are simple, and are easy to handle. Most important, visual aids are just that—aids. They should always be subordinate to the ideas they are meant to illustrate.

A skilled public speaker can make a significant impact in the public sphere. With this power, however, goes responsibility. Speakers who deal in false information or half-truths violate audience trust. Speakers who use their power to inflame an audience rob its members of the ability to make independent informed choices. Responsible speakers treat their audiences with respect.

KEY TERMS

Listed below are the key terms used in this chapter, along with the number of the page where each is explained.

public speech (263)	chronological order (269)	action step (271)
audience adaptation (264)	spatial order (270)	outline (272)
demographic analysis (265)	topical order (270)	impromptu speaking (273)
introduction (266)	causal order (270)	extemporaneous speaking (273)
thesis (267)	problem–solution order (270)	manuscript speaking (273)
conclusion (267)	motivated sequence (270)	speech anxiety (273)
body (267)	attention step (271)	cognitive restructuring (273)
preview (267)	need step (271)	
transitions (267)	satisfaction step (271)	physical relaxation (273)
internal summaries (269)	visualization step (271)	systematic desensitization (274)
stock organizational patterns (269)		

SUGGESTED READINGS

Lucas, Stephen E. (2004). *The art of public speaking* (8th ed.). New York: McGraw Hill.

    Lucas provides a nice discussion of how to use PowerPoint effectively in public speaking situations.

McKerrow, Raymie E., Gronbeck, Bruce E., Ehninger, Douglas, & Monroe, Alan H. (2003). *Principles and types of public speaking* (15th ed.). Boston: Allyn & Bacon.

    The fact that this basic public speaking text is in its fifteenth edition says it all. A solid introduction, this text presents everything you always wanted to know—and more—about how to speak in public.

Communication and the Media

I n a media culture, it is sometimes hard to distinguish fictional from factual reality.

After reading this chapter, you should be able to:

- Identify the characteristics of traditional media messages.

- List and explain the four classic functions of mass media.

- Give examples of ways in which the traditional media set agendas, create hegemonic messages, cultivate world views, and change expectations. Give examples of ways audiences resist media influence.

- Describe how consumers use newspapers, magazines, radio, and television and understand how the formats used by these media affect information processing.

- Identify the characteristics of new media.

- Be able to discuss the ways old and new media are converging and how convergence is making audiences more active.

- Understand how computer-mediated communication is used and how it enhances social interaction.

- Discuss how advances in cell phone technology are changing face-to-face communication.

- Be aware of ethical issues associated with computer-mediated communication.

I n the spring of 2009 researchers at Ball State University's Center for Media Design released a study demonstrating how important mediated communication is to the average American. According to these researchers, we spend approximately eight hours a day in front of screens: TVs, cell phones, computers, and the like, and the time spent is almost identical for every age group. Television accounted for the largest amount of time, followed by computer usage, radio, and print media in that order. Both as consumers and as producers of messages, we are deeply involved with the media, and it is unlikely that these figures will diminish in the near future.[1]

Media consumption allows us access to information we could never gather on our own. When Hurricane Katrina hit the Gulf Coast of the United States in 2005, people in every part of the country were glued to their TVs. Although rescue efforts stalled and relief agencies were unable to get through, camera crews from all the major networks were on the scene almost immediately. And in 2007, when a lone gunman opened fire at Virginia Tech, students turned to social networking sites to let their friends and relatives know they were okay. Media coverage is important not only during serious disasters, but also during more mundane events. Fans at sporting events may spend only part of their time watching what is going on before them. Many listen to the play-by-play on portable radios and watch game highlights on giant TV screens. Without "six different camera angles, slow-motion instant replay, expert (color) analysis, and constant action," spectators feel that something important is missing from the game.[2] In a media age, real-life events may not be as complete or satisfying as mediated events.

But we are no longer just passive consumers of media. People are anxious to be part of the show, either by taking part in reality TV or by creating their own media message. Would-be filmmakers can post their work directly on YouTube, and celebrity wanna-bes can dream about becoming stars of the latest reality TV show.

Reality TV is so big, in fact, that casting calls go out almost every week and text messages can alert potential contestants of the latest auditions. If the producers of reality programming have their way, everyone in the United States will get his or her "fifteen minutes of fame," as Andy Warhol predicated. In addition to talent shows, model searches, and survival ordeals, there are plenty of opportunities for "average people" to be on TV. As these words are being written, reality shows run the gamut from A (*Age of Love, America's Toughest Jobs,* and *Are You Smarter Than a 5th Grader?*) to W (*Wife Swap, Who Wants to Marry My Dad?,* and *World of Stupid*), with some amazing shows in between. For example, *Smile . . . You're Under Arrest* features criminals with outstanding arrest records being lured into elaborate comic stings before being arrested. And *America's Trashiest Weddings* allows the audience to watch engaged couples "miss the mark on creating classy ceremonies."[3] Why would people allow themselves to be on such a show? For many people today, being seen on national TV is the ultimate legitimating experience.

And it's not just average people who want to become media stars. Politicians also have been quick to recognize the importance of making their presence known either by mounting their own Websites, by twittering about their day-to-day activities, or by becoming guests on talk radio or TV. Quick to criticize negative media coverage, they also are quick to seize the limelight. Shortly after his election, for example, President Barack Obama used a guest shot on *The Tonight Show* with Jay Leno to explain his economic stimulus package, and a few days later, he held an online town-hall meeting to answer questions from the American public. Other politicians have appeared in commercials and have acted in skits on comedy shows like *Saturday Night Live.* In a media culture, it is sometimes hard to distinguish fictional from factual reality or politicians from performers.

These situations illustrate how important the mass media have become in our daily lives. Like it or not, we live in a media culture that affects how we experience the world and how we communicate with one another. In this chapter, we look at what it means to live in constant interaction with the traditional and emerging mass media.

THE TRADITIONAL MASS MEDIA

It has become common to distinguish between old and new media. The term old media refers to traditional one-to-many forms of mediated communication such as TV, radio, newspapers, and books. The label new media is used to describe digital information and telecommunication systems, including networked computing and mobile telecommunication.

Although this distinction is useful for organizational purposes, keep in mind that old and new media are rapidly converging, and that it won't take long for what we now consider new media to become old and for old media to take on new forms. In this chapter we'll start our discussion with the traditional media of mass communication and then turn our attention to some of the ways computer-mediated communication and mobile technologies are altering our lives and changing the nature of traditional media functions and formats. We'll then look at how old and new media are rapidly converging.

What Is Mass Communication?

Despite the attention that is currently being given to new media, traditional media are still an important and influential force in our lives. To understand how to interact with them more effectively, we have to begin by understanding what mass communication is and how it differs from other kinds of communication.

Defining Mass Communication

Mass communication is a form of communication through which institutional sources (often referred to as "the media") address large, diverse audiences whose members are physically separated from one another. Contact is indirect; devices for the transmission, storage, and reception of information are interposed between source and receiver. Mass communication is a powerful and pervasive mode of communication, and in modern societies, the media are important social institutions that reflect and affect the values and behaviors of large segments of the population.

Characteristics of Media Messages

Media messages are unique in at least three ways: (1) in major mass communication contexts, the source is a complex, profit-oriented organization rather than a single individual; (2) receivers are anonymous, dispersed in time and space, and heterogeneous in their interests and background; and (3) communication occurs through indirect channels that require specialized encoding and decoding technologies.

Institutional Sources.   In the communication contexts we have looked at in other chapters, the source has been a single individual who composes and delivers his or her own message. In mass communication contexts, messages are the products of complex organizations composed of individuals who perform specialized functions. To get a sense of how much internal specialization is involved in mediated communication, sit through the credits the next time you watch a film. You'll see that in addition to the director and actors, the film employs executive and associate producers, artistic directors, set dressers and costumers, lighting specialists, electricians, sound mixers, first- and second-unit camera operators, and a host of others. Making a movie costs millions of dollars, and production companies expect to make a profit. They must therefore appeal to the largest possible audience, a fact that is inevitably reflected in their products.

Invisible Receivers.   Another difference between interpersonal and mass communication lies in the relationship between source and receiver. Media sources have little, if any, direct contact with receivers. By the time audience members buy their popcorn and settle down in front of the screen, the cast and crew have long since packed up their equipment, struck the set, and moved on to other projects. In interpersonal contexts, sources and receivers are in direct contact; in mass contexts, feedback is indirect and delayed. Once a film or TV show is "in the can," the source's contribution is over. Media communicators must perform for invisible spectators.

Receivers are also invisible in another way: there are so many of them. Media audiences are huge. On a given night, 100 million viewers may watch a television special. These viewers represent a variety of ages and social classes; their backgrounds and interests may be extremely varied. Even with fairly specialized media, such as technical magazines, readers may number in the tens of thousands, and outside of the single shared interest that led them to purchase the magazine, they may have little in common. The problem of audience adaptation becomes particularly acute with such a heterogeneous public. Media messages cannot be individualized as can interpersonal messages. Being able to create messages that are widely acceptable is highly valued in the media industries.

> Being able to create messages that are widely acceptable is highly valued in the media industries.

A final characteristic of media receivers lies in the conditions under which reception takes place. With the exception of movie viewers, media receivers consume media messages alone or in small groups in fairly noisy environments. One source of noise is the competition of other mediated messages. It's important to remember that receivers' relationships with sources are voluntary and can be severed at any time. Audience members are free to turn off the radio if the DJ annoys them or to flip through TV channels until they find an image they like. When cable viewers have a choice of tuning in to any one of fifty different stations at a given time, the producers of a single program must work especially hard to capture an adequate share of the market.

Interposed Channels.   The use of interposed channels is a final characteristic of mass communication. Different media employ different technologies for the transmission and reception of messages, and these technologies make different demands on the resourcefulness of both source and receiver. Electronic media, for example, involve the use of special equipment to encode and decode messages. Not only does this equipment require a financial commitment, it may require technical expertise as well. Both producers and consumers must keep up with changing technologies.

Different media also require different cognitive skills. Books and magazines, for example, do not require costly equipment, but they do demand that the receiver be able to read the written word, an accomplishment that takes detailed instruction. The ability to "read" a message is actually demanded by every medium. To understand a TV drama, for example, viewers must be able to decode visual messages; they must accustom themselves to the language of camera angles, editing, scene composition, and so forth, just as directors must learn to tell a story in visual terms. Each medium has its own format, and successful media communicators understand their particular format.

How Audiences and Media Messages Interact

Mass communication is like every other form of communication in one way: sources and receivers form a relationship with one another. Since the beginning of the rise of the mass media in the United States, theorists have posed questions about this relationship, concerning themselves with the functions fulfilled by the media, the extent to which the media influence audiences, and the ways in which receivers process media messages. In this section, we look at some of the divergent viewpoints that have emerged as scholars have tried to understand the relationship between audiences and media messages.

Functions of the Media

Sociologist Charles Wright, expanding on a model first developed by political scientist Harold Lasswell, identifies four **media functions**: surveillance, correlation, cultural transmission, and entertainment.[4] Table 11.1 summarizes these functions.

The first media function is **surveillance**, the gathering and disseminating of information. Media sources affect receivers by providing them with news, by warning them of crises or dangers, and by giving them the instrumental information

Table 11.1 Media Functions

Surveillance	The gathering and disseminating of information
Correlation	The analysis and evaluation of information
Cultural Transmission	The education and socialization of receivers
Entertainment	The presentation of escapist material that provides enjoyment and gratification

they need to get through a day. When we speak of the media as the "watchdogs of a free society," we are referring to the surveillance function. In general, this function is fulfilled by newspapers and by radio and television news programming.

The second function of the media is correlation, the analysis and evaluation of information. In addition to reporting facts, the media affect receivers by interpreting news events and by analyzing social problems. The correlation function is most often found in the editorial pages of newspapers, on news analysis shows, and in magazine articles that analyze current issues.

The third function of the media is cultural transmission, or education and socialization. Not only do the media inform receivers about events, but also they socialize receivers. By observing what characters do in television dramas, we internalize behavioral norms; by viewing films, we learn about our culture's history; and by reading magazines, newspapers, and books, we confront questions of values. Media personalities act as role models for us. Often, our learning is prosocial learning; that is, it reinforces social ideals and passes on cultural understandings from one generation to the next. Sometimes, however, our learning is essentially antisocial learning, reinforcing socially destructive behavior. The debate about the effects of televised violence on the behavior of children indicates a very real concern—that culturally transmitted messages may inadvertently undermine cultural values.

> The debate about the effects of televised violence on the behavior of children indicates a very real concern—that culturally transmitted messages may inadvertently undermine cultural values.

The final function of the media is entertainment. The media offer receivers an escape from the problems of everyday life. Media provide enjoyment and gratification, help us to relax, allow us to experience vicarious adventure, and arouse our emotions. The entertainment function is fulfilled by almost every medium. Reading the newspaper, flipping through a magazine, and watching a TV show or a film are all ways that we give ourselves a break from the more serious aspects of our lives.

Of course, each of these functions can have negative side effects. Consider the surveillance function. News can as easily misinform as it can inform, and it can occasionally increase anxiety or cause panic. Too much information can even narcotize, or overwhelm and paralyze, an audience. When receivers are inundated with news reports, their knowledge of

Media offerings must appeal to mass audiences.

social problems may become superficial and their social concern may be replaced by apathy.[5]

The correlation, cultural transmission, and entertainment functions all have their negative sides as well. Simplistic commentary, for example, can increase passivity and can discourage social criticism. When anchors appear after every major broadcast to summarize what we have just heard, we may stop listening carefully or lose confidence in our own conclusions. Similarly, media socialization can reduce the ability of other institutions (such as families and schools) to set standards and can foster superficial, homogenized values. Finally, mindless entertainment can encourage escapism and can lower popular taste. The functions that the media fulfill appear to be mixed blessings.

Media Effects: An Overview

Do media messages brainwash a defenseless public, or are most people able to see through them? Do the media create desires, or do they simply give the public what it wants? Can the media instill values, or do they merely reflect values that already exist? The debate over these questions has resulted in two opposing schools of thought. According to the first, receivers are relatively passive; they accept media messages at face value and unconsciously allow media sources to tell them what to think. People who accept the first perspective believe in what has been called the powerful effects model.

According to the second point of view, far from accepting media messages as intended, audience members interpret messages according to their own preexisting beliefs and values and use these messages in unique ways. For people who hold this view, audiences are active processors who are quite capable of defending themselves against media influence. Those who accept this perspective employ a limited effects model.

During the last fifty years, the pendulum has swung back and forth between these extremes.[6] The earliest theories of mass communication tended to portray the media as extremely influential. Media influence was likened to a magic bullet or a hypodermic needle that could target unsuspecting audience members or inject them with a message. Receivers were seen as the passive victims of the all-powerful media.[7]

In the 1950s and 1960s, however, theorists began to take a closer look at the audience. They found that individuals were much more stubbornly resistant to media manipulation than had at first been assumed. According to the resulting obstinate audience theory, receivers were viewed as creative consumers who sought out media messages according to their own needs and interpreted messages in their own ways.[8] Media effects were thought to be mediated both by the receiver's personality and by his or her group allegiances.

Despite the popularity of this view, critics were left with a nagging feeling that audiences were not so resistant. Some theorists began to wonder just how much choice receivers really had. Therefore, beginning in the 1970s and continuing into the 1990s, theorists began to reconsider the power of the media to influence audiences. Of particular interest were the long-term effects of television viewing. Some theorists focused on uncovering hidden political agendas embedded in television programming; others looked at ways in which the media presented distorted views of society; and still others focused on specific effects like the correlation between media violence and aggressive behavior.

Adherents of each view still argue strongly for their own perspective. In the sections that follow, we'll take a brief look at some of the effects attributed to the media, as well as at characteristics that may make audiences at least somewhat resistant to media domination. After considering these arguments (which are summarized in Table 11.2), you be the judge.

What Media Messages Do to Receivers

Theories that argue for the power of the media generally argue one of four positions: that the media tell us what to think about, that the media tell us what not to think about, that the media present distorted views of the world, and that exposure to each new medium changes the way we process information and alters our expectations about how messages should be constructed.[9]

Media Agendas.   Very early on, critics identified the agenda-setting function of the media. According to this view, media gatekeepers select the issues they feel are most worthy of coverage and give those issues wide attention.[10] Receivers accept the gatekeepers' agendas without realizing that, somewhere along the line, an editor or producer is making choices about what to cover and what to ignore. As Norman Felsenthal remarks, "Neither an individual nor a society can give equal attention to everything. We are continually required to determine which problems get our immediate attention and which problems are simply endured or even ignored altogether."[11] The media often make decisions for us, alerting us today to a drug problem, tomorrow to a crisis in education, and the day after that to an erosion of family values. A movie-of-the-week about child abuse can trigger our

Table 11.2 Media Effects and Audience Resistance

How Media Affect Audiences	How Audiences Resist Media
Media influence receivers by:	Receivers resist influence by:
1. Agenda setting	1. Selective processing
2. Producing hegemonic messages	2. Conducting oppositional readings
3. Cultivating worldviews	3. Using media for individual gratification
4. Affecting cognitive practices and expectations	

interest in a normally overlooked problem, especially if it is followed up in other media. If, as a result of the movie, a weekly newsmagazine runs a feature about the problem and talk show hosts jump on the bandwagon, chances are that people will come to define child abuse as a serious issue. This is one way in which the media order our priorities.

Hegemonic Messages.   If media attention makes certain issues and information highly salient, it also makes some issues invisible. Critical theorists argue that the media reflect and reproduce only those ideas, meanings, and values that uphold the interests of the power elite and that they silence opposing views. According to these theorists, media messages are hegemonic; that is, media messages keep powerless groups from making their ideas known. Although the media may appear to present a variety of ideas and choices, this diversity is an illusion. Instead, the media reproduce and package a single message, or dominant ideology. Todd Gitlin, for example, argues that American TV encourages viewers to "experience themselves as antipolitical, privately accumulating individuals." Television supports the status quo and valorizes a consumer ethic while discouraging criticism of alternative economic or political arrangements.[12]

> Critical theorists argue that the media reflect and reproduce only those ideas, meanings, and values that uphold the interests of the power elite and that they silence opposing views.

The media also underrepresent and misrepresent certain social groups according to media watchdog site *Children Now*:

> As America's primary storyteller and chief cultural exporter, television provides messages and images that contribute to the worldviews of millions. When certain groups are privileged, others subjugated, and still others altogether excluded, prime time sends skewed messages to viewers—especially young ones—that these groups are valued differently.[13]

Does representation matter? Many would answer yes, arguing that media portrayals of gender, sexual orientation, race, ethnicity, age, disability, and so on affect how we see ourselves and others. If you're a person of color or member of another minority you know how frustrating it can be not to see yourself reflected realistically anywhere within the general culture. If you're not, it may not be too hard to imagine what it would feel like to be invisible.

Media content affects us in yet another way. Like other sources of stories and myths, the media convey not only what is normal and acceptable, but also what is irrelevant and wrong. As a result, people who disagree with the messages broadcast through the media often refuse to voice criticisms or objections for fear of being socially isolated or scapegoated. Elisabeth Noelle-Neumann's theory of the spiral of silence expresses this idea.[14] She believes that people who think their ideas are popular tend to express them; those who see themselves in the minority remain silent.

> Like other sources of stories and myths, the media convey not only what is normal and acceptable, but also what is irrelevant and wrong.

As a result, only one side of any given issue receives notice. And groups outside the mainstream have almost no chance of making themselves heard, because the media refuse to legitimate their ideas. Not only do the media tell us what to think about, they also tell us what not to think about. It is a bit frightening to realize that, for the first time in history, the stories we hear and the values we are taught do not come from parents, schools, or churches, but from "a group of distant conglomerates that have something to sell."[15]

Cultivated Worldviews.   In addition to creating hegemonic messages, media can affect the extent to which we feel comfortable in our social worlds. **Cultivation theory**, originally developed by George Gerbner and his colleagues at the Annenberg School for Communication at the University of Pennsylvania, draws our attention to ways in which individuals come to accept the televised world as an accurate reflection of the real world. Unlike the hypodermic needle theories, which focused on ways in which specific messages or genres directly affect audiences, cultivation theory looks at how long-term television viewing affects viewers' beliefs about social reality.[16] Instead of an injection metaphor, cultivation theorists liken TV's influence to the kind of slow buildup that occurs as stalagmites form. They argue that, just as stalagmites grow over time from the steady dripping of limewater in underground caverns, so our views of what the world is like are built up from the images and representations we are exposed to over long periods of time.

One effect of cultivation is called **mainstreaming**: like critical theorists, cultivation scholars believe that television viewing creates widely shared, middle-of-the road viewpoints that tend to support the status quo. Another effect of cultivation is a belief in what has come to be called the **mean world hypothesis**, the view that the world is a much more dangerous place than it actually is. For example, there is much more crime on TV than in the real world. As a result, viewers who spend a lot of time watching TV and don't have access to actual crime statistics come to view the world as violent and dangerous. According to cultivation theory, "heavy exposure to television violence cultivates insecurity, mistrust, and alienation, and a willingness to accept potentially repressive measures in the name of security."[17]

> There is much more crime on TV than in the real world. As a result, viewers who spend a lot of time watching TV and don't have access to actual crime statistics come to view the world as violent and dangerous.

Of course, not everyone is affected to the same degree. According to cultivation theory, it is **heavy viewers**, those who watch a lot of TV, who are most likely to experience cultivation. Light viewers, who presumably have alternative sources of information, are less affected. To date, research is somewhat mixed in its support for cultivation theory. However there is a general consensus that "television makes a small but significant contribution to the heavy viewers' beliefs about the world."[18]

Media Logics.   A final way in which the media may affect us has less to do with content and more to do with the form of media messages. According to this view, when new technologies emerge, they change the way we experience the world. They encourage certain kinds of messages and discourage others. Their very presence creates new social possibilities and changes existing power relations. For example, some critics argue that the electronic media have contributed to the emergence of an "imperial presidency." Elihu Katz sees the beginning of this trend in Franklin D. Roosevelt's "fireside chats." By broadcasting directly to the people, Roosevelt could bypass Congress.[19] Subsequent presidents adopted FDR's strategy, and modern presidents are now treated like media stars. Television focuses on "personalities," and it is easier to cast a single individual as a personality than it is to cast multiple characters, such as Congress or the judiciary.[20]

The creation of an imperial presidency is only one exemplification that media formats affect both the messages that are broadcast and the surrounding social structure. When Marshall McLuhan first stated that "the medium is the message," he was expressing the beliefs that the channel through which a message is transmitted is as important as the message itself and that the channel, in fact, often determines which messages will be transmitted and which will be ignored.[21] According to McLuhan's theory, each medium has its own internal logic, and each affects how we experience the world. For example, print media have linear logic; that is, they transmit information in an orderly sequence, word after word, idea after idea. Print media encourage rationality and individuality. Television, by contrast, has mosaic logic, bombarding us with changing bits of information that we must cognitively reassemble. Television encourages sensory involvement.

Because television is what McLuhan refers to as a cool medium, it demands that viewers fill in detail. Performers who are too hard-edged and direct are not "cool" enough to succeed on TV, although they may be perfect for a "hotter" medium, such as radio. In fact, McLuhan explains John F. Kennedy's success in the 1960 presidential debates in terms of his relative "coolness" compared to the "hotter" Richard Nixon.

Although not everyone has embraced McLuhan's cool–hot distinction, many critics accept the idea that form is as important as content in affecting audience responses. As we accustom ourselves to different media forms, our cognitive practices and expectations change. Exposure to a constant barrage of highly arousing and rapidly changing images (such as those found on TV) changes the way we think. We become impatient with nonpictorial stimuli and with nondramatic messages. People raised on a steady diet of television may expect all information to be condensed, simple, short, and rapidly changing. Linear and detailed information may be rejected out of hand both by receivers and by media sources. Some media critics believe that our

> Exposure to a constant barrage of highly arousing and rapidly changing images (such as those found on TV) changes the way we think.

definition of information has been changed by the advent of television and that we all think in the language of TV.

Robert P. Snow believes that our involvement with the language of television is so strong that it is changing the language of other media. Television viewers, used to the condensing and telescoping tendencies of TV, are demanding the same features in newspapers, books, and magazines, reading more tolerable for the TV generation.[22]

What Receivers Do with Media Messages

Our discussion so far has portrayed viewers as fairly passive recipients of media influence. But is this a fair portrayal? Many scholars argue that it is not. These scholars view receivers as selective, rational consumers of messages who are affected as much by their own needs and group memberships as by media goals and practices. To support this viewpoint, these scholars make three basic arguments: that audience members process messages selectively, that audiences are motivated to use media by private needs and desires, and that the meanings audience members assign to media messages are social constructions.

Selective Processing.   If everyone were to react to a given message in exactly the same way, the media would have very little trouble controlling receivers. Students of perception, however, know that this is not how perception works. People see the world in unique ways. As we saw in Chapter 3, we are capable of ignoring messages we don't like, of tuning out tedious or irrelevant details, of interpreting messages in original ways, and of forgetting inconvenient details. That is, we engage in selective exposure, attention, perception, and retention.

Selective exposure refers to people's tendency to avoid certain messages and to seek out others. Although we like to believe that we are open-minded and intellectually curious, many of us are not. Preexisting preferences guide us in the selection of media messages. Musical taste, for example, determines which radio station we listen to; a hard rock fan will not tune in to a station with an easy-listening format. Religious and political beliefs and values also affect media exposure; nonbelievers seldom watch televangelists, and political conservatives may refuse to read columns written by liberals. If we do expose ourselves to messages we usually avoid, we may do so to make fun of or criticize those messages, not to listen with an open mind. Most of the time, however, we don't go that far; we simply refuse to expose ourselves to messages we imagine we will not like. Media can hardly affect us if we don't tune in.

Even when we choose to process a message, we may engage in selective attention. That is, we may listen only to parts of the message. As we saw in Chapter 3, people's attention tends to wander, and messages must be vivid and novel if people are to process them. Advertisers, of course, are well aware of this fact and use music, color, sound effects, and other devices, to make us pay attention.

Receivers are also not immune from selective perception, the process of assigning meaning to messages in selective ways. Ask two different people to explain what a book or a movie is about. Chances are, the explanations will be very different and will be affected as much by preconceived notions as by the intention of the media source.

Finally, receivers engage in **selective retention**, remembering only a small portion of any message. Studies have shown that "viewers of the network newscast can seldom remember more than three or four stories, or approximately 20 percent, just an hour after seeing the news." The average viewer is often ill-informed, even on issues that receive heavy coverage.[23]

Need Gratification.   Why do receivers turn to the media in the first place? Many theorists argue that they do so to fulfill preexisting needs. **Uses and gratifications research** focuses on the needs that motivate media consumers. This research argues that receivers are active and goal directed. Receivers know what they need, and they look for ways to get it. The media are only one of a number of competing sources of gratification. In Katz's terms, this approach "does not assume a direct relationship between messages and effects, but postulates instead that members of the audience put messages to use, and that such usages act as intervening variables in the process of effect."[24]

One of the earliest studies in this tradition was Herta Herzog's investigation of why women listened to radio soap operas.[25] Herzog determined that listeners used the soaps for emotional release, fantasy escape, and advice on how to deal with their own problems. Denis McQuail and his colleagues argue that the media, in general, are chosen to provide (1) diversion and emotional release, (2) substitute companionship and a shared social experience, (3) identity and value reinforcement, and (4) surveillance.[26] As we shall see in the section on new media, uses and gratification research is being employed to understand how consumers use the Internet and cell phones.

Reading Media Texts.   A number of theorists have focused their research efforts on describing how receivers make sense out of what they see and hear. These scholars argue that media reception does not take place in a vacuum and that receivers are not blank slates waiting to have a message inscribed on them. Instead, receivers are members of "interpretive communities" who actively construct meanings in accordance with their own social experiences. The theorists refer to the process of assigning meaning to media messages as "reading" and to the messages themselves as "texts." Scholars who take this approach argue that receivers are quite able to read media texts in ways that oppose the dominant ideology. Thus, it is possible for feminists to do an oppositional reading of the ways in which women are portrayed in romance novels or for members of ethnic minorities to recognize ethnic biases in news reporting.

> Receivers are members of "interpretive communities" who actively construct meanings in accordance with their own social experiences.

Rather than a given text having one hegemonic message, it may have multiple meanings, a condition known as **polysemy**. In this sense, media exposure is a process of negotiating between what lies in the text itself and what lies in the social and cultural context in which the text is experienced.

The debate over how much the media affect us continues to rage. Although little doubt remains that media messages are influential, the question of just how much power they wield remains open. As media consumers, we should be aware of the potential of the media to affect our lives. One way to increase this awareness is to understand media formats, our next topic.

Media Formats and Logics

Each medium is unique not only in the conditions under which it is received, but also in the way it is structured and in its internal logic. As a result, each has a distinctive capacity for influence.[27] In this section, we'll look briefly at the formats employed in some of the major media. We'll focus on newspapers, magazines, radio, and television; follow with a few words about film and books; and end with a discussion of media ethics. Table 11.3 summarizes major points.

Newspapers

As this edition goes to press, American newspapers seem to be in decline, with a growing number of papers shutting down or switching to an online-only format. Although tens of millions of newspapers are still sold each day, projections aren't reassuring, with younger readers more likely to look for content through the Internet.[28] No one knows yet what the newspapers of tomorrow will be like,

---

Table 11.3 Media Formats and Logics: Media Uses and Effects of Media Logics

Newspapers

- *Used to:* pass time, find mundane information, keep in touch with events, identify self as reader
- *Formats encourage:* focus on single events, avoidance of detail, interest in crises and dramatic events

Magazines

- *Used to:* pass time, find detailed information, gain access to valued subgroups
- *Formats encourage:* knowledge of detail, identity-related knowledge, unrealistic expectations, pressures to consume

Radio

- *Used to:* pass time, find mundane information, regulate moods, ease loneliness
- *Formats encourage:* conservatism, apathy, venting of emotion (through talk radio)

Television

- *Used to:* pass time, provide companionship, keep in touch with events, relax, find escapist entertainment
- *Formats encourage:* impatience with long or detailed material, interest in dramatic material, belief in ideal norms, dismissal of news that is not visually compelling

but everyone agrees they will change. Michael Kinsley, writing in *Time* magazine, offers the following viewpoint:

> The *"me to you"* model of news gathering—a professional reporter, attuned to the fine distinctions between "off the record" and "deep background," prizing factual accuracy in the narrowest sense—may well give way to some kind of "us to us" communitarian arrangement of the sort that thrives on the Internet. But there is room between the New York Times *and myleftarmpit.com for new forms that liberate journalism from its encrusted conceits while preserving its standards, like accuracy.*[29]

Newspapers aren't dead yet, however; *USA Today* and *The Wall Street Journal*, for example, are still thriving. While we wait to see what happens in the future, let's look at the traditional functions and formats that have made newspapers an important source of detailed information since the early 1800s.[30]

In addition to providing news in more depth than is possible through radio or television, newspapers provide other uses and gratifications. Reading is, in part, a routine way to pass time during transitional periods; because newspaper reading is seen as a useful activity, it allows us to take a break without appearing lazy. Newspaper reading is also a way to search out mundane information; people look to see what's on sale at the local department store or what's playing at the nearest movie theater. As much as 60 percent of a newspaper may be devoted to ads. Readers don't complain, because the ads provide them with needed information.

Reading the paper is also a way of keeping informed on important news of the day, a way of taking advantage of the surveillance function that the press provides. People expect the press to act as watchdogs, and readership is especially strong when the community or nation is threatened by a crisis. Finally, reading a newspaper is an act of self-definition. When a reader opens the paper on the bus or in a local coffee shop, he or she sends the message "I am the kind of person who reads a newspaper."[31] So strong is this perception that one of the major goals of adults in literacy programs is to be able to read a paper in public.

Until recently, newspapers have taken the form of "hard copy." Information is laid out in two-dimensional space, and a variety of stories simultaneously compete for readers' attention. Readers skim the pages and select the items they find most useful or most appealing. News stories are typically written so that the most essential information appears in the first few paragraphs, leaving development to final paragraphs. This structure allows editors to cut a story from the end and readers to stop reading at any point without losing the most important information.

Newspaper format encourages certain kinds of communication: a focus on isolated events, a tendency to omit detailed analysis, and a temptation to focus on the unusual and the dramatic. The fact that the first paragraph of a news story must sum up the entire story leads to a focus on single events, and who, when, where, and what become more important than why. Coupled with the value placed on objective reporting, news stories tend to focus on concrete details that can be easily measured and counted: the size of a crowd, the number of days hostages have been held, the cost of a new bomber. News stories are less likely to explore why the crowd assembled, what sociopolitical factors led to the hostage taking, or whether the new bomber is needed.

In addition to providing a focus on events, newspaper stories search out the unusual and the dramatic. Although newspapers are designed to fulfill surveillance and correlation functions, they can't succeed unless they incorporate some level of entertainment as well. As any news reporter can tell you, "Dog Bites Man" is not news, but "Man Bites Dog" is. The more uncommon and sensational an event is, the more likely it will be reported. Reports of accidents and disasters are the most widely read of news stories, followed by reports of crime. As a result, "the world may seem more crime-ridden, conflict-filled, and/or absurd than it is."[32]

Kathleen Hall Jamieson and Karlyn Kohrs Campbell tell us that certain themes are considered especially newsworthy. These themes include (1) appearance versus reality (stories that uncover hypocrisy), (2) "little guys" versus "big guys" (accounts of conflict between the powerless and the powerful), (3) good versus evil (reports of crime and punishment), (4) efficiency versus inefficiency (exposures of waste and mismanagement), and (5) the unique versus the routine (the "Man Bites Dog" effect).[33]

In summary, the logic of newspaper discourse may result in events appearing isolated and separate, background information being overlooked and oversimplified, and crises and threats being exaggerated. The first two of these effects are partially offset by the analyses that appear in the editorial pages of a newspaper. It is here that the correlation function of the media is most evident. Given that TV news items are extremely short and concrete, receivers who want more thoughtful analysis of issues often turn to the print media for explanation and evaluation.

Magazines have always offered us glimpses into other worlds and images of who we could be.

Magazines

The typical magazine is written to attract young, middle-class, reasonably well-educated readers, the people demographic analyses show are heavy purchasers. To make any further generalizations about readers is difficult, however, because magazines tend to specialize. More than do newspapers, magazines speak to and for particular segments of society. With the possible exception of magazines such as *TV Guide, Family Circle,* and *People,* which are sporadically read by large segments of the population, most modern magazines orient themselves to specific subgroups within the mass audience. The loyal readers who buy *Seventeen, Modern Photography, Field and Stream,* or *Heavy Metal,* for example, do so because these magazines understand their interests and identifications.

Readers may choose to read a magazine for a variety of reasons. Some readers simply use magazines as a means of killing time. Other readers are more involved, choosing a magazine that reflects the groups to which they wish to, or actually do, belong. *Vogue,* for example, appeals to a cosmopolitan, style-conscious, sophisticated female reader who wants to know the latest fashions in both clothing and pop culture. *Sports Illustrated,* on the other hand, is written primarily for male sports fans. In general, the reader of *Vogue* is not the reader of *Sports Illustrated.*

Magazines often provide instructions about how to become a member of a given group. The woman who wants to improve her social standing reads *Vogue* to pick up hints on how to look and act the part. A novice tennis player purchases a tennis magazine in order to improve his or her skills. Robert Snow tells us that specialized magazines show readers how to "act like insiders, how to gain the respect of others already firmly entrenched, how to avoid being gauche, . . . and the emotional sensations that should be felt when one is achieving success."[34] Magazines reflect the norms and values of their readers. Thus *Playboy* legitimates one set of values, and *Ms.* legitimates another.

Magazines can also serve as channels of communication to others. By publicly displaying a magazine, one can send a message about one's tastes and values. A copy of the *New York Review of Books* or the *Advocate* casually tossed on one's coffee table can let visitors know intellectual and personal interests that may become channels for conversation or identification.

Magazines in their paper form are one of the least ephemeral of the mass media. Electronic messages disappear immediately after broadcast (unless they are taped for future reference). Newspapers are quickly discarded. Magazines, however, are kept for several weeks and read intermittently. In layout, they fall halfway between a newspaper and a book. Articles are generally arranged sequentially and are meant to be read all the way through, although the latter part of an article is usually separated from the first part and placed at the end of the magazine. Titles and vivid illustrations are used to catch the reader's attention and to move him or her through the text. In fact, many magazines are as much for looking at as for reading.

The writing style in magazines is more narrative and personalized, often involving the use of first-person narrative. The use of a more direct form of address is in keeping with the identity function that magazines serve for readers. Magazine designers work hard to create a unique style for their magazines. Typestyle, photos, illustrations, and even ads reflect an overall image. The serious, functional, non-flashy format of *U.S. News & World Report* tells the conservative businessperson who reads it, "We are here not to entertain but to inform you." In contrast, *Vanity Fair* celebrates the ephemeral, using a style that is trendy and irreverent and filling its pages with glossy color photos of the rich and famous.

Increasingly, magazines offer readers online Websites that encourage more interactive involvement with content and that, at the same time, encourage readers to subscribe to the hard-copy version. Magazine Websites also often allow readers to shop online.

Magazines can offer us needed information and can provide serious analyses of important problems. They can also pander to voyeurism and can make us miserable by setting up unrealistic expectations. Some magazines are little more than gossip mills, invading the privacy of celebrities and "real people" alike to show us the sordid and the sensational. Images in magazines can also make us discontented with who and what we are. When the models in magazines set up expectations for an unrealistic level of youth or beauty or physical prowess, we may find ourselves pursuing impossible goals.

Radio

Over the years, radio use has changed. In the early days of radio, families gathered together in their living rooms to listen as their favorite serials and soaps unfolded. Radio was a "communal storyteller" as well as a source of information and musical entertainment.[35] Now, most listening occurs outside the home. Today, radio is a kind of "portable friend" that helps us through the day by giving us useful information, matching our moods, and keeping us company. Radio is a comforting presence that we rely on more than we imagine, as Altheide and Snow suggest:

> Ask yourself if you can wash the car, clean house, study or read, or engage in a myriad of other activities without background radio noise. In these instances, radio is an integral part of the flow of the event. Indeed, without radio, some activity . . . would become awkward at best, and perhaps impossible.[36]

Radio keeps people in touch with the world. In the words of a respondent interviewed in the early 1960s, "To me when the radio is off, the house is empty. There is no life without the radio being on."[37] Radio communication has a strong interpersonal dimension. Not only does the music and talk provide a quasi-social interaction for lonely people, but also "radio binds people together through common shared experiences and provides subjects to talk about with others."[38] It can link people within a given subculture, validating their group identity.

Not only is radio a companion, it is a companion who shares our identity, understands our moods, and makes few demands on our attention. Radio stations work hard to create a personal identity that audience members will accept and find attractive. Country, Adult Contemporary, Religious, Golden Oldies, Classic and Alternative Rock, Top 50, and Urban Contemporary—all are identities that stations form to establish a relationship with receivers. In addition, each station programs its selections to match audience needs and moods. Thus, wake-up music uses a lively rhythm and a tempo designed to get the audience going, whereas late-night broadcasts air more mellow and more romantic sounds. Even within a given time segment, programmers vary tempo from one selection to the next and, on a Top 40 station, rotate the top ten songs throughout a two- or three-hour period. Thus, the radio listener knows with a high degree of precision what he or she will be getting by tuning in.

Although a large part of radio content consists of musical selections, talk radio is also popular. Talk radio is an excellent example of the quasi-interpersonal nature of radio. Talk hosts interact with listeners, creating a forum for the exchange of ideas. Altheide and Snow predict that "as urban life becomes more privatized and socially fragmented, talk radio will function both as an opportunity for vicarious and overt participation and as a source of information on issues. . . ."[39]

In many ways, radio is the most local and "demassified" of the mass media. Like magazines, radio stations tend to be specialized, catering to particular subcultures within a community. Because of this, the accusations of undue sociopolitical influence that are often leveled at the more "mass" of the mass media have not been made against radio. Perhaps the most serious charge leveled at radio is that it is conservative and uncommitted. "By creating the impression of abundance and unlimited fun, listeners may be encouraged to stand pat and go on blithely ignoring issues and controversies that are critical in the long run."[40]

When television first appeared, people were both fascinated and a bit fearful.

Television

In terms of audience penetration, "television is the *most mass* of all the mass media."[41] Despite earlier predictions that the Internet would rapidly surpass television in popularity, TV is still the medium of choice for most Americans.

Television fulfills many functions for its viewers. Like newspapers, it provides local and national news (although the amount and type of news provided are

> Despite earlier predictions that the Internet would rapidly surpass television in popularity, TV is still the medium of choice for most Americans.

characteristics unique to the medium). Like magazines and films, it gives viewers a glimpse into alternative worlds, and, like radio, it provides companionship. Like many other media, television teaches and socializes, although critics sometimes bemoan its content. Finally, television serves as the most popular medium for relaxation and escapist entertainment. Watching TV has become such a habit that viewers often sit through programs they don't like rather than turning off the set. When television reception is knocked out, viewers feel anxious and at loose ends, so accustomed are they to TV as background noise. In a 1992 survey reported in the October 10–16 issue of *TV Guide,* viewers were asked, "Would you take a million dollars to stop watching TV forever?" The answer for large segments of those surveyed was a resounding "No!"

Because television is both auditory and visual, it (along with film) is the most perceptually compelling of all the media. Although sound is an important aspect of television, music and dialogue are often subordinated to visual information. Television is something we watch more than listen to. Television images are in constant motion, and a fundamental part of the logic of TV is a valuation of movement and change. Television has given us an appetite for highly arousing visual stimuli.

> Television images are in constant motion, and a fundamental part of the logic of TV is a valuation of movement and change. Television has given us an appetite for highly arousing visual stimuli.

Television has also accustomed us to time compression. Shows that move slowly (such as annual awards shows) are generally criticized. The more rapid the tempo, the better received a program is.[42] In both entertainment and news programming, we expect unnecessary details to be edited out, so that a story about a week in the life of a character happens in half an hour, and the gist of an hour-long speech is summarized in a ten-second "sound bite."

Another defining characteristic of television is that it is a very intimate medium. The most frequent shots are medium close-ups and close-ups that personalize the audience–actor relationship.[43] This means that television encourages psychological identification. When we turn on the set, we want to identify with the characters and personalities we see. The fact that we view television in our homes rather than in more public spaces further emphasizes how personal our relationship is to this medium.

Entertainment Programming.   In his discussion of the logic of television, Snow remarks on three features of television programming: speed and simplicity, a tendency to dramatize material, and a need to stay within the bounds of ideal norms. We'll look at how these work, first in entertainment programs and then in news programs.

It's important to remember that television is a business. Advertisers pay networks in an effort to gain substantial numbers of consumers. Every successful program must seize audience attention and hold it through the commercials.

As viewers flip through the channels, a given show must be vivid enough to make them pause. The show must be simple enough that viewers can understand its premise immediately (even if they tune in halfway through the program), and it must be compelling enough to get viewers to stay tuned over commercial breaks. These factors affect the language of television.

Simplicity and brevity are important aspects of television discourse. Most programs have little time for detailed character or plot development. As a result, characters are stereotyped, and plots follow a simple beginning–middle–end structure. Situation comedies, for example, are organized around a simple problem or conflict that is inevitably resolved by the end of the show. Dialogue is written to ensure that viewers know exactly what is going on. Whereas in real life, a person might say, "Oh, there's Doug," a character on a TV soap says, "Look, there's Doug, Marcia's former husband who was falsely accused of the murder of old Doc Tyler and who's just been released from prison." Vocabulary must be simple and must convey plot intricacies instantly.

Extreme and dramatic situations are also a popular part of the logic of television entertainment. Characters are bigger than life, their lives more exciting or humorous or glamorous than ours. From the title to the final resolution, a show must maintain audience interest. In 1981, TV executive Ben Stein claimed that made-for-TV movie titles "must have sex, love, but especially human abuse. Human abuse works far better than sex. Sex can scare off people over 50. But roll it with abuse and you get everyone."[44] Other executives agreed that movies about love, sex, rape, or terror were surefire winners. Now, twenty years later, the principle remains the same. Just look through television listings during any sweeps week.

> Television producers can have it both ways: they can justify depiction of lurid and often ludicrous situations as long as these situations are placed in a moralistic frame. Television can titillate while remaining the most conservative of the major media.

The tendency to sensationalize material seems, at first glance, to contradict another important aspect of television content: reference to **ideal norms**. According to Snow, ideal norms are "the tradition of hard work, honesty, modesty, fidelity, and so on, which everyone upholds in principle."[45] A program such as the "Miss America Pageant" embodies the values of youth, feminine beauty, and love of God and country.

How do the sensational topics shown in TV movies fit in? The answer is that the resolution of sensational material always follows ideal norms: the rapist is punished, the drug user completes rehabilitation, the terrorist falls off a twenty-story building. The characters who commit crimes are evil, and the characters who solve crimes are noble. Television producers can have it both ways: they can justify depiction of lurid and often ludicrous situations as long as these situations are placed in a moralistic frame. Television can titillate while remaining the most conservative of the major media.

News Programming.   The values that inform entertainment programming can be found in nonentertainment shows as well. A perfect illustration is television news. A successful broadcast news item is brief, visually compelling, dramatic, and moralistic.

First, news reports are kept as short as possible—seldom longer than thirty seconds and usually about fifteen seconds long. In a fifteen-minute news broadcast, about twenty-five stories are told in about eighteen hundred words. Compare this figure to the one hundred thousand words found in an average daily newspaper, and you will see that television news skims the surface of events.[46] That this brevity leaves little time for detailed analysis or carefully explained background doesn't seem to bother news producers, whose concern is to keep viewers' attention throughout the newscast. Television executives assume that the average viewer is incapable of attending to a topic for long and that he or she will tune out if not kept constantly amused by slick production values—catchy theme music, colorful sets, reporters' happy talk, and the like.

Television news must also be highly visual, and a program usually leads off with the most visually interesting story. Thus, a fire may take precedence over a presidential press conference. Reporters and their subjects often go to unusual lengths to provide visuals. A reporter delivers news about the presidency while standing in the snow in front of the White House rather than sitting in the comfort of the studio, simply because location reporting is visually more interesting. A political candidate may announce a bid for a Senate seat while standing in front of Mount Rushmore, because doing so sends a visually symbolic message. During the war in Iraq, not only did reports from the field present dramatic visuals, but also specially designed graphics were used to lead into coverage, giving the war the look of a slickly produced action-adventure show.

Television reporters, like newspaper reporters, seek out the most dramatic stories they can find. The more unusual, conflict-filled, or violent a story, the more likely it is to be covered. Reuven Frank, former president of NBC News, has said, "Every news story should, without any sacrifice of probity or responsibility, display the attributes of fiction, of drama. It should have structure and conflict, problem and denouement, rising action and falling action, a beginning, middle, and an end."[47]

> Although it is tempting to believe that all reporting is governed by the norm of objectivity and that events can be separated from values, this is usually not true.

Although it is tempting to believe that all reporting is governed by the norm of objectivity and that events can be separated from values, this is usually not true. Media gatekeepers decide what is news and what is not and, in choosing what to report, tend to follow ideal norms. Driven by the need to create stories filled with conflict, reporters inevitably build their stories about "good guys" and "bad guys." International conflicts involving the United States are particularly open to oversimplified, "us-versus-them" reporting.

The Pervasiveness of TV Logic. In both entertainment and nonentertainment formats, television provides us with important services. It entertains, educates, and informs us. It can, however, be criticized on a number of levels. Perhaps the greatest criticism is that TV makes us want our everyday experience to come in short, vivid, entertaining form. According to an article in the *Los Angeles Times,* lawyers have had to change their style of presentation to more closely resemble a television courtroom scene. Some lawyers now call their strongest witnesses first and make their points in a rapid, dramatic way.[48] Members of the television generation are impatient with slow-moving events; with serious, detailed analyses of news events; and with narratives that deal with complex issues or personalities.

Television invites us into alternative realities. Unfortunately, these realities are seldom trustworthy. It oversimplifies, glamorizes, and sensationalizes everyday life. Some people buy into the glamorous lifestyles that they see, and they come to identify so strongly with favorite characters that they have difficulty separating fact from illusion. Soap opera actors frequently receive fan mail addressed to their on-screen personas.

Although most of us are not mesmerized by television to such a degree, we do regard media figures as role models. Children, especially, often take what they see quite literally. Joshua Meyerowitz has pointed out that one of the effects of television is to "obliterate childhood" by letting children see adult behavior that is otherwise kept from them and by showing children how to act like adults.[49] Children may also come to expect the adults in their world to act like those on TV. Today, when a young child can turn to her mother and ask, "Mommy, why can't you be like those ladies in the Pepsi commercial?," we have clear evidence that media images and values can affect everyday relationships.[50]

Another potential danger of television is the power of the visual image. When we see a picture of something, we assume that it is an objective representation of that thing. The fact that camera angle, shot composition, and the like might bias a perception seldom occurs to us. The possibility that people might be using the media to legitimate questionable causes is often ignored. One of the potential dangers of television is that we come to believe what we see on it.

NEW MEDIA: GOING GLOBAL AND MOBILE

Nowadays, we can communicate quickly and easily through networked computers and over cell phones. Most of us use these media in quite ordinary ways: to chat with friends, look up information, or make appointments. But some of the time, the new media are used in extraordinary ways. Consider the following examples.

In 2001, a young woman found herself stranded at sea off the coast of Bali. As her boat started to sink, she sent her boyfriend in England a text message asking for help, and he in turn contacted the U.K. coastguard, who made arrangements for an

Indonesian gunboat to come to her aid.[51] The new media can, quite literally, be lifelines.

In the Muslim Middle East, one can order a phone with a compass that points toward Mecca and an alarm to signal prayer time. In some Christian countries, subscribers can sign up for daily text messages from the Pope and can even have the entire Bible downloaded to their cell phones, although the verses are written in text-message shorthand.[52] New media are being adapted to every aspect of our lives.

Of course, in addition to making life easier, new media can be used in negative ways. For example, students in a Canadian high school created a Website entirely dedicated to humiliating a 17-year-old classmate, labeling him a pedophile and bombarding him with hate mail. As it turns out, this kind of cyberbullying is by no means an isolated incident. In one study, one-quarter of the seventh grade students in two Alberta schools reported being bullied via the Net.[53]

One of the newest uses of new media is the habit, popular among some teens, of **sexting**, using their cell phones to send nude pictures of themselves to others.[54] A nationwide survey conducted in 2009 revealed that one in twenty teens have used their phones in this way without realizing that it is against the law. In some areas of the country, officials have begun to prosecute participants, arresting them on child pornography charges. Whether or not you believe these photos are actually pornographic, they can certainly cause embarrassment, because the photos are often widely circulated, sometimes out of spite. Whereas most people believe that what they text or email is private, a moment's thought should show that is not the case. The new media raise important questions of privacy.

Finally, to offer another example, a man in Dubai sent his wife, who was late to meet him, a text message that read: "Why are you late? You are divorced." A court later ruled that the divorce was valid.[55] These are just a few examples of the inventive (and sometimes dismaying) ways in which individuals are adapting new media to meet their needs. As the new media become more accessible and powerful, people will undoubtedly think of even more unusual ways to integrate them into their lives.

In this section, we look at networked computing and mobile telecommunications, two of the most recent kinds of communication media. However, as we think about these communication technologies, we should keep in mind that they did not spring up overnight. New media are extensions of old media, and in the future, the personal computers and cell phones we use today will seem remarkably antiquated and will almost certainly have been revised, replaced, or reinvented.

> New media are extensions of old media, and in the future, the personal computers and cell phones we use today will seem remarkably antiquated and will almost certainly have been revised, replaced, or reinvented.

Characteristics of New Media

Despite the fact that new media develop out of old, today's new media also have characteristics that distinguish them from more traditional forms of mediated communication.[56] The fact that new media employ digital technology means, among other things, that it is now relatively easy to combine words, images, and sound in a single format. Digitization gives media consumers more control and freedom than they had in the past. It allows new patterns of access and offers greater possibilities for interactivity. Unfortunately, it can also lead to audience fragmentation and can erode privacy. Let's look at each of these characteristics in turn.

Digitization

As technology expert Nicholas Negroponte pointed out, new media are based on the "transmission of digital bits rather than physical atoms."[57] Think for a minute about the difference between snail-mail and email. Once upon a time, writing a letter to a friend overseas was a lengthy and laborious process. The message would have to be physically moved through space, and an overseas letter might take anywhere from a week to several months to get to the addressee. Now sending a message overseas is a much quicker process. When we type a greeting into our computer and hit the send key, the message is converted into digital bits that are processed almost instantaneously. Through the process of **digitization**, messages are converted into computer-readable electrical signals (or bits) that can be quickly processed, efficiently stored, and cheaply transmitted.

Multimedia Capability

One of the important results of digitization is the fact that, once converted to digital signals, different kinds of information—images, sounds, and words—can easily be combined in a single format. Of course, traditional media did some of this. Newspapers mixed written words and photos, and television merged images and sound. But digital technology allows us to combine diverse forms of information in very sophisticated ways. Any good Website will blend visuals and text, and most will provide access to video and audio content. To a generation raised with

> One of the important results of digitization is the fact that, once converted to digital signals, different kinds of information—images, sounds, and words—can easily be combined in a single format.

computers, it is hard to believe that people once lived in a world where combining media in sophisticated ways was difficult and, in some cases, impossible. Now our expectations about the use of multimedia are so great that we often lose patience with messages that rely on only one kind of input. To be successful today, communicators must master computer technology and be able to create compelling multimedia presentations.

New Modes of Consumption

Digitization has not only transformed *what* information we experience but also *how* we experience that information. Once upon a time, in the not so distant past, if you wanted to make sure you didn't miss your

> Time and space no longer act as barriers to communication and media receivers can set their own schedules.

favorite TV show, you stayed home the night it was broadcast. And before the advent of answering machines, cell phones, and text messaging, if you wanted to get in touch with a friend, you had to make sure he or she was near the (land line) phone to receive your call. Many new media messages are **asynchronous**, that is, receiver and sender do not have to be present at the same time in order to communicate. This means that you can contact friends at any time of day or night simply by texting or leaving a voice-mail or email message. It also means that you can consume traditional media messages when and where you want to. If you're busy when that TV show you want to see comes on, it's really not a problem. You can record it, view it whenever you want, rewind to see the parts you like again, bypass the boring bits, and even fast-forward through the commercials. Time and space no longer act as barriers to communication and media receivers can set their own schedules.

Interactivity

Recent computer applications have made it much easier for media users to become media producers. As a consequence, there is now a "more direct, interactive, and participative use" of computer-mediated communication than ever before.[58] On social networking sites like Facebook we can easily connect with others and share opinions; on Amazon.com we can rate and review products; on Wikipedia we can collaboratively edit information; and on community Websites like Second Life we can even construct virtual worlds. When we're not blogging or twittering, we can be remixing music, modding game content (using tools provided by game companies to design additional levels in game worlds), or creating short films for YouTube. This newfound ability to collaborate in the production of media content is often referred to as **Web 2.0**. This term refers more to the "explosion of creative and collaborative activity" that has occurred as a result of technical breakthroughs rather than to the breakthroughs themselves.[59] Admittedly, many of the traditional mass media have allowed some degree of audience involvement (think community TV stations and call-in radio shows), but nowadays the potential for audiences to become active has risen exponentially.

Whereas teenagers constitute the largest group of content creators and sharers, older users are also going online to blog, to publish photos or artwork, or even to create online profiles on social networking sites. When you log on to Facebook, don't assume everyone is your own age. Both MySpace and Facebook have several million users over the age of 65. Says one 88-year-old grandfather, "I don't browse Facebook much, but I see that it is a way to get to the nitty-gritty of a person's character. Also [it's] a way to do something late at night when I can't sleep." So next time you post a photo or create a profile, be aware that your grandparents may be browsing your Facebook page.[60]

As we've seen in previous chapters, the new media allow interpersonal self-presentation, enable groups to work together online, and make it possible for organizations to harness the collective intelligence of globally dispersed members.

The new media are also taking an increasingly important role in politics. During the 2008 election campaign, for example, 46 percent of Americans used the Internet to "get news about the campaigns, share their views, and mobilize others."[61] There were large increases in the viewing of online political videos and the use of social networking sites for political activity, with Americans not only going online to learn about the candidates, but also generating their own responses and promoting their own views. Campaigns have taken advantage of this activity by publishing talking points about their own and opposing candidates, "to give the public a tool kit they could use . . . in their conversations with friends and neighbors."[62]

Businesses and complex organizations are recognizing the advantages of connecting themselves with new media. Even the U.S. Army has gotten into the act. Recognizing that young Americans unfamiliar with the Army were unlikely to enlist, they developed an **MMOG** (massively multiplayer online game) called *America's Army* that allowed players to experience virtual military missions while exposing them to military values. Did it work? A 2004 marketing survey asked pro-military students the source of their favorable opinions. Nearly 30 percent cited their experiences playing *America's Army*.[63]

Interactivity is not without its perils. The online encyclopedia Wikipedia, for example, allows users to log on and add or edit existing entries. As the site explains, "Lots of people are constantly improving *Wikipedia,* making thousands of changes an hour, all of which are recorded on article histories and recent changes. Inappropriate changes are usually removed quickly, and repeat offenders can be blocked."[64]

Although the idea of a site that anyone can edit is appealing, it can also be open to abuse. In 2005, for example, a contributor anonymously posted false information in the biography of respected journalist John Seigenthaler, Sr. The bogus information suggested that Seigenthaler had been involved in the assassinations of both John F. and Robert F. Kennedy and had lived in the Soviet Union for many years. The hoax began as a joke but soon got out of hand. For several months, the libelous entry stood until a friend of Seigenthaler discovered it. In an editorial in *USA Today,* an obviously incensed Seigenthaler summed up his feelings:

> *And so we live in a universe of new media with phenomenal opportunities for worldwide communications and research—but populated by volunteer vandals with poison-pen intellects. . . . When I was a child, my mother lectured me on the evils of "gossip." She held a feather pillow and said, "If I tear this open, the feathers will fly to the four winds, and I could never get them back in the pillow. That's how it is when you spread mean things about people."*
>
> *For me, that pillow is a metaphor for Wikipedia.*[65]

User Choice and Audience Fragmentation

New media offer users greater freedom of choice. In previous times, media gatekeepers chose what the public read, saw, and heard. Now audience members can actively

> Some critics feel that as the people gain more control over what they see or hear, they will no longer be concerned with broad social issues.

search for the content they want, choosing to expose themselves only to ideas that match their values and interests. Although this situation gives receivers a great deal of freedom, it may have an unintended result: audience fragmentation. Audience fragmentation (or demassification, as it is sometimes called) refers to the fact that rather than being part of a single mass audience, people are now becoming members of separate, specialized audiences. As a consequence, they may no longer be exposed to information that could widen their knowledge, challenge their views, or create common ground with people who think differently. Some critics feel that as the people gain more control over what they see or hear, they will no longer be concerned with broad social issues.

Increased Surveillance

In earlier times, audiences were large and heterogeneous and, therefore, relatively anonymous. Media producers tried their best to gather information about audience members, but they often had to fall back on guesswork. And although skilled audience researchers could tell a lot about receivers, they had nowhere near the amount of knowledge that is available today. The technology that makes it easy for you to communicate by email or cell phone also makes it easy for large commercial or governmental organizations to monitor and predict your

> The technology that makes it easy for you to communicate by email or cell phone also makes it easy for large commercial or governmental organizations to monitor and predict your behavior.

behavior. The use of intelligent software programs that gather consumer data and the presence on computers of cookies (stored bits of data that allow Websites to authenticate user identity and track online choices) mean that very little that goes on online is private. And the GPS devices that are so useful when you want to use your cell phone to get directions to the nearest restaurant also mean that your presence can be constantly tracked, even when your phone is off.

Computers can also automatically "compile dossiers about individuals by piecing together countless tiny, otherwise harmless shards of information about transactions, medical conditions, buying habits, and demographic characteristics."[66] What are the results of living in a world where it is becoming difficult, if not impossible, to remain anonymous? Many critics, following the lead of philosopher Michel Foucault, fear that the presence of constant surveillance may make people more passive, willing to accept "regulations and docility as part of the way every 'normal' person thinks and behaves."[67]

CMC: Computer-Mediated Communication

In the last decades of the twentieth century, the Internet became the newest mass medium, opening up a world of computer-mediated communication that has revolutionized the way we live our lives. Its movement from invention to popular phenomenon has been faster than that of any other medium to date. Ray Hiebert and

Sheila Gibbons tell us that books took nearly 400 years to transform themselves from a curiosity for the elite to a mass medium. Newspapers took 200 years, while magazines required about 170 years. Sound recordings achieved mass popularity in about 60 years, movies in about 50, radio in about 40, and television in about 30 years. The Internet took even less time—about 15 years. In the early 1970s, the Internet, then called the ARPAnet, was a little-known network designed to link government computers so that scientists could exchange research data. By the mid-1990s, it was being used by millions of ordinary citizens around the world.[68]

By now, we use it "for almost any human activity you can imagine, from shopping to sex, from research to rebellion."[69] We use it to talk with family and friends, colleagues, and even animals. Koko, the mountain gorilla who has learned to use American Sign Language, has actually participated in live Internet chats. On Earth Day 1998, as her trainer Penny Patterson translated and an assistant typed in Koko's thoughts, Koko expounded on such topics as "motherhood, pets, food preferences, friendship, love, and the future."[70]

How Do People Use the Internet?

Earlier, we looked at uses and gratifications research as it applied to media in general and television in particular. It's time now to look at the ways in which people use computer-mediated communication.

The popularity of Internet communication has increased dramatically over the years. Today, email remains the most popular online activity, especially among older users, but instant messaging, social networking, and blogging have gained ground. A 2009 survey found that teens and members of Generation Y (those born between 1977 and 1990) use the Internet primarily for entertainment and social networking. They are much more likely than older users to look at online videos, play online games, visit virtual worlds, and download music. They are also more likely to keep in touch with others by writing and reading blogs and by logging on to social networking sites. Older generations use the Internet less for socializing and entertainment and more for seeking information, emailing, and shopping. Video downloads, online travel reservations, and work-related research, however, are pursued equally by both young and old.[71]

What general social functions does communication over the Internet fulfill? Hiebert and Gibbons discuss five in addition to *education*.[72] First, the Internet offers us *news and information;* most major newspapers now have online versions of their papers, including easily searched archives of articles in previous issues. Second, the Internet also serves as a site for *opinion, gossip, and rumor;* whether this function works to democratize information or to degrade it is a debatable issue. Certainly, on the Internet, people are free to disseminate all kinds of ideas. In fact, if you want to see the variety available, log on to one of the alt.aliens newsgroups on Usenet. A third function of the Internet is to deliver *entertainment.* A fourth function is *advertising* products, a function that is abundantly clear to anyone who has been spammed (and I don't know anyone who hasn't). Finally, a fifth function is to affect public opinion by serving as a conduit for *public relations* messages. In general, these five functions seem similar to those of other media, although the depth of involvement and amount of interactivity seem to go well beyond those in traditional media.

Does the Internet Lead to Social Isolation?

Whenever a new technology appears, it causes anxiety. As David Buckingham, an expert on the effects of media on children, points out, "new technology is often invested with our most intense fantasies and fears. It holds out the promise of a better future, while simultaneously provoking anxieties about a fundamental break with the past."[73] In the 1950s and 1960s, for example, when television was gaining hold, it was seen "both as a new way of bringing the family together, and as something which would undermine natural family interaction."[74] The same kind of fear has been attached to computer-mediated communication. Experts have worried about everything from physical damage (development of "Nintendo elbow" or epileptic seizures caused by computer games) and behavioral aberration (imitative violence, involvement with hate sites, or addiction to pornography). But the fear that has most captured the public's attention is the fear that individuals who use computers will become isolated, abandoning face-to-face interaction in favor of life lived in cyberspace.

> Although the inventors of networked computing assumed that it would be used for file sharing rather than interpersonal interaction, Internet communication has played out as fundamentally social.

The fact that email, which is used primarily for interpersonal contact, is the Internet's most popular application should allay these fears. Indeed, although the inventors of networked computing assumed that it would be used for file sharing rather than interpersonal interaction, Internet communication has played out as fundamentally social. "Even aspects of the Internet that do not seem particularly social, such as business sites, online magazines and information services, have integrated social opportunities such as chat spaces and bulletin boards into their sites."[75] Internet users, far from being social isolates, tend to enjoy interaction offline as well as online, often using computer-mediated communication to support face-to-face relationships. Research suggests that those who use the Internet frequently are also likely to engage in frequent phone and face-to-face contact.[76] Indeed, one study found that Internet users spend three times more time in social interaction than nonusers do.[77]

> Because there is less information about communicators' identities online, computer-mediated communication allows identity play and can result in a lowered sense of accountability.

Some social critics have even argued that the virtual worlds that occur in MMOGs (massively multiplayer online games) like *World of Warcraft* and MMORPGs (massively multiplayer online role playing games) like *Second Life* can actually serve as "third places," locations other than the home or workplace where people can congregate and interact socially as they do in offline brick-and-mortar neighborhood pubs or coffee shops. Although these cyberlocations do not provide deep emotional involvement, some argue that they provide "bridging social capital," relatively shallow social relationships that "expose the individual to a diversity to worldviews." Gaming, some suggest, allows "individual and collaborative problem solving, identity construction, apprenticeship, and literacy practices."[78]

Anonymity and the Net

One aspect of computer-mediated communication that cannot be so easily dismissed is its anonymity. Because there is less information about communicators' identities online, computer-mediated communication allows identity play and can result in a lowered sense of accountability. When no one knows who you are, you can be anyone you want to be. We are all familiar with cases of online deception. For the most part, however, identity deception does not seem to be widespread. Internet researcher Nancy Baym tells us that

> In some cases [CMC] offers the chance to explore untried identities or to falsify the self. In other cases, it offers the freedom to be more open and honest than one would otherwise be. In still other cases, anonymity is an obstacle to be overcome through various forms of self-disclosure. It is too often forgotten that in much—perhaps even most—CMC, however, anonymity is not an issue, as people are corresponding with people they also know offline and building online selves that are richly contextualized in their offline social networks.[79]

Websites as a Form of Communication

More and more of us are developing personal Websites. Whether the world needs any more Websites eating up bandwidth is debatable, but for now, they are a popular way to reach out to others. Patricia Wallace tells us that Internet Websites are an "inexpensive way to create an impression, polish your online persona, and tell the world something about yourself and your interests." By including photos, creative essays, poetry, and/or artwork, we can create an ideal self. By adding navigation links to our own favorite Websites, we can show off our interests and tastes.[80]

All of this assumes, of course, that our Websites are well designed and contain something interesting for others to view. This is not always the case for either personal or commercial sites. Jack Davis and Susan Merritt offer five design tips.[81] They believe that a well-designed Website is clear, visually and conceptually consistent, and uncluttered; uses contrast to make elements stand out; and employs cinematic techniques of storytelling such as personalization and emphasis on showing rather than describing. Other designers stress ease and simplicity.[82] If your Website has more than one page, it is important to provide easy links to these other pages as well as a quick way to get back to your home page. Most designers warn against using graphics that take too long to load because people lose patience after ten or fifteen seconds. Jacob Nielsen and Marie Takir, for example, recognize the temptation to include elaborate artwork or clever animation but point out that the home page (especially the commercial home page) is like a lobby through which people pass on their way to somewhere else. People who enter the site want to get to the information, not linger on the home page indefinitely. Nielsen and Takir stress that "web design is interaction design" and urge designers to invest more time and effort in thinking about usability rather than decorative elements.[83]

If you decide to use the free disk space your provider gives you to create a Web page, there are certain elements you should include. In addition to interesting and useful content, you will want to incorporate an attractive title at the top of the page that encourages visitors to scroll down, a clear site menu that tells visitors what you have to offer, useful navigation links that don't inadvertently strand your visitors in some remote outpost of cyberspace, and a way to contact you if they want to send a message. It is also a good idea to have some way to indicate new content, to give the date on which the site was last updated, and to provide copyright information where appropriate. The basic advice given by most designers is to keep it simple, organized, and clear—the same advice one might give about offline forms of communication.

Mobile Telephony

One of the most popular of the new technologies in general use today is the mobile or cellular phone. For many young people, being without a cell phone amounts to a kind of social death, a fate to be avoided at all costs. To members of "generation txt," having a cell phone is a necessity, not a luxury. So pervasive is the cell phone today, that "many urban song birds have become adept at impersonating mobile tones and melodies."[84]

> For many young people, being without a cell phone amounts to a kind of social death, a fate to be avoided at all costs. To members of "generation txt," having a cell phone is a necessity, not a luxury.

Uses and Gratifications

Mobile phones are an affordable, highly transportable way to stay in touch with friends and family. As Crispin Thurlow expresses it, "perhaps even more so than the telephone, the mobile phone and text-messaging are 'technologies of sociability.'"[85] In addition to their social functions, cell phones can be used to send and retrieve networked information. Many of today's cell phones have as much computing power as the largest and most expensive computers did only a generation ago.[86] Cell phones are not simply movable land lines. They have taken the networked computer and made it mobile. No longer is it necessary to be chained to one's desktop to retrieve information and send messages. Now access to the Internet is available anytime, anywhere.

Mobile technology, when coupled with its sister short messaging service (SMS) technology, has yielded some highly inventive applications. For example, demonstrators in a number of countries, including the United States, have used their cell phones to organize and coordinate political protests. In Sweden, roving gamers, who have created and armed "bots," receive SMS messages about the geographic location of other players. When they get within range, they can shoot, and if their "weapons" are strong enough, they are credited with a "kill" that is posted online. In Japan, similar technology is used for matchmaking. "Lovegety" keychain devices signal when another compatible Lovegety owner is within fifteen feet; in North America, a similar "Gaydar" device alerts members looking for same-sex matches. In Manhattan, a celebrity watch service makes it possible for fans to send one another sightings of favorite stars.[87]

Although they are interesting, these ingenious uses do not constitute the bulk of cellular communication. Most people use their cell phones to communicate with family and friends. In a survey on text messaging done in the United Kingdom, Crispin Thurlow found most messages consisted of "friendship work," for example, apologies, words of support, and thanks. Short greetings were also frequently sent, as were plans for getting together and specific requests for information.[88]

Social Effects and Social Challenges

Any technology presents social challenges. A cell phone may come with a user's manual that tells you how to operate the device, but social uses have to be figured out on the fly. One challenge of mobile technology is finding oneself in two different places at the same time. Talking to a distraught friend while walking along a busy sidewalk, for example, means negotiating two separate spaces: one physical and one psychological. Another problem comes in trying to allocate attention between the demands of one's copresent friends and one's ringing cell phone. Taking the call may signal to friends that they are unimportant, but not taking the call can lead to anxiety. The ability to handle these kinds of situations is becoming an important social skill.

> A cell phone may come with a user's manual that tells you how to operate the device, but social uses have to be figured out on the fly.

An interesting effect of cell phone use is a general devaluing of time and a redefinition of what it means to be present. The term aproximeeting has been used to describe the fact that when plans can easily be changed, they will be. People often no longer make specific time commitments. Instead, they make loose arrangements that are forever changing. Thus, it is possible for nights out to be "characterized by endless deferrals and reshufflings of meetings and events which might never occur."[89] To make things worse, people seem to feel that as long as they phone, they don't actually need to show up in person. Phoning in often counts as being there, allowing individuals to get out of dates they really don't want to keep.

If individuals can use cell phone calls to let people know where they are, they can also use such calls to lie about their whereabouts. It has been reported that individuals who are involved in illicit affairs find cell phones a boon, and suspicious spouses often check their partners' mobiles for signs of infidelity.[90] Other deceptive uses include stage-phoning, in which someone pretends to be making important calls to impress bystanders, or phone-shielding, in which someone pretends to take a call to avoid unwanted interactions.

Despite the challenges, most people would not give up their cell phones. In her research on cell phone use, cybertheorist Sadie Plant sums up this feeling:

> For all their reservations, the vast majority of the many contributors to this research found it impossible to imagine life without the mobile phone. . . . A young Afghan student in Peshawar said, "If I don't have my mobile with me, I feel as though I have lost something. I'm not OK. There's something missing. I turn off the ring tone when I take the bus, or when I'm in the mosque. But I never turn the mobile off."[91]

As we've seen throughout this chapter, technologies are never used quite the way their inventors intend. Initially, SMS technology was designed for purely commercial purposes. It was soon taken over for social purposes, however, in much the same way that email came to dominate the Internet. The popularity of texting is "yet another example of how the human need for social intercourse—a kind of 'communication imperative'—bends and ultimately coopts technology to suit its own ends."[92]

Today we are bombarded with media choices. Should we log on to MySpace, follow a celebrity Twitter, spend some time in *Second Life*, listen to our iPods, check out FriendFeed, surf through YouTube, or maybe just take a nap? It's no wonder some people are experiencing e-fatigue, a new term for media overload: "that mild, gnawing nausea that sets in once the marvels of a technology have worn off."[93]

One way to understand e-fatigue is to consider the life-cycle of new technologies. According to Gartner, an information technology consulting firm that offers yearly predictions about the potential of new media, public response to a given media product goes through a series of five predictable hype stages. In what is called the *technology trigger* stage, people first hear about the new technology and become intrigued. Next, during the *peak of inflated expectations* stage, they are overwhelmed with excitement and unrealistic expectations. When the technology doesn't quite live up to its press, during the *trough of disillusionment* stage, it falls out of favor. At this point, the technology enters the *slope of enlightenment* stage, where people begin to redefine its nature and true worth. Finally, at the *plateau of productivity* state, the technology discovers what it was meant to do and finds its audience, which may be very different from what the developers imagined. As Linton Weeks explains, "Eventually, people hold on to technologies that enrich their lives and jettison the rest."[94]

CONVERGENCE: THE INTERSECTION OF NEW MEDIA AND OLD

Media, whether new or old, are constantly converging with one another. Although we have looked at computer-mediated communication and mobile telephony sepa-rately, anyone with an iPhone or Black-Berry knows they are no longer separate. Media interact with and affect one another. Television, for example, has changed the design of newspapers. *USA Today* is print journalism's attempt to use the language of television, a language characterized by condensed information and visual contrast. Even textbooks are us-ing "multicolored graphics, photos, boxed inserts, bold-faced types, and summaries" to make reading more tolerable for the TV generation.[95]

As digitalization has taken hold in the new media, the traditional media have begun to realize its advantages and are busy converting from their traditional ana-log (nondigital) form. **Convergence** is the term used to describe this "coming to-gether of computing, telecommunications, and media in a digital environment," as well as to describe the merging of Internet and traditional media companies.[96] Now, for example, TV news channels have their own Websites that can add more detail to a broadcast news item as well as hyperlinks to other sources of information. And enter-tainment programs can increase interactiv-

Everything old is new again. 3-D movies and comics were once the latest fad; new technologies have made 3-D movies popular once more.

ity by inviting viewers to log onto connected Websites to chat with celebrities or to offer feedback through their cell phones. In its fourth season, for example, *American Idol* generated 41.5 million text messages as fans participated in *Idol* chat sessions, posted questions to contestants, and sent in their votes. And the figures have risen steadily since then.[97]

In *Convergence Culture,* author Henry Jenkins provides countless examples of the synergy that exists between the old and new media. *The Matrix,* for example, is more than the three movies most mainstream viewers are aware of. The story continues in a series of comics, a massively multiplayer game set in the world of the Matrix, and a program of short animated films, all of which interconnect. Fans may follow the story across media, and "the consumer who has played the game or watched the shorts will get a different experience of the movies than one who has simply had the theatrical film experience."[98]

In the case of *The Matrix,* the producers actively planned the intersecting storytelling and encouraged collaborative authorship. In other cases, fans take over and produce sequels and related material based on a film or book. Fans of *Star Wars* have made their own movies with names like *George Lucas in Love, The Jedi Who Loved Me,* and *Boba Fett: Bounty Trail.*[99] Similarly, the Harry Potter series has encouraged young writers to insert themselves into the world of Hogwarts and write their own stories.

BECOMING A MORE RESPONSIBLE COMMUNICATOR

In this last section of the chapter, we'll look at some of the ethical dilemmas that creators of media messages face, as well as the ethical responsibilities of media consumers.

Ethical Issues for Media Practitioners

Because the media are in business to make money and because media communicators are human, the potential for unethical practices is great. Hiebert and his colleagues present an excellent discussion of the kinds of ethical problems media communicators face on a daily basis.[100] Although many of the examples they provide are related to news reporting, the ethical conflicts they discuss arise in all forms of media messages.

One problem media communicators face is *conflict of interest,* a situation that occurs when a media communicator's professional role conflicts with a personal interest. Does, for example, a reporter have the right to march in a public demonstration, as a *New York Times* reporter who attended a pro-choice rally did? Does this kind of activity damage a reporter's ability to report events objectively or decrease his or her credibility? And, to consider a more extreme case, does a reporter have the right to send out letters in support of an issue or a candidate? A Florida pro-choice reporter sent small wire coat hangers to 160 legislators in an attempt to dramatize the restricting of women's access to abortion. Did the reporter have the right to express her own views? What would you have done if you had been these reporters' editor? Would you feel the same way if they had taken a pro-life stand? In these cases, the reporters' right to act as private citizens clashed with their role as objective news sources. In the first case, the reporter continued to work; in the second, the reporter was fired.[101]

Media communicators also face problems concerning *truth, accuracy, and fairness issues.* The use of composite characters and reenactments are two examples of techniques that either mislead or utterly fabricate, depending on your point of view. In 1981, *Washington Post* reporter Janet Cooke was awarded a Pulitzer prize for a compelling series about an eight-year-old heroin addict. Later, it was revealed that the child she described did not exist but was a fictionalized composite. Cooke's career as a journalist was ruined. She was fired, and she lost the Pulitzer. In another incident, ABC News came under fire for presenting a video segment showing a U.S. diplomat handing a briefcase to a Soviet agent. Ostensibly, the incident was taped during the actual transfer of secret information. In reality, however, the scene was a staged reenactment. What responsibility did ABC have to make clear to viewers that what was broadcast was not a real event?

Methods of information gathering also present potential ethical problems. To gather information, most journalists promise confidentiality to their sources. But what happens if, off the record, a reporter finds out about a source's criminal activity? What if a reporter feels that he or she is being used by an informant? Is it ever right for a reporter to reveal confidential sources? And how should a reporter treat a source? Overzealous reporters have ambushed sources during interviews, have lied about their own identity, and have bribed and threatened informants.

Reporters have even set out to break the law to demonstrate problems in law enforcement. Should a reporter be encouraged to smuggle a fake bomb onto a plane to show lax security measures or make a drug buy to show how available drugs are? Are there limits to how far a reporter should go to get a story?

Privacy and propriety issues are also ethically gray areas. In an effort to get a compelling picture, is it right to invade a grief-stricken victim's privacy? Is every aspect of a public figure's life open for scrutiny? Is it defensible to pry into the private domestic arrangements of political candidates and to publish detailed exposés of their sex lives? What rights do crime victims have to keep their identities hidden?

Sometimes, reporters know that reporting a story can lead to *physical or emotional harm* or can encourage dangerous practices. What if a story gives people ideas about how to commit a crime or how to hurt themselves? In this regard, critics have voiced concern about articles on teen suicide encouraging more suicides and about exposés on cheating serving as lessons on how to beat the system. Covering terrorist activities is probably the prime example of this kind of ethical dilemma, because terrorist acts are primarily symbolic and depend on publicity for their effectiveness.

Although our focus has been on the news, ethical decisions arise in other areas of the media. Advertising certainly provides an arena for unethical communication, as does entertainment programming. The latter has been criticized for violence and sexually explicit material and for stereotypical portrayals of members of minority groups. And there are sins of omission as well as of commission. R-rated movies, for example, often show people involved in sexual situations yet seldom depict any discussion of condom use. Social psychologists argue that the behavioral scripts individuals internalize as a result of this modeling encourage potentially dangerous sexual practices. In the age of AIDS, do screenwriters have a responsibility in their scripts either to model safer sex or to stop modeling unsafe sex altogether?

The ethical questions that are raised in regard to media practices are complex and difficult. Each communicator must resolve them in his or her own way. Clearly, however, thoughtless, irresponsible actions cannot be tolerated, and media communicators must examine their own practices and must make decisions based not on expediency but on values.

Using Traditional Media More Responsibly

Given the huge amount of time Americans spend with the media and given the potential for media abuse, it's clear that we could all benefit from becoming more thoughtful and responsible media consumers. Some guidelines follow; consider others you would add.

- The media can convey hegemonic messages that reinforce role inequality between genders, among races and classes, and so on. Often, these messages go unnoticed or, when noticed, they are dismissed as insignificant. The first step in becoming more thoughtful about media is to recognize that we are affected by media messages. As media consumers, we need to judge carefully the truth and fairness of what we hear and see.

- Most of us don't deconstruct and question media texts and "facts" as carefully as we should because media representations often fit so nicely with what we want to believe. When we process only what we already find acceptable, we become lazy processors, passively soaking up information. Questioning media ideologies and becoming more informed about events make us more mindful about the information we are given. When we consume news, for example, we should make a commitment to check out facts and demand accurate information. If we don't, then the quality of the information we receive will continue to be low.

- When we encounter objectionable media messages, we need to think about our reactions. We may find certain kinds of media messages objectionable, but many of us consume them every day, thus reinforcing the production of even more extreme and offensive materials. Blaming media producers for poor quality and then eagerly consuming their products will do nothing to raise standards.

- Finally, in addition to tuning out objectionable material, we could all bene-fit from exploring new sources of information and entertainment. A steady diet of "junk" media isn't going to challenge us. We should be open to ex-panding our tastes by sampling new, more complex, and varied media menus.

Ethics for the New Media

We end this chapter with some ethical guidelines for you to consider as you inter-act electronically.

- The first and most important point to remember is that the people with whom you communicate online are real people with real feelings. They can be hurt and betrayed as easily as the people you meet offline. Don't let the anonymity of the Net lead you to dehumanize your conversational part-ners. Online you should observe the ethical principles that guide real-world relationships.

- The standards of decency that apply to interpersonal, group, and public in-teractions apply in cyberspace as well. Because we communicate with face-less others, we may be tempted to think that our actions are innocent. But as Michael Heim so eloquently puts it:

  > Without directly meeting others physically, our ethics languish. Face-to-face communication, the fleshly bond between people, supports a long-term warmth and loyalty, a sense of obligation for which the computer-mediated communities have not yet been tested. . . . The physical eyes are the win-dows that establish the neighborhood of trust. Without the direct experience of the human face, ethical awareness shrinks. . . . The machine interface may amplify an amoral indifference to human relationships.[102]

- Unethical practices can also occur in the workplace. More than one em-ployee has been known to fire off foolish or insulting electronic memos without stopping to consider their effects. Not only is this bad form, it is dangerous. The "harmless joke" you sent to everyone about your boss may not seem so harmless when it's traced back to you. When email creates a hostile work environment, it is not only unethical, it is illegal. Think before you send messages that could annoy or insult coworkers.

- We know that gossip and misinformation thrive on the Net, perhaps because being "published" in cyberspace legitimizes information. Just remember that on a citizen's channel, anyone can say anything. We must therefore carefully evaluate the truth value of messages we receive and avoid posting information we have not checked for accuracy. When, simply by pressing a button, you can reach thousands of people who are primed to believe you, you take on addi-tional ethical responsibilities.

- Finally, when it comes to cell phones, try to remember that they can be intrusive and disturbing. Strangers shouldn't be forced to hear your private disclosures. And people sitting next to you at the theater or the movies shouldn't have to put up with interruptions. It has gotten so bad that the New York City Council passed a law banning cell phone use during live performances and in museums. And recently, Broadway actor Robert Griffin stopped a performance and threatened to walk off the stage if he heard one more cell phone ring. When in public, set your phone to vibrate or, better yet, turn it off.[103]

SUMMARY

This chapter looks at mediated communication. It begins by describing the language and logics of traditional mass media: newspapers, magazines, radio, and television. It then goes on to discuss the characteristics of new media with particular attention to computer mediated-communication (CMC) and mobile telephony.

In the traditional mass media, institutional sources address large, anonymous, heterogeneous audiences through interposed channels. Scholars usually talk about four functions of this form of mediated communication: surveillance, the gathering and disseminating of information; correlation, the analysis and evaluation of data; cultural transmission, the education and socialization of the audience; and entertainment. Although the impact of the mass media can be positive, it can also be negative by narcotizing audiences, increasing passivity, teaching antisocial behavior, and lowering popular taste.

There is lively debate about the extent to which mass media affect audiences. Early media theorists took a powerful effects view; they believed that audiences were largely powerless to resist media messages. Later theorists viewed audiences as more obstinate and resistant. Current theorists recognize that the media can set agendas, deliver hegemonic messages, cultivate erroneous world views, and change the way we think. But they also realize that audiences process media selectively, choose media according to their needs, and resist hegemonic messages with oppositional readings.

Consumers turn to different media for different reasons, some of which relate to the format of the medium. Newspapers are used to pass the time, gain practical information, keep in touch with public issues, and maintain a valued self-image. The newspaper format encourages focus on isolated events, a tendency to leave out detail, and a temptation to focus on the dramatic.

Magazines are more specialized and more personal than newspapers. They are read to pass the time, to gain information, and to learn how to live like "insiders." Radio has a strong interpersonal dimension, acting as a "portable friend" and binding people together through shared experience. Like magazines, radio is one of the most specialized of the media.

The medium of choice for most Americans is television. It provides news, gives us a glimpse of alternative worlds, and provides companionship. It also socializes us and provides entertainment. As a highly visual medium, it values movement, brevity, and intimate images. Entertainment programming favors speed and simplicity and tends to uphold ideal values. News programming tries to be brief, visuals oriented, dramatic, and moralistic.

It has become common to distinguish between traditional and new media. Six characteristics describe new media. First, they employ digital technology. Second, they make it easy to combine many different kinds of information in a single format. Third, time and space no longer act as barriers: media consumers can communicate anytime, anywhere. Fourth, new media allow new levels of interactivity; no longer are users passive receivers. Fifth, because media gatekeepers no longer have as much control over media content, consumers have more choice over what they see or hear. One result is audience fragmentation. Finally, new technologies make possible increased surveillance by commercial and governmental organizations.

Computer-mediated communication is the newest of the mass media, and its popularity has increased dramatically over time. Despite fears that CMC would isolate individuals from one another, it appears that it actually encourages interaction. Email is the most widely used form of CMC. Teens and Gen Ys use the Internet primarily for entertainment and social networking, whereas older users are more likely to seek information, email, and shop.

New technologies usually cause anxiety. In addition to unfounded fears that computer use would lead to social isolation, there is general concern about the anonymity offered by CMC. Although some people do explore different identities while online, others find it easier to be more open and honest over the computer than in face-to-face interactions. Anonymity is less of an issue than many fear, because most CMC is conducted between people who know one another offline.

Both private individuals and businesses use the Internet to publish personal Websites. Because Websites create a first impression, they must be well designed. A well-designed Website is clear, visually and conceptually consis-tent, uncluttered, uses contrast, and employs cinematic techniques. Most of all it is simple and easy to navigate, avoiding elaborate animation and art work. A personal Website should include interesting and useful content, an attractive title, a clear site menu, useful navigation links, and a way to leave messages. Like all messages, computer-mediated messages should be simple, organized, and clear.

Mobile phones are another offshoot of new media technologies. They are an affordable, highly transportable way to stay in touch. Along with SMS (short messaging service) technology, mobile telephony offers new ways to stay in contact as well as new communication challenges. Cell phones have changed notions of time and space. People who are not present can be treated as though they were, and plans and schedules no longer have to be made in advance. So pervasive is the hype surrounding new media offerings that overload or e-fatigue often sets in.

Each new medium changes the media that have gone before. In response to new media technology, old media are converting to digital formats and are finding new ways to connect with audiences. Traditional and new media are converging as networked computing, telecommunication, and mass media are finding new points of connection.

Because of the effects of the media, media communicators must be concerned with such ethical issues as conflict of interest, fairness, appropriate ways of gathering information, privacy and propriety, and the risk of abetting physical and emotional harm. Media programmers must also take responsibility. We must be aware of the power of traditional media and refuse to reinforce questionable media programming. We must also be responsible users of computer-based channels, remembering that the standards of decency that apply in the "real world" apply in cyberspace as well.

KEY TERMS

Listed below are the key terms used in this chapter, along with the number of the page where each is explained.

old media   (283)
new media   (283)
mass communication   (283)
media functions   (285)
surveillance   (285)
correlation   (286)
cultural transmission   (286)
prosocial learning   (286)
antisocial learning   (286)
entertainment   (286)
narcotize   (286)
powerful effects model
   (287)
limited effects model   (287)
magic bullet   (287)
hypodermic needle   (287)
obstinate audience   (287)
agenda-setting function   (288)

gatekeepers   (288)
critical theorists   (289)
hegemonic message   (289)
dominant ideology   (289)
spiral of silence   (289)
cultivation theory   (290)
mainstreaming   (290)
mean world hypothesis   (290)
heavy viewers   (290)
"the medium is the message"
   (291)
linear logic   (291)
mosaic logic   (291)
cool medium   (291)
selective exposure   (292)
selective attention   (292)
selective perception   (292)
selective retention   (293)

uses and gratifications research
   (293)
polysemy   (294)
ideal norms   (301)
sexting   (304)
digitization   (305)
asynchronous   (306)
Web 2.0   (306)
audience fragmentation   (308)
demassification   (308)
cookies   (308)
MMOG/MMORPG   (310)
aproximeeting   (313)
stage-phoning   (314)
phone-shielding   (314)
e-fatigue   (314)
hype stages   (314)
convergence   (315)

SUGGESTED READINGS

Campbell, Richard, & Martin, Christopher R. (2009). *Media and culture: An introduction to mass communication, 7th edition.* New York: Bedford/St. Martin's.
   A popular, comprehensive, and current introduction to the field.

Jenkins, Henry. (2008). *Convergence culture: Where old and new media collide.* New York: New York University Press.
   A fascinating look at ways in which converging media are making it possible for all of us to become media producers.

Intercultural Communication

In cross-cultural settings, even simple interactions can become complex.

For communication to work, people must have something in common. If communicators know and respect one another, communication is relatively easy. They can predict one another's moods and meanings, they know what topics to avoid, and they can sometimes even complete one another's thoughts. Uncertainty and stress are at a minimum; communication is spontaneous, open, and comfortable.

Communicating with strangers is more difficult. If the strangers come from our own culture, we can at least base our messages on shared attitudes, beliefs, and life experiences; but if the strangers are from another culture, we may be at a loss. In such a case, uncertainty is maximized. The actual forms, and even the functions, of communication may be strange to us.

In cross-cultural settings, even simple interactions can become complex. Imagine for a moment that you're working in Morocco. A colleague has invited you to his family home for dinner but is a little vague about when dinner will be served, and you have to ask several times before fixing the time. That evening, when you enter your host's home, his wife is nowhere to be seen, and when you ask when she'll be joining you, the host looks flustered and says that she's busy in the kitchen. When his little boy enters, you remark on how cute and clever the child is, but rather than being pleased, your Moroccan colleague looks upset. Before dinner is served, you politely ask to go to the washroom to wash up. During the meal, you do your best to hold up your end of the conversation, but it's hard going. Finally, after tea and pastry, you thank the host and politely leave. You have a feeling the dinner party wasn't a success, but you don't really know what went wrong.

As it turns out, according to Craig Storti, almost everything you did in this social situation was inappropriate.[1] In Morocco, an invitation to dinner is actually an invitation to come and spend time. At some point, food will be served, but what's important is being together. Therefore, discussing the specific time you should come to dinner is like asking your host how long he wants you around; it also implies that your major concern is to be fed. Your questions about his wife and your compliments to his son were similarly inappropriate. It is not customary for a Moroccan wife to eat with guests or even to be introduced, and praising a child is considered unlucky because it may alert evil spirits to the child's presence. Washing up in the washroom was also impolite. If you had waited, your host would have arranged for water to be brought in to you in an expensive decorative basin that would have shown his good taste as well as his concern for your comfort. Finally, it was rude to carry on a conversation during dinner. Talking interferes with the enjoyment of the meal and can be interpreted as a slight against the food.

An isolated incident such as this is not terribly serious, but people who spend time in other cultures may encounter many such small misunderstandings, which over time can take their toll. If cultural differences can get in the way of a simple meal between friends, you can imagine how they might seriously affect complicated business or diplomatic relations. Because cross-cultural contexts add another layer of complexity to normal interactions, some grounding in intercultural communication is essential for anyone who travels abroad or interacts with strangers in this country.

Although cultural differences can sometimes cause misunderstandings, intercultural communication need not be doomed to failure. As Harry Hoijer has remarked, "No culture is wholly isolated, self-contained, and unique. There are important resemblances between all known cultures. . . . Intercultural communication, however wide the differences between cultures may be, is not impossible. It is simply more or less difficult. . . ."[2] Intercultural communication is possible because people are not "helplessly suspended in their cultures."[3] By developing an openness to new ideas and a willingness to listen and to observe, we can surmount the difficulties inherent in intercultural interaction. In Chapters 9 through 11, we have already seen examples of ways in which culture affects communication. This chapter extends that discussion by directly examining ways in which people from different cultures can learn to communicate more effectively.

> By developing an openness to new ideas and a willingness to listen and to observe, we can surmount the difficulties inherent in intercultural interaction.

WHAT IS CULTURE?

According to anthropologist Ruth Benedict, we spend our lives following the patterns and standards handed down to us by our cultures:

> From the moment of birth the customs into which [an individual] is born shape his experience and behavior. By the time he can talk, he is a little creature of his culture, and by the time he is grown and able to take part in its activities, its habits are his habits, its beliefs his beliefs, its impossibilities his impossibilities.[4]

As Benedict points out, we are, in an important sense, the products of our cultures.

Defining Culture

But what exactly is culture? Donald Klopf gives a simple definition. For him, **culture** is "that part of the environment made by humans."[5] According to this definition, culture includes all the material objects and possessions that a social group invents or acquires. Even more important, it includes the group's less tangible creations: the shared customs and values that bind its members together and give them a sense of commonality. Thus, culture includes a group's "collective answer to the fundamental questions . . . 'Who are we?' 'What is our place in the world?' and 'How are we to live our lives?'"[6]

> Culture includes a group's "collective answer to the fundamental questions . . . 'Who are we?' 'What is our place in the world?' and 'How are we to live our lives?'"

Characteristics of Cultures

Cultures are "templates for living" that have certain basic characteristics. Cultures are learned, shared, multifaceted, dynamic, and overlapping.

Cultures Are Learned

The first point about cultures is that they are learned. Americans act like other Americans not because we are innately predisposed to do so, but because we learn to do so. Much of our early training is an attempt to make us fit cultural patterns. If we do not learn the lessons of our cultures, we pay—"through a loss of comfort, status, peace of mind, safety, or some other value. . . ."[7] We may even be imprisoned or labeled insane for acting in ways that would be perfectly acceptable in other cultures.

To those familiar with them, cultural practices embody important values and traditions; to outsiders they may seem inexplicable or exotic.

We are so well programmed that we seldom stop to think that culture is learned. Our cultural norms appear to be natural and right, and we can't imagine acting differently. Yet had we been brought up in Korea by Korean parents, an entirely different set of norms would appear natural. We would be culturally Korean. We would speak Korean, follow Korean norms and customs, and see the world in typically Asian ways. Although this point seems obvious, it is one we often forget. When we see someone from another culture act in ways we consider strange, our first impulse is to attribute the action to personality. For example, we label someone "pushy" who speaks more loudly and forcefully than we do; we seldom stop to realize that had we been brought up in that person's culture, we would probably express ourselves just as loudly and forcefully.

Cultures Are Shared

Another important characteristic of culture is that it is shared. Cultures are group understandings rather than individual ones, and belonging to a culture means acting according to group norms. For most people, fitting into a cultural group is very important. Being like others provides security, perhaps because we equate being alike with being right and being different with being wrong. Regardless of the reason, we learn very early to separate the world into "us" and "them," and we work very hard to make sure that others recognize which of the two we are. Little boys are mortified if they are mistaken for little girls; they will spend a good part of the rest of their lives living up to the masculine ideal. The wealthy do not wish to be thought poor; therefore, they act in ways that signal their status. Mistakes that mix "us" with "them" undermine our sense of self.

> We learn very early to separate the world into "us" and "them," and we work very hard to make sure that others recognize which of the two we are.

Because cultures are shared, we are not entirely free to act as we wish. Indeed, we spend a good deal of time proving who we are and living up to the expectations of others. This process of living out cultural rules is largely invisible and seldom difficult if we stay within a single culture. A white, middle-class, American male who associates only with others like himself seldom stops to think about the effects of national, racial, class, or gender rules on his beliefs and behaviors. Only when he steps outside his circle of friends, his neighborhood, or his country and experiences other cultures is he likely to see the extent to which culture affects him.[8]

People who frequently move between cultures are often more sensitive to the fact that culture is shared. Lawrence Wieder and Steven Pratt give an interesting example of the importance of shared cultural identity and the difficulties it presents for minority group members. In an article entitled "On Being a Recognizable Indian among Indians," Wieder and Pratt discuss ways in which Native Americans of the Osage people let one another know that they are "real Indians" rather than "White Indians." Wieder and Pratt's research not only illustrates the universal need to demonstrate cultural identity, but also shows how central communication style is to that demonstration.[9]

According to Wieder and Pratt, one of the primary differences between the communication styles of European Americans and Native Americans is the value the latter place on being silent. "When real Indians who are strangers to one another pass each other in a public place, wait in line, occupy adjoining seats, and so forth, they take it that it is proper to remain silent and to not initiate conversation."[10] Once Native Americans do engage in conversation with one another, they take on substantial obligations, among them the necessity of interacting whenever their paths cross. For students and businesspeople, this obligation may be burdensome, for it takes precedence over attending class or keeping appointments.

Talking like a "real Indian" also means being modest and not showing oneself to be more knowledgeable than other Native Americans. Being asked by a European American teacher to volunteer information in a group discussion in which other Native Americans are present puts a well-informed Native American student in a difficult bind. To avoid appearing arrogant, he or she may simply refuse to participate.

The desire to avoid seeming immodest occurs in public speaking situations as well, where speaking is reserved for tribal elders. Only certain individuals are entitled to speak, and they often speak for someone else rather than for themselves. It is customary to begin a speech with a disclaimer such as "I really don't feel that I am qualified to express [the wishes of the people I am speaking for] but I'm going to do the best I can, so please bear with me."[11] Compare this custom to the rule taught by most European American communication teachers that a speaker should build his or her credibility at the beginning of a speech, and you will see how communication styles across cultures can conflict.

The need to use Native American styles of communication in front of other Native Americans often means the "real Indian" is misunderstood or misjudged by European Americans. Steven Pratt, who collected the primary data for this research and who is himself a participating member of the Osage people, reported instances in which his identity as a graduate student conflicted with his identity as a Native American. He and Wieder conclude thus:

> *Being a real Indian is not a material thing that can be possessed and displayed. It consists of those patterns of appropriate conduct that are articulated in such a way that they are visible and recognizable to other Indians as specific Indian ways of conducting oneself. In the performance of these visible patterns, being a real Indian is realized.*[12]

Although deciding how to display one's cultural identity may be more problematic for the Native American communicator living in a predominantly European American society, each member of a culture must prove himself or herself to other members by acting in ways that are culturally approved. For another example, look ahead to the discussion of gang culture in Chapter 13.

Cultures Are Multifaceted

If we define culture as everything surrounding us that is not natural and biological in character, then culture clearly has many facets. At a minimum, culture affects language, religion, basic worldview, education, social organization, technology, politics, and law, and all of these factors affect one another.[13] As Edward Hall points out, if you touch a culture in one place, everything else is affected.[14]

> At a minimum, culture affects language, religion, basic worldview, education, social organization, technology, politics, and law, and all of these factors affect one another.

Table 12.1 gives an idea of the variety of interconnected activities that are found in virtually every culture. These activities are common to all people who live together in social groups and are thus examples of **cultural universals**, yet the enactment of these activities varies dramatically from culture to culture. In every culture, for example, people adorn their bodies, eat, educate their children, recognize family groupings, keep track of time, and so on. How people in a particular culture do these things, however, is unique. Although all people eat, what they consider edible and how they prepare food vary widely. The idea of eating dog, a food offered in many of the best hotels in South China, is considered revolting by most Americans. The idea of eating a ham and cheese sandwich, a perfectly acceptable meal for many Americans, is offensive to Arabs and Orthodox Jews. Thus, what is common practice in one culture may be taboo in another. To be functioning members of a culture, we must internalize rules governing a huge variety of activities; and to communicate with people from other cultures, we must recognize and learn to respect their customs.

Cultures Are Dynamic

Cultures are constantly changing. As economic conditions change, as new technologies are developed, and as cultural contact increases, old ways of doing things change and people must learn new behaviors. This important fact is one reason why memorizing lists of dos and don'ts is not the best way to prepare for intercultural

Table 12.1 A Partial List of Cultural Universals

Age grading	Cosmology	Family	Hygiene	Numbers
Athletics	Courtship	Folklore	Kinship	Puberty customs
Bodily adornment	Dancing	Funeral rites	Language	Rituals
Calendar	Education	Gestures	Law	Sex restrictions
Cleanliness	Ethics	Greetings	Magic	Surgery
Cooking	Etiquette	Hairstyles	Marriage	Toolmaking

Adapted from "The Common Denominator of Cultures," by George P. Murdock, 1945, in Ralph Linton, Ed., *The Science of Man in the World Crisis*. New York: Harcourt, Brace & World, p. 124.

contact. For just as soon as you've learned a rule about how to communicate with the "natives" of a culture, you'll find that the rule is obsolete. A better way to prepare for intercultural contact is to become sensitive to the kinds of differences that occur between cultures and to develop the ability to learn by observing.

> Memorizing lists of dos and don'ts is not the best way to prepare for intercultural contact. For just as soon as you've learned a rule about how to communicate with the "natives" of a culture, you'll find that the rule is obsolete.

Cultural Identities Are Overlapping

As our discussion of the communication patterns of some Native Americans showed, we belong to multiple overlapping cultures, some of which work together and some of which conflict. At a minimum, we all belong to national, regional, class, ethnic, religious, professional, age, and gender cultures. At various times, one or more of these identities may become crucial while the rest fade into the background.

If we are lucky, our overlapping identities fit together into a coherent whole. If we are less fortunate, we experience conflicts. The woman who believes in equal rights yet belongs to a traditional culture in which women are subservient to men feels pressure from each identity. The immigrant who wishes to assimilate into his adopted country but does not wish to abandon tradition also experiences stress. The adolescent who is no longer a child and yet is not an adult has difficulty determining how to act.

Although multiple cultural memberships can cause stress, they can also be a source of strength, allowing us to be unique individuals rather than cultural clones. Seldom are any two people members of exactly the same cultures, and none of us manages to follow all of the rules of the cultures to which we belong. As Marshall Singer points out, "that is precisely what makes each of us humans unique. And while that makes for a more rich, varied, and interesting world, it also makes generalizing about people . . . that much more hazardous and difficult."[15] The task that confronts each of us is to find a unique sense of self in the face of our own conflicting cultural identities and to recognize when we speak to others that their cultural identities are also complex and overlapping.

Why Communicate Cross-Culturally?

Admittedly, communication becomes more difficult when people do not share the same attitudes and values. Why, then, should we bother to communicate cross-culturally? The answer is that we cannot afford to ignore people from other cultures. There may have been a time when people could spend their entire lives communicating only with others who shared their own cultural identities. In such a time, learning how to communicate across cultural boundaries was a luxury rather than a necessity. Nowadays, it is impossible to remain isolated from others, and intercultural communication, communication wherein sender and receiver come from different cultures, cannot be avoided.

Living in the Global Village

One reason for the rise in importance of intercultural communication is that the world is shrinking daily. We live in a global village where intercultural encounters are commonplace. Advances in telecommunication and transportation technology have changed our sense of distance and of place. We can board a plane in New York and be in Hong Kong or Singapore within a day. We can walk to the corner store and find products from every part of the globe. We can go to a local movie house and see the latest film from France or Hungary. We can switch on CNN and watch a military campaign in Somalia or a civil war in Bosnia from the comfort of our living rooms. It is no longer possible to remain isolated—from events, ideas, or cultural products.

Many of you will travel internationally, either on business or for pleasure, at least once in your life (if you have not already done so). Whether you travel as a business representative, diplomat or technical adviser, member of the military, student, teacher, or tourist, you will find yourself communicating with people whose beliefs, values, and ways of existing may be vastly different from yours. The greater your understanding of intercultural communication, the richer this experience will be.

Even if you don't travel outside the United States, you may still find yourself interacting with people from other cultures, for just as Americans travel abroad more and more frequently, so foreign nationals come to the United States. As individuals from Vietnam, Cambodia, Cuba, Haiti, the former Soviet Union, and a host of other countries come here to escape political upheaval or to flee war or famine, "contacts with cultures that previously appeared unfamiliar, alien, and at times mysterious are now a normal part of our day-to-day routine."[16]

Familiarity with the problems that arise when people communicate interculturally can ease the adaptation that both immigrants and host nationals must make. For adjusting to the global village is by no means easy. As Richard Porter and Larry Samovar express it, "The difficulty with being thrust into a global village is that we do not yet know how to live like villagers; there are too many of 'us' who do not want to live with 'them.'"[17]

Coming to Terms with Diversity

Of course, we don't have to look to newly arrived immigrants to experience intercultural communication. We are a country of many coexisting cultures. Americans from different ethnic or religious backgrounds may seem as alien as someone "just off the boat." It is becoming increasingly difficult to ignore the presence of co-cultures within our own country. Groups that were outside the mainstream several years ago are now demanding recognition and respect from majority cultures. Even when we speak the same language, we may find overcoming cultural differences difficult. Yet if we are to live in harmony with our neighbors, overcoming differences is a necessity.

Intercultural Communication and Personal Growth

Intercultural understandings serve not only to make contacts more comfortable, but also to enrich us on a personal level. Communicating with people from other cultures allows us access to the experiences of other human beings. Intercultural contact shows us that there are other ways to act in the world than those we have been taught; it widens our field of choices and stimulates our imagination. Students of intercultural communication often talk about the development of an intercultural identity, a sense of belonging to an original and a new culture at the same time. People who achieve this identity are more open to change and are willing to transcend their own cultural premises. Young Yun Kim expresses it this way:

> Intercultural contact shows us that there are other ways to act in the world than those we have been taught; it widens our field of choices and stimulates our imagination.

> *Not all strangers may evolve this far in their adaptation process. Yet those who do will be able to enjoy a special kind of freedom, making deliberate choices for actions in specific situations rather than simply being bound by the culturally normative courses of action.*[18]

BARRIERS TO INTERCULTURAL COMMUNICATION

Despite its importance, learning to communicate interculturally is extremely difficult. A variety of barriers keep people from different cultures from understanding one another. In this section, we'll look at some of the attitudes that impede our ability to communicate clearly with one another—attitudes such as prejudice, ethnocentrism, and a refusal to acknowledge differences. But before we look at these barriers, we need to understand how culture affects communication.

How Culture Affects Communication

We have seen that culture is multifaceted, that it affects every aspect of our lives. That culture affects communication should therefore come as no surprise. Culture affects a number of aspects of communication: interpretation of reality, understanding of role relations, goal-oriented behavior, sense of self, and message making.

Culture and Perception

As we saw in Chapter 3, perception is not simply a matter of receiving what already exists: it is an active interpretive process. Meaning is "not extracted from Nature but projected by people on it. People's behavior can be understood only in terms of their own constructs," and many of these constructs are products of culture.[19] When we perceive events and people, we attach values to them and make attributions about them. Our values and attributions are culture-specific, as the following example, reported by Donald Klopf, shows.[20]

When we encounter a culture for the first time we may be puzzled about what is going on. Over time, we begin to understand what we see.

Nancy, a native Californian, moved with her husband, an executive with an oil company, to Iran. Because the climate was very hot and humid, Nancy often wore shorts and casual tops when she went to the local market to shop. As she walked alone to the market one day, an Iranian man grabbed her and made lewd suggestions. Upset, she shook herself free and called the police.

Nancy, working from an American point of view, saw the Iranian as a degenerate and his behavior as an attack. The Iranian, however, was astonished by her reaction. When he looked at Nancy, he saw a prostitute, for in Iran, no other woman would ever appear in public in shorts or walk alone. From an Iranian point of view, Nancy was giving clear signals that she was sexually available. The way each saw the other was influenced by cultural values and beliefs.

Had Nancy known more about the culture in which she was a guest, the incident might have been avoided. In *Beyond the Veil*, Fatima Mernissi describes the cultural codes that govern relations between the sexes in many Muslim countries. In these nations, she tells us, sexuality is territorial, and there are strict boundaries delineating the spaces belonging to each sex. Mernissi goes on to explain:

Women in males' spaces are considered provocative and offensive. If [a woman] enters [the male sphere], she is upsetting the male's order and his peace of mind. She is actually committing an act of aggression against him merely by being present where she should not be.[21]

With these cultural values in mind, the male's response to Nancy is logical, given his interpretation of her behavior as an example of aggressive sexuality and exhibitionism. Knowing the reasons behind the behavior of both parties does not necessarily lead to acceptance, however. The Iranian may still feel that behavior such as Nancy's is immodest, and Nancy may still find his behavior sexist. Nevertheless, cultural knowledge can place behavior in context and can reduce misunderstandings.

To communicate effectively, therefore, we have to be able to size up situations and people realistically. In an intercultural context, this means being aware of cultural conventions and familiarizing oneself with basic values and customs. Not knowing the values of another country can result in momentary embarrassment, as it did with Nancy, or can lead to the loss of millions of dollars and months of work, as the following story illustrates.[22]

An American engineering company spent months negotiating a huge contract with a Saudi Arabian firm. To signal the importance of the contract, the American executives bound their final proposal in costly leather. Unfortunately, they chose pigskin, unaware that Saudis consider the pig an unclean animal. Had the Americans wanted to insult their hosts, they could have found no better way. The proposal and binder were consequently burned, and the Saudi firm threw the American company out of the country. A cursory knowledge of religious custom could have averted this disaster. Unfortunately, however, no one had bothered to do basic research on Saudi beliefs.

Culture and Role Identities

Culture also tells us who to be and how to act. In every culture, people are classified according to factors such as age, status, occupation, gender, and so on. We do not expect the young and the old, princes and peasants, or men and women to act the same way; nor do we act the same way toward each of these groups. Being a good communicator means, in part, understanding role distinctions and adapting one's communication accordingly.

> We do not expect the young and the old, princes and peasants, or men and women to act the same way; nor do we act the same way toward each of these groups. Being a good communicator means, in part, understanding role distinctions and adapting one's communication accordingly.

An example of the way culture affects role identity can be found in varying attitudes toward age. The Ashanti of Ghana, for example, address all older men as "my grandfather," a title of respect.[23] The Maasai of East Africa also afford great honor to their elders. Lisa Skow and Larry Samovar explain that the Maasai equate age with wisdom and believe that those who are wise must be treated with special deference. Young people, no matter how clever, cannot reach the truth until they pass through all of life's stages.[24] The Chinese hold a similar view.

By comparison, Americans value youth more than age. Rather than welcoming old age, we see it as a time of diminished capacity. In fact, American beliefs about age may induce psychological states of "oldness." Carl Carmichael argues that "it is quite possible that many older people have aged prematurely by adopting the age-related characteristics they have come to believe must exist after a certain age."[25] If so, this is a dramatic example of the costs of false cultural beliefs.

Gender roles are also culturally derived. In parts of the Arab world, women do not work or drive cars, whereas in Israel and China, women do the same jobs as men. In parts of India, women must wait to eat until after men have finished, and in traditional Vietnamese households, women must eat smaller portions of food than men.[26] In modern America, these kinds of distinctions are seen as demeaning and offensive. Even the characteristics that we think are basic to the sexes may differ from culture to culture. According to Edward Hall, in Iran it is men who express their emotions freely, whereas women are considered to be coldly practical.[27]

Culture and Goals

Our cultures also affect us by telling us what goals we should pursue and how to pursue them. Americans have relatively high achievement motivation. We are generally characterized by **effort-optimism**, the belief that hard work will pay off. People in other countries may "expect to be rewarded on the basis of the social position of their family or clan" rather than on their own efforts, or in some cases, they may not expect to be rewarded at all.[28] K. S. Sitaram and Roy T. Cogdell explain the difference between the attitude in some countries that individuals can do little to change their future and the attitude in other countries, such as the United States, that people are able to control their fate:

> If you ask a Hindu why he got only ten bags of corn from his land while nearby farmers got much more, he would say it was the wish of God. An American farmer's answer to the same question would be, "Hell, I didn't work hard enough."[29]

The goal-oriented nature of middle-class American culture is evident in popular slogans such as "No pain, no gain," and "Just do it." It is also evident in high stress levels and burnout. To people in many countries, Americans are overly ambitious. What we think of as a healthy work ethic, they see as needless effort or even arrogance.

Culture and Images of the Self

In addition to affecting roles and goals, culture affects basic notions of human nature, including the extent to which the individual self is valued. Beliefs about the self are important because they are central to all other values and because they affect every aspect of behavior, including communication. Despite their importance, however, they often go unexamined.

Larry Samovar, Richard Porter, and Nemi Jain argue that most Americans hold three basic beliefs about human nature: that humans are, at heart, rational; that humans are perfectible; and that human nature is highly susceptible to social and cultural influence.[30] The **rationality premise**—the belief that most people are capable of discovering the truth through logical analysis—underlies many American institutions, including democracy, trial by jury, and free enterprise, all of which are based on the idea that the average person can be trusted to make good decisions. The **perfectibility premise** is based on the old Puritan idea that humans are born in sin but are capable of achieving goodness through effort and control. Finally, the **mutability premise** assumes that human behavior is shaped by environmental factors and that the way to improve humans is to improve their physical and psychological circumstances. A belief in universal education follows from this assumption.

> Most Americans hold three basic beliefs about human nature: that humans are, at heart, rational; that they are perfectible; and that human nature is highly susceptible to social and cultural influence.

Another important value related to human nature and the self is individualism, the belief that the most important social unit is the person, who acts in his or her own interest. American individualism is evident from the fact that Americans are encouraged "to make their own decisions, develop their own opinions, solve their own problems, have their own things, and, in general, learn to view the world from the point of view of the self."[31] In fact, researcher Geert Hofstede found the United States to be the most individualistic of the forty nations he studied. The countries highest in individualism were Western or European countries, while those lowest in individualism were Asian or South American.[32]

The opposite of individualism is collectivism. In collectivist cultures, people believe it is right to subordinate personal goals for the good of others. For collectivists, shared identity is more important than personal identity. Harry Triandis and his colleagues argue that naming practices may reflect where a culture stands on the collectivist–individualist continuum. In Bali, they report, a person is referred to by his or her position in the family (for example, "the first son of X family" or "mother of Y"). Similarly, in China, one's family name (what we call the last name) comes first, followed by a personal name. In more individualist cultures, the personal name comes first.[33]

People in collectivist cultures are comfortable in vertical relationships (relationships in which some people are afforded more status than others), whereas individualists feel most comfortable in horizontal relationships (relationships with status equals). Members of collectivist cultures rarely compete on a personal basis, although they will fight fiercely for the good of their group. The converse is true in individualist cultures. In a collectivist culture such as Japan, for example, workers feel strong loyalties to their work groups, and the qualities sought in a leader are patience and the ability to listen.[34] Leaders in individualist cultures are more likely to be prized for quick thinking and an ability to take the initiative.

According to Triandis and colleagues, the most important collectivist values are harmony, face-saving, duty to parents, modesty, moderation, thrift, equality in reward distribution, and the fulfillment of others' needs. The top values for individualists are freedom, honesty, social recognition, comfort, hedonism, and reward distribution based on individual performance. Table 12.2 outlines some other differences between collectivist and individualist cultures.

Culture and Language Style

It almost goes without saying that people from different cultures often speak different languages and that difficulties in making oneself understood are an important barrier to cross-cultural interaction. But the problem is not just that people from different cultures use different words to express their thoughts but also that the thoughts they express may be different. The world is filtered through our language habits, and it therefore stands to reason that people from different language communities may perceive the world differently.

One of the attitudes that most interferes with successful intercultural communication is the belief that everything that can be said in one language can be said in another, that meanings are directly translatable. This is simply not the case.

Table 12.2 Rules to Increase Cooperation between Collectivists and Individualists

Rules Collectivists Should Follow When Interacting with Individualists	Rules Individualists Should Follow When Interacting with Collectivists
1. Don't expect to be able to predict an individualist's attitudes and behavior on the basis of group affiliations. Although this works in your country, individualists have their own ideas.	1. Expect collectivists to abide by the norms, roles, and obligations of their groups. If group membership changes, expect members' values and personal styles to change as well.
2. Don't be put off when individualists take pride in personal achievement, and do not be too modest yourself.	2. Do not disclose personal information unless asked. Feel free, however, to disclose your age and salary.
3. Expect individualists to be less emotionally involved in group affiliations than is the norm for you. Do not interpret this as coldness or as a personality defect.	3. Do not criticize collectivists or openly refuse their requests. Expect them to be more sensitive to loss of face than you are.
4. Do not expect persuasive arguments that emphasize cooperation and conflict avoidance to be as effective as they are in your culture. Do not be offended by arguments that emphasize personal rewards and costs.	4. Persuasive arguments based on authority appeals or on the good of the group will be more effective than those based on personal rewards.
5. Do not interpret initial friendliness as a signal of intimacy or commitment. Expect relationships to be good natured but superficial and fleeting according to your own standards.	5. Spend a great deal of time getting to know others. Be patient, expect delays, and do not adhere to a rigid timetable.
6. Pay attention to written contracts. They are considered binding.	6. Do not be surprised if plans are changed after everything was seemingly agreed upon. Do not be surprised if negotiations take a lot longer than you consider necessary.
7. Do not expect to be respected because of your position, age, sex, or status. Do not be surprised if individualists lack respect for authority figures.	7. Let others know your social position, job title, and rank. A collectivist has a strong need to place you in an appropriate niche in the social hierarchy.
8. Expect individualists to be upset by nepotism, bribery, and other behaviors that give in-group members an advantage over others.	8. Gift giving is important, but do not expect to be paid back immediately.
9. Do not expect to receive as much help as you would in your own country. After initial orientation, you may be left to do things on your own.	9. Remember that for collectivists, family and social relationships are extremely important. Expect collectivists to take time off from work for family matters.
10. Do not expect an individualist to work well in groups.	10. Do not expect to be afforded as much privacy as you may be used to.

A concept that is central to the language of one culture may be translated into another language only with difficulty. The Japanese concept of *amae* is an example. According to Edward Hall and Mildred Reed Hall, *amae* comes from the verb *amaeru*, "to look to others for support and affection." As Hall and Hall explain, *amae* has its roots in the psychological relationship between a child and his or her mother, but the child later transfers *amae* to teachers, bosses, and other authority figures. Although *amae* may be translated as "dependence," it is more than that: it is a willingly assumed, reciprocal relationship that blurs the distinction between the world of work and the interpersonal realm.[35] Because English speakers have no exactly comparable term, we may have difficulty grasping the subtleties of the concept. This does not mean that we can't learn to use the word when it is explained to us (after all, Hall and Hall give us a detailed description written in English), but it does mean the concept won't seem natural to us. One of the reasons that learning a foreign language is both frustrating and exhilarating is that it opens up new ways of viewing the world.

> One of the attitudes that most interferes with successful intercultural communication is the belief that everything that can be said in one language can be said in another, that meanings are directly translatable.

Culture affects not only semantic content but pragmatic rules as well. It is important to keep in mind that language style is part of culture; what we do with language, how we use it, is a product of shared understanding. Speech forms such as teasing, flattery, charm, effusiveness, or directness have different values in different cultures. Even lying (which Americans tend to class as one of the worst possible sins) may be valued in a culture in which maintaining harmonious relations is more important than being certain about facts.

In general, Americans value plain, direct, efficient language use. In many other cultures, people are expected to circle around a point rather than to attack it directly. In cultures that value ambiguity, plain speaking may be shockingly rude. And whereas Americans tend to distrust anyone who "lays it on too thick," members of other cultures may believe in offering one another effusive praise.

It is important for people who intend to engage in intercultural communication to recognize the essential ambiguity of both verbal and nonverbal language and to realize that a single behavior may signify different meanings in different cultures. In some cultures, for example, looking away from or momentarily turning one's back and walking away from a speaker is a mark of respect and appreciation. It should not, therefore, be taken as an insult. As we saw in Chapter 5, shared behavior is an important hidden language that can affect the success of any interaction.

Because culture affects so many aspects of our lives, it can be a barrier to effective communication. This is especially likely if we hold negative attitudes about cultural differences. In the following section, we will look at some destructive beliefs that can guarantee intercultural misunderstandings.

If cross-cultural interaction involves mutual respect, understanding is possible. If not, cultures clash and exposure to new ideas can result in culture shock.

Attitudes That Diminish Understanding

Why are intercultural contacts so often frustrating rather than liberating? It is because we often enter them with preconceived attitudes that impede the possibility of understanding. Among these attitudes are stereotypes and prejudices, assumptions of similarity, a tendency to withdraw from novelty, and a deep belief in the superiority of one's own culture.

Stereotypes and Prejudices

The tendency to prejudge and stereotype members of other groups is one of the main barriers to intercultural understanding. Many people enter cross-cultural interactions with preconceived notions that make it impossible to find any common ground and that distort accurate perception. Stereotypes, which are "generalized 2nd-hand beliefs that provide conceptual biases from which we 'make sense' out of what goes on around us, whether they are accurate or fit the circumstances," are one kind of preconception.[36] Although stereotypes fulfill certain functions (for example, reducing the anxiety that comes with uncertainty and making the world seem more predictable), they interfere with objective perception. Once we have decided that Germans are obsessed with order, that Japanese are workaholics, or that Central Americans lack ambition, we stop thinking about people objectively.

A prejudice is a special kind of stereotype, a "negative social attitude held by members of one group toward members of another group," an attitude that biases perception and provides a rationale for discrimination.[37] Prejudices are the products of in-group interaction; very rarely are they the result of direct contact with out-group members. People learn prejudices from secondary sources and seldom make any attempt to check their validity. Having decided that members of a target group are dangerous, unintelligent, or lazy, people who hold prejudices avoid contact.

The purpose of prejudices is not to enable us to understand the world accurately but to "draw a line between in-group and out-group members, a line that divides those who are 'superior' from those who are 'inferior.' In drawing this line, people often use distorted data and unwarranted assumptions."[38] Table 12.3 shows some of the cognitive biases people use to keep their prejudices intact, biases that allow them to see differences where none exists or to distort differences that do exist.

> Prejudices are the products of in-group interaction; very rarely are they the result of direct contact with out-group members.

Assumed Similarity

Almost as serious a stumbling block to intercultural understanding as prejudice is an unwarranted assumption of similarity, a refusal to see true differences where they exist. Assuming that everyone is "the same under the skin" may reduce uncomfortable feelings of strangeness, but it may also result in insensitivity. By assuming that members of a different culture see the world in the same way we do, we overlook real differences. When, for example, an American sees a foreign visitor smiling and nodding as the two interact, the American may assume the interaction is a success. It may be the case, however, "that the foreigner actually [understands] very little of the verbal and nonverbal content and [is] merely indicating polite interest or trying not to embarrass him or herself."[39]

Smiling is a good example of an assumption of similarity, for this "universal expression" takes on quite different meanings in different cultures. In some countries, it is considered extremely impolite to smile at a stranger; a smile may be interpreted as a sexual invitation or as a sign of derision. Foreign travelers in the United States may be insulted or taken aback by the Americans' friendly smile, as is evidenced by this Japanese student's comment:

> On my way to and from school I have received a smile by non-acquaintance American girls several times. I have finally learned they have no interest for me; it means only a kind of greeting to a foreigner. If someone smiles at a stranger in Japan, especially a girl, she can assume he is either a sexual maniac or an impolite person.[40]

Table 12.3 Cognitive Biases Used to Maintain Prejudices

Negative Interpretation	Interpreting everything the target group does as negative
	Example: If we see "them" relaxing, we interpret their behavior as shiftless and irresponsible; when we relax, we are simply unwinding after a hard day.
Discounting	Dismissing information that doesn't fit a negative stereotype
	Example: If one of "them" succeeds, it must be due to favoritism or luck; their success is simply the exception that proves the rule.
Fundamental Attribution Bias	Interpreting another's negative behavior as internal rather than external
	Example: If one of "them" is rude, it's because they're that way by nature; if one of "us" is rude, it's because we're under stress.
Exaggeration	Making negative aspects of out-group behavior seem more extreme
	Example: A simple argument is seen as a violent confrontation; a demonstration is reported as a riot.
Polarization	Looking for differences and ignoring similarities
	Example: An immigrant who has assimilated in almost every respect is still seen as one of "them" and as fundamentally different from "us."

Adapted from *Communicating Racism: Ethnic Prejudice in Thought and Talk* by Teun van Dijk, 1987. Newbury Park, CA: Sage.

Conversely, an American sojourner whose greetings are not returned may consider host nationals rude or standoffish. These misinterpretations are a direct result of failing to acknowledge that cultural differences in nonverbal behavior exist.

Let's look at one more example.[41] An American woman working in Tunisia stops by the local newsstand to get a copy of the *International Herald Tribune*. The vendor tells the American that he'll have the newspaper the next day, and instinctively adds the phrase *"N'sha'llah"* (God willing). The next day, when the American returns, there's no paper. The American is upset, because she interpreted the vendor's words as a promise. A Tunisian would have heard something quite different. To a Tunisian, the vendor's statement would have clearly meant: "I don't know if there'll be a paper tomorrow; in fact I doubt it, but it's not for me to say what may or may not happen in the future. That is in God's hands." In short, when the vendor said, "Yes, *N'sha'llah*," he meant "no." We can only assume that, over time, this sojourner will come to realize that in Tunisia, at least, "yes" does not always mean "yes."

Anxiety and Withdrawal

Other potential barriers to intercultural understanding are anxiety and tension. Novel situations almost always cause stress. A small amount of tension and excitement can be energizing, but a large amount is extremely debilitating. If you have ever lived in a foreign country, you know how exhausting it is to decipher an unfamiliar language or to find your way around. When the tension rises too high, individuals experience **culture shock**, "the anxiety that results from losing all of our familiar signs and symbols of social intercourse."[42]

When we're in our own cultures, we depend on familiar routines. We feel secure because we know what to expect from those around us. As Craig Storti puts it, "if we were not instinctively sure that people would be civil unless provoked, stay on their side of the road and stop on red, that shopkeepers would give us goods in return for money—if we could not routinely depend on these things happening—the resulting uncertainty would immobilize us."[43] In new surroundings, we may not be able to depend on any of these things; thus, we begin to feel isolated and adrift. It's ironic that the conditioning that makes it so easy for us to function at home is the very thing that makes it difficult for us to function abroad.

> When culture shock is severe, individuals develop feelings of helplessness and lowered self-esteem, a desire to return home, insomnia, depression, and even physical illness.

When culture shock is severe, individuals develop feelings of helplessness and lowered self-esteem, a desire to return home, insomnia, depression, and even physical illness. They become almost completely dysfunctional and may have to withdraw from contact with the native culture. During severe culture shock, people are likely to distort perceptions and feel hostility toward members of the host culture.

Although severe culture shock can be devastating, mild periods of stress followed by withdrawal can be productive. In her **draw-back-to-leap model**, Young Yun Kim argues that brief periods of culture shock may be "a necessary precondition for adaptive change, as individuals strive to regain their inner balance by adapting to the demands and opportunities of their new life circumstances."[44]

As sojourners experience stress, they often withdraw (the draw-back phase), engaging in tension-reducing behaviors that allow them an opportunity to reorganize their thoughts and feelings. Once they have processed cultural differences, they have the strength to continue to adapt (the leap-forward phase). According to Kim, some degree of stress is to be expected. By taking it easy when stress occurs, the individual avoids complete withdrawal.

Ethnocentrism

A final barrier to intercultural understanding is **ethnocentrism**, the belief that one's own culture is superior to all others and the tendency to judge all cultures by one's own criteria. Although it may be natural to believe that anything different is wrong, this is not a very productive attitude. Blaming people for not behaving the same way we do is irrational, especially when economic or physical factors may explain the difference. An ethnocentric American may be aghast to find out that people in another culture "waste" two hours of the middle of the day in resting. He or she may fail to consider that in that location, the temperature often rises well above ninety degrees and there is no air-conditioning. An ethnocentric individual may look down on the "natives" for using "primitive" farming methods without understanding that they have no money to buy modern machinery. In many cases, the way "they" do things makes sense, given their circumstances.

Samovar and his colleagues argue that it is naive to believe that our culture has all the answers. They ask us to consider the following questions:

> *The Jew covers his head to pray, the Protestant does not—is one more correct than the other? In Saudi Arabia women cover their faces, in America they cover very little—is one more correct than the other? The Occidental speaks to God, the Oriental has God speak to him—is one more correct than the other? The American Indian values and accepts nature, the average American seeks to alter nature—is one more correct than the other? A listing of these questions is never-ending. We must remember, however, that it is not the questions that are important, but rather the dogmatic way in which we answer them.*[45]

Unless we can admit that differences do not always mean deficiencies and that our culture is not necessarily superior in all things, we will never be able to establish the trust and respect that are necessary counterparts of successful intercultural interaction.

ADAPTING TO NEW CULTURES

Despite all the difficulties we have described, people do manage to adapt to one another. In this section, we explore how people from different cultures accomplish this feat.

All individuals who leave their home countries and immerse themselves in strange new lands experience stress. Some overcome this stress better than others, finding ways to feel at home with people who are quite different. Research has identified a number of factors associated with successful adaptation. These include the nature of the host culture, the personal attitudes and predispositions of the newcomer, and, most important, the kinds of communicative bonds the newcomer makes. For just as one maintains contact with one's own culture through communication, one's ability to enter a new culture successfully is also determined by communicative behavior.

Nature of the Host Culture

Some cultures have more permeable boundaries than do others. Some make outsiders feel more at home than do others. One factor associated with successful adaptation is the host country's attitude toward foreigners. If citizens of a country consider outsiders barbarians and infidels, then adaptation will be rough going.

> Some cultures have more permeable boundaries than do others. Some make outsiders feel more at home than do others.

Generally speaking, **cultural distance**, the extent to which two cultures differ, affects ease of communication. This point is illustrated in Table 12.4, which ranks cultural exchanges in terms of their relative difficulty. At the top of the table are cultural pairings with maximal difference. Japan and the United States, for example, are quite different in a number of important dimensions; as we have already seen, one of these cultures is collectivist, and the other is individualist. In addition, Americans have what Hall and Hall call a **monochronic** sense of time: Americans tend to segment and sequence time and to value speed. Although on the surface the Japanese may seem monochronic, below the surface they are **polychronic**, especially when it comes to interpersonal behavior. People in polychronic cultures change plans often and easily and consider schedules as objectives to be met, not as definite commitments. Thus, in polychronic cultures, it may take a lot longer to do things than in monochronic cultures.[46]

Another difference between Japan and the United States is that Japanese and English are very different languages. The distinction between them is much greater than, say, the distinction between English and French or German. Aspects of material culture (housing, transportation, and so on), as well as artistic and literary conventions, are also quite distinct. Except for the fact that in both Japan and the United States, technology is quite advanced, these two countries exhibit large differences.

Germany and the United States, in contrast, may differ in some ways, but these countries share more similarities. Although their languages, educational systems, managerial styles, and problem-solving approaches exhibit some differences, people in these countries share common beliefs and impulses as well as mutually familiar material cultures.

Toward the bottom of Table 12.4 are cultural pairings of people who speak the same language and live side by side in the same country. People from the same nation show the smallest amount of difference. Unfortunately, this does not preclude volatile interactions. Although Catholics and Protestants coexist quite peacefully in the United States, this obviously has not been the case in Northern Ireland. And although homosexuals and heterosexuals may share almost all aspects of national identity, the one difference that separates them may be highly salient to some—so much so that some heterosexuals may commit vandalism and acts of violence against members of homosexual cultures. In general, the more aspects of a culture that differ, the more difficult intercultural communication becomes.

Table 12.4 Cultural Differences: Cultural Pairings Arranged According to Sociocultural Distance

Maximum Difference

Western/Asian

Italian/Saudi Arabian

U.S. American/Greek

U.S. American/French-Canadian

White Anglo American/Reservation Native American

White Anglo American/African American, Asian American, Mexican American, or Urban Native American

U.S. American/British

U.S. American/English Canadian

Urban American/Rural American

Catholic/Baptist

Male Dominance/Female Equality

Heterosexual/Homosexual

Environmentalist/Developer

Minimum Difference

Adapted from *Intercultural Communication: A Reader* (8th ed.) by Larry A. Samovar and Richard E. Porter, Eds., 1997. Belmont, CA: Wadsworth, p. 22.

Despite differences, people with open minds can learn from one another.

Personal Predispositions

Having an open mind is clearly a prerequisite for adaptation. This brings us to a second factor related to intercultural interactions: the newcomer's personality. Included here are such factors as one's openness, resilience, and self-esteem. Some people have a low tolerance for ambiguity and find being an outsider distressing. Others lack confidence and may displace their feelings of anxiety onto those around them. Still others have great difficulty handling tension. Since adapting necessitates change and is always accompanied by stress, people with these predispositions will experience difficulty in adaptation.

In addition to personality variables, education and preentry training are important. The more a newcomer knows about a culture ahead of time, the more prepared he or she is for contact. The traveler who reads about the host culture and makes contacts with host nationals before entering that culture will be more comfortable in the new setting.

Communication Bonds

The third factor affecting successful adaptation is the way in which the newcomer interacts once he or she is in the host culture. Although openness and confidence can help, these internal predispositions must be implemented in actual communicative behaviors. In discussing the communicative aspects of adaptation, Kim argues that a newcomer's exposure to communication networks in the host culture (what Kim refers to as **host social communication**) and his or her relationships with members of the home culture (**ethnic social communication**) are two important determinants of intercultural success.[47]

Kim believes that sojourners interested in **acculturation** (i.e., becoming part of a new culture) should expose themselves as much as possible to host social communication. They should make interpersonal contacts and familiarize themselves with mass communication within the host culture. They should also avoid depending too heavily on ethnic communication networks. The newcomer who interacts only with other foreigners, who refuses to make any attempt to learn the language, and who reads only books and newspapers from home needlessly isolates himself or herself. Although others who share the same ethnic identity can form a support group and can teach a newcomer the ropes, they often inhibit real cross-cultural contact.

Developing an open communication style is a key variable in successful adaptation. This means being willing to plunge in and explore new cultures with enthusiasm. It also means developing—often through trial and error—the behavioral competence to act in new ways that are more appropriate to one's new situation.

BECOMING A MORE OPEN COMMUNICATOR

As we have seen, misunderstandings occur not only between people from different countries, but also between people who live side by side. In fact, we may sometimes treat foreigners more respectfully and decently than we treat neighbors who, for one reason or another, we perceive as different. We end this chapter with some guidelines for becoming open- and fair-minded communicators, comfortable with both co-cultural and cross-cultural diversity.[48]

- Open yourself to new contacts. Remember that prejudiced people hold distorted and erroneous beliefs and seldom have any direct experience with members of the groups they target. Although contact can reinforce negative perceptions, it can also disconfirm negative expectations. The best way to find out that "they" are not all alike is through contact. Unfortunately, we tend to associate and feel most comfortable with others who are similar. Think of your own circle of friends. How many of them are from a different racial, ethnic, or religious background? If your answer is none or few, you might consider widening your field of experience.

- Learn about the history and experiences of people from diverse cultures. One of the major complaints of minority cultures is that their history has been rendered invisible by dominant groups. Most people know very little about other co-cultural groups, and this ignorance is a barrier to understanding. By taking a course about, or by experiencing on your own, the cultural history of another group, you can gain a deeper understanding of its members' perspectives.

- Examine yourself for possible stereotypes. Prejudices and stereotypes are insidious; although these barriers are all too apparent in others, we may not recognize them in ourselves. The first step in becoming more fair-minded and open lies in admitting the possibility that some of one's judgments are unfair.

- Responsible and open communicators are willing and able to role-take. Role-taking means seeing the world from another's perspective—imaginatively taking on another's viewpoint. It means actively trying to understand how others make sense of their world and actively trying to experience what they feel. Although complete empathy is impossible, getting a better sense of what others think and feel is possible.

- Finally, each of us should work on becoming more self-confident. The better we feel about ourselves, the more likely we are to feel good about others and the more able we are to learn from them.

SUMMARY

Now more than ever, learning to communicate across cultures is important. This chapter discusses how culture affects us and how we can become more effective cross-cultural communicators.

Culture consists of all those parts of the environment constructed by humans, including the shared customs and values that create community, as well as material objects and possessions. Cultural understandings are learned, shared, multifaceted, dynamic, and overlapping. Cultural norms are learned from and shared with others, and we spend substantial amounts of time and energy proving to others that we are "real" members of our cultures and that we are different from outsiders. Cultures control many interrelated facets of our lives. In this sense, it is true that if you touch a culture in one place, everything else is affected. Moreover, cultures constantly grow and change, and people belong to multiple overlapping cultural groups. All of these factors make learning the rules of a new culture difficult.

Understanding culture is important in today's global village. As international business becomes more common and as cultural groups within our own country demand recognition and respect, it is less and less possible to avoid intercultural interaction. By improving cross-cultural communication, we can make contacts with members of other cultures more comfortable and can enrich our own intercultural identities.

Intercultural communication is difficult for several reasons. First, people from different cultures perceive the world differently, attaching their own culture-specific values to events. Second, people from different cultures have different attitudes toward roles. Third, cultures differ in the goals their members value. Americans, for example, are characterized by effort-optimism, whereas people in other cultures may be more fatalistic. Fourth, cultures affect basic notions of self and humanity. Americans believe people are rational, perfectible, and mutable; for us, the most important social unit is the individual. Finally, language differences indicate that what can be said easily in one culture may be almost impossible to convey in another.

A number of attitudes diminish cross-cultural communication. When we stereotype, assume similarity while ignoring real differences, feel anxious about diversity, or take ethnocentric pride in the superiority of our own culture, we create blocks to understanding. Despite these barriers, intercultural communication can succeed. A number of factors are associated with successful adaptation to a foreign culture: the openness of the host culture and the degree to which it is culturally distant from one's own; the extent to which newcomers are open, resilient, and self-confident; and the willingness of newcomers to build bonds with members of host cultures.

Being comfortable with diversity is not easy. But by being as open as possible, by educating yourself on cultural issues, by challenging stereotypes, and by trying to see the world as others do, you will become a more confident and competent cultural communicator.

KEY TERMS

Listed below are the key terms used in this chapter, along with the number of the page where each is explained.

culture   (325)
cultural universals   (328)
intercultural communication
   (329)
co-cultures   (330)
intercultural identity   (331)
effort-optimism   (334)
rationality premise   (334)
perfectibility premise   (334)
mutability premise   (334)

individualism   (335)
collectivism   (335)
vertical relationships   (335)
horizontal relationships
   (335)
stereotypes   (338)
prejudice   (338)
assumption of similarity
   (339)
culture shock   (340)

draw-back-to-leap model   (341)
ethnocentrism   (341)
cultural distance   (342)
monochronic   (342)
polychronic   (342)
host social communication
   (344)
ethnic social communication
   (344)
acculturation   (344)

SUGGESTED READINGS

Samovar, Larry A., Porter, Richard E., & McDaniel, Edwin R. (2006). Communication between cultures. Belmont, CA: Wadsworth.

   A best-selling text that offers an overview of theory and research in intercultural communication.

Varner, Iris, & Beamer, Linda. (2004). *Intercultural communication in the global workplace* (3rd ed.). New York: McGraw-Hill/Irwin.

   Illustrates how intercultural differences play out in organizational contexts, offering real-life examples and cases for analysis.

13

Methods of Discovery

When people know how to communicate skillfully, the quality of their lives and the lives of those around them is improved; when people lack this knowledge, their social and personal worlds can crumble.

There is a close link between communication theory and communication practice. When people know how to communicate skillfully, the quality of their lives and the lives of those around them is improved; when people lack this knowledge, their social and personal worlds can crumble. In short, discoveries about communication are important.

This chapter is about methods of discovery—methods scholars use to further their understanding of communication as well as methods you can use to widen your own knowledge. We begin by reviewing some of the basic research methodologies used by critics and communication scientists. Although you may not plan on becoming a professional scholar, professional methods can guide your own efforts to understand communication and can make you a more critical consumer of communication research.

We also look at some sources you can turn to for information about communication once this class is over. First, we will describe the kinds of courses offered in communication departments at large universities. Although not all of these courses may be offered at your school, each draws on a rich body of literature that is readily available. Second, we will discuss ways you can learn about communication both inside and outside of class. Once you have learned where to look, you will find sources of discovery all around you.

HOW IS COMMUNICATION RESEARCH DONE?

Forming hypotheses about the social world and looking for evidence to test those hypotheses are everyday activities. Our lives are guided, to a large extent, by commonsense theories of human action. When we try to explain the success or failure of a relationship or think up a strategy for getting what we want, we are theorizing about communication. "We were so different; we never really had a chance" is a theory about relationships. "If I do a favor for her now, she'll have to repay me later" is a hypothesis about the way interpersonal influence works.

> When we try to explain the success or failure of a relationship or think up a strategy for getting what we want, we are theorizing about communication.

Problems with Commonsense Ways of Knowing

In everyday life, we often accept the first reasonable explanation we come across without asking whether there is another, better explanation for what is happening. Commonsense knowing is often biased. The first problem with commonsense knowledge is that we privilege our own experiences. Most people find it hard to accept generalizations that contradict what they have seen with their own eyes. Most project their own beliefs and motivations onto others. Thus, *our everyday models of human behavior are often models of our own behavior.*

We also let our own desires get in our way. We see what we want to see and turn a blind eye to information that makes us uncomfortable. Our prejudices make us dismiss anything that contradicts what we've decided is true. Our superstitions lead us to accept any message that gives us an illusion of control over unexplained events. Thus, *our everyday models of human behavior may also be models of what we wish were true rather than what is true.*

In everyday life, we also rely on simple heuristics, rules of thumb that allow us to avoid careful information processing.[1] When we encounter difficult information, we look for simple cues that tell us what to think. We may rely on authorities ("I didn't understand it, but my dad said it was true") or status cues ("The argument seemed odd, but after all, the author did go to Harvard"). We may look at formal aspects, rather than the content, of the message ("She used a lot of statistics and graphs, so she must know what she's talking about"). Too often, *our everyday models of human behavior are based on simplistic thinking.*

Systematic Ways of Knowing

Researchers try to avoid the errors that affect everyday thinking. In many ways, good researchers are like detectives or investigative reporters. They don't accept things at face value. They are suspicious.

> *To research is to search again, to take another, more careful look, to find out more. . . . What the research attitude presumes is that the first look—and every later look—may be prone to error, so that one must look again and again, differently and thoroughly each time.*[2]

To research is to search again, to look at the world systematically and repeatedly until we see what lies below the surface.

In many ways, good researchers are like detectives or investigative reporters. They don't accept things at face value. They are suspicious.

Researchers often set out to overturn commonsense beliefs. In this sense, researchers "are professional troublemakers: they must challenge old beliefs, create new ones, and then turn the challenge upon those new ones."[3]

Lawrence Frey and his colleagues offer an excellent discussion of the characteristics of scholarly research. This discussion is summarized in Table 13.1. According to these authors, research has six basic characteristics: it is question oriented, methodological, replicable, self-critical, cumulative and self-correcting, and cyclical.[4]

The first characteristic of research is that it is *question oriented*. Research begins when the researcher encounters a state of affairs that needs explanation. Rather than simply accepting the status quo, the researcher formulates questions about it and then tries to answer these questions. At heart, research "requires the capacity to ask the right questions as well as a sense of what form the answer should take."[5]

Research is also *methodological*; that is, it is systematic and ordered, with built-in guarantees that the findings will be as accurate as possible. As we shall see, researchers are guided by systematic methods and procedures during their investigations.

Table 13.1 Characteristics of Scholarly Research

- **Question Oriented**

"At the heart of all research is a question worth answering."

- **Methodological**

"Systematic procedures are used to ensure that researchers find and report what is accurate."

- **Replicable**

Other scholars must be able to "replicate, or reproduce, the entire inquiry process."

- **Self-Critical**

Scholarly researchers "openly evaluate the strengths and weaknesses of their own research studies."

- **Cumulative and Self-Correcting**

"The accumulation of information . . . allows for knowledge to evolve and grow."

- **Cyclical**

Research "ends up back where it started," with new questions emerging from previous answers.

Adapted from *Investigating Communication: An Introduction to Research Methods* by Lawrence R. Frey, Carl H. Botan, Paul G. Friedman, and Gary L. Kreps. (2000). Boston: Allyn & Bacon, pp. 13–17.

That research is as careful and as accurate as possible does not mean that researchers lack imagination. Researchers must often make counterintuitive leaps and think their way past cultural biases. They also must devise imaginative ways of gathering information and testing hypotheses.

When Frey and his colleagues say that research must be *replicable,* they mean that it must be repeatable. The methods employed must be so objective that if the research were conducted again, the same results would occur and the same conclusions would be drawn. A result that occurs only once in only one study may be due to some unusual aspect of the research (or the researcher) rather than to the underlying phenomenon the researcher is trying to explain. Scholars make an effort to test and retest their theories before they generalize about them.

> Researchers belong to a community of scientists and critics, a community that works together to correct old mistakes and to discover new information.

Scholarly research is also *self-critical.* This means that researchers make special efforts to disprove their own theories. A scholar should be his or her own most exacting critic. In addition, to make sure that research is replicated and criticized, researchers make their results public. They show their results to others for examination and questioning. To keep results secret violates the purpose of research, which is to further knowledge.

Another important characteristic of research is that it is *cumulative* and *self-correcting.* The first step in doing research is to review all of the previous studies on one's topic and to build on others' work. Researchers do not want to spend time and effort "reinventing the wheel." Researchers belong to a community of scientists and critics, a community that works together to correct old mistakes and to discover new information.

Scholarship is, then, ultimately *cyclical.* Just as good research begins with a question, it ends with another question. In the words of Frey and his colleagues,

> *a researcher begins with a sense of curiosity and a topic worth studying, asks questions and/or makes predictions, plans research carefully, carries out the planned research, analyzes the data to provide tentative answers, and starts all over again by posing new topics and questions worth asking.*[6]

Common Research Tasks

As we shall see shortly, researchers use a wide variety of methods in communication research. Some researchers rely on historical–critical methods, whereas others devise elaborate experiments. Nevertheless, all go through the basic activities shown in Table 13.2. The first task is to *find a subject of study and formulate a research question.* As Frey and his colleagues point out, inquiry is prompted by curiosity. The question a researcher attempts to answer in a given study is called a research question. The question should be specific and clear, for it will act as a guide throughout the research. Some researchers begin with a very specific question, whereas others start broadly and narrow the scope of their study as they proceed. For example, a researcher may be initially interested in political persuasion. The question "How do politicians persuade the public?" is so broad that a researcher could spend a lifetime on it and only scratch the surface. Researchers can narrow their focus by asking more specific questions. One interesting aspect of political communication is the use of surrogates, people who speak for a candidate. "What is the communicative role of surrogates in a political campaign?" narrows the focus, but the researcher must still decide which surrogates and which campaigns to study. An even more specific research question might be "What kinds of themes characterized the speeches of the vice presidential candidates in the last presidential campaign?"

An important part of framing a research question is defining key concepts and terms. The researcher who wishes to look at surrogates' roles must understand what a surrogate is and must be able to define the aspect of surrogates' communication behavior that he or she wants to investigate. The researcher who wants to study the effects of negative campaigning on a candidate's credibility and popularity must offer clear definitions of *negative campaigning, credibility,* and *popularity.*

Definitions are generally of two types: conceptual and operational. A conceptual definition explains the meaning of a term in a general, abstract way. *Credibility,* for example, might be conceptually defined as "the extent to which a candidate is seen by an audience as worthy of belief." An operational definition explains how a term will be measured in the study. An operational definition of *credibility* might be "the candidate's mean score on a ten-point rating scale of trustworthiness and expertness." An operational definition is necessary for measurement purposes. Although the researcher knows conceptually what negative campaigning means, he or she also has to know how to recognize specific examples of it. If a candidate refers to his opponent as "sleazy" and "dishonest," the characterizations are clearly negative. But what if the candidate refers to his opponent as a "liberal"? Is this a description or a slur? Before starting the study, the researcher must decide what to count as an instance of negative campaigning—an often quite difficult task.

In addition to formulating a research question and defining key terms, the researcher must *choose a particular research methodology.* Often, these tasks go

Table 13.2 Common Tasks in Communication Inquiry

Task 1	Formulate a research question
Task 2	Choose a research methodology
Task 3	Design a sampling strategy
Task 4	Gather and analyze data
Task 5	Interpret data and share results

hand in hand. The topic area may suggest a research methodology, or the methodology may guide formulation of the research question. Researchers use a variety of methodologies. Some researchers take a historical–critical approach. They might decide to investigate surrogate behavior by analyzing a given surrogate's public rhetoric. Other researchers might choose an ethnographic approach, actually joining a campaign to make behind-the-scenes observations. Still others might rely on survey methods, sending out questionnaires to track public opinion over the course of the campaign. Researchers with an experimental bent might even test whether certain kinds of information are more acceptable when attributed to a surrogate or when attributed to a candidate.

Having chosen a research approach, the researcher must *design a sampling strategy* to decide who or what to study. The researcher who has decided to do a rhetorical analysis of surrogates' public speeches must determine which surrogates are of interest and which speeches to analyze. One researcher might decide to focus on a single individual (say, a presidential candidate's running mate), comparing speeches at the beginning, middle, and end of the campaign to see how themes and topics evolve. Another researcher might be interested in a single speech given at the nominating convention.

The researcher who opts to conduct a survey must decide what questions to ask and whom to ask. Because it is impossible to ask everyone in the country all the possible questions related to political persuasion, the researcher must choose a small subset of people and items. This process of sampling occurs in every case of research, no matter what the approach is.

Once the researcher has decided whom or what to study, he or she must *gather and analyze data*. For one study, the researcher might analyze data by poring over transcripts of public speeches, searching for themes and metaphors. For another study, data gathering might involve exposing subjects to an elaborate experimental manipulation and measuring their responses, and analysis might use statistical tests of significance. Regardless of the form of the data-gathering and -analyzing process, the final research activity is to *interpret the data and report the results*. The researcher must attempt to make sense of the data, draw conclusions about them, and share those conclusions with others.

FIVE CONTEMPORARY RESEARCH METHODS

There are many research methodologies. Table 13.3 lists only a sampling. In the next five sections, we will look at five methodologies in particular: rhetorical criticism, ethnographic research, survey research, experimental research, and performance as research. As we discuss each methodology, we will first describe the goals and procedures researchers follow when using that methodology, and we will then look at a representative sample of research so that you can see how these methods are applied.

Rhetorical Criticism

In everyday life, we frequently act as critics, analyzing and evaluating messages. Most of us enjoy expressing opinions; after attending a lecture or seeing a film, we like to discuss what we experienced. Our response may be a fairly simple description of what we liked or disliked about the communication, or it may be a more detailed analysis of the intended and unintended effects of the message on the audience. In either case, by discussing a message critically, we increase our understanding and

Table 13.3 Popular Research Methodologies

Rhetorical Criticism

The rhetorical critic begins by choosing a rhetorical act to study. After describing its purpose, its audience, and its context, the critic examines the rhetorical strategies employed and evaluates their effectiveness.

Sample research questions:

- How did the president build audience identification in the last presidential campaign?

- How did the narrative structure that Spike Lee used in the film *Malcolm X* add to Malcolm's image?

- How did George W. Bush use metaphor to reach multiple audiences in his speech announcing the war in Iraq?

Content Analysis

Focusing on a text, the researcher systematically measures message content to determine how often a given unit of content occurs. The units studied may be general (themes, topics, viewpoints) or specific (kinds of words, grammatical forms). Results involve reporting the frequency of a given kind of content and relating frequencies to variables outside the text.

Sample research questions:

- What is the average number of violent acts on prime-time television shows on each of the major networks?

- Do Republican and Democratic senatorial candidates employ different kinds of symbols in campaign speeches?

- How do children's fairy tales portray family relationships?

Conversation Analysis

To describe the content, structure, and function of everyday spoken interaction, the researcher obtains a sample of talk, transcribes and examines it, and draws

inferences about it. Researchers frequently examine the sequential relationship, functions, and effects of the moves in a given conversation.

Sample research questions:

- What kinds of conversational moves do teachers use to encourage classroom participation?

- How are conversational openings and closings structured?

- What kinds of actions and utterances signal dominance in male–female interactions?

Ethnography

The researcher observes behavior in its natural setting. To describe the communication practices of a group of people, the researcher may actually "go undercover" as a participant. The researcher avoids imposing his or her own values and assumptions on the data. Instead of testing an existing hypothesis, he or she allows conclusions to emerge from observations.

Sample research questions:

- What are the primary functions of talk for male members of an urban, blue-collar neighborhood?

- How do middle-class mothers communicate to their children during play?

- How do established members of religious cults recruit and treat new members?

Unobtrusive Methods

Rather than openly observe people, researchers can opt to observe traces of their communicative behavior unobtrusively and draw conclusions from these observations. Researchers may focus on measures of erosion (how objects are worn down by use) or on measures of accretion (physical traces that build up over time).

appreciation of that message and of the communication process in general.

Rhetorical criticism is an extension and refinement of the everyday critical impulse; it is a systematic way of describing, analyzing, and evaluating a given act of communication. The kind of criticism we do in everyday life is often limited to a general description of how we personally react to a given message ("I really liked her

> Rhetorical criticism is an extension and refinement of the everyday critical impulse; it is a systematic way of describing, analyzing, and evaluating a given act of communication.

Table 13.3 *(continued)*

Sample research questions:

- What museum exhibits are most popular (measured by wear and tear on carpets or amount of dirt on floors)?
- Is racial tension increasing at a certain high school (measured by kinds of graffiti in the school's public areas)?
- Which of a series of cover designs makes a brochure most appealing (measured by the number of each brochure removed from racks)?

Survey Research

To survey groups of people, researchers use either written questionnaires or face-to-face interviews to question subjects and record and code their responses. Researchers question a representative sample so that findings will be generalizable.

Sample research questions:

- What issues were most important in influencing young people to vote in the last presidential election?
- What kind of parental advice do young adults remember as being most influential?
- What do college students report as the most significant factors in choosing a romantic partner?

Experimental Research

Researchers systematically manipulate causal variables and measure the effects of their manipulation on subjects' responses. Extraneous influences are controlled or held constant in order to discern the relationship between specific variables. Responses are normally converted to numerical form and analyzed statistically.

Sample research questions:

- Does watching violent cartoons lead children to act aggressively toward one another?
- Is a one-sided or two-sided argument more effective for persuading a hostile audience?
- Are women more likely to turn to other women or to men when they need advice about career moves?

Performance Research

Researchers focus on analyzing the social and/or aesthetic meanings of performances. Sometimes they write about performances they have observed; at other times they uncover the meanings of texts by actually performing them. Through the process of re-creating a text for an audience, the researcher discovers and shares his or her understandings and findings.

Sample research questions:

- How did the play *Waiting for Lefty* work to attract workers to the labor movement in the 1930s?
- How can protesters use street performances to raise the consciousness of an audience?
- In re-creating a transcript of an oral history interview, what performance decisions did the performer make?

Mixed Methods

Researchers may combine several methodologies in a single study. For example, within the framework of an experiment, samples of talk may be collected under different conditions and then content analyzed. Ethnographic observations may be followed up with surveys. The term used to describe the process of approaching a research question from multiple perspectives is **triangulation**.

speech. It was inspiring"). Although we may explain some of the things we liked about it ("The part where she described her childhood really hit home"), we seldom do so in much detail. Unless we are challenged, we do not spend a great deal of time making a strong case for our beliefs. We simply state our criticism and move on.

Rhetorical critics engage in a thorough examination of a given message and its effects, giving special attention to the situation that prompted the message as well as the social and personal constraints that affected the speaker. Rhetorical critics also examine the purpose, structure, and style of the message, evaluating the ways in which the speaker's rhetorical choices affected audience response.

Critics are careful to articulate the critical standards they use to judge a message. The same message may be evaluated in a number of different ways. One critic might look at arguments. Another might examine a speaker's metaphors. A third might look at the ideological values of a speech, and a fourth might analyze its social importance. Each evaluation can add to our understanding of how the message operates.

In their book *Communication Criticism,* Karyn Rybacki and Don Rybacki discuss the process of criticism. They argue that whatever the act being investigated is, the rhetorical critic has an obligation to do three things: to describe the significant qualities of a rhetorical act, to describe those aspects of the rhetorical situation that influenced the form of the rhetorical act, and to render a judgment about the quality and consequences of the rhetorical act.[7]

Steps in Rhetorical Criticism

Rhetorical criticism seeks to explain and evaluate a rhetorical act. A **rhetorical act** is any act of communication that influences the belief or behavior of an audience. Rhetorical acts can take many forms. An inaugural speech, a political cartoon, a propaganda film, a protest song, a satirical television show, an advertising campaign, an act of civil disobedience—all can influence an audience and may thus be classified as rhetorical acts.

In evaluating a given rhetorical act, the critic must take a critical approach. Each approach is based on a theory that defines rhetoric and the role of a critic, and each provides a slightly different set of criteria for judging rhetorical success. Table 13.4 gives a brief overview of some of the more popular contemporary critical approaches. Keep in mind, however, that critics may blend these approaches or develop new approaches in response to changing interests and ideologies.

Like all research, rhetorical criticism is designed to be shared. The rhetorical critic's goal is to increase understanding and appreciation of a rhetorical act. A rhetorical critic must make a strong case for his or her point of view by showing that he or she understands the context and the structure of the rhetorical act being judged and by providing support for critical claims. Rhetorical criticism is a rhetorical act in its own right, an act of argumentation that succeeds only when it enables us to understand and appreciate a message more fully.

Voting Rites: An Example of Rhetorical Criticism

We sometimes forget that it was only in 1920 that American women received the vote. Through a large part of our history as a nation, women have been disenfranchised. In their struggle for suffrage, women have used many rhetorical tactics. One of the most interesting is described by Angela G. Ray in her article, "The Rhetorical Ritual of Citizenship: Women's Voting as Public Performance, 1863–1875."[8]

After the Civil War, voting was a very public and communal activity. Voting often took place in public places such as town halls, shoemakers' shops, barbershops, or taverns, and in cases where voting was written rather than oral, voters supplied their own ballots. By all accounts, voting was a reasonably rowdy and often alcohol-fueled public ritual that offered "recurring, performative support for the myth of the ultimate authority of a sovereign people."[9]

Table 13.4 Contemporary Critical Approaches

Neo-Aristotelian Criticism

Using the concepts and principles set forth by Aristotle and other classical theorists, the rhetorical critic evaluates a speaker's rhetorical choices, examining modes of proof, structure and organization of arguments, and stylistic choices and delivery, as they affect audience response.

Genre Criticism

Critics discuss how a message fits into a genre, or specific type of communication. Traditional genres include the apologia (an apology, or defense of character), the eulogy, the political speech, the sermon, and so on. Rhetorical acts other than speeches also have their own genres—for example, the Western film or the romantic novel.

Burkean Dramatistic Analysis

Viewing symbolic acts as "drama," the critic analyzes how various aspects of a given "performance" (act, purpose, agent, agency, and scene) are symbolically represented and how they serve to evoke identification between speaker and audience.

Fantasy Theme Analysis

Working from the idea that we understand our world by telling stories about it, the critic examines the implicit narrative structure of rhetorical acts, describing the myths and fantasies that the acts convey. A fantasy theme analyst seeks to uncover fantasy themes (basic story lines and characters that dramatize a situation), fantasy types (recurring tales that embody the fears or values of a culture), and shared rhetorical visions (shared schemata for interpreting reality).

Social Movement Studies

The critic analyzes how a social cause gains adherents, how its members communicate to the public, and what their impact is on the culture at large. A social movement critic might study the rhetorical strategies of groups such as civil rights activists, the religious right, supporters of Jewish statehood, the right-to-life movement, and so on.

Cultural Ideological Criticism

The critic examines rhetorical acts for political messages and evaluates how these messages uphold or subvert existing power relations. Often, the critic evaluates what is left out of a message as well as what the message contains. Any political ideology, such as feminism or Marxism, may form the basis of criticism.

Social Values Criticism

Rhetorical critics look at the way cultural products (speeches, films, TV shows, etc.) represent a culture's basic values. Critics try to uncover ways in which rhetorical acts combine conflicting values. A social values critic might investigate how a rhetorical act synthesizes values such as individualism and community or morality and materialism.

During this period, hundreds of women across the country attempted to appropriate the male voting ritual by showing up at polling places and presenting themselves as voters. Knowing that their efforts would, in all likelihood, be denied, they persisted in what was clearly a symbolic act designed to induce an emotional response and draw attention to their cause. The women who took part in this ritual came from a variety of backgrounds, although the majority were well-to-do members of associations that promoted women's suffrage.

The performances varied. Women traveled to a polling place, often in groups, approached authorities, and asked to be registered. A lengthy debate might or might not occur. A few women were allowed to vote, but most were refused. In some cases, the women brought an alternative ballot box into which they placed symbolic ballots. A few used the occasion to make a statement. A woman in Richmond, Virginia, for example, was reported to have declaimed, "By the Constitution of the United States, I, Anne Whitehead Bodeker, have a right to give my vote at this election, and in vindication of it drop this note in the ballot-box, November 7, 1871." Another woman presented the election official with a vase of flowers and a scroll showing a crowd of women being welcomed by Columbia and the Goddess of Justice, while imps of darkness fled from the scene.[10]

As in any performance, participants were carefully costumed. Contemporary accounts described the costumes of the participants as conventionally feminine and their demeanor as quiet and dignified. One newspaper report, for example, described the dress of a would-be voter: "She wore a plaid shawl of quiet colors, a mink collar, black kid gloves and a black velvet bonnet," while another wrote: "If ever women illustrated the fact that devotion to principle and advocacy of a great cause are consistent with true womanliness, these women have done it."[11] The result of reports such as these was to construct suffragist voters as highly feminine, yet heroic, figures. Election officials were turned into co-actors, whose role was often confusing and uncertain. Bound to uphold the law, they were being asked to violate it, and many an alderman must have found it difficult to refuse "well-spoken, well dressed women of his own class or even of his acquaintance."[12] One election official was reported as being "covered in blushes" upon having to refuse a would-be voter, and an election judge in New Jersey even had to turn away his own wife. In any case, election officials had to confront their feelings and beliefs about citizens' rights to vote.

How successful was this ritual in changing public policy? In most parts of the country, woman's right to vote was legally denied. As Ray points out, "On the one hand, activist women's rhetorical rituals forced official, serious engagement with political arguments for inclusion . . . yet the backlash, buttressed by governmental power, produced new obstacles."[13] When the Supreme Court ruled that voting was not a privilege of citizenship, it was clear that securing the vote would take a constitutional amendment. If measured in terms of legal change, then, the tactic was not a success. However, if measured by the subjective experiences of the women involved, another story emerges. Although some women were discouraged and depressed by election refusals, many women experienced an increase in self-respect and a sense of what we would today call empowerment.

In summing up, Ray points out the contradictions inherent in this kind of public performance and the challenges of "enacting rituals that simultaneously venerated and undermined prior conventions." Discourses that seek change within existing systems," she tells us, ". . . are frequently bedeviled by the search for a balance between reverence and subversion."[14] And whereas dramatic performances can inspire and motivate actors, real social change requires hard, tedious work and a recognition that for every step forward there are setbacks and challenges that must be overcome.

Ethnographic Research

If in everyday life we often act as critics, we also often act as ethnographers. Whenever curiosity about human behavior motivates us to observe others, we are engaging in our own private version of ethnography. Watching people and trying to figure out the rules that guide their actions are basic mechanisms for survival; without them, we wouldn't be able to fit into our own culture.

> Whenever curiosity about human behavior motivates us to observe others, we are engaging in our own private version of ethnography.

Like the rest of us, professional ethnographers learn from observation. Their reasons for observing behavior, however, are scientific, not personal. Ethnographers want to understand how members of other cultures interpret their world. To do so, ethnographers immerse themselves in a culture in an effort to see it through the eyes of its members. As Howard Schwartz and Jerry Jacobs point out, the ethnographer has two goals:

> First, he wants to learn the actor's "definition of the situation"—to see what the actor sees, know what he knows, and think as he thinks. Second, having accomplished this reconstruction of the other's reality, the researcher hopes to transcend this view, to see what the actor does not see—the formal features, processes, patterns, or common denominators that characterize the actor's view and situation.[15]

To achieve these goals, the researcher must make direct contact with the individuals he or she wishes to observe. As J. Kirk and M. L. Miller explain, ethnographic research depends on "watching people in their own territory and interacting with them in their own language, on their own terms."[16]

Steps in Ethnographic Research

If the ethnographer is to observe people in their own territory, he or she must assume a role. One approach is to observe people without their being aware of one's presence. The ethnographer who chooses to take this covert role goes "undercover" by becoming a member of the group being studied. To understand how cult members are socialized, for example, a researcher might join a cult in the guise of being a spiritual seeker. Or to understand the culture of a New York City cab driver, a researcher might drive a cab for several months. The problem with this approach is that it is deceptive. As the researcher forms relationships with group members, he or she may feel uncomfortable about lying to them. Another problem is in becoming so emotionally involved that one's ability to make objective observations is threatened.

Another approach is to take a more overt role. Here, the ethnographer enters the field as a scientist, and people know full well that they are being observed. The problem here is that when people know they are being watched, they may try to impress the observer. The ethnographer who takes an overt role must make special efforts to gain the trust of group members and to blend into the background as much as possible.

The key to ethnographic research is the ability to make accurate and insightful observations. Observations take the form of field notes, a record of critical events and behaviors accompanied by the ethnographer's self-observations, feelings, and interpretations. Field notes can run to thousands of pages in a lengthy study. Because it is hard to tell what details will be significant in the final analysis, good ethnographers note as much as possible as it occurs.

To gather data, the ethnographer may work with an informant, a member of the culture who is willing to show the researcher around, to answer questions, and to set up interviews with other people. Interviews are an important part of ethnographic research. By talking to as many people as possible about their communicative experiences, the researcher can check his or her own perceptions and can begin to understand how people within the culture view their own experiences.

Ethnographers must constantly be on the lookout for prejudices that may bias their ability to understand a culture. Although ethnographic research strives to be presuppositionless research, the researcher's own norms and values are hard to set aside.

The final step in ethnographic research is making sense of the data. Most researchers analyze their data inductively. This means that their conclusions flow directly from the data themselves rather than from a preexisting theory. Frey and his colleagues offer four criteria for good, inductively generated results. Conclusions should be

> believable, in that they should seem plausible to the reader. They should be comprehensive or account for all (or most) of the data. They should be grounded or tied clearly to the data. Finally, they should be applicable and lead to testable hypotheses and additional investigation.[17]

Hook Up or Pull Up: An Example of Ethnographic Research

Communication scholar Dwight Conquergood provides a classic example of ethnographic research. In order to pursue his research, he moved into a Chicago tenement in the heart of gang territory and engaged in an intense period of participant observation during the late 1980s and early 1990s. In "Homeboys and Hoods: Gang Communication and Cultural Space," he describes how gangs use verbal and nonverbal messages to create solidarity and protect their boundaries.[18]

Gangs create strong bonds of solidarity. Members see themselves as families or teams. Their intense collectivism stands in opposition to the competitive individualism found in other aspects of American society. As one Latin King said, "We practice how to be together all the time. We think that that's our strength. Other people have money. We have each other." Someone who is not "hooked up," in other words, connected to others, might as well "pull up," or leave, because he or she has no protection, no family or team to belong to.

Many people think of gangs as isolated groups. But in Chicago, gangs are embedded within city-wide "nations." Nations are supergang confederations. The Chicago nations were developed in the Illinois prison system in order to organize and control intergang warfare. The creation of two major nations simplified boundaries by creating alliances, making it unnecessary for each individual gang to fight every other gang. In Chicago nations are not based on race, ethnicity, or geography. They are multiracial and multiethnic, and the city is a patchwork of alternating territories. Within the nations are the gangs themselves, which can have as many as 1,000 members. They in turn are subdivided into branches, which are made up of several age cohorts. The branch is the group that people identify with most deeply, for it provides "support, attachment, and solidarity against a hostile world."[19]

Conquergood argues that gang communication lies somewhere between group and organizational communication. Like other complex organizations, gangs have written constitutions or charters that explain their rules, rituals, and symbols. Common to many of these underground charters is a code of silence: a gang's affairs must not be revealed to anyone outside the gang. Some of the gang manifestos even contain organizational charts, showing power hierarchies.

The basis of gang communication is *reppin'*, short for representing. It is through reppin' that gang members reveal their gang identity. To represent themselves, members use a complex blend of both verbal and nonverbal signs. "Reppin' encompasses everything from wearing the signifying gang colors, throwing up hand signs, and calling out code words to inscribing elaborate graffiti murals."[20] The Latin Kings, for example, might show their identity by tilting their baseball caps to the left to indicate membership in the Folks Nation, by using choreographed handshakes, by placing their first on their heart with their fingers in the shape of a crown, by lacing their shoes in gang-approved style, and by creating elaborate graffiti.

Verbal, as well as nonverbal, communication is often camouflaged. Maintaining a boundary between insider and outsider, between us and them, necessitates secrecy and circumspection. Gangs use street slang to distinguish themselves from mainstream society. In addition, they use terms and phrases that belong only to their group. For example, "take your V" is a way of commanding someone to submit to punishment, the *V* being short for *violation*. Among the Latin Kings, "Amor!" is a common greeting. In addition to being the Spanish word for "love," *amor* is an acronym for Almighty Masters of Revolution. The Black Gangster Disciples' identification is "BOS," which stands for Brothers of the Struggle. "Secret acronyms as well as special argot are thus developed and designed precisely to circumscribe group boundaries, heighten in-group consciousness, and exclude outsiders."[21]

Elaborate greetings are repeated whenever gang members meet. Not to take part in these "rites of affiliation" is to commit the greatest sin of life in the hood—disrespect. And one of the worst forms of disrespect is to "leave someone hanging" by failing to return a handshake. These communication rites "help restore respect, repair the loss of face, and redress the daily humiliations of poverty and prejudice."[22]

Like all participant observers, Conquergood encountered ethical dilemmas. For example, the gang charters that he was shown are secret; yet he felt it was important to describe their existence in order to counter media portrayals of gangs as simply disorganized bands of drug-crazed killers. "Conducting and publishing research on an underground, somewhat secret social group," he tells us, involves negotiating "the delicate boundary between respect and sensitivity to my field consultants, and the need to write the fullest, most complex ethnographic account of their communication practices that my data support."[23]

Conquergood ends his article by discussing what can be done about the "gang problem." He argues that instead of stigmatizing individual gang members, "communication needs to be redirected toward rallying and awakening communities and public policymakers to a sense of social justice and responsibility to these youngsters and their families. An initial, concrete step would be to think about jobs, instead of jails."[24]

Survey Research

Perhaps the most direct and straightforward way to learn about other people is to ask them questions. Survey research does just that. In **survey research**, an investigator chooses a sample of people to question, decides what to ask and how to ask it, and administers the questions in either written or oral form. He or she then codes responses and looks for meaningful patterns. Finally, the survey researcher draws conclusions from the data.

> Perhaps the most direct and straightforward way to learn about other people is to ask them questions. Survey research does just that.

Surveys may be used to describe a population or to test a hypothesis. They may be used to build theories of social behavior or to solve practical problems. Surveys are part of public opinion research, marketing studies, and program evaluations. Because surveys are used in so many contexts, you will likely be asked to design and conduct a survey someday.

Steps in Conducting a Survey

Survey researchers are often interested in describing the attitudes and communication behaviors of large groups of people. A pollster's ideal is to know how every American will vote. Practically, however, a pollster can question only a small fraction of the voting public. Luckily, it is not necessary to question every member of a population (the entire group a researcher wants to study) to get a good idea of what the population is like. By examining a sample (a small group of people representative of the population), the researcher can often draw very accurate conclusions about population characteristics.

There are good and bad ways to draw a sample; generalization is possible only if an unbiased sample has been chosen. To choose a representative sample, the researcher first chooses a sampling plan, a systematic method for choosing respondents for a study. Researchers use two general kinds of sampling plans: probability and nonprobability. Probability sampling allows generalizations because it assures the researcher that the sample is representative. In a probability sample, the researcher knows the exact probability that each member of a population will be included in a sample. For example, in simple random sampling, each member of the population has an equal chance of being in the sample. Nonprobability sampling does not give the researcher the same assurance. In nonprobability samples, some members of the population may have virtually no chance of being included whereas others may be overrepresented. A common form of nonprobability sampling is accidental sampling, whereby the researcher uses the most convenient people available.

There are many ways to find out about others. Careful observation and systematic questioning are two "lenses" we can use to discover insights about human communication.

Using nonprobability samples is risky. Imagine that you've been assigned to cover a presidential election for your college broadcasting station. Your task is to report the political views of students on your campus. With little time left before the election, you take the easy way out: you call all your friends and ask them how they intend to vote. The likelihood that this accidental sample will be accurate is very low because friends often share political views.

Simple random sampling, although costly in time and effort, significantly improves your chances of drawing a representative sample. If you were to use this method in our example, you would need a list of every student at your school as well as a computer-generated list of random ID numbers. You could then match the random numbers on your list to the student IDs, choosing for your survey only those students whose numbers came up. If you were to generate a sufficiently large sample (and if you could convince everyone in the sample to take part in the study), your results would closely approximate population figures.

Deciding whom to question is only the first step. A survey researcher must also frame questions and organize the survey. These steps are not as easy as they might seem. Like any other form of communication, questions can be misunderstood and misinterpreted. A researcher must take care that questions are answerable, unambiguous, and as nonthreatening as possible; that they focus on a single issue at a time; and that they do not lead the respondent to give a desired answer.

First, questions should be answerable; that is, they should avoid asking for information that the respondent does not know. "How many hours did you spend talking to friends last week?" is a difficult question; although some respondents might be able to give you a fairly accurate estimate, many would have no idea. Unfortunately, respondents often make up answers rather than admitting their ignorance, making data from this kind of question suspect.

Questions should also be unambiguous; that is, what the researcher is asking should be clear. "How many channels of communication do you use in your job?" is ambiguous. "I am going to read off a number of ways in which people communicate on the job. As I mention each one, tell me whether you have used it during the last week: memo, telephone, fax, . . ." is a much clearer way to ask the same question.

Questions should be as nonthreatening as possible; that is, they should avoid making the respondent feel guilty or incompetent. Questions about drug use, sexual behavior, or academic dishonesty are examples of topics that respondents may be unwilling to discuss. Explaining why these questions are necessary and assuring confidentiality may help respondents to overcome their reluctance. Sometimes, asking the question in an indirect form increases a respondent's willingness to respond. "Why do you think some students cheat?" may be more effective than "Why do you cheat?"

Double-barreled questions should be avoided. A double-barreled question asks several questions at once. "Do you believe that Governor Smith should be elected president because of her stand on the environment?" is really several questions rolled into one: "Do you believe that Smith should be elected?" is one question; "Do you approve of Smith's stand on the environment?" is another; and "Will Smith's environmental stand affect whether or not you vote for her?" is a third.

Another kind of question that should be avoided is the leading question. Leading questions are questions that indicate a preferred response. "Don't you think the depiction of women on MTV is shameful?" is a leading question. Generally, any question that starts with "Do you agree that . . ." is leading. A better phrasing would be "Consider the following statement. Do you agree or disagree with it?"

In addition to carefully considering the way in which a question is worded, the survey researcher is also concerned with the way questions are ordered.

In general, easy-to-answer questions should be placed early in the questionnaire, and questions on sensitive topics should go toward the end. In addition, questions on a single topic should be grouped together.

Like other forms of communication, the survey interview should have a beginning, a middle, and an end. As Frey and colleagues point out, "how interviews are begun often determines whether, and then how fully, respondents cooperate."[25] In the beginning of a survey, the researcher must introduce himself or herself and state the purpose of the interview, the topic, how much time the survey will take, and whether the data will be confidential. At the end, he or she should thank the respondent for cooperating.

Researchers administer surveys in two general ways: through a face-to-face interview or through a self-administered questionnaire. Each method has advantages and disadvantages. Interviews allow the researcher to control what goes on during the survey and to clarify ambiguous questions. On the other hand, interviewers can inadvertently bias responses, and interviewers are relatively expensive to train and use. Mailed questionnaires are cheap and have the advantage of being anonymous, but there is no way to control for distractions. In addition, the response rate is often low, and the responses may not be statistically valid because those who choose to respond may differ in some important respect from those who do not respond.

Generally speaking, survey researchers convert responses into categories or numbers so that the responses can be statistically analyzed. Although this is relatively easy to do with responses to closed-ended questions (whereby respondents choose from a finite set of answers provided by the researcher) or rating scales (whereby the respondent rates an idea or an attitude on a numerical scale), it is more difficult to do with responses to open-ended questions (whereby the respondent is free to answer in his or her own words). With responses to open-ended questions, the researcher must find a way to categorize and compare responses. The researchers described in the next section used both responses to rating scales and content analysis to categorize responses to open-ended questions.

The Tribe Has Spoken: Two Examples of Survey Research

Reality programming has become commonplace on broadcast TV. For many people, including college students, viewing reality TV is a "guilty pleasure." What makes this kind of entertainment so compelling? In this section we look at two surveys that seek to answer this question. In the first, "Why People Watch Reality TV," Steven Reiss and James Wiltz use a standardized questionnaire to create a motivational profile of reality TV viewers.[26] In "Simply Irresistible: Reality TV Consumption Patterns," Lisa K. Lundy, Amanda M. Ruth, and Travis D. Park employ a focus group approach to explore the rationales college students give for watching.[27] Like other "uses and gratifications" research, these studies focused on understanding audience motives for using mass media.

In the first study, Reiss and Wiltz gave 121 working adults and 117 college students a written questionnaire. In addition to providing information on age, sex, and viewing habits, respondents rated the importance of 16 fundamental motives. The researchers then compared motive scores of people who watched no reality TV with those who watched one or two of the reality shows identified in the study (*Survivor, Big Brother, Temptation Island, The Mole, and The Real World*). Results showed that the motive most associated with reality viewing was status, defined as the need to feel self-important. The authors argue that not only does reality TV enhance viewer esteem by implying that ordinary people are important, it also allows viewers to feel superior to on-screen characters. A second related motive was the desire to get even, a motive associated with the enjoyment of competition. In addition, the researchers found that sociable people were more likely than nonsociable people to watch reality programming and that people who score low on the desire to obey traditional moral codes enjoy reality programs more than their more ethical counterparts. The authors interpret this latter effect as due to the fact that reality television shows frequently "champion expedience over ethics."

In the second study, college students were divided into small groups and asked to discuss their opinions and perceptions of reality TV. Their discussions were guided by a moderator, and they were encouraged to respond to and build on one another's ideas. After the discussions, Lundy and her colleagues reviewed tapes and transcripts to identify dominant themes in the discussion. The researchers begin their analysis by noting that respondents watched more reality TV than they were initially willing to admit. At least 25 shows were discussed, the most common among them being *The Bachelor, The Bachelorette, American Idol, The Real World, Trading Spaces, The Swan, Survivor, Joe Millionaire, Average Joe, Extreme Makeover, The Simple Life,* and *American Chopper.*

Lundy and her colleagues found that escapism was a major reason for reality television viewing. As one respondent said, "I don't think it is real life but that is the point. Real life is boring and you watch reality shows to live vicariously through others."[28] Although students recognized that reality programming can be ridiculous, they still consumed it. As one individual remarked, "It's like a train wreck—horrible but (you) can't turn away." Respondents were especially critical of shows that humiliated or hurt participants and found the shows' deception, immorality, and materialism troubling. As one respondent noted, "when you put money at the end of the road . . . people lose track of what is important and . . . that is when I have a problem with the reality issue; when people start doing things they normally wouldn't do in order to win."[29] Despite these criticisms and the recognition that, far from being real, reality TV is often contrived, students continued to watch, and many took an active role by voting for winners and losers.

In addition to investigating reasons for viewing, Lundy and her colleagues looked at how students watch. They found that social affiliation is an important part of the viewing experience. Students view programs in groups and discuss reality TV with friends. Some even watch shows they don't particularly like so as not to be "left out" of conversations. Although most felt conversation about reality TV was shallow and silly, all of the respondents indicated having at least one discussion about an episode. It appears that reality TV is a topic that serves an important social function for college-aged adults.

Despite the fact that they used quite different methods to survey student attitudes, both studies found that sociability is an important aspect of reality viewing, and that reality programming provides gratifications for young adults. Whether viewing is an attempt to enhance feelings of self-worth, or whether it is simply a form of escapist entertainment, a large portion of 18- to 24-year-olds regularly watch and enjoy reality TV.[30] In the words of Susan Murray and Laurie Ouellette, "what ties together all the various formats of the reality TV genre is their professed ability to more fully provide viewers an unmediated, voyeuristic, yet often playful look into what might be called the 'entertaining real.'"[31]

Experimental Research

In everyday life, we frequently have hunches about cause and effect. To test these hunches, we run naive experiments: we manipulate what we think might be the cause and wait to see the effect of this manipulation. A parent, for example, may decide that arguing with a child reinforces the child's negative behavior. To test this idea, the parent may stop arguing and see what happens. If the child's bad behavior ceases, the parent will probably conclude that it was caused by too much attention. Although not very scientific, this is an instance of everyday experimentation.

In **experimental research**, researchers are also interested in cause and effect. The effect they want to explain is called the **dependent variable**, whereas the suspected cause is called the **independent variable**. If, for example, a researcher believes that giving an employee praise will cause that employee to feel more satisfied with his or her work, praise is the independent variable and satisfaction is the dependent variable.

> In everyday life, we frequently have hunches about cause and effect. To test these hunches, we run naive experiments: we manipulate what we think might be the cause and wait to see the effect of this manipulation.

All experiments involve manipulation, comparison, and control. To find out whether praise leads to satisfaction, for example, a researcher must **manipulate** the independent variable, praise. One way to do this is to choose two groups of workers, praise one group and not the other, and then **compare** the groups to find out which group was most satisfied. If the researcher carefully **controls** the experiment by making sure no other independent variables are at work, then any change in satisfaction is necessarily due to the effects of praise.

Steps in Doing an Experiment

Like survey researchers, experimental researchers want to generalize their findings. They want to discover general laws of cause and effect that apply in many different situations. To do this, they must choose the best possible sampling plan. A probability sampling plan is best, but if this is impossible to implement, the researchers must devise a sampling strategy that controls for as much bias as possible.

The way the researcher sets up a study is called the research design. In designing a study, the researcher must decide how the independent variable, or treatment, is to be administered and when the dependent variable is to be measured. The measurement of the dependent variable before the treatment is called a pretest; the measurement after the treatment is called a posttest. Some research designs are faulty and allow no conclusions to be drawn. Others are logically valid and can be used to demonstrate causal relationships.

To see what constitutes a faulty design, let's return to the praise–satisfaction experiment. Assume, for a moment, that the researcher did the experiment on a single group of workers. The researcher measured workers' satisfaction level, praised the workers at least once a day for two weeks, and then measured their satisfaction again. Assume also that satisfaction was greater after the two-week period than before. Would the researcher be justified in concluding that the change in satisfaction was due to the praise? The answer is no. The change might well have been due to other factors—perhaps the workload lightened during that period or rumors of a wage increase circulated. Because this design (called a one-group pretest–posttest design) used only one group, it is impossible to rule out alternative explanations.

The research design can be improved by adding a second, control group, which is equivalent to the first group in every way except that it does not receive the experimental treatment. If the satisfaction level of the control group stays the same over the two weeks while the satisfaction level of the treatment group rises, then the researcher can rule out alternative explanations. To ensure that the control and treatment groups are equivalent, the researcher should not use existing groups, for they may be different to begin with. Instead, he or she should randomly assign subjects to the experimental and control groups. The design used in this example is called a pretest–posttest control group design and is one of the strongest and most popular of the experimental designs.

In any experiment, the researcher must devise a way to measure the dependent variable. In the example we have been using, the researcher must measure satisfaction. To do so, he or she might use a simple yes-or-no question ("Are you satisfied with your job, yes or no?") and compare the percentages of workers in each group saying yes before and after the treatment. On the other hand, the researcher might use a more elaborate rating scale ("On a scale from one to ten, where ten indicates high satisfaction, how would you rate your feelings about your job?") and compare the average rating before and after the treatment. In any case, a measurement method must meet two criteria. It must be reliable (i.e., it must consistently yield the same results), and it must be valid (i.e., it must actually measure the dependent variable). If, for example, employees know that the boss will receive their answers to the satisfaction question, the results might not be valid; the results might reflect the employees' desire to please the boss and protect their jobs rather than the employees' actual degree of satisfaction.

Experimental researchers depend on statistical methods to help them analyze their data. They compute statistics that tell them whether their findings are due to random variation or to the presence of the independent variable. Although statistics provide an objective, numerical method for analyzing differences, it is still up to the researcher to interpret what these differences mean.

The Social Presence of Social Robots: An Example of Experimental Research

Robots no longer belong only in science fiction. They currently aid humans in a variety of ways from therapy to entertainment. As "social robots" become more common, communication scholars are turning their attention to a new form of communication: human-robot interaction. In "Can a Robot Be Perceived as a Developing Creature?" Kwan Min Lee and colleagues investigate some of the factors that lead to successful human-robot interaction.[32]

Previous research has shown that the more robots look and act like social actors with individual, friendly personalities, the more willing humans are to interact with them. Building on this research, the authors wanted to identify other variables that might affect human-robot interaction. One such variable is the extent to which a robot is capable of change. The authors reasoned that the ability to develop should make robots appear more human. After all, a hallmark of living creatures is that they develop and learn. A second variable of interest is the extent to which the presence of other humans might affect human-robot interaction. The authors point out that many of today's robots are helper robots used in public museums, hospitals, and schools. Despite this fact, most previous research has looked only at individual rather than group human-robot interactions.

To test their reasoning, the authors devised an experiment. They hypothesized that humans would be more positive about and would feel more social presence (i.e., feel more personally connected) when interacting with a developing robot than with a robot that was fully developed. They also hypothesized that people who interacted with a robot individually would have greater feelings of social presence and would respond more positively than people who interacted with a robot in a group setting. Finally, they predicted that people's social responses toward a robot would be related to the amount of social presence they felt during interaction.

Their first task was to find a suitable robot. They chose Sony's AIBO, an entertainment robot that looks like a small dog. In order to compare reactions to a developing robot as opposed to an already developed robot, they programmed the AIBO to go through four developmental stages, from "puppy" to "adult dog." In the first stage, the AIBO was only capable of understanding its name and saying goodbye. By the time it reached adulthood, it could sit, stand, lie down, walk, turn, cheer up its master, sing a song, shake its front legs, make clapping sounds, and dance a happy dance.

Forty students took part in the study over a four-week period. Half of the students interacted individually with a developing AIBO; their AIBO started as a puppy and learned new behaviors each week until it became an adult. The other half interacted with an adult AIBO. Within each group, ten students interacted with the AIBO individually and the other ten in a group setting. To measure social presence and psychological involvement, students indicated on a ten-point scale their responses to questions like, "How much did you feel as if you were interacting with an intelligent being?" "How much attention did you pay to the AIBO?" and "How much did you feel involved with [the AIBO]?" The authors also collected ratings of attraction toward the AIBO, perceived closeness to the AIBO, and buying intentions.

After analyzing the data, the researchers found that students who interacted with the developing AIBO felt it was more lifelike and experienced more social presence than the students who experienced the fully developed AIBO. The former also were more attracted to their robot, felt closer to it, and had higher buying intentions than did the latter.

The results for the second variable were not as clear. Although students who experienced the AIBO alone felt closer to the robot and had higher buying intentions than those who experienced it with others present, when it came to social presence and attraction the amount of people present did not seem to make any difference. Finally, using a statistical method known as path analysis, the researchers were able to determine that social presence plays a large role in people's social responses to robots. When social presence is high, attraction, closeness, and buying intentions are also high.

Not only does the study add to our general understanding of the importance of social presence in human-robot interaction, it also has practical implications. It shows that even small changes in the way robots function can produce large response differences. It also demonstrated that strong feelings of social presence occur even in group situations. Furthermore, it suggests that "equipping a robot with a full functional capability from the beginning of interaction might not be a good choice for the design of social robots."[33] Finally, this study points out the importance of taking an interdisciplinary approach to robotics. Together engineers and social scientists can share understandings in order to improve human-robot interaction.

Performance as Research

In everyday life, we perform more than you might think. We tell stories, often imaginatively taking on the roles of the characters involved. We do impressions to amuse (or to mock). We take part in rituals, ceremonies, or religious rites. Often, these performances are liberating, allowing us to try on new identities and express unfamiliar emotions. They allow us to explore and work through feelings and ideas we may not even know we have. Our everyday performances are often acts of discovery.

In the field of **performance studies**, communication scholars focus on a wide range of performances. Some researchers study the meanings in the performances of others, and others may perform themselves in order to gain insights into the meanings of texts and to share these insights with an audience. The performances researchers in this field study and enact are wide-ranging. They may study aesthetic products such as stage productions or performance art, but they may also choose to look for the meaning in everyday performances such as pageants, rites, and rituals. Those who choose to perform may create readings of plays, poems, or novels, but they may also perform folktales, enact natural conversations, or interpret oral histories.

> Our everyday performances allow us to explore and work through feelings and ideas we may not even know we have.

Many researchers in this area use performance as a tool for research. They take a text, embody it with voice and movement, and share the product with an audience; as a result of actively engaging with the text, they come to understand the intricacies of its language and the power of its meanings. For these researchers, performing is a mode of inquiry as well as an aesthetic activity.

Steps in Performance Research

As in all of the methods we've looked at so far, the first step for performance researchers is one of *selecting*, of identifying a communication act or text for study. Performance researchers choose a text that has significance for them, whether that text is a literary work, a public speech, an autobiography, or the like. Ron Pelias calls the second step *playing*.[34] In this step, the researcher experiments with a variety of ways of interpreting the work. He or she tries on different voices and movements to see what these have to say about the meaning of the text. When the researcher feels that he or she has fully explored a number of possibilities, it is time to go on to the third step: *testing*. Here, the researcher tests interpretation against the evidence contained in the text. Says Pelias, "The researcher uses the other's text to guide his or her vocal and body work, and the researcher's vocal and body work help reveal textual dimensions."[35]

The fourth step involves *choosing*. Here the performer chooses a performance vision, a particular way of performing the text that will convey meaning to an audience. The performance may be very simple and direct, allowing the text's author to speak through the performer's voice and body. Alternatively, the performance may comment on the text so that distance is put between the author, the performer, and the audience. The fifth step is *repeating*. The performer repeats and rehearses the piece until it flows naturally, learning more in each iteration. Finally, step six is *presenting*. Here the researcher displays for others what he or she has come to understand. Following public presentation, the researcher often decides to write about what he or she has experienced. Pelias concludes:

> *Whether the researcher elects to report findings through public performance or*
> *written essay, the steps of selecting, playing, testing, choosing, repeating, and*

presenting are a method for examining the communication acts of others. They position the researcher to learn about others' discourse experientially, to come to know others by becoming them, to live in complete empathy, at least for a time, in the voice and body of others.[36]

Voices from Katrina: An Example of Performance Research

In August of 2005 when Hurricane Katrina hit the Gulf Coast, many people lost everything. Families were separated and neighborhoods were destroyed. In Saint Bernard Parish over 95 percent of the parish structures were destroyed. Danielle Sears Vignes experienced Katrina first-hand. As a performance scholar and storyteller, she understood that in a disaster as devastating as Katrina, it is not just houses that must be rebuilt. When disasters occur, she tells us, the stories that make up the living history of a community must also be salvaged. As the outside world began to dismiss the experiences of Katrina's survivors, urging them to move on, Vignes became convinced that the voices of the people in her community needed to be heard. She therefore began to collect material for a performance to commemorate the anniversary of Katrina.

She began by taking snapshots of images that convey not only devastation but also hope—messages spray-painted on the front of homes, salvaged items, laundry lists of objects, photos of survivors, ruined homes, and businesses that have reopened. After collecting the images, she sat down and talked with friends and neighbors, recording on videotape the experiences she would later re-create on stage. Many interviews later, she began to write about her own experiences as well.[37] The result is a one-woman show that blends music, slides, and the oral histories of Katrina survivors. The performance script describes the staging and transcribes the stories of each of the characters that Vignes embodies. During the transitions between stories, as Vignes moves across the stage, she repeats the phrases "scrubbin' and rinsin'," "oh my God, what has happened?" and "pick up and move on".[38] In his review of the piece, David Terry reads these repetitions as emblematic of the past-oriented impulse to restore (scrubbin' and rinsin'), the present-oriented desire to understand the unimaginable ("oh my God, what has happened?"), and the future-oriented need to replace ("pick up and move on").[39] Framing the production, Vignes sings a plaintive decima, one of the folk narrative songs from Spanish-speaking Islenos, inhabitants of the marshy islands east of New Orleans. Like the victims of Katrina, the Islenos culture is in danger of erasure, preserved in the stories that make up this unique form of narrative. Thus, Vignes connects the oral histories she presents to other stories, stories that can be traced back through time, stories that help performers and listeners commemorate and re-create their cultures.

Vignes's commentary, her performance script, and a review of her performance can be found in volume 28 of *Text and Performance Quarterly*. Reading the script can give us an idea of how performance can give voice to the thoughts and feelings of actual people whose stories would otherwise be lost, but, of course, it fails to represent the actual, embodied performance by Vignes. We can only imagine what would be added by this talented actress reaching out to a live audience.

LEARNING MORE ABOUT COMMUNICATION

The research studies we've looked at represent only a few of the ways scholars and critics gather new information and draw conclusions about communication. The five studies reviewed in the last section were taken from scholarly journals in the field of communication. Table 13.5 lists some additional journals that publish research in the field. One way to learn more about communication studies is to look through these journals for interesting articles. Doing so will give you a good sense of the kinds of topics that interest communication researchers today.

Subject Areas in Speech Communication

If you're not familiar with the field of communication—if this is your first exposure to the study of human message making—you may not be aware of the courses offered in departments of communication. Table 13.6 lists some of the major subject areas that make up this discipline, along with the kinds of courses that are offered at either the undergraduate or graduate level.

Table 13.5 Communication Journals

Here is a listing of some of the scholarly journals that publish articles about communication. The association that publishes each journal is listed, along with the Web address of that association's home page.

National Communication Association
[http://www.natcom.org]

- *The Quarterly Journal of Speech*
- *Communication Monographs*
- *Communication Education*
- *Critical Studies in Media Communication*
- *Text and Performance Quarterly*
- *Journal of Applied Communication Research*
- *Communication and Critical/Cultural Studies*
- *Communication Teacher*

International Communication Association
[http://www.icahdq.org]

- *Human Communication Research*
- *Communication Yearbook*

- *Communication Theory*
- *Journal of Communication*

Eastern Communication Association
[http://www.ecasite.org]

- *Communication Quarterly*
- *Qualitative Research Reports in Communication*
- *Communication Research Reports*

Central States Communication Association
[http://www.csca-net.org]

- *Communication Studies*

Southern States Communication Association
[http://www.ssca.net]

- *Southern Communication Journal*

Western States Communication Association
[http://www.westcomm.org]

- *Western Journal of Communication*
- *Communication Reports*

Table 13.6 Subject Areas in Speech Communication

Interpersonal Communication

The study of verbal and nonverbal exchanges in everyday interaction. Specialists in interpersonal communication study topics such as interpersonal influence, relational development and maintenance, impression formation, interpersonal attraction, gender and communication, and communication and the development of the self.

Courses include Interpersonal Communication, Gender and Communication, Family Communication, Conflict Management, and Therapeutic Communication.

Small-Group/Organizational Communication

The study of how communication helps people in groups accomplish goals and maintain group identity; the study of how communication operates in complex organizations. Specialists in small-group/organizational communication study topics such as group problem solving, conflict resolution, leadership, mediation and negotiation, superior/subordinate relationships, and organizational culture.

Courses include Small Group Decision Making, Business and Professional Communication, Leadership, and Employment Interviewing as well as courses in specialized professions, such as Health Communication or Legal Communication.

Public Communication

The study of communication in face-to-face, one-to-many communication settings. Specialists in the rhetoric of public communication study topics such as persuasion, propaganda, political communication, the history of public address, social movements, freedom of speech, and the ethics of speaking.

Courses include Public Speaking, Theories of Persuasion, Public Address, Rhetorical Theory, and Argumentation and Debate.

Performance Studies

The study of the ways people perform personal, cultural, or artistic scripts before audiences. Specialists in performance studies study topics such as folklore and oral traditions; storytelling; performance art; the work of individual performers, such as stand-up comics or cultural icons; and the performance of literature.

Courses include Oral Interpretation, Readers' Theatre, Performance of Literature and Folklore, as well as courses specializing in a given author or genre, such as Performing Joyce or Performance and Analysis of Prose.

Mass Communication

The study of mediated messages created for a wide public audience. Specialists in mass communication study topics such as the history of the media, prosocial effects of the media, television and the family, media law, nonfiction film, and politics and the media.

Courses include Advertising, Public Relations, Broadcast Production, Introduction to the Mass Media, Journalism, and Media Criticism.

Intercultural Communication

The study of communication across cultural boundaries. Specialists in intercultural communication study topics such as interethnic and interracial conflict, verbal and nonverbal differences across cultures, forms of talk unique to a given culture, and ways to increase cross-cultural understanding.

Courses include Cross-Cultural Communication and a variety of specialized courses examining given cultures.

Language and Semiotic Systems

The study of code systems used to create messages in any of the contexts listed above. Topics include nonverbal message systems, semantic and pragmatic rules and their effects, dialect differences and social class, bilingualism, gender differences in language use, and conversational structures.

Courses include Language and Social Action, The Psychology of Language, Language Development, American Dialects, and Phonetics.

As you can see, the types of courses offered in departments of communication are both theoretical and applied. Some, such as public speaking, argumentation, and group discussion, help you improve your organizational and delivery skills. Others, such as interpersonal, family, and gender communication courses, focus on understanding and analyzing everyday interaction. You may choose courses that explore the history of our field (e.g., Classical Theories of Rhetoric), courses that develop your critical and analytic skills (e.g., Rhetorical Theory, Analysis, and Performance of Literature), or courses that prepare you for a specific communication-related career (e.g., Public Relations, Broadcast Production, Health Communication). The areas covered in departments of communication are far-reaching and varied.

Other Sources of Discovery

Although taking formal courses or reading books written by communication experts can increase your knowledge, you can learn more about communication in many other ways. One way is to explore other subject areas. There are connections between all of the humanities and sciences. Psychology and sociology can offer insights into communication by illuminating human and group behavior, and anthropology can show us how communication practices differ from culture to culture. Literary criticism and linguistics can tell us more about how meanings are created and shared, whereas the study of music, art, and architectural design can help us see how different media transform expression. History and politics show us how events in the public sphere affect the subjects we communicate about as well as the ways we communicate about them. Indeed, it is difficult to think of any course in the humanities or social sciences that is not related to communication.

Another way you can understand communication more fully is through reading novels and viewing plays and films. Not only are these forms of expression examples of rhetorical acts in their own right, they also illuminate our understanding of human behavior and therefore make us more sensitive to one another.

Curiosity about the world is the basic impulse behind all research. It is an impulse we are born with and one that guides us throughout our lives. Only when we no longer find the world interesting do we stop learning.

Finally, you can gain insight into communication by observing human interaction. This takes a willingness to stand aside and to watch and wonder. Curiosity is at the heart of all discovery—a curiosity that is initially attracted by anything odd or different and that proceeds to celebrate regularities in the "life that flows beneath the surface of things." If you develop that curiosity, you cannot help but learn about communication theory and practice.

SUMMARY

This chapter discusses methods of discovery: it describes the research process, examines five contemporary approaches to communication study, and outlines the structure of communication as an academic field.

Research is not exotic; it's something we do every day. Commonsense methods of discovery, however, are often biased. We privilege our own experiences, engage in wishful thinking, and rely too much on simple heuristics. Systematic research is more accurate and less biased; it is question oriented, methodological, replicable, self-critical, cumulative and self-correcting, and cyclical. Regardless of approach, researchers accomplish four tasks: they ask questions and define key concepts; they choose a method to guide their inquiry; they gather and analyze samples of communication acts; and they interpret these samples, sharing the results.

Five representative research methods are rhetorical criticism, ethnographic research, survey research, experimental research, and performance research. Rhetorical criticism is a systematic way of describing, analyzing, and evaluating rhetorical acts. In criticizing acts of influence, rhetorical critics use methods such as neo-Aristotelian criticism, genre criticism, Burkean analysis, fantasy theme analysis, social movement criticism, ideological criticism, and social value criticism. Ray's article on voting as a rhetorical ritual is an example of rhetorical criticism.

A second and very different kind of research is ethnography. Ethnographers try to understand how members of other cultures interpret their worlds. Ethnographers do this by observing behavior in natural surroundings to uncover rules that guide action. Ethnographers bracket their preconceptions and try to see the world without bias. Conquergood's research on communication in gangs is an example of ethnographic research.

A third research method is survey research. Survey researchers describe populations by asking questions of systematically chosen samples. The questions must be answerable, unambiguous, and nonthreatening; researchers must avoid double-barreled and leading questions. The articles on reality TV by Reiss and Wiltz and Lundy, Ruth, and Park are examples of survey research.

A fourth research method is experimental research. Experimental researchers manipulate independent variables to discover their effects on dependent variables. Experiments are controlled so that no unexpected factors invalidate conclusions about causal relationships. Measurement must be reliable and valid. The article by Lee, Park, and Song on robots is an example of an experiment.

A final research method involves either critically observing the performance of others or actively engaging in performance in order to understand the meanings of a text. By selecting, playing, testing, choosing, repeating, and presenting a text, the researcher learns more about the communication acts of others and shares this knowledge with an audience. The Vignes article and script about Hurricane Katrina illustrate performance research.

The field of communication encompasses many interesting topics to study and many ways to study them. Whether your interest is in interpersonal, small-group/organizational, public, mass, or intercultural communication or in performance studies or language, you will find large bodies of research available and a variety of courses to take. But taking a course in speech communication is not the only way to learn more about communication. By reading and studying related topics or by simply observing life around you, you can continue to make discoveries about human communication.

KEY TERMS

Listed below are the key terms used in this chapter, along with the number of the page where each is explained.

heuristics (349)	sampling plan (363)	dependent variable (367)
research question (351)	probability sampling (363)	independent variable (367)
conceptual definition (352)	simple random sampling (363)	manipulate (367)
operational definition (352)	nonprobability sampling (363)	compare (367)
rhetorical criticism (355)	accidental sampling (363)	controls (367)
triangulation (355)	double-barreled questions (364)	research design (368)
rhetorical act (356)	leading question (364)	treatment (368)
ethnographers (359)	interview (365)	pretest (368)
covert role (359)	questionnaire (365)	posttest (368)
overt role (360)	closed-ended questions (365)	one-group pretest–posttest design (368)
field notes (360)	rating scales (365)	control group (368)
informant (360)	open-ended questions (365)	pretest–posttest control group design (368)
presuppositionless research (360)	experimental research (367)	reliable (368)
survey research (362)		valid (368)
population (363)		performance studies (371)
sample (363)		

SUGGESTED READINGS

Frey, Lawrence R., Botan, Carl H., & Kreps, Gary L. (2005). *Investigating communication: An introduction to research methods* (3rd ed.). Boston: Allyn & Bacon.

An excellent, interesting, and comprehensive introduction to understanding and using research methods.

Foss, Sonja K. (Ed.). (2004). *Rhetorical criticism: Exploration and practice* (3rd ed.). Long Grove, IL: Waveland Press.

Offers a clear explanation of a variety of critical methods, followed by sample essays by both undergraduate students and experts in the field.

Notes

CHAPTER 1

1. Shands, Harley C. (1968). Crystallized conflict: Semiotic aspects of neurosis and science. In Carl E. Larson & Frank E. X. Dance (Eds.), *Perspectives on communication*. Milwaukee: The University of Wisconsin, Milwaukee, Speech Communication Center, 128.

2. Lynch, John Patrick. (1972). *Aristotle's school: A study of a Greek educational institution*. Berkeley: University of California Press, 57, 93.

3. Bryant, Donald C. (Ed.). (1968). *Ancient Greek and Roman rhetoricians: A biographical dictionary*. Columbia, MO: Artcraft, 15–16.

4. Aristotle. (1954). *Rhetoric and poetics* (W. Rhys Roberts, Trans.). The Modern Library. New York: Random House, 1355b 26.

5. The material on the history of rhetoric is taken from two sources: Thonssen, Lester, Baird, A. Craig, & Braden, Waldo W. (1970). *Speech criticism* (2nd ed.). New York: The Ronald Press; and Harper, Nancy. (1979). *Human communication theory: The history of a paradigm*. Rochelle Park, NJ: Hayden Book Company.

6. Cicero. (1939). *Orator* (H. M. Hubell, Trans.). Cambridge, MA: Harvard University Press, 101. For a summary of Cicero's attitudes toward style, see Harper, 46–47.

7. Cicero, II. xliii, 182.

8. Plato. (1952). *Phaedrus, Gorgias* (Benjamin Jowett, Trans.). Oxford: Clarendon, 261.

9. Harper, 70.

10. Augustine. (1952). *On Christian doctrine* (J. F. Shaw, Trans.). Great Books of the Western World: Vol. 18. Chicago: Encyclopaedia Britannica, IV.2.

11. *Ibid.*, II.l; Capes, W. W. (1877). *University life in ancient Athens*. London: Longmans, Green, and Co.

12. Augustine, II.2.

13. Arnold, Carroll C., & Frandsen, Kenneth D. (1984). Conceptions of rhetoric and communication. In Carroll C. Arnold & John Waite Bowers (Eds.), *Handbook of rhetorical and communication theory*. Boston: Allyn and Bacon, 27.

14. Golden, James L., Berquist, Goodwin F., & Coleman, William E. (1976). *The rhetoric of Western thought*. Dubuque, IA: Kendall/Hunt Publishing Company, 85.

15. Ehninger, Douglas. (1952, September). Dominant trends in English rhetorical thought, 1750–1800. *Southern Speech Journal*, 3–11.

16. For the original discussion see Hugh C. Dick (Ed.). (1955). *Selected writings of Francis Bacon*. New York: The Modern Library. For an excellent commentary, see Golden et al., 81–82. A new edition with a 2000 publication date is available.

17. Quotations from Bacon are taken from Golden et al., 82.

18. Leff, Michael C., & Procario, Margaret Orgen (1985). Rhetorical theory in speech communication. In Thomas W. Benson (Ed.), *Speech communication in the twentieth century*. Carbondale: Southern Illinois University Press, 4.

19. For a similar but more sophisticated example of source credibility research, see Bernstein, Arla G. (2000). The effects of message theme, policy explicitness, and candidate gender. *Communication Quarterly, 48*(2), 159–174.

20. Bormann, Ernest G. (1980). *Communication theory*. New York: Holt, Rinehart & Winston, 10.

21. From the reference list accompanying Gregg, Richard B. (1985). Criticism of symbolic inducement: A critical–theoretical connection. In Benson, 380–381.

22. From the table of contents of Arnold & Bowers, v–vi.

CHAPTER 2

1. Dance, Frank E. X. (1970). The "concept" of communication. *Journal of Communication, 20,* 201–210.

2. Dance, Frank E. X., & Larson, Carl E. (1972). *Speech communication: Concepts and behavior*. New York: Holt, Rinehart & Winston, 1–16.

3. Book, Cassandra, et al. (1980). *Human communication: Principles, contexts, and skills*. New York: St. Martin's, 31–34.

4. For a general discussion of communication perspectives, see Fisher, B. Aubrey. (1978). *Perspectives on human communication*. New York: Macmillan.

5. Gergen, Kenneth J., & Davis, Keith E. (1985). *The social construction of the person*. New York: Springer-Verlag.

6. Fisher, B. Aubrey. (1982). A view from system theory. In Frank E. X. Dance (Ed.), *Human communication theory: Comparative essays*. New York: Harper & Row.

7. Watzlawick, Paul, Bavelas, Janet Beavin, & Jackson, Don D. (1967). *Pragmatics of human communication*. New York: Norton.

8. Aune, James Arnt. (1999). Catching the third wave: The dialectic of rhetoric and technology. In Thomas Rosteck (Ed.), *At the intersection: Critical studies and rhetorical studies*. New York: Guilford, 84–100, 85.

9. Condit, Celeste Michelle. (1999). The character of "history" in rhetoric and cultural studies: Recoding genetics. In Rosteck, 168–185, 169.

10. Sloop, John M., & Olson, Mark. (1999). Cultural struggle: A politics of meaning in rhetorical studies. In Rosteck, 248–265, 250.

11. Brummett, Barry, & Bowers, Detine L. (1999). Subject positions as a site of rhetorical struggle: Representing African Americans. In Rosteck, 117–136, 117.

12. Condit, 1999, 170; Nelson, Cary. (1999). The linguisticality of cultural studies: Rhetoric, close reading, and contextualization. In Rosteck, 211–225, 213.

13. Condit, 1999, 173.

14. The origins of cultural studies can be found in Williams Raymond. (1973). *The country and the city*. New York: Oxford University Press; and Thompson, E. P. (1966). *The making of the English working class*. NY: Vintage. For other influential sources, see Hall, Stuart, et al. (1978). *Policing the crisis: Mugging, the state, and law and order*. London: Macmillan; Grossberg, Lawrence, Nelson, Cary, & Treichler, Paula A. (Eds.) (1992) *Cultural studies*. New York: Routledge Fiske, John. (1989). *Understanding the popular*.

Boston: Unwin Hyman; and Fiske, John. (1994). *Television culture*. London: Routledge.

15. Hymes, Dell. (1974). *Foundations in sociolinguistics: An ethnographic approach*. Philadelphia: University of Pennsylvania Press.

CHAPTER 3

1. The original study is reported in O'Brien, Brian. (1959). How much can we see? In Robert S. Daniel (Ed.), *Contemporary readings in general psychology*. Boston: Houghton Mifflin, 270. It is retold and related to communication in Brooks, William D. (1974). *Speech communication* (2nd ed.). Dubuque, IA: William C. Brown, 23–24.

2. This definition is taken from the home page of the International Listening Association Website. Retrieved 11/29/2005 from www.listen.org.

3. Nichols, Ralph G., & Stevens, Leonard. (1957). *Are you listening?* New York: McGraw-Hill, 12–13.

4. Wolff, Florence I., Marsnik, Nadine C., Tacey, William S., & Nichols, Ralph G. (1983). *Perceptive listening*. New York: Holt, Rinehart & Winston, 29.

5. Cooper, L. O. (1997). Listening competency in the workplace: A model for training. *Business Communication Quarterly, 60*(4), 75–84, cited in Brownell, Judi. (2006). *Listening: Attitudes, principles, and skills* (3rd ed.). Boston: Allyn & Bacon, 9.

6. Salopek, J. (1999). Is anyone listening? *Training & Development, 53*(9), 58–59, cited in Brownell 9.

7. Brownell 10. See also Bentley, S. C. (1998). Listening better. *Nursing Homes, 47*(2), 56–60; Anderson, D. A. (2000). Effective communicative and listening skills revisited. *Marine Crops Gazette, 84*(3), 60–61; Goby, J., & Lewis, H. (2000). The key role of listening in business: A study of the Singapore insurance industry. *Business Communication Quarterly, 63*(2), 41–51; Kemp, M. (2000). Listening skill saves time, increases effectiveness. *The American Salesman, 45*(9), 3–8; Feiertag, H. (2002). Listening skills, enthusiasm top list of salespeople's best traits. *Hotel & Motel Management, 217*(13), 20; Render, M. (2000). Better listening makes for a better marketing message. *Marketing News, 34*(19), 22; Steil, L. K., & Brommelje, R. K. (2004). *Listening leaders: The ten golden rules to listen, lead, and succeed*. St. Paul, MN: Beaver's Pond Press.

8. James, William. (1890). *Principles of psychology*. New York: Holt; Neisser, Ulrich. (1967). *Cognitive psychology*. New York: Appleton-Century-Crofts.

9. Schneider, David L., Hastorf, Albert, & Ellsworth, Phoebe C. (1979). *Person perception* (2nd ed) Reading, MA: Addison-Wesley.

10. For a brief description and comparison of social cognitive schemata, see Chapter 3 in Trenholm, Sarah, & Jensen, Arthur (2004). *Interpersonal communication* (5th ed.). New York: Oxford University Press. For a fuller discussion of some of the issues in schema theory as applied to media perception, see Wicks, Robert H. (1992). Schema theory and measurement in mass communication research: Theoretical and methodological issues in news information processing. *Communication Yearbook, 15,* 115–145. See also

Garramone, Gina M. (1992). A broader and "warmer" approach to schema theory. *Communication Yearbook, 15,* 146–154.

11. Canter, Nancy, & Mischel, Walter. (1979). Prototypes in person perception. In Leonard Berkowitz (Ed.), *Advances in experimental social psychology* (Vol. 12). New York: Academic Press. See also Pavitt, Charles, & Haight, Larry. (1985). The "competent communicator" as a cognitive prototype. *Human Communication Research, 12,* 225–240.

12. For the original expression of construct theory, see Kelly, George A. (1955). *The psychology of personal constructs, Vol. I: A theory of personality*. New York: Norton.

13. Bargh, John A. (1988). Automatic information processing: Implications for communication and affect. In Lewis Donohew, Howard E. Sypher, & E. Tory Higgins (Eds.), *Communication, social cognition, and affect*. Hillsdale, NJ: Lawrence Erlbaum Associates, 18.

14. *Ibid*.

15. Crockett, Walter H. (1965). *Cognitive complexity and impression formation*. In Brendan A. Maher (Ed.), *Progress in experimental personality research, Vol. II*. New York: Academic; Delia, Jesse G., Clark, Ruth Anne, & Switzer, David E. (1974). Cognitive complexity and impression formation in informal social interaction. *Speech Monographs, 41,* 299–308; and Hale, Claudia, & Delia, Jesse. (1976). Cognitive complexity and social perspective-taking. *Communication Monographs, 43,* 195–203. For examples of studies on the impact of cognitive complexity in interpersonal relations, see Burleson, Brant R., & Samter, Wendy. (1990). Effects of cognitive complexity on the perceived importance of communication skills in friends. *Communication Research, 17*(2), 165–182; Samter, Wendy. (2002). How gender and cognitive complexity influence the provision of emotional support: A study of indirect effects. *Communication Reports, 15*(1), 5–16; Koesten, Joy, & Anderson, Karen. (2004). The influence of family communication patterns, cognitive complexity and interpersonal competence on adolescent risk behaviors. *Journal of Family Communication, 4*(2), 99–121.

16. Schank, R., & Abelson, Robert. (1977). *Scripts, plans, goals, and understanding: An inquiry into human knowledge structures*. Hillsdale, NJ: Lawrence Erlbaum Associates.

17. Sypher, Howard E., Donohew, Lewis, & Higgins, E. Tory. (1988). An overview of the roles of social cognition and affect in communication. In Donohew, Sypher, & Higgins, 35.

18. Bower, G. H., Black, J. B., & Turner, T. J. (1979). Scripts in memory for text. *Cognitive Psychology, 11,* 177–220; Loftus, E. F., & Zanni, G. (1975). Eyewitness testimony: The influence of the wording of a question. *Bulletin of the Psychonomic Society, 5,* 86–88; and Picek, J. S., Sherman, S. J., & Shiffrin, R. M. (1975). Cognitive organization and encoding of social structures. *Journal of Personality and Social Psychology, 31,* 758–768.

19. Petty, Richard E., Cacioppo, John T., & Kasmer, Jeff A. (1988). The role of affect in the elaboration likelihood model of persuasion. In Donohew, Sypher, & Higgins, 119. See also McGuire, William. (1985). Attitudes and attitude change. In G. Lindzey & E. Aronson (Eds.), *The handbook of social psychology* (3rd ed., Vol. 2). New York: Random House, 233–346; and Taylor, S. E. (1981). The interface of cognitive

and "social" psychology. In J. H. Harvey (Ed.), *Cognition, social behavior, and the environment*. Hillsdale, NJ: Lawrence Erlbaum Associates.

20. Bargh, 28.

21. Langer, Ellen J. (1989). Minding matters: The consequences of mindlessness-mindfulness. In Leonard Berkowitz (Ed.), *Advances in experimental social psychology* (Vol. 23). New York: Academic, 137–173.

22. Baddeley, Alan. (1991). *Your memory: A user's guide*. New York: Macmillan, 82.

23. Weaver, Richard. (1953). *The ethics of rhetoric*. Chicago: Regnery.

24. Pratkanis, Anthony, & Aronson, Elliot. (2000). *The age of propaganda: The everyday use and abuse of persuasion*. New York: W. H. Freeman and Company, 75.

25. Henderson, John R. ICYouSee: T is for thinking, Ithaca College Library. Retrieved 12/19/2005 from www.ithaca.edu/library/training/think1.html.

26. Barnes, Susan. (2003). *Computer-mediated communication: Human to human communication across the Internet*. Boston: Allyn & Bacon, 125–126.

27. Henderson, op cit., www.ithaca.edu/library/training/think4.html.

28. Gudykunst, William B., & Kim, Young Yun. (1997). *Communicating with strangers: An approach to intercultural communication* (3rd ed). New York: McGraw-Hill, 265–266.

29. Chen, Guo-Ming, & Starosta, William J. (1998). *Foundations of intercultural communication*. Boston: Allyn and Bacon, 183.

30. Pratkanis & Aronson, 60–64.

31. Loftus, Elizabeth F. (1993). The reality of repressed memories. *American Psychologist, 48,* 518–537; Loftus, Elizabeth, and Loftus, G. R. (1980). On the permanence of stored memories. *American Psychologist, 35,* 409–420.

32. Brownell, 2006, 157–162.

33. Zuckerman, Marvin. (1988). Behavior and biology: Research on sensation seeking and reactions to the media. In Donohew, Sypher, & Higgins, 173.

34. *Ibid.,* 174.

35. Bargh, John A. (1984). Automatic and subconscious processing of social information. In Robert S. Wyler, Jr., & Thomas K. Srull (Eds.), *Handbook of social cognition* (Vol. 3). Hillsdale, NJ: Lawrence Erlbaum Associates.

36. Nisbett, R., & Ross, L. (1980). *Human inference: Strategies and shortcomings of social judgment*. Englewood Cliffs, NJ: Prentice-Hall.

37. An early statement of the cognitive response model can be found in Petty, Richard E., Ostrom, Thomas M., & Brock, Timothy C. (1981). *Cognitive responses in persuasion*. Hillsdale, NJ: Lawrence Erlbaum Associates.

CHAPTER 4

1. Orwell, George. (1949). *1984*. New York: Harcourt, Brace & World, 311. See also the appendix on Newspeak.

2. Lutz, William. (1989). *New double-speak*. New York: Harper & Row, 9.

3. Fromkin, Victoria, & Rodman, Robert. (1988). *An introduction to language* (4th ed.). New York: Holt, Rinehart and Winston, 4.

4. Saussure, Ferdinand de. (1966). *Course in general linguistics*. London: McGraw-Hill.

5. Chen, Guo-Ming, & Starosta, William J. (1998). *Foundations of intercultural communication*. Boston: Allyn and Bacon, 36.

6. Aristotle. (1963). *De interpretatione* (J. L. Ackrill, Trans.). Clarendon Aristotle Series. Oxford, UK: Oxford University Press, 43; Arnauld, A., & Lancelot, C. (1968). *Grammaire de Port-Royal* (R. Alston, Ed. and Trans.). Menston, UK: Scolar, 22; cited and discussed in Sperber, Dan, & Wilson, Deirdre. (1986). *Relevance: Communication and cognition*. Cambridge, MA: Harvard University Press, 5–6.

7. Carmichael, L., Hogan, H. P., & Walter, A. A. (1932). An experimental study of the effect of language on the reproduction of visually perceived forms. *Journal of Experimental Psychology, 15,* 73–86; Slobin, Dan. (1971). *Psycholinguistics*. Glenview, IL: Scott, Foresman, 103.

8. Mandelbaum, D. B. (Ed.). (1958). *Selected writings of Edward Sapir in language, culture and personality*. Berkeley: University of California Press, 162.

9. Slobin, 129.

10. Cohn, Carol. (1987). Sex and death in the rational world of defense intellectuals. *Signs: Journal of Women in Culture and Society, 12*(4), 690.

11. The latter example is taken from Lutz, 176. For additional examples, see 175–177.

12. Cohn, 713.

13. The originators of CMM theory are Vernon Cronen and W. Barnett Pearce. One of the many sources on CMM is Cronen, Vernon, Pearce, W. Barnett, & Harris, Linda. (1982). The coordinated management of meaning. In Frank E. X. Dance (Ed.), *Comparative human communication theory*. New York: Harper & Row.

14. Lakoff, Robin Tolmach. (1992). *Talking power: The politics of language in our lives*. New York: Basic, 28.

15. McLaughlin, Margaret L. (1984). *Conversation: How talk is organized*. Beverly Hills, CA: Sage, 271.

16. My discussion of the differences between public and private forms of talk is based in part on Lakoff's discussion, but her ideas have been modified. For a discussion of this distinction as applied to relationships, see Trenholm, Sarah, & Jensen, Arthur. (1992). *Interpersonal communication* (2nd ed.). Belmont, CA: Wadsworth, chapter 2.

17. Grice, H. P. (1975). Logic and conversation. In P. Cole & J. Morgan (Eds.), *Syntax and semantics* (Vol. 3). New York: Academic, 41–58.

18. Lakoff, 45.

19. The four sets of questions were suggested by, but are not identical to, those used by Lakoff, 140.

20. Tannen, Deborah. (1990). *You just don't understand: Women and men in conversation*. New York: Ballantine.

21. Condry, John, & Condry, Sandra. (1976). Sex differences: A study of the eye of the beholder. *Child Development, 47,* 812–819; cited in Tannen, 1990, 228.

22. See, for example, Weatherall, Ann. (1998). Re-visioning gender and language research. *Women and language, 21*(1), 1–9. Electronic full-text version. Retrieved September 15, 2003, from http://infotrac-college.thomsonlearning.com; and

Kyratzis, Amy. (2000). Tactical uses of narratives in nursery school same-sex groups. *Discourse processes, 29*(3), 269–299.

23. Tannen, 1990, 44; Maltz, Daniel N., & Borker, Ruth A. (1982). A cultural approach to male-female miscommunication. In John J. Gumperz (Ed.), *Language and social identity*. Cambridge, UK: Cambridge University Press.

24. Tannen, 1990, 177–178.

25. Kramer, Cheris, Thorne, Barrie, & Henley, Nancy. (1978). Perspectives on language and communication. *Signs: Journal of Women in Culture and Society, 3*(3), 638–651, 638.

26. Crawford, M., & English, L. (1984). Generic versus specific inclusion of women in language: Effects on recall. *Journal of Psycholinguistic Research, 13*, 373–381.

27. Kitto, J. (1989). Gender reference terms: Separating the women from the girls. *British Journal of Social Psychology, 28*, 185–187.

28. Weatherall, 2.

29. Cameron, Deborah (1998). Gender, language, and discourse: A review essay. *Signs, 23*(4), 945. Electronic full-text version retrieved from http://infotrac-college.thomson learning.com on September 25, 2003, 2. See also, Wareing, Shan. (1996). What do we know about language and gender? Paper presented to the Eleventh Sociolinguistic Symposium, Cardiff, September 5–7, cited in Cameron.

30. Aries, Elizabeth. (1996). *Men and women in interaction: Reconsidering the differences*. New York: Oxford, vii.

31. Ibid., viii.

32. Ibid., 205.

33. West, Candace, & Zimmerman, Don. (1987). Doing gender. *Gender and society, 1*(2), 125–151, 140.

34. Tannen, Deborah. (1994). *Gender and discourse*. New York: Oxford University Press, 198.

35. Cameron, 6.

36. Aries, 204.

37. The discussion here is modeled after that in Brake, Terence, Walter, Danielle Medina, & Walker, Thomas (Tim). (1995). *Doing business internationally: The guide to cross-cultural success*. New York: Irwin Professional Publishing, 54–59.

38. Brake, 54.

39. Lustig, Myron W., & Koester, Jolene. (1996). *Intercultural competence: Interpersonal communication across cultures* (2nd ed.). New York: HarperCollins, 125.

40. Brake, 57; see also, Stewart, Edward C., & Bennett, Milton J. (1991). *American cultural patterns: A cross-cultural perspective* (rev. ed.). Yarmouth, ME: Intercultural Press, 97–98.

41. Quoted in Lustig, p. 253; the original source is Beeman, William O. (1986). *Language, status, and power in Iran*. Bloomington: Indiana University Press, 86.

42. Eisenberg, Eric M. (1984, September). Ambiguity as strategy in organizational communication. *Communication Monographs, 51*, 227–241.

43. Bavelas, Janet Beavin, Black, Alex, Chovil, Nicole, & Mullett, Jennifer. (1990). *Equivocal communication*. Newbury Park, CA: Sage. Situations are modified from those used by Bavelas (68, 69); response alternatives are verbatim.

44. Ibid., 260.

45. Mehrabian, Albert. (1967). Attitudes inferred from nonimmediacy of verbal communications. *Journal of Verbal Learning and Verbal Behavior, 6*, 294–295.

46. *San Francisco Chronicle*, 30 January, 1984.

47. Berger, Charles R., & Bradac, James J. (1982). *Language and social knowledge: Uncertainty in interpersonal relations*. London: Edward Arnold, 203–204.

48. Tannen, Deborah. (1984). *Conversational style*. Norwood, NJ: Ablex.

49. Lakoff, 180.

50. Lakoff, George, & Johnson, Mark. (1980). *Metaphors we live by*. Chicago: The University of Chicago Press, 4.

51. Ibid., 5.

52. Huxley, Aldous. (1962). Words and their meanings. In Max Black (Ed.), *The importance of language*. Englewood Cliffs, NJ: Prentice-Hall, 4–5.

CHAPTER 5

1. Ekman, Paul, & Friesen, Wallace. (1975). *Unmasking the face: A guide to recognizing emotions from facial expressions*. Englewood Cliffs, NJ: Prentice-Hall.

2. Mehrabian, Albert. (1970). A semantic space for nonverbal behavior. *Journal of Counseling and Clinical Psychology, 35*, 248–257.

3. Ekman, Paul. (1965). Communication through nonverbal behavior: A source of information about an interpersonal relationship. In S. S. Tompkins & C. E. Izard (Eds.), *Affect, cognition, and personality*. New York: Springer; Knapp, Mark. (1980). *Essentials of nonverbal communication*. New York: Holt, Rinehart & Winston, 11–15.

4. Knapp, 14.

5. Weimann, John M. (1977). Explication and test of a model of communication competence. *Human Communication Research, 3*, 195–213. See also Spitzberg, Brian H., & Cupach, W. R. (1988). *Handbook for interpersonal competence research*. New York: Springer-Verlag; and Spitzberg, Brian H. (1990). Perspectives on nonverbal communication skills. In Joseph A. DeVito & Michael L. Hecht (Eds.), *The nonverbal communication reader*. Prospect Heights, IL: Waveland Press.

6. Rubenstein, C. (1980, August). Body language that speaks to muggers. *Psychology Today*, 20.

7. Ekman, Paul, & Friesen, W. V. (1969). The repertoire of nonverbal behavior: Categories, origins, usage, and coding. *Semiotica, 1*, 49–98; and Trager, G. L. (1958). Paralanguage: A first approximation. *Studies in Linguistics, 13*, 1–12.

8. Johnson, H. G., Ekman, P., & Friesen, W. V. (1975). Communicative body movements: American emblems. *Semiotica, 15*, 335–353.

9. Burgoon, Judee K., Buller, David B., & Woodall, W. Gill. (1995). *Nonverbal communication: The unspoken dialogue*. New York: McGraw-Hill, 28, 187–189.

10. Ekman, Paul, & Friesen, W. V. (1974). Detecting deception from the body or face. *Journal of Personality and Social Psychology, 29*, 288–298; Ekman, Paul, & Friesen, W. V. (1975); Zuckerman, Miron, DePaulo, Bella M., & Rosenthal, Robert. (1981).Verbal and nonverbal communication of deception. In Leonard Berkowitz (Ed.), *Advances in experimental social psychology* (Vol. 14).

New York: Academic Press; Zuckerman M., & Driver R. E., (Eds.). (1985). Telling lies: Verbal and nonverbal correlates of deception. In A. W. Siegman & S. Feldstein (Eds.), *Multichannel integrations of nonverbal behavior*. Hillsdale, NJ: Lawrence Erlbaum Associates.

11. Burgoon, Buller, & Woodall, 281–287.

12. Charlesworth, W. R., & Kreutzer, M. A. (1973). Facial expressions of infants and children. In Paul Ekman (Ed.), *Darwin and facial expressions: A century of research in review*. New York: Academic Press; Eibl-Eibesfeldt, I. (1975). *Ethology: The biology of behavior*. New York: Holt, Rinehart & Winston.

13. Ekman, Paul, & Friesen, W. V., 1975.

14. Chen, Guo-Ming, & Starosta, William J. (1998). *Foundations of intercultural communication*. Boston: Allyn and Bacon, 90.

15. Buck, Ross. (1979). Individual differences in nonverbal sending accuracy and electrodermal responding: The externalizing-internalizing dimension. In R. Rosenthal (Ed.), *Skill in nonverbal communication: Individual differences*. Cambridge, MA: Oelgeschlager, Gunn & Hain.

16. Donaldson-Evans, L. (1980). *Love's fatal glance: A study of eye imagery in the poets of the Ecole Lyonnaise*. University, MS: *Romance Monographs, 8*, 21; cited in Grumet, Gerald W. (1983). Eye contact: The core of interpersonal relatedness. *Psychiatry, 28*, 172–180, and reprinted in DeVito & Hecht, 126–137, 129.

17. Grumet, 129.

18. Hess, E. H. (1975). *The tell-tale eye*. New York: Van Nostrand; Andersen, P. A., Todd-Mancillas, W. R., & Clementa, L. D. (1980). The effects of pupil dilation on physical, social, and task attraction. *Australian SCAN of Nonverbal Communication, 7–8*, 89–96; Malandro, Loretta A., & Barker, Larry L. (1983). *Nonverbal communication*. Reading, MA: Addison-Wesley, 170–172.

19. For an interesting discussion of the function of the stare in initiating interpersonal relationships, see Wilmot, William. (1979). *Dyadic communication* (2nd ed.). Reading, MA: Addison-Wesley, 9–10.

20. Grumet, 133.

21. Miller, Patrick W. (1988). *Nonverbal communication* (3rd ed.). Washington, DC: National Education Society, 14.

22. Heinberg, P. (1964). *Voice training for speaking and reading aloud*. New York: Ronald; Burgoon, Buller, & Woodall, 68–70, also offer a good discussion of vocal qualities.

23. Malandro & Barker, 281–283; Burgoon, Buller, & Woodall, 68.

24. Bruneau, Thomas. (1973). Communicative silences: Forms and functions. *Journal of Communication, 23*, 17–46.

25. Basso, Keith H. (1992). "Speaking with names": Language and landscape among the Western Apache. In George E. Marcus (Ed.), *Rereading cultural anthropology*. Durham, NC: Duke University Press, 230; see also, Basso. (1990). "To give up on words": Silence in Western Apache culture. In Donal L. Carbaugh (Ed.), *Cultural communication and intercultural contact*. Hillsdale, NJ: Erlbaum, 303–320.

26. Gonzalez, Alexander, & Zimbardo, Philip G. (1985, March). Time in perspective. *Psychology Today*, 21–26.

27. Burgoon, Buller, & Woodall, 145. See also Hall, Edward T. (1959). *The silent language*. Garden City, NY: Doubleday.

28. Gonzalez & Zimbardo, 26.

29. Lyman, Stanford M., & Scott, Marvin B. (1967). Territoriality: A neglected sociological dimension. *Social Problems, 15*(2), 236–249. An abridged version is available in DeVito & Hecht.

30. Adams, R. S., & Biddle, B. (1970). *Realities of teaching: Exploration with video tape*. New York: Holt, Rinehart & Winston; Sommer, Richard. (1969). *Personal space: The behavioral basis of design*. Englewood Cliffs, NJ: Prentice-Hall; Milandro and Barker, 202–203.

31. Feilor, Bruce S. (1991). *Learning to bow: Inside the heart of Japan*. New York: Ticknor and Fields, 19; for another discussion of Japanese and American use of space, see Brake, Terrence, Walter, Danielle Medina, & Walker, Thomas (Tim). (1995). *Doing business internationally: The guide to cross-cultural success*. New York: Irwin Professional Publishing, 60–61.

32. Feilor, 20.

33. Burgoon, Buller, & Woodall, 77–79.

34. Burgoon, Judee, & Saine, Thomas (1978). *The unspoken dialogue: An introduction to nonverbal communication*. Boston: Houghton Mifflin, 70.

35. David, F. (1978, September 27). Skin hunger—An American disease. *Woman's Day*, 48–50, 154–156; cited in Milandro & Barker, 253.

36. Milandro & Barker, 253.

37. Knapp, 119.

38. See, for example, Wells, W., & Siegel, B. (1961). Stereotyped somatypes. *Psychological Reports, 8*, 77–78.

39. Knapp, 107.

40. Milandro & Barker, 74–75.

41. Smith, Lawrence J., & Malandro, Loretta A. (Eds.). (1985). *Courtroom communication strategies*. New York: Kluwer.

42. Ruesch, Juergen, & Kees, W. (1956). *Nonverbal communication: Notes on the visual perception of human relations*. Berkeley: University of California Press.

43. Becker, Franklin D. (1977). *Housing messages*. Stroudsburg, PA: Dowden, Hutchinson & Ross, 4.

44. Becker, 5.

45. Burgoon & Saine, Chapter 4.

CHAPTER 6

1. Miller, Gerald R., & Steinberg, Mark. (1975). *Between people: A new analysis of interpersonal communication*. Chicago: Science Research Associates.

2. Trenholm, Sarah. (1991). *Human communication theory* (2nd ed.). Englewood Cliffs, NJ: Prentice-Hall, 161.

3. Allen, Woody. (1982). *Four films of Woody Allen*. New York: Random House, 105.

4. Gilbert, Paul. (2005). Social mentalities: A biopsychosocial and evolutionary approach to social relationships. In Mark W. Baldwin (Ed.), *Interpersonal cognition*. New York: Guilford Press, 299. See also, Cacioppo, J. T., Berston, G. G., Sheridan, J. F., & McClintock, M. K. (2000). Multilevel integrative analysis of human behavior: Social neuroscience and the complementing nature of social and biological approaches. *Psychological Bulletin, 126*, 829–843; Wearden, A. J., Tarrier, N., Barrowclough, C., Zastowny, T. R., & Rahil,

A. A. (2000). A review of expressed emotion research in health care. *Clinical Psychology Review, 5,* 633–666; and Luecken, Linda J., Appelhans, Bradley M., Kraft, Amy, & Brown, Ana. (2006). Never far from home: A cognitive-affective model of the impact of early-life family relationships on psychological stress responses in adulthood. *Journal of Social and Personal Relationships, 23*(2), 189–203.

5. Cooley, Charles Horton. (1969). The social self: On the meaning of "I." In Chad Gordon & Kenneth J. Gergen (Eds.), *The self in social interactions, I: Classic and contemporary perspectives.* New York: Wiley, 87–91.

6. Rosenberg, Morris. (1967) Psychological selectivity in self-esteem formation. In Carolyn W. Sherif & Muzafer Sherif (Eds.), *Attitude, ego-involvement, and change.* New York: Wiley, 26–50; cited in Wilmot, William. (1987). Dyadic communication (3rd ed.). New York: Random House.

7. Rawlins, William. (1983). Openness as problematic in ongoing friendship: Two conversational dilemmas. *Communication Monographs, 50,* 1–13; Baxter, Leslie A. (1990). Dialectical contradictions in developing relationships. *Journal of Social and Personal Relationships, 7,* 69–88.

8. Wilmot, William. (1987). *Dyadic communication* (3rd ed.). New York: Random House, 169.

9. Cupach, William R., & Metts, Sandra. (1994). *Facework.* Thousand Oaks, CA: Sage, 3.

10. Brown, Penelope, & Levinson, Stephen C. (1987). *Politeness: Some universals in language usage.* Cambridge, UK: Cambridge University Press.

11. For some recent research on face needs and politeness, see Johnson, Danette I. (2007). Politeness theory and conversational refusals: Associations between various types of face threat and perceived competence. *Western Journal of Communication, 71*(3), 196–215; Johnson, Danette I., Roloff, Michael E., & Riffee, Melissa A. (2004). Politeness theory and refusals of requests: Face threat as a function of expressed obstacles. *Communication Studies, 55*(2), 227–238; Adrianne D. Kunkel & others. (2003). Identity implications of influence goals: Initiating, intensifying, and ending romantic relationships. *Western Journal of Communication, 67*(4), 382–412.

12. Sieburg, Evelyn. (1975). *Interpersonal confirmation: A paradigm for conceptualization and measurement.* San Diego: United States International University. (ERIC Document Reproduction Service No. ED 098 634).

13. Wilmot, 148.

14. Knapp, Mark L., & Vangelisti, Anita L. (1992). *Interpersonal communication and human relationships* (2nd ed.). Boston: Allyn and Bacon; Wood, Julia T. (1982). Communication and relational culture: Bases for the study of human relationships. *Communication Quarterly, 30*(2), 75–83.

15. Knapp & Vangelisti, 39.

16. Baxter, Leslie A., & Wilmot, William. (1984). "Secret tests": Social strategies for acquiring information about the state of the relationship. *Human Communication Research, 11,* 171–202.

17. Altman, Irwin, & Taylor, Dalmas A. (1973). *Social penetration: The development of interpersonal relationships.* New York: Holt, Rinehart and Winston.

18. Duck, Steve. (1973). Interpersonal communication in developing acquaintance. In Gerald R. Miller (Ed.), *Explorations in interpersonal communication.* Beverly Hills, CA: Sage, 127–148.

19. Zhang, Shuangyue, & Stafford, Laura. (2007). Paper delivered at the annual meeting of the International Communication Association; available online from EBSCOhost. For a discussion of a range of relational maintenance strategies, see also Guerrero, Laura K., Andersen, Peter A., & Afifi, Walid A., *Close encounters: Communicating in relationships* (Mt. View, CA: Mayfield, 2001), 230–231. See also, Dainton, Marianne, & Gross, Jamie. (2008). The use of negative behaviors to maintain relationships. *Communication Research Reports, 25*(3), 179–191.

20. Canary, Daniel J., & Stafford, Laura. (1992). Relational maintenance strategies and equity in marriage. *Communication Monographs, 59,* 243–268.

21. Stafford, Laura, Dainton, Marianne, & Haas, Stephen. (2000). Measuring routine and strategic relational maintenance: Scale revision, sex versus gender roles, and the prediction of relational characteristics. *Communication Monographs, 67*(3), 306–323. See also, Myers, Scott A., & Glover, Natica P. (2007). Emerging adults' use of relational maintenance behaviors with their parents. *Communication Research Reports, 24*(3), 257–264.

22. Weigel, Daniel J., & Ballard-Reisch, Deborah S. (2008). Relational maintenance, satisfaction, and commitment in marriages: An actor-partner analysis. *Journal of Family Communication, 8*(3), 212–229; Stafford, Laura, & Canary, Daniel J. (2006). Equity and interdependence as predictors of relational maintenance strategies. *The Journal of Family Communication, 6*(4), 227–254; Johnson, Amy Janan, Haigh, Michel M., Becker, Jennifer A., Craig, Elizabeth A., & Wigley, Shelley. (2008). College students' use of relational management strategies in email in long-distance and geographically close relationships. *Journal of Computer-Mediated Communication, 13,* 381–404; Buoy Kissick, Amana, & Yum, Young-Ok. (2007). Differences in relationship quality and maintenance behaviors between active parents and empty nesters. Conference paper delivered at the Annual Meeting of the International Communication Association; available online from EBSCOhost. See also Canary & Stafford, 1992.

23. Guerrero, Laura K., & Chavez, Alana M.(2005). Relational maintenance in cross-sex friendships characterized by different types of romantic intent: An exploratory study. *Western Journal of Communication, 69*(4), 339–358; Canary, Daniel J., Stafford, Laura, Hause, Kimberley S., & Wallace, Lisa A. (1993). An inductive analysis of relational maintenance strategies: Comparisons among lovers, relatives, friends, and others. *Communication Research Reports, 10*(1), 5–14.

24. Myers, Scott A., Brann, Maria, & Rittenour, Christine E. (2008). Interpersonal communication motives as a predictor of early and middle adulthood siblings' use of relational maintenance behaviors. *Communication Research Reports, 25*(2), 155–167; Serewicz, Mary Claire Morr, Dickson, Fran C., Morrison, Jennifer, Huynh Thi Anh, & Poole, L. Lori. (2007). Family privacy orientation, relational maintenance, and family satisfaction in young adults' family

relationships. *The Journal of Family Communication, 7*(2), 123–142. Myers, Scott A., & Glover, Natica P. (2007). Emerging adults' use of relational maintenance behaviors with their parents. *Communication Research Reports, 24*(3), 257–264.

25. Goodboy, Alan K., & Myers, Scott A. (2008). Relational maintenance behaviors of friends with benefits: Investigating equity and relational characteristics. *Human Communication, 11*(1), 71–86.

26. Yum, Young-Ok, & Li, Han Z. (2007). Associations among attachment style, maintenance strategies, and relational quality across cultures. *Journal of Intercultural Communication Research, 36*(2), 71–89; Guerrero, Laura K., & Bachman, Guy F. (2006). Associations among relational maintenance behaviors, attachment-style categories, and attachment dimensions. *Communication Studies, 57*(3), 341–361.

27. Henson, Donna F., Dybvig-Pawelko, Kristin C., & Canary, Daniel C. (2004). The effects of loneliness on relational maintenance behaviors: An attributional perspective. *Communication Research Reports, 21*(4), 411–419.

28. Afifi, Tamara, Caughlin, John, & Afifi, Walid. (2007). The dark side (and light side) of avoidance and secrets. In Brian H. Spitzberg & William R. Cupach (Eds.), *The dark side of interpersonal communication*. Mahwah, NJ: Lawrence Erlbaum, 68; See also Smyth, Joshua M., & Pennebaker, James W. (2001). What are the health effects of disclosure? In Andrew S. Baum, Tracey A. Revenson, & Jerome E. Singer (Eds.), *Handbook of health psychology*. Mahwah, NJ: Lawrence Erlbaum.

29. Braithwaite, Dawn O., & others. (2001). "Becoming a family": Developmental processes represented in blended family discourse. *Journal of Applied Communication Research, 29*, 221–247; Caughlin, John P., & others (2000). Intrafamily secrets in various family configurations: A communication boundary management perspective. *Communication Studies, 51*, 116–134.

30. Johnson, David W. (1993). *Reaching out: Interpersonal effectiveness and self-actualization* (5th ed.). Boston: Allyn and Bacon, 179. Johnson gives excellent sample problems and responses, as well as good advice on how to respond helpfully.

31. *Ibid.,* 181.

32. *Ibid.,* 183–184.

33. *Ibid.,* Chapter 8, 205–265.

34. *Ibid.,* 222.

35. *Ibid.,* 231.

36. Chen, Guo-Ming, & Starosta, William J. (1998). *Foundations of intercultural communication*. Boston: Allyn & Bacon, 128. For a full discussion of the use of intermediaries, see Ma, R. (1992). The role of unofficial intermediaries in interpersonal conflicts in the Chinese culture. *Communication Quarterly, 40,* 269–278.

37. Reeves-Ellington, Richard H. (1993). Using cultural skills for cooperative advantage in Japan. *Human Organization, 52,* 203–215; quoted in Lustig, Myron W., & Koester Jolene. (1996). *Intercultural competence: Interpersonal communication across cultures* (2nd ed.). New York: HarperCollins.

38. Trenholm & Jensen, 327–328.

39. Lea, Martin, & Spears, Russell. (1995). Love at first byte? Building personal relationships over computer networks. In Julia Wood & Steve Duck (Eds.), *Understudied relationships: Off the beaten track*. Thousand Oaks, CA: Sage, 201.

40. *Ibid.,* 206.

41. Rosenberg, M. S. (1992). Virtual reality: Reflections of life, dreams and technology. *Electronic Journal on Virtual Culture, 1.*8; quoted in Lea & Spears, 204.

42. Walther, Joseph B. (1996). Computer-mediated communication: Impersonal, interpersonal, and hyperpersonal interaction. *Communication Research, 23,* 3–44.

43. Anderson, Traci L., & Emmers-Sommer, Tara M. (2006). Predictors of relationship satisfaction in online romantic relationships. *Communication Studies, 57,* 153–172.

44. Walther, 1996; Walther, Joseph B. (1993). Impression development in computer-mediated interaction: A relational perspective. *Communication Research, 19,* 52–90.

45. Wallace, Patricia. (1999). *The psychology of the Internet.* New York: Cambridge University Press, 135. See also Parks, Malcolm, & Floyd, Kory. (1996). Making friends in cyberspace. *Journal of Communication, 46*(1), 80–97, and Anderson & Emmers-Sommer, 2006.

46. Switzer, Jamie. (2007). "I picture short sentences coming from short people": Creating impressions in CMC. Paper presented at the annual meeting of the International Communication Association. Available on EBSCOhost.

47. Stern, Lesa A., & Taylor, Kim. (2007). Social networking on Facebook. *Journal of the Communication, Speech, and Theatre Association of North Dakota, 20,* 9–20.

48. Toma, Cataline, Hancock, Jeff, & Ellison, Nicole. (2007). Separating face from fiction: An examination of deceptive self-presentation in online dating profiles. Paper presented at the annual meeting of the International Communication Association. Available on EBSCOhost.

49. Walther, Joseph, & others. (2008). The role of friends' appearance and behavior on evaluations of individuals on Facebook: Are we known by the company we keep? *Human Communication Research, 34,* 28–49, 32. See also, Ellison, N., Heino, R., & Gibbs, J. (2006). Managing impressions online: Self-presentation process in the online dating environment. *Journal of Computer-Mediated Communication, 11*(2), Article 2. Retrieved 10/10/2008 from http://jcmc.indiana.edu/vol11/issue2/ellison.html; Ellison, Nichole B., Steinfield, Charles., & Lampe, Cliff. (2007). The benefits of Facebook "friends": social capital and college students' use of online social networks sites. *Journal of Computer-Mediated Communication, 12*(4). Retrieved 10/10/2008, from http://jcmc.indiana.edu/vol12/issue4/ellison.html.

50. Tong, Stephanie Tom, Van deer Heide, Brandon, Langwell, Lindsey, & Walther, Joseph B. (2008). Too much of a good thing? The relationship between number of friends and interpersonal impressions on Facebook. *Journal of Computer-Mediated Communication 13,* 531–549.

51. Johnson, Amy Janan, & others. (2008). College students' use of relational management strategies in email in long-distance and geographically close relationships. *Journal of Computer-Mediated Communication, 13,* 381–404, 383.

52. Wang, Hua, & Andersen, Peter A. (2007). Computer-mediated communication in relationship maintenance: An

examination of self-disclosure in long-distance friendships. Paper presented at the annual meeting of the International Communication Association, 22. Available on EBSCOhost.

53. Johnson & others, 385.

54. Kramer, Melinda. (2001). *Business communication in context*. Upper Saddle River, NJ: Prentice Hall, 428. See also Harcourt, Jules. (1990). Developing ethical messages. *The Bulletin of the Association for Business Communication*. 53(3), 19; and Dreilinger, Craig, & Rice, Dan. (1991). Office ethics. *Working Woman*, 35.

CHAPTER 7

1. Jensen, Arthur D., & Chilberg, Joseph C. (1991). *Small group communication*. Belmont, CA: Wadsworth, 5.

2. Pittinger, R. E., Hockett, C. F., & Danehy, J. J. (1960). *The first five minutes: A sample of microscopic interview analysis*. Ithaca, NY: Martineau, 223.

3. Cited in Rothwell, J. Dan. (1992). *In mixed company: Small group communication*. New York: Harcourt Brace Jovanovich, 39.

4. For a good discussion of the problems of triads, see Wilmot, William W. (1987). *Dyadic communication* (3rd ed.). New York: Random House, 21–32.

5. Bormann, Ernest. (1990). *Small group communication: Theory and practice*. New York: Harper & Row, 2.

6. Rothwell, 41.

7. Schutz, William. (1958). *Firo: A three-dimensional theory of interpersonal behavior*. New York: Holt, Rinehart & Winston.

8. Johnson, David W., & Johnson, Frank P. (1994). *Joining together: Group theory and group skills*. Boston: Allyn and Bacon, 254.

9. Moreland, Richard, & Levine, John. (1982). Socialization in small groups: Temporal changes in individual-group relations. In Leonard Berkowitz (Ed.), *Advances in experimental social psychology* (Vol. 15). New York: Academic; and Moreland, Richard, & Levine, John. (1987). Group dynamics over time: Development and socialization in small groups. In J. McGrath (Ed.), *The social psychology of time*. Beverly Hills, CA: Sage.

10. Hollander, Edwin. (1958). Conformity, status and idiosyncrasy credit. *Psychological Review*, 65, 117–127.

11. There are many analyses of the *Challenger* case. See Anatomy of a tragedy. (1987). *IEEE Spectrum*, 24, 44–51; Jaksa, James, Pritchard, Michael, & Kramer, Ronald. (1988). Ethics in organizations: The *Challenger* explosion. In James Jaksa & Michael Pritchard (Eds.), *Communication ethics: Methods of analysis*. Belmont, CA: Wadsworth; Kruglanski, A. (1986, August). Freeze-think and the *Challenger*. *Psychology Today*, 48–49; Hirokawa, Randy Y., Gouran, Dennis S., & Martz, A. E. (1988). Understanding the sources of faulty group decision making: A lesson from the *Challenger* disaster. *Small Group Behavior*, 19, 411–433; Renz, M. A., & Greg, J. (1988). Flaws in the decision making process: Assessment of risk in the decision to launch flight 51-L. *Central States Speech Journal*, 39, 67–75.

12. Janis, Irving. (1972). *Victims of groupthink*. Boston: Houghton Mifflin.

13. Hogg, Michael A. (2005). The social identity perspective. In Susan A. Wheelan (Ed.), *The handbook of group research and practice*. Thousand Oaks, CA: Sage Publications, 136.

14. Miller, D. T., Downs, J. S., & Prentice, D. A. (1998). Minimum conditions for the creation of a unit relationship: The social bond between birthdaymates. *European Journal of Social Psychology*, 28, 475–481. See also Bourhis, R. Y., Sachdev, I., & Gagnon, A. (1994). Intergroup research with the Tajfel matrices: Methodological notes. In Mark Zanna and J. Olson (Eds.), *The psychology of prejudice: The Ontario symposium*. (Vol. 7). Hillsdale, NJ: Lawrence Erlbaum.

15. Abrams, Dominic, Frings, Daniel, & deMoura, Georgina Randsley (2005). Group identity and self-definition. In Wheelan, 343.

16. Hogg, 141; Hogg, Michael A. (2004). Uncertainty and extremism: Identification with high entitativity groups under conditions of uncertainty. In V. Yzerbyt, C. M. Judd, & O. Corneille (Eds.), *The psychology of group perception: Perceived variability, entitativity, and essentialism*. New York: Psychology Press.

17. Abrams, Frings, & deMoura, 342; Marques, J. M., & Paez, D. (1994). The black sheep effect: Social categorization, rejection of ingroup deviates, and perception of group variability. In W. Stroebe & M. Hewstone (Eds.), *European review of social psychology* (Vol 5). Chichester, UK: Wiley, 37–68; Marques, J. M., & others (1998). The role of categorization and in-group norms in judgments of groups and their members. *Journal of Personality and Social Psychology*, 75, 976–988.

18. Tuckman, Bruce W. (1965). Developmental sequence in small groups. *Psychological Bulletin*, 63, 384–399.

19. Fisher, B. Aubrey. (1970). Decision emergence: Phases in group decision making. *Speech Monographs*, 37, 53–66. See also Fisher, B. Aubrey. (1980). *Small group decision making*, 2nd ed. New York: McGraw-Hill.

20. Wheelan, Susan A. (2005). The developmental perspective. In Wheelan (Ed.), *The handbook of group research and practice*, 130.

21. Poole, Marshall Scott. (1981). Decision development in small groups I: A comparison of two models. *Communication Monographs*, 48, 1–24; Poole, Marshall Scott. (1983). Decision development in small groups II: A study of multiple sequences in decision making. *Communication Monographs*, 50, 206–232; Poole, Marshall Scott. (1983). Decision development in small groups III: A multiple sequence model of group decision development. *Communication Monographs*, 50, 321–341; Poole, Marshall Scott, & Roth, Jonelle. (1989). Decision development in small groups V: Test of a contingency model. *Human Communication Research*, 15, 549–589.

22. Wheelan, 2005, 123.

23. Northhouse, Peter G. (2001). Trait approach. In Northhouse (Ed.), *Leadership: Theory and practice*, 2nd ed. Thousand Oaks, CA: Sage. For an overview of theories of leadership see Gouran, Dennis S. (2003). Leadership as the art of counteractive influence in decision-making and problem-solving groups. In Randy Y. Hirokawa, Robert S. Cathcart, Larry A. Samovar, & Linda D. Henman (Eds.), *Small group communication theory and practice: An anthology*. Los Angeles: Roxbury.

24. Gouran, 172. See also Aviolo, Bruce J. (1999). *Full leadership development: Building the vital forces in organizations.* Thousand Oaks, CA: Sage.

25. Hirokawa & others, 170. For the original article see Geier, J. G. (1967). A trait approach to the study of leadership in small groups. *Journal of Communication, 17,* 316–323.

26. See Lewin, Kurt, Lippitt, Ronald, & White, R. K. (1939). Patterns of aggressive behavior in experimentally created "social climates." *Journal of Psychology, 10,* 271–299; Blake, R. R., & Mouton, Jane S. (1964). *The managerial grid.* Houston, TX: Gulf; and Blake, Robert Rogers, & McCanse, Ann Adams. (1991). *Leadership dilemmas—Grid solutions.* Houston, TX: Gulf.

27. Hershey, Kenneth, & Blanchard, Paul (1969). Life-cycle theory of leadership. *Training and Development Journal, 23,* 26–34.

28. House, Robert J., & Dessler, Gary (1974). The path-goal theory of leadership: Some post hoc and a priori tests. In James G. Hunt & Lars L. Larson (Eds.), *Contingency approaches to leadership.* Carbondale: Southern Illinois University Press.

29. Fiedler, Fred E. (1964). A contingency model of leadership effectiveness. In Leonard Berkowitz (Ed.), *Advances in experimental social psychology* (Vol. 1). New York: Academic Press, 149–190.

30. Graen, George B., & Ulh-Bien, Mary. (1991). Relationship-based approach to leadership. Development of leader-member exchange (LMX) theory over 25 years: Applying a multi-level multi-domain perspective. *Leadership Quarterly, 6,* 219–247.

31. Gouran, 172–182.

32. *Ibid.,* 181–182.

33. Fisher, 1980, 223–225.

34. For the original formulation of this research and review, see Stasser, Gerald, & Titus, William. (2003). Hidden profiles: A brief history. *Psychological Inquiry, 14,* 304–313.

35. Wittenbaum, Gwen M., & Bowman, Jonathan M. (2004). A social validation explanation for mutual enhancement. *Journal of Experimental Social Psychology, 40,* 40–169; Wittenbaum, Gwen M., & Park, Ernest S. (2001). The collective preference for shared information. *Journal of Personality and Social Psychology, 10,* 10–70.

36. Wittenbaum, Gwen M., Hollingshead, Andrea B., & Botero, Isabel C. (2004). From cooperative to motivated information sharing in groups: Moving beyond the hidden profile paradigm. *Communication Monographs, 71*(3), 298, 301. For a different model of information sharing see Bonito, Joseph A. (2007). A local model of information sharing in small groups. *Communication Theory, 17,* 252–280.

37. Brodbeck, Felix C., & others (2002). The dissemination of critical, unshared information in decision-making groups: The effects of pre-discussion dissent. *European Journal of Social Psychology, 32*(1), 35–56.

38. Wittenbaum, Hollingshead, & Botero.

39. Gibb, Jack R. (1961). Defensive communication. *Journal of Communication, 11,* 141–148.

40. Bormann, 243.

41. Dewey, John. (1910). *How we think.* Lexington, MA: Heath. For a complete and detailed discussion of the standard agenda, see Wood, Julia T., Phillips, Gerald M., & Pedersen, Douglas J. (1986). *Group discussion: A practical guide to participation and leadership.* New York: Harper & Row.

42. Johnson & Johnson, 269.

43. Rothwell, 223–224.

44. Johnson & Johnson, 272–273; Lewin, Kurt. (1944). Dynamics of group action. *Educational Leadership, 1,* 195–200.

45. Johnson & Johnson, 320–321. The Johnsons draw their discussion from David, G., & Houtman, S. (1968). *Thinking creatively: A guide to training imagination.* Madison: Wisconsin Research and Development Center for Cognitive Learning.

46. Delbecq, A. (1975). *Group techniques for program planning.* Glenview, IL: Scott Foresman.

47. Brilhart, J. K., & Galanes, G. J. (1989). *Effective group discussion.* Dubuque, IA: Brown.

48. For a good discussion of different formats, see Barker, Larry L., Wahlers, Kathy J., Cegala, Donald J., & Kibler, Robert J. (1991). *Groups in process: An introduction to small group communication* (4th ed.). Englewood Cliffs, NJ: Prentice-Hall, especially Chapter 10.

49. Hollingshead, Andrea B., & Contractor, Noshir S. (2006). New media and small group organizing. In Leah Lievrouw & Sonia Livingstone (Eds.), *Handbook of new media: Social shaping and social consequences of ICTs.* (Updated student ed.). Thousand Oaks, CA: Sage Publications, 116.

50. Parker, Robyn E. (2003). Distinguishing characteristics of virtual groups. In Randy Y. Hirokawa, Robert S. Cathcart, Larry A. Samovar, & Linda D. Henman. *Small group communication theory and practice: An anthology.* Los Angeles: Roxbury.

51. Hollingshead & Contractor, 127.

52. *Ibid.,* 121.

53. *Ibid.,* 1, 126–128.

54. Baym, Nancy K. (2006). Interpersonal life online. In Lievrouw & Livingstone, 46.

55. Poole, Marshal Scott, & Zhang, Huiyan. (2005). Virtual teams. In Wheelan, 365–366, Susan A. Wheelan presents an excellent review of many of the factors affecting virtual teams, including personal characteristics.

56. *Ibid.,* 374.

57. Hollingshead & Contractor, 128.

58. See, for example Contractor, Noshir, and Monge, Peter R. (2002). Managing knowledge networks. *Management Communication Quarterly, 16,* 249–258; Katz, Nancy, et al. (2004). Network theory and small groups. *Small Group Research, 35,* 307–332; and Katz, Nancy, et al. (2005). The network perspective on small groups: Theory and research. In Marshall Scott Poole & Andrea B. Hollingshead (Eds.), *Theories of small groups: Interdisciplinary perspectives.* Newbury Park, CA: Sage, 2005.

CHAPTER 8

1. Weber, Max. (1969). Bureaucracy (H. H. Gerth & C. W. Mills, Trans.). In J. A. Litterer (Ed.), *Organizations: Structure and behavior.* New York: John Wiley & Sons.

2. Daniels, Tom D., Spiker, Barry K., & Papa, Michael J. (1997). *Perspectives on organizational communication* (4th ed.). Boston: McGraw Hill, 3.

3. Poole, Marshall Scott, & McPhee, Robert D. (1983). A structurational analysis of organizational climate. In Linda L. Putnam & Michael E. Pacanowsky (Eds.), *Communication and organizations: An interpretive approach*. Beverly Hills: Sage.

4. Giddens, Anthony. (1993). *Sociology*. Cambridge: Polity Press, 18. For a detailed explanation of structuration theory, see Giddens, Anthony. (1984). *The constitution of society: Outline of the theory of structuration*. Berkeley and Los Angeles: University of California Press.

5. Redding, Charles, as quoted in DeWine, Sue. (1994). *The consultant's craft: Improving organizational communication*. New York: St. Martin's Press, xxiii.

6. Conrad, Charles. (1994). *Strategic organizational communication: Toward the twenty-first century* (3rd ed.). New York: Harcourt Brace, 3.

7. *Ibid.*, 5.

8. Yates, Joanne, & Orlikowski, Wanda J. (1992). Genres of organizational communication: A structurational approach to studying communication and media. *Academy of management review, 17*(2), 299–326.

9. Feilor, Bruce S. (1991). *Learning to bow: Inside the heart of Japan*. New York: Houghton Mifflin, 24–25.

10. Daniels, Spiker, & Papa, 115.

11. *Ibid.*, 116.

12. Callan, Victor J. (1993). Subordinate–manager communication in different sex dyads: Consequences of job satisfaction. *Journal of Occupational and Organizational Psychology, 66*, 13–27.

13. Krivonos, P. D. (1976). Distortion of subordinate-to-superior communication. Paper presented at the annual meeting of the International Communication Association, Portland, Oregon.

14. Downs, Cal, & Conrad, Charles. (1982). Effective subordinancy. *Journal of Business Communication, 19*, 27–37.

15. Milgram, Stanley. (1967). The small world problem. *Psychology Today, 1*(1), 60–67. Travers, Jeffrey, & Milgram, Stanley. (1969). An experimental study of the small world problem. *Sociometry, 32*(4), 425–443.

16. Conrad, 180.

17. Davis, Keith. (1980). Management communication and the grapevine. In Steward Ferguson & Sherry Devereaux Ferguson (Eds.), *Intercom: Readings in organizational communication*. Rochelle Park, NJ: Hayden Books, 55–66. Quoted in DeVito, Joseph A. (1997). *Human communication: The basic course*. New York: Longman, 348. See also Hellweg, Susan A. (1992). Organizational grapevines. In Kevin L. Hutchinson (Ed.), *Readings in organizational communication*. Dubuque, IA: Wm. C. Brown, 159–172.

18. Conrad, 310.

19. Perrow, Charles. (1984). *Normal accidents*. New York: Basic Books.

20. Daniels, 124.

21. For a discussion of the importance of structural diversity, see Cummings, Jonathon N. (2004). Work groups, structural diversity, and knowledge sharing in a global organization. *Management Science, 50*(3), 352–364. See also Cummings, Jonathan N., & Ancona, Deborah G. (2005).

The functional perspective. In Wheelan, *The handbook of group research and practice*.

22. Littlepage, Glenn E., Hollingshead, Andrea B., Drake, Laurie R., & Littlepage, Anna M. (2008). Transactive memory and performance in work groups: Specificity, communication, ability differences, and work allocation. *Group Dynamics: Theory, Research and Practice, 12*(3), 223–241.223. For an early formulation of the theory, see Wegner, D. M. (1987). Transactive memory: A contemporary analysis of the group mind. In B. Mullen & G. R. Goethals (Eds.), *Theories of group behavior*. New York: Springer-Verlag.

23. Garner, Johny T. (2006). It's not what you know: A transactive memory analysis of knowledge networks at NASA. *Journal of Technical Writing and Communication, 36*(4), 329–351.

24. Ellis, Kathleen, & Shockley-Zalabek. (2001). Trust in top management and immediate supervisor: The relationship to satisfaction, perceived organizational effectiveness, and information receiving. *Communication Quarterly, 49*(4), 382–398; and Lau, Dora C., & Liden, Robert C. (2008). Antecedents of coworker trust: Leaders' blessings. *Journal of Applied Psychology, 93*(5), 1130–1138.

25. Stewart, Charles J., & Cash, William B., Jr. (1991). *Interviewing: Principles and practices*. Dubuque, IA: William C. Brown, 3.

26. *Ibid.*, 5.

27. Much of the material about interview preparation is taken from "A Guide to Resume Writing," "Successful Interviewing," and "How to Write a Cover Letter," brochures prepared by Ithaca College Career Services. If your college does not provide similar guides, there are many popular books on the subject. See, for example, Medley, Anthony. (1992). *Sweaty palms: The neglected art of being interviewed*. Berkeley, CA: Ten Speed Press, or Krannich, Caryl. (1998). *Interview for success: A practical guide to increasing job interviews, offers, and salaries*. Manassas Park, VA: Impact Publications.

28. Kreps, Gary. (1984). Organizational culture and organizational development: Promoting flexibility in an urban hospital. Paper delivered at the meeting of the International Communication Association, San Francisco; quoted in Goldhaber, Gerald M. (1993). *Organizational communication* (6th ed.). Dubuque, IA: Brown and Benchmark, 69.

29. Louis, Meryl Reis. (1980). Surprise and sense making: What newcomers experience in entering unfamiliar organizational settings. *Administrative Science Quarterly, 25*, 226–251.

30. Louis, 247.

31. Pacanowsky, Michael E., & O'Donnell-Trujillo, Nick. (1982). Communication and organizational cultures. *Western Journal of Speech Communication, 46*, 115–130.

32. Stohl, Cynthia. (1995). *Organizational communication: Connectedness in action*. Thousand Oaks, CA: Sage, 11.

33. Conrad, 86.

34. Conrad, 80–81.

35. Trice, Harrison M., & Beyer, Janice M. (1984). Studying organizational cultures through rites and ceremonials. *Academy of Management Review, 9*, 655.

36. *Ibid.*

37. *Ibid.*, 666.

38. Weick, Karl E. (1979). Cognitive processes in organizations. In Barry M. Staw (Ed.), *Research in organizations* (Vol. 1). Greenwich, CT: JAI Press, 42.

39. Wall, Bob. (1999). *Working relationships: The simple truth about getting along with friends and foes at work.* Palo Alto, CA: Davies-Black, 12.

40. Wall, 21.

41. Dillard, James. (1987). Close relationships at work: Perceptions of the motives and performance of relational participants. *Journal of Social and Personal Relationships, 4,* 179–193; Buzzanell, Patrice. (1990). Managing workplace romance. Paper presented at the annual convention of the Speech Communication Association, Chicago. See also DeWine.

42. Fox, Grace. (1998). *Everyday etiquette: A guide to modern manners.* New York: Berkeley Books, 78.

43. Fine, Gary Alan. (1986). Friendships in the workplace. Originally printed in Derlaga, Valerian J., & Winstead, Barbara A. (Eds.), *Friendship and social interaction.* New York: Springer-Verlag, 186–206. Quote is taken from version excerpted in Galvin, Kathleen M., & Cooper, Pamela (Eds.). (1996). *Making connections: Readings in relational communication.* Los Angeles: Roxbury, 274.

44. www.eeoc.gov/facts/fs-sex 6/15/00.

45. Conrad, 400. See also Conrad, Charles, & Taylor, Bryan. (1994). The contexts of sexual harassment: Power, silences and academe. In Shereen Bingham (Ed.), *Conceptualizing sexual harassment as discursive practice.* Westport, CT: Greenwood Publishing.

46. Daniels, 232.

47. Doheny-Farina, Stephen. (1996). *The wired community.* New Haven, CT: Yale University Press, 93.

48. *Ibid.,* 89.

49. *Ibid.,* 90.

50. See Noble, Barbara Presley. (1994, June 15). Electronic liberation or entrapment? *New York Times,* D4; cited in Doheny-Farina, 95.

51. Shellenbarger, Sue. (1993, December 16). I'm still here! Home workers worry they're invisible. *Wall Street Journal,* B1; cited in Doheny-Farina, 95.

52. Poole, Marshall Scott, & Zhang, Huiyan. (2005). Virtual teams. In Wheelan, *The handbook of group research & practice.*

53. *Ibid.,* 374.

54. Jarvenpaa, Sirkka L., & Leidner, Dorothy E. (1999). Communication and trust in global virtual teams. *Organization Science, 10,* 791–815; Jarvenpaa, Sirkka L., Shaw, Thomas R., & Staples, D. Sandy. (2004). Toward contextualized theories of trust: The role of trust in global virtual teams. *Information Systems Research, 15*(3), 250–267; also see Jarvenpaa, Sirkka L., & Tanriverdi, Huseyn. (2003). Leading virtual knowledge networks. *Organizational Dynamics, 31*(4), 403–412.

55. Poole & Zhang, 365. Kirkman, B. L., & others (2002). Five challenges to virtual team success: Lessons from Sabre, Inc. *Academy of Management Executive, 16,* 67–79; Kirkman & others (2004). The impact of team empowerment on virtual team performance: The moderating role of face-to-face interaction. *Academy of Management Journal, 47,* 175–192.

56. See O'Connell, S. E. (1988). Human communication in the high tech office. In Gerald M. Goldhaber & George A. Barnett (Eds.), *Handbook of organizational communication.* Norwood, NJ: Ablex, 473–482.

57. Kramer, Melinda G. (2001). *Business communication in context.* Upper Saddle River, NJ: Prentice Hall, 69.

58. Zaremba, Alan Jay. (2003). *Organizational communication: Foundations for business & management.* New York: Thomson/South-Western, 112.

59. Kiesler, Sara, & Sproull, Lee. (1991). *Connections: New ways of working in the networked organization.* Cambridge, MA: The MIT Press.

60. Zaremba, 2003, 112; see also, Zaremba, Alan. (1996, January). Effects of e-mail availability on the informal network. *International Journal of Technology Management,* 151–161.

61. Deetz, Stanley. (1999). Multiple stakeholders and social responsibility in the international business context: A critical perspective. In Philip Salem (Ed.), *Organizational communication and change.* Cresskill, NJ: Hampton Press, 289.

62. Conrad, 330.

63. Banner, D. K., & Gagne, T. E. (1995). *Designing effective organizations: Traditional and transformational views.* Thousand Oaks, CA: Sage, 97; quoted in Salem, 25.

64. Deetz, 313.

CHAPTER 9

1. Darrow, Clarence. (1924, August 22). "Closing Argument: The State of Illinois v. Nathan Leopold and Richard Loeb." Retrieved 1/26/2006 from www.law.umkc.edu/faculty/projects/ftrials, or do a Web search on "famous trials UMKC School of Law."

2. Roosevelt, Franklin Delano. (1933, March 4). "First Inaugural Address." Retrieved 1/26/2006 from www.americanrhetoric.com/speeches/fdrfirstinaugural.html.

3. Nixon, Richard. (1952, September 23). "Checkers." Retrieved 1/26/2006 from www.americanrhetoric.com/speeches/richardnixoncheckers.html; and Nixon, Richard. (1974, August 8). "Resignation Speech." Retrieved 1/26/2006 from www.americanrhetoric.com'speeches/richard nixon resignationspeech.html.

4. King, Martin Luther, Jr. (1968, March 3). "I've Been to the Mountaintop." Retrieved 1/26/2006 from www.americanrhetoric.com/speeches/mlkivebeentothe mountaintop.html.

5. Glaser, Elizabeth. (1992, July 14). "Address to the 1992 Democratic National Convention." Retrieved 1/26/2006 from www.americanrhetoric.com/speeches.elizabethglaser1992dnc.html.

6. Cooper, Martha. (1989). *Analyzing public discourse.* Prospect Heights, IL: Waveland Press, 5–6.

7. *Ibid.,* 5.

8. Lightner, Candy, & Hathaway, Nancy. (1990). *Giving sorrow words: How to cope with grief and get on with your life.* New York: Warner Books. Numerous Web pages give details of Ms. Lightner's work against drunk driving and her relationship to MADD.

9. Plato. (2004). *Gorgias* (Walter Hamilton and Chris Emlyn-Jones, Trans.). London: Penguin Books.

10. Herrick, James A. (2005). *The history and theory of rhetoric: An introduction*. Boston: Allyn & Bacon, 16.

11. *Ibid*. In making this point, Herrick also cites Perelman, Chaim, & Olbrechts-Tyteca, Lucy. (1969). *The new rhetoric: A treatise on argumentation* (John Wilkinson and Purcell Weaver, Trans.). Notre Dame, IN: University of Notre Dame Press.

12. Herrick, 18.

13. *Ibid.*, 23.

14. *Ibid.*, 20.

15. van Oosting, James. (1985). *The business speech: Speaker, audience, and text*. Englewood Cliffs, NJ: Prentice-Hall, 9.

16. Andrews, James R., Leff, Michael C., & Terrill, Robert. (1998). *Reading rhetorical texts: An introduction to criticism*. New York: Houghton Mifflin, 37.

17. *Ibid.*, 30–31.

18. Bitzer, Lloyd. (1968). The rhetorical situation. *Philosophy and Rhetoric, I*(1), 1–14.

19. *Ibid.*, 14.

20. Rokeach, Milton. (1968). *Beliefs, attitudes, and values*. San Francisco: Jossey-Bass.

21. For a discussion of current thinking about the three dimensions of attitudes, see Gass, Robert H., & Seiter, John S. (2003). *Persuasion, social influence, and compliance gaining*. Boston: Allyn & Bacon, 43–44, note 1, 70.

22. Rokeach.

23. Kelman, Herbert. (1961). Processes of opinion change. *Public Opinion Quarterly, 25,* 57–78; and McGuire, William J. (1985). Attitudes and attitude change. In Gardner Lindzey & Elliot Aronson (Eds.), *Handbook of social psychology* (3rd ed., Vol. 2). New York: Random House.

24. Zajonc, Robert B. (1968). The attitudinal effects of mere exposure. *Journal of Personality and Social Psychology, 9*(1), 1–27.

25. See Trenholm, 39; and Smith, Mary John. (1982). *Persuasion and human action*. Belmont, CA: Wadsworth, 202.

26. Jones, Edward E., & Wortman, Camille. (1973). *Ingratiation: An attributional approach*. Morristown, NJ: General Learning. For a discussion of ingratiation as a negotiation tactic, see Pruitt, Dean G., & Rubin, Jeffrey Z. (1986). *Social conflict: Escalation, stalemate, and settlement*. New York: Random House.

27. French, John, & Raven, Bertram. (1959). The basis of social power. In Dorwin Cartwright (Ed.), *Studies in social power*. Ann Arbor, MI: University of Michigan Press.

28. See Adorno, Theodor W., et al. (1950). *The authoritarian personality*. New York: Harper & Row.

29. Toulmin, Stephen Edelston. (1958). *The uses of argument*. Cambridge, UK: Cambridge University Press.

30. This argument is taken from Rottenberg, Annette T. (1985). *Elements of argument*. New York: St. Martin's, 118–126.

31. Brockreide, Wayne, & Ehninger, Douglas. (1960). Toulmin on argument: An interpretation and application. *Quarterly Journal of Speech, 46,* 44–53.

32. Maslow, Abraham H. (1970). *Motivation and personality* (2nd ed.). New York: Harper & Row, 35–58.

33. The distinctions between arguments from cause, sign, generalization, and analogy are standard, as are the tests of their validity. The present discussion is taken from three sources: Bradley, 226–237; Ross, Raymond S. (1985).

Understanding persuasion: Foundations and practice (2nd ed.). Englewood Cliffs, NJ: Prentice-Hall, 165–169; and Trenholm, 232–235.

34. Fearnside, W. Ward, & Holther, William B. (1959). *Fallacy: The counterfeit of argument*. Englewood Cliffs, NJ: Prentice-Hall, 25.

35. Sears, David O., & Funk, Carolyn L. (1991). The role of self-interest in social and political attitudes. In Mark P. Zanna (Ed.), *Advances in experimental social psychology* (Vol. 24). New York: Academic.

36. For research on lazy processors and heuristics, see Eagly, Alice H., & Chaiken, Shelly. (1984). Cognitive theories of persuasion. In Leonard Berkowitz (Ed.), *Advances in experimental social psychology* (Vol. 17). New York: Academic; Langer, Ellen J. (1978). Rethinking the role of thought in social interaction. In John H. Harvey, William J. Ickes, & Robert F. Kidd (Eds.), *New directions in attribution research* (Vol. 2). Hillside, NJ: Lawrence Erlbaum Associates; and Petty, Richard E., & Cacioppo, John T. (1986). The elaboration likelihood model of persuasion. In Leonard Berkowitz (Ed.), *Advances in experimental social psychology* (Vol. 19). New York: Academic.

37. For additional information on fallacies, see Fearnside & Holther; Rottenberg; and Lee, Alfred M., & Lee, Elizabeth B. (1979). *The fine art of propaganda*. San Francisco: International Institute for General Semantics.

CHAPTER 10

1. Lucas, Stephen E. (2004). *The art of public speaking* (8th ed.). New York: Random House. Material cited is taken from the second edition, published in 1986, p. 72.

2. See Bradley, Bert E. (1991). *Fundamentals of speech communication: The credibility of ideas* (6th ed.). Dubuque, IA: Brown, 93–95, for an excellent discussion of sources to pursue in analyzing audiences.

3. For a complete discussion of the motivated sequence, see any edition of *Principles and types of speech communication*. The latest edition (the 15th) is authored by Raymie E. McKerrow, Bruce E. Gronbeck, Douglas Ehnirger, & Alan H. Monroe and was published by Allyn & Bacon in 2003.

4. Ross, Raymond S. (1983). *Speech communication: Fundamentals and practice*. Englewood Cliffs, NJ: Prentice-Hall, 193–199.

5. Stephen E. Lucas, 2004, 337.

6. Andersen, Kenneth E. (1991). A history of communication ethics. In Karen Joy Greenberg (Ed.), *Conversations on communication ethics*. Norwood, NJ: Ablex.

7. Campbell, Paul N. (1972). *Rhetoric-ritual*. Belmont, CA: Dickenson. For an overview of approaches to ethics, see also Johannesen, Richard L. (2002). *Ethics in human communication* (5th ed.). Prospect Heights, IL: Waveland Press.

CHAPTER 11

1. Stelter, Brian. (2009). 8 hours a day spent on screens, study finds. Article retrieved 3/30/2009 from http://www.nytimes.com/2009/03/27business/media/27abco.html?scp=1&sq=&st=nyt. If no longer at this URL, available through New York Times online archive.

2. Snow, Robert P. (1983). *Creating media culture.* Beverly Hills, CA: Sage, 29.

3. For a description of Fox television network's reality programming, see http://www.foxreality.com/show.php?id=1759.

4. Lasswell, Harold D. (1948). The structure and function of communication in society. In Lyman Bryson (Ed.), *The communication of ideas.* New York: Institute for Religious and Social Studies; Wright, Charles R. (1960). Functional analysis and mass communication. *Public Opinion Quarterly, 24,* 605–620; Wright, Charles R. (1975). *Mass communication: A sociological perspective* (2nd ed.). New York: Random House, 8–22.

5. Lazarfeld, Paul F., & Merton, Robert K. (1971). Mass communication, popular taste, and organized social action. In Wilbur Schramm & Donald F. Roberts (Eds.), *The process and effects of mass communication* (Rev. ed.). Urbana: University of Illinois Press, 565. For a good brief review, with examples, of the functions of the media, see Felsenthal, Norman. (1976). Orientations to mass communication. In Ronald L. Applbaum & Roderick P. Hart (Eds.), *Modules in speech communication.* Palo Alto, CA: SRA, 6–8.

6. For a summary of some of the major effects theories, see Littlejohn, Stephen W. (1989). *Theories of human communication* (3rd ed.). Belmont, CA: Wadsworth, Chapter 13.

7. Schramm, Wilbur. (1971). The nature of communications between humans. In Schramm & Roberts, 8.

8. Bauer, Raymond. (1971). The obstinate audience: The influence process from the point of view of social communication. In Schramm & Roberts. See also Klapper, Joseph. (1960). *The effects of mass communication.* Glencoe, IL: Free Press; and Weiss, Walter. (1969). Effects of the mass media of communication. In Gardner Lindzey & Elliot Aronson (Eds.), *Handbook of social psychology.* Reading, MA: Addison-Wesley.

9. Katz, Elihu. (1987). Communications research since Lazarfeld. *Public Opinion Quarterly, 51*(4), S25–S45, suggests this typology, although his examples differ.

10. See, for example, Shaw, Donald L., & McCombs, Maxwell E. (1977). *The emergence of American political issues.* St. Paul, MN: West Publishing.

11. Felsenthal, 31.

12. Gitlin, Todd. (1979). Prime time ideology: The hegemonic process in television entertainment. *Social Problems, 26*(3), 251–266; also reprinted in Horace Newcomb (Ed.), *Television: The critical view* (4th ed.). Oxford, UK: Oxford University Press, 510.

13. Children Now. (2000, May). *Highlights: Prime time diversity report, 2001–02.* Retrieved 8/31/2003 from http://www.childrennow.org/medoa/fc2002/fc-2002-highlights.htm, 2.

14. Noelle-Neumann, Elisabeth. (1984). *The spiral of silence: Public opinion—Our social skin.* Chicago: University of Chicago Press.

15. Gerbner, George. (1993). *Women and minorities on television: A study in casting and fate.* Philadelphia: University of Pennsylvania, Annenberg School of Communication, 1; the portions of this report pertaining to gender are summarized and analyzed in Michael R. Real. (1996). *Exploring media culture: A guide.* Thousand Oaks, CA: Sage, 181.

16. See, for example, Gerbner, George, Gross, Larry, Morgan, Michael, & Signorelli, Nancy. (2002). Growing up with television: The cultivation perspective. In Jennings Bryant & Dolf Zillmann (Eds.), *Media effects: Advances in theory and research.* Hillsdale, NJ: Lawrence Erlbaum Associates, 43–68.

17. The Museum of Broadcast Comunications. Audience research: Cultivation analysis. Retrieved 5/30/2006 from http://www.museum.tv/archives/etv/A/htmlA/audienceresec/audienceresec.htm.

18. *Ibid.,* 2.

19. Katz.

20. Felsenthal, 33.

21. McLuhan, Marshall. (1964). *Understanding media: The extensions of man.* New York: McGraw-Hill.

22. Snow, 162–163.

23. Book, Cassandra, et al. (1980). *Human communication: Principles, contexts, and skills.* New York: St. Martin's, 206; and Booth, Alan. (1970–1971). The recall of news items. *Public Opinion Quarterly, 34,* 604–610.

24. Katz, Elihu, Blumer, Jay, & Gurevitch, Michael. (1974). Uses of mass communication by the individual. In W. Phillips Davidson & Frederick Yu (Eds.), *Mass communication research: Major issues and future directions.* New York: Praeger, 12. For a brief summary and critique of uses and gratifications research, see Littlejohn.

25. Herzog, Herta. (1944). What do we really know about daytime serial listeners? In Paul Lazarfeld & Frank Stanton (Eds.), *Radio research, 1942–43.* New York: Dull, Sloan & Pearce.

26. McQuail, Denis, Blumer, Jay G., & Brown, J. R. (1972). The television audience: A revised perspective. In Denis McQuail (Ed.), *Sociology of mass communications.* Middlesex, UK: Penguin, 155–161.

27. Jamieson, Kathleen Hall, & Campbell, Karlyn Kohrs. (1992). *The interplay of influence: News, advertising, politics, and the mass media.* Belmont, CA: Wadsworth, 2.

28. Kawamoto, Dawn. (January 27, 2009). Online newspaper reading climbs 16%. Retrieved 3/27/2009 from http://news.cnet.com/8301-1023_3-10150884-93.html.

29. Kinsley, Michael. (September 26, 2006). Do newspapers have a future? Retrieved 3/27/2009 from http://www.time.com/time/printout/0,8816,1538652,00.html.

30. Vivian, John. (2009). *The media of mass communication, 9th ed.* Boston: Pearson, 80.

31. Snow, 53.

32. *Ibid.,* 59.

33. Jamieson & Campbell, 24.

34. Snow, 91.

35. Hiebert, Ray Eldon, Ungurait, Donald F., & Bohn, Thomas W. (1991). *Mass media VI: An introduction to modern communication.* New York: Longman, 288.

36. Altheide & Snow, 21.

37. Mendelsohn, Harold. (1964). Listening to radio. In A. Lewis Dexter & David M. White (Eds.), *People, society, and mass communication.* London: Collier-Macmillan, 91.

38. Snow, 101.

39. Altheide & Snow, 26.

40. Snow, 121.

41. Felsenthal, 11.

42. Altheide & Snow, 31.

43. Jamieson & Campbell, 63.

44. Stein, Ben. (1981, July 25). Love, rape, highway, diary. *TV Guide,* 34–35; cited in Snow, 137.

45. Snow, 142.

46. Hiebert, Ungurait, & Bohn, 428.

47. Cited in Epstein, Edward J. (1974). *News from nowhere.* New York: Hastings, 4.

48. Ferguson, E. B. (1980, July 20). Media hype for fun and profit. *Los Angeles Times,* part VII, p. 5.

49. Meyerowitz, Joshua. (1983). Television and the obliteration of "childhood." In Sari Thomas (Ed.), *Studies in mass communication and technology.* Norwood, NJ: Ablex.

50. Snow, 157.

51. Tobin, Hugh. (2006). Fear of txt. *Institute of Public Affairs Review, 58*(1), 41. Full text also available online. Retrieved 5/30/2006 through Academic Search Premier, 20449474.

52. The almighty cell phone. (2006). *Wilson Quarterly, 30*(1). Full text also available online. Retrieved 5/18/2006 through Academic Search Premier, 03633275.

53. Gillis, Charles. (2006). Cyberbullying is on the rise. Who can stop it? *Maclean's, 119*(2). Also available online. Retrieved 5/18/2006 through Academic Search Premier, 00249269.

54. Teen "sexting" worries parents, schools. (Feb. 4, 2009). Retrieved 3/13/2009 from http://www.cbsnews .com/stories/2009/02/04/tech/main4776708.shtml, "Sexting" shockingly common among teens. (Jan. 15, 2009). Retrieved 3/13/2009, from http://www.cbsnews.com/stories/2009/01/15/national/main4723161.shtml; Associated Press. (March 26, 2009). Girl, 14, faces porn charges for nude photos. Retrieved 3/31/2009 from http://www.npr.org/templates/story/story.php?storyId=102386952.

55. The almighty cell phone.

56. Discussion of the characteristics of the new media is taken from a number of sources. See, for example, Pavlik, John, & McIntosh, Shawn. (2004). *Converging media: An introduction to mass communication.* Boston: Allyn & Bacon, 15. See also McMillan, Sally J. (2006). Exploring models of interactivity from multiple research traditions: Users, documents and systems. In Leah A. Lievrouw & Sonia Livingstone (Eds.), *Handbook of new media: Social shaping and social consequences of ICTs* (Updated student ed.). Thousand Oaks, CA: Sage, 205–229.

57. McMillan, 206. For original discussion, see Negroponte, Nicholas. (1995). *Being digital.* New York: Knopf.

58. Harrison, Teresa M., & Barthel, Brea, (2009). Wielding new media in Web 2.0: Exploring the history of engagement with the collaborative construction of media products. *New Media & Society, 11,* 155–178, 157.

59. *Ibid.,* 157. See also, Madden, Mary, & Fox, Susannah. (October 5, 2006). Riding the waves of "Web 2.0": More than a buzzword, but still not easily defined. Pew Internet & American Life Project. Retrieved 4/2/2009 from http://www.pewinternet.org/Reports/2006/Riding-the-waves-of-Web-20.aspx.

60. DeFalco, Beth. (March 11, 2009). Grandpa is browsing your Facebook page. Associated Press. Retrieved 3/16/2009 from http://www.google.com/hostednews/ap/article.

61. Smith, Aaron, & Rainie, Lee. (June 15, 2008). The Internet and the 2008 election. Pew Internet & American Life Project. Retrieved 4/5/2009 from http://www.pewinternet .org/Press-Releases/2008/The-internet-and-the-2008 -election.aspx.

62. Jenkins, Henry. 2008. *Convergence culture: Where old and new media collide.* New York: New York University Press, 229.

63. *Ibid.,* 77. See also Au, Wagner Jame. (April 13, 2004). John Kerry: The video game. *Salon,* at http://www.salon .com/tech/feature/2004/04/13/battlefield_vietnam/. See also America's Army Website.

64. Retrieved 6/14/2006 from http://en.wikipedia.org/ wiki/Wikipedia:Introduction.

65. Retrieved 6/14/2006 from http://www.usatoday.com/ news/opinion/editorials/2005-11-29-wikipedia-edit_x .htm.

66. Rheingold, Howard. (2002). *Smart mobs: The next social revolution.* New York: Basic Books, 188.

67. *Ibid.,* 189. See also Foucault, Michel. (1977). *Discipline and punish: The birth of the prison.* London: Tavistock; and Foucault, Michel. (1980). *Power/knowledge: Selected interviews and other writings, 1972–1977.* (Colin Gordon, Ed.). New York: Pantheon.

68. Hiebert, Ray Eldon, & Gibbons, Sheila Jean. (2000). *Exploring mass media for a changing world.* Mahwah, NJ: Lawrence Erlbaum Associates, 306.

69. Wallace, Patricia. (1999). *The psychology of the Internet.* New York: Cambridge University Press, 1.

70. *Ibid.,* 1.

71. Jones, Sydney, & Fox, Susannah. (January 28, 2009). Pew Internet Project Data Memo: Generations online in 2009. Pew Internet & American Life Project, 3. Retrieved 4/4/2009 from http://pewinternet.org/~/media//Files/Reports/2009/PIP_Generations_2009.pdf.

72. Heibert & Gibbons, *Exploring mass media,* 317–321.

73. Buckingham, David. (2006). Children and new media. In Lievrouw & Livingstone, 75.

74. *Ibid.*

75. Baym, Nancy K. (2006). Interpersonal life online. In Lievrouw & Livingstone, 35.

76. *Ibid.,* 48. See also Baym, Nancy K., Zhang, Yan Bing, & Lin, Mei-Chen. (2004). Social interactions across media: Interpersonal communication on the Internet, telephone, and face-to-face. *New Media & Society, 6*(3), 299–318; and Copher, J. I., Kanfer, A. G., & Walker, M. B. (2002). Everyday communication patterns of heavy and light e-mail users. In Barry Wellman & Carolyn A. Haythornthwaite (Eds.), *The Internet in everyday life.* Malden, MA: Blackwell, 263–290. (Cited in Baym, 51.)

77. Robinson, J. P., Kestenbaum, M., Neustadtl, A., & Alvarez, A. S. (2002). The Internet and other uses of time. In Wellman and Haythornthwaite, 244–262. (Cited in Baym, 53.)

78. Steinkuehler, Constance A., & Williams, Dmitri. (2006). Where everybody knows your (screen) name: Online games as "third places." *Journal of Computer-Mediated Communication, 11,* 885–909, 888. For further discussion of gaming and online role playing, see Diehl, William C., &

Prins, Esther. (2008). Unintended outcomes in Second Life: Intercultural literacy and cultural identity in a virtual world. *Language and Intercultural Communication, 8*(2), 101–118; Woods, Mathew. (2007). Login for love: Defining intimacy in the metaverse of Second Life. Convention paper presented at the National Communication Association annual meeting. Retrieved 3/30/2009 from EBSCOhost; Demetrious, Kristin. (2008). Secrecy and illusion: Second Life and the construction of unreality. *Australian Journal of Communication, 35*(1), 1–13; Shaw, Patrick, LaRose, Robert, & Wirth, Christina. (2006). Reaching a new level and other pleasures of massive multiplayer online games: A social cognitive theory of MMO usage. Paper presented at the International Communication Association annual meeting. Retrieved 4/4/2009 from EBSCOhost.

79. Baym, 2006, 43; McKenna, K. Y. A, & Bargh, J. A. (2000). Plan 9 from cyberspace: The implications of the Internet for personality and social psychology. *Personality and Social Psychology Review, 4*(1), 57–75; Pew. (2000). Tracking online life: How women use the Internet to cultivate relationships with family and friends. Washington, DC: Pew Internet and American Life Project. Retrieved 6/25/2006 from http://www.pewinternet.org.

80. Wallace, 32.

81. Davis, Jack, & Merritt, Susan. (1998). *The Web design wow! book.* Berkeley, CA: Peachpit Press.

82. See, for example, VanderVeer, Emily, et al. (2002). *Creating Web pages: All-in-one desk reference for dummies.* New York: Wiley Publishers, 16–22.

83. Nielsen, Jakob, & Takir, Marie. (2002). *Homepage usability: 50 Websites deconstructed.* Indianapolis, IN: New Riders Publishing. A related Website can be found at http://www.useit.com/homepageusability.

84. Plant, Sadie. (2001). On the mobile: The effects of mobile telephone on social and individual life. Retrieved 6/19/2006 from www.motorola.com/mot/doc/0/234_MotDoc.pdf., 29. Original news report is from Gray, Chris. (2001, May 18). Now birds brag by mimicking mobiles. *The Independent.*

85. Thurlow, Crispin. (2003). Generation txt? The sociolinguistics of young people's text-messaging. Retrieved 9/20/2005 from http://www.shu.ac.uk/daol/articles/v1/n1/a3/thurlow1001003-paper.html, 15.

86. Plant, 22.

87. Reingold, 164–165.

88. Thurlow, 10.

89. Plant, 65.

90. *Ibid.,* 55.

91. *Ibid.,* 65.

92. Thurlow, 2.

93. Weeks, Linton. (2009). It's not you, it's me: Breaking up with technology. Broadcast on NPR March 31, 2009, and retrieved from http://www.npr.org/templates/story/story.php?storyID=101409144 on the same date.

94. *Ibid.*

95. Snow, 19.

96. Pavlik, 19–20.

97. Cingular expects to top the charts with the number of text messages sent this season on "American Idol."

(2006). Retrieved 6/24/2006 from http://techweb.com/showPressRelease.jhtml?articleID=X440758.

98. Jenkins, 104.

99. *Ibid.,* 147.

100. Hiebert, Ungurait, & Bohn.

101. Saul, Stephanie. (1989, July–August). Judgment call: Do reporters have a right to march? *Columbia Journalism Review,* 51; and Gersh, Debra. (1989, August 19). Question of conflict. *Editor and Publisher,* 11.

102. Heim, Michael. (1993). *The metaphysics of virtual reality.* New York: Oxford University Press, 78–79.

103. Krotz, Joanna L. Cell phone etiquette: 10 dos and don'ts. Retrieved 6/4/2006 from http://www.microsoft.com/smallbusiness/resources/technology/communications/cell_phone_etiquette_10_dos_and_donts.mspx; Stage actor Richard Griffith berates young man in audience for cell phone disturbance. (2006, January 2). Retrieved 6/20/2006 from http://www.textually.org/textually/archives/cat_cell_phone_etiquette.htm.

CHAPTER 12

1. Storti, Craig. (1990). *The art of crossing cultures.* Yarmouth, ME: Intercultural Press, 25.

2. Hoijer, Harry. (1954). The Sapir-Whorf hypothesis. In Harry Hoijer (Ed.), *Language in culture.* Chicago: University of Chicago Press, 94; cited in Singer, Marshall R. (1987). *Intercultural communication: A perceptual approach.* Englewood Cliffs, NJ: Prentice-Hall, 7.

3. The phrase comes from Diamond, C. T. Patrick. (1982). Understanding others: Kellyian theory, methodology and applications. *International Journal of Intercultural Relations, 6,* 403; cited in Singer, 8.

4. Benedict, Ruth. (1946). *Patterns of culture.* New York: Penguin, 2.

5. Klopf, Donald W. (1991). *Intercultural encounters: The fundamentals of intercultural communication* (2nd ed.). Englewood, CO: Morton, 31.

6. Trenholm, Sarah, & Jensen, Arthur. (1992). *Interpersonal communication.* Belmont, CA: Wadsworth, 368.

7. Klopf, 33.

8. For a discussion of cultural identity, see Singer, 46.

9. Wieder, D. Lawrence, & Pratt, Steven. (1990). On being a recognizable Indian among Indians. In Donal Carbaugh (Ed.), *Cultural communication and intercultural contact.* Hillsdale, NJ: Lawrence Erlbaum Associates, 45–64.

10. *Ibid.,* 51.

11. *Ibid.,* 61.

12. *Ibid.,* 63.

13. Samovar, Larry A., & Porter, Richard E. (1991). *Communication between cultures.* Belmont, CA: Wadsworth, 15.

14. *Ibid.,* 20.

15. Singer, 53.

16. Porter, Richard E., & Samovar, Larry A. (1991). Basic principles of intercultural communication. In Larry A. Samovar & Richard E. Porter (Eds.), *Intercultural communication: A reader* (6th ed.). Belmont, CA: Wadsworth, 6.

17. *Ibid.,* 6.

18. Kim, Young Yun. (1988). *Communication and cross-cultural adaptation: An integrative theory.* Philadelphia: Multilingual Matters, 145–146.

19. George Kelly, as cited in Diamond, 396–397.

20. Klopf, 57.

21. Mernissi, Fatima. (1975). *Beyond the veil: Male-female dynamics in modern Muslim society.* Cambridge, MA: Schenken, 81–86. For a discussion of a similar incident, see Storti, 66–67.

22. Klopf, 20.

23. Dodd, Carley H. (1987). *Dynamics of intercultural communication* (2nd ed.). Dubuque, IA: Brown, 44.

24. Skow, Lisa, & Samovar, Larry A. (1991). Cultural patterns of the Maasai. In Samovar & Porter, *Intercultural communication,* 90.

25. Carmichael, Carl W. (1991). Intercultural perspectives on aging. In Samovar & Porter, *Intercultural communication,* 130.

26. For examples of these kinds of differences, see Samovar, Larry A., Porter, Richard E., & Jain, Nemi C. (1981). *Understanding intercultural communication.* Belmont, CA: Wadsworth, 119; and Dodd, 45.

27. Hall, Edward T. (1959). *The silent language.* Garden City, NY: Doubleday, 67.

28. Argyle, Michael. (1991). Intercultural communication. In Samovar & Porter, *Intercultural communication,* 40; reprinted from Stephen Bochner (Ed.), *Cultures in contact: Studies in cross-cultural interaction.* Oxford, UK: Pergamon, 61–79.

29. Sitaram, K. S., & Cogdell, Roy T. (1976). *Foundations of intercultural communication.* Columbus, OH: Merrill, 51; cited in Samovar, Porter, & Jain, 94.

30. Samovar, Porter, & Jain, 73–74.

31. *Ibid.,* 76.

32. Hofstede, Geert. (1982). *Culture's consequences.* Newbury Park, CA: Sage.

33. Triandis, Harry C., Briskin, Richard, & Hui, C. Harry. (1988). Cross-cultural training across the individualism-collectivism divide. *The International Journal of Intercultural Relations, 12;* reprinted in Samovar & Porter, *Intercultural communication.*

34. Hall, Edward T., & Hall, Mildred Reed. (1987). *Hidden differences: Doing business with the Japanese.* Garden City, NY: Doubleday, Anchor.

35. *Ibid.,* 54–56, 157.

36. Barna, Laray M. (1991). Stumbling blocks in intercultural communication. In Samovar & Porter, *Intercultural communication,* 348.

37. Trenholm & Jensen, 386.

38. *Ibid.,* 388.

39. Barna, 346.

40. *Ibid.,* 345.

41. Storti, 26, 64–65.

42. Oberg, Kalvero. (1985). Culture shock: Adjustment to new cultural environments. *Practicing Anthropology, 7,* 170–179.

43. Storti, 52.

44. Kim, 56–57.

45. Samovar, Porter, & Jain, 195.

46. Hall & Hall, 18–20, 115.

47. Kim.

48. Trenholm & Jensen, 404–405.

CHAPTER 13

1. Selltiz, Claire, Wrightsman, Lawrence S., & Cook, Stuart W. (1976). *Research methods in social relations* (3rd ed.). New York: Holt, Rinehart & Winston, 2.

2. For a good discussion of heuristic rules as they apply to persuasion, see Cialdini, Robert B. (1984). *Influence: How and why people agree to things.* New York: Morrow. For a more formal discussion, see Eagly, Alice H., & Chaiken, Shelly. (1986). Cognitive theories of persuasion. In Leonard Berkowitz (Ed.), *Advances in experimental social psychology* (Vol. 19). New York: Academic, 123–181.

3. Selltiz, Wrightsman, & Cook, 5.

4. Frey, Lawrence R., Botan, Carl H., & Krebs, Gary L. (2000). *Investigating communication: An introduction to research methods,* (2nd ed.) Boston: Allyn & Bacon, 13–17.

5. Poole, Marshall Scott, & McPhee, R. D. (1985). Methodology in interpersonal communication research. In Mark L. Knapp & Gerald R. Miller (Eds.), *Handbook of interpersonal communication.* Newbury Park, CA: Sage, 100.

6. Frey, Botan, & Krebs, 17.

7. Rybacki, Karyn, & Rybacki, Don. (1991). *Communication criticism: Approaches and genres.* Belmont, CA: Wadsworth, 16.

8. Ray, Angela G. (2007). The rhetorical ritual of citizenship: Women's voting as public performance, 1863–1875. *Quarterly Journal of Speech, 93*(1), 1–26.

9. *Ibid.,* 2.

10. *Ibid.,* 13.

11. *Ibid.,* 9.

12. *Ibid.,* 11.

13. *Ibid.,* 15–16.

14. *Ibid.,* 18.

15. Schwartz, Howard, & Jacobs, Jerry. (1979). *Qualitative sociology: A method to the madness.* New York: Free Press, 48.

16. Kirk, J., & Miller, M. L. (1986). *Reliability and validity in qualitative research.* Newbury Park, CA: Sage, 9.

17. Frey, Lawrence R., et al. (1991). *Investigating communication: An introduction to research methods.* Englewood Cliffs, NJ: Prentice-Hall, 247.

18. Conquergood, Dwight. (1994). Homeboys and hoods: Gang communication and cultural space. In Lawrence R. Frey (Ed.), *Group communication in context: Studies of natural groups.* Hillsdale, NJ: Lawrence Erlbaum Associates.

19. *Ibid.,* 39.

20. *Ibid.,* 40.

21. *Ibid.,* 28.

22. *Ibid.,* 42–43.

23. *Ibid.,* 28.

24. *Ibid.,* 55.

25. Frey, et al., 1991, 191.

26. Reiss, Steven, & Wiltz, James. Why people watch reality TV. *Media Psychology, 6,* 363–378.

27. Lundy, Lisa K., Ruth, Amanda M., & Park, Travis D. (2008). Simply irresistible: Reality TV consumption patterns. *Communication Quarterly, 56*(2), 208–225.

28. *Ibid.*, p. 214.

29. *Ibid.*, p. 214.

30. Gardyn, R. The tribe has spoken. *American Demographics, 23*(9), 34–40.

31. Murray, Susan, & Ouellette, Laurie. (Eds.). (2004). *Reality TV: Remaking television culture.* New York: New York University Press, 4.

32. Lee, Kwan Min, Park, Namkee, & Song, Hayeon. (2005). Can a robot be perceived as a developing creature? *Human Communication Research, 31*(4), 538–563.

33. *Ibid.*, 558.

34. Pelias, Ronald J. (2000). Performance as method. In Frey, Botan, & Krebs, 253.

35. *Ibid.*, 234.

36. *Ibid.*, 255.

37. Vignes, Danielle Sears. (2008). "Hang it out to dry": Performing ethnography, cultural memory, and Hurricane Katrina in Chalmette, Louisiana. *Text and Performance Quarterly, 28*(3), 344–350.

38. Vignes, Danielle Sears. (2008). "Hang it out to dry": A performance script. *Text and Performance Quaterly, 28*(3), 351–365.

39. Terry, David. (2008) Surfacing, homing, and belonging in "hang it out to dry." *Text and Performance Quarterly, 28*(3), 366–368.

Author Index

Subject Index

Photo Credits